COURVOISIER'S
BOOK OF THE
BEST

C ognac Courvoisier is renowned worldwide for its unique Napoleonic connection.

The story dates back to the early 19th century when the enterprising Emmanuel Courvoisier became a supplier of cognac to Emperor Napoleon I. By 1811, when Napoleon visited Courvoisier's warehouses in Bercy, Paris, the association was proving a commercial success.

Soon after this, Napoleon tried to escape to America in a ship stocked with his favourite cognac, Courvoisier. However, he had to abandon his plans, and surrendered to the British. While the ship was being unloaded, British naval officers sampled the haul of cognac and were so impressed that they referred to it as the 'Emperor's Cognac', or 'Le Cognac de Napoleon'.

By 1869, the much-expanded business was proclaimed, by special appointment, purveyor to the court of another Emperor and Courvoisier aficionado, Napoleon III. From this association evolved the famous Courvoisier trademark, the silhouette of Napoleon, and the slogan 'Le Cognac de Napoleon'. To complement the cognac, Courvoisier created the distinctive 'Josephine' bottle.

Today, the bust of Napoleon appears on the bottle of all styles of Courvoisier cognac, and is the recognized symbol of cognac excellence throughout the world.

♣ The silhouette of Napoleon has been used in this book to denote a person or establishment that has been highly recommended by several of our contributors.

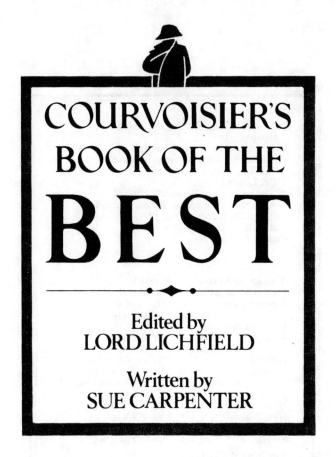

COURVOISIER'S
BOOK OF THE
BEST

Edited by
LORD LICHFIELD

Written by
SUE CARPENTER

Sterling Publishing Co., Inc. New York

Published 1993 by Sterling Publishing
  Company, Inc.
387 Park Avenue South, New York, N.Y. 10016
Originally published in Great Britain by
Vermillion an imprint of Random House
  UK Limited
© 1992 by Random House UK Limited
Distributed in Canada by Sterling Publishing
c/o Canadian Manda Group, P.O. Box 920,
Station U, Toronto, Ontario
Canada M8Z 5P9

Managing Editor	Sarah Bailey
Senior Researcher	Sophie Lance
Researchers	Oliver Morgan
	Selina Higgins
Foreign Editors:	
America (East Coast)	Sarah Owens
(West Coast)	Britta Lee
Australia	Susan Westwood
Canada	Freda Colbourne
France	Anne-Elisabeth Moutet
Far East	Claudia Cragg
Hong Kong	Catherine Gaynor
New Zealand	Vic Williams
Italy	Logan Bentley
Singapore	Ch'ng Poh Tiong
Additional written material	Sophie Lance
	Oliver Morgan
Design	Harry Green

Courvoisier's Book of the Best is a regularly
updated and totally independent guide. We accept
no advertising or payment of any kind from the
establishments included in the book. We would
welcome your views on our current selection, in
writing, to Courvoisier's Book of the Best,
Vermilion, Random House, 20 Vauxhall Bridge
Road, London SW1V 2SA.

The information contained in this book was
checked as rigorously as possible before going to
press. The publisher accepts no responsibility for
any changes which may have occurred since, nor
for any other variance of fact from that recorded
here in good faith.

**Library of Congress Cataloging in
Publication Data Available**

10 9 8 7 6 5 4 3 2 1

Manufactured in the United States of America

Sterling ISBN 0-8069-0363-5

Contents

♟ Art and museums ♟ Ballet ♟ Bars and cafés ♟ Clubs ♟ Fashion designers
♟ Festivals ♟ Film ♟ Gardens ♟ Historic houses ♟ Hotels ♟ Music
♟ Restaurants ♟ Shopping ♟ Ski resorts ♟ Theatre ♟ Tours ♟ Wine

FOREWORD
by
LORD LICHFIELD

When *Courvoisier's Book of the Best* was first published in the mid-1980s, no one could foretell just how well established the book would become among discerning travellers, foodies and all-round connoisseurs. It takes time to build up a reputation for reliability, and I am pleased to say that I believe *Courvoisier's Book of the Best* has well and truly earnt its reputation as an accurate, entertaining and original guide to all that is best around the world.

For anything to become established and withstand the test of time, it has to be of the highest quality. Quality is something that we uphold as a top priority for *Courvoisier's Book of the Best*, not just in our own standards of writing and research, but in the establishments we write about.

The past few years have been among the hardest on record for many businesses, and many have fallen victim to the recession. But those that have maintained high standards of service and provided true value for money have endured and are set to flourish once again. Such hotels as The Oriental in Bangkok and Claridge's in London have never stopped providing the very best service in the very best surroundings, and their continuing position in our world best lists reflects that consistency.

It is not an easy task to remain at the top. Once you are recognized as a leader in your field, you have to work twice as hard to maintain standards. A by-product of the recession is that people are more discerning and demanding than ever. They will not be fobbed off with sub-standard goods or food or service, nor with paying extortionate sums for the sake of fashion.

Thus we have seen such fads as nouvelle cuisine truly dead and buried. Hungry diners are simply not satisfied with an artistic arrangement of, say, three minuscule médaillons of lamb in a raspberry coulis, however tasty they may prove as an amuse-gueule. Portions are heartier and, above all, healthier, as international chefs learn

World's Best Ballet Companies

1	L'OPERA BALLET · Paris
2	BALLET OF THE MARIINSKY THEATRE · St Petersburg
3	ROYAL DANISH BALLET · Copenhagen
4	ROYAL BALLET COMPANY · London
5	THE BIRMINGHAM ROYAL BALLET · Birmingham, England
6	NEW YORK CITY BALLET · New York
7	AMERICAN BALLET THEATER · New York
8	AUSTRALIAN BALLET · Melbourne
9	NATIONAL BALLET OF CANADA · Toronto
10	HOUSTON BALLET FOUNDATION · Houston

LORD LICHFIELD was educated at Harrow and spent 7 years in the Grenadier Guards. In the 60s he became a photographer, working for *Life*, *Queen* and American *Vogue*. Advertising and editorial work now takes him all over the world, travelling some 250,000 miles a year, staying 150 nights in hotels and eating out virtually every day of the year. Co-owner of the successful restaurant chain, Deals, he has homes in London, Shugborough in Staffordshire and Mustique. His books include the autobiographical *Not the Whole Truth* and *Lichfield in Retrospect*. He has recently launched his own range of gentlemen's fragrance, *Lichfield*.

from each other and from experimentation how best to please the eye, the appetite – and the medical profession.

Most of the restaurants listed in the book reflect this new trend in dining. At the same time many leading restaurateurs have opened up second strings to bring sensational cuisine to more people at more affordable prices. Now you can sample cooking by Claude Terrail (La Tour d'Argent, Paris) at La Rôtisserie du Beaujolais, for example; by Michel Rostang (Michel Rostang, Paris) at Bistrot d'à Côté among others; and by Marco Pierre White (Harvey's, London) at Harvey's Canteen.

The fashion trade has been going through testing times, too. As one of our leading fashion contributors, Bruce Oldfield, points out: "The reason why fashion is so weird and wonderful and pulling every which way at the moment is the desperation of a dying industry. Clothes have become very, very, very, very expensive. That's OK if they are very special and exclusive, but expensive clothes for the sake of being expensive are finished." So, while couture hangs on by a silken thread for the élite, fashion designers are having to be more realistic and provide better value for money. Thus virtually all the top names now have diffusion lines – Donna Karan's DKNY, Christian Lacroix's Luxe, Jean-Paul Gaultier's Junior Gaultier, Rifat Ozbek's O for Ozbek.

All this is good news for the forward-looking aficionado. Style is not good enough without substance. The establishments recommended in the fourth edition of *Courvoisier's Book of the Best* represent better value, better service, more effort and more originality than ever before.

Which brings us back to the eternal question, exactly what is 'the best'? And how can I pronounce this place or that to be the best? 'Best' is, of course, partly a matter of opinion. For me it represents enduring quality and uncompromising attention to detail, but often it is a personal experience that can tip the scales – a certain

World's Best Restaurants

1	JAMIN (ROBUCHON) · Paris
2	GIRARDET · Crissier, Switzerland
3	L'ARPEGE · Paris
4	LE MANOIR AUX QUAT' SAISONS · Great Milton, England
5	LAI CHING HEEN · Hong Kong
6	AUREOLE · New York
7	ARZAK · San Sebastián, Spain
8	DA FIORE · Venice
9	TAILLEVENT · Paris
10	HARVEY'S · London

World's Best Hotels

1	THE ORIENTAL · Bangkok	
2	HOTEL CIPRIANI · Venice	
3	CLARIDGE'S · London	
4	MANDARIN ORIENTAL · Hong Kong	
5	HOTEL DE CRILLON · Paris	
6	THE CARLYLE · New York	
7	GRAND HYATT · Hong Kong	
8	THE REGENT · Sydney	
9	HOTEL SEIYO · Tokyo	
10	THE REGENT · Hong Kong	

atmosphere, a favourite dish, special service. That is where this book is unique, because the editorial opinion is formed by collecting the ideas and views of over 200 style-setters and experts, whose opinions are informed and respected. Together their thoughts form an invaluable anthology of the best. The result is a global guide that is thoroughly researched, with the added attraction of word-of-mouth recommendations from people who know.

One thing our contributors do know is that the best need not be élitist. Indeed, some of the best things in life really are free – and if not free, certainly affordable. Wander with this book around the markets of Chiang Mai or Aswan, the museums and galleries of Amsterdam or Frankfurt, the stately gardens of England, a tropical oasis in Marrakech, and the hurdy-gurdy rooftops of Barcelona.

You can discover where best to find ravioli in Florence, chocolate in Paris, contraband caviare in Russia, fish and chips in London, cigars in Geneva, lorgnettes in Hong Kong, whales in New Zealand, a 16th-century Venetian ceiling and a Tahitian couple waltzing.

As always, our horizons continue to expand. As new areas open up for visitors, our travellers report back with their experiences. Thus we have Robin Hanbury-Tenison on Romania and Czechoslovakia, Dan Topolski on Bhutan, Cuba and China, Carol Wright on Irian Jaya in Indonesia, Sir Peter Parker on Iceland, and Michael Gebicki on Papua New Guinea. New recommendations have come in for countries such as Hungary and Poland, while other countries such as Spain have received greater coverage to reflect their rise in world prominence.

While enduring quality is our watch-word, we keep abreast of trends and innovation, and you will find that new young chefs, hoteliers, fashion designers and shops are given the

World's Best Fashion Designers

1	KARL LAGERFELD at CHANEL · Paris	
2	GIANNI VERSACE · Milan	
3	GIORGIO ARMANI · Milan	
4	GIANFRANCO FERRE at DIOR · Paris	
5	YVES SAINT LAURENT · Paris	
6	DONNA KARAN · New York	
7	AZZEDINE ALAIA · Paris	
8	RALPH LAUREN · New York	
9	VIVIENNE WESTWOOD · London	
10	CLAUDE MONTANA · Paris	

World's Best Galleries and Museums

1	MUSEE DU LOUVRE · Paris
2	MUSEO DEL PRADO · Madrid
3	GALLERIA DEGLI UFFIZI · Florence
4	MUSEI VATICANI · Rome
5	KUNSTHISTORISCHES MUSEUM · Vienna
6	RIJKSMUSEUM · Amsterdam
7	METROPOLITAN MUSEUM OF ART · New York
8	NATIONAL GALLERY · London
9	THE HERMITAGE · St Petersburg
10	MUSEE D'ORSAY · Paris

World's Best Opera Companies

1	LA SCALA · Milan
2	ROYAL OPERA HOUSE · London
3	METROPOLITAN OPERA · New York
4	ENGLISH NATIONAL OPERA (ENO) · London
5	PARIS OPERA · Paris
6	LYRIC OPERA OF CHICAGO · Chicago
7	BAVARIAN STATE OPERA · Munich
8	NEW YORK CITY OPERA · New York
9	DEUTSCHE OPER · Berlin
10	VIENNA STATE OPERA · Vienna

recognition they deserve. The familiar Courvoisier symbol, the silhouette of Napoleon, continues to be bestowed upon highly recommended establishments. Following the success of the last edition's awards ceremony, we have again given awards to those British establishments voted best in their category.

Since the genesis of this book, the name 'Courvoisier' has become inextricably linked with the title 'Book of the Best'. I have noticed on my travels that the book is sometimes referred to simply as 'Courvoisier'. It has proved a natural marriage between the producers of the finest cognac and a publication about the finest things in life.

Never content to rest on their laurels, Courvoisier continue to develop their product year by year. In 1992, the 100th anniversary of Erté's birth, the exquisite Cognac Courvoisier Collection Erté is more than ever a collector's item. The newly released limited edition Succession JL, a very old and very rare cognac of exceptional quality, is on every connoisseur's shopping list – while stocks last.

Courvoisier's Book of the Best will continue to be updated every two years. While some establishments remain timeless, others fluctuate. We will be constantly assessing what deserves to be included in the book, and we again welcome your suggestions and comments. One of our contributors once said that the best was best kept to oneself. Some secrets deserve to be shared, however, and I hope that you will enjoy sampling both the secret and the celebrated establishments that we consider to be the best.

_____ *written by* _____

SUE CARPENTER, a freelance writer and journalist for various national newspapers and magazines. Her world travels have provided a rich source of material for *Courvoisier's Book of the Best*. Formerly with *Harpers & Queen* she edited *St Moritz* magazine, and is author of *The Good Wedding Guide* and *Harrods Wedding Book*.

_____ *with contributions from* _____

STEPHANIE ALEXANDER Top Australian chef whose namesake restaurant is one of Melbourne's best and whose books include *Stephanie's Australia*.

LADY ELIZABETH ANSON Founder of Party Planners, which has organized parties for most of the British royals. Her books include *Lady Elizabeth Anson's Party Planners*.

JEFFREY ARCHER Bestselling author and playwright whose books include *First Among Equals*. Recently made a peer.

GIORGIO ARMANI One of Italy's top fashion designers and style gurus.

JOHN ARMIT London-based owner of fine wine suppliers, John Armit Wines, partner of 192 restaurant and director of the Groucho Club.

JANE ASHER Actress, author and owner of the successful London shop, Jane Asher Party Cakes.

TONY ASPLER Canadian wine writer and consultant.

SUE AVERY BROWN Boston-based writer and reporter for *People* magazine.

LISA BARNARD Editor of the British-based magazine *Inside Hotels*.

STEPHEN BAYLEY Design expert, owner of Eye-Q design consultancy and author of *Taste – the Hidden Meaning of Things*.

ROSS BENSON Social columnist and former foreign correspondent for the *Daily Express*. Educated at Gordonstoun, where he was a contemporary of Prince Charles.

LOGAN BENTLEY Long-time resident of Rome, Italian

correspondent for *People* magazine and Italian editor of *Courvoisier's Book of the Best*. Her other identity is Countess Lessona.

LIZ BERRY MW Owner of the London-based wine merchants La Vigneronne.

MARK BIRLEY Restaurateur and businessman. Owner of London's famous Annabel's, Harry's Bar and Mark's Club.

BIJAN Persian-born menswear designer based in America.

PETER BLAKE British artist best known for his Pop Art of the 1960s.

RAYMOND BLANC French chef-owner of the acclaimed Le Manoir aux Quat' Saisons, Oxfordshire, whose most recent book is *Cooking for Friends*.

MARC BOHAN Former design head of Christian Dior, now fashion designer for Hartnell.

JOHN BOWMAN Dublin-based wine writer, author and television presenter.

BARBARA TAYLOR BRADFORD Novelist and journalist whose most recent bestseller is *Remember*.

SEYMOUR BRITCHKY American author of the annual guide *The Restaurants of New York* and the periodical *Seymour Britchky's Restaurant Letter*.

MICHAEL BROADBENT MW Head of Christie's Wine Department. President of the International Wine and Food Society and author of *Wine Tasting* and *The Great Vintage Wine Book*.

JOHN BROOKE-LITTLE CVO, Norroy & Ulster King of Arms British heraldry and genealogy expert and author at the College of Arms in London.

BONNIE BROOKS Toronto-based socialite and fashion expert.

JOAN BURSTEIN Owner and chief buyer of Browns, the directional London fashion store.

SALLY BURTON Writer and television producer/presenter; widow of the late Richard Burton.

GEORGINA CAMPBELL Food writer for the Irish *Sunday Press* and author of *Good Food in Ireland*.

JOAN CAMPBELL Influential food editor of *Vogue Australia*, based in Sydney.

AMANDA DE CADENET Best known as the former presenter of the British pop television programme, *The Word*. Married to John Taylor of Duran Duran.

DAME BARBARA CARTLAND The most famous romantic novelist in the world. She has written over 560 books and sold over 650 million copies, making her the world's bestselling author.

CHAMBERTIN Restaurant critic of *Le Soir* in Brussels, covering Belgium and Luxembourg.

GLYNN CHRISTIAN New Zealand-born television chef and food writer, based in England. His many books include *Edible France* and *The Gourmet's Kitchen*.

VICTORIA COLLISON Senior fashion editor of *Vogue Australia*.

JOAN COLLINS British-born television, stage and film star. International traveller and author.

RICHARD COMPTON-MILLER Author of the insider's guide *Who's Really Who*. Senior feature writer at the *Daily Express* in London.

SIR TERENCE CONRAN Businessman, designer, style-leader, restaurateur and owner of the Conran shop, whose latest project is The Gastrodome in London.

JILLY COOPER Journalist and author of many books including the bestselling novels *Riders*, *Rivals* and *Polo*.

LEO COOPER Publisher specializing in military books; husband of Jilly Cooper.

JUDITH COOK Fashion director of *Vogue Australia* and avid traveller.

CLAUDIA CRAGG Journalist, Tokyo Editor of *Harpers & Queen* and Far East editor of *Courvoisier's Book of the Best*. Her books include *Hunting with the Tigers*, about business in the Asian Pacific.

HENRY CRAWFORD Successful Australian film producer turned hotelier. Now owns Vatulele Island Resort in Fiji.

QUENTIN CREWE British writer, restaurateur and traveller. His books include his recent autobiography *Well, I Forget the Rest*.

QUENTIN CRISP British-born author of *The Naked Civil Servant*, based in New York.

ALAN CROMPTON-BATT Leading food and restaurant consultant, based in London.

RAFFAELLA CURIEL Couturier who dresses many of Milan's most prestigious ladies. Also a passionate antique collector.

TESSA DAHL Daughter of the late Roald Dahl and Patricia Neal, her books include *Babies, Babies, Babies* and *Working for Love*.

DAVID DALE Journalist, broadcaster and author of *The Obsessive Traveller*.

SERGE DANSEREAU Acclaimed chef of Kable's at The Regent Hotel, Sydney.

ELIZABETH DAVID The late and highly respected journalist and author whose many inspiring and influential cookery books include *French Provincial Cooking*.

GREG DANIEL Dynamic head of Australia's most influential advertising agency, Clemengers.

LON DIAMOND Los Angeles-based television and film producer.

DOMIX London-based rave DJ.

VICTOR EDELSTEIN Fashion couturier working in London.

ROBERT ELMS British-based style writer and journalist who contributes to Channel 4's *Travelog*. His most recent book is *Spain – A Portrait after the General*.

ROLAND ESCAIG French food expert and journalist based in Paris. Publishes the magazine *National 7* and works both behind and in front of the camera on Channel 2.

MEREDITH ETHERINGTON-SMITH British-based international journalist and author of a forthcoming biography of Salvador Dalí.

JOE EULA World-class fashion illustrator who contributes to French and Italian *Harper's Bazaar*, based in Italy. Co-owned the Greene-Eula studio in partnership with Marilyn Monroe.

DOUGLAS FAIRBANKS JR Legendary Hollywood actor, who has appeared in over 75 films. Also a film, TV and theatre producer, knight, writer and businessman.

SUE FAIRLIE-CUNINGHAME Well-known Australian food and wine expert and the managing editor of *Vogue Entertaining*.

SERENA FASS British founder of the travel company, Serenissima, she now arranges private cultural tours for groups of clients.

CARLA FENDI Daughter of Adele Fendi who founded the famous fur and fashion empire. With her sisters,

she works in the Rome-based family business.

MARCHESA FIAMMA DI SAN GIULIANO FERRAGAMO Eldest child of the renowned Italian shoe designer Salvatore Ferragamo, she follows in her father's footsteps as head of shoe production, based in Florence.

DUGGIE FIELDS Artist whose work has evoked controversy and cult admiration. He lives in London and is an avid nightclubber.

MATTHEW FORT Food and wine editor of *The Guardian*.

CLARE FRANCIS Famous as a skilled yachtswoman – she crossed the Atlantic single-handed and sailed around the world – she is now a bestselling author.

MARCHESA BONA FRESCOBALDI Italian aristocrat whose Tuscany estates yield some of Italy's best wines.

SIR CLEMENT FREUD Writer, broadcaster, ex-restaurateur and Member of Parliament 1972–87.

CATHERINE GAYNOR Editor-in-chief of *Elle Decoration*, Hong Kong. Hong Kong editor of *Courvoisier's Book of the Best*.

DAVID GLEAVE MW A director of the London wine merchant Winecellars and an authority on Italian wine.

MICHAEL GEBICKI Sydney-based travel writer who contributes to *Gourmet Traveller* among other publications.

DAVID GIBBONS General manager of the Drake Swissotel Boston.

VALERIE GIBSON Fashion editor of Canada's *Toronto Sun*.

JOHN GOLD British co-founder and host of Tramp nightclub in London.

HARVEY GOLDSMITH Top music promoter whose clients have included Madonna, the Rolling Stones and Pavarotti.

DAVID GOWER Former England cricket captain, player for Hampshire and bon viveur.

LORD GOWRIE Chairman of Sotheby's auctioneers in London and former Minister for the Arts.

SOPHIE GRIGSON Cookery columnist for the *Evening Standard* and writer for major magazines. Her books include *Food for Friends* and *Ingredients*.

LOYD GROSSMAN American-born restaurant critic, design expert and television broadcaster. Host of BBC's *Masterchef*.

ROBIN HANBURY-TENISON Traveller and writer whose books include *A Ride Along the Great Wall*, *Worlds Apart* and the recent *The Pilgrimage to Santiago*.

ANTHONY HANSON MW Wine expert and a director of Haynes Hanson & Clark wine merchants. Author of *Burgundy*.

BRUCE HARING Los Angeles-based New Yorker who is the music editor of *Daily Variety*.

MARGARET HARVEY MW New Zealand wine expert, she runs Fine Wines of New Zealand in London and is the first New Zealand woman to gain the title Master of Wine.

DOUGLAS HAYWARD Celebrated London-based tailor whose clients include Ralph Lauren, Roger Moore and Michael Caine.

MARCELLA HAZAN Italian food expert. Based in Venice, she has a cookery school in Bologna and a home in New York. Her books include the *Classic Italian Cookbook* and *Marcella's Kitchen*.

MARIE HELVIN American top model, originally from Hawaii, now based in London. She has written on fashion and beauty, is a television presenter and actress and has her own fashion label.

LYN HEMMERDINGER Los Angeles-based film and theatre writer and producer whose many involvements include the founding and funding of the Museum of Contemporary Art.

ANOUSKA HEMPEL Australian-born actress-turned-fashion designer and hotelier, she designs clothes for royalty and owns Blakes hotel in London.

CHARLES HEIDSIECK Great-, great-, great-grandson of the original "Champagne Charlie". He is currently working on the launch of a new scent by Oscar de la Renta.

PAUL HENDERSON Hotelier who runs the renowned Gidleigh Park hotel in Devon.

JEAN-MICHEL HENRY The leading hairdresser at Carita, the No 1 salon in Paris.

DON HEWITSON New Zealand-born wine expert and writer who owns several top London wine bars. His books include *Enjoying Wine* and *The Glory of Champagne*.

SANDRA HIRSH Top fashion stylist and woman about town, based in Melbourne.

TERRY HOLMES Vice-president and managing director of Cunard Hotels, based at the Ritz in London.

KEN HOM American cookery expert and food consultant with bases in California and Hong Kong. Bestselling books include *Ken Hom's Chinese Cookery* and *Ken Hom's East Meets West*.

CAROLINE HUNT Based in Texas, she is the head of the Rosewood Corporation which runs some of America's most exclusive hotels and the Lanesborough in London.

DAVINA JACKSON Architecture editor for Australia's *Vogue Living*.

MADHUR JAFFREY Actress and leading Indian cookery writer based in New York.

TAMA JANOWITZ New York-based author of the bestselling *Slaves of New York*. Her other books include *American Dad* and the most recent, *The Male Cross-Dresser Support Group*.

JEAN-MICHEL JAUDEL International businessman and art collector based in Paris.

IAIN JOHNSTONE British film critic for *The Sunday Times*, author of *Cannes* and *Wimbledon 2000*.

STEPHEN JONES British milliner who has created collections for fashion designers such as Claude

Montana. He has also designed a cosmetic range for Shiseido in Japan.

BARBARA KAFKA American food expert and author. President of her own New York-based food consultancy, she travels extensively.

KAREN KAIN Prima Ballerina of the National Ballet Company of Canada based in Toronto.

JENNY KEE Australian fashion designer who specializes in fabrics and knitwear.

ANGELA KENNEDY London-based fashion expert.

MARGARET KEMP Paris-based British freelance journalist. She has travelled widely in India, America and Australasia and is currently working on a book of profiles, *The Last Fantasy*.

BETTY KENWARD Former social editor of *Harpers & Queen* (writer of Jennifer's Diary for over 45 years), she is currently writing her autobiography.

DAN KOMAR Owner of the world's largest collection of Swatches, author of *A Guide to Swatch Watches* and world traveller in search of rare Swatches.

IRVING SMITH KOGAN 'Smitty' Kogan is director of the Champagne News and Information Bureau, based in New York.

JUDITH KRANTZ American novelist and francophile. Her many bestsellers include *I'll Take Manhattan* and *Dazzle*.

SUSAN KUROSAWA Travel editor of the national daily *The Australian*.

ELISABETH LAMBERT ORTIZ London-born food writer of award-winning cookery books such as *The Book of Latin American Cooking* and *The Food of Spain and Portugal – The Complete Iberian Cuisine*.

COLIN LANCELEY Leading Australian contemporary artist.

ELEANOR LAMBERT Head of her own top fashion PR company based in New York, she initiated the Best Dressed lists.

KENNETH J LANE American jewellery designer whose many illustrious clients include Barbara Bush. He has shops throughout America and in London and Paris.

MARQUIS DE LASTOURS Holder of a French title that was created in the 11C. Member of the prestigious Order of the Cincinatti and man about town.

ALEXANDRE LAZAREFF Food advisor to the French Minister for Culture, Jack Lang. Author of *Paris Rendez-Vous* and *Guide to Other European Cities*. Food critic for *Le Figaro*.

ROBIN LEACH Co-creator and presenter of *Lifestyles of the Rich and Famous* in the USA. His books include *Lifestyles of the Rich and Famous* and *Entertaining with the Rich and Famous*.

LIS LEIGH London-based journalist, food writer and author. *Greed*, her first novel, gives the low-down on haute cuisine.

PRUE LEITH London-based food expert, author and businesswoman. She runs the prestigious Leith's Cookery School of Food and Wine, Leith's Restaurant and the Leith's Good Food caterers.

DOTTORESSA ROSA MARIA LETTS Chairman of the *Accademia Italiana delle Arti e delle Arti Applicate* in London and the Italian government's advisor on visual art and design.

MAUREEN LIPMAN British stage and television actress, comedienne and bestselling author and columnist.

ALASTAIR LITTLE Top British chef whose namesake restaurant is one of London's most fashionable.

ANDREW LLOYD WEBBER Composer of such box-office blockbuster musicals as *Evita, Cats, The Phantom of the Opera* and *Joseph and the Amazing Technicolour Dreamcoat*. Recently knighted.

JULIAN LLOYD WEBBER Acclaimed cellist who has played with all the major British orchestras, and tours worldwide.

SAUL LOCKHART An American writer who has lived in Hong Kong for over 20 years. His books include the *Insight Guide to Hong Kong* and *A Diver's Guide to Asian Waters*.

SIMON LOFTUS Director of top wine merchants Adnams of Southwold and author of their wine list. His books include *Puligny-Montrachet*.

SEAN MACAULAY British journalist and avid restaurant-goer, he is assistant features editor of *The Sun*.

SKYE MACLEOD National PR manager for top Australian department store David Jones and keen party-goer.

STEVEN HENRY MADOFF Executive editor of *Art News* in New York.

STANLEY MARCUS American chairman emeritus of top Dallas store Neiman-Marcus. He is also a lecturer and marketing consultant.

MARK MCCORMACK American-born managing director of the No 1 international sports' management company IMG.

LADY MACDONALD OF MACDONALD Author of many cookery and entertaining books, including *The Harrods Book of Entertaining, Celebrations* and *Claire MacDonald's Scotland*.

JONATHAN MEADES Restaurant critic for *The Times*, novelist and television presenter.

PATRICIA MERK French-born fashion editor of *Elle*, based in Sydney. Married to top fashion photographer Graham Shearer.

GEORGE MELLY Professional blues singer and modern art enthusiast, based in London.

NANDO MIGLIO Top art director and image consultant, based in Milan.

RODNEY MILNES Editor of *Opera Magazine*.

JUSTIN MILLER Dynamic young general manager of Sotheby's auctioneers in Australia.

ALESSANDRO MODENESE Milan-based public relations executive and man about town. Nephew of the man who put Ferre on the fashion map, Beppe Modenese.

LORD MONTAGU OF BEAULIEU He created the National Motor Museum at his seat in Beaulieu. Former chairman of the Historic Buildings and Monuments Commission.

INDRO MONTANELLI Leading Italian journalist and founder of his own Milan-based daily, *Il Giornale*, one of Italy's most prestigious newspapers.

ANTON MOSIMANN Swiss-born chef-owner of the private dining club Mosimann's in London, author and TV presenter.

ANNE-ELISABETH MOUTET Paris bureau chief for *The European* and French editor of *Courvoisier's Book of the Best*.

JILL MULLENS Travel writer and book reviewer who contributes to many Australian publications including *Gourmet Traveller, Elle* and *Vogue Entertaining*.

MICHAEL MUSTO Nightlife columnist for *The Village Voice* in New York.

GRAEME MURPHY Acclaimed director of the Sydney Dance Company.

ROBERT NOAH American food writer living in Paris. He runs Paris en Cuisine, a company specializing in gastronomic tours of France.

BRUCE OLDFIELD Top British fashion designer whose clients include the Princess of Wales.

SIR PETER PARKER Highly successful businessman, best known for his 8 years as chairman of British Rail. He is now chairman of Mitsubishi Electric.

ELISE PASCOE Australian food writer, TV presenter, consultant and lecturer.

MARK PATRICK Former fashion designer and editor-at-large of *Mode Australia*.

BOB PAYTON American restaurateur, writer and broadcaster whose Chicago Pizza Pie Factory is famous across Europe. Currently the proprietor of

Stapleford Park country-house hotel in Leicestershire.

PALOMA PICASSO Daughter of Pablo Picasso, she is an international name in jewellery design, accessories and perfume.

NANCY PILCHER American-born journalist who sets the style for *Vogue Australia* as its editor.

DOMINIQUE PIOT Paris-based member of the Societé des Gastronomes. Co-chairman of Communication et Développement, a market research and PR company.

STEVE PODBORSKI A World Cup downhill ski champion and president of Pod Enterprises. He is a TV celebrity in Canada and author of 2 books on skiing.

MADELEINE POULIN TV personality based in Montreal; co-anchor of *Le Point* for Radio Canada.

GREG DUNCAN POWELL Leading Australian wine expert and writer.

ANDRE PREVIN World-famous conductor based in New York State.

PRINCESS PUCCI SALAMEH Born in Naples and based in Rome, she is married to Sheik Salameh who is Ambassador of Liberia.

GILLES PUDLOWSKI Respected food and travel writer, literary critic and novelist. *Guide Pudlowski de l'Alsace Gourmande* is the latest in his Guide Pudlowski series.

ROBERT RAMSAY Toronto-based communications consultant and feature writer for most of the Canadian press.

FREDERIC RAPHAEL British/American novelist and writer of screenplays, biographies and reviews. Novels include *The Glittering Prizes* and *After the War*, both adapted for TV. He lives in England and the Dordogne in France.

GEOFFREY ROBERTS Pioneer of California wines in Britain, he runs Les Amis du Vin in London.

GAIL ROLFE London-based fashion editor of the *Daily Mail*.

MARY ROSSI Head of her own

pioneering travel agency, Mary Rossi Travel, and Australian representative for Relais & Châteaux.

CLAUDIA ROSSI HUDSON Director of Mary Rossi Travel.

CATHY ROSSI HARRIS Head of her own PR company and a director of Mary Rossi Travel.

HILARY RUBINSTEIN Former literary agent and editor of *The Good Hotel Guide*.

JOHN RUDD Chairman of the world-famous wine merchants, Berry Bros & Rudd.

GIOVANNI SANJUST Rome- and Siena-based man about town, painter, garden architect, sculptor and furniture maker.

ROBERT SANGSTER British racehorse owner and breeder. Son of pools founder Vernon Sangster and director of the family business.

GIOVANNI SANTANGELETTA Influential head concierge of the Principe di Savoia in Milan. Known as the man who can solve any problem and find anything.

MIWAKO SATO Senior editor of the glossy magazine *Kateigaho*, based in Tokyo.

DONALD L SAUNDERS Boston-based property developer and hotelier, married to Liv Ullman.

LEO SCHOFIELD Australia's best-known public stomach, a PR and advertising expert, food and travel writer. He edits *The Sydney Morning Herald Good Food Guide*.

SEBASTIAN SCOTT Former New York and European correspondent for the BBC programme *Eyewitness*, he is now editor of Channel 4's flagship youth programme *The Word*.

ROSEMARY SEXTON Toronto-based socialite and social columnist for *The Globe & Mail* in Canada.

BRIAN SEWELL Art critic for the *Evening Standard*.

GILES SHEPARD Managing director of the Savoy Group of hotels in

London, and world traveller.

NED SHERRIN Film, theatre and TV producer, director and writer. Host of BBC Radio 4's *Loose Ends* and author of *Ned Sherrin's Theatrical Anecdotes*.

DAVID SHILLING A British milliner, he also designs clothes, fabric and china.

MARTIN SKAN Proprietor of the celebrated Chewton Glen in Hampshire.

YAN-KIT SO Hong Kong-born food writer whose bestselling cookery books include *Yan-Kit's Classic Chinese Cook Book* and the most recent, *Yan-Kit So's Classic Food of China*.

STEVEN SPURRIER British wine expert. Founder of L'Académie du Vin, Paris's first wine school, his books include the academy's *Wine Course* and *French Country Wines*.

WILLIAM STADIEM Los Angeles-based writer. Former Hollywood columnist for Andy Warhol's *Interview* magazine; author of *Too Rich (The High Life and Tragic Death of King Farouk)* and *Marilyn Monroe Confidential*.

DANIEL STOFFMAN Canadian writer, ex-*Toronto Star* and *Vancouver Sun*, now working on a variety of national magazines.

SHARYN STORRIER-LYNEHAM Sydney-based editor of *Vogue Entertaining*.

SERENA SUTCLIFFE MW International wine consultant and head of Sotheby's wine department. Her books include *The Wine Drinkers' Handbook, The Pocket Guide to the Wines of Burgundy* and *A Celebration of Champagne*. She is a Chevalier dans l'Ordre des Arts et des Lettres.

EDWARD THORPE Ballet critic for the *Evening Standard*.

CH'NG POH TIONG Lawyer, wine consultant and journalist, he publishes *The Wine Review* and lives in Singapore. Singapore editor of *Courvoisier's Book of the Best*.

DAN TOPOLSKI British journalist,

former international rower and Olympic coach. Son of the late Feliks Topolski, the Polish artist, he has travelled extensively and written books on his expeditions.

JOHN TOVEY Chef-owner of top English country-house hotel Miller Howe in Cumbria. He makes frequent TV and radio appearances and his books include *The Miller Howe Cookbook* and *John Tovey's Country Weekends*.

JEREMIAH TOWER Top American chef and pioneer of Californian cuisine. Brought up in Europe, his acclaimed restaurants include *Stars* in San Francisco.

CASEY TOLAR London head of The Fashion Group and international fashion consultant.

SIR PETER USTINOV Multi-talented international actor, author, traveller, director and producer, star of countless films and plays. He lives in Switzerland and Paris.

ED VICTOR American literary super-agent who divides his time between London, New York and LA.

NICHOLAS VILLIERS British-based international banker who travels constantly and has lived in America and Switzerland.

COUNT GIOVANNI VOLPI Italy's most eligible bachelor. Based in his family palazzo on the Grand Canal in Venice and a pillar of the international social scene.

WARWICK VYNER Top Australian travel consultant. Based in Sydney, he is a director of Travellers.

STANLEY WEISER Los Angeles-based script-writer and producer. Writing credits include *Wall Street*; he is currently co-producing *A Hole in the World* with Oliver Stone.

SANDY WEYLAND A long-time resident of Florence, she has travelled extensively in Italy. She is administrative director of Studio Arts Centers International, which runs art study programmes.

MARCO PIERRE WHITE Acclaimed chef-owner of Harvey's restaurant in London.

LESLEY WILD Publisher of *Vogue Australia*, based in Sydney.

SIMON WILLIAMS British stage and screen actor famous for his role in the long-running *Upstairs, Downstairs*.

VIC WILLIAMS New Zealand wine and food writer and broadcaster. His TV programmes include *Weekend* and *Summer Cooking with Vic Williams* and books include *The Penguin Good New Zealand Wine Guide*. New Zealand editor of *Courvoisier's Book of the Best*.

FAITH WILLINGER Freelance journalist based in Italy. Her books include *Eating in Italy*.

CAROL WRIGHT British journalist specializing in travel. Most recent book is *A Taste of the Ritz*.

ACKNOWLEDGEMENTS

Lord Lichfield, Sue Carpenter and the publishers would especially like to thank the following people for their invaluable help in compiling this book:

Joanna Bailey, Karla Bonoff, Ivar Braastad, Bartholomew Broadbent, Kathy Dignan, Daniel de Villeneuve, Linsay Firman, Fred and Kathie Gill, Brenda Glover, Stephen Harthog, Ian Jesnick, Roger Jupe, Sarah Lance, Carolyn Lockhart, Julia McGrath, Harry O'Neill, Deirdre Pierce, George Sitwell, Tim Tweedie.

AMERICA

BOSTON

— *Art and museums* —

BOSTON INSTITUTE OF CONTEMPORARY ART, 955 Boylston St, MA 02115 ☎ (617) 266 5152
Versatile space for contemporary arts both static and dynamic: new painting, sculpture, video, music, dance, photography, film and performance art. SUE AVERY BROWN rates it most highly.

♠ ISABELLA STEWART GARDNER MUSEUM, 2 Palace Rd, MA 02115 ☎ (617) 566 1401
Replica 15C Venetian palazzo designed around Mrs Gardner's eclectic collection and built around a gloriously pretty courtyard. Over 2,000 objects, from Italian Renaissance and 17C Dutch and Flemish paintings (Rembrandt, Van Dyck) to tapestries and sculptures as well as the odd Sargent and Whistler (Mrs Gardner's generous friends). More recent admirers include BRIAN SEWELL, LOYD GROSSMAN, LORD GOWRIE and TESSA DAHL. "*Its Sunday classical concert series in the grounds is an ongoing favourite of Bostonians*" – SUE AVERY BROWN.

♠ MUSEUM OF FINE ARTS, 465 Huntington Ave, MA 02115 ☎ (617) 267 9300
Boston's finest gallery with an authoritative collection of Asian art and artefacts (the largest number under one roof), French Impressionists (the most Monets outside Paris), a comprehensive display of contemporary American painting and decorative arts. The new Nubian Gallery traces the history of the neglected black pharaohs. Lively exhibitions.

— *Ballet* —

BOSTON BALLET, 19 Clarendon St, MA 02116 ☎ (617) 695 6950
Innovative and diverse. The fourth largest ballet company in America. Under artistic director Bruce Marks the rep shows classic story ballets such as *The Nutcracker* alongside the most contemporary of contemporary – Mark Morris's *Mort Subite* and avant-garde works. Home-grown talent is spiced up with international dancers, choreographers and designers. "*The ballet is superb and becoming one of the best in the country – there's a tremendous emphasis on bringing children into the company through the school, located in a $12 million reconstructed building*" – DONALD L SAUNDERS.

— *Bars and cafés* —

BULL & FINCH/CHEERS, 84 Beacon St, MA 02116 ☎ (617) 227 9600
Where everybody might not know your name, but you're always glad you came. Set on Beacon Hill, overlooking the public gardens, this American bar with burgers and sandwiches is "*so popular you can't get in*" – DONALD L SAUNDERS.

— *Clubs* —

AVENUE C, 120 Boylston St, MA 02116 ☎ (617) 423 3832
In Boston's nightclub quarter, this NY loft-style space is the fun one. College yuppies-in-training and all-purpose groovers mingle to a progressive dance beat.

VENUS DE MILO, 11 Lansdowne St, MA 02215 ☎ (617) 421 9595
Armlessly eccentric fusion of 60s day-glo psychedelia and brothelesque baroque. The serious dance-crowd changes with the nights: Wed is gay hip-hop, Thurs an alternative, progressive rave, Fri hip-hop and deep house, Sat techno-industrial funk.

ZANZIBAR, 1 Boylston Place, MA 02116 ☎ (617) 451 1955
Upmarket tropicana: all is palm and rattan and faux-marble. Besuited thirtysomethings get down to Top 40-style music. Next-door's **Crescent Club** is the place for billiards, more serious drinks and private functions.

— *Hotels* —

THE BOSTON HARBOR HOTEL, 70 Rowes Wharf, MA 02110 ☎ (617) 439 7000
For a room with a view, it can't be bettered. Newish luxy hotel with instant establishment appeal – antique maps in the lobby, generic oil portraits, mahogany repro furniture. "*I really rate it, the staff are as good as I've seen anywhere*" – BOB PAYTON.

THE CHARLES HOTEL, 1 Bennett St, Cambridge, MA 02138 ☎ (617) 864 1200
Low-key comforts of Shakeresque furniture, patchwork quilts and bowls of red apples at reception belie the high-tech of **Le Pli** health spa and sophisticated cooking of the highly rated **Rarities**. **Regatta Bar** "*offers an ongoing menu of top-flight jazz performers in a spacious and elegant setting with a sound system that can't be beat*" – SUE AVERY BROWN.

♠ RITZ-CARLTON, 15 Arlington St, MA 02117 ☎ (617) 536 5700
Where the heads of state rest their heads. Tight security, high-priority service (staff:guest ratio is the top in town) and the old-fashioned charm of French provincial furnishings have attracted the

Prince of Wales, the Kennedys, Katharine Hepburn and a gaggle of Euroroyals. *"It's got that Brahmin elegance and a perfect Back Bay location"* – SUE AVERY BROWN. The **Dining Room** is an institution – discreet, elegant and just slightly unadventurous in accordance with its clientele.

——— *Music* ———

🐟 BOSTON SYMPHONY ORCHESTRA, Symphony Hall, 301 Massachusetts Ave, MA 02115
☎ (617) 266 1492
This world-renowned orchestra doesn't rest on its laurels. Forward-thinking music director Seiji Ozawa maintains a classical repertoire as well as commissioning works from contemporary composers. The Boston Pops (May to mid-July) and summer at Tanglewood are much-loved institutions. *"A wonderful treat with conductor John Williams, who is increasingly known for his Oscar-winning and nominated film scores – Raiders of the Lost Ark, Star Wars, etc"* – SUE AVERY BROWN. ANDRE PREVIN is a fan of Symphony Hall itself.

HANDEL & HAYDN SOCIETY, 300 Massachusetts Ave, MA 02115
☎ (617) 266 3605
Founded in 1815, the oldest continuously active performing music society in the country. Under famed artistic director Christopher Hogwood the orchestra and choir perform a historically informed repertoire of baroque and classical music (expanding from Messrs H & H to Mozart, Bach, Gesualdo and Monteverdi).

🐟 TANGLEWOOD MUSIC FESTIVAL, Tanglewood, Lenox, MA 01240 ☎ (617) 266 1492; July/Aug ☎ (413) 637 1600
The BSO's summer abode, where al fresco aficionados listen to classics from Mozart through to Copland and Knussen. Frequent guest artists include James Galway, John Williams, Jessye Norman and Midori; performances by high-flying students give a preview of the next generation's biggies.

——— *Restaurants* ———

See also Hotels.

AUJOURD'HUI, Four Seasons Hotel, 200 Boylston St, MA 02116 ☎ (617) 338 4400
Understated dining room where power lunchers' plots are muffled by thick plush carpet. Young chef Michael Kornick has an inventive hand with New England produce and far-flung influences: acorn squash and Maine lobster bisque and swordfish sandwich with aioli.

BIBA, 272 Boylston St, MA 02116
☎ (617) 426 5684
Lydia Shire's (ex-Jasper's) cheerful, perma-packed restaurant has established itself as a Boston hot spot. Non-conformist menu (divided into fish, offal, meat, starch, legumes, sweets and specials) encourages grazing on little courses: calves' brains with crisp-fried capers, roasted sugar-cane chicken and garlic sausage and bitter broccoli pizza among them. Adventurous wine list eschews the obvious.

🐟 CAFE BUDAPEST, 90 Exeter St, MA 02116 ☎ (617) 734 3388
If it was ever a café, it's sure hiding it now. *"One of the 10 best restaurants in the US. It is, of course, Hungarian, and very, very good. A beautiful place, it has several dining rooms and cocktail lounges, white silk-covered walls, exquisite tables and chairs – probably the most expensively furnished restaurant I've ever seen. My favourite dishes are chicken paprika and, of course, Hungarian beef goulash"* – DONALD L SAUNDERS. SUE AVERY BROWN favours the cold celery soup and stroganoff, but ventures further with her superlatives: *"One of the best restaurants in the world."*

> **❝ *I've found the best beach at Ipswich, north of Boston: Crane Beach – it's a couple of miles long and gorgeous. Finding an empty beach in America is not easy* ❞**
>
> 🐟 DAVID GIBBONS

THE CAPITAL GRILL, 359 Newbury St, MA 01115 ☎ (617) 262 8900
A New American restaurant of the old school – and making ground where the faddish have failed. Best for huge (24oz) slabs of meat, dry-aged on the premises. *"A steakhouse with everything, including lobster; one of the best in Boston"* – DONALD L SAUNDERS.

🐟 JASPER'S, 240 Commercial St, MA 02109 ☎ (617) 523 1126
Restrainedly modern dining room houses the city's finest restaurant. With missionary zeal, Jasper White has reworked trad New England dishes into contemporary classics. There's little recognizably puritan about pan-roasted lobster with chervil and chives or a salad of grilled duck with spiced pecans, but no one's complaining.

LEGAL SEA FOODS, 35 Columbus Ave, MA 02116 ☎ (617) 426 4444
The truth of the catch phrase 'if it isn't fresh, it isn't legal' is borne out by the constant queues of patient piscophiles outside the Boston Park Plaza Hotel. Out of the sea and into the sauté pan. *"Stupendous"* cries DONALD L SAUNDERS. Next-door's café is more casual.

**LOCKE OBER, 3 Winter Place, MA 02101
☎ (617) 542 1340**
Trad, slightly stuffy Bostonian where the food is
as rich as the clientele. Solid mahogany panelling is a suitable foil for the cream-lashed lobster savanna. "*A bastion of the Brahmin set.
The food is wonderful and the lush, Victorian
setting transports one to another era*" – SUE
AVERY BROWN. Behind the restaurant,
Yvonne's nightclub (known to the cognoscenti
as the Harvard Club) is exclusive and masculine
with a library, billiard room and sitting room.
Members only.

**SEASONS, Bostonian Hotel, 1 Faneuil
Hall, MA 02101 ☎ (617) 523 4119**
One of Boston's best, this skyline restaurant has
been the breeding ground for the city's crop of
top chefs. Outstanding seasonal (of course) New
American menu: swordfish with chickpeas,
aubergine and taramasalata, and caraway venison with wood mushrooms suggest the style.

**798 MAIN, 798 Main St, Cambridge, MA
02139 ☎ (617) 492 9500**
Fun bistro with more emphasis on food than formality. Chef-owner Bruce Frankel has winning
ways with local produce and a good eye for
creating a well-balanced wine list. A permanent
feature of his creative, modern menu is the Hub-
bardstan chèvre with grilled flat-bread – you
might follow it with sautéed scallops with olive
butter sauce or grilled venison with roasted
garnet yams.

———— *Shopping* ————

The best shopping areas for high fashion and hip
boutiques are **Newbury St, Boylston St** in
the Back Bay, ye olde **Beacon Hill** (at the bottom, on **Charles St**); and **Harvard Square**
and **Brattle St** in Cambridge. The indoor **Copley Place Mall** houses top-drawer Euro and
US shops: "*A major success, any name you
think of is there*" – DONALD L SAUNDERS.

**ALAN BILZARIAN, 34 Newbury St, MA
02116 ☎ (617) 536 1001**
A converted town house (one floor for his, one
for hers), with some of the most exciting fashion
in town. Husband and wife team turn their
hands to designing the classics – silk and cashmere sweaters, blazers and trousers – that
underpin their stock of innovators: Hamnett,
Gaultier, Miyake, Yamamoto, etc. "*A very smart
store with a great combination of things*" – DUG-
GIE FIELDS.

**SARA FREDERICKS, Copley Place, MA
02116 ☎ (617) 536 8766**
Couturiers to Cabots and Lowells (and the rest
of the Boston Brahmins). Stronger on attentive,
old-fashioned service (with an extensive in-
house alteration team) than innovation, it carries the designs of the top of the US and Euro

---

Saunders Saunters
♟
DONALD L SAUNDERS waves his umbrella
and shows you where to strut forth in
Boston. "*Follow the red bricks in the side-
walk from Back Bay to Quincy Market,
absolutely a must – you get a tour without
the guide. Quincy Market is a major complex of around 60 restaurants and shops,
also known as Faneuil Hall marketplace.
Also not to be missed are the Boston Public Gardens across from the Ritz-Carlton,
where they have boats in spring and summer and ice skating on the pond in the
winter. It's the most beautiful public garden, supported by private contributions.*"

establishment: Blass, Lagerfeld, Valentino, La
Croix, de la Renta, Mackay, Scaasi and Ungaro.

———— *Theatre* ————

**AMERICAN REPERTORY THEATRE,
Loeb Drama Center, 64 Brattle St,
Cambridge, MA 02138 ☎ (617) 547 8300**
Go-ahead company with a base in the classics
and an eye to the future. Many a Broadway hit
had its birth here.

CHICAGO

———— *Art and museums* ————

♟ **THE ART INSTITUTE OF CHICAGO,
Michigan Ave at Adams St, IL 60603
☎ (312) 443 3600**
Among America's best national collections with
nearly 200,000 works. "*It is a favourite, a very,
very good collection*" – JEAN-MICHEL JAUDEL.
Pre-Renaissance to Post-Impressionist works.
"*The best collection of Impressionist paintings
in the world*" – BOB PAYTON. Oriental and classical pieces, photographs, architectural drawings,
textiles, European decorative arts and sculpture. 17C–19C American arts and 20C American
painting and sculpture are housed in the Rice
Building, a $23 million extension. Recently reno-
vated Asian Galleries are worth a squint.

———— *Bars and cafés* ————

**POPS FOR CHAMPAGNE, 2934 N
Sheffield St, IL 60657 ☎ (312) 472 1000**
Champagne bar off the beaten track grabs

Chicago's after-dinner crowd, including IRVING SMITH KOGAN – "*More than 100 champagnes are offered by the glass and by the bottle, along with unusual finger foods and a live jazz band. On weekends it is packed to the eaves.*" Jeans and cowboy boots mosey in alongside Karans and Ferragamos – the bubbles do the trick whatever you're wearin'.

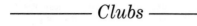

Clubs

CAIRO, 720 N Wells St, IL 60610
☎ (312) 266 6620
Mummy's boys (and girls) wind up on 3 floors of rockin' sound – live bands on one and DJs on the other two. Hieroglyphics and pyramids feature on the walls. It gets the nod from MICHAEL MUSTO.

KABOOM CLUB, 747 N Green, IL 60622
☎ (312) 243 8600
This one's Ka-booming. 4 rooms on 3 floors provide an outsize dance area, cabaret and live jazz, pool tables and a VIP lounge. The one celebs go to – Bill Murray, Robert De Niro, James Woods. "*A big dance club, very good*" – MICHAEL MUSTO.

KINGSTON MINES, 2548 N Halsted, IL 60631 ☎ (312) 477 4646
Seamy blues in the kickin' Chicago style. Aficionados and ravers scramble for places to hear serious vocal and 4-string chords from Chuck Rogers, Sugar Blue, the Casey Jones Band, Shirley King . . . 2 acts nightly.

LEGEND'S, 754 S Wabash St, IL 60611
☎ (312) 427 0333
Buddy Guy – one of the very greatest Chicago blues guitarists – is a partner, which means he plays here regularly. If that doesn't entice you in, the good southern cooking might.

Hotels

🍷 THE DRAKE, 140 E Walton Place, IL 60611 ☎ (312) 787 2200
Still bowling them over – high-flying execs follow the British royal lead and lay down their heads in this Renaissance-style palace. "*My favourite hotel in Chicago, it's a terrific hotel, huge but it feels like a town house*" – BOB PAYTON. Spectacular views over the lake.

FOUR SEASONS, 120 E Delaware Place, IL 60611 ☎ (312) 280 8800
Seventh heaven for high flyers – the lobby takes up the 7th floor of a striking Chicago skyscraper and the 18C English-style bedrooms hold floors 30 to 46 in suspended animation and regulars in awe. Understandably terrific city and lake views and good health facilities too.

LE MERIDIEN, 21 E Bellevue Place, IL 60611 ☎ (312) 266 2100
High chic (granite, glass, metal, Mapplethorpe

photos), high tech (CDs and videos in the rooms) and high profile (John Malkovich, Harrison Ford check in). So does BOB PAYTON: "*I like it very much, it's avant-garde, modern, for the more sophisticated, European clientele.*" Taste budding chef Remy Brigaudin's celebrated cooking at **Brasserie Bellevue**.

> # Music Box
>
> Amid the clash and clang and clank and clamour of this jostling world we live in, LORD GOWRIE finds solace in the purer sounds lilting forth from first-class hifi equipment. "*Painkillers and music in your home are among the compensations of our violent century. Audiophiles rejoice in the genius of Mr Sugano, whose Koetsu needle can cost as much as $5,000 but is the Stradivarius of gramophone styli. Linn turntables; Quad, Apogee, Sonus Faber or Wilson Watt loudspeakers; Naim or Meridian compact disc players; Jadis, Audio Research or Music Fidelity amplifiers all have the same clout in their respective fields. A good gramophone should cost as much as a good car. The pleasure is intense; the musical journey unending.*"

MAYFAIR REGENT, 181 E Lake Shore Drive, IL 60611 ☎ (312) 787 8500
"*The most European of Chicago's hotels*" in BOB PAYTON's opinion, though this peaceful lake-fronter borrows, US-style, from all over with Chinese murals, classical friezes, Queen Anne pieces and French haute cuisine in the penthouse restaurant, **Le Ciel Bleu**.

RITZ-CARLTON, 160 E Pearson St at Water Tower Place, IL 60611
☎ (312) 266 1000
Confusingly one of the Four Seasons chain, this splendid hotel takes up floors 10 to 31 of the 74-storey Water Tower Place shop/restaurant/theatre complex. The private **Carlton Club** has health spa, indoor pool, sun terrace and great food, as does the regular **Dining Room**.

Music

CHICAGO OPERA THEATER, 20 E Jackson Blvd, IL 60604 ☎ (312) 663 0555
Intimate opera – small productions in small spaces. Specializes in neglected classics such as Rossini's *Count Ory* and works of living composers – Menotti's *The Medium*, with a strong

emphasis on Americans. Visually exciting shows, sung in English. After 18 years, singers, designers, artists are still hired production by production.

🏃 **CHICAGO SYMPHONY ORCHESTRA, Orchestra Hall, 220 S Michigan Ave, IL 60604 ☎ (312) 435 6666**
Over 100 years old, this orchestra is one of the best in the States, under the new directorship of Henry Fogel.

🏃 **LYRIC OPERA OF CHICAGO, 20 N Wacker Drive, IL 60606 ☎ (312) 332 2244**
Consistently heralded as America's best opera company. From the most contemporary works to standards such as *Madam Butterfly* and *The Marriage of Figaro*. Under artistic director Bruno Bartoletti's reign, seasons sell out before the curtain goes up. Strong commitment to 20C opera in a 10-year programme, Toward 21st. Some 8 operas in each Sept-Feb season.

—————— *Restaurants* ——————

See also Hotels.

AMBRIA, 2300 N Lincoln Park W, IL 60614 ☎ (312) 472 5959
Art Nouveau nouvellerie with stylish Spanish fare from the adventurous Gabio Sotelino. Lots of dark wood, plenty of dark suits, upmarket fish and deep sea food.

CHARLIE TROTTER'S, 816 W Armitage St, IL 60614 ☎ (312) 248 6228
Charlie Trotter is one of Chicago's top chefs, his American/French/Asian experiments keep gastrofolk on the edge of their seats.

THE EVEREST ROOM, 40th Fl, 440 S La Salle, IL 60605 ☎ (312) 663 8920
Rarefied lunching and dining on the 40th floor of a financial district skyrise – Jean Joho's marvellous Alsace-accented cuisine makes this the best French restaurant in town.

🏃 **THE FRONTERA GRILL, 445 N Clark St, IL 60610 ☎ (312) 661 1434**
Chef Rick Baylis *"does wonderful Mexican food, really superb"* – BARBARA KAFKA. Try his turkey breast in red mole sauce, or carne asada. **Topo Lobampo**, next door, is a posher nosher with upscale dishes from the same team.

MORTON'S, 1050 North State St, IL 60610 ☎ (312) 266 4820
Beefeaters dream about the mega-steaks here, some punters rate it the best in the States (though New Yorkers wouldn't). BOB PAYTON avoids the issue: *"The best in town."*

—————— *Shopping* ——————

The big boys line up on **Michigan Avenue's** Magnificent Mile – Bloomingdale's, Lord & Taylor, I Magnin and Hammacher Schlemmer; the best shopping complex is the 74-floor **Watertower Place**, but the highest fashion is on **Oak St** – where you'll find Armani, Rykiel, et al.

MARSHALL FIELD, 111 N State St, IL 60602 ☎ (312) 781 5000
Ahead of the field in department stores. US bests (Lauren, Karan, Klein) rack up with top Euros (Lacroix, Rykiel, Dior). Stacks of china, crystal, furniture and food shops too. Try Field's own famous chocolate Frangos – mint, raspberry or peanut butter.

STANLEY KORSHAK, 940 N Michigan Ave, IL 60611 ☎ (312) 280 0520
US design stars crammed into this former couture house include de la Renta, Blass, Klein and Kors. Slip into Krizia or Steiger shoes; try on Cerruti, Genny and Basile.

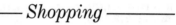 **Buzzz Street eating:** IRVING SMITH KOGAN dives into **Montana Street Café**, 2464 N Lincoln St ☎ (312) 281 2407, for *"gourmet American, it is quite different, with a very interesting presentation"* 🏃 . . . . . . Tokyo, Illinois: Taste the Japanese experience here in the USA at the **Hotel Nikko**, 320 N Dearborn St ☎ (312) 744 1900, where you can sleep on tatami mats and walk in a trad Japanese garden, or be chicly Chicagoan in contemporary Western-style rooms 🏃 . . . . . . Reach for the sky: **The 95th**, 875 N Michigan Ave ☎ (312) 987 9596, has to be the loftiest dining experience in town, at the top of Chicago's third-tallest building 🏃 . . . . . . Best bartender: José McClure, who mixes the drinks at **Crickets**, 100 E Chestnut ☎ (312) 280 2100, an elegant town-house restaurant 🏃 . . . . . . Haute dining: **Le Français**, 269 S Milwaukee Ave, Wheeling ☎ (708) 541 7470, is the place for an upscale blow-out 🏃 . . . . . . Pretty as a picture: Feast the body before the eyes at the **Art Institute of Chicago Dining Room** (see Art and museums) . . . . 🏃

ULTIMO, 114 E Oak St, IL 60611
☎ **(312) 787 0906**
Design fiends make a beeline here – for chicly chosen Valentino, Gigli, Ferré, Gaultier, Mugler, Alaïa selections and the best from Japan and the USA. In-house Ermegildo Zegna boutique, Sonia Rykiel at 106 E Oak St and Armani at 113.

DALLAS

—— Art and museums ——

DALLAS MUSEUM OF ART, 1717 N Harwood, TX 75201 ☎ **(214) 922 1200**
Strong collection, including the marvellous re-creation of Emery and Wendy Reves's Mediterranean villa complete with original contents, and good temporary exhibitions. *"A wonderful museum which is noted for 2 things: decorative art and the Reves collection. The most valuable things are the French Impressionists but it is eclectic. Winston Churchill was a good friend of theirs, so there is a nook for all the things that he gave them"* – CAROLINE HUNT. Also excellent collections of African and Pre-Columbian art, and Thomas Church's pricy painting *Iceberg*.

🔱 **KIMBELL ART MUSEUM, 3333 Camp Bowie Blvd, Fort Worth, TX 76107**
☎ **(817) 332 8451**
Louis Kahn's highly acclaimed classically-designed modern museum is a work of art in its own right. Innovative use of natural light and space show off the wealth of the second richest museum in the land (after the Getty). Outstanding works include Caravaggio's The Cardsharps, Picasso's Nude Combing her Hair, Duccio's The Raising of Lazarus, Matisses, Rembrandts, El Grecos, Tintorettos . . . Old Masters galore. Also Chinese paintings, Japanese screens and Southeast Asian sculpture.

—— Bars and cafés ——

SFUZZI, 2504 McKinney Ave, TX 75201
☎ **(214) 871 2606**
Buzzy Italian bistro-bar chain, Dallas-born and rapidly spreading throughout the States. The Frozen Sfuzzi is their signature drink (champagne, peach schnapps, peach nectar plus a secret ingredient). *"Northern Italian cuisine with the best bits of southwestern cuisine, the blue corn, the wood-smoke oven and wonderful décor, faded frescos "* – GLYNN CHRISTIAN.

—— Clubs ——

BILLY BOB'S TEXAS, 2520 Rodeo Plaza, Fort Worth, TX 76106 ☎ **(817) 624 7117**
The world's largest country 'n' western club. Rhinestone cowboys and gals toe-tap to the greats. Rip-roaring rodeo on Fri and Sat.

DALLAS ALLEY, Market at Monger, TX 75202 ☎ **(214) 988 0581**
Bigger than Texas – a 9-nightclub complex in 2 restored buildings in the historic West End district. The grand tour whisks you through **Tilt** – a games room; **Alley Cats** – duelling piano bar; **Alley Oops** – sports bar with TVs and pool; **Take 5** – dance room with live music; **Foggy Bottoms** – R & B, blues, jazz; **Bobby Sox** – 50s and 60s music; **Backstage** – quiet bar; **Plaza Bar** – country 'n' western bar; and the **Boiler Room** – a massive techno-pop disco.

—— Hotels ——

🔱 **HOTEL CRESCENT COURT, 400 Crescent Ct, TX 75201** ☎ **(214) 871 3200**
Part of the Rosewood necklace (far more up-market than a chain) and grand centrepiece of the Crescent Complex, hailed by GLYNN CHRISTIAN: *"The most beautiful modern complex . . . shops, hotel and the best health club I've seen bar none – the most glamorous, the most caring. The lobby of the hotel is the best room just to stand in that I know – lots of space and marble, French-style furniture and big paintings. And beg, borrow or steal an invitation to the Crescent Club dining room so that you can watch the sun go down through the Venetian window over the Dallas skyline."* Those who don't make the Club don't do too badly with the **Beau Nash** for open-kitchen char-grilling or the glass-pavilioned **Conservatory** for seafood.

🔱 **MANSION ON TURTLE CREEK, 2821 Turtle Creek Blvd, TX 75219**
☎ **(214) 559 2100**
Flagship of Caroline Hunt's Rosewood Hotels and still a contender for America's best. Omnipresent service (staff outnumber guests 2:1) lends personality to the 1925 Italian Renaissance-style mansion. *"It's the most genuinely hospitable place I've ever stayed. They actually say 'Welcome home' each time you return and you think 'Mmmm, yes, I am' "* – GLYNN CHRISTIAN (MARY ROSSI and LISA BARNARD find it homely too). He hums with pleasure about **The Restaurant** ☎ (214) 559 2100: *"Dean Fearing is one of the creators of southwestern cuisine and there is great pleasure in eating in the main restaurant, in the wonderfully coffered-ceilinged drawing room of the original house – I call it Spanish Gasp Deco. You wear jacket and tie in a very formal atmosphere, but then there's this wonderful raunchy, upfront, spectacular food – blue corn, red pepper and hot chillis. I love the contrast."*

—— Music ——

🔱 **MORTON H MEYERSON SYMPHONY CENTER, 2301 Flora, TX 75201**
☎ **(214) 954 1700**
Having stretched budgets, deadlines and plan

ners' patience, the modernist home of the Dallas Symphony Orchestra seems to justify the wait. *"You hear of architects building monuments to themselves – I M Pei is generally that way. It is a very fine hall acoustically and a very unusual building . . . a square within a circle, all glass and limestone. The square arch given by Wendy Reves is part of the architectural glory. Very difficult to get a ticket"* – CAROLINE HUNT.

Hunt's Haunts

The woman with Dallas in her palm points the finger at simple pleasures in her city. They may not be Rosewood-owned, but they get the Rosewood stamp of approval from CAROLINE HUNT: *"We have a place called* **Old City Park** ☎ *(214) 421 5141 – a museum of early times with log cabins, barns and root cellars, everything that Dallas used to be.* **Dallas Zoo** ☎ *(214) 670 6825 has been expanded and there is a little tram that takes you around . . . they've re-created a rainforest so all the animals are in their natural environment. We have the wonderful* **Dallas Arboretum** ☎ *(214) 327 8263, which is two estates joined together. One is a Texas-style house, the other an Art Deco house, both with gardens, flowers and fountains."*

——— *Restaurants* ———

See also Hotels.

ACTUELLE, The Crescent, 500 Crescent Court, Suite 165, TX 75201
☎ **(214) 855 0440**
New architectural setting for New American cuisine. Sleekly contemporary with soaring ceilings, glassed-in bar, open kitchen and sophisticated comfort food: braised lamb shanks with basil and tomato and turnip mashed potatoes or steak with red pepper ketchup and polenta fritter. *"Very good food with a French twist"* – CAROLINE HUNT.

CITY CAFE, 5757 W Lovers Lane, TX 75209 ☎ **(214) 351 2233**
Casual, homy restaurant with food you wished you got back home. A weekly-changing menu encompasses the game in season and appeals to such power-players as the Governor, the Mayor, and George Bush Jr. *"Very comfortable. I recommend particularly their hot/cold tomato soup, crab cakes and grilled breast of chicken"* – STANLEY MARCUS.

THE FRENCH ROOM, The Adolphus, 1321 Commerce St, TX 75202
☎ **(214) 742 8200**
Consultant chef Jean Banchet's elegant, modern French menu includes lobster sausage with pistachios and lobster sauce followed by Dover sole with morels in a champagne and crawfish sauce and crème brûlée in flaky pastry with berries.

THE RIVIERA, 7709 Inwood Rd, TX 75209
☎ **(214) 351 0094**
The place for dining *à deux* or *a due*. Franco-Italian fusion under the hands of husband and wife Lori and David. OK, so the chefs aren't from the Med but the atmosphere is homely and the food gutsy: wild mushroom and lobster agnolotti, roasted tomato and crab soup, and veal chops with polenta and gorgonzola.

ROUTH STREET CAFE, 3005 Routh St, TX 75201 ☎ **(214) 871 7161**
A bastion of SW foodism with an ever-changing, ever-inventive menu under Stephen Pyle. Art techo dining room, all peach and grey and stainless steel, and a taste of modern Texas in dishes such as tenderloin of beef with chipotle barbecue, caciotta relleno and an ancho-corn salsa. *"Continues to be one of the star restaurants in Dallas. For those who do not want the full-sized meal and quicker service, the bar proves to be an excellent place to dine"* – STANLEY MARCUS. Its more laid-back child, **Baby Routh**, 2708 Routh St ☎ (214) 871 2345, continues in the same vein, playing to a younger, noisier bunch.

YORK STREET RESTAURANT, 6047 Lewis St, TX 75206 ☎ **(214) 826 0968**
"This is a tiny restaurant with about 10 tables with an intimacy that is not duplicated elsewhere in Dallas. The food is excellent" – STANLEY MARCUS.

——— *Shopping* ———

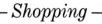

The Crescent remains the most stupendous and exclusive mall, with **The Galleria** hot on its heels for serious spenders. **North Park Center** is *"fabulous – miles and miles of enclosed marble"* – GLYNN CHRISTIAN.

THE GAZEBO, 8300 Preston Rd, TX 75225
☎ **(214) 373 6661**
The Dallas design showcase with all the big names: Karan, Kors, Genny, Ozbek, Lacroix. Staff know regulars' taste and keep an eye on collections for them. Karan and Kors have their own boutiques with regular runway shows.

LADY PRIMROSE'S SHOPPING ENGLISH COUNTRYSIDE, 2200 Cedar Springs, TX 75201 ☎ **(214) 871 8333**
Mirage-like apparition in downtown Dallas – a row of thatched cottages towered over by a Baronial Hall. Best of British bits and pieces, antique furniture and Lady P's real cream tea

with proper scones. Also **Shopping Texas Country Style**, for silver buckles and other handcrafted Texan gear.

THE NATURE COMPANY, 317 North Park Center, TX 75225 ☎ (214) 363 7441
Nature boy GLYNN CHRISTIAN rambles: *"A chain that's spreading all over America and it's more fun than anything I've been into for years. They only sell things to do with nature, from little collections of rocks to the re-creation of Galileo's thermometer which is the most beautiful thing you've ever seen. Every book, every video, every bit of camping gear, everything to do with the enjoyment of the country. I've never been in a shop where there were more things I wanted."*

NEIMAN MARCUS, 1618 Main St, TX 75201 ☎ (214) 741 6911
Forget the racks of designer labels, the shoes, the accessories, the rest of this department store's accoutrements – Neiman Marcus's fame rests squarely on its extraordinary, extravagant Christmas book. Fancy an assorted bag of loose diamonds? Howzabout a set of his and hers ostriches, hot air balloons, Egyptian mummy cases or ermine bathrobes? Buy 'em here but don't expect 'em cheap.

STANLEY KORSHAK, 500 Crescent Court, Suite 100, TX 75201 ☎ (214) 871 3600
Big-label outfitters from top to toe for men and women: Versace, Boss and Armani for him, Lagerfeld, de la Renta, Karan for her. All right, she owns it, but CAROLINE HUNT thinks it's a buzz: *"One of the most exclusive shops in Dallas. It's a specialty store, a very smart shop. The service is excellent, the best."*

HAWAII

— Hotels —

COLONY SURF HOTEL, 2895 Kalakaua Ave, Honolulu, HI 96815 ☎ (808) 923 5751
Under the volcano (the extinct Diamond Head), on Waikiki beach, sits this splendid small hotel. Over-enthusiastic décor in the self-contained rooms, but service is impeccable – you can even leave your 'I only wear it in Hawaii' beach shirt with the staff when you leave – and they'll keep it till your next visit. Best room is the penthouse at adjoining **Colony East Hotel**. Best food on the island at **Michel's** French restaurant: *"Consistently voted most romantic in America"* – MARIE HELVIN.

HALEKULANI, 2199 Kalia Rd, Honolulu, HI 96815 ☎ (808) 923 2311
Highly bred hybrid – a traditional stop-over for bon viveurs, it's now a place for deal-doers to do deals (3 phones per room) and unwind as well, as MARIE HELVIN does. Oceanside pool, myriad beach sports, slabs of marble, yards of dark wood and 2 of Honolulu's top restaurants (one is **La Mer**, for *"expensive but fab French food"* – MARIE H), render its name (Halekulani = 'house befitting heaven') more than an idle boast.

🐚 HOTEL HANA-MAUI, Maui, HI 96713 ☎ (808) 248 8211
A million and one things to do in this resort hotel: hiking, biking, riding, surfing, kayaking, messing around in jeeps . . . . *"One of my favourites. A laid-back resort-cum-ranch hidden away on Maui's little-visited eastern coast.*

🕵 Buzz The best of the rest of US:
Best in the West? *"The* **Excalibar**, *3850 Las Vegas Blvd S, Las Vegas, CA 89109* ☎ *(702) 597 7777, seems like the largest hotel in the world – over 4,000 rooms – and it was wonderful because I lost my car in the car park, it was so big, and missed my plane"* – STEPHEN JONES 🐚 . . . . . . Feast in the East: *"Off the beaten track and absolutely worth the pilgrimage is a restaurant called* **Windows**, *Suite 500, 1801 Robert Fulton Drive, Reston, Virginia* ☎ *(703) 758 2000. It's all estuaries, so he's famous for incredible crab"* – DAVID GIBBONS 🐚 . . . . . . Virginian Virtues 2: **"Nick's Seafood Pavilion**, *Water St, Yorktown* ☎ *(804) 887 5269, is an institution. The fish is fabulous as is the mountain of Greek salad they automatically bring to you"* – LOGAN BENTLEY 🐚 . . . . . . Soothed in the South: *"One of the most beautiful gardens in the world is* **Middleton Gardens**, *Charleston, South Carolina. It has the most wonderful oak trees and azaleas and the shape of the 2 ponds by the Ashley River is wonderful"* – GIOVANNI SANJUST 🐚 . . . . . . Cerebral in the centre: *"The best bookshop in the world is* **The Tattered Cover Bookstore**, *2955 East 1st Ave, Denver* ☎ *(303) 322 7727; there are chairs and coffee, so you can browse and read the morning papers. They have a gift for making you want to go there and you end up carrying 3 or 4 books away"* – JEFFREY ARCHER . . . . 🐚

Wooden sea ranch cottages overlook the surf and feature private spa tubs on wide decks" – SUSAN KUROSAWA. PAUL HENDERSON unwinds there – *"the most relaxing resort hotel"*. The best health and beauty facilities too, in the **Wellness Clinic**.

KAHALA HILTON, 5000 Kahala Ave, Honolulu, HI 96816 ☎ (808) 734 2211
The hotel with its own dolphin lagoon. Cabaret, sport and fab rooms as well are reason enough for MARIE HELVIN to stay.

❝*The beaches are spectacular, the north shore is the best for windsurfing in the world. In my mind Hawaii is paradise – you can have a tropical holiday yet you are in a civilized country* ❞**

STEVE PODBORSKI

MAUNA KEA BEACH HOTEL, 19 Queen Kaahumanu Highway, Kohala Coast, HI 96743 ☎ (808) 882 7552
Coastland resort with volcanic activity – a Trent Jones golf course, 13 tennis courts and fitness centre – all in the spectacular shadow of Mauna Kea, the world's highest volcano. Arty eyes feast on the Rockerfeller collection of art from the Pacific Rim.

MAUNA LANI BAY, Kohala Coast, HI 96743 ☎ (808) 885 6622
Top 5-star. Earthly delights include oceanside golf (the course is built on lava), 10 tennis courts and activities aplenty. Lagoons, pools, emerald grass and the whitest sand.

—— *Restaurants* ——

ROY'S, 6600 Kalanianaole Highway, HI 96825 ☎ (808) 396 7697
Roy Yamaguchi is certainly Hawaii's most celebrated chef; MARIE HELVIN reckons he's the best too: *"Specialities include mesquite-smoked Peking-style duck and candied pecans in ginger sauce – to die for!"* Watch the sun set over the ocean from the simple, elegant dining room.

HOUSTON

—— *Art and museums* ——

THE MENIL COLLECTION, 1511 Branard, TX 77006 ☎ (713) 525 9400
Renzo (Centre Pompidou) Piano's uncharacteristically anonymous grey and white structure does nothing to detract from Dominique de Menil's $150 million private art collection of about 10,000 pieces. Antiquities, Byzantine and Mediterranean art, tribal and modern art, including Picasso, Ernst, Warhol and Magritte.

—— *Ballet* ——

🐾 HOUSTON BALLET FOUNDATION, 1921 W Bell, TX 77019 ☎ (713) 523 6300
One of the best companies in the States, able to flourish thanks to healthy funding; EDWARD THORPE would now put them in his world top 10: *"They've increased their repertoire in the last few years and have developed rather a lot."* Under directorship of Ben Stevenson, choreographer Christopher Bruce and artistic associate Kenneth MacMillan, the repertoire is indeed diverse – all 3 take turns in the driver's seat steering such productions as *Sleeping Beauty, Gloria, Manon* and *Journey*. Young Texan dancers are reared at their own school. Performances at the Wortham.

—— *Hotels* ——

THE LANCASTER, 701 Texas Ave, TX 77002 ☎ (713) 228 9500
Centre stage for businessmen – (4 phones in each room), the small hotel in the theatre district packs in the big oilers for breakfast at the **Lancaster Grille**. Euro-style rooms are swathed in chintz, stacked with repro antiques, and fed with the clearest artesian water; guests are ferried around in the hotel's silver London taxi. TERRY HOLMES is keen.

🐾 RITZ-CARLTON, 1919 Briars Oak Lane, TX 77027 ☎ (713) 840 7600
The former Remington is still the top stop for hot shots – workaholics will even find a business research library. Service is nigh on faultless; there are antiques and objets d'art scattered high and low, and the pastel rooms are big – try to get one on the 2nd floor for sundeck and pool. *"An extremely good hotel. I think Englishmen feel at home there – there's a European stateliness and calm"* – LORD LICHFIELD.

—— *Music* ——

HOUSTON GRAND OPERA, Wortham Theater Center, 510 Preston Ave, TX 77002 ☎ (713) 546 0200
Renowned for commissioning and performing new work, while nurturing American artists and composers. World premieres include Leonard Bernstein's *A Quiet Place*, Carlisle Floyd's *The Passion of Jonathan Wade* and Robert Moran's *Desert of Roses*. General director David Gockley created Opera New World – new musical theatre influenced by diverse Houston cultures. RODNEY MILNES thinks *"they're really rather*

good". The Spring Opera Festival in Hermann Park is a complimentary complement to the regular season.

──────── *Restaurants* ────────

See also Hotels.

CADILLAC BAR, 1802 Shepherd St, TX 77007 ☎ (713) 862 2020
'Check your morals at the door when you come to the Cadillac Bar,' advises the management. Just about anything goes in the graffiti-walled bar-diner – dancing on the tables, etc. Shooter Girls wander around with tequila-shot glasses looped into bandoliero belts. Good Mexican food – mesquite-grilled quail, cabrito, fresh fish, and a kickin' mule of a margarita.

☘ PICCOLA CUCINA, 5015 Westheimer St, Suite 2220, TX 77056 ☎ (713) 622 4544
Fresh Gulf fish, home-baked focaccia bread – scented with rosemary and kosher salt – pizzas with Cucina's own mozzarella Puck-ishly prepared in Pino Luongo's new open-plan 'little kitchen'. Have the yellow-fin tuna Livornese, or the panzotti spinach, then let the tiramisu pull you under.

──────── *Shopping* ────────

THE GALLERIA, 5075 Westheimer, TX 77056 ☎ (713) 621 1907
Barney's is the latest addition to Houston's most exclusive shopping mall. Other names in lights include Lord & Taylor, Gucci, Neiman Marcus, Tiffany, Marshall Field and Fendi – there are over 300 shops in all. There's a massive ice rink to cool down on after spending all those dollars.

STELZIG'S, 3123 Post Oak Blvd, TX 77056 ☎ (713) 629 7779
The oldest Western store there is – it's been in the family since 1870. They can make you a pair of boots from almost anything – sting-ray, frog, hornback lizard, kangaroo – and their saddles, belts, Indian silver buckles and harnesses are the best. Shoeshiner TC is no longer there, but his successor brings a gleam to Texan eyes and boots. Also at 9511 South West Freeway.

LOS ANGELES

──────── *Art and museums* ────────

CALIFORNIA MUSEUM OF SCIENCE AND INDUSTRY, 700 State Drive, Exposition Park, CA 90037 ☎ (213) 744 7400
Gee-whizz gadgetry with a green tinge. Consciousness-raising exhibitions range from **Aids and the Immune System** to waste recycling in a giant trash can. Also live broadcasts from space, invisible forces, electricity and magnetism, earthquakes and scientific principles of toys. Imax screen is 5 storeys high, 70ft wide with a booming sound system.

☘ J PAUL GETTY MUSEUM, 17985 Pacific Coast Highway, Malibu, CA 90265 ☎ (310) 459 7611
Rich in funds and Roman and Greek antiquities, the Getty collection resides in a spectacular museum. A wealth of European paintings, drawings, sculpture, illuminated manuscripts, decorative arts and photographs. Check out Getty's famous bronze statue, the Victorious Athlete, complete save the feet. "*Brilliant. Architecturally it is very interesting, built on the theme of a Roman villa with extensive gardens, so it is a really lovely experience*" – DAVID SHILLING. "*Getty's a great getaway. The outdoor restaurant's like being in a European café at lunchtime*" – LYN HEMMERDINGER. All bar the antiquities will move in 1996 to the new Richard Meier-designed Getty Center, tipped to be one of this century's great architectural creations. Visitors with cars must book ☎ (310) 458 2003.

☘ LOS ANGELES COUNTY MUSEUM OF ART, 5905 Wilshire Blvd, CA 90036 ☎ (213) 857 6000
The city's most prestigious museum, whose fine collection of art spans cultures and eras. The **Anderson Building** holds all the 20C US giants (Lichtenstein, Warhol et al), the permanent collection (European painting, Eastern artefacts, 18C–19C American works) resides in the **Ahmanson Building**, while the **Armand Hammer Building** is devoted to all things photo- and, simply, graphic. "*I go for the movie festivals mostly and fell in love with the* **Japanese Pavilion**" – LYN HEMMERDINGER.

MUSEUM OF CONTEMPORARY ART, 250 S Grand Ave at California Plaza, CA 90012 ☎ (213) 621 2766
The LA chic shuttle between Arata Isozaki's rose sandstone building and Frank Gehry's renovated warehouse. MOCA is devoted exclusively to art from 1940 to the present – painting, sculptures, drawings, prints and photographs. Permanent collection features Rothko, Kline, Pollock, Stella and Warhol. At Gehry's **Temporary Contemporary**, 152 N Central Ave, CA 90013, check out an up-to-the-second combination of dance, theatre, performance, film, video and music: "*Best of all the museums and one of Frank Gehry's best designs*" – LYN HEMMERDINGER.

MUSEUM OF NEON ART, 704 Traction Ave, CA 90013 ☎ (213) 617 1580
A fluorescent tribute to neon, electric and kinetic art. Major exhibitions each year show works of contemporary artists. Also night-time tours to see one of the best living lights shows – on LA's streets.

**NORTON SIMON MUSEUM OF ART, 411
W Colorado Blvd, Pasadena, CA 91105
☎ (818) 449 6840**
Perhaps the finest collection of Old Masters on
the West Coast – Rembrandts, Raphaels and
Goyas. Dodge between sculptures in beautiful
landscaped gardens before being outnumbered
by them in the Sculpture Garden. Also view
Impressionists, Post-Impressionists and episto-
lary offerings by Gauguin, Matisse, Rubens and
Van Gogh.

———— *Arts centres* ————

**LA COUNTY MUSIC CENTER, 135 N
Grand Ave, CA 90012 ☎ (213) 972 7200**
3 top venues under one roof. Oscar winners
would just like to thank their host, the glitzy
Dorothy Chandler Pavilion, which is also home
to the LA Philharmonic. The Ahmanson Theater
shows blockbusting Broadway hits; new directors and plays experiment in the round at the
Mark Taper Forum: *"lively – but operas need
improvement"* – LYN HEMMERDINGER. Plans for
a 4th concert hall are under way.

———— *Bars and cafés* ————

See also Hotels.

**CAFFE LATTE, 6254 Wilshire Blvd, CA
90048 ☎ (213) 936 5213**
Aromatherapy via on-the-spot roasted coffee
beans. Spot cappuccino quaffers from The
Industry such as LON DIAMOND: *"The best – best
coffee, muffins, pancakes and bizarre but delicious herb teas. And great eavesdropping. If
you're doing a study of the Jewish screenwriter
in Hollywood, do your research here."*

**GORKY'S CAFE & RUSSIAN BREWERY,
536 E 8th St, CA 90014 ☎ (213) 627 4060**
Trendy caff with its own brewery – 20 different
types on offer including Russian Stout, Arctic
Ale, Red Star Ale and Baltic Light. Also cappuccinos, stuffed cabbage, kasha (*"if you're horny*

for kasha, go here" – LON DIAMOND), live jazz,
R&B and acoustic music.

**HIGHLAND GROUNDS, 742 N Highland
Ave, CA 90038 ☎ (213) 466 1507**
Offbeat café/performance space where hipper
Hollywood (Winona Ryder, Johnny Depp) flings
for fresh-ground coffee and nightly jazz, poetry,
folk and improv. *"Good little blues room –
finding it could be a problem but, then again,
let's keep it our secret"* – BRUCE HARING.

**JAVA, 7286 Beverly Blvd, CA 90036
☎ (213) 931 4943**
A comfortably Bohemian environment – all
over-stuffed velvet sofas and changing art exhibitions – for its inhabitants, scriptwriters who
linger, hunched over coffee and notepads.

**LULU'S ALIBI, 1640 Sawtelle Blvd, CA
90025 ☎ (310) 479 6007**
Espresso bar/art forum (curated by the contemporary art gallery B-1's Robert Berman), open
till 4am for a late, late Brazilian supper. Cher
and Eddie Murphy might drop in for Portuguese
sausage with black bean stew.

**TRUMPS, 8764 Melrose Ave, CA 90069
☎ (310) 855 1480**
The fashionable denizens of LA think it's a bar,
though it's actually a great restaurant too. STAN-
LEY WEISER gets it the other way round: *"Food
consistently good. Bar scene is like a bad
episode of Dynasty."* What does he mean? *"The
most gold chains and foreign accents per square
foot"* explains KARLA BONOFF. Contemporary art
and Eric Orr's water sculptures give such quaffers as DAVID SHILLING a talking point.

———— *Clubs* ————

**BAR ONE, 9229 Sunset Blvd, CA 90049
☎ (310) 271 8355**
The toughest club in LA to get into – though
JOHN GOLD manages. It's worth the effort he
reckons; Springsteen-, Stallone-, Coppola- and
Idol-idolizers would agree. Pretty tough once

 Buzz Coffee grounds: Laid-back
Los Angelinos get a jolt at **Il Fornaio**, 633 W 5th St ☎ (213) 623 8400, where *"the coffee's so strong it could stand up on its own"* – STANLEY WEISER 🕺 . . . . . . **Stomping
grounds:** BRUCE HARING's haunts include **Molly Malone's**, 575 Fairfax Ave ☎ (213)
935 1577, *"one of the few Irish bars in LA that make a New Yorker feel at home. 3-
nights-a-week house band, Garrison White, is one of the city's best unsigned acts"* and
El Compadre, 7408 W Sunset Blvd ☎ (213) 751 7148, *"is a secret love of the city's
musicians – good food, great traditional Mexican music from a 3-piece band"* 🕺 . . . . . .
Grounds for popularity: somewhere over the **Double Rainbow**, 73 Melrose Ave
☎ (213) 655 1986, *"is a great teenybopper hang-out – who has the tightest jeans, etc"* –
LYN HEMMERDINGER (jeans get tighter after their sensational ice cream) . . . . 🕺

you're in there too: *"Urban biker heaven"* – WILLIAM STADIEM. *"A NY attitude, filled with women in little black dresses pretending to be European"* – BRUCE HARING. And tougher still: *"This is it, the Bimbo Equinox"* – LON DIAMOND.

THE ROXBURY, 8225 Sunset Blvd, CA 60069 ☎ (310) 656 1750
Streets ahead on Sunset, Roxbury puts the rest of LA clubland in the shade. Celeb behinds – Arsenio Hall's, Sean Penn's, Sinead O'Connor's, Ringo Starr's among them – park themselves in the gold leaf chairs. Hear veteran bluesman Roy Gaines downstairs in **Johnny's Joint**. Try the pineapple vodka, then get cued up in the pool room or sweat it out on the dance floor. Arouses loathing and devotion in equal measures – JOHN GOLD and WILLIAM STADIEM rock on, but hark at LON DIAMOND (*"Go once so you can see how lucky you are not being a regular"*).

VERTIGO, 333 S Boylston St, CA 90012 ☎ (213) 747 4849
The dizzy heights of hip – but in a very un LA-way ("What, no doorman?"). Inside it's serious warehouse décor and high-energy dancing. *"Not a bad concert hall – no one's in charge at the door, even though 14 people have walkie-talkies. You're never 'on the list'"* – BRUCE HARING.

—— *Fashion designers* ——

BOB MACKIE, 8636 Melrose Ave, CA 90069 ☎ (310) 657 7377
No 1 for the sort of theatrical glamour only stars can carry off. Plunging necklines, backlines and soaring hemlines joined by a few strategic sequins demand the body of an 18-year-old (which in LA ain't so hard to come by).

GALANOS ORIGINALS, 2254 S Sepulveda Blvd, CA 90064 ☎ (213) 272 1445
X-rated designer: exclusive, expensive little *ex*tras for social X-rays (Nancy Reagan, Gloria Vanderbilt . . .). His handcrafted, beautifully finished outfits might not be highly original but you can be sure they are originals (at $30,000 a dress, the embarrassment would be ruinous).

NOLAN MILLER, 241 S Robertson Blvd, CA 90211 ☎ (213) 655 7110
Ultra-glam evening wear beloved by model *femmes d'un certain âge* (Sophia Loren, Joan Collins, Elizabeth Taylor). Luxuriant ballgowns of velvet, lace and beaded silk, a new retail line, plus a sense of humour: tongue in chic, he dressed the soap queens in *Soapdish*.

TYLER TRAFFICANTE, Studio enquiries ☎ (213) 931 5769
Fine, handmade workmanship for the hip and famous. Regular customers include Susan Sarandon, Laura Dern and Julia Roberts (rumour is that Richard Tyler created a volumi-

nous white *peau de soie* wedding gown for the ill-fated Roberts/Sutherland wedding which, although paid for, still hangs in his salon . . .).

—— *Film* ——

Century 14 in Century City is the place to see and be seen – get there yesterday and avoid the crush. After all the hype, Hollywood's newly refurbished **El Capitan Theater** is wunderbar. The biggest complex in the US, **Universal City 18 Cinemas**, Universal City Plaza, is massive enough to guarantee a seat – and a good flick. **Fox Village**, Westwood, has booming speakers – which they really crank up – that befit a big movie. LA's 10 **Cineplex Odeons** each have between 10 and 18 screens each to keep you out of mischief.

OM/AFI WORLD FEST, American Film Institute, 2021 N Western Ave, CA 90027 ☎ (213) 856 7707
Still a youngster, started in 1986, directed by Ken Wlaschin. International and non-competitive, its venue is the Cineplex Odeon Century Plaza Cinemas. Catches the stars when they're in town for the Oscars, around April.

—— *Hotels* ——

BEVERLY HILLS HOTEL, 9641 Sunset Blvd, Beverly Hills, CA 90210 ☎ (310) 276 2251
The legendary pink Spanish villa, set in unreal greenery, has long been a hang-out of the stars, the epitome of casual, glitzy Hollywood style. Recently annexed to the Sultan of Brunei's empire, it's due to close for a major overhaul à la London Dorchester. Meanwhile, **The Coffee Shop** is where ED VICTOR breaks his fast. JOHN GOLD makes reservations; JOHN BROOKE-LITTLE has reservations: *"Living on their reputation a bit."* BRUCE OLDFIELD doesn't care: *"Fab – I love the Tinseltown glamour."*

CHECKERS HOTEL KEMPINSKI, 535 S Grand Ave, CA 90071 ☎ (213) 624 0000
Owned by the Ayala Group (Campton Place Kempinski, San Francisco), the revamped Mayflower retains its olde worlde values and gives them a shot of adrenaline. Old-fashioned service, understatedly comfortable rooms and a cosy library are splashed with modern touches: each room has 2 phone lines and voice mail, pets get top service, beds have the luxury of Belgian sheets and the eclectic New American **Checkers** restaurant rates highly under Thomas Keller, *"a great chef"* – WILLIAM STADIEM.

FOUR SEASONS, 300 S Doheny Drive at Burton Way, CA 90048 ☎ (310) 273 2222
In 5 years it's established itself as the place to stay with those who prefer its charming solidity

to some of the glitzier LA offerings. A good location, keen service and a homely sense of decoration (well-stuffed sofas, fresh flowers and antiques), as well as bits and pieces such as TVs in the bathroom and free limo service to Beverly Hills, keep President Bush, ANDRE PREVIN and JOHN GOLD happy. WILLIAM STADIEM tips the bar as the place to meet *"rich Iron-Curtainers".*

 **HOTEL BEL-AIR, 701 Stone Canyon Rd, CA 90077 ☎ (310) 472 1211**
Luxurious, celebrity-studded and irresistible, this is still LA's finest. The warm terracotta villa with hideaway suites for the publicity-shy, amid bougainvillaea and hibiscus-filled gardens, is under well-tuned Rosewood management. *"Of course, the best hotel in LA"* – ROBIN LEACH. *"I would consider selling all my estate and moving into the Bel-Air and letting them take care of me until I die. You get the feeling of being in a resort yet you are in a top-of-the-line-service hotel; they take care of all your business needs, yet you are in a gorgeous tropical garden. Anyone who stays there becomes an addict"* – ED VICTOR. PAUL HENDERSON echoes: *"Like a country hotel in the city."* ANDREW LLOYD WEBBER and MARY ROSSI rate it, as does LISA BARNARD: *"For the best service."* Al fresco power-breakfasts at **The Restaurant** while the sun rises over LA are the attraction for locals: *"Delightful breakfasts. The piano and fireplace are best for midnight rendez-vous"* – LYN HEMMERDINGER; *"Gardens of paradise and power breakfasts are the order of the day. The city's moguls gather early here"* – BRUCE HARING.

America's Best Hotels

1	THE CARLYLE · New York
2	MANSION ON TURTLE CREEK · Dallas
3	THE MARK · New York
4	HOTEL BEL-AIR · Los Angeles
5	FOUR SEASONS CLIFT · San Francisco
6	THE PLAZA · New York
7	FOUR SEASONS . Los Angeles
8	THE WILLARD INTER-CONTINENTAL · Washington, DC
9	WINDSOR COURT HOTEL · New Orleans
10	RITZ-CARLTON · Houston

L'ERMITAGE, 9291 Burton Way, Beverly Hills, CA 90210 ☎ (310) 278 3344
With so much class it's almost passed over for its more upfront neighbours – but with so much class, it's the one to visit. Original Impressionist artwork gives the original impression of luxury – confirmed by the swags of fine freebies, from strawberries and wine to limo rides in Beverly Hills/West Hollywood. The rooftop garden has a heated pool (unnecessary if you're in a suite – some have vast Jacuzzis). Le Petit Ermitage, next door and part of L'Ermitage, is just the job for post-job (nose, lip) recuperation – there's a cinematic Who's Who behind the bandages.

THE PENINSULA BEVERLY HILLS, 9882 Santa Monica Blvd, Beverly Hills, CA 90212 ☎ (310) 273 4888
Classically designed luxe hotel with a top-of-the-trees roof garden health spa. Conveniently located opposite super-agent Mike Ovitz for a steady stream of celebrity callers.

 **THE REGENT BEVERLY WILSHIRE, 9500 Wilshire Blvd, Beverly Hills, CA 90212 ☎ (310) 275 5200**
Grand old West Coaster with Far Eastern efficiency, this one's outsmarting the others with outsized rooms, outnumbered guests (one attendant per room), outstanding decoration (Brocatelle marble, Aubusson tapestries), and outrageously luxurious Presidential suite. Appeals to mad hatters STEPHEN JONES and DAVID SHILLING: *"It's brilliant since they renovated, I love it – so plastic."* ROBIN LEACH reckons: *"It closely follows the Bel-Air; each room is about twice the size of an average hotel room and has 2 phone lines."* KEN HOM's another fan: *"They've done a good job renovating the place and they also have a terrific gym, which is absolutely necessary when you travel and eat as much as I do."* Following its supporting role in the film, they now offer *Pretty Woman* packages (roses, champagne and *discretion*).

Music

WILTERN THEATER, 3790 Wilshire Blvd, LA 90010 ☎ (213) 380 5005
Home to the Los Angeles Chamber Orchestra, this Art Deco hall also hosts the latest groovers and rockers – though the future is less clear, following the tragic death of owner/promoter Bill Graham. BRUCE HARING likes it: *"Acoustics can be a pain at times, but generally it's comfortable, clean, secure."*

Restaurants

See also Hotels.

 **CA'BREA, 346-348 S La Brea Ave, CA 90036 ☎ (213) 938 2863**
Bigger, newer, more fashionable restaurant from Antonio Tomassi of Locanda Veneta fame, appealing to Italophiles from Tom Cruise to Charlton Heston. Just as noisy, just as good.

Hobby Horses

Kevin Costner has a lot to answer for – born-again equestrians all over LA are taking the bit between their teeth and hustling on down to riding school. Jockeying for position as the hottest of the lot is the **Los Angeles Equestrian Center**, 480 Riverside Drive, Burbank, CA 91506 ☎ (818) 840 9063. It ain't exactly unbroken broncos and beans by the fire – more private boarding, polo and a little smoked Indian salmon steak in the centre's **Equestrian Bar and Grill**. And a pride worse off for a run-in with a recalcitrant mare might be soothed by the **Classroom Restaurant**'s chef (one of 47 International Culinary Certified Master Chefs in the US). Good to see they've got their priorities in order – if young Kevin never does his own stunts at least he'll know his way around a contemporary American menu.

🐎 **CAMPANILE, 624 S La Brea Ave CA 90036 ☎ (213) 938 1447**
Named after the tower topping this 1926 landmark and pretty damn stylish itself. KEN HOM is bowled over: *"The hottest place in LA. Superb food, Californian/Mediterranean, cooked by the most wonderful couple. They have their own bakery next door. It's a wonderful place to go even for breakfast, and for dinner I would just eat all the appetizers because they're so good. It's a real people-watching place too."*

CHASEN'S, 9039 Beverly Blvd, CA 90048 ☎ (310) 271 2168
Clubby old-timer with a similarly well-preserved Hollywood establishment clientele (Liz Taylor, James Stewart, Ron and Nancy) whose jaded palates keep returning for honest hobo steaks and chilli. ROBERT SANGSTER can't blame them; LYN HEMMERDINGER recognizes its attractions: *"A good place to take someone's parents who want to star-gaze."*

🐎 **CHAYA BRASSERIE, 8741 Alden Drive, CA 90048☎ (310) 859 8833**
3 centuries of restaurant know-how of the Tsunoda family have been brought to bear on this most 20C of restaurants. Casually stylish room designed by Grinstein-Daniels packed with vociferous celebrities picking at platefuls of Japanese-accented Franco/Cal food. *"My personal favourite for food, service and décor. Let's not forget stars: Eddie Murphy, Madonna,* Arnold and Maria Schwarznegger. If I'm going to spend some money, that's where I enjoy doing it most" – LYN HEMMERDINGER. *"Friendly service, decent food – European without the pretension"* – BRUCE HARING.

🐎 **CITRUS, 6703 Melrose Ave, CA 90038 ☎ (213) 857 0034**
Chef-owner Michel Richard keeps a watchful eye on his ever-successful eatery and it shows: spotlessly white enclosed patio, gleamingly glassed kitchen and encyclopaedically well-informed staff. The best of Californian cooking – combinations are clever rather than smart-alec, as KEN HOM recognizes: *"Really terrific food."*

IL MITO, 11801 Ventura Blvd, Studio City, CA 91604 ☎ (818) 762 1818
Tomassi-trained Michael Fekr has set up shop in a 20s tile factory and dishes out similarly concise, no frills, Italian cooking – regulars swear there is no better grilled veal chop.

🐎 **THE IVY, 113 N Robertson Blvd, CA 90048 ☎ (310) 274 8303**
Thrilling grills and cakes galore – of the fishy kind. ED VICTOR goes crustacean: *"Great crab cakes, that is what to eat at the Ivy."* WILLIAM STADIEM echoes, AMANDA DE CADENET sidesteps: *"They're the best salmon fish cakes in the world I've ever had"* (spot her eating them at lunch and dinner). DAVID SHILLING is hooked too, as is LON DIAMOND: *"Great food, great service, class in a not always classy city."* Move on to great puddings and swig the frothiest cappuccinos from outsize, hand-painted coffee cups. Good name spottin' – Selleck, Shapiro, Lemmon, Foster. **Ivy at the Shore**, 1541 Ocean Ave, Santa Monica ☎ (310) 393 3113, is a Sunday lunchtime treat – Californian cooking with cajun and creole spice.

KATSU, 1972 Hillhurst Ave, Los Feliz, CA 90027 ☎ (213) 665 1891
High-tech, lab-style sushi bar, where Katsu continues to boldly go . . . Fill out what you want on the form, savour beyond-fantastic Japanese food, and keep an eye on the dollars. *"Still the best sushi in town. His other restaurants are tops too"* – LYN HEMMERDINGER. The rest of the family includes **Café Katsu**, 2117 Sawtelle Ave, and **Katsu 3rd** 8636 W 3rd St.

LE CHARDONNAY, 8284 Melrose Ave, CA 90046 ☎ (213) 655 8880
Gossipy, buzzy French bistro where lip reading is an advantage if you wish to talk. More than lip service paid to the food though – good, French, and plentiful. FREDERIC RAPHAEL mouths *oui*. Reliably good service: *"Nicest waiters and you don't have to be famous to get a good table"* – KARLA BONOFF.

LE DOME, 8720 Sunset Blvd, CA 90069 ☎ (310) 659 6919
Big deals over fab meals – LA's power-lunch hot

Puckish Pleasures

In fickle, faddish LA, chefs come and go as quickly as psyches in a self-transformation class, but not the wily Wolfgang, who sets the trends that others spot: *"Of course the star chef in California is still Wolfgang Puck"* – ROBIN LEACH. First showing his prescience in pizzas, designer-style, at **Spago**, 1114 Horn Ave, W Hollywood, CA 90069 ☎ (310) 652 4025. Baseball-capped bright young things have been dishing out startling combinations of haute fast-food for near 10 years (legendary smoked salmon pizza, *"caviare pizza, delicious"* – KENNETH LANE) to the determinedly casual rich and famous like Dustin Hoffman, Steven Spielberg, Donald Sutherland, STEPHEN JONES, KARLA BONOFF (*"food is still outstanding despite tourist clientele"*), ROBIN L (*"still in but very informal"*), ED VICTOR (*"great atmosphere, it's the theatre, the buzz"*) and KEN HOM (*"still a favourite of mine"*). Then came

Chinois on Main, 2709 Main St, Santa Monica, CA 90405 ☎ (310) 392 9025, leading the Pan-Pacific invasion with imaginative Franco/Oriental food: *"The best meal I ever had was here"* – LON DIAMOND; *"still crazy for this food after all these years"* – LYN HEMMERDINGER; *"inventive and fun"* – PAUL HENDERSON. Back to honest-to-God sausages and beer at **Eureka**, 1845 S Bundy Drive, CA 90025 ☎ (310) 447 2916 where *"you can actually watch beer being made"* – ROBIN L, though LYN H reckons it's *"too noisy"*. The whimsical neo-industrial-styled interior is *"quite beautiful to look at, the beer quite lethal"* – ED V. **Granita**, 23725 W Malibu Rd, Malibu, CA 90265 ☎ (310) 456 0488, catches the drift to Mediterranean-style seafood: *"Excellent food, great ambience and not expensive"* – HARVEY GOLDSMITH. ED V sums it up: *"Anything Wolfgang Puck does is interesting and exciting."*

spot still fuels film and showbiz execs. *"A good celebrity watch. Try the mixed vegetable salad with chicken. Attentive service is always first rate"* – BRUCE HARING. The bar/bistro burns on late at night too. STEPHEN JONES and ED VICTOR are familiar faces there. For ROBERT SANGSTER, *"it's still very good"*. Great crab cakes, popular conservatory/terrace.

L'ORANGERIE, 903 N La Cienega Blvd, CA 90069 ☎ (213) 652 9770
French/international cuisine of the highest order. Décor and prices to match. *"The No 1 gourmet restaurant in LA, where you really dress for dinner. You will always find Roger Moore and Michael Caine there together when they are in town, with their wives"* – ROBIN LEACH.

🍴 MATSUHISA, 129 N La Cienega Blvd 90211 ☎ (310) 659 9639
Chef Nobu Matsuhisa has extraordinary ways with raw and cooked fish, among other Japanese creations. Read the testimonies: *"The best Japanese restaurant, if not the best restaurant in the world. Stunning monkfish liver pâté. It is brilliant to see major film stars standing in a queue to get in"* – SIR CLEMENT FREUD; *"I, who do not like Japanese food, was converted to whatever this was"* – ANDREW LLOYD WEBBER; *"way beyond sushi, though that's good too. Ser-*

vice is sometimes a bit too helpful, but portions are ample and first-rate" – BRUCE HARING; *"the Disneyland of sushi – worth fighting the crowd for"* – STANLEY WEISER.

MORTONS, 8800 Melrose Ave, CA 90069 ☎ (310) 276 5205
Astronomy meets gastronomy. Sit down, gaze at the stars – Lemmon, Oxenberg, Collins – then tuck in to marinated grills and delicious puddings. ED VICTOR likes going, and IAIN JOHNSTONE doesn't think twice: *"One eats, fairly obviously, in places like Mortons – it's consistently good."*

ORSO, 8706 W 3rd St, CA 90048 ☎ (310) 274 7144
One of the NY/London gang. Renowned for their thin pizzas, served on splendid handcrafted and -painted pottery. *"A shiny little salted-away gemstone. Good and not overcrowded"* – LON DIAMOND. Romantic, softly lit patio. ROBERT SANGSTER is the man who says *"Si"*.

🍴 PATINA, 5955 Melrose Ave, CA 90038 ☎ (213) 467 1108
Super eclecticizer Joachim Splichal puts together dishes like a soufflé of grits with Herkimer cheddar and an apple and smoked-bacon sauce. Foodies just can't get enough.

ROCKENWAGNER, 2435 Main St, Santa Monica, CA 90405 ☎ (310) 399 6504
Teutonic tucker from chef Hans Rockenwagner joined by compatriot baker Dietmar, served in a dining room in the guise of an old German town square. It's less hearty than one might expect: *"Excellent food, but you'll need to stop for a hamburger afterwards"* – BRUCE HARING. Lunchers and fast-breakers roll up for great fresh-baked bread, and a good deli.

72 MARKET ST, 72 Market St, Venice, CA 90261 ☎ (310) 392 8720
Glitzy crowd-puller part-owned by Dudley Moore and Liza Minnelli. Vamped-up everyday American classics, like meat-loaf, go down well, and Dud's fave warm scallop salad and crab cakes get him going on the ol' pianer. LYN HEMMERDINGER loves the design, STANLEY WEISER loves it all: *"A favourite – class all the way. Best combination ambience-cuisine and, by default, one of the only happening bar scenes – proof that one of LA's greatest liabilities is its lack of down-home neighbourhood bars."*

VALENTINO, 3115 Pico Blvd, Santa Monica, CA 90405 ☎ (310) 829 4313
Mooted by some to be the finest Italian restaurant in the city, if not the whole of the USA, Piero Selvaggio's restaurant draws lustful foodie palates. Others find the coolness of décor and absence of trattoria buzz decidedly not to their taste.

WEST BEACH CAFE, 60 N Venice Blvd, Venice, CA 90291 ☎ (310) 823 5396
Great seafood and ultra-fresh Californian cuisine from artsy/foodie doyen Bruce Marder gets the Venice beachcombers crooning: *"Best French fries outside Belgium"* – WILLIAM STADIEM. Sculpture and contemporary paintings are exhibited, drawing a *"Venice art mafia scene"* – LYN HEMMERDINGER.

Shopping

Rodeo Drive is still the most famous drag in Beverly Hills – glossy, international, expensive and soulless. **Brentwood Gardens** on San Vicente Blvd is a great new one-stop shop (48 boutiques, 4 restaurants). **Sunset Plaza** remains a chic place to shop – at Gallay, Lisa Norman, Rosenthal Truitt, Joan Vass, Oliver Peoples. **Sherman Oaks Galleria** is the original mall that Valley Girls sprang from. The maxiest mall in LA is the **Beverly Center**, a glassy complex with 2 exterior escalators, 20 restaurants, 13 movie theatres and shops like Bullocks, Abercrombie & Fitch, Banana Republic, The Gap. **Melrose** is still the beat of the young, zany crowd in LA, sons and daughters of the rich and famous. **Montana Avenue** has a 'neighbourhood atmosphere' (ie you can walk along it); browse from trad (Lanz) to trendy (Savannah).

FREDERICK'S OF HOLLYWOOD, 6608 Hollywood Blvd, CA 90028 ☎ (213) 466 8506
So serious about lingerie that it became a museum for it. Desirable, purchasable bits and pieces, as well as famous knickers on display: Marilyn Monroe's bra (and she said *diamonds* were a girl's best friend), and Greta Garbo's peignoir, which she wore ven she vas alone. As BRUCE HARING says: *"Any place that has Madonna's bra on the wall can't be all bad."*

Well-bread

The staff of life becomes the stuff of fantasy in if-it-exists-it-can-be-designer LA. Fathoms-deep queues, $8-a-loaf shell-outs and ingredients more familiar on an antipasto platter make the white sliced nutritionist's nightmare seem, well, stale. Bread baked by **La Brea**, 524 S La Brea Ave ☎ (213) 939 6813 carries the most clout – germinated from hybrid European yeast, flourishing into loaves studded with Greek olives, rye and currants: *"Hat rolls, potato rolls, basil rolls – I hate them, they've ruined bread for me at all normal restaurants"* – LON DIAMOND. *"Bread here is the best thing"* – KARLA BONOFF. Old standby **Il Fornaio**, 301 N Beverly Drive, Beverly Hills ☎ (310) 550 8330, holder of the best baguette in town title, holds its own (*"Dependable breads, though cookies and cakes can be too rich"* – LYN HEMMERDINGER") but new bread is rising and may prove worthy competition. **Breadworks**, 7961 W 3rd St ☎ (310) 930-0047, is hauling in dough in return for sun-dried tomato, pomegranate and jalapeño cheddar breads. But the highest-rising newcomer (by a nose) looks to be **Cyrano** on Sunset Blvd, from the people who brought you **Bread Only**, 3022 Cochran Ave ☎ (213) 933 5586, which at just over a year old is already supplying Citrus, Champagne, Locanda Veneta and Olive.

Hidden Fruit

Remember the restaurant-booking scene in *LA Story*? LA restaurants don't *really* demand your credit rating, date of birth, CV and mother's maiden name; LA restaurants want to *encourage* customers, don't they? And LA diners wouldn't subject themselves to such treatment .... One might wonder, especially when the greatest success story in town is **Olive**, a restaurant so exclusive, so very *in* that it has no sign, no windows, no telephone listing and there are *still* queues outside, just waiting to be turned away. What's the attraction? There's the star-spotting, of course (David Bowie, Iman, Madonna, you name it) but that's *de rigueur* round here; there's the food (dishes of architectural daring like the seafood springtime booster box or seared tuna under a towering potato 'gate'); there's the fact that, in a town that winds down at 11pm, it gets going at 2am; but the important thing is the minimal chance of ever getting a table and, in a masochistic town like LA, that makes the place pretty damned attractive. (By the way, it's on Fairfax Ave but exactly where, we can not reveal ...)

FRED HAYMAN, 273 N Rodeo Drive, Beverly Hills, CA 90210 ☎ (310) 271 3000
International designerdom plus expensive Hayman parfum for those who shun common scents. Having tired of their bottles of '273', Beverly Hills wives now can't do without ' ... with Love'. Top designer clothes, accessories and leather goods. Blow the froth and shoot some pool in Hayman's **Cappuccino Bar**.

FRED JOAILLIER, 401 N Rodeo Drive, Beverly Hills, CA 90210 ☎ (310) 278 3733
Spectacular contemporary designs in fine jewellery. Richard Gere 'borrowed' a magnificent ruby and diamond necklace to give to Julia Roberts in *Pretty Woman*.

GALLAY, 8711 Sunset Blvd, W Hollywood, CA 90069 ☎ (310) 858 8711
Here, life is beautiful. Mere mortals are left pressed to the windows while film stars flock to the satin, lycra and shimmering silk by Alaïa, Gigli, Kamali and La Perla. Also hats, jewellery, belts and shoes. LYN HEMMERDINGER loves it: *"The nicest sales girls."*

MAXFIELD, 8825 Melrose Ave, CA 90069 ☎ (310) 274 8800
Room upon room of the ultimate designers – Miyake, Mugler, Sybilla, Gigli, Byblos, Comme des Garçons, Alaïa, Gaultier, Hamnett, Jean Muir, Yohji Yamamoto and Dolce & Gabbana. *"If I had the money . . . "* sighs LYN HEMMERDINGER. Covetable collection of reproduction Pierre Chareau-designed furniture – pieces of the 20s and 30s that paved the way for full-blown modernism. Also shoes, hats and fab jewellery.

TRASHY LINGERIE, 402 N La Cienega Blvd, CA 90048 ☎ (213) 652 4543
Sensuous snippets of silk and business suits that reveal more than they conceal in this red plush and very lush store. What they might reveal is a Trashy trademark leather bra or bustier. The place for stars to pick up their barely there evening wear for the Academy and Grammy Awards, and purveyors of raunchy gear to films from *9½ Weeks* to *Whore*. Its critics deplore over-commercialization: *"Has the nerve to charge admission,"* sniffs BRUCE HARING.

🕵 **Buzzz** Have a close encounter of the kosher kind at Spielberg's mother's **Milky Way**, 9108 W Pico Blvd ☎ (310) 859 0004, with cheese blintzes, chimichangas and potato pancakes 🕵 ...... At **Santa Monica Mall**, 3rd St Promenade, Santa Monica ☎ (310) 393 8355, the action starts post-shopping hours with street musos, 4 cinemas, 40-odd restaurants and Scissorhands-esque topiary dinosaurs 🕵 ...... Fastidious celebs entrust silks and sequins only to **Brown's Cleaners**, 1223 Montana Ave, Santa Monica ☎ (310) 451 8531, and pay through the well-modelled nose for the privilege 🕵 ...... The rarest of creatures in LA, **Samuel French**, 7623 Sunset Blvd, Hollywood ☎ (213) 876 0570, *"is a little Hollywood bookstore miracle"* – LON DIAMOND 🕵 ...... SHARYN STORRIER-LYNEHAM digs up her treasure at **Tesoro**, 319 S Robertson ☎ (310) 273 9890: *"They have huge damask table napkins in the best bright colours – the ultimate napkin"* .... 🕵

MIAMI

—— Clubs ——

❝Miami is the best club town outside of New York. It is becoming a very youthful and exciting city instead of somewhere people go to die. South Miami Beach, the Art Deco district, is mainly where the action is ❞

 MICHAEL MUSTO

TORPEDO, 634 Collins Ave, FL 33139 ☎ (305) 538 2500
Fetish-inspiring leather, vinyl and metal bar/nightclub with a high-energy mix of moustachioed leather-boys, cross-dressers and Don Johnson types. Every night is happy hour and the legendary Sunday tea-dances start at 4pm and end in Monday's wee hours. MICHAEL MUSTO shoots in.

America's Best Clubs

1	TATOU · New York
2	WARSAW BALLROOM · Miami
3	COPACABANA · New York
4	NELL'S · New York
5	DV8 · San Francisco

🎩 **WARSAW BALLROOM, 1450 Collins Ave, FL 33139 ☎ (305) 531 4555**
Poles apart from the other Floridans. A wildly way-out crowd (*"Similar to the Roxy in NY in energy and spirit"* – MICHAEL MUSTO) gets into whatever's happening: *"Extraordinary – they had flavoured smoke, in lovely tropical flavours. It was quite weird and it's only because I was tiddly that it seemed nice – the next day my outfit stank of strawberries"* – STEPHEN JONES. Regular host to Suzanne Bartsch's outrageous parties: *"Try to catch it then"* – SEBASTIAN SCOTT.

—— Hotels ——

CENTURY HOTEL, 140 Ocean Drive, FL 33139 ☎ (305) 674 8855
Not officially in the Deco district but one of Miami's first Art Deco buildings. *"A small hotel which has been redone in good taste and very*

charming people run it, very helpful. All the hotels I really like nowadays tend to be almost like small family-run hotels; even in large cities I search them out. This one's wonderful" – STEPHEN JONES. White meat and seafood Med/minceur menu in the restaurant.

—— Restaurants ——

CASA JUANCHO, 2436 SW 8th St, FL 33135 ☎ (305) 642 2452
A truly Spanish restaurant – only the deeply provincial would enter before 9pm. *"Be prepared for festively dressed locals – this is not a place for blue jeans – a tapas bar and the most extensive list of Spanish wines I have ever seen, including those in Spain. If you are feeling lavish try the thread-sized imported baby eel in olive oil and garlic, a great delicacy brought out in one of the attractive, shallow, earthenware casseroles used for all of the stewed dishes such as a marinated cabretto, simmered until the meat is falling off the bone"* – BARBARA KAFKA.

CHEF ALLEN'S, 19088 NE 29th Ave, N Miami Beach, FL 33180 ☎ (305) 935 2900
Pastelly Art Deco restaurant with vibrant, strong cooking. Chef Allen Susser knows his fish and puts them to good use on his ever-changing menu. *"World class with absolutely no pretension. The cobia, a local fish, is truly terrific, grilled and served with a fresh redcurrant chutney and bell peppers of many colours. I'm running out of superlatives but the wahoo encrusted with white peppercorns and broiled and served with black ink linguine in a lobster and tomato broth is fabulous"* – BARBARA KAFKA.

JOE'S STONE CRABS, 227 Biscayne St, FL 33139 ☎ (305) 673 0365
In its fourth generation and still going strong. Slightly touristy and long waits might make you crabby, but the restaurant is still the best and surest place to taste this speciality. Keep your order simple.

❝One of the more stunning transformations of a culinary desert into a food Mecca has taken place in greater Miami, a transformation on every level: food shops, little places to snack, elegant restaurants, bars with a beat ❞

 BARBARA KAFKA

🎩 **MARK'S PLACE, 2286 NE 123rd St, N Miami, FL 33181 ☎ (305) 893 6888**
Marksman Militello has hit bullseye with this spot-on post-modernist place. Lively and vocif-

erously appreciative crowd go for his light, contemporary cooking. "*My favourite dish is a local seafood first course of fried Gulf oysters with salsa, ancho butter and lime. The hot crisp and tender oysters – a neat technical trick – are replaced in their shells, layered with the melting butter and the cold salsa. My favourite main course is a thick and very rare tuna steak whose rim has been rolled in black and white sesame seeds served with cold soy-noodles and pickled ginger. This mixture of East and West may be a cliché but this was not a cliché dish*" – BARBARA KAFKA. Hits the mark with ROBERT ELMS too.

🏠 YUCA, 177 Giraldo, Coral Gables, FL 33135 ☎ (305) 444 4448
Cuban inspiration, Big Orange interpretation with a cheerfully bilingual crowd and menu. Bright, informal interior in a clean-as-paint shopfront; truly innovative food. Yuca (starchy, white-fleshed tuber) turns up in sour dough and wholewheat bread, in blinis with caviare, in cold Vichyssoise-like soup, and in a warm spinach and papaya salad with lamb. "*One of my favourite restaurants in the world – YUCA stands for Young Upwardly-mobile Cuban Americans. Kind of nouvelle Cuban – pork and beans and rice and fish tarted up into quite an alto cuisine, brilliant*" – ROBERT ELMS.

NEW ORLEANS

—— Bars and cafés ——

NAPOLEON HOUSE, 500 Chartres St, LA 70130 ☎ (504) 524 9752
Trad, not jazz. Sip cocktails and listen to piped classical music in an old French Quarter building. Afternoon or late night is the best time, Pimm's is their No 1 cup.

PAT O'BRIEN'S, 718 St Peter St, LA 70116 ☎ (504) 525 4823
3 choices here: jazz/pop twin piano singalong bars, one with a juke box, and drinks on the patio outside for those who like the sound of silence – relatively speaking. The new **Annexe Bar** on Bourbon Street expands the empire.

—— Clubs ——

PRESERVATION HALL, 726 St Peter St, LA 70116 ☎ (504) 522 2841
Sawdust-floored birthplace of Delta jazz and blues. It's packed out, it's smoky, sweaty and seamy, and it rings with the grand ol' brass and bass sound, played by men who remember how it all began. Serious – no food, no bar, just jazz.

SNUG HARBOR, 626 Frenchmen St, LA 70116 ☎ (504) 949 0696
Lively mix of out-of-towners and regulars ship

in to listen to the best local musos plus big, big names: Charmaine Neville, Harry Connick Jr and the Marsalis family are among them.

TIPITINA'S, 501 Napoleon Ave, LA 70115 ☎ (504) 895 8477
Cajun fiddle-dee-dee-ers, R & B-ers and rock 'n' rollers come along to hear the best bands live. Listen up, swig beer and hang loose.

—— Festivals ——

NEW ORLEANS JAZZ AND HERITAGE FESTIVAL, PO Box 2530, LA 70176 ☎ (504) 522 4786
The Delta fiesta – a bayou burlesque drawing 4,000 musicians and cooks together in late April to lay on southern food and play on till the small hours. 300,000 pilgrims feast on spicy fare: filé gumbo, alligator piquante, jambalaya; and hear just about anything that's thrown at them – zydeco, cajun, blue grass, blues, country, R & B, Gospel, calypso, salsa, ragtime, folk and straightforward jazz.

—— Hotels ——

🏠 WINDSOR COURT HOTEL, 300 Gravier St, LA 70140 ☎ (504) 523 6000
One of America's frontrunners. *Real* Old Masters (Gainsborough, Reynolds, Van Dyck, Canaletto), antiques, Chinese lacquer, four-posters and leather-bound books give this big hotel the grand old Euro feel, though it's a relative youngblood. Tea is the best in town – nibble crustless sandwiches and lemon tart while a chamber group play. Save space for dinner in the **Grill Room** – updated creole dishes and harlequin mask pudding.

—— Restaurants ——

See also Hotels.

BAYOU RIDGE CAFE, 5080 Pontchartrain Blvd, LA 70118 ☎ (504) 486 0788
Creative creolerie kept contemporary with a light sleight of hand – pasta with fried oysters and mozzarella plus the city's best crème brûlée.

BISTRO AT MAISON DE VILLE, 733 Toulouse St, LA 70130 ☎ (504) 528 9206
Tasteniks drop everything to fill this chic 40-seat bistro and try John Neal's modern Euro/American dishes. Oysters with corn cakes and garlic mayonnaise, and a crème fraîche lemon tart have them crying out for more.

BRENNANS, 417 Royal St, LA 70130 ☎ (504) 525 9713
Early risers get the most famous creole breakfast in town – eggs benedict, sautéed fish, Cana

Mardi Gras
♣

Pancake blow-outs dwindle into insigni-
ficance next to the show put on in New
Orleans, host of the fattest Tuesday of all.
Months of preparation on gaudy floats,
costumes and jazz parades culminate in an
exuberant 2-month-long celebration of
hedonism – Carnivale – which in turn
peaks at Mardi Gras: the feast before the
famine – when death by cirrhosis is seen to
be one of natural causes. Bacchantes line
the streets, yelling for masked float-riders
to throw them a token (doubloons, plastic
jewellery or toys), black Mardi Gras Indians in elaborate feathered costumes strut
their stuff and a high-profile citizen in a
pageboy wig is king of the day. It's a mad
mixture of commercialism, Catholicism
and superstition – raucous, touristy, traditional and infectiously fun. The next morning, half the population totters off to Mass
to accept the sign of the cross on their
forehead; the purgatory of Lent begins.

dian bacon; diners get some of the best seafood –
fabulous oysters Rockerfeller (their version
misses out the spinach).

**BRIGTSEN'S, 723 Dante St, LA 70118
☎ (504) 861 7610**
Simple cottage restaurant with dynamic cooking
from ex-K'Paul's Frank Brigtsen. Try the cream
of oysters Rockerfeller soup and the blackened
prime rib; the crawfish and shrimp are great any
which way.

**CHARLIE G's, 3809 Ambassador Caffery
Parkway, Lafayette, LA 70503
☎ (318) 981 0108**
It's more than a hike from New Orleans (over 2
hours), but people come from all over Acadiana
for Charlie's creole concoctions. Wood-grilled
seafood a speciality, plus *"the best gumbo I've
had in Louisiana. They do a stunner of a duck
gumbo, really dark and unctuous. Also melting
pecan pralines"* – SOPHIE GRIGSON.

**CHEZ HELENE, 1540 N Robertson St,
Bywater, LA 70116 ☎ (504) 945 0444**
The original Helene is 80 now but nephew
Austin Leslie has been doing very nicely thank
you since 1964. Famed throughout the country
for his soul food (with creole, cajun and French
accents) and best for down-home specialities like
filé gumbo and fried chicken.

♟ **COMMANDER'S PALACE, 1403
Washington Ave, LA 70130
☎ (504) 899 8221**
Magnificent, massive mansion in the Garden
District – this is one of New Orleans's grandest
restaurants. Dine upstairs in the glass-walled
Garden Room on imaginatively spiced cajun and
creole – turtle soup, poached oysters in cream
sauce with Oregon caviare and bread pudding
soufflé.

**GALATOIRE'S, 209 Bourbon St, LA 70130
☎ (504) 525 2021**
Unchanged turn-of-the-century establishment
with old-style French/creolities which hold the
standards others aspire to. The red rémoulade
sauce is justly famed.

**LA PROVENCE, US Highway 190 (exit 1-
12), Meedanville (Lacombe), LA 70445
☎ (504) 626 7662**
One hour's drive from the city, Chris Kerageor-
giou cooks provincial French food overlooking
Lake Pontchartrain. Spectacular menu includes
French – rabbit in lavender gravy – and creole –
quail gumbo with rice.

NEW YORK
—— *Art and museums* ——

**THE CLOISTERS, Fort Tryon Park, NY
10040 ☎ (212) 923 3700**
Set on a skyscraperless grassy hill, the Met's
Cloisters are a peaceful jaunt uptown. Con-
structed from the ruins of several European
cloisters, they are filled with medieval art, sculpture, illuminated manuscripts and architectural
relics from AD 1000 onwards.

**COOPER-HEWITT MUSEUM, 2 E 91st St,
NY 10128 ☎ (212) 860 6868**
The Smithsonian's decorative arts collection is
housed in the Georgian-revival former home of
Andrew Carnegie (of the Hall fame). It also
serves as a design reference centre. Regularly
changing exhibits.

♟ **FRICK COLLECTION, 1 E 70th St, NY
10021 ☎ (212) 288 0700**
Beaux Arts mansion built to show off art collected by industrialist Henry Clay Frick. *"It's a
rich man's taste at a particular period so it has
a marvellous coherence"* – BRIAN SEWELL. *"It's
wonderful, go there to see Rembrandt's Polish
Rider and the Fragonard Room. It's an evoca-
tion of the great collecting and money at the
turn of the century. Spectacular collection of
French furniture"* – MEREDITH ETHERINGTON-
SMITH. Also Turners, Constables, Gainsbor-
oughs, Renoirs and Vermeers. Stroll around
the colonnades, in the cool pooled courtyard. *"I*

suppose my favourite building is the Frick. Absolutely a classic little jewel, a gem" – DOTT ROSA MARIA LETTS. Firm favourite of LORD LICHFIELD and JEFFREY ARCHER.

America's Best Galleries and Museums

1	METROPOLITAN MUSEUM OF ART · New York
2	NATIONAL GALLERY OF ART · Washington, DC
3	THE ART INSTITUTE OF CHICAGO · Chicago
4	PHILADELPHIA MUSEUM OF ART · Philadelphia
5	MUSEUM OF MODERN ART · New York
6	FRICK COLLECTION · New York
7	MUSEUM OF FINE ARTS · Boston
8	LOS ANGELES COUNTY MUSEUM OF ART · Los Angeles
9	MUSEUM OF CONTEMPORARY ART · Los Angeles
10	SMITHSONIAN INSTITUTION · Washington, DC

METROPOLITAN MUSEUM OF ART, 5th Ave/82nd St, NY 10028
☎ **(212) 879 5500**
Bafflingly large, bursting with more than 2 million works of art spanning 5,000 years. *"I can't wait to get into the Metropolitan. I will spend a day in there easily. I am never bored"* – JOHN TOVEY. Stroll through the reconstructed room sets and galleries of the Americas, Africa, Europe, Asia, Islam, Oceania. Excellent Dutch and Flemish paintings; great Impressionists and Post-Impressionists; a celebrated 20C art wing; fine antiquities, sculptures and decorative art. Check out the recently renovated Costume Institute. A big hit with ANDRE PREVIN, MARK PATRICK, LORD MONTAGU OF BEAULIEU, JEFFREY ARCHER and BARBARA TAYLOR BRADFORD. BRIAN SEWELL recognizes its worth, and its pitfalls: *"One of the world's great museums but the whole thing is so glossy, so hygienic, that it looks more like a commercial gallery."*

MUSEUM OF MODERN ART, 11 W 53rd St, NY 10019 ☎ **(212) 708 9480**
The world's most comprehensive survey of 20C art, including unparalleled collections (over 100,000 works) of paintings, sculpture, drawings, prints and photography. Also film, architecture, industrial and graphic design. A large number of Picassos, Mirós, Mondrians; major works by Van Gogh, Hopper, O'Keeffe, Pollock, Johns, Rothko, Rauschenberg, Warhol et al. Check out the Abbey Aldrich Rockerfeller Sculpture Garden and films in state-of-the-art theatres. Excellent exhibitions.

SOLOMON R GUGGENHEIM MUSEUM, 1071 5th Ave, NY 10218
☎ **(212) 423 3500; (212) 360 3500**
Restoration and renovation of Frank Lloyd Wright's provocative structure (1957–59), an icon of modern architecture, has transformed the gallery, doubling the space. *"Fantastic, totally helical. In a strange way it has the effect of heightening, it makes you feel as if you are going up towards the sky, and so with modern art you lift yourself in a totally functional manner"* – DOTT ROSA MARIA LETTS. As with all great buildings, it's still controversial: *"Thoroughly bad design – you can't hang flat things on a curving wall. It's got marvellous works but it seems to be an ankle-breaking business to see them"* – BRIAN SEWELL. Works are viewed from a spiral ramp that descends into the museum. Survey Degas, Gauguin, Vuillard, outstanding avant-garde art, the largest Kandinksy collection in the world, Klee, Chagall, Delaunay, Léger, Mondrian, Braque and fine sculptures. Downtown, the new **Guggenheim SoHo**, 575 Broadway, NY 10012, a converted warehouse, *"is very exciting, great works of 20C art in SoHo for the first time"* – STEPHEN HENRY MADOFF. STEPHEN JONES loves it.

WHITNEY MUSEUM OF AMERICAN ART, 945 Madison Ave, NY 10021
☎ **(212) 570 3600**
Tops for American contemporary art. Edward Hopper's oils, watercolours, drawings and prints, Jasper Johns's *Three Flags*, work by Reginald Marsh, Alexander Calder, Arshile Gorky and Georgia O'Keeffe. Film and video works too. Progressive, up-to-date exhibitions of abstract painting, photographs, figurative sculpture.

--- *Arts centres* ---

LINCOLN CENTER, Broadway btwn 62nd and 65th St, NY 10021
☎ **(212) 875 5000**
One for the hall's hall of fame – the nucleus of NY's cultural life. The world's largest arts complex spreads itself over 14 acres and takes in the Metropolitan Opera; the New York Philharmonic (one of ANDRE PREVIN's favourite orchestras *"on a good day"*); the New York City Ballet and the New York City Opera – both housed in the New York State Theater; the Film Society (in the new Walter Reade Theater); the Chamber Music Society in Alice Tully Hall; a first-rate

Broadway theatre, the Vivian Beaumont; the School of American Ballet, and The Juilliard School (of music, drama and dance).

———— *Ballet* ————

🏛 **AMERICAN BALLET THEATER, 890 Broadway, NY 10003 ☎ (212) 477 3030**
Under strong directorship of Oliver Smith and Jane Hermann the company flows along in an exuberant and spirited fashion, appealing to EDWARD THORPE. Sensational productions of everything from classics – *Swan Lake, Giselle, Sleeping Beauty* – to the work of new young choreographers such as John Selya's *Moondance* and Ulysses Dove's *Serious Pleasures*.

THE JOFFREY BALLET, 130 W 56th St, NY 10019 ☎ (212) 265 7300; LA ☎ (213) 487 8677
Distinctly American, the bicoastal troupe of 40 dancers celebrated the company's 35th anniversary in 1991. Its future, however, is uncertain: *"Joffrey is dead and they've had to lose a lot of dancers"* – EDWARD THORPE. They're still known for innovative new ballets by contemporary American choreographers. Catch them in autumn at the City Center Theater, New York; in spring in Los Angeles County Music Center; and the rest of the year on tour.

🏛 **NEW YORK CITY BALLET, New York State Theater, Lincoln Center, NY 10023 ☎ (212) 870 5500**
The most important and largest ballet company in America, founded by Lincoln Kirstein and George Balanchine. Under the directorship of Peter Martins, the repertoire is diverse and dancers dynamic. *"My favourite, they do a lot of new things as well as old"* – KEN LANE. Spectacular performances in the magnificent New York State Theater of Balanchine classics, Martins premieres and Robbins ballets such as *Glass Pieces* and *Quiet City*. In EDWARD THORPE's world top 10.

———— *Clubs* ————

AMAZON VILLAGE, Pier 25, West St, NY 10013 ☎ (212) 227 2900
Summer club (mid-May to mid-Oct) on TriBeCa beach, run on eco-conscious lines, for outdoorsy downtown types. Al fresco clubbing under 5 big tents, amid palm trees, a waterfall and a real sand volleyball court. DJs and live Afro-Caribbean sounds; restaurant serving southwestern/French/Italian/New American cuisine, plus an oyster bar. Go boating, or gaze at the aquarium. Open noon till the wee hours.

AU BAR, 41 E 58th St, NY 10022 ☎ (212) 308 9455
Drawing-room décor – bookshelves and deep leather armchairs, massive bowls of caviare, but dancing for sardines only. Rather Trampish, reckons an avuncular JOHN GOLD: *"A very successful operation."*

🏛 **COPACABANA, 10 E 60th St, NY 10022 ☎ (212) 755 6010**
Drag yourself along to Suzanne Bartsch's Love Ball on the last Thursday of the month for the kinkiest cross-dressing-up box in town. *"She hires all these drag queens with brilliant headdresses and sequins to dance on go-go boxes for entertainment. You could stand there and be in awe all night"* – MICHAEL MUSTO. *"She always has the best, most interesting mixture of people"* – DUGGIE FIELDS. Bankers groove to 70s music next to muscle men and strippers. Fashion designers such as Gaultier flock down to get inspiration from the Big Apple's weirdest and most wonderful one-nighter. STEPHEN JONES and SEBASTIAN SCOTT stand in awe too.

CRANE CLUB, 408 Amsterdam Ave, NY 10024 ☎ (212) 877 3097
Low-key dining and dancing. Eat to jazz slicksters – Sinatra, Harry Connick Jr – then shake it off to funk and rock sounds after 12. Wood-panelled rooms, oil paintings, old photos, etc . . . .

🕵 **Buzzz Art for money's sake:** STEVEN HENRY MADOFF tips where to hand over the cash: Larry **Gagosian**, 980 Madison Ave ☎ (212) 744 2313, *"is shaping up to be the major dealer of the 90s – a place to go if you're looking to buy and have a lot of money in your wallet"* 🏛 . . . . He turns up some cheaper tricks further downtown: **Flynn**, *113 Crosby St ☎ (212) 966 0426, is interesting and her shows run for months and are always quirky and wonderful"* 🏛 . . . . . . Head down to the old US Customs Building for a pow-wow at the **Museum of the American Indian**, 1 Green Bowling St, NY 10004 ☎ (212) 283 2420. Here is the greatest collection of its kind in the world: artefacts and information about native Americans from the North Pole to Tierra del Fuego. Directional temporary exhibitions; for *Points of View*, one of the inaugural exhibitions, 32 native Americans chose objects that told the story of their peoples . . . . 🏛

Outlawed

Beyond clubs, beyond cool; what can you do if you tire of Tatou? *"There are these outlaw parties that are held outdoors in different locations – on a bridge or on a sanitation pier or in a park. The word gets out and everyone shows up. The police always come and break it up, so it's the only time that people show up on time for anything"* – MICHAEL MUSTO.

Over the other side of the Atlantic, outlaw parties have become depressingly inlaw. Called raves (post-acid house parties), they attract a younger crowd and start later, but some of the old magic has gone. *"In the early days, you'd hear about a rave on your local pirate radio station and half the excitement was not knowing if it was on or off till you got there,"* tips our roving raver DOMIX. *"Now the music's better than ever – lots of British hard-core techno stuff and music from Europe, but the atmosphere's not the same. A real raver (mostly the younger kids who've only just started) wears baggy jeans, a floppy hat, baggy jumper, huge trainers and a baby's dummy. Up north some of the kids wear mouth masks, like couriers wear, with Vicks rubbed inside, for a bit of a buzz. But mostly the emphasis is on music and PAs (personal appearances) now – unlike the old illegal days when there'd be 8,000 in a hangar."*

LAURA BELLE, 120 W 43rd St (6th Ave at Broadway), NY 10036 ☎ (212) 819 1000
New York's retro mood has locked into the supper club. This one's the choice for ultra-beautiful people – Naomi Campbell had her birthday party here, Madonna, Diana Ross and Liza Minnelli just partied. The marble entrance hall leads through to a 40 ft neo-classical façade overlooking the dance floor. Dancers take time out to dine on Japanese-accented dishes designed by exec chef Mitsu Kikuchi (ex-Connaught, River Café, NY). *"A huge, brilliant place"* – SEBASTIAN SCOTT.

🎩 NELL'S, 264 W 14th St, NY 10011 ☎ (212) 675 1567
Little Nell's is still the first night stop-off for jet-lagged Brits (MEREDITH ETHERINGTON-SMITH, IAIN JOHNSTONE, DAVID SHILLING) – though it reminds them less and less of home as the crowd gets blacker and funkier. But New York's original gentlemen's clubby club is the natural place for a post-Mortimer's drink and boogie, and Village people like MICHAEL MUSTO still rate it.

REX, 579 6th St, NY 10009 ☎ (212) 741 0080
Dinner/dancing club that pulls the best-looking bods in town. French style, cool jazz. *"Fun, for beautiful people – models. Short people may be advised to wear platform heels, I am 6 ft tall and I feel short in there"* – DAVID SHILLING. Justine Bateman tore it up for hours on the dance floor here.

THE SUPPER CLUB, Edison Hotel, 240 W 47th St, NY 10036 ☎ (212) 921 1940
The talk of the town – a cavernous dining and dancing club that heralds a swing back to the swing era of the 1940s. Big bands trumpet their stuff on a vast stage, while diners (up to 400) sit at grand round tables in the blue and gilt ballroom, tucking into chef Wayne Nish's dishes. Hearty food with a modern touch is the order of the day – confit of duck, herb-roast chicken (turn up when the joint is jumping on Saturday for the best food and service, when staff adrenaline's running high). Supping sorts include Claudia Cardinale, Joan Collins and Tony Bennett. Music from 7.30 pm, but the action doesn't start till 11 pm.

SIN-E, 122 St Mark's Place, 8th Ave, NY 10009 ☎ (212) 982 0370
Laid-back, pass-the-guitar-style live music venue/café with spontaneous improvisation by talented audiences. Coffee's great and so's the Irish soda bread.

🎩 TATOU, 151 E 50th St, NY 10022 ☎ (212) 753 1144
Cabaret, jazz, dance and supper club that's the talk of the chattering classes, ROBIN LEACH for one: *"The hottest nightlife restaurant that everyone is raving about."* A nightclub of old, where Edith Piaf first performed in America, Tatou has been restored to its former glory. *"A nice place to eat – the food is excellent"* – MICHAEL MUSTO. SEBASTIAN SCOTT's sentiments exactly. 2 floors full of loopy entertainments – swing along to the 20-piece all-girl orchestra, and jive to serious jazzmen. DUGGIE FIELDS looks in when he's after *"a more upmarket, straighter scene"*. If he went out on Sunday he could have a gospel brunch – if he went to LA or Aspen he'd find Tatous there too.

TRAMPS, 45 W 21st St, NY 10010
☎ (212) 727 7788
Best new addition to Manhattan's live scene,
often hosting 2 live shows a night – rock 'n' roll,
rhythm 'n' blues – to jam packed list 'n' ers.

WETLANDS, 161 Hudson St, NY 10002
☎ (212) 966 4225
They've been back in NY for a while now – kaf-
tans, afghans and flares – and this is where
you'll find them. Greenery sprouts up in the
Earth Station, a psychedelic VW bus brim-full
of environmentalia. You can groove to 60s
sounds or drink downstairs in the Inner Sanctum. Hear live bands from Mon to Sat, but on
Sun you save the planet – at least talk about it.

—— *Fashion designers* ——

ADOLFO, 36 E 57th St, NY 10022
☎ (212) 688 4410
Neat little day suits with more than a hint of
Chanel made to order for women who like to
order (Nancy Reagan, Jean Tailor, Carol
Petrie). The right silk dress for the races too, or
an evening dress for the charity do.

**ADRIENNE VITTADINI, 1441 Broadway,
NY 10018 ☎ (212) 921 2510, and at major
department stores**
Casual, sporty designs – perfect for a 90s city
lifestyle. Known best for her knits: "*A fantasti-
cally talented designer, in the Klein/Karan
mode*" – CASEY TOLAR (SKYE MACLEOD's a fan
too). The biggest hit at the moment's her Home
collection. Also boutiques all over the States.

**ARNOLD SCAASI COUTURE, 681 5th
Ave, NY 10022 ☎ (212) 755 5105**
NY's great couturier manages to escape the current passion for understated fashion. Scaasi creates confections for the Occasion with a capital O
(Jackie, that is, as well as Ivana and Barbra and
others whose first names are instantly recognizable) – silk taffeta and tulle, to be worn once
only. Also ready-to-wear at 530 7th Ave.

🛡 BILL BLASS, 550 7th Ave, NY 10018
☎ (212) 221 6660
Blass blasts a path through fashion's vagaries
with 3 constants: terrific fabrics, unerring
design and masterly craftsmanship. Lately, the
look leans to downhome Americana mixing
lumberjack and picnic checks and flippy cheer-
leader skirts. Courts (and is courted by) the
ladies of the Social Register – an eminently
satisfactory situation for both parties.

**🛡 CALVIN KLEIN, 205 W 39th St, NY
10018 ☎ (212) 719 2600**
Klein's signature of casual chic looks set to flourish throughout the 90s. Little silk print dresses,
soft-tailored trouser suits and gossamer chiffon
etched with plaid beading sum up his wearable,
very marketable blend of comfort, understate-

ment and ein Klein kinda class. NANCY PILCHER
goes for it.

**CAROLINA HERRERA, 19 E 57th St, NY
10022 ☎ (212) 355 3055**
Still in there, but more low-key than of yore, as
the lunch-a-lot set lunches a lot less. The perfect
little day suit and cocktail dress are perennial
favourites with society queen bees.

———— 🛡 ————
America's Best Designers

1	DONNA KARAN
2	RALPH LAUREN
3	CALVIN KLEIN
4	BILL BLASS
5	ISAAC MIZRAHI

**CHRISTIAN FRANCIS ROTH, 336 W 37th
St, NY 10018 ☎ (212) 239 0130**
One of NY's most directional young designers,
unafraid to make a statement. Classic tailoring
with witty touches – cocktail dresses come not
with a twist but a cherry and umbrella, tuxedos
are worn back to front. Fun, and one to watch.

**🛡 DONNA KARAN, 14th Fl, 550 7th Ave,
NY 10018 ☎ (212) 302 1680**
Karan's unfussy, perfectly put together separates never pall. The woman who put the body
on the agenda still does them best and the short
draped skirt remains a city winner teamed with
her long-line jacket. Fluidity's the thing, but
then a crisp Jermyn Street shirt with satin
collar also carries unmistakable Karan clout –
it's a matter of simplicity and proportion which,
for MARIE HELVIN, is "*luxurious*" and, for JOAN
BURSTEIN, "*wonderful*". "*She has done more for
the working woman's wardrobe than any other
designer, because she was totally realistic about
what woman wanted to wear – at a price*" – GAIL
ROLFE. DKNY brings the look, if not to the
masses, at least to a wider set of fans.

**GEOFFREY BEENE, 783 5th Ave, NY
10022 ☎ (212) 935 0470**
The quiet achiever, Beene's been there, done
that and gets on with his own thing. The sleek
lacquer and marble shop in the Sherry-Nether-
lands accommodates the full range – sportswear
through superbly cut suits to sculpted evening
gowns. Mutterings have been heard that he's
playing it a little safe in recent collections.

**🛡 ISAAC MIZRAHI, 104 Wooster St, NY
10012 ☎ (212) 334 0055**
The fashion prodigy of the States leads the way
forward. His discipline is obvious in beautifully
tailored classics, his sense of fun is apparent in
seasonal flourishes of poppy-printed chiffon

dresses or rhinestone cowgirl campery. JOAN BURSTEIN applauds, as does GAIL ROLFE: "*He and Michael Kors are the two hot young names of the 80s that are likely to last. They have fashion sense and business sense.*"

MICHAEL KATZ, 13 E 17th St, NY 10003 ☎ (212) 929 3976
A new and highly individual individual to watch. "*He's really a painter but he handpaints Matisse-looking pictures on lengths of fabric and cuts them into shirts and pyjamas. They're very amusing conversation pieces but they've attracted quite a following – purely couture*" – ELEANOR LAMBERT.

🦺 MICHAEL KORS, 119 W 24th St, NY 10001 ☎ (212) 620 4677
Kors' recipe of sexiness and simplicity is one of the most palatable to non-US fashion folk. Co-ordinated separates are the basis of the Kors woman's wardrobe – more head-turning numbers are long, slim skirts, slashed to the thigh, and lingerie-inspired lace evening dresses. "*Probably my favourite American designer at the moment – really nice blazers, trousers and skirts . . . clothes we want to buy*" – GAIL ROLFE.

NORMA KAMALI at OMO, 11 W 56th St, NY 10019 ☎ (212) 957 9797

The shop's initials stand for On My Own and Kamali is: a woman of the 90s designing for women of the 90s. Cotton jersey/lycra mixes and swimwear won't show the day's wear and tear, long-line linen suits are just the ticket for the office, transparent chiffon print dresses leave the office far behind. Couture and bridal wear in extravagant fabrics from this shop only.

🦺 OSCAR DE LA RENTA, 550 7th Ave, NY 10018 ☎ (212) 354 6777
No 1 for NY's doyennes – with the sort of disregard for understatement that suits Agnellis and Rothschilds. Lots of beadwork and ornament – glittery sweaters and ra-ra skirts catch eyes on the catwalk. "*Along with Bill Blass, he dresses real American women, who actually do buy the clothes from the catwalk*" – GAIL ROLFE.

RALPH LAUREN, see Shopping

TODD OLDHAM, 499 7th Ave, NY 10018 ☎ (212) 629 6100
A bright newcomer to a rather restrained scene, gathering plaudits from all over. Style-watchers sat up and noticed his black 'Alteration' shift dress with seams picked out in contrasting colours, and his dress made from a man's shirt (the sleeves are used as a belt). "*He's very talented*" – ELEANOR LAMBERT.

Burrowing
—— 🦺 ——

A modern-day Donne would have something to say about current social trends ("Read my lips, buddy – *no* man is an island") but New Yorkers wouldn't hear a word of it ("Quit that bell tolling, it's disturbing my island fortress"). After the hectic activity of the 80s – networking, ladder-climbing, interfacing, aerobicizing – the 90s is a time (they say) for domestic values, a time, as ELEANOR LAMBERT says, for "*going back to homely settings and family life. They know the other way of living is harmful, people now realize there have to be rules.*" Well, yes, tell that to the boys at the 19th precinct who probably haven't noticed a drop in crack dealing or homelessness but then, isn't that the point? City life has become so threatening that the middle classes have give up the fight for the streets, hence 'cocooning' themselves in the comfort and safety of home, or as the new catch-phrase has it,

'burrowing'. Those who can afford it are heading for the country (or at least reading *Countryside* instead of *Vogue*), others are staying home, baking cookies and decorating with chintz. And who needs to venture on to the streets? Not New Yorkers – they can dial it all from home. Want sushi? **Hatsuhana ☎** (212) 661 3400 delivers. Want a new bed in 2 hrs? Try **Dial-a-Mattress ☎** (1-800) MATTRES (the last S is left off for extra savings – geddit?). Or you could have your whole house overhauled without moving more than your index finger – **Bloomingdale's Home Shoppers ☎** 1 (800) 888 8840 will bring swatches of fabric, furniture, the works. "*People are furnishing homes rather than adorning their bodies, so home furnishing and food industries are prospering when all else is in recession*" – ELEANOR L. But it couldn't possibly all be a marketing ploy . . . could it?

——— *Hotels* ———

🍴 **THE CARLYLE, 35 E 75th St, NY 10021**
☎ **(212) 744 1600**
Caring, discreet and well endowed is this perfect mistress of a NY hotel. Despite former
manager Frank Bowling's departure, under Dan
Camp the chic Upper East Sider *"remains
excellent"* – GILES SHEPARD. MEREDITH ETHER-
INGTON-SMITH catalogues the charm: *"Incredibly
pretty with Aubusson carpets, wonderful food
and a proper pianist – Bobby Short – in the
cocktail bar. The best hotel in America."* KEN
HOM lists his priorities: *"It is a very nice, discreet
place which has good food and superb service"* –
KEN HOM. BARBARA TAYLOR BRADFORD visits, and
she's a New Yorker. LISA BARNARD thinks it's a
winner for execs.

THE LOWELL, 28 E 63rd St, NY 10021
☎ **(212) 838 1400**
Small (by NY standards) well-bred suite hotel.
Open fireplaces, shelves crammed with books,
and proper kitchens make it *"homely, not in a
shabby way but as you'd like your house to be.
It's always immaculate and the staff are wonderful"* – VICTOR EDELSTEIN. TESSA DAHL and
TERRY HOLMES applaud its class.

🍴 **THE MARK, 25 E 77th St, NY 10021**
☎ **(212) 744 4300**
A classic hotel created, it seems, overnight.
Comfortable, stylish post-neo-classical décor,
keen-as-mustard service (managers get a piece
of the action), and a tip-top East Side residential
location. *"The manager, Raymond Bickson, is
outstanding and has made a 200-bedroom-plus
hotel seem like a very small, highly personalized boutique hotel"* – MARTIN SKAN. *"One of the
new hot spots"* – BOB PAYTON. *"Brilliantly run,
great restaurant and with the best bathrooms
I've ever been in"* – ALAN CROMPTON-BATT.
*"Incredibly well put together and they are so
nice to children in the restaurant which is rare
in NY"* – TESSA DAHL. MARY ROSSI stands by
that, as does TERRY HOLMES: *"It's very much in
the European tradition."*

🍴 **MAYFAIR REGENT, 610 Park Ave, NY
10021 ☎ (212) 288 0800**
Still No 1 among those who enjoy Euro charm
and style. Lauded by its regulars for personal
attention and warmth, where you're a valued
name, not a number. Known to its intimates
(such as SKYE MACLEOD and LISA BARNARD) as
Dario's (Dario Mariotti is general manager), it
can't go wrong as long as it houses Sirio's (**Le
Cirque** – see Restaurants). It's *"still one of the
best hotels in the city"* for ROBIN LEACH; for
PRINCESS PUCCI SALAMEH it is too: *"We love it
and its manager."*

**THE PARAMOUNT, 235 W 46th St, NY
10036 ☎ (212) 764 5500**
Similarly Starck younger sibling of the Royal-

ton. At first glance, cold planes abound; at the
second, intriguing fixtures and a new sense of
design become apparent. The **Whisky Bar** has
rapidly become the biggest scene in the city for
the ex-Brat Packers – Matt Dillon, Julia
Roberts, Kevin Bacon. *"Fun, the later the better.
If you can't find a pair of chairs that match it
may not be that you've drunk too much, they
just don't"* – DAVID SHILLING. *"A combination of
futuristic, nostalgic, 50s, science fiction . . . very
elegant and very minimal"* – MICHAEL MUSTO.

THE PENINSULA, 700 5th Ave, NY 10019
☎ **(212) 247 2200**
Dynamic outpost of the Hong Kong-based group
with Eastern-attentive service, Art Nouveau-
style furnishings and state-of-the-art health
club. *"Today, people want proper health clubs in
hotels and the Peninsula takes the cake for that
facility – an incredible swimming pool and spa
on the top 3 floors. It really is extraordinary to
work out with the view of the Manhattan
skyline"* – ROBIN LEACH. The **Pen-Top Bar
and Terrace**'s city views draw a happening
music crowd. *"Still as fabulous"* – KEN HOM.

THE PIERRE, 2 E 61st St, NY 10021
☎ **(212) 838 8000**
One of the Four Seasons' clutch of prime properties, a good, solid 20s building with the glamour
of that era. *"Its elegance is quite unique. To stay
in a hotel is very sad – you must find something
that resembles a house"* – DOTT ROSA MARIA
LETTS. DAVID SHILLING admires it for reasons of
his own: *"I like it because it has its own Bulgari,
and Tiffany is just a stone's throw away."* Low-
turnover, long-time staff make the difference for
SHARYN STORRIER-LYNEHAM.

🍴 **THE PLAZA, 768 5th Ave, NY 10019**
☎ **(212) 759 3000**
The grandest of NY's old hotels, Trump's baby
has survived the ups and downs of the past few
years and is stronger for it. *"The refurbishment
is exceptional, a total transformation – if you
like being in the centre of things it couldn't be
more perfect. Even though it is a big hotel, the
staff remember you"* – TERRY HOLMES. Original
1907 mouldings and crystal chandeliers are
matched by fine old-fashioned service. Join the
suits for dinner in the panelled **Oak Room** or
listen to piano and violin in the gilded **Palm
Court**. *"Still a key landmark"* – ROBIN LEACH.
JOHN GOLD likes it too.

**RITZ-CARLTON, 112 Central Park S, NY
10019 ☎ (212) 757 1900**
A slice of England, Manhattan-style – country
life in 19C repro furniture and hunt prints,
clubby respectability in the wood-panelled
Jockey Club dining room. Chef Craig Henne's
deftly reworked classics (tenderloin with foie
gras and red onion marmalade, scallops on
Japanese seaweed) and wine-paired tasting
menus are tipped for the top. LORD MONTAGU OF
BEAULIEU backs a winner.

THE ROYALTON, 44 W 44th St, NY 10036
☎ (212) 869 4400
The peak of designerdom's achievement, Philippe Starck's temple of steely minimalism makes pop stars and fashion gurus (Lisa Stansfield, Dolce & Gabbana) feel at home and everyone else feel out of place. *"The ground floor is the best modern room I know. It's got a wonderful sense of space, colour and furnishing which makes people look very glamorous"* – SIR TERENCE CONRAN. It's even got the most designer address (44 W 44). VCRs and cassette decks in every room go down well (especially with BONNIE BROOKS), as does the food, consumed conspicuously, of course. The vodka bar is the clear complement to the Paramount's **Whisky Bar**.

THE ST REGIS, 2 E 55th St, NY 10022
☎ (212) 753 4500
A year into its new incarnation and the 3-year, $100 million refit shows no signs of wear. The grand Beaux Arts building's decoration boasts impressive statistics: 600 crystal chandeliers (each taking 2 days to install), 3.2 acres of bathroom marble, as well as Louis XV furniture and the famous Maxfield Parrish *Old King Cole* mural. Under Gray Kunz (Girardet-trained), **Lespinasse** looks set to become one of NY's top hotel restaurants.

─────── *Music* ───────

CARNEGIE HALL, 154 W 57th St, NY 10019 ☎ (212) 247 7800
Entering its 2nd century, the Carnegie remains New Yorkers' favourite concert hall. It's also one of the 5 best halls in the world, according to ANDRE PREVIN.

🎔 **METROPOLITAN OPERA, Metropolitan Opera House, Lincoln Center, NY 10023 ☎ (212) 362 6000**
The 800-strong company is the top US stop for all the great voices, though priority given to the best vocal chords money can hire – Pavarotti's, Domingo's, Te Kanawa's – can take the edge off the production, say critics. None the less, it's widely seen as the America's best – and world premieres of, say, the new Philip Glass, or a new Puccini or Verdi production, maintain it's prestigious status. Tickets go like hot cakes. The Met Opera House has the most glamorous sweeping staircase in NY, 2 massive Chagalls (hung the wrong way round) and chandeliers which withdraw into the ceiling when the lights go down.

NEW YORK CITY OPERA, New York State Theater, Lincoln Center, NY 10023 ☎ (212) 870 5570
Dynamic counterpoint to the dynastic Met. Challenging modern productions – eg Zimmermann's *Die Soldaten* – run along side *Madam Butterfly*, *Tosca* and co, musicals, and up-to-the-minute contemporary. Superb set and costume design. July-Nov season.

92nd STREET Y, 92nd St at Lexington Ave, NY 10128 ☎ (212) 427 6000
One of America's most important new venues. It attracts the world's greatest performers – Perlman, Zuckerman, Jessye Norman – to year-round concerts. Don't miss the Schubertiade if you're in town in January, and the summer jazz festival. JULIAN LLOYD WEBBER's favourite hall in New York: *"It has the most beautiful acoustic . . . it holds about 600 people and it has a good deal more atmosphere than most concert halls."*

─────── *Restaurants* ───────

See also Hotels.

ALISON ON DOMINICK STREET, 38 Dominick St, NY 10013 ☎ (212) 727 1188
A small, romantic town house, A on D serves fare from SW France. Local artists and voracious Wall Streeters rub shoulders as they tuck into such hearty provençalities as braised lamb shank with fava beans, white beans and chicory, or roast guinea fowl with wild mushroom risotto.

AQUAVIT, 13 W 54th St, NY 10019 ☎ (212) 307 7311
Architectural dining room soars with Christer Larsson's sophisticated Scandinavian cooking. *"Its enclosed atrium is a well-bred chamber of stone, steel and glass that, by the addition of a bit of nature's art and man's art has been softened into an enfolding glade, and the Scandinavian food is of rare purity"* – SEYMOUR BRITCHKY. Wash down near-mythological beasties (snow goose, Arctic venison) with the fiery water of life, Aquavit.

🎔 **ARCADIA, 21 E 62nd St, NY 10021 ☎ (212) 223 2900**
New American cooking, with gutsy flavours and a deceptive air of simplicity. *"Anne Rosenzweig is a wonderful young cook, and it's a charming small restaurant with a beautiful mural of the seasons. Her cooking is seasonal and in the autumn she has the most miraculous chocolate bread pudding with brandy custard sauce – you can't resist it. All her cooking is inspired but this hits a special high"* – ELISABETH LAMBERT ORTIZ. Et in Arcadia go GILES SHEPARD, KEN HOM and MARK MCCORMACK: *"My favourite place to have lunch."*

🎔 **AUREOLE, 34 E 61st St, NY 10021 ☎ (212) 319 1660**
Charlie Palmer's flower-filled power-dining room has established his place as leader in progressive American cooking. French bases, American ingredients and world influences fuse in dishes such as tea-smoked squab or pepper-seared quail, and inspire high praise from foodies: *"Charlie Palmer's place is fantastic. He makes the most original food in NY; he really is superb"* – KEN HOM. Just desserts from BARBARA

KAFKA: *"One of the few places I know where people actually eat dessert. There'll be a whole plate of different caramel desserts or fruit or chocolate in sort of architectural shapes which might sound contrived but aren't."* DOUGLAS FAIR-BANKS JR is a regular.

🍴 BOULEY, 165 Duane St, NY 10013
☎ (212) 608 3852
David Bouley's seriously French restaurant has transformed a warehouse into a vaulted cathedral to gastronomy. Seasonal decorations of fruit baskets and herbs highlight the food's freshness: guinea hen with an autumn risotto and julienned organic vegetables or fish (flown in daily) with tomato water. *"He's a fabulous cook, it is §nouvelle but very personal nouvelle"* – MADHUR JAFFREY. *"Very highly rated, very French"* – BARBARA KAFKA. JOE EULA eulogizes.

CAFE LUXEMBOURG, 200 W 70th St, NY 10023 ☎ (212) 873 7411
Buzzy, Art Deco bistro (cream and blue tiles, zinc bar) with high energy level and straightforward French food draws in a good mix of people – smart pre-theatre crowd early on; hipper downtown artists, musos (Mick Jagger, David Bowie), etc, as the night wears on. *"I love it"* – DUGGIE FIELDS.

CHANTERELLE, 2 Harrison St, NY 10013
☎ (212) 966 6960
Soaring post-modernism in TriBeCa's landmark Mercantile Exchange Building. The room's imposing starkness is softened by glorious floral arrangements; modern provençal food, infallible home-baked breads and comprehensive wine list. *"One of my favourites in NY, really terrific food"* – KEN HOM.

🍴 COCO PAZZO, 23 E 74 St, NY 10021
☎ (212) 794 0205
Another grand success for man with a mission Pino (Le Madri) Luongo. Bringing regional Italian food to NY, the Madri concept has expanded to a famiglia feed: Fri-Sun you get what's in the pot, from the pot, and no one's complaining. *"Sensational, good pasta, great service and a nice atmosphere"* – MARK MCCORMACK. *"Very lively, hot and happening. A lot of glamorous jetsetters, a lot of good-looking men and women go there"* – ROBIN LEACH. *"Everything is really very good"* – MARCHESA DI SAN GIULIANO FERRAGAMO. Echoes from DAVID SHILLING and KEN HOM.

DAWAT, 210 E 58th St, NY 10022
☎ (212) 355 7555
Authentic regional Indian cookery in a peach and aqua dining room a mere chapatti's throw from Bloomingdale's. Of the menu which she oversees, MADHUR JAFFREY declares: *"You will find foods here that you don't get in any other Indian restaurant – a lot of the dishes are family dishes from all over India, from Kashmir, from my family in Delhi. Very good value."*

ELAINE'S, 1703 2nd Ave, NY 10022
☎ (212) 534 8103
More literary than glittery, publishers and their protégés remain faithful to Elaine's long-standing diner. A spare table's a rare thing, a spare power table (along the wall, right-hand side) is something to write about. *"Still the old standby for the journalists, the writers here in New York"* – ROBIN LEACH. *"I still love going to Elaine's, they have been running a supper club for the last 25 years, a very interesting group of people turns up – it's like going to a party every night"* – ED VICTOR. Woody Allen joins the party.

America's Best Restaurants

1	AUREOLE · New York
2	BOULEY · New York
3	STARS · San Francisco
4	GALILEO · Washington, DC
5	LE CIRQUE · New York
6	CHEZ PANISSE · Berkeley
7	MARK'S PLACE · Miami
8	MATSUHISA · Los Angeles
9	THE FRONTERA GRILL · Chicago
10	FOUR SEASONS · New York

ELIO'S, 1621 2nd Ave, NY 10028
☎ (212) 772 2242
Cheerfully cliquy café/restaurant, good for fish and seafood. *"I love going to Elio's, a very buzzy Italian restaurant. It's just a hot spot, a lot of people one knows are there and the food is excellent"* – ED VICTOR.

🍴 FOUR SEASONS, 99 E 52nd St, NY 10022 ☎ (212) 754 9494
The major-league lunch-spot for hard ball players. *"Every year it gets better . . . a restaurant that has great food, great service and great theatre, packed with people you either know or know of. I think the **Bar Room** is one of the greatest restaurant rooms in the world, panelled in the most beautiful wood with an amazing grain. The tables are very well spaced so you can never overhear conversations"* – ED VICTOR. *"It's managed to keep its glamour, a wonderful place"* – SIR TERENCE CONRAN. *"An institution, beautifully run"* – DAVID GIBBONS. The institution lives on for STEPHEN JONES, MARCHESA DI SAN GIULIANO FERRAGAMO, ROBIN LEACH, CAROLINE HUNT and PAUL HENDERSON (who prefers the Pool Room), but the prices stick in some

throats: *"I can't afford to go there any more, it's gone mad"* – JOHN TOVEY. He should try the pre-theatre cheapo deal. ED V has the last word: *"It's one thing to go because it's a power place but the fact is you eat there terribly well."*

GOTHAM BAR & GRILL, 12 E 12th St, NY 10003 ☎ (212) 620 4020

Ultra-designed, beautiful people's restaurant with an inspired, eclectic menu under Alfred Portale. Intelligent lighting and walls blasted with paint form a backdrop for such far-flung offerings as veal carpaccio, duck choucroute or the bravado-stamped black bass in port sauce.

🍴 JO JO'S, 160 E 64th St, NY 10021 ☎ (212) 223 5656

Jean-Georges Vongerichten's disciples followed in his wake from Lafayette to this most uptown of restaurants. *"Looks as though it's filled with many a mistress but quite groovy"* – SEBASTIAN SCOTT. DAVID SHILLING goes *"not for the food but for the fun"*. *"Very in, I think they are a little snooty but I also like it very much"* – MARK MCCORMACK. Can they all be talking about the same place? MADHUR JAFFREY knows why she goes, for inventive, forward-thinking food: *"He specializes in sauces and oils that he makes from vegetables; he cooks in them or dribbles them over food and it is quite wonderful."*

🍴 LA GRENOUILLE, 3 E 52nd St, NY 10022 ☎ (212) 752 1495

Old-fashioned French grandee rigorously maintains its haut-prix, haute-cuisine standards as attested by devotees BARBARA TAYLOR BRADFORD, ANDREW LLOYD WEBBER, MARCHESA DI SAN GIULIANO FERRAGAMO, MARC BOHAN (*"for food, atmosphere, all that sort of thing"*), MEREDITH ETHERINGTON-SMITH (*"very grand old-fashioned food"*) and KENNETH LANE (*"delicious French food"*). Outstanding floral arrangements, hovering service.

🍴 LE BERNARDIN, 155 W 51st St, NY 10019 ☎ (212) 489 1515

Still NY's biggest catch for spanking fresh seafood, surrounded by the sharks of the business district. Solid, teaky room hung with seascapes is kept ship-shape by family duo Maguy and Gilbert Le Coze. *"The best fish I have eaten in my life. It gets two bests because it's the best fish and the best-looking brother and sister who run it"* – SALLY BURTON. *"Fantastic fish, but also other things . . . it is very, very good"* – MARCHESA DI SAN GIULIANO FERRAGAMO. CAROLINE HUNT and LORD LICHFIELD say aye.

🍴 LE CIRQUE, 58 E 65th St, NY 10021 ☎ (212) 794 9292

Tables at the Mayfair Regent's gastronomic grandee are filled as ever with the very rich and very famous, as ROBIN LEACH has noticed: *"Probably the only restaurant in the world where you could sit down for dinner and see 3 former US presidents."* Fabulous French/Italian food from chef Daniel Boulud: kick off with lobster risotto rosemary, green onions and pea pods; on to paupiette of black sea bass in red barolo wine sauce – then the famous crème brûlée. Woody Allen, Richard Nixon, Joan Collins and Mick Jagger and Nancy Reagan are hooked. So are MARC BOHAN, BIJAN (*"elegant chic"*), BARBARA KAFKA (*"first rate"*), ANDREW LLOYD WEBBER (*"still very good"*) and MEREDITH ETHERINGTON-SMITH (*"you'd fall into Le Cirque for fantastic grand Italian food"*). *"Le Cirque? Certainly,"* confirms DOUGLAS FAIRBANKS JR.

🍴 LE MADRI, 168 W 18th St, NY 10011 ☎ (212) 727 8022

Housewife/mother turned chef, Marta Pulini epitomizes the Madri phenomenon: homely, authentic and successful. Under Pino Luongo's unerring management, this Tuscan-based trat is still at the top. *"The best Italian restaurant I've ever been to outside Italy"* – ALAN CROMPTON-BATT. *"Really quite remarkable. A very, very fine restaurant in a sort of relaxed, hip way"* – STEPHEN HENRY MADOFF. MARK MCCORMACK and JOAN BURSTEIN think *la madre* knows best.

🍴 LUTECE, 249 E 50th St, NY 10022 ☎ (212) 752 2225

Serious French cuisine and superlative service. *"Chef/proprietor André Soltner is the simple, clear voice of a Mozart amid the cacophony of a million restaurants clamouring for trade. But here, in civilization preserved, in a landmark institution, Soltner's outpouring of dishes is on the culinary front line"* – SEYMOUR BRITCHKY. PAUL HENDERSON (who always asks M Soltner to choose the meal and the sommelier to choose Alsatian wine) and MEREDITH ETHERINGTON-SMITH agree with such eloquence.

MONDRIAN, 7 E 59th St, NY 10022 ☎ (212) 935 3434

The great Dutch painter of blocks painted on this block, hence the name. Exciting cooking, drawing on worldwide traditions with flair. *"Here is wood-panelled, clubby solidity that actually achieves grandeur and food that speaks fluently and expressively in an international language all its own"* – SEYMOUR BRITCHKY. Try the house speciality and stint not on the pud.

MORTIMER'S, 1057 Lexington Ave, NY 10021 ☎ (212) 517 6400

The sanctum for Euro toffs, Upper Easties, jet-setters and Brits abroad, run in clubbish style by Glenn Bernbaum. *"I love Mortimer's . . . nanny food, hamburgers for 10-year-olds"* – KENNETH LANE. MEREDITH ETHERINGTON-SMITH thinks the window table is New York's smartest and *"not expensive, but a very chic place to go"*. *"One sticks with the Brits a bit and eats at Mortimer's,"* says IAIN JOHNSTONE.

ODEON, 145 W Broadway, NY 10013 ☎ (212) 233 0507

Bistro buzzing with artspeak; trendy film and

fringe folk eat upmarket French brasserie fare in the original McNally Bros dinery. Well-designed neon/chrome space – good late at night and for brunch. An obvious choice for STEVEN HENRY MADOFF.

OYSTER BAR, Grand Central Terminal, Lower Level, NY 10017 ☎ (212) 490 6650

The noisiest lunch in town: don't go for a power-wow but expect a super-abundance of the best fresh fish, chowders and oysters. Chase them with a Great White (wine) from the large list. "*It just buzzes. If you are going to New York just once, you must go there*" – TERRY HOLMES. "*I think it is marvellous*" – JEAN-MICHEL JAUDEL.

PETROSSIAN, 182 W 58th St, NY 10019 ☎ (212) 245 2214

The caviare house. "*When you get stuck with a stack of large bills you are unable to launder and when caviare, smoked fish, foie gras and champagne are what you crave, this place has no peer*" – SEYMOUR BRITCHKY. Art Deco-r, mink-lined kid-skin banquettes, mammoth bill. MICHAEL BROADBENT is attracted by its "*refinement and miniature luxury*".

PROVENCE, 38 MacDougal St, NY 10012 ☎ (212) 475 7500

Authentic provençale cuisine – tarte à l'oignon, bouillabaisse, gâteau d'aubergine – cooked beautifully, in a *very* busy eaterie. "*It's a wonderful restaurant. I think it's the most consistent downtown bistro*" – STEPHEN HENRY MADOFF. The bar is crammed with huge glass bowls of scented wines and fiery marcs de Provence – worth the challenge. Pretty garden.

THE QUILTED GIRAFFE, AT&T Arcade, 550 Madison Ave, NY 10022 ☎ (212) 593 1221

Wins the Most Expensive Restaurant in New York award by a neck. Old-timers return ad infinitum to the stainless steel-walled dining room where chef/owner Barry Wine's inventive New American cooking breaks new ground.

RUSSIAN TEA ROOM, 150 W 57th St, NY 10019 ☎ (212) 265 0947

The whitest Russian nosh for NY bluebloods, newbloods and SEYMOUR BRITCHKY: "*All the glitter of today in a posh 19C café bedecked with 20C art. The vigorous Russian food these days has been relieved of its weight but not of its pungent flavour.*" Vodka, blinis, caviare, Russian tea . . . na starove!!!

SAN DOMENICO, 240 Central Park S, NY 10019 ☎ (212) 265 5959

Glamorous Italian restaurant with "*the most wonderful northern Italian food*" – KENNETH LANE. So say ROBIN LEACH and BARBARA KAFKA: "*It's very refined with great food – things like baby rabbit.*" Other specialities are red bean soup, foie gras and all things Bolognese.

SANDRO'S, 420 E 59th St, NY ☎ (212) 355 5150

Italian for Italians like MARCELLA HAZAN – "*There's something he does – and I don't know anyone else who does it in New York – carciofi alla Giudea, which are fried artichokes that look like chrysanthemums and the bottom is very creamy and the tiny leaves are crispy like potato chips. When I eat there, it's like I eat in Rome.*" The Roman lamb and bucatini all'amatriciana also carry seals of approval.

SHUN LEE PALACE, 155 E 55th St, NY 10017 ☎ (212) 371 8844

Sichuan/Cantonese specialities that are among the best in New York. Plunge your chopsticks into the crispiest Peking duck or aromatic rack of lamb. **Shun Lee Café**, 43 W 65th St, is the cheaper version.

SISTINA, 1555 2nd Ave, NY 10028 ☎ (212) 861 7660

Heard the one about the 4 Italian brothers? There's one to cook, one to make the drinks, and 2 to oversee the dining room. The rustic food and rustic décor gets BARBARA KAFKA'S vote: "*Very clean, very clear, it's a place to eat the*

🐟 **Buzzz** NY hot spots: spot SALLY BURTON getting to grips with the big bagel at **PJ Clarke's**, 915 3rd Ave ☎ (212) 759 1650: "*It's very buzzy. A bloody mary and eggs benedict and I really know I'm in New York*"; DOUGLAS FAIRBANKS JR likes it too 🐟 . . . . . . Spot STEPHEN JONES spinning along to **The Rainbow Room**, 30 Rockerfeller Plaza ☎ (212) 632 5100 – "*extraordinary for a drink*" – and a dance on the revolving floor 🐟 . . . . . . Spot well-connected Italians at **Campagnola**, 1382 1st Ave ☎ (212) 861 1102, "*where the food is unbelievably good. It's frequented by people like Tony Quinn and Rod Stewart, it's very Frank Sinatra if you know what I mean*" – TESSA DAHL 🐟 . . . . . . The name says it all at **EAT**, 1064 Madison Ave ☎ (212) 772 0022: "*You walk through a bread shop-cum-salad bar to the dining room out the back and feast on the best bread outside France and wonderful salads*" – JILL MULLENS; SALLY B eats to that beat too . . . . 🐟

specials – *the fish or the wild mushrooms they got in that day.*" Hope for snapper, roasted on the bone with balsamic vinegar, or the trio of grilled mushrooms, for example. ELISE PASCOE loves it "*to bits – terrific food*".

SPARKS STEAK HOUSE, 210 E 46th St, NY 10017 ☎ (212) 687 4855

Hunky red meat – the best cuts in NY – and hulky red wine – the best Italian cellar in NY – set the sparks flying for MICHAEL BROADBENT and TERRY HOLMES: "*It is the best steakhouse in the world without a doubt.*" That goes for DAVID GIBBONS ("*my favourite NY steakhouse*") and PAUL HENDERSON, who advises: "*Always have simple foods like clams and steaks; spinach is first class. Ask Pat Cetta to choose American or Italian wines to accompany the meal.*"

TRATTORIA DELL'ARTE, 900 Seventh Ave, NY 10019 ☎ (212) 245 9800

The great NY Italian experience – it's where BOB PAYTON stops off first. "*The No 1 thing there is the antipasto bar with more antipasti than you could think of and it all tastes fresh and right. It's a real scene – close to Carnegie Hall so it's full of celebrities*" – ELISE PASCOE.

🐾 UNION SQUARE CAFE, 21 E 16th St, NY 10003 ☎ (212) 243 4020

High-flying Flatiron folk – admen and publishers – cram into Danny Meyer's casual, bustling Italian/American diner. So does JOHN TOVEY: "*It's the best because it is all-American simple country food. My favourite dish is corn-fed chicken, just roasted – just superb.*" ELISE PASCOE thinks "*they're doing everything properly, especially their tuna steaks – hardly cooked but with a gorgeous crust.*"

──────── *Shopping* ────────

See also Fashion designers.

The glossiest, most expensive shopping strips are still **Fifth** and **Madison** avenues – home to some of the biggest and best stores in the world. Fifth and 57th is aglitter with jewellers – Harry Winston, Tiffany, Van Cleef & Arpels, Bulgari, Cartier. **Lower Fifth Avenue**, **SoHo** and **Greenwich Village** (particularly **Bleecker Street**) are the best for offbeat original clothes, contemporary art and for street life. On the West Side, **Columbus Avenue** is still on the up and yup – lots of smart little shops and cafés.

AMY DOWN HATS AT THE DRESS, 103 Stanton St, NY 10002 ☎ (212) 473 0237

"*Gorgeous hats and a cute little store like a doll's house. You won't find the hats anywhere else, she designs and makes them herself – quirky, different, in fun, bright colours*" – TAMA JANOWITZ. Open Wed to Sat.

🐾 BALDUCCI'S, 424 Ave of the Americas, NY 10011 ☎ (212) 673 2600

One of the world's great food shopping experiences, guaranteed to produce ravenous hunger. "*It's just so crowded and there's this wonderful sense of generosity and abundance*" – SOPHIE GRIGSON. Whether you want baby salad leaves, marscapone, prepared Italian dishes or fresh fish, Balducci'll have it and they'll only have the best. "*I rely on it for everything – from meat to cheese to vegetables*" – MADHUR JAFFREY.

🐾 BARNEYS, 106 7th Ave at 17th St, NY 10011 ☎ (212) 929 9000

Style-setting store for an image-conscious crowd. Directional designers for woman (from Armani to Zoran), man (trad Huntsman to avant-garde Dolce & Gabbana) and child. Designer tableware too, one-off signed vases, crystal, china. Lauren Hutton, Cindy Crawford and Lucy Ferry are Barnstormers. So are MARK PATRICK, DAVID SHILLING and SHARYN STORRIER-LYNEHAM: "*They've started getting items from the Young Barbarians from Paris, fantastic coloured resin candlesticks that everyone's copying now.*" "*A lovely store*" – JOAN BURSTEIN.

🐾 BERGDORF-GOODMAN, 754 & 745 5th Ave, NY 10019 ☎ (212) 753 7000

The least stressful, most successful of the uptown department stores with floors of beautifully displayed, directionally bought designer wear. Stylish chaps now catered for at No 745

🎩 **Buzzz** Chop chop: ED VICTOR gets in and out without a fleecing at his favourite pub/bar **Billy's**, 948 1st Ave ☎ (212) 753 1870, where "*they serve the best grilled lamb chop, quite wonderful*" 🐾 ...... For "*a very good shepherd's pie made with real shepherds*", QUENTIN CRISP joins the flock at the **Telephone Bar and Grill**, 149 2nd Ave ☎ (212) 529 5000 🐾 ...... GILES SHEPARD trots off to **Bice**, 7 E 54th St ☎ (212) 688 1999, for a quiet bite in the mod Milanese manner 🐾 ...... DUGGIE FIELDS veges out at **Dojos**, 24 St Mark's Place ☎ (212) 674 9821, "*a wholefood, brown rice and stir-fry place. You can sit outside and people-watch*" 🐾 ...... TESSA DAHL keeps it strictly organic at the **Healthy Candle**, 972 Lexington Ave ☎ (212) 472 0970: "*It's divine and the man who runs it is called Bart*" .... 🐾

with Armani, Lauren, Jeffrey Banks . . . . *"For conservative menswear, the new store is great"* – DAVID SHILLING. SHARYN STORRIER-LYNEHAM picks up stylish bits and pieces on the 7th floor. JOAN BURSTEIN kicks up her heels.

BIJAN, 699 5th Ave, NY 10022 ☎ (212) 758 7500
The glittering centre of a menswear empire that spans the world, many of its crowned heads and most of its more affluent presidents. From diamond-inlaid rings to a mink-lined, bullet-proof cashmere overcoat, the energetic Bijan has men's bare essentials covered. If Mohammed can't make it to the mountain, the mountain will wing his jet to your private airstrip.

BLOOMINGDALE'S, 59th St and Lexington Ave, NY 10022 ☎ (212) 705 2000
The Big Brown Bag of this landmark New Yorker hangs from all the best wrists. Bagfuls of goodies, designer and edible, and Bloomies' own classics like 3-packs of cotton knickers.

BROOKS BROTHERS, 346 Madison Ave, NY 10017 ☎ (212) 682 8800; Liberty Plaza, 1 Church St, NY 10006
By appointment to Wall Street, the only place for timeless, preppy men's clothes. The signature blue button-down Oxford shirt is still the mark of the Brooks Bro, but they do the full kit (for Brooks Sis too) – cricket jerseys, cotton knits, ties, off-the-peg suits, plaid skirts, shoes.

CHARIVARI, 18 W 57th St, NY 10019 ☎ (212) 333 4040; branches at 2315 Broadway, 201 W 79th St, 257 and 441 Columbus Ave
Fashion cache with contemporary cachet. Well-selected European-leaning collections of men's (Armani, Versace, Montana, Byblos, Casely-Hayford, Matsuda, Dominguez) and women's (Gigli, Sybilla, Gaultier, Dolce & Gabbana).

DE VECCHI at Bergdorf-Goodman, I Magnin, Neiman Marcus
Innovative bags, belts and briefcases by Hamilton Hodge (ex-Ferragamo and Donna Karan). Rare skins and leathers – Louisiana alligator,

lizard, kid – are hand-woven around wooden blocks for seamless, organic shapes.

🐾 DEAN & DELUCA, 560 Broadway, NY 10012 ☎ (212) 431 1691
In foodies' holy trinity (with Balducci's and Zabar's of course) with the most edible array of luxury bits and pieces from around the globe. SALLY BURTON feasts *"the eyes, the imagination, the senses, everything. Just to wander around is inspirational. It's got the most wonderful fresh fish and espresso bar and the most gorgeous vegetables."* SOPHIE GRIGSON stocks up there when she wants *"to go upmarket – it has a very chic feel"*, which might be why JOAN BURSTEIN likes it.

F A O SCHWARTZ, 767 Fifth Ave, NY 10153 ☎ (212) 644 9400
The most famous toy shop in the world, especially after the movie *Big*. The floor piano *is* for sale (special order only) or you could buy the more practical life-sized stuffed cow. Big kids DAVIDS GIBBONS and SHILLING think it's neat.

FRANK OLIVE, 9th Fl, 134 W 37th St, NY 10018 ☎ (212) 947 6655
Kentucky Derby fillies get their flower-bedecked headpieces here. Tailored straw titfers, beaded evening numbers, woven metallic caps can be found on the heads of Joan Collins and Claudette Colbert and on the collections of de la Renta and Bob Mackie.

FRED LEIGHTON, 773 Madison Ave, NY 10021 ☎ (212) 288 1872
Probably the world's best selection of Art Deco jewels. Signed pieces by all the heavyweights: Cartier, La Cloche, Van Cleef and Boucheron commanding KO prices (starting at $10,000 and soaring into the stratosphere).

HAMMACHER SCHLEMMER, 147 E 57th St, NY 10022 ☎ (212) 421 9000
No 1 cult home of high-class gadgetry (they were the first ever to stock the pop-up toaster and the electric shaver). Trinkets for the Christmas stocking: a Palladian doll's house (sadly unfurnished) for a mere $12,000 or a $5,200 Soda Fountain CD Jukebox.

🐾 **Buzzz** The chic-est bite of the Big Apple: MARCHESA DI SAN GIULIANO FERRAGAMO's choice is homy: **Danny Alessandro/ Edwin Jackson**, 307 E 60th St ☎ (212) 421 1928, *"for fireplaces and accessories"*; **L'Antiquaire & The Connoisseur**, 36 E 73rd St ☎ (212) 517 9176, *"for absolutely wonderful antiques and interior decoration"*; **Handblock**, 487 Columbus Ave ☎ (212) 799 4342, *"for Mezzeri and oriental fabrics"* 🐾 . . . . . . JEREMIAH TOWER's choice is crystal clear: **Nesle Chandelier Shop**, 151 E 57th St ☎ (212) 755 0515, is the *only* place to light up 🐾 . . . . . . DAVID DALE's soars to the **Chrysler Building**, *"a spiky silver tower with chrome leopard gargoyles and magnificent murals – it shows there was a time when capitalists put beauty ahead of greed"* . . . . 🐾

More Flash than Cash

The big Bs (Barneys, Bergdorf Goodman and Bendel's) are all very well but, as anyone interested in their cred rating (credit and credibility) knows, canny cost-cutting carries the clout. We follow TAMA for some bargain glamour: **Dollar Bill**, 99 E 42 St ☎ (212) 867 0212, *"does really heavily discounted men's and women's designers – beautiful stuff for men, like Armani.* **Century 21**, *21 Courtland St* ☎ *(212) 227 9092, has big-brand designers, American and European.* **Last Call for Neiman Marcus**, *off Route 23, Wayne Town Center, New Jersey* ☎ *(201) 812 1100, has everything that didn't sell at Neiman Marcus – Romeo Gigli clothes for $300, casual clothes and beautiful evening cloaks.* **The Rainbow Shop**, *2 Penn Plaza, 7th Ave* ☎ *(212) 594 3235 is a good cheapo – they have the best shoes for about $20 – Italian knock-offs and dress-up shoes. I got some great goofy red and purple velveteen platform shoes for $10. On Sundays, the market on 81st and Columbus Ave has clothes by struggling artists where I just bought a red velvet dress for $45 – friends said it looks like Comme des Garçons for $900"* – TAMA JANOWITZ.

HARRY WINSTON, 718 5th Ave, NY 10019 ☎ (212) 245 2000; at Trump Tower
Serious jewels for serious buyers. Expect rocks in classic settings, like Marla Maples's 7-carat engagement ring from Donald Trump.

♠ HENRI BENDEL, 712 5th Ave, NY 10019 ☎ (212) 247 1100
Classy, ultra-designed addition to the NY fashion scene. *"Brilliant. Just wonderful things, a wonderful spiral staircase leads you to the most glamorous evening wear in the world. They do everything, they've got a small home section, it's like Fortnum's without the food"* – DAVID SHILLING. A **New Creators** department celebrates the rising stars of the US and Europe. Complexion perfectionists trek from afar for the MAC make-up range.

JOAN & DAVID, 816 Madison Ave, NY 10021 ☎ (212) 772 3970; in major stores
Husband and wife team supplying hand-crafted shoes with a Western lilt to a stellar clientele: Cher, Madonna (staid loafers wouldja credit it?)

and the Duchess of York among them. Also bags, belts and Armani-esque sportswear.

KENNETH COLE, 95 5th Ave, NY 10003 ☎ (212) 675 2550; 353 Columbus Ave
Fashion forward but classic shoes, sparing animals and consciences, from Mario Cuomo's son-in-law. Kid, croc and buck are all fab forgeries – the real McCoy would not sit easily with Cole's right-on advertising campaign.

KENNETH JAY LANE, Trump Tower, 725 5th Ave, NY 10018 ☎ (212) 868 1780
Fabulous fakes to adorn the necks, wrists and lapels of the style- and insurance-conscious. Black, white and brown pearls are perennially popular (see them on Barbara Bush); seasonal departures might include enormous Byzantine earrings or bright metallic brooches.

LINDA DRESNER, 484 Park Ave, NY 10022 ☎ (212) 308 3177
Minimalist showpiece for a cleverly pared-down selection of the top crop of designers: Jil Sander, Lagerfeld, Lacroix, Mugler, Montana, Alaïa, Gigli, Muir.

LUC BENOIT, 720 5th Ave, NY 10019 ☎ (212) 397 1005
Belts and bags of alligator, crocodile, lizard and ostrich, signature diamond-dotted or Renaissance-patterned leather, the exclusive on Byblos bags and baubles and Ferré jewels as well.

MACY'S, 151 W 34th St, NY 10001 ☎ (212) 695 4400
The world's biggest, if not its chic-est, department store won't be kept down. Not a bone of understatement in its 2 million sq ft body, its over-the-top, nationally broadcast Thanksgiving Day parade, or wholehearted embrace of all things Christmassy (when Santaland and Holiday Lane take over the 8th and 9th floors). Still good for cosmetics and basics, it also has its share of designer boutiques (Klein, Armani, Mizrahi, Lempicka) and an abundant food hall, with superb take-home goodies.

♠ MARTHA, 475 Park Ave, NY 10022 ☎ (212) 753 1511
A cluster of great names in Martha's vineyard, strong both for US and OS labels. Bill Blass, Bob Mackie and Carolina Herrera, Valentino, Hanae Mori and Christian Lacroix give an idea of the selection. Younger, fast-forward fashion next door at **Martha International**, including the rising stars of the US design world, Todd Oldham and Christian Francis Roth. Impeccable service makes it just that bit easier to slide into a new outfit.

PATRICIA UNDERWOOD, 242 W 36th St, NY 10018 ☎ (212) 268 3774
Wearable, stylish hats that flatter rather than flatten. Has topped the collections of Calvin Klein and Rifat Ozbek. *"Divine"* – TESSA DAHL.

🏆 **POLO/RALPH LAUREN, 867 Madison Ave, NY 10021 ☎ (212) 606 2100**
One-stop shop for a complete designer lifestyle: *"The best shop in the whole world"* – BOB PAYTON. The Madison Ave mansion is the heartbeat of a world-spanning empire of romantic, homy knick-knacks, classic children's and womenswear and, of course, menswear for the urban country gentleman. *"He has had an enormous impact on the way we live, our whole lifestyle"* – GAIL ROLFE. Plaudits from fellow rag-traders: *"Lauren has had more influence on menswear than anyone in the last 20 years"* – DOUGLAS HAYWARD. *"I always buy my ties from Ralph Lauren and I always buy them in NY because it's a brilliant shop and they are double the price in London"* – VICTOR EDELSTEIN. Alongside the designer chic of women's day and evening wear is the mass-market peak of Polo – producer of the collared T-shirt essential to most chaps' wardrobes.

ROBERT LEE MORRIS GALLERY, 409 W Broadway, NY 10012 ☎ (212) 431 9405; ARTWEAR GALLERIES, 456 W Broadway, NY 10012 ☎ (212) 673 2000
Art more than decoration: bold, minimalist shapes – oversized arm cuffs, smooth knuckle rings, pre-Christian amulets. Has worked in conjunction with Donna Karan, Yamamoto, Lagerfeld and Calvin Klein; his Artwear Galleries have fostered a new generation of jewellers. JOAN BURSTEIN is an admirer.

SAKS FIFTH AVENUE, 611 5th Ave, NY 10022 ☎ (212) 753 4000
A big department store, stocking all the big designers. Make your way up through the levels of Adolfo, Blass and Beene, Armani, Saint Laurent and Ungaro but don't even *think* about it at sale or Christmas time. **Café SFA** is a great place for lunch and, after a hard day's card-flexing, you can retire to the beauty salon for fashion consultation, make-up and manicure.

SULKA, 430 Park Ave, NY 10022 ☎ (212) 980 5200
Originally clothiers to butlers and policemen, Sulka now provides the male smart set with made-to-measure from the skin outwards (underwear to suit). The store's nigh-on 100 years of service has seen clients as disparate as Al Capone and JFK.

SUSAN BENNIS WARREN EDWARDS, 22 W 57th St, NY 10019 ☎ (212) 755 4197
Exclusive outlet for the most outrageously extravagant shoes in the world. Handmade from the finest of materials, satin to lizard, these shoes cosset the feet of the fastidious.

TENDER BUTTONS, 143 E 62nd St, NY 10021 ☎ (212) 758 7004
Diana Epstein and Millicent Safro's world-beating treasure trove of buttons has pieces from 75 cents to $1,200. Not a zippy place but LOGAN BENTLEY loves it.

🏆 **TIFFANY, 727 5th Ave, NY 10022 ☎ (212) 755 8000**
A place where all New Yorkers go-lightly, with a grin on their face and a hand on their wallet. The world's most famous jewellery store is also a source of expensive little knick-knacks (JEREMIAH TOWER's friends love the engraved silver photo frames he gives them) and now a fabulous, and growing, line of accessories.

🏆 **ZABAR'S, 2245 Broadway, NY 10007 ☎ (212) 787 2000**
The gastronomic great is top of the tree of the deli 3. Over 30,000 customers a week so don't expect a refined ambience, *"it's down to earth and unpretentious and the quality is what counts"* – SOPHIE GRIGSON. Pick up such exotica as cajun crab boil spicing or root vegetable crisps. SIR CLEMENT FREUD does: *"Wonderful deli, great for Sunday shopping."*

——————— *Theatre* ———————

BROADWAY
The world's toughest stage – audiences don't give new work its best chance. Even Arthur Miller didn't gamble his latest play on Broadway – it opened in London last year. Sadly it's only sure-fire successes – *Les Mis, Cats* and co – and

🕵 **Buzzz** Essential esoterica: TESSA DAHL tracks down some creature comforts. **John Chianciolo** ☎ (212) 751 8428, *"visits people in hospital with chicken soup, a sort of mobile Jewish father;* **Judyth van Amring**, *107 Green St ☎ (212) 925 4749, makes her own scent – heady and the sort of thing sirens would wear;* **Anoushka**, *241 E 60th St ☎ (212) 355 6404, is a beauty salon run by very large Romanian women in white overalls who do wonderful treatments for cellulite"* 🕵 . . . . . . Esoterica 2: LOGAN BENTLEY seeks the pen-ultimate thrill at **Vito Giallo**, 966 Madison Ave ☎ (212) 535 9885, *"great for little antiques, especially fountain pens; or try the market on Sun at 26th St and 6th Ave; for fixing those sick old pens, there's the* **Fountain Pen Hospital**, *10 Warren St ☎ (212) 964 0580"* . . . . 🕵

new drama that's been tested in Britain and pre-mièred around the States that makes Broadway. Critics are notorious – shows can boom or crash on the word of one man (his name is Frank Rich of *The New York Times*). Tickets are hideously expensive and many stage lovers are forced to look elsewhere. Broadway does not mean that theatres are actually on Broadway, neither does **Off-Broadway** mean they are just round the corner. Off-Broadway refers to smaller venues – 400 seats and below – in less rent-racked areas – SoHo, the villages, TriBeCa. The productions are more experimental, often the hits of tomor-row: find updatings of classics, classics to be, the avant-garde and the frankly way out. **Off Off-Broadway** ventures even further – students, street theatre, the weird and zany.

NEW YORK SHAKESPEARE FESTIVAL, 425 Lafayette St, NY 10003 ☎ (212) 598 7100
First-class summertime Shakey – for free. Top actors (Hurt, Kline, Raul Julia), hot artistic direction under Joanne Akalaitis, and first-come-first-served seating at the Delacorte The-ater in Central Park.

PHOENIX

—— *Hotels* ——

ARIZONA BILTMORE, 2400 E Missouri Ave, AZ 85016 ☎ (602) 955 6600
Grand old Phoenician resort, designed by Albert Chase McArthur and recently brought up to scratch inside. *"You must see it if only for the décor – it was built by Frank Lloyd Wright's col-league and it is absolutely glorious architecture with great huge grounds – 17 tennis courts, 3 pools and so on"* – BARBARA KAFKA.

🏊 **THE PHOENICIAN, 6000 E Camelback, Scottsdale, AZ 85251 ☎ (602) 941 82003**
In fashionable downtown Scottsdale and under the capable management of Hans Turnovszky.

MARY ROSSI is one of its new-found fans, as is ELISE PASCOE: *"It's a huge resort like a small curved theatre built into the Camelback Moun-tain, all black slate and cacti growing out of the shale. An oasis in the middle of the desert with a fabulous golf course and a restaurant,* **Win-dows on the Green,** *whose chef understands southwestern cooking. The flagship restaurant is* **Mary Elaine's,** *where the chef, Alessandro Stratta, is cooking very nicely."*

—— *Restaurants* ——

🏊 **VINCENT ON CAMELBACK, 3920 E Camelback Rd, AZ 85018 ☎ (602) 224 0225**
Hailed master of southwestern cuisine, Vincent Guerithault has a solid base in French technique and is a dab hand at new combos – try lobster with chipotle chilli pasta. *"A chef who's doing very good Franco-American food and is rather prestigious"* – BARBARA KAFKA.

PHILADELPHIA

—— *Art and museums* ——

🏊 **PHILADELPHIA MUSEUM OF ART, 26th St and Benjamin Franklin Parkway, PO Box 7646, PA 19101 ☎ (215) 763 8100**
Set in Fairmont Park, this Graeco-Roman revival building is one of the greatest art institu-tions in the world, housing over 350,000 works from 500 BC to Richard Prince's untitled silk screen and acrylic work of 1991. European Old Masters; American painting (including the largest collection of Thomas Eakin's oils), sculp-tures, sketches and photographs; furniture – a splendid sweep from American 17C to contem-porary; Renaissance art; Impressionists and Post-Impressionists, including Cézanne's *Bathers*. Also Chinese antiquities and recon-structed period rooms. The **Rodin Museum,** 22nd St and Benjamin Franklin Pky ☎ (215) 787 5431, has casts of most of his great sculptures, plus studies, drawings and memorabilia.

🧥 **Buzzz** Arizonan horizons: BARBARA KAFKA phinds phun in Phoenix: **"John Gardiner's Tennis Ranch,** *5700 E McDon-ald St ☎ (602) 948 2100, is very hot* 🏊 . . . . . . **Gallery 10,** *7045 3rd Ave ☎ (602) 994 0405, and* **Lovina Ohl Gallery,** *4251 N Marshall Way ☎ (602) 945 8212, are both great places for Indian artefacts and jewellery"* 🏊 . . . . . . Indians 2: Follow the smoke signals to **Guadelupe,** a Yaqui Indian reservation within the urban area. Wander among hand-built houses, a mission church, craft shops and terrific little restaurants 🏊 . . . . . . MARY ROSSI susses Scottsdale: *"A shopper's paradise – more than 2,500 boutiques and shops in malls – Borgata of Scottsdale, Camelview Plaza, Fifth Avenue Shops and Scottsdale Mall, to name a few"* . . . . 🏊

**WINTERTHUR MUSEUM & GARDENS,
Route 52, Winterthur, DE 19735**
☎ **(302) 888 4600**
Henry F du Pont's country estate, 30 mins from
Philadelphia and set in a delightful gardens. A
fine collection of American decorative arts from
mid-17 to mid-19C: furniture, textiles, ceramics
and silverware, including 6 tankards made by
Paul Revere.

———— Hotels ————

🖋 **ATOP THE BELLEVUE, 1415
Chancellor, PA 19102** ☎ **(215) 893 1776**
The upper crust – floors 12 to 19 house one of
Philadelphia's grandest old hotels – sandwiched
below are the best shops in the city – Lauren,
Gucci, Dunhill, Tiffany. The turn-of-the-century
building was recently completely overhauled –
two-tiered ballroom and all. *"It has got some of
the greatest shops underneath, you never have to
go out"* – TERRY HOLMES. Federal period furniture, good food in the **Founders** restaurant.

**FOUR SEASONS, 1 Logan Square, PA
19103** ☎ **(215) 963 1500**
Overlooking one of the prettiest squares in town
(actually a circle), this one's crammed with fresh
flowers, polished marble, etc, à la Four Seasons
group – with polished service to match. Good
power breakfasts in the **Fountain Restaurant**; keep in trim in the fitness centre.

———— Restaurants ————

🖋 **LE BEC-FIN, 1523 Walnut St, PA 19102**
☎ **(215) 567 1000**
One of the East Coast's best French restaurants. Louis Quinzerie galore: peach walls, chandeliers, gleaming silver, mirrors and damask.
Magnificent 6-course tasting menu. The sweetbreads on cabbage with a black truffle sauce,
and the scallops on black trumpet mushrooms
with petit pois mousse, sesame wafers and
lemongrass sauce are extraordinary.

**RESTAURANT ODEON, 114 S 12th St, PA
19107** ☎ **(215) 922 4399**
Bustling mirrored restaurant on 2 levels with
variations on regional French dishes – sautéed
crab cakes with lemon butter sauce, salmon in a
lobster sauce, fillet of beef with shallot sauce.

SAN FRANCISCO

———— Ballet ————

**SAN FRANCISCO BALLET, 455 Franklin
St, CA 94102** ☎ **(415) 861 5600**
Classics – *Swan Lake* et al – line up with up-to-
the-minute prods – eg David Bentley's *The Sons*

of Horus. This is the USA's oldest company, and
it uses only dancers from its own ballet school,
directed by Helgi Tomasson.

———— Bars and cafés ————

**THE CARIBBEAN ZONE, 55 Natoma St,
CA 94105** ☎ **(415) 541 9465**
Grab a mammoth drink, hop into the plane that's
conveniently crash-landed by the bar and take
off to the Caribbean. Videoed aerial island
scenery flashes by the window, getting closer
and closer, until you crash. Stagger out the
other end into the palm-dotted, waterfall-
splashed restaurant. Great gimmick, great fun.

**RASSELAS ETHIOPIAN CUISINE AND
JAZZ CLUB, 2801 California St, CA 94115**
☎ **(415) 567 5010**
Indigo blues on Friday nights make up for the
dubious idea of Ethiopian cuisine. Best nights
are when larger-than-life E C Scott sings.

**TRADER VIC'S, 20 Cosmo Place, CA
94109** ☎ **(415) 775 6300**
The original and best. Polynesian décor, powerful drinks and party atmosphere. The Captain's
Bar's where all the action is – buy a goldfish
bowl-sized cocktail with 10 straws and see why.

———— Clubs ————

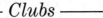

DNA LOUNGE, 375 11th St, CA 94103
☎ **(415) 626 1409**
Still a hit with the mixed-leather crowd – men in
peaked leather caps shaking their booties with
girls in micro-minis. Theme nights keep interest
levels high – go from 70s disco to heavy metal to
deep funk.

🖋 **DV8, 55 Natoma St, CA 94105**
☎ **(415) 957 1730**
Dr Winkie's wonderdome – a converted warehouse on several levels. Groove out to a progressive beat in the main section (black clothes com-
pulsory) or do your damnedest to get into the
private club (easiest if you claim friendship with
the great Winkie). Upstairs is the **Pleasure
Zone**, where you can play pool or loll about on
four-poster beds. Strange but true . . . .

SLIM'S, 333 11th St, CA 94103
☎ **(415) 621 3330**
Big-time blues bar, co-owned by 70s crooner Boz
Scaggs. Still the place to drop in very late for a
burger, a beer and great live music.

**SWEETWATER, 153 Throckmorton St,
CA 94941** ☎ **(415) 388 2820**
Across the Golden Gate in Mill Valley. It's a bit
of a hike and pretty basic once you get there, but
it's the happening scene for folk, blues and rock.
Packed to the rafters when big names are in
town – John Lee Hooker, Carlos Santana.

Film

SAN FRANCISCO INTERNATIONAL FILM FESTIVAL, 1560 Fillmore, CA 94115 ☎ (415) 567 4641
Held in March. Movies from America, Asia, Africa, Europe and Australia, animations, documentaries and more.

Hotels

🛏 **CAMPTON PLACE KEMPINSKI, 340 Stockton St, CA 94108 ☎ (415) 781 5555**
Small, central hotel with bags of European style. A 19C façade conceals upbeat service and decoration with oriental leanings. ELISE PASCOE noticed the little things: *"There was an appalling drought and they put a little cactus in your bathroom with a note that, although it mightn't have been thirsty, California was – nicely and subtly done."* *"Very nice with a good restaurant and a superb Napa Valley wine list. Lovely bathrooms"* – CAROL WRIGHT.

THE DONATELLO, Pacific Plaza Hotel, 501 Post St, CA 94102 ☎ (415) 441 7100
Intimate, personal hotel with an eye for original details. Marvellous lobby juxtaposes antiques with 20C paintings; acres of Italian marble, Fortuny fabrics, hand-painted arabesque panels, Salviati glass. **Ristorante Donatello**, kitted out in rococo splendour, dishes out fine northern Italian cooking.

🛏 **FOUR SEASONS CLIFT, 495 Geary St, CA 94102 ☎ (415) 775 4700**
One of the best: a dignified grande dame with impeccable personal service. SIR PETER USTINOV tries to pin down the charm: *"One doesn't know why it's so good but it is . . . the way things vanish when they're not wanted and are replaced without you asking – it's obviously good management."* The fine French dining room and redwood-panelled Art Deco bar can be experienced by non-residents too.

HUNTINGTON HOTEL, 1075 California St, CA 94108 ☎ (415) 474 5400
Elegantly traditional, family-run hotel atop prestigious, panoramic Nob Hill. Rooms all artfully and expensively undesigned and touches such as enormous truffles by the bed and courtesy limo make reclusive celebs feel at home. Modern, complex food in clubby opulence at **The Big Four**.

🛏 **MANDARIN ORIENTAL, 222 Sansome St, CA 94104 ☎ (415) 885 0999**
Soaring above the city are the Mandarin's twin peaks, linked by a glass skybridge. Immaculately designed and managed as befits the group, with unbeatable views (rooms start at the 38th floor). *"The most extraordinary bathrooms, in the tub you can see all San Francisco"* –

MARCELLA HAZAN. Service is smooth at **Silks**; food a much-lauded fusion of East and West. *"Not only does it have good food but fantastic views of Golden Gate Bridge, Asian service and the sense that you are in Asia"* – KEN HOM.

STOUFFER STANFORD COURT, 905 California St, CA 94108 ☎ (415) 989 3500
Stouffer Hotels haven't let standards slip at this very grand former residence of Governor Leland Stanford. Nothing home-like about 402 bedrooms, complimentary Rolls-Royce limo service, Tiffany glass-domed courtyard and 20,000-bottle-strong cellar, but who needs home when you can brunch in the glass-enclosed pavilion in **Fournou's Ovens** (*"Terrific chef"* – KEN HOM) watching the cable cars social-climbing Nob Hill.

Music

OPERA IN THE PARK, Music Concourse, Golden Gate Park
A free al fresco concert, held on the Sunday after the opening of the autumn season. Picnic under the stars and gaze at the stars from the opening night production.

🛏 **SAN FRANCISCO OPERA, War Memorial Opera House, 301 Van Ness Ave, CA 94102 ☎ (415) 565 6431**
One of the USA's finest, under the inspirational directorship of Lotfi Mansouri. Many of the world's great artists made their début here, from Solti to Schwarzkopf. Operas are sung in their original language with English surtitles. Also recitals, concerts and visiting ballet (has played host to the Kirov and Bolshoi). A programme of refurbishment is under way to repair the damage caused by the 1989 earthquake.

🛏 **THE SAN FRANCISCO SYMPHONY, Davies Symphony Hall, Van Ness Ave, CA 94102 ☎ (415) 552 8011**
One of the best orchestras in the States, under the baton of Herbert Blomstedt. A forward-thinking company, they champion young up-and-coming artists and commission new work every season.

Restaurants

See also Hotels.

CHINA MOON CAFE, 639 Post St, CA 94109 ☎ (415) 775 4789
Barbara Tropp's hot-to-trot eatery is beloved for its Sino/Americano collision cooking and reasonable prices. *"Very original and very good. I can rely on it absolutely because she's always in the kitchen"* – MADHUR JAFFREY.

FLEUR DE LYS, 777 Sutter St, CA 94109 ☎ (415) 673 7779
Elegant, unCalifornianized classic French cook-

ing as created by ex-Auberge de l'Ill's Hubert Keller. This a serious gastronomic experience and diners are suitably reverential – leave unseemly mirth at home. *"The best restaurant in San Francisco; marvellous"* – SIR PETER USTINOV.

GREEN'S, Building A, Fort Mason, CA 94123 ☎ (415) 771 6222

A meat-free institution worldwide – veg haute here. Not a sign of tired nut cutlets, this is the new wave of vegetarianism – fresh, creative and gutsy. Great karma, great cooking and a view of the Golden Gate Bridge.

MONSOON, 601 Van Ness Ave, CA 94102 ☎ (415) 441 3232

Outstanding in the monsoonal deluge of Sino/Cal cooking round town, run by Bruce Cost. *"He is not Asian but he cooks some of the most delicious Asian-inspired food and it really is fantastic. Steamed fish, wonderful Monterey prawns, lots of seafood – all light and tasty and wonderful"* – KEN HOM.

🍴 POSTRIO, 545 Post St, CA 94102 ☎ (415) 776 7825

LA bigwig Wolfgang Puck's SF diner has wooed and wowed locals – try getting a table without a week's notice. Sweeping staircase, open kitchen and 3 levels (best is lowest for people-peeking) crank up the energy and volume. The trio of chefs (1/3 is Puck, occasionally) serve honest, gutsy Californian food with flair. *"An incredible restaurant"* – GEOFFREY ROBERTS. *"Still terrific"* – ROBIN LEACH.

SQUARE ONE, 190 Pacific St, CA 94111 ☎ (415) 788 1110

Joyce Goldstein's Med-meets-Cal food and airy restaurant is still top for foodie folk. *"A lovely restaurant, very, very good food. It's always cramped"* – ELIZABETH DAVID. Tip-top wine list.

🍴 STARS, 150 Redwood St, CA 94102 ☎ (415) 861 7827

A lodestar of California cooking, Jeremiah Tower's buzzing eatery draws high praise and glitzy crowds: *"The Langan's of San Francisco – still wonderful"* – GEOFFREY ROBERTS. Predictably unpredictable – lots of mesquite grilling, wild funghi, fresh flavours and gee-whizz combos. *"Our favourite restaurant in SF"* – PAUL HENDERSON.

YUJEAN'S, 843 San Pablo Ave, Albany, CA 94706 ☎ (415) 525 8557

Eclectic Chinesery, taking the best from all provinces and giving them a modern edge. Reworked peasant food such as Chinese polenta sits alongside the celebrated tea-smoked duck and is backed by a surprisingly strong, lovingly chosen wine list.

🍴 ZUNI CAFE, 1658 Market St, CA 94102 ☎ (415) 552 2522

Light and white and very bright with the expected open kitchen and most unexpected food from young chef-co-owner Judy Rodgers (partner is Billy West). *"A lovely restaurant. It started off as a café and grew into a full-blown restaurant but it still isn't like any other. They bake their own bread and it's the most inventive, wonderful food"* – ELIZABETH DAVID. She's not the only foodie to darken Zuni's door: JEREMIAH TOWER goes with ELISE PASCOE, who sighs over *"the wood-fired oven, which sends out wonderful aromas of whatever's being cooked – vegetables, pizzas, fish or bread. I had a wonderful roasted chickpea salad on top of field greens and they had a chicken and beef bollito misto which worked really well."*

—— *Shopping* ——

Landmark **Union Square** has the big department stores. The 9-storey **San Francisco Center**'s spiral escalator leads onwards and upwards to over 100 shops. Chinatown coils 24 blocks around **Grant Ave** (SF has the biggest Chinese community outside Asia) – check out Shanghai Bazaar (Chinese bargains, antique and new) and Long Boat Enterprises Co (for Rosita Young's oriental jewellery).

GUMPS, 250 Post St, CA 94108 ☎ (415) 982 1616

Gumps is no frump but a favoured institution. Treasure trove of jade and pearls, antique furniture, wonderful gifts and home furnishings.

I MAGNIN, 135 Stockton St, CA 94108 ☎ (415) 362 2100

Puts the cover-up on movie moguls and rag-traders. Top designers – Dior, Chanel, Ungaro, Saint Laurent, Valentino, Oscar de la Renta. Exclusive international boutique with classy Underwood and Olive hats. *"It's got so many good services. You can call them from your hotel and say 'I'm size 10 and I want everything in blue' and they'll send it round. Lovely rooms and an amazing Art Deco loo"* – CAROL WRIGHT.

NORDSTROM'S, 865 Market St, CA 94103 ☎ (415) 243 8500

Directional fashion specialists with all the top Euro and US designers. Good for diffusion and bridge (more expensive than diffusion, less exclusive than the main collection) lines of Armani, Donna Karan, Oscar de la Renta et al with an emphasis on sportswear. Footsore shoppers can retire to one of 4 restaurants (the 'English' pub is cunningly placed next to the menswear) or the spa for shiatsu and an aromatherapeutic body wrap.

WILKES BASHFORD, 375 Sutter St, CA 94108 ☎ (415) 986 4380

Stylish, expensive menswear – beautifully tailored suits from Brioni and Kitan – and a hipper designer loft for Gigli, Dolce & Gabbana, Richard Tyler and Katharine Hamnett. Wom-

Spa Attractions

Spa life California-style is more like an Outward Bound camp; luxuriating is out – work that body, don't just pamper it. At **Cal-a-Vie**, 2249 Somerset Rd, Vista ☎ (619) 945 2055, the day starts with a 3-mile spa trek up into the hills, before being catapulted into stretch class, body contour, Reebok Step, weight-training, etc. All that and a dose of hydrotherapy, thalassotherapy or aromatherapy hook Christie Brinkley, Larry Hagman, Oprah Winfrey, Barbra Streisand, Alexander Godunov and Dyan Cannon. Two Bunch Palms, 67-425 **Two Bunch Palms** Trail, Desert Hot Springs ☎ (619) 329 8791, is for those who don't want to be marshalled around by the spa police. No set diet plan (you can even get *alcohol*), exotic treatments (floating water shiatsu massage, clay cabana mud baths – love birds book early for side-by-side baths), and plenty of wallowing in geothermal pools fed by natural hot springs from Miracle Hill. South of the border, at **Rancho la Puerta**, PO Box 69, Tecate, Baja California ☎ (619) 744 4222, you can integrate body, mind and spirit under relentlessly blue skies at the foot of a sacred mountain. But if you want to feel like the starlet of some big-spend movie, **Doral Saturnia International Spa Resort**, 8755 NW 36th Street, Miami ☎ (305) 593 6030, is the one, a $33 million film-set version of the Terme di Saturnia in Tuscany with American mod-cons. Ritzy suites, Italian pleasure gardens, Tuscan volcanic mud treatment . . .

enswear is more along the ladies-who-lunch lines. Look out for the new WilkesHome department or functional (and perishable) art – signed vases and plates, antique tapestry cushions.

· REST OF ·
CALIFORNIA

Hotels

MEADOWOOD RESORT & COUNTRY CLUB, 900 Meadowood Lane, St Helena, CA 94574 ☎ (707) 963 3646
Quiet, Napa Valley resort where frazzled Franciscans unfurl. Its own wine school, croquet lawns (PAUL HENDERSON reckons it's *"a good place to learn to play"*), golf, tennis, swimming pool and 2 restaurants. MARK MCCORMACK and CAROL WRIGHT escape the hustle here.

VENTANA, Highway 1, Big Sur, CA 93920 ☎ (408) 667 2331
Location, location, location – a shack would be successful in *these* hills with *that* oceanscape. This comfortably woodsy inn (handmade quilts, lots of pine and tiles) sensibly doesn't compete with the outdoor grandeur, the dining terrace positively revels in its natural setting. Worldly pleasures of sauna, massage, Japanese hot tubs, manicure, etc, are at hand. At atmosphere of unadulterated romance prompts many couples to marry here each year.

Restaurants

🔦 **AUBERGE DU SOLEIL, 180 Rutherford Hill Rd, Rutherford, CA 94573 ☎ (707) 963 1211**
Rustic sophisticate in the splendid surrounds of the Napa Valley. Spanking fresh local ingredients deftly given modern Cali-French treatment keep things sunny for MARK MCCORMACK, MARY ROSSI, PAUL HENDERSON and TERRY HOLMES. *"Extremely provençale-looking, whitewashed, and you can eat out virtually all year round"* – CAROL WRIGHT. You can stay there too.

🔦 **CHEZ PANISSE, 1517 Shattuck Ave, Berkeley, CA 94709 ☎ (415) 548 5525**
A legend in California's lunchtime, Alice Waters's ground-breaking restaurant spawned the CA cuisine which has changed the world's tastes, and a bright new generation of chefs. Others might copy the formula but the mould is hers – you still have to book a month in advance to sample her uncompromising 5-course, no-choice menu. *"Some of the best food in the USA, it's my neighbourhood restaurant"* – KEN HOM. No bookings for **Café Chez Panisse** upstairs; an hour's wait adds an indefinable something to the famous Sonoma goat's cheese calzone. *"It's good, it's fun. I like to go at lunchtime and I like to go to the café upstairs"* – ELIZABETH DAVID.

LARK CREEK INN, 234 Magnolia Ave, Larkspur, CA 94939 ☎ (415) 924 7766
Only 20 mins from San Francisco, Bradley Ogden's regional American restaurant among

the redwoods soothes the souls of city folk. Be there for brunch – scrambled eggs with house-cured gravad lax and fries; or drop in at dinner – spit-roasted rabbit with creamy polenta, braised greens and golden chanterelles.

MUSTARD'S GRILL, 7399 St Helena Highway, Yountville, CA 94558 ☎ (707) 944 2424

This Napa noshery will be drawing crowds of oenologists for aeons. The mesquite grill's the thing, try roasted cured pork shoulder with apple butter and red bean chilli, or Thai-style snapper for those inclined to the brine. Wine list concentrates on California but spreads to other states and beyond.

TABLE 29, 4110 St Helena Highway, Napa ☎ (707) 224 3300

A Spanish stucco set-up for Jonathan Waxman's talents. The menu doesn't tie itself into Californian combination knots – it highlights good produce, honestly dealt with (red pepper pancakes with caviare and crème fraîche, tenderloin of pork with oven-roasted vegetables). Comprehensive (350-odd-strong) wine list.

TRA VIGNE, 1050 Charter Oak St, St Helena, CA 94574 ☎ (707) 963 4444

Mustard's fratello Italiano. Food from the North finds focus in the Napa: all is rigorously authentic from the daily-made mozzarella to their home-cured prosciutto. In summer, *si mangia al fresco*, as PAUL HENDERSON and GEOFFREY ROBERTS do.

—————— Wine ——————

"The experimentation with new grape varieties continues. People are planting Sangiovese (the Chianti grape), Viognier (a white grape more usually associated with the Rhône, what we call Condrieu, an appellation in France), Grenache, Syrah. They are in the upper price levels because they are being produced in such small quantities – obscure wines in a way but very interesting: wines escaping from the dominance of Chardonnay and Cabernet, which is rather nice. Very prestigious and very experimental and absolutely typical of California always to be wanting to experiment and try something different.

"The final thing is a trend towards blended wines, for example 50% Cabernet Sauvignon, 30% Merlot and 20% Cabernet Franc – as they can't be called by a single grape name they have made-up names and are often grouped under a new category called Meritage" – GEOFFREY ROBERTS.

Carneros

A hilly sprawl between the Sonoma and Napa valleys, whose coastal proximity gives it an advantageous couple of degrees – warmer in winter, cooler in summer – over the big duo.

ACACIA

Small estate producing elegant Chardonnays – their own Marina vineyard is the best (*"They make very good wines"* – GEOFFREY ROBERTS) – and Pinot Noirs from St Clair, the Iund and Madonna vineyards. *"Go for the 88 or 90, not 89, which was tricky due to rain during the vintage"* – ANTHONY HANSON.

SAINTSBURY

The Saintsbury stables – home to the splendidly buttery, oaky Chardonnay and bright, fruity Pinot Noir – go *"from strength to strength"* – ANTHONY HANSON. GEOFFREY ROBERTS agrees.

California's first winery, **BUENA VISTA**, while in Sonoma, is *"the largest vineyard owner in Carneros. Not in the same breath as Acacia and Saintsbury but sound, good quality wines"* – GEOFFREY ROBERTS.

Napa Valley

The leader of the 70s wine revival, its top position is no longer unassailable.

BEAULIEU VINEYARD

Famous old winery still under the eye of André Tchelistcheff. *"The 90-year-old guru of California winemaking has been making wine since before the war –* **Georges De Latour Private Reserve** *Cabernet Sauvignon is the wine he made his reputation on and is still good"* – GEOFFREY ROBERTS.

DOMINUS

"The Moueix (owners of Chateau Pétrus) wine of the Napa – Cabernet Sauvignon-based and terrific" – SERENA SUTCLIFFE. Those of the late 80s will repay long, *long* cellaring.

DUNN VINEYARD

Small winery producing extraordinary Cabernet Sauvignon, especially the **Howell Mountain**, whose 1982 has beaten Lafite, Mouton and Haut Brion in a blind tasting.

GROTH VINEYARD

Accomplished producers of Cabernet Sauvignons that do consistently well at blind tastings: *"The 1988 achieves a balance and finesse all too rarely seen. This is surely worth cellaring"* – ANTHONY HANSON.

JOE HEITZ

Joe Heitz sets high standards with his Cabernet Sauvignons: *"One of the most extraordinary red wines is the Heitz Cabernet Sauvignon, which comes from a single vineyard, Martha's Vineyard (not to be confused with the one in Massachusetts). The 1974 is absolutely sensational, comparable to any wine you care to mention – to a first-growth claret in a great year"* – GEOFFREY

ROBERTS. DON HEWITSON echoes: "*It is so complex and yet that is its attraction, and it's made by one of the characters of the world of wine.*"

JOSEPH PHELPS

Well-made wines with a wide range: fine Chardonnay, Syrah, superlative late-harvest Riesling, and Cabernet Sauvignon: "*I was tasting their 1989 reds out of a barrel, I thought they were very good*" – GEOFFREY ROBERTS.

Sparkling Success

♠

GEOFFREY ROBERTS toasts the effervescence of the new contenders. "*A lot of French champagne houses have invested in California recently and their releases are now coming out, very successfully. The ones that spring to mind are* **Mumm's Cuvée Napa**, *Roederer's operation in the Anderson Valley* (**Roederer Estate**), **Domaine Chandon** *and* **Taittinger**, *who have built a huge château called Domain Carneros, producing good sparkling wine. The Californians were there first –* **Schramsberg Blanc de Noirs** *is one to look out for and the* **Iron Horse Blanc de Blancs** *is very good. So all the French producers thought they'd better come in. It's the first time we've really seen a concerted effort to produce good-quality sparkling wine outside Champagne. And it's succeeding in a way that's really frightening to Champagne.*"

ROBERT MONDAVI

The great innovator, man behind the rise and rise of the Napa. One of the biggest producers, yet still setting standards for Cabernet Sauvignon (especially the **Reserve**, according to LIZ BERRY), Pinot Noir, botrytis Semillon and, to a lesser extent, Fumé Blanc and Chardonnay. "*I think their reds are much better than their whites, what they've been particularly successful with is their Pinot Noirs, the 88 and 90* **Reserve Pinot Noirs** *are extremely good*" – GEOFFREY ROBERTS. DON HEWITSON tips the Reserve Cabernet Sauvignon 82 and 84: "*Californian winemaking at its finest. A serious wine.*" Also partners in a joint venture with Mouton-Rothschild to produce **Opus 1**, one of California's greatest red wines.

STAG'S LEAP WINE CELLARS

A cluster of whites (Chardonnay, Riesling and Sauv Blanc) but it is Cabernet that made Stag's

Leap famous and Cabernet that's king for LIZ BERRY. Top of the range **Cask 23** challenges and beats many Médocs.

TREFETHEN

A fine old winery, producing long-living Chardonnays, good dry Riesling and, sometimes, top Cabernet Sauvignon, on LIZ BERRY's short-list.

Other reliable Napa names are **CHAPPELLET**, whose hillside vineyard gives good, long-lived results in Cabernet Sauvignon, Chardonnay and Chenin Blanc; **FREEMARK ABBEY**, whose stylish Cabernet Sauvignons and late-picked Riesling, **Edelwein**, are good advertisements for their type; the French-run **CLOS DU VAL**, which makes Cabernet Sauvignons and Merlots of distinction, and the aesthetically inclined **HESS COLLECTION**, whose modern art collection vies for attention with its supple, balanced Cabernet Sauvignon and 1989 Chardonnay, which is "*fine quality without breaking the bank*" – ANTHONY HANSON.

Santa Barbara

AU BON CLIMAT

Small, exciting winemaker whose rich, darkly fruity Pinot Noirs show a great deal of promise and whose Chardonnays appeal to LIZ BERRY and ANTHONY HANSON: "*Jim Clendenen is the name to follow around Santa Barbara. His Chardonnays are buttery and luscious and he is an imaginative and inspired winemaker with other grape types (Pinot Noir, Syrah).*"

SANFORD

Since Richard Sanford split away from his original partner, Michael Benedict, he has gone from strength to strength with his mouth-filling Chardonnays, aromatic Sauvignon Blancs and full, earthy Pinot Noirs. "*He has just regained control of one of the best Pinot Noir vineyards in California, the Benedict. The resulting wines should be extraordinary*" – GEOFFREY ROBERTS.

Santa Clara

RIDGE

Draws magpie-like from Napa, Sonoma and Santa Clara for the wonderful, unusual **York Creek Petite Sirah**, Zinfandel from Geyserville ("*in very small quantities. Rich, round, elegant – a wine to drink after about 5 years and as good as many Cabernet Sauvignons. Very good value*" – GEOFFREY ROBERTS), and Bordeaux-like **Monte Bello Cabernet Sauvignon** ("*One of the top 6 of California*" – GEOFFREY R).

Monterey

CHALONE

A contender for California's top winery; non-conformist winemaker-in-chief Dick Graff gets spectacular results in Burgundian-style Chardonnay and Pinot Noir. *"Both great after at least 5 years in bottle. They also make a very interesting Pinot Blanc, which is not widely produced"* – GEOFFREY ROBERTS.

San Benito

CALERA
Unpredictable (both in crop size and quality) but frequently brilliant. *"Josh Jensen's Calera is often outstanding. Calera is located slap on the San Andreas fault, so buy the wines (Chardonnay and Pinot Noir) before they slip into the primeval magma. The yields are low, the flavours concentrated"* – ANTHONY HANSON. Look out for the single-vineyard wines from Jenson, Reed and Selleck.

Sonoma Valley

"Great things are happening here, where the cool airstreams flow in from San Francisco Bay" – ANTHONY HANSON.

CHATEAU ST JEAN
Suntory-owned but retaining its individuality. A clutch of single-vineyard whites (*"very good white-wine producer"* – GEOFFREY ROBERTS): Chardonnays, Fumé Blancs and, LIZ BERRY's favourite, sweet botrytis Riesling.

KISTLER VINEYARDS
Recently branching out into Cabernet and Pinot Noir but best known for their smoky Chardonnays, *"at the top of the quality league and priced to match"* – ANTHONY HANSON.

SONOMA-CUTRER VINEYARDS
Chardonnay is all they do, but they do it very well, as GEOFFREY ROBERTS recognizes. **Les Pierres** is No 1 (*"Beautifully crafted, elegant and yet full of flavour"* – DON HEWITSON), **Russian River Ranch** a worthy second-stringer.

Desert Rose

Bob Zimmer (ex-Rosewood Hotels) has zoomed into the hotel hall of fame with his homy southwesterner near the main square of Santa Fe: **The Inn of the Anisazi**, 113 Washington Ave, NM 87501 ☎ (505) 988 3030. *"It's small and very reasonably priced but the best thing is you can feel the atmosphere of Santa Fe. The wooden floorboards feel warm and earthy, they have the proper beehive-shaped fireplaces (kivas) and near the fireplace there will be a winged chair with a hand-woven shawl draped nonchalantly over it. Beautiful pristine beds and everywhere there are local flowers, and all the soaps are made to Pueblo Indian recipes"* – ELISE PASCOE. It brings out the mystic in CAROLYN LOCKHART: *"Indian gods of ancestors have blessed this place."* Zimmer's son Peter runs the kitchen and very fine it is too, according to STANLEY MARCUS: *"Specialities are chilli-seared T-bone steak, crabmeat pancakes and broiled free-range chicken. The food has a southwestern flavour and the presentations are beautifully designed."* ELISE P is bowled over by breakfast: *"No American, no Continental – it's all southwestern – Mexican eggs and beans, local grain cereals and good fruit juices."*

Buzzz HANSON's hands-on Sonoma: *"A name to watch is* **Chalk Hill Winery**, *1990 onwards. The winemaker is David Ramey, Pomerol-trained with Ets Jean-Pierre Moueix, and surely one of California's most determined and perceptive winemakers* ...... **Matanzas Creek** *frequently make immaculately balanced Sauvignon Blanc and their Chardonnays age well. The 87 Merlot is one of the richest, finest Merlots of its vintage* ...... *Russian River valley and vineyards around Sebastopol are areas we'll hear more of. For Pinot Noir,* **Williams Sellyen Winery** *brings true Burgundian passion to the making of red wine"* – ANTHONY H ...... HANSON and ROBERTS rave about the **Ravenswood** Zinfandel ...... Try to get your hands on a little something from **Kalin Cellars**, which produces a mere 6,000 cases a year: *"Brilliant wines made by a micro-biologist – for the insider trade connoisseur"* – SERENA SUTCLIFFE ...... Overproduction of sparklers means *"Great values from some of the wineries, particularly* **Domaine Mumm** *(maybe ahead of the sometimes disappointing French Mumm)"* – ANTHONY H ....

SANTA FE

— *Music* —

⚑ SANTA FE OPERA, Box 2408, NM 87504 ☎ (505) 982 3851
For supremacy of setting and music, this one is top of the league in the States. The summertime festival stages 40-odd performances of 5 operas. No resident company and few big names, just a progressive spirit under founder and general director John Crosby. Open-air amphitheatre in the foothills of the Sangre de Cristo mountains Impresses ANDREW LLOYD WEBBER no cnd.

— *Restaurants* —

COYOTE CAFE, 132 W Water St, NM 87501 ☎ (505) 983 1615
A howling success for ex-Chez Panisse's Mark Miller. *"The No 1 place. He's doing imaginative food, based on authentic use of Mexican food but not your chilli and beans. It's a whole trend of upscale, upmarket food"* – BARBARA KAFKA. Hits the spot for CAROLYN LOCKHART too.

WASHINGTON, DC

— *Art and museums* —

HIRSHHORN MUSEUM & SCULPTURE GARDEN, Independence Ave at 7th St SW, DC 20560 ☎ (202) 357 2700
The Smithsonian's extensive collection of modern and contemporary art. Best known for sculpture – a garden and plazaful of Rodin, Moore (including his *King and Queen*), Calder, Giacometti and co. Inside are Matisse, Degas and Daumier, plus Cubists, Nihilists and contemporary American, and Latin masters.

⚑ NATIONAL GALLERY OF ART, 4th St and Constitution Ave NW, DC 20565 ☎ (202) 737 4215
One of the best art galleries in the States, with an outstanding collection of European and American art, from the 13C onwards. Hot favourites include Leonardo's *Ginevra de' Benci*, John Singleton Copley's *Watson and the Shark*, Renoir's *A Girl with a Watering Can* and Henry Moore's *Knife Edge Mirror Two Piece*. Investigate Alexander Calder's giant organically shaped mobile, *Untitled*, in the monumental atrium of the I M Pei-designed East Building. Brilliant special exhibitions.

PHILLIPS COLLECTION, 1600 21st St NW, DC 20009 ☎ (202) 387 2151
One of the most distinguished small museums in the USA. Large representation of American and European paintings from Impressionists to the present day: Modigliani, Picasso, Kandinsky, Klee, Matisse, Cézanne, Renoir, Avery, Braque. Sunday-afternoon chamber music in the Music Room, in a beautiful setting hung with paintings. Informative lectures by journalists, art historians and artists.

⚑ SMITHSONIAN INSTITUTION, 1000 Jefferson Drive W, DC 20560 ☎ (202) 357 2700
A mammoth organization with 13 museums here in Washington and 2 in New York. Although there are more than 78 million works, you'll be lucky to get to see 1%. At various addresses around town are the **National Museums of American Art** and **American History** (stacks of Hollywood memorabilia and the First Ladies' restored gowns), **National Portrait Gallery**, **Renwick Gallery** (American crafts and decorative arts), the Freer Gallery (19C-20C American art; Oriental art). In the **Museum of Natural History** lies the beautiful blue Hope Diamond, the largest of its kind. Check out the Apollo 11 Command Module in the **National Air and Space Museum**, along with the 1903 Wright Flyer, hot-air balloons, planets and stars in a chain of thematic galleries.

🧥 **Buzzz Santa comes to town:** it's like Christmas all year round for STANLEY MARCUS at **The Compound**, 653 Canyon Rd ☎ (505) 982 4353, *"the only restaurant in Santa Fe providing classical Continental cuisine, not a single bit of bell pepper in evidence. Service is the most professional of any Santa Fe restaurants"* ⚑ ...... Celebration 2: ELISE PASCOE has a topping time at **Café Escalera**, 130 Lincoln Ave ☎ (505) 989 8188, *"A great new restaurant at the top of an escalator in a shopping centre,"* which is more Med than Mex ⚑ ...... **Mud pack:** according to the DAVID DALE scale, *"The best pre-20C building is the **Taos Pueblo**, about 1,000 years old, built of mud, looking like half-melted apartment blocks. Still houses the descendants of the original Native Americans, except they now enter through doors at ground level instead of by ladders through the roof"* .... ⚑

Arts centres

THE JOHN F KENNEDY CENTER, 2700 F St NW, DC 20566 ☎ (202) 416 8000
Top in the USA after NY's Lincoln Center. The **Eisenhower Theater** stages major shows such as the Paul Taylor Dance Company and some productions of the Washington Opera, while the **Opera House** stages the rest, as well as international and national ballets and musicals. At the Terrace, see music, dance, performance artists and small-scale plays, at the **American Film Institute Theater** new films and retros, and at the small **Theater Lab** cabaret and comedy. The **Concert Hall** is proud home of the National Symphony Orchestra. At New Year the Vienna Waltz takes place in the red-carpeted Grand Foyer. And here are presented the Kennedy Center Honors.

Clubs

BAYOU CLUB, 31–35 K St NW, DC 20007 ☎ (202) 333 2897
Nightclub-cum-performance space for cabaret, comedy and concerts. College-kid crowd.

BLUES ALLEY, 1073 Wisconsin Ave NW, DC 20007 ☎ (202) 337 4141
Jumping joint for serious jazz. All the greats have strutted their stuff here – Ella Fitzgerald, Bradford and Wynton Marsalis and Dizzy Gillespie among the roll-call.

FIFTH COLUMN, 915 F St NW, DC 20004 ☎ (202) 393 3632
Washington's hippest hopper – a club-cum-art gallery over 3 floors. A young, streetwise crowd mixes to house, rave and Euro-dance music. The 3rd floor is more laid-back with R & B CDs in the VIP lounge. MICHAEL MUSTO goes when he's in town.

9.30 CLUB, 930 F St NW, DC 20004 ☎ (202) 393 0930
Little-known bands with tongue-twisting names and a strictly savvy crowd.

PISCES, 3040 M St NW, Georgetown, DC 20007 ☎ (202) 333 4530
Discreet, established, members' only club where congressmen and ambassadors can let their thinning hair down. Glitzy Art Deco space – mirrored walls, etched glass, mauve and silver furnishings – with a small stage for the once-a-month dinner-dance bands. Pall Mall-ish grill room is the spot for lunchtime assignations.

RIVER CLUB, 3223 K St NW, DC 20007 ☎ (202) 333 8118
Grown-up dinner-dancing club with live jazz and a nostalgic DJ. The rather formal restaurant has a casual approach to its Amer-Asian menu which allows grazing on little courses.

1492 and all that

Seville and Barcelona aside, Washington's the city at the heart of Christopher Columbiana (it's a real ticket in electioneering). Whether Columbus et al were dashing explorers or dashed exploiters (and some commentators bring it down to the level of whether potato chips and cocoa have truly enriched the Old World's diet) it's all here at the *Seeds of Change* exhibition at the Smithsonian's **National Museum of Natural History**. Until April 1993, enter through gates of corn (14,000 ears-worth) to see the $2.5 million show which illustrates the 5 seeds – sugar, corn, the potato, the horse and disease – that altered both worlds in the culture collision – for ever. Then you can hold your own at dinner parties.

Hotels

HAY ADAMS, 1 Lafayette Sq, DC 20006 ☎ (202) 638 6600
Restored 20s building with anachronistic appeal – arched Italian Renaissance lobby complete with Medici tapestry and leather-bound tomes, the pseudo-Tudor John Hay Room. All bedrooms are of the English country house variety and are the resting place for many a polly who can keep an eagle eye on the White House from South Side windows. Big biz takes place over breakfast in the sunny yellow **Adams Room**.

THE MADISON, 15th and M Sts NW, DC 20005 ☎ (202) 862 1600
Impeccably run by Marshall Coyle, and bearing the stamp of his love for European antiques throughout. In the financial district with a fab health club for city fat cats and a fine haute American restaurant, **Montpelier**, to undo all the benefits.

PARK HYATT, 24th and M Sts NW, DC 20037 ☎ (202) 789 1234
More than just one of a chain, this is of the abundant-fresh-flowers-and-ornate-furniture boutique variety. "*A Hyatt that's a personal hostelry thanks to the British general manager, Paul Limbert. Authentic afternoon tea in a drawing room. Kenneth Juran cooks inventive New American cuisine*" – DEIRDRE PIERCE.

♠ RITZ-CARLTON, 2100 Massachusetts Ave NW, DC 20008 ☎ (202) 293 2100
Low-key Euro-elegance in this meeting place of

the mighty. English paintings and antiques abound, making LORD MONTAGU OF BEAULIEU feel at home. The **Fairfax Bar** is your place for a genteel afternoon tea. The **Jockey Club** crackles with power, 3 meals a day. Among the make-or-break, see-and-be-seen crowd lining the walls (for optimum viewing) is a Who's Who of Washington – Nancy Reagan comes for the chicken salad, others choose more adventurously from Fabrice Cannelle's modern Ameri-Franco menu.

🐦 THE WILLARD INTER-CONTINENTAL, 1401 Pennsylvania Ave, DC 20004 ☎ (202) 628 9100

'The residence of presidents', sending forth for inauguration each one from Polk (the 11th) to Cleveland (the 24th). Big hotel with small hotel values, old-fashioned chandeliered opulence and a historical roll-call like none other – here Martin Luther King wrote his 'I have a dream' speech, Lincoln hid from an assassin. . . . The historic **Round Robin** bar has acquired a **Nest** lounge, the Viennese-style **Café Espresso** waltzes along and the **Willard Room's** American/French cooking is matched by a most patriotic wine list spanning 39 US states.

—— *Restaurants* ——

See also Hotels.

BOMBAY CLUB, 815 Connecticut Ave NW, DC 20006 ☎ (202) 659 3727

Echoes of Empire in this rattan- and brass-accented Indian restaurant. Besuited ambassadorial types are calmed by *"the soothing sounds of a white baby grand. Have the crab starter, tandoori prawns or lamb chops, rogan josh and scrumptious mint paratha"* – DEIRDRE PIERCE.

CHRISFIELDS, 8012 Georgia Ave, Silver Springs, MD 20910 ☎ (301) 589 1306

Simply the best seafood. In reverse-snobbery gear, townies head out of their element for *"marvellous seafood. It's like eating in a diner, sort of interesting and out of the way and you get wonderful oysters"* – DEIRDRE PIERCE. Even the Reagan double act venture forth.

DUKE ZEIBERTS, 1050 Connecticut Ave NW, DC 20036 ☎ (202) 466 3730

Good ol' American food for good ol' Washington boys. Politicians and quarterbacks rub powerful shoulders over the legendary Duke's ribs, steaks and fish.

🐦 GALILEO, 1110 21st St NW, DC 20036 ☎ (202) 293 7191

Chef-owner Roberto Donna's astronomically successful *ristorante* offers fresh, regional Italian fare – lots of grilling, great pasta, wild mushrooms in season. *"He's really a comer. He was chosen by Food and Wine Magazine as one of the 10 hot new young chefs in America"* – DEIRDRE PIERCE.

I MATTI, 2436 18th St NW, DC 20009 ☎ (202) 462 8844

Galileo's cheaper sister in hyper-hip Adams-Morgan. Pastas, pizzas and grills. Hot choices are the gorgonzola and prosciutto pizza, quadrucci with basil cream, and beef and sausage stew with polenta.

🐦 THE INN AT LITTLE WASHINGTON, PO Box 300, Washington, VA 22747 ☎ (703) 675 3800

More than a restaurant, this inn is consistently ranking up there with America's best, for food, décor, accommodation, the whole deal. At the foot of the Blue Ridge Mountains, it's a trek from Washington proper but one which proper Washingtonians make whenever owners Lynch and O'Connell can squeeze them in. *"A beautiful place, all done up like an English country inn. New American cuisine which borrows heavily from the French – I know nouvelle is a dirty word now but it is that lighter style of French cooking – using Virginia products, Smithfield ham rather than prosciutto"* – DEIRDRE PIERCE. It also gets the MARY ROSSI seal of approval.

🐦 JEAN-LOUIS AT WATERGATE, Watergate Hotel, 2650 Virginia Ave, DC 20037 ☎ (202) 298 4488

Washington's one remaining hot-shot French chef presides over the capital's finest dining room. Jean-Louis Palladin's multi-course, prix-fixé meals enliven the tastebuds of the élite with fabulous ingredients given the master's treatment. *"The best restaurant in Washington – definitely French. The chef is eccentric but a genius"* – TERRY HOLMES.

LE CAPRICE, 2348 Wisconsin Ave NW, DC 20007 ☎ (202) 337 3394

Alsatian chef Edmond Foltzenlogel makes DC's best French bistro a gathering of all regions. Good choices are a light choucroute with grated cured turnips, poached fillet of beef à la ficelle and small roasted chicken on a rösti.

OBELISK, 2029 P St NW, DC 20030 ☎ (202) 872 1180

Peter Pastan's tiny Italian restaurant manages to turn out a new 4-course, fixed-price menu nightly. Remarkable quality and a comprehensive, good-value Italian wine list.

NOTTE E LUNA, 809 15th St NW, DC 20005 ☎ (202) 408 9500

Buzzing modern Italian restaurant a couple of blocks from the White House. Fabulously fresh pasta might include saffron fettucine or crab ravioli, washed down with a predominantly Italian wine list. Night and day it is the one for ELISE PASCOE: *"Absolutely spot on. The Americans are doing Italian so well that you can't go past this one."*

OCCIDENTAL, 1475 Pennsylvania Ave NW, DC 20014 ☎ (202) 783 1475
A power hub-club of the occidental world, where statesmen from Roosevelt to Churchill have dined, re-created with the same mahogany bar and vintage elevator. Solid and very American.

RED HOT & BLUE, 1600 Wilson Blvd, Arlington, VA 22209 ☎ (202) 276 7427
Rib-sticking, finger-licking Memphis barbecue restaurant specializing in brisket, smoked pork roast, chicken and ribs. Opened by the late Lee Atwater, Bush's chief campaign strategist; spot the big boys on their days off.

TWENTY-ONE FEDERAL, 1736 L St NW, DC 20036 ☎ (202) 331 9771
Now into its second wind and as noisy and fashionable as ever. Robert Kinkead's New Americana, based in France and leaning to the southwestern, inspires jaded palates with fresh combos – swordfish gazpacho or lobster and crab cakes with a corn/okra relish. Great bar.

Shopping

SAKS JANDEL, 5510 Wisconsin Ave, Chevy Chase, MD 20815 ☎ (301) 652 2250; SAKS AT WATERGATE, 2522 Virginia Ave, DC 20037 ☎ (202) 337 4200 and branches
Ernest and Henry Marx's forward-thinking fashion flair has made this No 1 for the first ladies of the capital. The exclusive on Saint Laurent, Valentino, Lagerfeld, Laroche and Dior boutiques plus Rykiel, Montana, Chanel, Féraud et omnes. **The Right Stuff** boutique focuses on fast fashion for the diplomatic brat pack.

SHARPER IMAGE, 529 14th St NW, DC 20045 ☎ (202) 626 6340 and branches
Wannabe James Bonds stock up here for the latest gadgets. Automated hairbrushes, chess pieces that move themselves, squirt-guns with a 50 ft range.

SUTTON PLACE GOURMET, 3201 New Mexico Ave NW, DC 20016 ☎ (202) 363 5800 and 4872 Massachussetts Ave NW ☎ (202) 966 1740
Fabulous foodstuffs in DC's answer to Balducci's. Terrific gourmet-to-go array of prepared meals. The Mass Ave shop is smaller and concentrates more on delicatessen and bakery than fresh goods. At the branch on 600 Franklin St, Alexandria, Virginia ☎ (703) 549 6611, the **Sutton Place Café** has become a rather smart little restaurant for regional American cooking.

Theatre

ARENA STAGE, 6th St and Maine Ave SW, DC 20024 ☎ (202) 554 9066
Front-running regional company, based in a 3-theatre complex. Classics to contemporary American pieces. The company tours from time to time – it was the first from the USA to play in Moscow.

NATIONAL THEATER, 1321 Pennsylvania Ave NW, DC 20004 ☎ (202) 628 6161
DC's oldest cultural institution (estab. 1835) is a top pre-Broadway tester. Strong on musicals, comedy and drama.

· REST OF ·

AMERICA

Festivals

SPOLETO FESTIVAL USA, PO Box 157, Charleston, SC 29402 ☎ (803) 722 2764
Exuberant cousin of the Italian festival under the same direction of Gian Carlo Menotti. In its 17th year – with more than 100 performances of opera, theatre, dance, music and visual artistry over 18 summery days. Showcases new or obscure works and vamps up the classics. Carnival atmosphere prevails – dinners, dances, gallons of bubbly, and fireworks on the harbour.

Film

TELLURIDE FILM FESTIVAL, PO Box 6, Telluride, CO 81435 ☎ (303) 728 4401
Leading US festival set in the middle of the Rockies. It's worth booking in advance (PO Box B1156, Hanover, NH 03755) – there's no guarantee of a ticket, and *all* top celluloidites want to be there, including IAIN JOHNSTONE: "*It has an opera house and in summer they show films in the opera house and the open-air square beside it. A very fashionable film festival – the people who go to Robert Redford's Sundance Institute are the sort of people who turn up there, the intelligentsia of American films.*"

Shopping

LL BEAN, Main St, Freeport, ME 04033 ☎ (207) 865 4761; mail order ☎ (207) 865 3111
Outdoor doodle dandies go for waders, docksiders, silk turtlenecks, etc, from America's great outdoors catalogue's HQ. The chamois shirts are the same as they were in 1927, and so are some of their customers.

Ski resorts

ALTA/SNOWBIRD
For the tingle factor: these twin resorts in the

Utah Rockies have skiing up to 11,000 ft, and powder snow that is so sifted-soft and light that you feel you're floating. Alta is an old mining town whose boisterous saloons are a thing of the past – now it's one of the most peaceful and pally resorts in the States.

ASPEN
Still the most snocial ski resort in the USA, this old mining town is athrong with folk such as powder-hound John Denver, Jack Nicholson, Don Johnson, Goldie Hawn, Christie Brinkley and Billy Joel, who either own a place or have a friend who does. *"Hollywood empties at Christmas and it all moves to Aspen. It is the night life and the slopes life"* – ROBIN LEACH. Elevated skiing, too, the highest in the USA at over 13,000 ft in the Imperial Bowl. Non-chalet-owners stay at the **Ritz-Carlton** – rev up on their ice rink or the cross-country skiing track, wind down in a Jacuzzi, sauna or steam room.

SUN VALLEY
Idaho's top ski resort, a Tinseltown Tyrol, tests the best off-piste turns – Margaux Hemingway and Brooke Shields turn heads. Demanding skiing for experts, US powder at its best. *"A bit of heaven. Really rough and ready, you don't have to get dressed up"* – NANCY PILCHER.

TELLURIDE
Now that Sylvester Stallone has bought land here, this one-horse town, south-west of Aspen, is poised (reluctantly) to become a millionaire's playground. Scene of Butch Cassidy's first bank robbery, the little mining town has survived intact, down to the Last Dollar Saloon. Demanding skiing.

VAIL
Purpose-built in the Alpine style, known variously as Instant Tyrol and Plastic Bavaria, Vail has the fastest lifts in the world, supreme back-bowl skiing and some of the best-kept pistes. *"The No 1 ski area in America"* – STEVE PODBORSKI. Not the best-kept secret though – see ex-President Ford and top Texan families like Wyatt, Murchison and Bass whizzing down the mountain. Check in to the Orient-Express-run **Lodge**.

———— Wine ————

See also Rest of California.

Oregon

"Interesting things are happening in Oregon – probably the most interesting is that the Burgundy house of **JOSEPH DROUHIN** *have invested there. They've just released their first Pinot Noirs, which are certainly the most exciting produced in Oregon and, bearing in mind that it's their first attempt, it's very exciting"* – GEOFFREY ROBERTS. And more seals of approval for the area, he continues: *"The other significant thing is that Brian Croser has come to Oregon to start a winery called* **ARGYLE**, *principally to make sparkling wines which are a little more austere and elegant than some of those from California."* Try also the pioneering **EYRIE VINEYARDS** – *"Fine Pinot Noirs and smoky-flavoured rich yet lively Pinot Gris"* – ANTHONY HANSON. Another Oregon tip from HANSON: *"In 1989, many Oregon Pinot Noirs beat those of Carneros for fruit, balance and length of flavour*

Opera Argentina

Tango-lovers and Fitzcarraldo eat your hearts out – the **Teatro Colón**, Avenida 9 de Julio, Buenos Aires ☎ (01) 355414, is the cultural institution of Argentina and the No 1 opera house in South America. Built at the turn of the century, a night here turns back the clock as slick-haired men in tuxedos and mahogany-skinned women in jewels and furs arrive at the floodlit theatre. Lavish red and gold décor, a massive stage and the incomparable romance of the place have attracted nightingales from around the world – Caruso, Callas, Domingo et al. The orchestra plays from individual velvet armchairs, and audience seating for 2,400 expands to standing for 4,000 when a big

name sings. Ballet performances too, which have prompted Mikhail Barishnikov to declare the Colón the most beautiful of all theatres he knows. Below stage are 3 floors of underground workshops, a replica stage for rehearsals, and store rooms that would have Imelda Marcos slavering at their doors (30,000 pairs of dainty shoes, zillions of costumes and wigs). The Colón borders on the unique in that you can get tickets – just turn up 3 days before a performance, and you don't even need to tell the bank manager. PS Post-Colonic entertainment? *"If you like to dance, the place to go is Buenos Aires –* **La Bocca** *is the sleaziest tango club but it's the most fun"* – JOE EULA.

– *look out for* **ADELSHEIM VINEYARD,**
PONZI, BETHEL HEIGHTS *and*
DOMAINE DROUHIN."

Washington State

Bordeaux to Oregon's Burgundy, the Cabernet
Sauvignon grape wins the laurels in Washington
State. LIZ BERRY's money's on *"single estates*
like the **WOODWARD CANYON,** *which is*
superb, and the **Otis Vineyard** *from*
COLUMBIA WINERY, *a single vineyard, old*
vines, starting to produce some very good
wines." GEOFFREY ROBERTS recommends
CHATEAU STE MICHELLE (big, reliable
producers) and **HOGUE CELLARS,** whose
elegant Chardonnays and Cabernet Sauvignons
are beginning to make a stir.

AUSTRALIA

ADELAIDE

—— *Art and museums* ——

ART GALLERY OF SOUTH AUSTRALIA,
North Terrace, SA 2000 ☎ **(08) 223 7200**
Interesting collection of Oz and Euro art – with
some eccentric British works such as Edward
Lear's drawings – and the history of South
Australia thrown in.

—— *Arts centres* ——

ADELAIDE FESTIVAL CENTRE, King
William St, SA 5000 ☎ **(08) 213 4788**
Renowned around the world as a modern architectural masterwork – beautiful clean lines – and
for its pin-sharp acoustics. Brilliant sight lines,
too. *"Really good, we liked it a lot"* – FREDERIC
RAPHAEL. Regular classical concerts, ballet and
theatre.

—— *Bars and cafés* ——

UNIVERSAL WINE BAR, 285 Rundle St,
SA 5000 ☎ **(08) 232 5000**
Michael Hill-Smith's (he of winemaking fame)
inviting parquetry-floored drinkery/eatery has
proved hugely popular with stylish Adelaide.
Decently priced and imaginatively chosen wines
by the glass and homy plats-du-jour sort of food
(salad of lardons, soft-poached egg, lettuce and
mange-touts, and duck leg with shredded
parsnip) are the rewards of patient queuing.

—— *Fashion* ——

GAY NAFFINE, 270 Unley Rd, Hyde
Park, SA 5061 ☎ **(08) 272 0099**
Adelaide's numero uno is among CAROLYN LOCK-
HART's favourites – for *"classics with an inter-*
esting twist". Modern lines with their own lean
energy are none the less softly tailored and sensual.

—— *Festivals* ——

ADELAIDE FESTIVAL OF ARTS, GPO
Box 1269, SA 5001 ☎ **(08) 216 8600**
Big international festival, held biennially in Feb-
March of even years. Broad and deep sweep of
multi-cultural arts – theatre, dance, exhibitions
and concerts under maestros like Solti, Tilson
Thomas and Boulez. 50,000 attend the opening
spectacular, watching and drinking around the
massive outdoor stage, 60 international writers
attend Writers' Week to debate, read and perform. Hungry arties dine happily at Lyrics
restaurant on festive fare from guest chefs.

—— *Hotels* ——

 **HYATT REGENCY, North Terrace, SA**
5000 ☎ **(08) 231 1234**
Grandiose new block. Granite and marble encase
the HR's 4-atria section of the Adelaide Plaza,
which also contains SA's first casino and the festival centre. All the Hyatt trimmings, including
the Regency Club. *"It really has become one of*
the best hotels in Australia. They have top-
quality service. What is more impressive is
Fleurieu [see Restaurants]. *They have a very*
young, enthusiastic staff, which is really impor-
tant" – KEN HOM. Try out the tepanyaki at
clover-leafed counter in the brill Japanese
Shiki. As for STEPHANIE ALEXANDER, she says:
"I'm always extremely well looked after at the
Hyatt in Adelaide," while CAROLYN LOCKHART
reckons it has *"the best kind of service and*
attention to detail".

THE TERRACE ADELAIDE, 150 North
Terrace, SA 5000 ☎ **(08) 217 7552**
Euro-style hotel opposite Parliament House and
the Casino, sleeping the trad pack and with a big
reputation for service. The weary traveller who
can't tolerate another night of air-conditioning
will appreciate windows that actually open.

—— *Restaurants* ——

See also Hotels.

CHLOE'S, 36 College Rd, Kent Town, SA
5067 ☎ **(08) 422574**
Great game, poultry and seafood – crab and
abalone a speciality – boned, shelled or filleted at

the hands of trendsetting Nick Papazahariakis. Relax in the converted villa, marvel at the presentation, and order some top grog from the rather large cellar to accompany Chloe's signature dish: duck breast with game wonton.

🐟 **FLEURIEU, Hyatt Regency, see Hotels**
Dynamic dining – supremely high-class Aussie/Gallic cooking by Swiss chef Urs Inauen, faultless service and deep, deep cellar. *"Wonderful, their chef is wonderful – really special"* – ELISE PASCOE. KEN HOM pays homage, too: *"The chef is really fabulous, his food is really very interesting, a combination of European cooking techniques and the best of Australian ingredients. He cooks it in a manner which is extremely light and flavoursome."* And from STEPHANIE ALEXANDER: *"The chef is brilliant, but the restaurant is often overlooked – it suffers from being a hotel restaurant though the food is of the greatest distinction."*

MANDARIN DUCK BISTRO, 110 Flinders St, SA 5000 ☎ (08) 223 2370
A busy, casual bistro with a strong lunchtime following. *"Of the restaurants that set out to be serious and charge top-of-the-market prices for fairly simple food, I would say it is the best. In Adelaide, unlike everywhere else in Australia, the chefs are Eastern, cooking in a Western way, rather than the other way round. The chef there is Cedric Eu, from Malaysia, and he creates lovely things"* – STEPHANIE ALEXANDER.

MEZES, 287 Rundle St, SA 5000 ☎ (08) 223 7384
Modern Med: influences from Italy, Greece and Spain combine in dishes like pigeon breast carpaccio with capers, capsicum, olive oil and garlic paste, or sugar bacon with duck liver sausage on brioche with orange glaze. Run by the Kathreptis family – Elias cooks, Anthony and Irene front the neo-classical house. SUE FAIRLIE-CUNINGHAME goes, *"because the chef really is amazing . . . his food has wonderful taste and texture".*

🐟 **MISTRESS AUGUSTINE'S, 145 O'Connell St, N Adelaide, SA 5006 ☎ (08) 267 4479**
Bold, straightforward cooking, with real invention by owner-chef Ann Oliver. Presentation is spot-on, colours are terrific, flavours punchy: Coffin Bay oysters on Sichuan pepper noodles and braised duck leg stuffed with dates and green ginger are classic examples. Décor is a little austere – in contrast to the food. *"I admire Ann Oliver because she tries so hard, she has worked alongside such greats as Paul Prudhomme and Marc Meneau, she engenders so much enthusiasm in her patrons, her staff – people admire her"* – SUE FAIRLIE-CUNINGHAME.

🐟 **NEDIZ TU, 170 Hutt St, SA 5000 ☎ (08) 223 2618**
Every influence imaginable goes – Oriental,

Western, Oz . . . *"one of my favourites, it really is superb food"* – KEN HOM. Chefs Kate Sparrow and Vietnamese Le Tu Thai collaborate on dishes like millefeuille of scallops with coriander butter sauce, and venison with a crisp crêpe filled with parsnip purée and served with a lemon ginger glaze. MARY ROSSI eats well there, CAROLYN LOCKHART says they're *"the dearest people"*. Dinner only.

URAIDLA ARISTOLOGIST, Cnr Greenhill and Basket Rds, Uraidla, SA 5142 ☎ (08) 3901995
A taste of Tuscany in the Adelaide Hills where ventures the amateur aristologist (student of dining, not *Debrett's*) to learn about great produce, simply cooked in rustic Franco-Italian style. Some vegetables are picked from the kitchen garden when the water is already boiling – things don't come fresher than that.

· REST OF ·

SOUTH AUSTRALIA

—— *Hotels* ——

THE LODGE, RSD 120, Seppeltsfield, SA 5355 ☎ (085) 628277
The original Seppelts winemakers' family homestead in the Barossa Valley. A charming 1900 bluestone villa, it is *"small scale, run by restaurateurs Aaron Penley and Graham Butler, with nice attention to detail, lovely food. It's very welcoming, not glamorous, but very well done"* – CAROLYN LOCKHART. *"One of the prettiest gardens you'll ever see, and it's smack in the middle of the finest wine-growing area"* – MICHAEL GEBICKI.

MOUNT LOFTY HOUSE, 74 Summit Rd, Crafers, SA 5152 ☎ (08) 339 6777
Grand old 19C house in the Adelaide hills – rebuilt after a fire – blending mod cons and trad style (croquet lawn, good service, etc). *"Very appealing"* – CAROLYN LOCKHART; MARY ROSSI agrees. Convenient too: *"You can be in Adelaide in 45 minutes. The setting, the gardens and the atmosphere are magnificent"* – MICHAEL GEBICKI.

PADTHAWAY ESTATE, Padthaway, Coonawarra, SA 5271 ☎ (087) 655039
Laceworked to the nines, in the back of beyond, this is the place to lounge on verandahs, sip the homespun bubbly and look out at the Padthaway vineyards. A handful of comfy colonial rooms, splendid food, crystal, porcelain and silver.

THORN PARK COUNTRY HOUSE, College Rd, Sevenhill, SA 5453 ☎ (088) 434304
"Everything a country house should be – warm,

Great Escapes

There's no getting away from it, when it comes to getting away from it all, Aussies have a world of choice in one continent. Some don't even need to leave home: *"I'm funny about resorts because I feel that I live in one. I think, 'why go away when I've got the beach at my front door?' – the best beaches, the best restaurants"* – NANCY PILCHER. And no one needs to leave the country: *"We've all gone to Europe but do I really want to sit on a plane for 24 hours . . . I used to go to Hawaii a lot but what extra benefit am I going to get from going there than I am from Port Douglas? Answer – very little"* – GREG DANIEL. A trip away from the coast yields getaways in the proper pioneering spirit. COLIN LANCELEY is inspired by *"Sofala, an old gold mining town west of the Blue Mountains – the pub's immortalized by Russel Drysdale's painting – a true escape to a frontier village of the 1850s."* JENNY KEE finds multiple inspirations: *"Walking through the Tasmanian wilderness; exploring the extraordinarily intricate paintings inside the aboriginal cave at Laura in North Queensland; my own retreat in the Blue Mountains."* A trip right into the red centre sorts out the trackers from the slackers: *"Kakadu is a fabulous rain forest and the Kimberley Ranges are phenomenal, in the heart of the red desert – you wonder how anyone could ever live there"* – SKYE MACLEOD.

welcoming, it's got good books and a great record library – it's the sort of place where you can just curl up in an armchair and read all day. The food is wonderful – dinners tend to be long and boozy" – MICHAEL GEBICKI. CAROLYN LOCKHART stays there too.

Restaurants

PETULUMA'S BRIDGEWATER MILL, Mount Barker Rd, Bridgewater, SA 5155 ☎ (08) 339 4227

Gourmet hot spot – owned by the he-can-do-no-wrong Petaluma wine guru Brian Croser. The restored 1860s stone flour mill is home to fabulous foodie inventions by Catherine Kerry – minced Thai-style fish cooked in banana leaf, kangaroo fillet and anchovy butter, leek and parmesan pie with white pepper butter – washed down with a drop of the patron's own nectar. *"Transports you to Californian food . . . Chez Panisse, very upmarket, unexpected"* – SUE FAIRLIE-CUNINGHAME.

PHEASANT FARM, Samuel Rd, Nuriootpa, SA 5355 ☎ (085) 621286

For phantasmagorical phood and sensational setting, this has rocketed to No 1 in Australia. Pheasant and duck home-reared by the Beers, local rabbit and kangaroo (the roo prosciutto is incroyable) bought in, and all cooked by Maggie B with ultimate inspiration and invention. *"She is a great success, always cooks what she knows she does best. She's a brilliant game cook. It's on the side of a dam, so it's a natural outdoorsy, Australian timber building. It really is quite surprising to go into the country and eat so well. And she is lovely, everyone loves her"* – ELISE PASCOE. More praise from STEPHANIE ALEXANDER, MARY ROSSI and CAROLYN LOCKHART: *"Unpretentious, with perfect ingredients and detail."* The salad of smoked kangaroo with keta caviare is legendary.

THE VINTNERS RESTAURANT, Nuriootpa Rd, Angaston, SA 5353 ☎ (085) 642488

Everything is home-made here, from kangaroo carpaccio to the puds (divine ice cream). Front-of-house Don Coats and his chef-wife Marjorie know their vino and dash it aplenty in the food – try the Shiraz-steeped claret jelly or the Peter Lehmann Semillon Sauternes ice cream. The rest is in the ample cellar.

BRISBANE

Art and museums

MUSEUM OF CONTEMPORARY ART, 164 Melbourne St, Qld 4101 ☎ (07) 846 2255

Newish gallery in a 1930s building. See the large modern collection, watch out for visiting exhibitions.

Arts centres

QUEENSLAND CULTURAL CENTRE, South Bank, Qld 4000 ☎ (07) 840 7229

Tripartite centre on a sleek modern design,

housing the Queensland Museum, Queensland Art Gallery and the **Brisbane Performing Arts Complex** ☎ (07) 846 4444 – incorporating the Lyric Theatre and the 2,000-seat Concert Hall, which JULIAN LLOYD WEBBER thinks is one of the best there is. Also houses the excellent riverside **Fountain Room** restaurant.

—— Bars and cafés ——

MOCAFE, Museum of Contemporary Art, 164 Melbourne St, S Brisbane, Qld 4101
☎ (07) 844 8924
Attached to the MOCA, with its own collection of original art on the walls. Go for *"salads, pastas, very good coffee . . . it's nicely done, with lovely paintings – you can tell that there are enthusiastic people behind it all"* – STEPHANIE ALEXANDER. Spiced-up pumpkin and scallop soup is a winner; there's a decently priced short wine list too.

———— Hotels ————

🐾 **THE HERITAGE HOTEL, Cnr Edward and Margaret Sts, Qld 4001**
☎ (07) 221 1999
The newest in town, though in a restored 19C building, next to the Botanical Gardens, with views out over the river. NANCY PILCHER raves: *"I didn't want to leave. I got to my hotel room, thought 'this is it!'. It's so comfortable, service is fantastic, location fantastic, right on the river, decoration in the rooms is fantastic, bathrooms and dressing rooms are huge, and in the bathroom they've got these little TVs that rotate, so you can have this gorgeous bath and watch a movie."* For MARY ROSSI, *"who manages a hotel or restaurant makes all the difference to its mood. The Heritage has charm, just like John and Lyn Parche, who are the ultimate hosts."* Fine dining at **Siggi's**, see Restaurants.

🐾 **SHERATON BRISBANE HOTEL & TOWERS, 249 Turbot St, Qld 4000**
☎ (07) 835 3535
The swankiest hotel in town, boasting a sparkling entrance hall with glass-panelled, extra-speedy lifts. *"It has got to be the best place in Brisbane. A great restaurant, and downstairs in the basement there is a bar/restaurant/club that heaves. Great sound system and videos. The bar is an entertainment in itself, just watching the people"* – TERRY HOLMES. *"It is a very good hotel"* – JULIAN LLOYD WEBBER. The Sheraton Towers is a super-exclusive hotel within a hotel – at the very top.

—— Restaurants ——

BAGUETTE, 150 Racecourse Rd, Ascot, Qld 4007 ☎ (07) 268 6168
A culinary T-junction – here, Queensland is introduced to Mediterranean and Oriental cooking prepared by Thai chef Timmy Kemp and Oz chef David Pugh. Try Queensland scallops with mango, cashew and coconut and a spicy lime dressing or marinade of Western Australian goat's cheese on grilled focaccia with capsicum, avocado, tomato, and olive purée.

CZARS, 47 Elizabeth St, Qld 4002
☎ (07) 221 3486
Russian of the old style – samovars, coloured lamps and fairy pictures rather than queues and cabbage soup. SIR PETER USTINOV thinks it *"the best I've ever been to, run by people who have come from there fairly recently. I was amazed at how authentic it all was. They serve blinis, frightfully well done, and things I hadn't expected in the Russian cuisine, which are never taken up in posh restaurants elsewhere. Kuliabaka, for example, a kind of moussaka made of salmon, is absolutely marvellous."*

MICHAEL'S, Riverside Centre, 123 Eagle St, Qld 4000 ☎ (07) 832 5522
Changes are afoot – Asian influences are creeping into the splendid seafood menu and there's a new champagne bar, both well received by a business clientele. Great views, excellent wine cellar, definitely one of the top noshers in Brissy.

RUMPOLES, Cnr of North Quay and Turbot Sts, Qld 4000 ☎ (07) 236 2877
Improvisational, inspirational modern cooking in the city's legal district. Order lots of little bits – taste the designer pizzas or crocodile meat and save space for the bread and butter pud with whisky sauce. Designer food, designer crowd, design your day around it.

> **❝** *I love the informal eating places in Port Douglas for great Australian produce laced with Asian herbs and spices. The seafood is fighting fresh and the atmosphere very Aussie-casual* **❞**
>
> 🐾 SUSAN KUROSAWA

SIGGI'S, The Heritage Hotel, see Hotels
☎ (07) 221 4555
Sophistiqués swan in for haute-Euro in posh surroundings. They like the wine cellar as well, and, presumably, the gold cutlery and just a tad over-attentive service. Seafood dominates – dishes might include coral trout cured with ginger and aniseed or puff pastry filled with scallops, oysters and a wasabi buerre blanc.

TWO SMALL ROOMS, 517 Milton Rd, Toowong, Qld 4066 ☎ (07) 371 5251
Two small rooms doing big, big business. Run by

Island Idylls

Blend the Crusoe credo with the Cartland principle, add 1,200 miles of live coral reef, a sprinkling of 1,900 varieties of tropical fish, stretches of squeaky white sand and surroundings of deep blue, and you have the best of Australia – the island resorts of the Great Barrier Reef. The appeal is as great for honeymooners (empty beaches, all comforts) as for sportifs (scuba diving, snorkelling, deep-sea fishing, sailing). In the far north, on the fringe of the Outer Reef, **Lizard Island** (3 islands form the resort) is a diver's paradise, drawing ROSSIS CLAUDIA and MARY and HENRY CRAWFORD (*"the best of the Barrier Reef resorts, very good"*). The discreet house-party atmos and 24 private beaches have scored points with British royalty (there's an island named after the PoW) and Bob Hawke. Palm trees rule on **Bedarra Island**, where, rather than chop or avoid 'em, the architects designed some cabins *around* them. Here, the all-in price (no cash changes hands) includes as much champagne as you can cope with and some t'riffic tropical tucker. **Orpheus Island** has a lazy tropical/colonial atmosphere, with wicker furniture, ceiling fans and muslin drapes. 50 guests (including royals and politicos) spread themselves around 7 beaches, walk in the National Parkland and dream up their Desert Island Discs in peace. Book via Australian Airlines Holiday Travel Centre (see Tours and charters).

---

a trio of twentysomethings who know what they're doing with clever, ungimmicky flavour combinations. A glance over the weekly-changing menu might reveal barramundi with Pernod and fennel butter or black bean and kid sausage on rösti; all puddings are sublime, especially Andrew Mirosch's heavenly ice cream.

· REST OF ·

QUEENSLAND

—— *Hotels and resorts* ——

CAPE WILDERNESS LODGE, c/o Air Queensland Resorts, 62 Abbott St, Cairns, Qld 4870 ☎ (070) 504305
Aptly named, its the northernmost mainland retreat resting right on the tip of Cape York. North = hot, tropical swimming, diving, deep-sea fishing and snoozing.

HAYMAN ISLAND, N Qld 4801 ☎ (079) 469100
Top resort – millions of dollars turned the idyllic spot into a lagooned haven the size of 5 Olympic pools. Eat French at **La Fontaine** – you must wear a tie. Rupert Murdoch likes it, so do MARY ROSSI and SKYE MACLEOD, and though dressing up sticks in HENRY CRAWFORD's gullet he says it's *"a very good resort"*. It's a must for ROBIN LEACH, and ELISE PASCOE notes a sea-change: *"It has done a total about-face. At first it didn't let families come and made you wear a jacket and tie, but the new manager has changed all that. I was knocked out by the quality of the food, the service, and the resort in general."*

HYATT REGENCY, Warran Rd, Coolum Beach, Qld 4573 ☎ (071) 461234
Hot place to put a spring back in weary steps. Spa baths, health treatments, fitness programmes, Tai Chi, tennis, golf, 8 swimming pools, the Noosa beaches (with coloured sands) and a Creative Arts Centre. It's where the Rossi clan gets together, says CLAUDIA ROSSI HUDSON: *"It was as good as having our own private home, yet we didn't have to do a thing."*

SHERATON MIRAGE, Port Douglas Rd, Port Douglas, Qld 4871 ☎ (070) 985888
Good food, great lagoon. . . . *"It's fantastic. All your rooms are around a man-made lagoon – you walk out of your room and you just fall into this lagoon. But you have actually got the beach with real surf, just behind a line of palm trees. It*

Australia's Best Resorts

1	SHERATON MIRAGE · Port Douglas
2	CABLE BEACH CLUB · Broome
3	HAYMAN ISLAND · Queensland
4	LIZARD ISLAND · Queensland
5	BEDARRA ISLAND · Queensland

is idyllic, like you are in a mirage. Very good food and very good cooks" – SKYE MACLEOD. *"I had an image of it as a dreadful glitzy place but it's just fantastic, relaxing and not overdone. It's a world-standard resort hotel"* – GREG DANIELS. *"Everything it promises to be; in terms of the quality of the service and the all-over atmosphere, I thought it was just about as good as it could be"* – FREDERIC RAPHAEL.

SHERATON MIRAGE GOLD COAST, Seaworld Drive, Main Beach, Surfers Paradise, Qld 4217 ☎ (075) 911488
Similar to its lagooned-out Port Douglas twin. Sydneysiders like it because it's nearer home. Marvellous ocean suites and a butler service second to none.

CANBERRA

— Art and museums —

AUSTRALIAN NATIONAL GALLERY, Parkes Place, ACT 2600 ☎ (06) 271 2411
No 1 for Australian and Aboriginal; and good on foreign artists working in Australia. More than 70,000 pieces all told. *"Despite the unsuitable architecture it has the only chronologically hung collection of Australian art, demonstrating its historical development and incorporating furniture and decorative arts of the period"* – COLIN LANCELEY. Look out over the lake from the terrace and gaze at modern sculpture.

— Hotels —

PARK HYATT HOTEL, Commonwealth Ave, Yarralumla, ACT 2600 ☎ (06) 270 1234
Update of the capital's old hotel – in the best Hyatt style – with a structuralist incorporation of the old Deco design. King-sized beds and marble bathrooms entice the insomniac and fastidious. Dine finely in the **Oak Room**, Sunday brunch at the **Promenade Café**.

— Restaurants —

See also Hotels.

BLUNDELL'S, The Capital Parkroyal Hotel, 1 Binara St, ACT 2600 ☎ (06) 247 8999
Beautifully presented, immaculately served food in a split-level hotel dining room. Look for game on the menu – wash it down with wine from the carefully chosen, rather idiosyncratic wine list.

FRINGE BENEFITS BRASSERIE, 54 Marcus Clarke St, ACT 2600 ☎ (06) 247 4042
Political thriller – Libs, Labs and Dems in the Brussels of the South tuck in here. Up-to-the-minute brasserie food – cassoulet, mod pasta and pizza, warm quail salad and fab puds. The golden chips and Italian bread are constants – they dare not risk the uproar of removing them.

HILL STATION RESTAURANT, Shepard St, Hume, ACT 2620 ☎ (06) 260 1393
An original colonial homestead with 5 dining rooms, each with an open fire (Canberra can be mighty nippy in winter). Fine dining and an art gallery with temporary exhibitions.

THE LOBBY, King George Terrace, Parkes, ACT 2600 ☎ (06) 273 1563
A jolt of electricity in a town still running on gas, Fiona Wright's menu injects pan-Pacific influences and a 90s direction into plain fodder – barramundi, oysters. Overlooking the parks in front of the old Parliament House. The strong wine list carries bottles from every wine-growing area in Oz, including the ACT.

DARWIN

— Hotels —

BEAUFORT HOTEL, The Esplanade, NT 5790 ☎ (089) 829911
Housing the Darwin Performing Arts Centre, the soft blues and ochres of the hotel echo the

Buzzz Mud-slingers: check out the new **Parliament House**, Capital Hill ☎ (06) 277 5101, those with delicate minds or ears can concentrate on the displayed work of Australian artisans, including a remarkable tapestry in the Great Hall ...... Paint-flingers: the National Trust-classified **Lanyon Homestead**, Tharwa Drive, Tharwa ☎ (06) 237 5136, on the banks of the Murrumbidgee is home to a major collection of Sidney Nolan works ...... Buzzer ringers: it's all bells and lights at the **National Science and Technology Centre**, Parkes ☎ (06) 270 2800, a hands-on museum of all things high- and low-tech ....

contrasting colours of the NT. 196 rooms surrounded by palms and water gardens and Darwin's largest pool and spa area. It comes recommended by MARY ROSSI.

· REST OF ·
NORTHERN TERRITORY

CLOUDY'S RESTAURANT, Glen Helen Gorge ☎ (089) 567489
Where else but the NT would you drive 133 km to try out a restaurant? Judging by the awards and accolades, the hike is worth it for such unexpected pleasures as creamy beetroot soup with smoked salmon and wasabi croûtons, followed by saffron rice with octopus, orange roughy (deep-sea perch) and olives in a lemon thyme sauce. Safari-style accommodation nearby.

SEVEN SPIRIT BAY, Coburg Peninsula, Arnhem Land Reserve ☎ (089) 816844
The most remote resort in Oz, reached by light plane and boat. Only 24 cabins, with all creature comforts. This is the wild wilderness as you have never seen it before. With Aboriginal trackers as your guides, go walking, hunting, or sailing from deserted white beach to beach.

SHERATON AYERS ROCK, Yulara Drive, PO Box 21, Yulara, NT 0872 ☎ (089) 562200
Bang in the centre of the continent, this resort sails forth with its windmill-like panels sheltering the hotel from the blistering heat. Great pool, tennis and dining: in the cool of the evening try venison fillet on a fig. *"The rock itself is so surprising and the design of the resort is spectacular too"* – CATHY ROSSI HARRIS.

MELBOURNE
—— Art and museums ——

NATIONAL GALLERY OF VICTORIA, 180 St Kilda Rd, Vic 3000 ☎ (03) 618 0222
Impressive Impressionism from the Heidelberg school – Australia's answer to the Parisian pals – hangs out with the broadest collection of contemporary Oz art in the world. Funded by state and individual purses, it's a cathedral to New World aesthetics – complete with stained glass roof atop the towering Great Hall.

—— Arts centres ——

VICTORIAN ARTS CENTRE, 100 St Kilda Rd, Vic 3004 ☎ (03) 617 8211
Colossal visual and performing arts centre which NED SHERRIN thinks *"very impressive. They were having a Loudon St Hill exhibition when I was there. A great Australian design."* You'll find the **National Gallery, Museum of Victoria**, a 2,600-seat ultra-acoustic concert hall, 3 theatres (**Playhouse** tops the bill for drama, the **State Theatre** for opera) a performing arts museum, a children's museum and massive outdoor entertainment area. Architecturally intriguing, it burrows 6 storeys down into the old bed of Yarra River.

—— Ballet ——

♠ AUSTRALIAN BALLET, 11 Mount Alexander Rd, Flemington, Vic 3031 ☎ (03) 376 1400
Strong classical and contemporary company which EDWARD THORPE includes in his worldwide top 10: *"Last time I saw them they were on fine form."* Artistically directed by Maina Gielgud, niece of Sir you know who.

—— Bars and cafés ——

♠ CAFE DI STASIO, 31 Fitzroy St, St Kilda, Vic 3182 ☎ (03) 525 3999
Concentrated Italiana, run by ebullient Ronnie di Stasio. Test top Tuscan wines, carpaccio and al dente spaghetti. *"The chef feels free to draw on all regions of Italy, so I've had a very good bollito misto from the north and a Sicilian sardine pasta"* – STEPHANIE ALEXANDER. *"Italian food by Italy's standards. It is what Mario's is to Sydney but smaller, more intimate. The quality is forever consistent"* – SANDRA HIRSH. *"Transports you to Milano, a lot of Italians go there . . . young and fashionable"* – SUE FAIRLIE-CUNINGHAME. LEO SCHOFIELD is transported.

CAFE FLORENTINO, 80 Bourke St, Vic 3000 ☎ (03) 663 1811
"The stand-up coffee bar is very Italian, very Milanese," and certainly MARK PATRICK's cup of tea. ROBERT SANGSTER is a regular, and WARWICK VYNER drops in too.

CAFE IGUANA, 564 Chapel St, S Yarra (3141) ☎ (03) 826 6055
Heading the hip list of Melbourne's trendy bars – good tucker (Mexican, Spanish, Italian influences), groovy crowd and upbeat grooves.

♠ CAFFE E CUCINA, 481 Chapel St, S Yarra ☎ (03) 827 4139
A constant stream of concentrated espressos, lashings of fisherman's risotto and crusty bruschetta delight regulars (who know each other by name) and Italian cognoscenti. *"Very popular – it's a tiny Italian place with wonderful coffee and a very fast turnover. They keep things simple – it's mainly the coffee/cake/focaccia thing people go for"* – STEPHANIE ALEXANDER. Anyone who's anyone has been, including LEO

The Ustinov Philosophy

'Flawless' and 'immaculate' are all very well, but when SIR PETER USTINOV seeks out the best, he's looking for a little something extra. "*I think I look for a standard of human contact as well,*" he explains. "*I've always admired Mercedes motor cars but they're always, to me, a little like a waiter serving you at a large banquet and you drop a pea on the table cloth and you look up apologetically and he pretends not to have seen. I prefer the waiter to say, for example, as he serves you, 'take the bit from the middle, it's the best part'. It is rare and it depends on how the staff are instructed. When they're told it's a grand hotel and they have to behave in a certain way, then I find it cold and forbidding.*"

SCHOFIELD: "*Great – very Melbourne feel. I like the breeze of it all, like an Italian restaurant but much nicer because the people are nicer.*"

THE DOG'S BAR, 54 Acland St, St Kilda, Vic 3182 ☎ (03) 525 3599
Laid-back designerie packed with designery types (architects, artists). The bar adjoins a pâtisserie which adjoins a deli – it's a stylized all-at-your-fingertips kinda place. At weekends it really is *it*.

—————— Clubs ——————

THE CLUB, 132 Smith St, Collingwood, Vic 3066 ☎ (03) 417 4425
Best wannabe bands all wanna play here – it's a wired-up livewire club with 2 stages showing non-stop music till late. Run by ex-Skyhook Rob Stakey.

THE IVY, 145 Flinders Lane, Vic 3000 ☎ (03) 650 5377
Level best – Glen Wheatley's A\$5 million, 4-floored hot spot stacks the VIPs on top (see local TV, film and radio hot shots on their way up), the noshers a floor below, boozers in the ground-floor bar, and ravers in the basement club.

THE METRO, 20 Bourke St, Vic 3000 ☎ (03) 663 4288
The tallest in town, 5 floors crammed with fab light/video show, beautiful people, and very little breathing space.

THE RED HEAD, Aughtie Drive, S Melbourne, Vic 3205 ☎ (03) 690 7877
Lively live sound venue set in an antique football stand. Bop on the black-and-white-tiled floor, amid antique mirrors and paintings, listening to hip sounds from The Bitch Magnets and co. Non-members and unwelcomes kept outside – strict door policy. SANDRA HIRSH gets in.

—————— *Fashion designers* ——————

ADELE PALMER, 671 Chapel St, S Yarra, Vic 3141 ☎ (03) 240 0611
Balmy, palmy casuals and smart sportswear. Bold prints and Australia's best jeans, Jag. Everyone had their Jag flares in the 70s, now everyone (Redford, Newman, Cher included) has their laid-back button-flies.

JENNY BANNISTER, Studio enquiries ☎ (03) 510 8932
Original party numbers for the original party girl. Her young, exuberant, energetic styles liven up sometimes stuffy Melbourne society. "*Jenny Bannister's designs are wild, wonderful. She is creating divine party dresses for all the Melbourne girls – dresses for the anti-débutante*" – VICTORIA COLLISON. SANDRA HIRSH applauds her style: "*I find her inspired. As well*

Buzz Coffee society: if you like it à la español, ramble off to **Café Ramblas**, 37 Toorak Rd, for trad Spanish food and good coffee ...... Coffee only: That's what to sample at **Rosati**, 95 Flinders Lane ...... Espress yourself: Everyone knows **Mietta's**, but go downstairs for a mean espresso ...... Hard Rock Coffee: **Le Monde**, 18 Bourke St, draws le monde for good music and a strong dose ...... HRC 2: SANDRA HIRSH takes in a brew at the **Botanical**, Domain Rd, S Yarra, or the **Cherry Tree**, 53 Balmain St, Richmond – architect of the year Tom Kodak designed the inside, hot sound merchants Patois and Freaked Out Flower Children play in it ...... Rock 3: Funk rats head to S Melbourne for the best pubs such as the rocked-out **Water Rat**, cnr Moray and Park Sts ☎ (03) 690 2116, for a 50s and 60s beat ....

as designing the ultimate party dress, she is brilliant when given leeway creatively to do other things. She always has incredible fabric and from it creates something perfect."

🐚 JODIE BOFFA, Studio enquiries ☎ (03) 361 5867; at Riada, Hampshire & Lowndes, Daimaru

Great newcomer, wowing the style-watchers with her unstreety, intelligent clothes. "Wonderful tailored clothes, not too structured, low-key style" – JUDITH COOK. NANCY PILCHER thinks she's "very, very clever, bridging that gap between the young creative and established manufacturer/designer." "Australia's answer to Jasper Conran (she worked with him for a time in London). Has greatly impressed everyone with her impeccable tailoring, beautiful fabrics, lovely subtle colours" – VICTORIA COLLISON. "An individual signature, hers is an elegant minimal style. Beautiful fabrics are very important to her" – PATRICIA MERK.

🐚 SCANLAN AND THEODORE, 539 Chapel St, S Yarra, Vic 3141 ☎ (03) 241 2449

Inspired, youth-oriented designs which have the Melbourne fashion scene wrapped up. "Original, witty, feminine, very soft, fluid clothes. A lot of stripes and colour. Many of Fiona Scanlan's shapes are quite organic – for instance, a big white shirt with a round collar, a rounded edge on a jacket. Unexpected detailing makes her designs stand out" – PATRICIA MERK. "One of the best innovative young designers in Australia, she has proved you can be a successful fringe designer – up and coming and a commercial success as well" – SANDRA HIRSH. NANCY PILCHER wishes her well.

───── Festivals ─────

SPOLETO FESTIVAL, 6th Level, 1 City Rd, S Melbourne, Vic 3205 ☎ (03) 614 4484

Australian wing of Menotti's Italian fiesta. International contemporary and classical dance, drama, musicals and classical concerts set the Victorian Arts Centre and surrounding churches and halls abuzz for 2 weeks in Sept.

───── Hotels ─────

HILTON INTERNATIONAL MELBOURNE ON THE PARK, 192 Wellington Parade, E Melbourne, Vic 3002 ☎ (03) 419 3311

Cricketing cache – bang next to the Melbourne Cricket Ground (biggest in the world), and overlooking Fitzroy Gardens, this is where the likes of Imran Khan have stayed. Good for power travellers and folk who expect good service (Margaret Thatcher, Prince Philip). Dining at the oak-panelled **Cliveden Room** is a treat too.

🐚 HOTEL COMO, 640 Chapel St, S Yarra, Vic 3141 ☎ (03) 824 0400

This chic boutiquer is hitting the top of the trendy Melbourne scene. "Unique in the world – modern, comfortable, well designed" – PATRICIA MERK. "My favourite city hotel in Australia, because it's got a very young attitude, very hip – they leave you to yourself. Not 5 star in the sense of extraordinary room service, but the facilities are very good and you feel part of the city" – MARK PATRICK. For NANCY PILCHER it has "the most comfortable beds of any hotel I've stayed in ever". Rockers like U2 seem to think so too.

🐚 HYATT ON COLLINS, 123 Collins St, Vic 3000 ☎ (03) 657 1234

The most opulent, gleaming, polished hotel in Australia, this is very big and very grand. Over 6 acres of Veronese marble (tons of it in the massive, massively decadent bathrooms), skylit galleried atria with the chic Collins Chase shopping complex, bars, the splendid **Max's Seafood Restaurant**, **Monsoon's** night club and the ultra-exclusive Regency Club – a 4-floor hotel-within-a-hotel – for a total blow-out. MARY ROSSI thinks it's grand, WARWICK VYNER agrees, and SHARYN STORRIER-LYNEHAM stays because "if I'm in a city for a short time I want to be where the action is".

🐚 THE REGENT OF MELBOURNE, 25 Collins St, Vic 3000 ☎ (03) 653 0000

Gaze down on the world or on glamourites vacating their limos from the 50-storey atrium skyscraper. Floor-to-ceiling windows in the spacious suites are eye-openers, regular rooms have less elbow room. Massive auditorium tops excellent business facilities. GREG DANIEL reckons it is "the best hotel in town, without a doubt, in terms of service and style. For a big hotel it's got a really personalized feel and that's what people want." It's what MARY ROSSI and JEFFREY ARCHER want, at any rate.

ROCKMAN'S REGENCY HOTEL, Cnr Exhibition and Lonsdale Sts, Vic 3000 ☎ (03) 662 3900

Chic boutique hotel where snazzocrats sip (at the **Regency Bar**), dine (at Iain Hewitson's fab restaurant) and sleep (in sleek rooms – videos in all regulars, Jacuzzis in suites). "A very, very cultivated hotel and a very personal hotel" – SIR PETER USTINOV. Whitney Houston, John McEnroe, James Taylor, Sean Connery and MARY ROSSI rock up too. Pool and spa polish things off.

🐚 SEBEL OF MELBOURNE, 321 Flinders Lane, Vic 3000 ☎ (03) 629 4088

Baby sister of Sydney's Sebel Town House – first birthday was summer 92 – it's the new place to see and be seen in Melbourne, reckons ELISE PASCOE. Renaissance-styled gardens, business bits – fax, PC, etc – and real choice in the restaurant – eat what you like, they say, the menu's only a guideline.

**TILBA HOTEL, Cnr Toorak Rd W and
Domain St, S Yarra, Vic 3141**
☎ (03) 867 8844
A rare town-house hotel, with a clubbish air and
only 15 beautifully presented rooms and suites,
including a garden cottage. Arties and rag-
traders book early.

WINDSOR, 103 Spring St, Vic 3000
☎ (03) 653 0653
Old Victorian hotel, full of *"whimsical eccentric-
ities. It may not be as brisk and efficient as some
of the modern monoliths that went up during
Melbourne's hotel boom, but it has character
and that's far more important"* – DAVID DALE.
Restored by the Oberoi group, it's kept its old-
fashioned values and clientele.

——— Restaurants ———

See also Hotels.

🐟 **BROWN'S, 1097–1111 High St,
Armadale, Vic 3143** ☎ **(03) 822 3188**
Roux brothers-trained Greg Brown treats his
diners well and his dinners seriously. Alongside
the smart restaurant is the cheaper **Brown's
Bistro**. *"Certainly one of the top restaurants in
Melbourne. It's pretty fabulous"* – KEN HOM.
*"Greg Brown is really serious about food, his
basis is French, obviously using wonderful local
ingredients. The ambience there is lovely, so
pretty, like being in someone's house. Very good
cellar. What's so clever is the kitchen is shared
with the bistro"* – CAROLYN LOCKHART. SUE FAIR-
LIE-CUNINGHAME likes the pair of them. LEO
SCHOFIELD prefers a different approach: *"Like
transposed French. The food is good but I want
my favourites to be more Australian."*

FANNY'S, 243 Lonsdale St, Vic 3000
☎ (03) 663 3017
On the boil – as ever. Life upstairs is a polished,
top-notch, posh affair, downstairs punters watch
their brill bistro fare prepared in the open
kitchen. Cooking is constantly revised, seasonal
dishes are always on, past diners include Bacall,
Dietrich, MARY ROSSI and WARWICK VYNER.

**FLOWER DRUM, 17 Market Lane, Vic
3000** ☎ **(03) 662 3655**
Celebrated Chineserie, mooted as Oz's best.
GREG DANIEL goes one further: *"The best Chinese in the world."* It's haute cuisine, grand prix,
and très chic – private salles lead away from the
main dining room. Chef Anthony Lui beats the
field with his egg noodles, stuffed crab shell and
Peking duck.

FRANCE SOIR, 11 Toorak Rd, S Yarra
☎ (03) 866 8569
Cacophonic, Gallic brasserie packed with oyster-
swallowers, steak-chewers, frite-nibblers, etc.
One of NANCY PILCHER's top 2 (along with
Marchetti's Latin): *"I really like it because it's*

❝We can now target one area
of Australia and get all the
produce from that region:
Tasmanian salmon, lamb from
Gippsland, beautiful grass-fed beef
from Victoria, stone fruit and
berries so beautiful, luscious,
delectable. . . . **❞**

 SERGE DANSEREAU

*silly, so much action, it's crowded and the food's
kind of basic. Pommes frites, chicken, salad,
steak frites. I don't like fussy food."* SHARYN
STORRIER-LYNEHAM agrees.

**JACQUES REYMOND'S RESTAURANT,
259 Lennox St, Richmond, Vic 3121**
☎ (03) 427 9177
On-the-pulse French cooking from ex-Mietta's
chef JR wows Melbournian taste buds. This
is a purely foodie place – formal décor is a bit
intimidating, some say.

**KENZAN, Lower Gr Fl, Collins Place, 45
Collins St, Vic 3000** ☎ **(03) 654 8933**
One of Melbourne's Japanese pioneers, a first-
rate restaurant under the Regent hotel, with
splendid sushi, the best kaiseki (traditional
banquet) and nabe ryori (cooked in the pot).

**THE LAST AUSSIE FISHCAF, 256 Park
St, S Melbourne, Vic 3205** ☎ **(03) 699 1942**
Brash caff with rock 'n' roll atmos (co-owners
Tim Connell, Russell Brandon and John Flower
mime along to oldies doin' the bar stool leap),
décor (lino floor, chrome-edged tables, retro
jukebox) and clientele. Fish is creole/Orient-
inspired – blackened fillets, boudin of char-
grilled seafood, tempura, and good old paper-
wrapped fish and chips. Branches out to
Adelaide, Brisbane and Sydney.

**LYNCH'S, 133 Domain Rd, S Yarra, Vic
3141** ☎ **(03) 266 5627**
Old-style Parisian – feel like a guest in the
fin-de-siècle dining rooms (there are 3 plus a
covered winter garden), dine on Paul Lynch's
versions of classic French dishes, but book well
ahead, it's full full full.

🐟 **MARCHETTI'S LATIN, 55 Lonsdale St,
Vic 3000** ☎ **(03) 662 1985**
On-form Italian. Though it's been around a
while, ground-glued ears give it 3 cheers – MARK
PATRICK, for example: *"Melbourne's very strong
on Italian, I love the Latin because of the quality of the food, and it's a very sophisticated
restaurant which we don't really have as they
do in Sydney."* Squid ink spaghetti, pumpkin
ravioli are the things to munch. *"Just fantastic.
Wines are great, waiters are great, ambience is*

great – it's got everything going for it and a good crowd of people" – GREG DANIEL. SHARYN STOR-RIER-LYNEHAM goes latino, NANCY PILCHER doesn't mince words: *"I love the Latin,"* says she. Ditto LEO SCHOFIELD.

MASK OF CHINA, 115-117 Little Bourke St, Vic 3000 ☎ (03) 662 2116
No MSG here, but they have got a licence – the former brill BYO now has an exciting wine list as well as top-rating Chiu Chow cooking (similar to Cantonese), and swish modern styling. From an adventurous menu try shark's fin soup, abalone, soy goose and live lobster or mud crab. *"The standard is very high"* – SIR PETER USTINOV.

Australia's Best Restaurants

1	PHEASANT FARM . Nuriootpa, SA
2	STEPHANIE'S . Melbourne
3	BEROWRA WATERS INN . NSW
4	ROCKPOOL . Sydney
5	KABLE'S . Sydney
6	CLAUDE'S . Sydney
7	BROWN'S . Melbourne
8	FLEURIEU . Adelaide
9	MERRONY'S . Sydney
10	OASIS SEROS . Sydney

MIETTA'S, 7 Alfred Place, Vic 3000 ☎ (03) 654 2366
Dignified dining upstairs in a former gentlemen's club. Hovering waiters a-plenty, rare wines (a memorable stash of burgundies) and Alsatian-born chef Romain Bapst's classy French seasonal cuisine (savour his pastry, petits fours and cheeses). *"Absolutely fabulous, it would certainly get 2 stars in the Michelin guide without any difficulty"* – FREDERIC RAPHAEL. Relax with a drink or a cup of tea downstairs and listen to singers or readers. It's a favourite with MARY ROSSI.

SHARK FIN INN, 50 Little Bourke St, Vic 3000 ☎ (03) 662 2552
Real Chinese packed out with delighted yum cha-ing dim sum-ers. SIR PETER USTINOV goes to its younger brother, the quadruple-decker **Shark Fin House**, 131 Little Bourke St ☎ (03) 663 1555: *"My wife's a great expert on shark's fin soup and she said it was the greatest – splendid."* The egg noodles with shredded crab aren't too bad either.

STEPHANIE'S, 405 Tooronga Rd, Hawthorn East, Vic 3123 ☎ (03) 822 8944
Oz wizardry continues to lead the gastro race in Melbourne. Stephanie Alexander grafts modern Australian, Oriental and French styles together to delight serious foodies, including JOAN CAMPBELL, MARY ROSSI and SERGE DANSEREAU: *"I like to follow what she's doing. I have great admiration and respect for her."* The Victorian mansion setting draws admiring comments, too.

TANSY'S, 555 Nicholson St, Carlton North, Vic 3054 ☎ (03) 380 5555
Light bright dining for trendy foodies. Mousses, game and poultry get the new-style Oz treatment, diners the old – relax in fresh, understated surroundings on a Victorian terrace. Informal fun, at a price. LEO SCHOFIELD thinks it's fine.

Shopping

DAIMARU, 221 Latrobe St, Vic 3000 ☎ (03) 660 6666
The in department – owned by the Japanese. Spectacular building in the centre of the Melbourne Central complex, stacks of top fashion (the only Melbourne store with Agnès B, Claude Pierlot, Max Mara, Kenzo, Basile and Gianfranco Ferré), furniture, food and fab service – thanks to the inverted pyramid theory.

❝*I found the standard of all sorts of things better in Melbourne than in most places. I find it a more integrated city than Sydney, but Sydney's fascinating of course, it's so beautiful***❞**

SIR PETER USTINOV

GEORGES, 162 Collins St, Vic 3000 ☎ (03) 283 5555
Old-fashioned fashionability – treat yourself to Genny, Kenzo, Laurel, Liberty, Montana, Rykiel, YSL and Valentino, get served by polite, long-standing staff. Go to the loo and use a free telephone, sit on an old sofa, read a magazine by chandelier-light and smell the flowers. MARK PATRICK and NANCY PILCHER like all that.

HENRY BUCK'S, 320 Collins St, Vic 3000 ☎ (03) 670 9951 and branches
Highly bespoken tailor. Trad cuts, opulent surroundings – Persian carpets, polished floors – this is the place where the upper crust kit themselves out. *"He made the suit for my knighting, and I've worn it with great satisfaction ever since"* – SIR PETER USTINOV. Great bow ties.

Shoe Shiners

Kickin' away the competition, **Stephen Davies Designer Shoes**, 65 Gertrude St, Fitzroy ☎ (03) 419 6296, sweeps Melbourne dames off their feet. A man of distinction, *"Stephen Davies is king of the mule. He does divine jewelled mules. He is also doing beautiful high-heeled shoes with velvet ankle ribbons and diamanté ankle straps!"* – VICTORIA COLLISON. *"His mules are modern in style, romantic, pure and simple,"* sighs PATRICIA MERK. Hot on his heels with their serried ranks of imports are **Evelyn Miles**, Shop 1, Tok-H Centre, 459 Toorak Rd, Toorak ☎ (03) 827 5844 (for Walter Steiger, Robert Clergerie, Maud Frizon, Charles Jourdan and Philippe Model) and **Miss Louise**, 471 Toorak Rd, Toorak ☎ (03) 240 1984, and at the Hyatt on Collins ☎ (03) 654 7730, who keeps in step with the big names. Fleet feet shoehorn into **McCloud's**, 120 Queen St ☎ (03) 670 3386, for street-sharp imports in hand-tooled leather and well-sought hides, and walk out on McAir.

LE LOUVRE, 74 Collins St, Vic 3000 ☎ (03) 650 1300
Leopard-skinned chic shack where Euro imports claw in Melbourne's gotta-have-its. Pull the stops out for evening and wedding dresses.

MASON'S, 111 Toorak Rd, S Yarra, Vic 3141 ☎ (03) 266 5106
Collections from the sexiest and smartest stables. Slip on a Gigli or Kamali, but get there early in the season, otherwise someone else'll be wearing what you should be. . . .

SABA, 131 Bourke St, Vic 3004 ☎ (03) 654 6176
TV screens flash supermodels on catwalks to get you in the mood, Saba's own-label racks up with Yohji Yamamoto and Comme des Garçons. *"Saba is a bit like Joseph in London. They do wonderful essentials, every essential under the sun. For daywear definitely – great T-shirts, sweaters, trousers, jackets"* – SANDRA HIRSH.

TAMASINE DALE, Shop 1, 94 Flinders St, Vic 3000 ☎ (03) 650 7122
The most creative, consummate milliner in town. *"She does hats which are witty, quirky, classical, all at the same time"* – PATRICIA MERK.

WENDY MEAD HATS, Shop 11, 521 Toorak Rd, Toorak, Vic 3142 ☎ (03) 240 9093
Top crowns are topped here – she makes 300 or so hats for the Melbourne Cup – and her extravagant ready-to-wear and custom-made designs are seen at all the right places.

Theatre

MELBOURNE THEATRE COMPANY, 19 Russell St, Vic 3000 ☎ (03) 654 4000
New Australian plays line up with the classics and hits from Broadway and the West End. The best company in Melbourne, and perhaps in Oz, due to its very high rep standard.

· REST OF ·

VICTORIA

Hotels

BURNHAM BEECHES COUNTRY HOUSE, Sherbrooke Rd, Sherbrooke, Vic 3789 ☎ (03) 755 1903
A nautical retreat for landlubbers – the gleaming Art Deco mansion is styled like an ocean liner, complete with sundecks. Cooking is fabulous, the gardens beautiful, it's in the spectacular Dandenong Hills and MARY ROSSI loves it: *"How great that it has gained the stamp of approval of the prestigious Relais & Châteaux."*

 **DELGANY COUNTRY HOUSE HOTEL, Delgany Ave, Portsea, Vic 3944 ☎ (059) 844000**
Dreamland 35-room castle, built in 1920s and run by restaurant partners the Schneiders, now under Japanese ownership. The place for MARY ROSSI and for STEPHANIE ALEXANDER: *"The kitchen is run by Herman Schneider, who is one of our most famous chefs, he's Swiss. It's a beautiful restaurant, really top of the market."*

HOWQUA DALE GOURMET RETREAT, Howqua River Rd, PO Box 379, Mansfield, Vic 3722 ☎ (057) 773503
Very exclusive dining à la country-house weekend for no more than a dozen out-of-town gourmets. STEPHANIE ALEXANDER has this to say: *"It's marvellous, it fits 12 people very comfortably. It's known as a gourmet retreat and it*

is that, but it's also a place for bush-walking or riding or staring at the river. One of the reasons for its success is its residential cooking schools – I go about once a year and so do other chefs to take cooking classes."

THE QUEENSCLIFF HOTEL, 16 Gellibrand St, Queenscliff, Vic 3225 ☎ (052) 521066
If you do like to be beside the seaside – and you like white lacework verandahs, stained glass, tessellated floor tiles, dark wood furniture, bunches of violets, and lavender bags under the pillow – this is your place. Run by Mietta's sister Patricia O'Donnell, whose chef, Xavier Robinson, turns out cutting-edge Oz fare – chargrilled Tasmanian salmon; warm salad of quail.

PERTH

—— *Hotels* ——

🐾 **HYATT REGENCY, 99 Adelaide Terrace, WA 6000 ☎ (09) 225 1234**
A smart link in the Hyatt chain near the banks of the Swan River. Space-age lobby of pink Italian granite and 13-storey soaring atrium with tubular steel and glass domed roof. 2 floors are given up to the exclusivity of the Regency Club. The musically themed **Gershwin's** is kitted out like a 50s Manhattan apartment and dishes out the best the West Coast waters can offer.

PARMELIA HILTON, Mill St, WA 6000 ☎ (09) 322 3622
Distinguished, well-run old favourite. The service and atmosphere belong to a smaller, older hotel which makes it a winner with JULIAN LLOYD WEBBER: *"I think it's very good – it has enormous rooms."* The Garden Restaurant's French cuisine has an accent on regional dishes and perfect presentation. Weighty wine list.

PERTH INTERNATIONAL, 10 Irwin St, WA 6000 ☎ (09) 325 0481
Top-drawer modernist, with views over the

Governor's garden and an outback colour scheme. Much-vaunted restaurant, the **Irwin**, serves modern French food with a strong line in game and interesting seafood dishes.

SHERATON PERTH HOTEL, 207 Adelaide Terrace, WA 6000 ☎ (09) 325 0501
Another big, swanky, modern hotel, with fabulous views of the Swan River and city from every room. VIPs get astonishing butler service, others are on the receiving end of the expected Sheraton professionalism.

—— *Music* ——

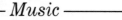

PERTH ENTERTAINMENT CENTRE, Wellington St, WA 6000 ☎ (09) 322 4766
Mixed-use music venue. The main auditorium is the largest in Australia – a winner with big rock stars. The smaller, more intimate Concert Hall hosts the classics and is known by those in the trade – such as JULIAN LLOYD WEBBER – for its crystalline acoustics.

—— *Restaurants* ——

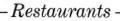

See also Hotels.

CHANTERELLE RESTAURANT, 210 Rokeby Rd, Subiaco, WA 6008 ☎ (09) 381 4637
Andrew Peaston's modern French menu is raking in accolades in the foodie biz. Uses the best of local produce and has a light touch with soufflés, sweet and savoury.

CO-CO'S, Cnr Mends St and The Esplanade, S Perth, WA 6151 ☎ (09) 474 3030
Co-Co loco – and what a location. Fabulously popular bright and breezy restaurant on the banks of the Swan. Oversized steaks are the thing here, but seafood also gets a look in. *"Glitzy, bright, fun place, plenty of seafood, good wines, varied menu. It's well cooked, not fancy fancy"* – DAVID GOWER.

🐾 **Buzzz** The pick of the bunch in Melbourne, according to MARC PATRICK, is brilliant garden designer **Paul Bangay**, 595 Malvern Rd, Toorak ☎ (03) 827 0792: *"Even though he doesn't really do flowers, he will on request"* 🐾 . . . . . . Flower power 2: **Lavender cheese**? No laughing matter, it comes from the people who make Gippsland Blue cheese and is seriously good. Ask **Butterfields** ☎ (03) 482 3176 where to find it 🐾 . . . . . . *"Australian cheeses are second to none in the world"* says SUE FAIRLIE-CUNINGHAME who tips **Milawa Cheeses** ☎ (057) 273588 as a name to watch 🐾 . . . . . . The corner shop as gourmet stop: *"Almost every suburb has a specialty food store – some do prepared food, some catering, some might have coffee shops – it's a feature of life here"* – STEPHANIE ALEXANDER . . . . 🐾

**THE MEDITERRANEAN, 414 Rokeby Rd,
Subiaco, WA 6008 ☎ (09) 381 2188**
Still the place for the big boys to eat well
(property developers, lawyers, flash Harrys),
especially with the introduction of the A$20
business lunch. Seasonal, West Coast (USA that
is) menu and an extensive wine list, for imported
as well as home-grown varieties.

**ORIEL CAFE, 483 Hay St, Subiaco, WA
6008 ☎ (09) 382 1886**
Bright and breezy Sloane clone brasserie.
*"Exactly like the one in Sloane Square, even
down to its chairs. Unusual for Perth – Perth
doesn't really have those big, bustling places like
other cities"* – STEPHANIE ALEXANDER.

🐟 **SAN LORENZO, 23 Victoria Ave,
Claremont, WA 6010 ☎ (09) 384 0870**
Reincarnated under new, forward-thinking
ownership. Gary Jones's innovative, seasonal
menu nods to France (fillet of hare), to his native
Yorkshire (black pudding and pig's cheeks) and
to his adopted country (terrine of Fremantle
sardines). *"Fabulous, grapevines over the ceiling, live yabbies in the pond. Very Italian, I
really want to live in it. The food is very good – a
great young chef"* – CAROLYN LOCKHART.

———— *Shopping* ————

**ELLE, 56 Weld St, Nedlands, WA 6009
☎ (09) 386 6868**
The best in the West – taking in the established
leaders (YSL, Armani, Lagerfeld) as well as
walking on the wilder side with young Japanese

Swept away by Broome

*"If you want the ultimate Australian ex-
perience – of its isolation yet rich desert
culture – Broome is the place to be, on the
edge of the continent"* – MARK PATRICK. Its
wonders are not confined to the safety of
Cable Beach Club (see Hotels). *"The
best, most undiscovered area of the world.
It really is an adventure. You discover
wonders that make Ayers Rock look like
Luna Park. It's a tiny little town with a
couple of streets, still with the Chinese
influence, still with Aborigines living there.
And then you go out and discover places
like the petrified forest. The missions were
outside Broome and I saw an entire church
made from pearl shells – fantastic. Everyone should go there. But maybe we don't
want them to"* – NANCY PILCHER.

---

designers. Complete the look with a fab range of
hats, shoes, bags and baubles.

**SCARPERS, Shop 13, City Arcade, WA
6000 ☎ (09) 321 6941**
Great collection of fancy footwear imported
from all parts of the globe: Robert Clergerie,
Christian Dior, Rayne, Sonja Bettine, Charles
Jourdan, Sergio Rossi, Amalfi and further
Italian-crafted showy shoes.

· REST OF ·

WESTERN AUSTRALIA

———— *Hotels* ————

**CABLE BEACH CLUB, Cable Beach Rd,
Broome, WA 6725 ☎ (091) 922505**
The only hotel on 24 km of white sand. Lord
McAlpine's getaway resort fuses Asian and Australian, the natural and the man-made. Oriental
antiques, garden pagodas alongside *"very
Australian architecture with ripple-iron walls
festooned with Sidney Nolan paintings and colonial verandahs"* – JILL MULLENS. Wonderful food
(pearl meat in lime juice, olive oil, herbs and pink
peppercorns is a classic) and tropical heat may
induce torpor – shake it off with a brisk camel
ride along the beach. *"It's amazing, unique and
wonderfully designed"* – SHARYN STORRIER-
LYNEHAM. And so says LORD LICHFIELD.

———— *Music* ————

**LEEUWIN CONCERTS, Leeuwin Estate,
Gnarawary Rd. Tickets: 1st Fl, 1B High
St, Fremantle, WA 6160 ☎ (09) 430 4099**
A cultural highlight on the WA and international calender is the well-attended al fresco
classical concerts in late summer (Feb/Mar).
Entrepreneur Denis Horgan lures top performers such as Dame Kiri Te Kanawa and James
Galway to his estate, where guests picnic on the
grounds casually or with full accompaniment of
champagne and crystal. Be warned – book early,
or not at all.

———— *Restaurants* ————

**LEEUWIN ESTATE RESTAURANT,
Gnarawary Rd, Witchcliffe, WA 6286
☎ (097) 576253**
Set in Denis Horgan's lush vineyard, half a day's
drive south of Perth. Fresh, local produce
(freshwater marrons, plump young asparagus)
and, of course, Leeuwin Estate wines. The
views from the verandah are wonderful.

Sydney Moca Glory

MOCA is Mecca in some of the sleekest international cities. Sydney, at last, joins the select coterie, with its very own **Museum of Contemporary Art**, Circular Quay, The Rocks, NSW 2000 ☎ (02) 252 4033 – a first for Australia (and known here as MCA rather than MOCA). The A\$4 million bequest in 1939 to the University of Sydney by John Power (Professor of Fine Arts and pretty fine artist himself) has since funded a collection of over 3,000 paintings which has finally been given a home in the old Maritime Services Board Building, slap bang on the harbour. *"A wonderful historic setting"* – MARY ROSSI. All the big contemporary names are represented – Warhol, Hockney, Christo, Lichtenstein, Beuys, Duchamp, Gilbert and George – as well as Powell's own (mostly Cubist) work and ever-changing mixed media installations. *"I love the MCA because it's very offbeat for a contemporary gallery and I think it'll shock a lot of people"* – MARK PATRICK. SKYE MACLEOD is keen, CAROLYN LOCKHART likes Neil (Rockpool) Perry's bright and breezy **MCA Café** (*"a great venue to have functions in"*) as does ELISE PASCOE: *"I trust Neil Perry implicitly – I know whatever he serves will be right for the market."* What's right *from* the market has a sunny Mediterranean accent – focaccia with prosciutto or roast peppers, risotto, pasta. . . . All as contemporary as the collection and, one hopes, as permanent. GRAEME MURPHY sums up: *"The building is wonderful, the view is superb and the restaurant just what the Rocks needed."*

SYDNEY

—— *Art and museums* ——

ART GALLERY OF NEW SOUTH WALES, Art Gallery Rd, NSW 2000 ☎ (02) 225 1700
Under Edmund Capon's directional directorship, Sydney's cultural heartbeat gets stronger and stronger. All the best from Australia (ancient Aboriginal artefacts through to Brett Whitely) and, somehow, Capon always manages to scoop all the top international exhibitions – the homeless Guggenheim collection lived here for 4 months. *"Fabulous"* – SKYE MACLEOD (GRAEME MURPHY agrees). Wonderful extensions by Andrew Andersons, who was responsible for the transformation of Macquarie St, have *"vastly improved it. Works look wonderful in the light airy spaces"* – COLIN LANCELEY.

POWERHOUSE MUSEUM (Museum of Applied Arts and Sciences), 500 Harris St, Ultimo, NSW 2007 ☎ (02) 217 0111
Hands-on powerhouse of all things technical, scientific, industrial and decorative, Lionel Glendinning's architecture has transformed a derelict power station into a dramatic testament to the 20C. *"It is a museum of scientific things over the years, the first steam train ever in Australia is housed there and then models of steam trains and electric trains right up to the present day. And it is not just science but also art,* design, clothing . . . a fabulous museum" – SKYE MACLEOD. Pull levers and press buttons to bring the past and future to life. *"I love the Powerhouse because it's so functional"* – MARK PATRICK.

—————— *Ballet* ——————

SYDNEY DANCE COMPANY, Pier 4, Hickson Rd, Walsh Bay, NSW 2000 ☎ (02) 221 4811
Graeme Murphy's company has put Australia on the modern dance circuit. Innovative and highly successful productions have gained renown with both local and international audiences.

—————— *Bars and cafés* ——————

See also Hotels.

BAR COLUZZI, 322 Victoria St, Darlinghurst, NSW 2010 ☎ (02) 357 5420
The grooviest caff in Sydney with no pretensions to chicness (unlike some of its espresso-downing crowd). Fab focaccia for all, seats for a dedicated few who stake them before the breakfast rush. MARK PATRICK is one of them.

THE BURDEKIN HOTEL, 2 Oxford St, Darlinghurst, NSW 2010 ☎ (02) 331 3066
Once a rather seedy pub, now the most happening scene in the city. *"It is full of lawyers, advertising execs – a good-looking young bunch of*

Cafe Deli-cacies

Sydney's latest meeting places are where dining and shopping collide. It's a perfect marketing strategy: sample the wares before you buy and no one minds being taken for this particular ride. The warm and cheerful **Gastronomia Chianti**, 444 Elizabeth St, Surry Hills ☎ (02) 319 4748, is a biggie, co-owned by the wonderful Armando Percuoco of Buon Ricordo. The clutch of tables in front of the deli counter is perma-packed (*"You can book at night, otherwise just trust to luck"* – ELISE PASCOE) with besuited biz types and professional lunchers sampling fabulous pasta. From the deli (*"the best in Sydney"* –

CAROLYN LOCKHART) they can take away duck neck and Lyonnaise sausages or local sun-dried tomatoes. Sheltering behind a giant fig tree, **Bar Paradiso**, 7 Macquarie Place ☎ (02) 241 2141. It is clattery and gossipy, with city folk downing espressos (*"The best coffee in town"* – CAROLYN L) at the counter alla Milanese, or more substantial repasts al fresco. Famous focaccias such as the one with smoked chicken, roasted capsicum, bocconcini and tapenade, and cakes of distinction. The gourmet on the run can pick up a bag of olive oils, dried pasta, cured meats and pickles to re-create paradise at home.

---

people. *The best cocktails"* – SKYE MACLEOD. *"The 2 bars are never-to-be-forgotten scenes on Friday evenings: loud, loose and saturated with exotic people. For a very tight squeeze in a crowd of fashion, film and design people, go to the* **Dug Out Bar** *– formerly the basement toilets (with original 30s tiles still on the walls). Another option is the public bar . . . with an elliptical serving counter as the centrepiece and bar seats like rugby balls"* – DAVINA JACKSON. SANDRA HIRSH digs.

DOV, 252 Forbes St, Darlinghurst, NSW 2010 ☎ (02) 360 9594
Unpretentious and madly popular with those with more dash than cash. *"Very interesting, very small, serving astonishingly cheap food with real character. Very good breakfasts, proper home-made jam in preserve pots with crusty bread. . . . A strong Jewish influence, good chopped liver, Russian salad, herrings, that sort of thing"* – STEPHANIE ALEXANDER. *"Great for casual lunches and suppers. Eclectic clientele and the fact that Darlinghurst is a pretty seedy suburb means that the rent-a-crowd stays away, leaving the true appreciators of style in control here. Restrained décor, spectacular food and unlicensed. Outside are rings on which to tie up one's dogs while you eat . . . unique in Sydney, where one never sees a dog near a restaurant (we have very keen health inspectors)"* – JILL MULLENS.

LA PASSION DU FRUIT, 100 Oxford St, Paddington, NSW 2021 ☎ (02) 361 5487
Paddo caff attracting a healthy crowd for fitting salads and puds. *"Chrissie Juillet still insists on using a mortar and pestle to make fresh pesto for her pasta, she uses the best olive oils, parmigiano, etc. This is the closest thing we have in*

Sydney to an academic hangout" – SUE FAIRLIE-CUNINGHAME. JENNY KEE is keen on her *"fresh Mediterranean salads"*.

TROPICANA COFFEE LOUNGE, 110 Darlinghurst Rd, Kings Cross, NSW 2011 ☎ (02) 331 6486
Packed to the glass walls with film/fashion/media/model types downing doses of Darlo street-cred and shot-in-the-arm coffee. MARK PATRICK appreciates the grooviness within, if not the down-and-outs without.

Clubs

THE CAULDRON, 207 Darlinghurst Rd, Darlinghurst, NSW 2010 ☎ (02) 331 1523
Bubbly young things join the melting pot here before graduating to Rogues (here, dresses are shorter and trousers less roomy). *"Probably the second-best club, it attracts a different, much younger clientele"* – SKYE MACLEOD. A good spot for a late-night bop; Gary Skelton's (ex-Kables and Paddington Inn) Italian-leaning bistro food offers an alternative to the sweaty dance floor.

THE FREEZER, 11 Oxford St, Paddington, NSW 2010 ☎ (02) 332 2568
Exclusive little club with decadent décor all cracked and artfully distressed. Thurs is jazz night, Fri Canned (can of food gets you in), Sat the hip Icebox, Sun soul night.

KINSELA'S, cnr Bourke and Campbell Sts, Darlinghurst, NSW 2010 ☎ (02) 331 3299
The old funeral parlour has risen from the dead once again and buzzes with a good-looking, unghoulish crowd. Ground floor's a pool bar with

Cruise-ing sharks; upstairs, a cocktail bar and spacy, functional dance floor.

NEO PHARAOH'S, Nikko Hotel, 161 Sussex St, NSW 2000 ☎ (02) 299 1231
Sleek, Japanese-owned sophisticate in the flash new Nikko. Ultra-designed from its hard-edged wooden bars to the thoughtfully placed lighting. Great, if expensive cocktails and safe music.

♣ ROGUES, 16 Oxford Square, Oxford St, Darlinghurst, NSW 2010 ☎ (02) 332 1718
Still going strong, though no one's quite sure why. The discerning doorman lets in members only . . . unless you happen to be an exceptionally pretty girl or a celebrity that is. *"The most popular club . . . it's kind of fun"* – HENRY CRAWFORD. Cosy rooms and a very intimate dance floor where the city rubs shoulders with visiting stellar types: Mick Jagger, Sylvester Stallone, INXS. Wednesday's *All Souled Out* nights pack in the punters for pacy black dance music in one room, laid-back soul in another and so-laid-back-it's-horizontal music in the **All Souled Out Café** (before midnight known as **Streetons** – see Restaurants).

SIGHT, 171 Victoria St, Kings Cross, NSW 2011 ☎ (02) 358 6511
A high cool quotient necessary to pass the doorman's muster. Inside all is metal and distressed paint and a seriously hip crowd getting down to progressive dance music. Next-door's **Soho Cocktail Bar** gives fuel for the night ahead.

—— *Fashion designers* ——

CARLA ZAMPATTI, 435A Kent St, NSW 2000 ☎ (02) 264 8244
Still a first choice for thirtysomethings to pick up pastelly, flattering clothes, draped or tailored to advantage. Double Bay society dames love her, as does Olivia Newton-John.

GEORGE GROSS & HARRY WHO, c/o Viva, 19-27 Cross St Plaza, Double Bay, NSW 2028 ☎ (02) 322485
Bold, sexy gear for women who mean business. George (sharp bright day suits and glam, plunging evening wear) and Harry's (more natural, less vampish) collection is storming the international scene – you'll even find them at Harrods. *"In recent seasons it's all been brights . . . the jewel colours. They work in silks, cotton, linen – pretty, easy fabrics for the Australian climate"* – SKYE MACLEOD.

JENNY KEE, Flamingo Park, Suite 102, 2F, Strand Arcade, George St, NSW 2000 ☎ (02) 231 3027; Shop 53 QVB, George St ☎ (02) 267 3230
More wearable artist than designer, her signature is bold knitwear in singing colours, and prints that define Australia.

♣ LEONIE LEVY, Studio ☎ (02) 327 2610; at Riada, Hampshire & Lowndes
New designer with an eye to the past. *"More sophisticated than streetwise, she uses incredible fabrics, like shot taffetas in rich, jewelled purples and deep emeralds and brocades – they have an opulence reminiscent of Romeo Gigli"* – VICTORIA COLLISON. JUDITH COOK is a Levy lover, too: *"Innovative, there is a twist to her contemporary designs, they are more eclectic in mood."*

MARCUS TUSCH, 51-63 O'Connor St, Chippendale, NSW 2008 ☎ (02) 318 0477
Classic, work-wise gear for the young woman around town. Soft, Armani-esque trouser suits and businesslike, feminine separates take the Tusch woman to the office and beyond.

♣ PETER MORRISSEY & LEONA EDMISTON, Shop 63, Strand Arcade, NSW 2000 ☎ (02) 221 5616 (men); Shop 74, Strand Arcade ☎ (02) 232 7606 (women)
Since the days of designer-ripped jeans, Morrissey and Edmiston have been *"right on the cutting edge of fashion"* – VICTORIA COLLISON. *"It's a trendy-retro sort of look. Very short miniskirts, the cut-away jacket. It's a really fresh, young, wonderful look. Leona designs for Kylie Minogue when she comes back to Sydney"* – SKYE MACLEOD; JUDITH COOK echoes: *"Wonderful modern clothes: the colours, the sequins."* PATRICIA MERK sums up the style: *"Streetwise, contemporary and wearable."*

Australia's Best Designers

1	ROBERT BURTON
2	TRENT NATHAN
3	PETER MORRISSEY & LEONA EDMISTON
4	JODIE BOFFA
5	LEONIE LEVY
6	SCANLAN AND THEODORE

♣ ROBERT BURTON, 729 Elizabeth St, Zetland, NSW 2017 ☎ (02) 319 0177; at David Jones
Perfect renditions of classic styles from the master of tailoring and fabrics. *"The Robert Burton suit is the most classic suit you could ever buy. Not casual, but for the executive woman it is a perfect suit. Beautiful fabrics, a lot of them imported – stunning"* – SKYE MACLEOD. *"He has his own strong, distinctive signature, his clothes are of superb quality. A lot of our designers follow trends from overseas, but Robert is his own man"* – PATRICIA MERK.

JENNY KEE, NANCY PILCHER and CAROLYN LOCKHART admire the work and the man.

SIMONA, 736 Military Rd, Mosman, NSW 2088 ☎ (02) 969 6843; at David Jones
Modern spirited designs, just right for smart Sydneysiders. *"Doing great collections, very young but established clothes"* – NANCY PILCHER.

STEPHEN GALLOWAY, Studio enquiries ☎ (02) 361 3939; at Riada
Bridging the gap between young blood and establishment, Galloway *"has a great sense of style"* – JENNY KEE. *"I like his designs for their originality. They have good proportions, good tailoring. He has a distinctive, romantic style, always beautiful fabrics"* – PATRICIA MERK.

❝The ride to Manly on the ferry is lovely and certainly the best value journey – beats first class on Qantas ❞

 FREDERIC RAPHAEL

⚓ TRENT NATHAN, 220 Henderson Rd, Alexandria, NSW 2015 ☎ (02) 550 3355
After 30 years, Nathan's timeless designs for men and women are forever fresh. NANCY PILCHER and MARY ROSSI admire his stamina, as does SKYE MACLEOD: *"One of Australia's oldest designers – going unbelievably well. He does absolute classics: navy blue jacket, blazers, the tailored suit with a Chanel influence."*

WEISS, c/o Weiss Pringle, Shop G12, Gallery Level, Centrepoint, NSW 2000 ☎ (02) 232 7894
Breezy casuals for the Australian clime. Adele and Peter Weiss's unfussy, brightly coloured separates and streamlined knitwear win praise from all, including MARY ROSSI. Weiss-Art shops with their minimalist black and white Australiana squiggles are a welcome alternative to the ubiquitous Ken Done.

—— Festivals ——

FESTIVAL OF SYDNEY, 175 Castlereagh St, NSW 2000 ☎ (02) 267 2311
"The Festival of Sydney, ged into it" and Sydney does, every January. It all happens, all over Sydney – buskers at the Quay, parades in the street, funfairs in the park . . . every theatre, stadium, open space becomes a performance space for sunburnt Sydneysiders. Undoubted highlight is the free concert series in the Domain – pack a picnic, and pack in (with about 100,000 others) for Midsummer Jazz, Symphony in the Park (ending in the 1812 Overture and fireworks) and the beloved Opera in the Park.

—— Hotels ——

⚓ INTER-CONTINENTAL, 117 Macquarie St, NSW 2000 ☎ (02) 230 0200
Most charming of the big hotels, the 3-storey 1851 Treasury building surrounds a soaring atrium and is dwarfed by its 28-storey extension. Cracking views over the harbour and Royal Botanic Gardens, warm, updated colonial furniture and smooth service appeal to JEFFREY ARCHER *("excellent")*, SKYE MACLEOD and CAROLYN LOCKHART: *"I always feel extremely comfortable."* Gerard Madani (ex-Troisgros and Waterside Inn) gives food the Midas touch in the **Treasury** restaurant.

⚓ PARK HYATT, 7 Hickson Rd, The Rocks, NSW 2000 ☎ (02) 241 1234
Boutiquey harbourside hotel which has established itself in its short history as one of Sydney's stars. Personal, *discreet* service (round-the-clock butlers, check-in on every floor) appeals to such luminaries as Placido Domingo, Cher, Julio Iglesias, Frank Sinatra and Elizabeth Taylor. *"The best hotel, right on Circular Quay so every room has a magnificent view of the Opera House and the waterfront. It is the best located (but not necessarily the best food)"* – HENRY CRAWFORD. *"The view looks straight on to the Opera House and down the harbour . . . an exquisite location"* – SKYE MACLEOD. *"Brilliant harbourview setting – small, immaculate and the city's favourite"* – MARY ROSSI. *"Expensive but lavish"* – MARK PATRICK. *"I love it. I like the way the design of the building draws your eye to the beauty of the harbour and the fact you can open your windows in your room"* – SHARYN STORRIER-LYNEHAM. CAROLYN LOCKHART, CLAUDIA ROSSI HUDSON and NANCY PILCHER intake breath simultaneously.

RAMADA RENAISSANCE, 30 Pitt St, NSW 2000 ☎ (02) 259 7000
High-rise high-flyer down on the Quay. A stone's throw from the Exchange, attracting loads of money people, and musos: *"It overlooks the Opera House so it's obviously very convenient for the opera . . . very good. Excellent food, very prompt room service. They were just extremely helpful and they like people who are working at the Opera House to stay there. They came to concerts, it was a very good atmosphere"* – JULIAN LLOYD WEBBER.

⚓ THE REGENT OF SYDNEY, 199 George St, NSW 2000 ☎ (02) 238 0000
The hotel with it all: great views, service, food and General Manager Ted Wright. *"It's just going from strength to strength . . . the food and quality of everything continue to make it world class. They've renovated all the rooms, most have their own fax, every room has a video. Stupendous view of the harbour . . . a lot of things are good because of the General Manager, he provides the impetus and sets the tone"* – KEN

HOM. BOB PAYTON echoes: *"Everyone rates Ted Wright."* Sydney-style service finds favour with PRUE LEITH (*"the professionalism, nothing ever goes wrong. One of the nicest things is you can talk to the lift boys as equals, there's none of that bowing and scraping that you find in oriental hotels nor that distant British hauteur"*), though it leaves a little to be desired for JILL MULLENS: *"Remains my Australian favourite but I still really don't need to know the name of my waitress/waiter/sommelier. Food terrific, especially in the lobby coffee shop."* For TERRY HOLMES, *"It probably has two of the most spectacular suites overlooking the harbour."* The new health club and outdoor pool attract the fit set; **The Don Burrows Supper Club** remains the coolest spot for hot jazz, **Kable's** (see Restaurants) the most serious spot for dining. *"There's just a good buzz about the whole place"* – SHARYN STORRIER-LYNEHAM. Others who've buzzed in include Tom Cruise, Michael Jackson, LORD LICHFIELD, Dan Quayle, ROBIN LEACH, Pavarotti, STEPHANIE ALEXANDER, CAROLYN LOCKHART, NANCY PILCHER, JENNY KEE, SKYE MACLEOD (*"still fabulous"*), LISA BARNARD and HENRY CRAWFORD: *"You have to accept it for all-round service, food and everything else."*

Australia's Best Hotels

1	THE REGENT · Sydney
2	THE REGENT · Melbourne
3	PARK HYATT · Sydney
4	HYATT ON COLLINS · Melbourne
5	HYATT REGENCY · Adelaide
6	HOTEL COMO · Melbourne
7	INTER-CONTINENTAL · Sydney
8	THE HERITAGE HOTEL · Brisbane
9	HYATT REGENCY · Perth
10	SEBEL OF MELBOURNE · Melbourne

RITZ-CARLTON, 93 Macquarie St, NSW 2000 ☎ (02) 252 4600
Newish, small hotel with inclinations towards the old and the grand. Crystal chandeliers, 18C and 19C oil paintings and furniture, marble floors, baby grands in suites and *determinedly* personal service. *"Excellent, a very smart hotel. I'm slightly ashamed to say that they're a bit over-friendly, very sweet but every time they open a door they tend to say, 'How's it going, are you having a great time?' We had a wonderful suite overlooking the harbour and in every other respect, it's absolutely first class"* – FREDERIC RAPHAEL. Sydneysiders such as NANCY PILCHER and SKYE MACLEOD are keen.

RITZ-CARLTON, DOUBLE BAY, 33 Cross St, NSW 2028 ☎ (02) 362 4455
The new nerve centre for ritzy Double Bay, where ex-PM Bob Hawke has a ritzy pad. A French provincial-styled building over a 'promenade' of glam shops. *"It looks fabulous and it's absolutely right for Double Bay. Lovely sandstone façade, pale ochry colours and a lovely sweeping driveway"* – ELISE PASCOE.

♠ SEBEL TOWN HOUSE, 23 Elizabeth Bay Rd, Elizabeth Bay, NSW 2011 ☎ (02) 358 3244
From the gaggles of groupies outside, it can only be the Sebel, home from home of megastars. Sanguine staff know how to pamper their guests and when to turn a blind eye – parties in the tiny **Ricky May Bar** can reach legendary proportions. *"Immaculate service – nice rooms, nice situation – they just make one feel very welcome"* – NED SHERRIN. *"A media hotel to which people inevitably gravitate. It's like having your own apartment on top of the Groucho Club"* – IAIN JOHNSTONE. SIR PETER USTINOV likes their style and they like his – they named a suite after him. But the bar's the thing: *"A real poky little affair, covered in photographs of performing artists – either you like the fact that it's small and intimate, or you hate it. I like it"* – DAVID GOWER. Dire Straits, Elton John, Tina Turner, Bob Dylan, Paul Simon are regulars.

Music

♠ AUSTRALIAN OPERA, 480 Elizabeth St, Surry Hills, NSW 2010 ☎ (02) 699 1099
The AO continues to play to packed houses, recession or no. Under Donald McDonald's direction, the company's rendering of classics and avant-garde (occasionally a bit too adventurous) premieres *"gets better and better, though still needs stronger male voices, the women have always been terrific"* – COLIN LANCELEY. *"Why anyone in Australia thinks they have to travel to Europe is beyond me. I saw Il Trovatore and it looked spectacularly good and sensible, no converted motorbikes like you get in Europe, and just wonderful, wonderful singing. I can't say how superb it was"* – GLYNN CHRISTIAN.

SYDNEY OPERA HOUSE, Bennelong Point, Circular Quay, NSW 2000 ☎ (02) 250 7111
Architectural marvel or New South Whale, the curving white sails/shells against the harbour are *the* Sydney landmark. Showcases the cream of Australian opera, music, ballet, theatre and film: *"I'm a big fan . . . 2 fabulous groups perform the opera and the ballet"* – SKYE MACLEOD. *"A spectacular building but the concert hall just doesn't live up to the exterior"* – JULIAN LLOYD WEBBER. *"It is an architectural wonder but it leaks! And they forgot to build parking"* – CAROLINE HUNT. The future looks rosier – plans are under way for a major overhaul.

Restaurants

See also Hotels.

ARMSTRONG'S BRASSERIE, 1 Napier St, N Sydney, NSW 2060 ☎ (02) 955 2066
Everyone's favourite chef and best-loved brasserie. Mark Armstrong's place sums up the Sydney spirit – informal, inexpensive, unfussy and with great food. *"We go from the office and get a quick, delicious meal. A perfect Caesar salad. He has all the new things; when there are new mushrooms they are at Mark's. Wonderful steaks, he has a room for ageing the beef there"* – JOAN CAMPBELL. CAROLYN LOCKHART and MARY ROSSI favour strong-arm tactics too.

ATLAS BAR AND BISTRO, 95 Riley St, Darlinghurst, NSW 2010 ☎ (02) 360 3811
Buzzy new bistro from the Centennial Park Café team, Duncan Ackery and Angus Krane, who seem to have the whole world in their hands. Try sizzling boned spatchcock with herbs and spices, ricotta cheesecake, poached fruits with mascarpone. *"Fabulous – it showcases the best local produce, like whole grilled fish with salsa verde, and it's cheap. Staff are more groovy than the crowd"* – JUSTIN MILLER.

🦞 BATHER'S PAVILION, 4 The Esplanade, Balmoral Beach, NSW 2088 ☎ (02) 968 1133
The best place for a sunny summer lunch; Victoria Alexander's fresh, eclectic menu is a match for the view. *"A simple 20s or 30s pavilion, no grand architecture, but it takes people's breath away – this earthy, unpretentious place on the beach serving lovely, uncomplicated Australian food"* – ELISE PASCOE. SHARYN STORRIER-LYNEHAM and CAROLYN LOCKHART hold it dear as well; JUDITH COOK enjoys *"the beautiful setting"*.

🦞 BAYSWATER BRASSERIE, 32 Bayswater Rd, Kings Cross, NSW 2011 ☎ (02) 357 2749
Sydney's watershed brasserie is better than ever. Still a media Mecca, still packed to the rafters, in spite of the no-bookings rule. *"An institution, largely because of Tony Papas, who started it and is still in the kitchen – an extraordinarily broad range of food"* – STEPHANIE ALEXANDER. *"A terrific place. It does a mixture of East and West and really does it right"* – KEN HOM. In true brasserie fashion, you can drop in any time of day. *"Tony Papas ensures the place always jumps, is always sparky. He's always there, never stops developing new ideas"* – SUE FAIRLIE-CUNINGHAME. *"I know for Sunday brunch I will go to Bayswater Brasserie – I know they will give me the same table, I always eat the same thing. I feel comfortable there"* – SERGE DANSEREAU. Deft combinations such as farm curd toasts with poached leeks or black cuttlefish pasta appeal to SHARYN STORRIER-LYNEHAM and PATRICIA MERK.

BEACH ROAD RESTAURANT, 1 Beach Rd, Palm Beach, NSW 2108 ☎ (02) 974 1159
A simple beachside BYO with sensationally fresh food (Anthea Parmentier and Steve Bennett grow their own veg). *"I can't go past Beach Road, it's the best food, the atmosphere's great and relaxed"* – NANCY PILCHER. A local hero with CATHY ROSSI HARRIS too: *"Annie Parmentier acknowledges what people want to eat at the beach. The setting is simple, uncontrived, with wooden tables on wooden floors. Service is relaxed yet attentive. I just love it."*

BEPPI'S, Cnr Stanley and Yurong Sts, E Sydney, NSW 2000 ☎ (02) 360 4558
Beppi Polese's 35-year institution isn't allowing the 90s to pass it by. Lighter touches have given a lift to Italian standards and the service remains a great pre-theatre show. *"The best restaurant in Australia, you get the best Italian food almost anywhere in the world and Beppi's great patter. You can choose what you would like cooked – great fun, a terrific atmosphere"* – ROBERT SANGSTER.

BUON RICORDO, 92 Hargrave St, Paddington, NSW 2021 ☎ (02) 363 3706
Armando Percuoco's serious Italian restaurant with northern leanings is the stuff of good memories. He reworks the classics – figs and prosciutto might be baked with a gorgon-

zola sauce – and serves them impeccably to appreciative tasters, JOAN CAMPBELL and CAROLYN LOCKHART among them.

🍴 BURDEKIN DINING ROOM, 2 Oxford St, Darlinghurst, NSW 2010 ☎ (02) 331 1046

A triple-decker of style: the **Dug Out Bar**, **Public Bar** and, topping the lot, the **Burdekin Dining Room**. Reached by a rickety, manned elevator, the understated Deco restaurant has doubled in size and now seats a couple more handfuls of well-behaved, well-dressed diners, sending them out comforted by untricked-up, well-executed food and sensibly priced wines. *"Very smart. On top of a pub – that pub culture interests me"* – LEO SCHOFIELD. *"Wonderful – it's been redone very well. Everything Nigel Hannigan does is done with great panache and style"* – ELISE PASCOE. CAROLYN LOCKHART echoes: *"terrific."*

CENTENNIAL PARK CAFE, Grand Drive, Centennial Park, NSW 2021 ☎ (02) 360 3355

A glassy conservatory slap bang in the great lung of Sydney. Joggers and equestrians provide the entertainment as you tuck into light pasta dishes or sensational Caesar salad and a bloody mary. ELISE PASCOE takes overseas visitors here, as does LEO SCHOFIELD: *"This place simply can't exist anywhere else. It is peculiarly and particularly Australian and I like it for that reason."*

CHEZ OZ, 23 Craigend St, Darlinghurst, NSW 2010 ☎ (02) 332 4866

The No 1 80s media lunch spot is enjoying a renaissance, thanks to its 90s recession-led prices. Still noisy, gossipy and fun. *"Probably the chic-est restaurant in Sydney. One of the hot things is deep-fried whiting with chips . . . they do chips fabulously – big and thick and crunchy"* – SKYE MACLEOD. *"Helen Spry always has the best flowers in Sydney, extravagant, exotic and they complement the room and garden. Full of good-looking people, well-groomed women . . . the acoustics are so bad you can talk about the people at the next table without them hearing you"* – WARWICK VYNER.

CHOYS JIN JIANG, 2nd Fl, Queen Victoria Bldg, Cnr Market and George Sts, NSW 2000 ☎ (02) 261 3388

Glam black and turquoise Chinesery, dynasties away from the corner take-away. Perfect service, an unusually strong wine list and dishes not seen elsewhere: yin yang prawns, tea and camphorwood-smoked squab.

🍴 CLAUDE'S, 10 Oxford St, Woollahra, NSW 2025 ☎ (02) 331 2325

The most seriously serious dinner in Sydney. Damien Pignolet's tiny shop-front restaurant maintains formidable standards of cooking and service. *"I have the greatest respect for him as a chef, for his single-mindeness in pursuing a clear idea of classic French cooking which is often more classic than the original. For example, I have had a fish soup there better than any I've had in France"* – STEPHANIE ALEXANDER. *"His food is beautiful, very studied"* – SERGE DANSEREAU. Book far ahead, and dust off your finest bottles – it's unlicensed.

DARCY'S, 92 Hargrave St, Paddington, NSW 2021 ☎ (02) 363 3706

Reliable Italian cooking and a glitzy clientele – if the formula works, why change it? A mixed media crowd – Rupert Murdoch, Jana Wendt, Mike Gibson – and Paddo locals like their carpaccio, quail with polenta and tiramisu. So do ROBERT SANGSTER (*"Still very good"*) and WARWICK VYNER: *"They look after you like family."*

DARLEY STREET THAI, Botany View Hotel, 597 King St, Newtown, NSW 2042 ☎ (02) 550 6650

Top of the Thais right now. *"A sparse, bistro-style place. The chef, David Thompson, lived in Thailand and he makes everything from scratch – they grate the coconut for their coconut cream and make all their own bases. He's serving the most authentic Thai food and it's from a Western pair of hands"* – ELISE PASCOE.

🍴 KABLE'S, The Regent, 199 George St, NSW 2000 ☎ (02) 238 0000

Still a front-runner in the culinary field, but a change of image means the old formality has gone; in its place a warm, lively, inviting dining room with menus that catch the mood of the markets. *"The chef, Serge Dansereau, is fabulous – he sources all these farms and really supports them, so people grow things just for him. So you get food as if it was done in a petite restaurant rather than hotel food. Really top notch"* – KEN HOM. *"Consistently very, very good"* – ELISE PASCOE. And so say MARY ROSSI and CAROLYN LOCKHART: *"Still has that Australian touch, not too stitched up."* LEO SCHOFIELD sums up: *"There will always be a place for it because it is a special-occasion restaurant."*

LA STRADA, 95 Macleay St, Potts Point, NSW 2011 ☎ (02) 358 1160

A grandly formal establishment serving traditional, *expensive* fare (caviare, oysters and beautifully aged meats) with the attendant trimmings of crystal and silver. *"Fabulous, but a bit awe-inspiring for the price"* – MARK PATRICK.

LUCIO'S, 47 Windsor St, Paddington, NSW 2021 ☎ (02) 380 5996

Old Paddo standby with a fresh lick of paint and a new lease of life. *"Feels like Rome, decorated in lovely colours, terracotta and pinks, with delicious food and a young oriental waiter who is quite unique"* – WARWICK VYNER. MARY ROSSI loves Lucio for *"authentic Italian cuisine"*. Try the famed gamberi e fagioli (prawns, cannellini beans and caviare).

On the Waterfront

If you've got it, flaunt it. And one thing Sydney ain't short of is waterfrontage. Peter Doyle was one of the first to stake his claim with **Doyle's on the Beach** (no ambiguities there), 11 Marine Parade, Watsons Bay ☎ (02) 337 2007. The colonial house has great charm, though waits for your rock oysters can be so long you could shuck them yourself. The Brit pack flock along – spot IAIN JOHNSTONE, DAVID GOWER (*"I always love eating at Doyle's, it has good fish and chips and a good man who looks after you, Peter Doyle"*) and TERRY HOLMES (*"lots of locals go there, it is where everyone goes for fun"*). Also leaving paddling punters in no doubt as to the brininess of their location are **Bather's Pavilion, Beach Road Restaurant** (for both, see listings) and **Pier**, 594 New South Head Rd, Rose Bay ☎ (02) 327 4187, where the Steve Hodge/Greg Doyle (no relation) partnership proves peerless. With clean, spare lines, naïve paintings and spanking fresh seafood (Sydney rock oysters on crushed ice, prawn ravioli, seared Asian-spiced squid), no wonder it's a winner. **Imperial Peking Harbourside**, 13–17 Circular Quay W, The Rocks ☎ (02) 223 1128, crowns the quintet with its priceless view, priced-up food and a devotee in JULIAN LLOYD WEBBER: *"One of the best Chinese restaurants in the world."*

MACHIAVELLI RISTORANTE, 123 Clarence St, NSW 2000 ☎ (02) 262 4816
Il principe of power-lunches, run by the daughters of Giovanna Toppi of La Strada. Politicians' and media stars' photos adorn the walls – the celebs themselves might be at the next table.

MACLEAY STREET BISTRO, 73A Macleay St, Potts Point, NSW 2011 ☎ (02) 358 4891
Busy, bright and with no bookings. The blackboard menu changes monthly but there'll always be interesting tarts, Caesar salad, char-grills and the definitive bread and butter pudding.

MARIO'S, 73 Stanley St, Darlinghurst, NSW 2021 ☎ (02) 331 4945
Minimally decorated ristorante – the glitterati provide the colour. Everyone's a regular – staff remember what you like and provide it. Wonderful seafood on Mon, Wed and Fri, a happening atmosphere every night. PATRICIA MERK and Graham Shearer are keen, as are fashion folk.

🍴 **MERRONY'S, 2 Albert St, Circular Quay, NSW 2000 ☎ (02) 247 9323**
From the Cricketer's Arms, via Craigend and the Paddington Inn, Paul Merrony has now reached eponymity and establishment. The crowd is better shod with décor to match but Merrony's signature still flourishes on gutsy old favourites such as beef carpaccio with fried onion rings and melting lamb shanks. *"Where the Australian table is heading in the next century – light, clever but without ostentation. The restaurant is lovely, very Mediterranean, and the food is Mediterranean-inspired with Australian produce. His side-dishes are fabulous – the best creamed potatoes and to-die-for beet-root"* – ELISE PASCOE. *"I like Paul Merrony because his food is honest and the restaurant has a good feel. He seems to make food for people who love wine too"* – SUE FAIRLIE-CUNINGHAME.

MEZZALUNA, 123 Victoria St, Potts Point, NSW 2011 ☎ (02) 357 1988
Stark, stylish newcomer from the Beppi Polese (of Beppi's) fold, spilling on to a luna-lit terrace. *"A special-event restaurant, because of the view, the food, the price"* – JUSTIN MILLER.

🍴 **OASIS SEROS, 495 Oxford St, Paddington, NSW 2021 ☎ (02) 361 3377**
The cutting edge of the culinary knife. Phillip Searle's daring combinations of flavours go far beyond the simple East-meets-West formula and his desserts elicit gasps of amazement. *"The squared-off ice cream checkerboard is undoubtedly the most extraordinary dessert I have ever had"* – FREDERIC RAPHAEL. *"Phillip Searle is brilliant – his star anise dessert is a stand-out"* – JOAN CAMPBELL. LEO SCHOFIELD is an admirer.

PARAGON HOTEL, 1 Loftus St, Circular Quay, NSW 2000 ☎ (02) 363 9839
Chef Christine Manfield (ex-Oasis Seros) is a paragon of patriotic virtues. All Australian produce at this airy first-floor dining room of a revamped hotel. Signature dishes such as eggplant, chèvre and pesto 'sandwich' and a judicious use of Asian spicing appeal to LEO SCHOFIELD.

THE RESTAURANT, 88 Hackett St, Ultimo, NSW 2007 ☎ (02) 211 5895
A *vera famiglia* affair with Stefano and Franco

Manfredi in the kitchen, Stefano's wife Julie front-of-house and mamma Franca churning out the pasta and starters. Straight Italian cooking has become more flexible to exploit local produce (try warm smoked Atlantic salmon lasagne for example) but the flavour still finds favour with SUE FAIRLIE-CUNINGHAME, LEO SCHOFIELD and GRAEME MURPHY.

✦ ROCKPOOL, 109 George St, The Rocks, NSW 2000 ☎ (02) 252 1888

Glossy showcase for Neil Perry's ever-increasing genius. *"The food's brilliant but it's also worth a visit to see the splendid interior by a precocious trio called D4 design. The 2 floors are furnished to a degree of luxury reminiscent of the Jazz Age, updated in the style of Philippe Starck. Finishes include exotic timber veneers, silvery metals and mirrors, deep carpets and velvet walls"* – DAVINA JACKSON. Foodie folk eschew the flash and chew the fish. *"Neil Perry is really excellent, he uses a lot of Asian ingredients"* – KEN HOM. *"He serves fish and shellfish straight from the ocean on to the plate. One of my favourite meals is his totally simple grilled whole snapper – it's sensational"* – SHARYN STORRIER-LYNEHAM. Other Perry-winkles clinging to the Rockpool are LORD LICHFIELD, MARY ROSSI, MARK PATRICK, SUE FAIRLIE-CUNINGHAME, CAROLYN LOCKHART, HENRY CRAWFORD and JILL MULLENS. The less expensive **Oyster Bar** is a winner pre- or post-theatre. *"If I'm looking for something fun and jazzy I might go there to have something simple"* – SERGE DANSEREAU.

✦ ROGUES STREETONS, 16–18 Oxford St, Darlinghurst, NSW 2010 ☎ (02) 332 1718

Its name inspired by the Arthur Streeton painting, *The Coffee Set*, which hangs out of reach on a back wall, the brash brasserie above the club is the city's most happening scene. *"It really jumps at lunch when it's got the media mafia there. At night, whenever there's a big evening function on, Streetons later takes off. Peter Simpson is the ultimate host, he always gives you a drink or sits at your table and talks to you. Very Sydney, we're all a bit gauche, tend to make it known we know everyone in the restaurant"* – MARK PATRICK. *"Very popular with the movers and shakers. They have the best Thai chicken curry"* – SKYE MACLEOD. *"Peter Simpson's a guy with lots of style and taste"* – HENRY CRAWFORD. TERRY HOLMES drops in, CAROLYN LOCKHART actually notices the food above the crowd: *"The best menu: broad beans, shaved parmesan, asparagus, absolutely delicious."*

TAYLOR'S, 203-205 Albion St, Surry Hills, NSW 2010 ☎ (02) 361 5100

Charming, restful northern Italian restaurant based in a pair of colonial houses. *"On a good night you can eat like a prince there"* – LEO SCHOFIELD. A splendid antipasto selection is matched by the extensive wine list (more than 20 wines in half bottles).

✦ TETSUYA'S, 729 Darling St, Rozelle, NSW 2039 ☎ (02) 555 1017

"The word unique was made for the cooking of Tetsuya Wakuda – calling it a French/Japanese blend doesn't begin to convey how combinations that look bizarre on paper can turn into ecstasy in the mouth. You might encounter a consommé of eggplant with potato and leek purée and Sevruga caviare or another luscious soup made with Japanese-farmed turtles, or a salad of Blue Swimmer crab with avocado, sushi rice and wasabi mayonnaise. It's worth making the journey to Australia for Tetsuya's alone" – DAVID DALE. LEO SCHOFIELD makes it all the way from the Eastern Suburbs.

TRE SCALINI, 174 Liverpool St, E Sydney, NSW 2000 ☎ (02) 331 4358

Pasta con brio. Fashionable Italian trat with a glitzy clientele and gutsy specials. *"Their antipasto is the freshest and best. Beautiful seafood, carpaccio . . . everything's so fresh. Very much a restaurant for top business people, they know they can have a beautiful meal at a relatively reasonable price and it's trendy, it has a buzz . . . they have 2 special tables, you really know you are in if you get one"* – LESLEY WILD. SKYE MACLEOD climbs 3 steps, too.

✦ TRIANON CHALLIS AVENUE, 29 Challis Ave, Potts Point, NSW 2011 ☎ (02) 358 1353

Serene, flower-filled dining room and a vine-canopied terrace. Peter Doyle (not he of Doyle's, but the bro of Pier's Greg D) concocts neo-classical French food that appeals to STEPHANIE ALEXANDER, SERGE DANSEREAU and CAROLYN LOCKHART. *"The food is very classically based, very soundly executed. He's a marvellous cook, committed to a classic style and doing it well"* – LEO SCHOFIELD. GREG DANIEL applauds the Doyles: *"Finally getting the following they deserve. The ambience is wonderful – it is just one of those restaurants."*

—————— *Shopping* ——————

Sydney has a number of shopping areas. **Double Bay – Cross St, Bay St, Knox St** in particular – is still the place for international designers and middle-European pavement cafés. **Queen St, Woollahra**, is the only place to find your colonial antiques. In the city, **Castlereagh St** has all the biggest names – Chanel, Hermès, Vuitton . . . . The **QVB (Queen Victoria Building)** has all the best chains (Esprit, Country Road, Adele Palmer) and the most beautiful façade. **The Strand Arcade** has great charm, glitzy jewellers and young designers. **Mosman**'s villagy shopping area is the best in the north for home-grown and imported fashion. A roam down Paddington's **Oxford St** shows innovative clothes shops, healthy caffs and, on Saturday, **Paddington Markets** for the next generation of designers, ethnic gear and tat.

**ANNABEL INGALL, 24 Oxford St,
Woollahra, NSW 2025 ☎ (02) 331 2626**
Marvellous milliner for the Cup and le Cap now
covers bright young things from top to toe.
*"Wonderful summer and winter hats, the best
swimsuits in lycra and cotton knit, breezy resort
shirts and other body-conscious separates for a
sunny, relaxed resort/city lifestyle in one"* –
VICTORIA COLLISON.

ANNE LEWIN at David Jones
Up-market Down Underwear, Lewin's lingerie
is Australia's No 1 fashion export. Her unfrilly
slinks of silk may be found on the best bods at
home and in the US.

**THE CHEESE SHOP, 797 Military Rd,
Mosman, NSW 2088 ☎ (02) 969 4469**
David and Kate Herbert's products raise a grin
for the camera. The eponymous dairy stuff from
Australia and beyond is *"even better than before.
It has Eastern Suburbs Sydney green with
envy"* – ELISE PASCOE.

🎒 **COUNTRY ROAD, 742 Military Rd,
Mosman 2088 ☎ (02) 960 4633**
The biggest in the world – a Ralph Lauren-style
emporium for ever-expanding men's, women's
and Homewear lines. *"It encompasses our
lifestyle perfectly. They do Workwear for the
weekend, then they have city dressing for men
and women, so you can get a beautiful suit to
wear to work or a great dress to wear to lunch"* –
MARK PATRICK. Homewear covers everything
from lamp-stands to armchairs.

**DAVID JONES, Elizabeth St, NSW 2000
☎ (02) 266 5544, and branches
countrywide**
'The most beautiful store in the world' goes the
blurb; it's certainly the finest department store
in Oz. A grand piano tinkles over the marble
floors, wonderful window displays attract credit
cards like magnets up to the hushed 7th floor,
where reside Armani, Chanel, Valentino et al.

Good, proper tailoring and all the best clobber for
chaps in the Market St store; a famously tempt-
ing food hall: *"I enjoy being at DJs and I love
being in their food hall"* – CAROLYN LOCKHART.
The Oyster Bar is the place for a civilized
lunch and a glass of cold white.

**DINOSAUR DESIGNS, 73 Strand Arcade,
NSW 2000 ☎ (02) 223 2953**
Brilliant, affordable jewellery in translucent
jujube-bright resin and perspex which catches
the eye and holds it. *"I love their jewels because
they are bold, colourful – and much copied"* –
PATRICIA MERK.

**FIVE WAY FUSION, 205 Glenmore Rd,
Paddington, NSW 2021 ☎ (02) 331 2828**
The only place for the Europhile Sydney man.
Shoot-to-kill dressing from all the big guns:
Armani, Montana. . . .

**HAMPSHIRE & LOWNDES, 12 Cross St,
Double Bay, NSW 2028 ☎ (02) 327 2834;
16 Transvaal Ave, Double Bay**
No longer ersatz Laura Ashley, linens and lace,
H&L's clean, pared-down clothes and range of
perfect accessories are forging a new identity
for the 90s.

**HUNT LEATHER, MLC Centre, King St,
NSW 2000 ☎ (02) 233 1681; 141 George St,
The Rocks, NSW 2000 ☎ (02) 241 2918**
The finest in non-fetishist leather goods – hand-
bags, overnighters, suitcases and Filofaxes – at
decent prices and with *very* helpful staff.

**IN RESIDENCE, 30 Oxford St, Woollahra,
NSW 2025 ☎ (02) 361 5476**
Fabulous stuff from the sisters Zubani, everything you need to make the home sweet. The
best pure cotton sheets with ribbon trim, crisp,
fringed damask pillowcases, jewel-bright tablecloths and napkins, eclectic decorative pieces
from South-east Asia and paintings by well-
loved Oz artist James Gordon.

🎒 **Buzzz** Floral art: **Alison Coates**, 92
William St, Paddington ☎ (02) 360 2007, doesn't, according to DAVINA JACKSON, merely
arrange flowers. *"Her specialty is spectacular displays of natural materials – including fresh-snipped branches, pods and nuts, leaves, fruits, dried blooms and vegetables,
usually wrapped up in old-fashioned brown wax paper, tied with naturally dyed rope"*
🎒 . . . . . . Toujours Provence: **Appley Hoare**, 55 Queen St, Woollahra ☎ (02) 362 3045,
is the person to drop in on for wonderful antique armoires, tables, chairs, mirrors,
tablewear. *"A dazzling collection of French and Spanish peasant wares and furniture;
a must-see shop for anyone planning to decorate in European provincial style"* –
DAVINA J 🎒 . . . . . . Boarding in 5 minutes? Slither into the **Rainbow Serpent** in the
Departure Terminal, Kingsford Smith Airport ☎ (02) 669 5881, first. No souvenir shop
tat here. A seriously stylish shop: glorious Aboriginal art and artefacts, hand-painted
silk scarves, enamelled jewellery and one-off canvases to roll up in your baggage . . . . . 🎒

J H CUTLER, Level 3, 33 Bligh St, NSW 2000 ☎ (02) 232 7351
Proper, old-fashioned Savile Row-style tailoring from the long-established Cutler family. Current Cutler John dresses patriotic pollies with flair and discretion and does a cover-up on LEO SCHOFIELD and DORIAN WILD.

JOHN SERAFINO, 20 Bay St, Double Bay, NSW 2028 ☎ (02) 363 9884
Flamboyant tailor/designer whose styles nod to Italy and whose clients appear on the small screen.

MARC'S, P203 Mid-City Centre, Pitt St, Sydney 2000 ☎ (02) 221 5575; and branches
A gleaming white shop by brilliant modern architect Leigh Prentice. Displays all-Australian designs, though warming to global trends. Men's and women's gear includes Italian-inspired classics, Gaultier-esque sportswear – all in natural fabrics. NANCY PILCHER is keen.

PASSELLO, 27 Bronte Rd, Bondi Junction, NSW 2022 ☎ (02) 389 3304
Saviour of the last-minute dinner party – wonderful fresh pasta, sauces, Italian salads, breads and cakes (the Siena cake's a knock-out) – all made in the shop's kitchen.

PURL HARBOUR, 92 Gould St, Bondi, NSW 2026 ☎ (02) 365 1521
The effervescent John Macarthur's breezy shop is first port of call for his hand-knits and designs. Inspired cotton knits in summer, chunky pure wool in winter.

READS, 130 Queen St, Woollahra, NSW 2025 ☎ (02) 328 1036
Sue Read's tiny shop has fashion sewn up. *"My favourite shop apart from David Jones – she just has the best mix, all Australian designers. She buys incredibly well so instead of looking at a pair of pants and wondering if the rest of Syd-*ney will have them, you just buy them because they look wonderful"* – SKYE MACLEOD.

🔥 REMO, Oxford St at Crown St, NSW 2010 ☎ (02) 331 5544
A design museum of a general store – the best of everything from Tabasco sauce to Zippo lighters. NANCY PILCHER and SHARYN STORRIER-LYNEHAM love it, as does DAVINA JACKSON: *"Well-designed wares – chosen around the world for their high quality and classic styling. A more eclectic range than the usual giftware store: including hats, Kiehl's handmade cosmetics from NY, T-shirts and pyjamas, jewellery, leather goods, penknives, cards, games, obscure art and design journals."*

RIADA FASHION BOUTIQUE, 618A Military Rd, Mosman, NSW 2088 ☎ (02) 969 4269
Best looks from leading Australian designers both established (Robert Burton) and ascendant (Leonie and Jodie Boffa). Flairful collections from individual French and Italian designers, Robert Clergerie and Stephane Kélian shoes and bags, and a glittering selection of Italian costume jewels.

RM WILLIAMS, 389 George St, NSW 2000 ☎ (02) 262 2228
It doesn't come more fair dinkum than this – the original bushman's outfitter. Moleskins, riding coats, plaid shirts and the great RM Williams boot appeal to PATRICIA MERK's earthier instincts. The mail-order catalogue is a hoot – where else can you find a junior tanning kit?

ROX JEWELLERY, 31 Strand Arcade, Pitt St, NSW 2000 ☎ (02) 232 7828
From serious rocks to not-exactly rock-bottom costume pieces – chosen with a fresh, modern eye for design. A necessary drop-in for visiting glamour merchants: Tina Turner, Boy George, David Bowie and Olivia Newton-John have Rox in their heads.

🍖 Buzzz Thumbs up: **Four Fingers**, 150 Victoria St, Potts Point ☎ (02) 358 3707, is the hippest joint in town – go gamy/eclectic on, eg, crespinette of pheasant and pork 🍖 . . . . . . Despite Paul Merrony's departure, Sydney's brightest progeny still cram into the **Paddington Inn Bistro**, 338 Oxford St ☎ (02) 361 4402, to sit on painted nursery-school chairs and study the blackboard for mod Aussie fare 🍖 . . . . . . Looking for **Mr Bonaventura's**? It's one and the same place as **George's Delicatessen**, 2 Hopetoun St, Paddington ☎ (02) 332 3395. Barrels of wonderfully salty anchovies, prosciutto like none other, capers as beady as caviare 🍖 . . . . . . Best stock-up shops in food-mad Sydney: **The Bay Tree**, 40 Holdsworth St, Woollahra ☎ (02) 328 1101, for cooking essentials (Apilco, Le Creuset, Sabatier, etc) and **Accoutrement**, 611 Military Rd, Mosman ☎ (02) 969 1031, which also offers cooking classes led by star chefs (Damien Pignolet, Maggie Beer . . .) . . . . 🍖

————— *Theatre* —————

SYDNEY THEATRE COMPANY, Pier 4, Hickson Rd, Walsh Bay, NSW 2000
☎ **(02) 250 1700**
Fabulous harbourside showcase for Australia's top company. Lots of Australian premieres as well as revamped productions of the classics. Airy warehouse-space with a great, casual restaurant for before and after the show.

———————————————
· REST OF ·
———————————————
NEW SOUTH WALES
———————————————
— *Hotels and restaurants* —

BELLTREES COUNTRY HOUSE, Scone, NSW 2337 ☎ (065) 461119
Pretty, self-contained guest house on the squattocratic Whites' Belltrees Estate. Ride along picturesque trails or brush up your polo skills with Anto (5 goals) White and let the big boys show you how it's really done down the road at Kerry Packer's Ellerston Polo Centre. MARY ROSSI mosies along.

🍴 BEROWRA WATERS INN, Berowra Waters, NSW 2082 ☎ (02) 456 1027
Barely out of Sydney, but if you travel by sea-plane it feels further. Wonderfully tranquil setting and Gay Bilson's highly polished, imaginative cooking make it *"the finest in the country and one of the best in the world"* – JILL MULLENS. Signature dishes of bone marrow en brioche and tripe lyonnaise will usually be on the menu and anything wrapped in a wonton is wonderful. *"Expresses a kind of Australian informality along with very, very grand food"* – LEO SCHOFIELD. STEPHANIE ALEXANDER would choose it for an occasion, as would COLIN LANCELEY: *"A special trip for special occasions."* CAROLYN LOCKHART likes the fact that *"it is of the Australian style – informal/grand."* BRUCE OLDFIELD is mad on the setting: *"It's in a prehistoric forest on part of a river and you're very much open to the elements – suddenly the heavens can open and there will be an incredible deluge. The food is excellent too."* DAVID GOWER just likes the pleasant rigmarole of getting there. Open weekends only.

CARRINGTON HOUSE, 130 Young St, Carrington, NSW 2294 ☎ (049) 613564
Revamped after the earthquake, now the decoration is as good as what's on your plate. Barry Meiklejohn and Paul Garman's unrustic country restaurant might offer griddled tuna served with a peanut sauce and black rice or doublesmoked salmon with radicchio, sun-dried tomatoes and a poached egg.

CASUARINA, Hermitage Rd, Pokolbin, NSW 2321 ☎ (049) 987888
Small, eccentric guest house set in an established vineyard with themed suites: British Empire, Colonial, Asian, French Bordello. Great Orient-meets-Occident restaurant.

🍴 THE CONVENT PEPPERTREE, Halls Rd, Pokolbin, NSW 2321 ☎ (049) 987764
The meeting of 3 sets of great minds: Mike and Suzie O'Connor (she's an interior designer), Sally and Robert Molines (restaurateur and chef) and Murray Robson (winemaker). Accommodation is in an old convent which is now *most* unpurgatorial: 17 suites lead out of French windows on to private verandahs, beds are covered by filmy mosquito nets. **Robert's Restaurant** is housed in an old, antique-filled cottage and leans gently towards modern French food – poached salmon and rocket, woodfired loin of pork with diced apple. . . . *"A real benchmark for Australian country hotels, very tasteful, not too ritzy. Their restaurant features a huge wood-fired oven which is their pride and joy. The accommodation in the old convent is decorated beautifully"* – CAROLYN LOCKHART.

KIM'S BEACHSIDE RETREAT, Charlton St, Toowoon Bay, NSW 2261 ☎ (043) 321566
Sydneysiders' escape. Snug bungalows in a coastal Norfolk Pine forest an hour from the big smoke and seconds from the deep blue sea. *"The accommodation is superb. There's dripping greenery everywhere and little decks outside your room with spas in the middle of them and peacocks that wake you up in the morning. The buffet meals are a visual treat as well as a gastronomic one – a kind of showcase of all that Australia does best"* – MICHAEL GEBICKI. MARY ROSSI is a fan.

MILTON PARK, PO Box 676, Hordern's Rd, Bowral, NSW 2576 ☎ (048) 611522
A healthy hideaway for jaded city folk. All you need to realign body and soul: indoor pool, golf course, equestrian centre, fabulous food and fine art and antiques. MARY ROSSI takes time out.

PEPPERS GUEST HOUSE, Ekerts Rd, Pokolbin, NSW 2321 ☎ (049) 987596
Springboard for the vineyards of the Hunter. Return from a hard day's tasting to the charming cream and green colonial house, comfortably chintzy rooms, fine food and, of course, more wine.

POKOLBIN CELLAR RESTAURANT, Hungerford Hill Wine Village, Broke Rd, Pokolbin, NSW 2321 ☎ (049) 987584
The best restaurant in the valley. Relaxed, with homely, old-fashioned touches (generous flowers, open wood fires) and fresh, comforting food: game pies in the autumn, soufflés in winter. Dreamy summer lunches under the Italian market umbrellas.

Resorts

PINETREES LODGE, Lagoon Rd, Lord Howe Island, NSW 2898 ☎ (02) 632177
A short hop by plane from Sydney and you're on a World Heritage-listed island with its own coral reef, beaches and palm forests. Don't expect luxury or all-night partying – this is a homely resort for lovers of the bush and the briny blue.

THREDBO
Most fashionable ski resort in Australia; the lower slopes might only get man-made snow but June to end-Sept always sees a happening crowd of snow bunnies and year-round European ski-bums. Varied and variable pistes from beginner to expert level – if you can duck gum trees and dodge wombats on the snow, you can ski anywhere in the world. Best hotel: **Bernti's Alpine Lodge**. Best glühwein/schnapps/night-life: at the **Keller**.

TASMANIA

Hotels

LAUNCESTON INTERNATIONAL HOTEL, 29 Cameron St, Launceston, Tas 7250 ☎ (003) 343434
In the style of a grand old European manor house, and your last chance of comfort before trekking in the Cradle Mountain/Lake St Clair National Park.

LENNA OF HOBART, 20 Runnymede St, Battery Point, Tas 7004 ☎ (002) 232911
A small 19C hotel, with all the historic, villagy atmosphere of Battery Point. No finer springboard from which to sample Hobart's best – restaurants, Constitution Dock, galleries and markets are all a brisk stroll from your door.

PROSPECT HOUSE, Richmond, Tas 7025 ☎ (002) 622207
Owned and operated by the great-great-grandson of the original 1830s owner. A handful of guest rooms in the converted stables and a well-loved restaurant with a strong line in game.

Restaurants

🍴 DEAR FRIENDS, 8 Brooke St, Hobart, Tas 7000 ☎ (002) 232646
Tassie's finest restaurant – a warmly converted warehouse showcasing the pick of her seafood – Mercury Passage oysters, home-cured gravad lax. Carnivores get their teeth into King Island smoked beef with sun-dried tomatoes, capers and parmesan.

🍴 MOORILLA WINE CENTRE, Moorilla Estate, 655 Main Rd, Berriedale, Tas 7011 ☎ (002) 492949
Lovely place for an outdoor lunch at the Moorilla Vineyard. *"A marvellous set-up where you can drink their wines. They have absolutely, exclusively concentrated on serving Tas produce, they do not serve anything from the mainland. I love that"* – LEO SCHOFIELD.

MURE'S FISH CENTRE, Victoria Dock, Hobart, Tas 7000 ☎ (002) 311999
Double-decker piscatorium. Downstairs is a simple café, the Upper Deck more upmarket. *"A wonderful fish restaurant overlooking the harbour – you can imagine the fish swimming around there"* – SIR PETER USTINOV. *"Run by a wonderful people who are popularizing fresh fish – cooking very fresh fish and plainly at that. Very good"* – STEPHANIE ALEXANDER.

PROSSER'S ON THE BEACH, Sandy Bay Regatta Pavilion, Beach Rd, Sandy Bay, Tas 7005 ☎ (002) 252276
Casual seafood diner with views over the Derwent Estuary and influences from the South of France and West Coast USA.

· REST OF ·

AUSTRALIA

Tours and charters

AUSTRALIAN AIRLINES ☎ 131313 Australia-wide
Sets up holidays and flies you to Bedarra, Lizard, Orpheus, Daydream, Great Keppel, Heron and other islands.

ANSETT HOLIDAY TRAVEL ☎ 131344 Australia-wide
If Australian Airlines doesn't handle it, you can bet Ansett does: holidays to Hayman and Hamilton Islands, Cairns, Port Douglas and all the smartest coastal resorts (Reef House, Club Tropical, Mirage). And they fly too.

CRADLE MOUNTAIN HUTS ☎ (03) 312006
Take a walk on the wild side through the listed wilderness areas of Tassie following the Overland track from Cradle Valley to Lake St Clair through some of the world's most spectacular scenery. It's a 60km, 6-day guided walk, staying at night in cosy huts.

QUICKSILVER CONNECTION, Marina Mirage, PO Box 171, Port Douglas, Qld 4871 ☎ (070) 995455; bookings: (070) 995500
For the quickest, smoothest ride to the Reef, in

new Wavepiercer catamarans. Daily cruises to the Low Isles (a coral cay) and the Outer Reef; trips by helijet, semi-submersible and glass-bottomed boats; scuba and snorkelling.

SEAIR PACIFIC, Whitsunday Airport, Air Whitsunday Rd, Whitsunday, N Qld 4802 ☎ (079) 469133
Seaplane charter and scheduled air services to island resorts; scenic flights; flying boat and 'submareef' trips to the Great Barrier Reef.

SYDNEY IN STYLE, 1 Wharf Rd, Longueville, NSW 2066 ☎ (02) 427 5471; 427 0213
Exclusive tour service for visitors organized by wised-up duo, Penelope Wise and Kate Weir. Individually planned tours give you a (privi-leged) Sydneysider's view of the city. Lunches in private harbourside homes, sailing, special views of art galleries, collections and private houses. All fed and cultured, you can then follow stockmen's cattle trails through mountain river country or the grapie scent through the Hunter.

WALKABOUT GOURMET ADVENTURES, PO Box 2179, Brighton, Vic 3186 ☎ (03) 571 8910
As the name says: holidays created for (and by) trekkers who value their tucker. You explore the beautiful bush on foot (walks from 1 to 11 days) and Gabriela and Graeme Clarke bring up the rear with your luggage and the feasts.

—————— *Wine* ——————

"With only a couple of centuries of viticulture in Australia, Europe has a couple of thousand years' head start. Despite that, it is becoming apparent surprisingly quickly what grapes grow best where. The New World is challenging the old with the same grape varieties" – GREG DUNCAN POWELL. Chardonnay and Cabernet Sauvignon, the super-grapes of the 80s, are ubiquitous, but there's also a swing toward the less fashionable grapes such as Semillon, Riesling and Shiraz (Syrah), all traditionally successful in Australia.

New South Wales

The warmest of the wine-producing states comes up with year after year of great wines, especially white, from the Hunter Valley and Cowra regions. *"A great old Semillon from the Hunter Valley can be a real classic wine.* **TYRELL'S** *or* **LINDEMAN 65** *you would die for, or* **ROTHBURY'S** *or* **TYRELL'S 76**, *they can be lovely at any time but with age are trans-formed into something quite different from any-thing in the world"* – LIZ BERRY. GREG DUNCAN POWELL tips **MT WILLIAMS' Elizabeth and REYNOLD'S Wybourg Estate** (whose Upper Hunter Winery is a former prison). NB: Semil-lon sometimes is misleadingly called Riesling.

Chardonnays find form too; the unctuous **ROSEMOUNT Show Reserve** almost single-handedly put the Hunter on the international wine map and the limy **LAKE'S FOLLY**s of the late 80s seem set to lead another revolution. **LAKE'S FOLLY** also produces an outstanding **Cabernet** made from the difficult Petit Verdot. And another NSW oddity – the area around Griffith regularly produces great botrytized Semillon. *"***DE BORTOLI Semillon Sauternes** *is Australia's answer to Chateau Coutet"* – GREG DUNCAN POWELL. LIZ BERRY just despairs that its import into Britain is illegal.

Victoria

Cooler climate, older vineyards, Victoria is pro-ducing some of Australia's most exciting wine, especially from the Yarra Valley and Mornington Peninsula (*"the latest 'in' region in Australia"*, according to LIZ BERRY). **YARRA YERING** is a new star: *"A good winery, he just does Syrah* [**Dry Red Wine No 2**], *Chardonnay and Cabernet* [**Dry Red No 1**]*"* – LIZ B. Close neigh-bour **COLDSTREAM HILLS** is another. *"The Yarra Valley is becoming Australia's Bur-gundy. The* **DIAMOND VALLEY 1990 Pinot Noir** *will convince any doubters.* **COLD-STREAM HILLS** *and* **YARRA RIDGE 1990** *are also stand-outs"* – GREG DUNCAN POWELL. On the Mornington Peninsula, LIZ BERRY reckons *"***MERRICK** *is probably the best estate there"*, while GREG DUNCAN POWELL and DON HEWITSON agree that **DROMANA ESTATE Chardon-nay** is becoming a byword for a restrained, cool-weather example of the grape: *"I am drinking some of the 1990 now and keeping a few bottles for later years.* **TARRAWARRA** *is another Victorian beauty – beautifully balanced, rich and honeyed"* – DON H.

NE Vic is certainly where sticky Tokays and Muscats come into their own. *"The liqueur Mus-cats have to be some of Australia's best because they make a pure Muscat, unlike any other in the world.* **CHAMBERS** *is probably the best;* **MORRIS** *and* **STANTON AND KILLEEN** *are good. Most of the commercial ones are 5–8 years old, but there are still small amounts of wines that are 25-50 years old mixed into the blends and they have just such an intensity of flavour"* – LIZ BERRY. GREG DUNCAN POWELL adds to the list: *"***CAMPBELLS** *and* **BAILEYS** *of Glenrowan, a town made famous not by its fortified wine but by Australia's most famous bush ranger, Ned Kelly."*

South Australia

SA is dominated by the big boys of winemaking but its wines are no less individual for that. Indeed, some of Australia's most outstanding wines – red, white and sparkling – come from the areas of Coonawarra, Padthaway, the Clare Valley and, of increasing importance, the Adelaide Hills. **PENFOLD'S**, of course, is the biggie (and it in turn is owned by the SA Brewing Company), a vast producer whose Grange is *"the greatest ever Shiraz and should be drunk either very, very young or very, very old"* – LIZ BERRY (it's a desert island wine for DAVID DALE too). *"The only Australian wine that has really penetrated the prestigious London wine auction scene"* – SERENA SUTCLIFFE. Of the striplings, the 1986 is *"a wonderful wine"* – GREG DUNCAN POWELL (**PENFOLD'S Bin 707** – Cabernet Sauvignon – is no slouch either and in top years such as 1982/3 it is a very good wine indeed). Other Shiraz to watch: *"The relatively simple but charming* **CORIDE 1989** *and the rich and wonderful* **CHARLES MELTON 1990"** says GREG DP. LIZ BERRY tips **LINDEMAN'S** (another branch of the SA Brewing Clan) and **LIMESTONE RIDGE.**

The Coonawarra region and the Cabernet Sauvignon grape is a *"classic combination and* **PETALUMA Coonawarra 1988** *exemplifies this match"* – GREG DP. Brian Croser's wonder winery also goes from strength to strength in a superbly balanced Chardonnay, Riesling (both sweet and dry can be splendid) and the pace-setting sparkling wine, Croser (*"Really superb"* – LIZ B). **MOUNTADAM's** voluptuous, nutty Chardonnay and fruit-packed Pinot Noir make it a close contender as SA's new star. Back to Cab Sauv, and the Coonawarras warranting LIZ B and GREG DP's attention are **WYNN'S John Riddoch** and **LINDEMAN'S St George.** GDP also recommends the small **BOWEN ESTATE.**

Bucking the white = Chardonnay trend, SA's Rieslings are not to be sniffed at, rather to be savoured for their flowery aromatic qualities underpinned by good acidity. GREG DUNCAN POWELL'S tip? *"The classic limy Clare Valley style is hard to beat. Try the* **TIM KNAPP-STEIN 1990 Rhine Riesling."** LIZ BERRY goes for **"LEO BURING** *and* **QUELLTALER**, *which would age very well if you ever got the chance to find them".*

Western Australia

The wines of the Margaret River continue to increase in importance and, disproportionately, price. *"There's a cluster of good producers which are among my favourites –* **CAPE MENTELLE** *and* **MOSS WOOD** [a BERRY favourite too] *which both make good Chardonnays.* **CAPE MENTELLE** *also makes a very good Semillon/Sauvignon blend and a Zinfandel, the real, red McCoy but quite elegant"* – SIMON LOFTUS. **MOSS WOOD** also produces, according to GREG DUNCAN POWELL, an exceptional Pinot Noir, which proves that Yarra Valley doesn't have the monopoly on good Pinots. Chardonnays coming out of the technocratic **LEEUWIN ESTATE** are better and more expensive than ever. The most promising new area, Mount Barker, on WA's southern tip, *"has born stunning Rieslings from wineries such as*

CASTLE HILL, HOWARD PARK, ALKOOMI *and* **FOREST HILLS"** – GREG DP.

Tasmania

The smallest, coolest, dampest, most European of states – producing only a tiny fraction of Australia's output but with a growing reputation for classic winemaking. *"There's one top-quality producer, Dr Andrew Pirie,* **PIPERS BROOK**, *making a really fantastic Pinot Noir and a great Chardonnay"* – SIMON LOFTUS. Even further south, **MOORILLA ESTATE** finds success with Chardonnay, Pinot Noir and *"delicate, aromatic Riesling"* – GREG DUNCAN POWELL.

AUSTRIA

SALZBURG

Festivals

🏛 **SALZBURG FESTIVAL, Postfach 140, Hofstallgasse 1, A-5010 ☎ (0662) 8045**
Annual homage to Mozart (and friends) held in his home town from end-July to end-Aug. A month of opera, symphony, chamber music, recitals, theatre and open-air candlelit concerts. Top brass, strings and vocal chords under mega maestros' batons – such names as Haitink, Abbado and Mutter. Ultra-knowledgeable audiences keep them up to scratch. Serious music lovers can't stay away, which makes for serious traffic jams and ticket shortages. Pick up yours by Jan, or clear up the leftovers in Mar–Apr, otherwise it's up to friendly hotel doormen. ANDRE PREVIN and ANDREW LLOYD WEBBER are old fans.

Hotels

HOTEL OSTERREICHISCHER HOF, Schwarzstrasse 5, A-5020 ☎ (0662) 88977
Nummer ein in central Salzburg. Christmas-card views over the old town from the banks of the Salzach, meticulous service – it's under the same ownership as Vienna's Sacher.

GOLDENER HIRSCH, Getreidegasse 37, A-5020 ☎ (0662) 8485110
A hostelry since 1407, though the present incarnation dates from WWII. Small, not especially grand, but with excellent service and a good restaurant, it is for NICHOLAS VILLIERS: *"The best hotel – old-fashioned, family-run and certainly the place to stay in walking distance of the opera. And yet it's very sort of . . . local."* Breakfasts are famous nationwide.

VIENNA

—— *Art and museums* ——

**ALBERTINA, Augustiner Strasse 1,
A-1010 ☎ (0222) 534830**
Over a million works make this the world's
greatest collection of graphic art. Dürer tops the
bill; Raphael, Rubens, Poussin lead a strong supporting cast. ANDRE PREVIN applauds the show.

**🦺 KUNSTHISTORISCHES MUSEUM,
Burgring 5, A-1010 ☎ (0222) 934 5410**
Massive and massively important collection
amassed by centuries of Hapsburg Holy Roman
and Austro-Hungarian emperors. Paintings,
sculpture and decorative arts date from antiquity to Post-Impressionism. Famous court
portraiture (emperors will be emperors) and
other works from the great masters – Raphael,
Titian (Charles V's court painter), Caravaggio,
Velázquez and Hals. See famous Mannerist and
hyperbolist Benvenuto Cellini's salt cellar. 19C
and early 20C works are housed in the **Neue
Galerie** at Stallburg Palace.

—— *Bars and cafés* ——

**🦺 CAFE CENTRAL, 1 Herrengasse 14,
A-1010 ☎ (0222) 533 37630**
A Viennese extravaganza, as decorative and
indulgent as the cakes on offer. Sigmund Freud
and Leon Trotsky were among the regulars ear-
lier this century. *"One of the great famous cafés
where people still read newspapers on those
cane newspaper racks, sit on very comfortable
chairs and are served delicious coffee and a
glass of water on marble-top tables. You can
just sit there for hours and write your letters
and they don't mind"* – SIMON WILLIAMS.

**🦺 DEMEL, Kohlmarkt 14, A-1010
☎ (0222) 533 5516**
Former Hapsburg favourite – Emperor Franz

Josef used to chin-chin over the famous coffee
back in the 19C; they serve one kind (only the
best). Cakestand upon cakestand tempt you
with Mozartbombas, tortes, pralines and cheese
crackers – the stuff diets are abandoned for.

—— *Hotels* ——

**HOTEL BRISTOL, Kärntner Ring 1,
A-1015 ☎(0222) 515160**
Fin de siècle splendour across from the opera
house, where musicians and buffs pack in
for late-night bites. Antique furnishings, Old
Master paintings and jolly good service mean
"the Bristol remains the best hotel in Vienna" –
SERENA FASS.

**HOTEL SACHER WIEN,
Philharmonikerstrasse 4, A-1015
☎ (0222) 51456**
Home to one of the world's most famous (and
many would say best) cake – the Sacher Torte.
Tuck into it in the gossipy café / pâtisserie; get
tucked-in amid lashings of rococerie in the bedrooms – splendid views of the castle and the
town – and relish the old-world service. It's an
obvious choice for LORD MONTAGU OF BEAULIEU.

**IMPERIAL, Kärntner Ring 16, A-1015
☎ (0222) 50110**
The one that makes visiting royalty – including
the Queen of England – feel at home. Opened in
1873 by Emperor Franz Josef, the palatial building, marble halls, crystal chandeliers and rococo
furniture make SIMON WILLIAMS come over all
lordly: *"A proper old brocade-walled, heavy pine
Austrian hotel . . . beautiful, it does everything
in the proper Viennese style."* *"I like it very
much"* – SIR CLEMENT FREUD; ANDRE PREVIN
and BARBARA TAYLOR BRADFORD say aye to that.

**PALAIS SCHWARZENBERG,
Schwarzenbergplatz 9, A-1030
☎ (0222) 784515**
Another grand old hotel – part of the palatial
home of a Schwarzenberg prince (the family
Rubens collection is dotted about the vast

🦺 Buzzz Burger king: Trot along to the
Hofburg, city residence of the Hapsburgs, if only to see the **Spanish Riding School**
(where the Lippizaner stallions perform dressage in a baroque ballroom); also the 18C
library and imperial apartments, though Franz Josef's rooms lack the expected
grandeur or even creature comforts 🦺 . . . . . . If it's grandeur you're after, the baroque
Belvedere, Prinz-Eugen-strasse 27 ☎ (0222) 784 1580, supplies it by the sackload –
wonderful gardens and Austrian art, medieval to modern (*"I'm quite entranced with all
the Klimts and things"* – SIMON WILLIAMS) 🦺 . . . . . . The place the music died: pay your
respects to Beethoven, Brahms and Schubert in **Musician's Square** in the Central
Cemetery 🦺 . . . . . . Where death loses its sting: the **Undertakers' Museum**, Goldeg-
gasse 19 ☎ (0222) 5019 5227, is a celebration of that noble and underrated profession . 🦺

rooms). Long-serving, loyal staff and imposing grounds near the city centre. The restaurant of the same name is reliable, if not adventurous, where fresh fish is always a good bet.

Music

MUSIKVEREIN, Bösendorfer Strasse 12, A-1010 ☎ (0222) 5058 6810
"The greatest hall in the world. A musician is always going to like a hall for the way it sounds, other people like the way a hall looks, but unfortunately there are a great many halls scattered around the world that look great but sound terrible. With the Musikverein, which is by light years the best, you've got the best of both worlds because it's gorgeous and sounds incomparably good" – ANDRE PREVIN. It's home to the Vienna Philharmonic (*"the world's greatest orchestra"*, adds AP).

> **❝ The diet in Vienna is famously catastrophic. Too much strüdel takes its toll, but the whole café society thing is part of the city's history ❞**
>
> SIMON WILLIAMS

VIENNA FESTIVAL, Wiener Festwochen, Lehargasse 11, A-1060 ☎ (0222) 586 1676
Important festival with carnival atmosphere. The whole town gets on down to classical and contemporary music, jazz, theatre, proms, ballet, puppet shows and exhibitions from mid-May to end-June.

♠ VIENNA STATE OPERA, Opernring 2, A-1010 ☎ (0222) 514440
The stunning opera house built in 1887 puts on terrific productions of classics under the direction of Eberhard Waechter. Hugely admired and attended, it's top of the Euro-pile for many opera buffs. The best standing room in the world in the central pit. MARY ROSSI loves it for its *"fine artistic standards in a beautiful historic building."* BARBARA TAYLOR BRADFORD just loves it. On New Year's Eve, the Vienna State Opera holds the spectacular Vienna Imperial Ball in the state rooms of the Hofburg.

Restaurants

12 APOSTEL KELLER, Sonnenfelsgasse 3, A-1010 ☎ (0222) 512 6777
Nothing fancy here – locals come for a hearty blast of good old-fashioned Austrian nosh – blood pudding, sausages, sauerkraut with caraway seeds. Wine is served in beer glasses, hence the merry atmos.

♠ STEIRER ECK, Rasumofskygasse 2, A-1030 ☎ (0222) 713 3168
Adventurous revisions of Viennese classics – wood and meadow mushroom gratiné, lamb in basil sauce, duck timbale with goose liver and mushrooms – line up with stalwarts such as Vienna café dessert. Bins full of fine wine, impeccable service – all in all the best in Austria.

ZU DEN DREI HUSAREN, Weihburggasse 4, A-1010 ☎ (0222) 512 1092
Romantic gourmanderie with Austrian haute cuisine – chicken filled with goose liver in filo pastry, cheesecake dumplings with walnut butter – and a very thick list of the best Austrian and French wines. Candlelit tables and tinkling piano set the tone.

· REST OF ·

AUSTRIA

Hotels

SCHLOSS DURNSTEIN, A-3601 Dürnstein an der Donau, Wachau ☎ (02711) 212
An old hotel on the banks of the Danube, with a liltingly beautiful view from the leafy terrace. Renowned cuisine and wine cellar. Wonderful high rococo churches in the region to visit.

Music

BREGENZER FESTSPIELE, Festspiel-und-Kongresshaus, Platz der Wiener Symphoniker, A-6900 Bregenz ☎ (05574) 49200
The one that walks on water – well, floats on a spectacular stage on Lake Constance. Evening sky backdrops and fireworks lend the medieval town's Jul-Aug festival of opera and symphony concerts some knockout drama. Indoor theatre for the chilly.

BRUCKNERFEST, Brucknerhaus, Postfach 57, Untere Donaulände 7, A-4010 Linz ☎ (0732) 76120
'Cloud of sound' open-air recitals and concerts surround audiences mainly with the heroic post-Wagnerian strains of the Austrian composer Anton Bruckner but also everything from Haydn to Bartók. Lasts a week in late summer.

MORBISCH LAKE FESTIVAL, c/o Femdenverkehrsbüro der Gemeinde, A-7072 Mörbisch am See ☎ (02685) 8430
Lakeside operetta festival on the Hungarian border. Every July and August the resort town holds night-time operas on a floating stage lit by

flaming torches – swimmers, windsurfers, sailors and waterskiers take over during the day. BARBARA TAYLOR BRADFORD admires.

SCHUBERTIADE HOHENEMS, Postfach 100, Schweizer Strasse 1, A-6845 Hohenems ☎ (05576) 2091
Staged in the courtyard and rooms of the old Palasthof – a castle opened once a year for the purpose – this June festival celebrates the music of Franz Schubert.

———— *Ski resorts* ————

KITZBÜHEL
"My heart is in Kitzbühel" says STEVE POD-BORSKI – he probably left it there as he skied down its infamous Hahnenkamm faster than almost anyone alive. Grand, trad resort in and around a medieval walled city with casino and sports centre for posh Munich weekenders. **Praxmair**'s hot chocolate is legendary, as is the unreliability of decent snow on lower slopes, thanks to the low altitude.

LECH
Lech's a cul-de-sac – the road up from St Anton ends at the fave Austrian resort for chic winterers. Set in a wide valley with crystal river and little church, bejewelled designerfolk stay in pricy hotels like the **Almhof** or **Hospiz**, or personal ones like the **Hotel Gasthof Post**. On a clear day, you can hear bands playing on hotel roof terraces from the mountaintops.

ST ANTON
Extreme skiing for extremely good skiers and nutters. Scream down from Valluga Mountain, stay in the **Post Hotel** or **St Antoner Hof** to escape screaming Brits and Swedes after dark in the town centre. Rejoin them in the **Krazy Kanguruh**.

BELGIUM

BRUSSELS

———— *Hotels* ————

HOTEL AMIGO, 1–3 rue de l'Amigo, 1000 ☎ (02) 511 5910
A slice of Brussels charm in this Spanish Renaissance-style hotel. Privately owned, it stands on the site of the old city jail, a stone's throw from Grand'Place and Town Hall. Ornately furnished rooms with touches of Louis XV. Discreet personalized service.

HILTON INTERNATIONAL, 38 blvd de Waterloo, 1000 ☎ (02) 513 8877
Leagues ahead of the Hilton norm, this one's a distinctive city landmark, renowned for its individual service, mod cons and trad values. Catch snippets of power gossip over coffee and croissants in the **Café d'Egmont**, lounge about in black lacquer chairs, relax in steam cabinets, use personal computers and video (one in every suite). Throw open the windows on to magnificent Egmont Park. The **Maison de Boeuf** is one of the best hotel restaurants in town – misleading because it's famous for fish.

METROPOLE, 31 place de Brouckère, 1000 ☎ (02) 217 2300
Jazzy modern rooms swank up the Eurocapital's grand fin de siècle hotel. The **Alban Chambon restaurant** hits the spot for diners – step outside the marble hall into the centre-ville.

SAS ROYAL HOTEL, 47 rue Fossé aux Loups, 1000 ☎ (02) 219 6262
One of town's newer kids has gone down a treat with locals and Eurocrats – red eyes rest in seriously snazzy rooms. No guesses what the **Sea Grill** serves – very fresh, very tasty.

STANHOPE, 9 rue du Commerce, 1040 ☎ (02) 506 9111
Charming new arrival on the scene – opened in autumn 1991 – the rooms are very pretty (and pretty small). Young, multilingual staff provide jump-to-attention service. Get glam at **Caviar Bar** or over a drink in the terraced garden.

———— *Restaurants* ————

 **BRUNEAU, 73 ave Broustin, 1080 ☎ (02) 427 6978**
Market-scourer Jean-Pierre Bruneau hunts for tip-top ingredients to flavour his ultra-inventive experiments in taste. Cognoscenti consistently make the pilgrimage for food *"of a rare delicacy"* – CHAMBERTIN.

🍴 **COMME CHEZ SOI, 23 place Rouppe, 1000 ☎ (02) 512 2921**
Simply the best in Belgium – book a month ahead to get into culinary high priest Pierre Wynants's Art Deco gastro temple; if you make it to the tabernacle – his table d'hôte served *in the kitchen* – you know you are one of the very favoured few. Tuck into mousse of Ardennes ham and sole with mousseline of Riesling and drunken prawns. Service in the 50-seater remains friendly and unintimidating. BOB PAYTON likes it not least for the seconds ladled out of their copper pots.

DE BIJGAARDEN, 20 Beverenstraat, 1720 Groot-Bijgaarden ☎ (02) 466 4485
Relaxed service, top-notch Belgian cooking, and a loyal following of foodies, who go for such delicacies as coquilles St Jacques with béarnaise

sauce or caramelized veal sweetbreads with truffle sauce. Out of the hustle of the town centre, businessmen and women throw off their busy personae and relax in rustic surroundings in leafy suburbia.

🏊 DELICES DE LA MER, 1020 chaussée de Waterloo, 1080 ☎ (02) 375 5467
Rising star Michel Beyls attracts a constellation of similarly twinkling folk – the word on the street is he just gets better and better. He prides himself on using the freshest, first-class ingredients, with game in season and fish and seafood specialities.

L'ECAILLER DU PALAIS ROYAL, 18 rue Bodenbroek, 1000 ☎ (02) 512 8751
Dead chic, offering live – or as near to it as poss – fish and seafood, considered the best in Brussels (there's absolutely no meat on the menu). Set in Le Sablon district, this is the most spectacularly refined dinerie, for the beautiful on a beautiful night out. Get there before the crowds (of celebs) do.

VILLA LORRAINE, 75 ave du Vivier d'Oie, 1180 ☎ (02) 374 3163
For country-house style in town, a classic restaurant with glass-covered terrace, next to the quiet Bois de la Cambre. Freddy Vandecasserie blends hearty cuisine d'Escoffier with cuisine du marché, using seasonal market produce for his ever-changing menu, which *"it is the diner's privilege to delect"* – CHAMBERTIN.

· REST OF ·

BELGIUM

—— *Restaurants* ——

SIR ANTHONY VAN DIJCK, 16 Oude Koornmarkt, 2000 Antwerp ☎ (03) 231 6170
Red herring, wild geese – this culinary treasure is the one to track down. Eat classical cooking in the 17C house with appreciative locals.

WEINEBRUGGE, 242 Koning Albertlaan, 8000 Bruges ☎ (050) 384440
Contemporary cooking in a modern villa in the ancient city of Bruges. Worth the trip, and the cash: *"A bit expensive but excellence has no price"* – CHAMBERTIN.

FILIP BOGAERT, 5 Munster Tacklaan, 8500 Koprtrijk ☎ (056) 203034
Filip Bogaert's haute cooking – 10 years at Comme Chez Soi taught him a thing or two – is packed with invention, subtlety and surprise. Beautiful setting in an 18C house.

SCHOLTESHOF, 130 Kermstraat, 3512 Stevoort ☎ (011) 250202
Hidden in a charming small village near Hasselt, Roger Souvereyns – artist, antique collector and host par excellence – manages his superb hotel-restaurant. Each room is different, the cooking is a tour de force.

BOTSWANA

Twin habitats – the inland Okavango Delta and the Kalahari Desert – make Botswana the most diverse and fascinating safari land. The remarkable Okavango flows away from the sea into the heart of the country and fans out into a system of thousands of navigable capillaries. Watch the magnificent animals from a hollowed-out canoe or camp-hop by plane and stay in some of the world's wildest outposts. *"For total freedom from phones, faxes and dramas, head for the*

❝ *The Okavango is unspoilt, very unspoilt. There are crocodiles, elephant, buffalo, wildebeest, baboons, eagles. And there are lions – but we didn't see any* **❞**

 DAVID GOWER

African bush. A safari in Botswana arranged through Ker & Downey, including tented accommodation in the Okavango Delta and elephant-back game-viewing, could qualify as the most exhilarating escape on earth" – SUSAN KUROSAWA. Contact K&D at 13201 Northwest Freeway, Houston, TX 77040 ☎ (713) 744 5222.

🕵 Buzzz Euro sweet teeth get stuck in early at fab pâtisserie, **Dandoy**, 31 rue au Beurre ☎ (02) 511 0326 – sink them into speciality speculoos and pain à la Greque 🏊 ...... World-beating encounters of the chocoholic kind happen at **Maison Leonidas**, 46 blvd Anspach ☎ (02) 720 5980, and **Godiva Chocolatier**, Grand'Place ☎ (02) 511 2537 (in that order). Be warned – it really is addictive .... 🕵

The Kingdom of Bhutan

"The most romantic country you could ever visit – visually, but not for comfort" – SERENA FASS. The absolutely unspoilt Himalayan Bhuddist Kingdom is a challenge to get into – it only issues 4,000 tourist visas a year – and very expensive (US$220 a day is demanded of every tourist, wherever you stay). But it's the trip of a lifetime. Known as Druk Yul – Kingdom of the Thunder Dragon – just getting there took DAN TOPOLSKI's breath away, flying up to Kathmandu, passing Everest on the way, before landing some 30 minutes later in the capital, Thimphu. The place itself is *"the size of Wales, and has literally come out of the Middle Ages. They still wear traditional dress, a type* of coloured dressing gown. The young king has married his 4 sisters, his parents are very powerful, but there is not very much corruption. The people are very accueillant, open, and they speak English. Accommodation is comfortable and there is running water – it's a trekking, wildlife, climbing, outward-bound kind of holiday"*. Visit the dzongs – half-temple, half-administrative centres, or venture up to Tak Sang Monastery – the mythical 'tigers' nest' where Buddha first entered the Kingdom. **Steppes East**, Castle Eaton, Swindon, Wiltshire, England ☎ (0285) 810267, will get you there, organize trekking among remote tribes and a Himalayan safari in the south.

CHOBE GAME LODGE, PO Box 32, Kasane ☎ 250340
High life in the wilderness – look out over the Chobe River while you swim in safer waters (the pool), relax in airy rooms, hire a boat, spot leopard from land cruisers and get back in time for a splendid candlelit supper – antelope dishes are de rigueur.

DELTA CAMP, Chief's Island, PO Box 39, Kasane, or c/o Okavango Tours and Safaris (see Travel Directory)
Small, exclusive camp in the middle of the Okavango Delta, surrounded by the network of streams. *"Good, very nice and very isolated"* – DAVID GOWER. Paddle a *mokuro* into the Moremi Wildlife Reserve, watch spectacular birds – emerald green Swallow-Tailed Bee Eaters – and return to hot-running water, fine cooking and your very own lethaka-reed chalet.

BRAZIL

RIO DE JANEIRO

Clubs

HIPPOPOTAMUS, Rua Barao da Torre 354 ☎ (021) 247 0351
Just the place to wallow. *"The discothèque is* down in the bowels of the club and it really is jam-packed in there, tremendous atmosphere, quite electric. Very good, plain food . . . you eat upstairs away from the discothèque"* – JOHN GOLD. Late start, late finish – the restaurant doesn't even start taking *orders* until 10.30pm.

Hotels

COPACABANA PALACE, Av Atlantica 1702 ☎ (021) 255 7070
Difficult to imagine doing anything other than flaking out by the pool at **Bar do Copa**, one eye on your cocktail and the other checking out the famous Copacabana beach scene. Traditional Brazilian *feijoada* lunch (rice, black beans and meat stew) on Sat, international cuisine in **Bife de Ouro**, excellent wine list. Long restoration programme and plans to build a health club.

HOTEL INTER-CONTINENTAL, Av Prefeito Mendes de Morais, 222 Sao Conrado, PO Box 33011 ☎ (021) 322 2200
Classic large-scale extra-modern hotel. Sip the sugar cane and lemon caipirinha cocktail at the **Ocean Bar** overlooking the beach or snack out on seafood at **Captain Cook's**. Plunge into more of a native scene with samba show and Brazilian buffet lunch on the **Veranda**. 3 pools, tennis courts, nearby golf courses and a tropical garden.

RIO PALACE HOTEL, Av Atlantica 4240, Copacabana ☎ (021) 521 3232
Perfectly located at the junction of Copacabana and Ipanema beaches. Zip up the external glass

elevator, stopping off at pools, bars, health club and restaurants. Art and antiques, tapestries and modern sculpture add gravitas to the ephemeral beach scene. **Le Pré Catelan** offers excellent French cuisine. Nip into **The Horse's Neck** to hear gossip from the horse's mouth over a pre-Pré cocktail. Take traditional tea in **Tea and Sympathy**.

────── *Restaurants* ──────

ANTIQUARIUS, Rua Aristides Espínola 19, Leblon ☎ (021) 294 1049
Arty, but not old hat, selling sculptures and antiques out the front and serving Portuguese-accented food out the back. Drop in between noon and 2am for grilled shrimp or shredded fish and scrambled eggs.

LE SAINT HONORE, Hotel Meridien, Av Atlantica 1020, Leme ☎ (021) 257 1834
As haute as it gets here, with a Paul Bocuse-designed menu, no less. Super-rich French standards – snails in garlic butter, duck emincé in honey and herbs – wreak havoc with a beach-going bod (and it's right on Copacabana too).

────────── *Tours* ──────────

TURISMO CLASSICO, Ave N S Copacabana 1059, Office 805 ☎ (021) 287 3390
Made-to-measure holidays for one or a group of 100, anywhere within Brazil – eg, to Manaus, 1,000 miles up the Amazon and starting point for the heart of the jungle, on by plane to the island of Marajo, or stay in Pantanal and see hundreds of beautiful species of bird and crocodiles aplenty. Hotel reservations, transfers, tours.

· REST OF ·
BRAZIL

────────── *Hotels* ──────────

POUSO DO CHICO REY, Rua Brigadeiro Musqueira 90, Ouro Preto ☎ (031) 551 1274
Between Brazil's first opera theatre and the Praça Tiradentes and pretty damn historic itself. A perfect old colonial house with simple but authentic furniture, warm polished floors and 18C art throughout. They still don't accept bookings – why would they need to when people eagerly turn up on spec?

POUSADA PARDIEIRO, Rua Tenente Francisco Antonio 74, Parati ☎ (0243) 711370
This small but stylish, low, rambly, red-tiled

hotel is set in one of the most important and beautifully preserved colonial towns in the world, a fashionable weekend getaway for fraught arty types. Rooms blend colonial Brazil (hammocks as well as beds) with such swish ideas as foie gras and champagne in your fridge. Lovely gardens, small pool and sauna.

BRITAIN

BATH

Bath Festival (May/June) runneth over with music and fringe events. The **Theatre Royal** is a favourite for MAUREEN LIPMAN and SIMON WILLIAMS: *"It can't be bettered, it's like a Toulouse-Lautrec bordello backstage."*

────── *Art and museums* ──────

John Wood père et fils revolutionized town planning in Britain with their 18C scheme for Bath. The town is now littered with museums that reflect life in Roman and Regency Britain. Wallow in the **Roman Baths** and **Roman Museum**; see life as it was in the 18C at: the **Pump Room**, social centre of the spa; the authentically furnished Georgian house at **No 1 Royal Crescent**; and the **Carriage Museum** (the finest in the country). Dedicated followers of fashion can pursue their love from the 17C to the present day at the **Museum of Costume** in the Assembly Rooms. Don't miss the charming **American Museum** at Claverton Manor, with its collection of folk art, furniture and hand-made patchwork quilts. *"To spend a day in Bath is most agreeable. There's an enervating atmosphere of doziness, you take the waters and listen to chamber music in the Pump Room and go to the races at one of the prettiest courses in the land"* – SIMON WILLIAMS.

HOLBURNE MUSEUM, Great Pulteney St ☎ (0225) 466669
This fine example of Regency architecture holds the Holburne family's collection of 17C–18C decorative and fine art (including Gainsborough and Stubbs) as well as an extensive art library and pieces by contemporary craftsmen.

────────── *Hotels* ──────────

BATH SPA HOTEL, Sydney Rd ☎ (0225) 444424
Raking in rhapsodies from the hotel hawks is this many-starred wonder, set in an extremely fine neo-classical house, carefully restored over

4 years. All the tranquillity of a large country house (with 8 acres of landscaped gardens), only minutes from the town centre. Warm, friendly service is earning loyal guests.

THE QUEENSBERRY HOTEL, Russel St ☎ (0225) 447928
Typically Bath – a row of John Wood-designed buildings commissioned by the Marquis of Q himself. A fair fight to land one of the 24 double rooms, decorated in unfrilly contemporary style. *"The best hotel in Bath"* – BOB PAYTON. *"Really comfortable bedrooms at a reasonable price and a friendly efficient staff"* – PAUL HENDERSON. Sit under **The Olive Tree** for modern bistro-ish food at more than reasonable prices.

ROYAL CRESCENT HOTEL, Royal Crescent ☎ (0225) 319090
Resplendent centrepiece of the famous crescent, this golden oldie looks over vast lawns to the front and its own gardens to the rear. The Regency life to a tee (talking of which, tea here is a treat). Sumptuous four-poster suites come with personal hot spring spa bath and stupendous views: *"You see the whole crescent in front of you"* – SIR CLEMENT FREUD.

CAMBRIDGE

This small historic city is home to the famous university, rival to Oxford. Only some 40 years its junior (dating back to 1209), among its notable colleges are **Peterhouse** (the oldest, founded c. 1280 – the original hall survives), St John's (spectacular Tudor gateway and its own Bridge of Sighs), **Corpus Christi** (whose Old Court is in fact the oldest in town), **Trinity** (the largest court and the prized Wren Library). Unmissable is **King's**, for the Chapel, a high point of Gothic architecture with spectacular fan-vaulting. Visit **Magdalene** for the celebrated Pepys Library (he was an undergrad) complete with diary. One of the loveliest walks in Britain is along the **Backs**, where the college lawns meet the River Cam. The jewel of Cambridge's gardens is the stone-walled **Fellow's Garden of Clare College**. The **Cambridge Festival** (July) makes use of the most beautiful buildings in the town.

—— *Art and museums* ——

FITZWILLIAM MUSEUM, Trumpington St ☎ (0223) 332900
A delightful museum, well set out and thought out, whose prize is a fine collection of Old Masters. Rubens, Van Dyck and the Dutch school (including prints and drawings by Rembrandt) are well represented. Renaissance and Impressionist works too, plus ceramics, glass, textiles, weaponry, sculptures, manuscripts and Greek and Roman antiquities. *"A beautiful museum"* – SERENA FASS.

LONDON

—— *Art and museums* ——

BRITISH MUSEUM, Great Russell St, WC1 ☎ (071) 636 1555
A neo-classical temple to antiquity, under new directorship that is destined to shake up any old fossils. One of the world's greatest collections boasts the Rosetta Stone, the Portland Vase, the tug-of-love Elgin Marbles.... *"You can get a clear picture of all the civilization in the eastern Mediterranean basin and further east which almost eliminates the need to go anywhere else"* – BRIAN SEWELL. Well-preserved old-timers include ancient Egyptian mummies and the Lindow Man, who's pushing 2,200 years old. Also medieval, Renaissance, Oriental collections, and marvellous prints, drawings and watercolours.

COURTAULD INSTITUTE GALLERIES, Somerset House, Strand, WC2 ☎ (071) 872 0220
Uniting William Chambers's neo-classical Thames-side building with a picture gallery of international standing. *"Exceptional"* – SERENA FASS. Mostly from private bequests, paintings include household names in Impressionism and Post-Impressionism – Manet's *A Bar at the Folies-Bergère*, Renoir's *La Loge*.... Also Flemish, Dutch and Italian Old Masters, 20C British paintings, 18C decorative arts. *"It has a very good collection but its exhibiting space is minute"* – BRIAN SEWELL. The gallery rotates its 8,000 prints, drawings and watercolours.

DULWICH PICTURE GALLERY, College Rd, SE21 ☎ (081) 693 5254
Designed by Sir John Soane in 1817, it's England's oldest public picture gallery. *"The part built by Soane is so rigorous"* – DOTT ROSA MARIA LETTS. The huge response to the architectural competition for a new pavilion resulted in a sympathetic, low-slung design by Christopher J Grasby which remains on the drawing board until a future time of plenty. 17C and 18C art predominates through Poussin, Claude, Rembrandt, Rubens, Van Dyck, Gainsborough and Lawrence. Pay your respects to the founders in the amber glow of the domed mausoleum.

IMPERIAL WAR MUSEUM, Lambeth Rd, SE1 ☎ (071) 416 5000
The latest technology allows you to experience the Blitz (see it, smell it, hear it) and interact with audio-visuals. Survey war planes, arms, paintings and memorabilia. Harrowing photographs and films depict the liberation of Belsen in a new gallery; more recent wars become exhibitions through journalists' dona-

tions. *"One of the best museums"* – LEO COOPER. LORD MONTAGU OF BEAULIEU agrees.

MUSEUM OF THE MOVING IMAGE,
South Bank Centre, SE1 ☎ (071) 401 2636
A real hands-on experience, with levers, pulleys and buttons galore. A cast of actors ushers you through the history of the moving image from shadow plays of 2,000 BC to 20C laser technology. Youngsters can step through the Tardis into Dalek land or shriek at Frankenstein in the Hammer Horror. You have been warned.

🕵 NATIONAL GALLERY, Trafalgar
Square, WC2 ☎ (071) 839 3321
The National Gallery continues to rule the roost, maintaining its high standards through continual refurbishment and chronological rehanging. With highlights from all the European schools of painting, it houses *"an extraordinary collection"* – MEREDITH ETHERINGTON-SMITH. *"For permanent exhibitions, only the National matters"* – BRIAN SEWELL. The Sainsbury Wing is now hailed as a triumph – internally, at least – with its fine customized display of the gallery's oldest, most fragile works: the early Renaissance collection. *"The paintings were such a surprise and such a delight. The interior colour is fabulous – the paintings look so bright and lively"* – STEPHEN JONES. *"I think the new extension is great, fab, brilliant"* – DAVID SHILLING. *"Totally exceptional, the whole architectural layout . . . the pale grey makes all the colours of the paintings sing"* – SERENA FASS. MARY ROSSI and LORD MONTAGU OF BEAULIEU are both admirers.

NATIONAL PORTRAIT GALLERY,
Trafalgar Square, WC2 ☎ (071) 930 1552
Britain's history depicted from the Tudors to today through portraits of its leading figures. A

new Resource Centre, planned to open in 1993, will unite the library and archives; new exhibition space will be created for 20C portraits, a video and photographic gallery.

🕵

Britain's Best Galleries and Museums

I	NATIONAL GALLERY · London
2	BRITISH MUSEUM · London
3	WALLACE COLLECTION · London
4	VICTORIA AND ALBERT MUSEUM · London
5	COURTAULD INSTITUTE GALLERIES · London
6	TATE GALLERY · London

ROYAL ACADEMY OF ART, Burlington
House, Piccadilly, W1 ☎ (071) 439 7438
Some of the most sparkling international exhibitions destined for London alight here. *"If it's exhibiting space you're looking for, the Royal Academy has no competition"* – BRIAN SEWELL. The renowned Summer Exhibition (mid-June to mid-Aug) continues to be contentious for not being contentious enough, but such shows as *Pop Art* pack enough punches to make up. *"Pop Art signalled a new era for the RA. It bodes well for future exhibitions"* – DAVID SHILLING. Norman Foster's successful transformation of the Sackler Galleries provides bright new exhibition

🕵 **Buzzz** If you like your animals huge, fast and rare, spring along to the **Natural History Museum**, Cromwell Rd, SW7 ☎ (071) 938 9123, stuffed with uncuddly creatures. Robotic reptiles now challenge the famous dinosaur skeletons. The all-glass Ecology Gallery woos stimulus-cravers with videos and computer games 🕵 . . . . . . Stand where time begins, at longitude 0, at the **National Maritime Museum**, Greenwich, SE10 ☎ (081) 858 4422. Observe life through Britain's biggest refracting telescope at Christopher Wren's Old Royal Observatory, see marine paintings, Royal barges and Lord Nelson's blood-stained uniform from the Battle of Trafalgar at the museum, and, down on the river, the Cutty Sark, fastest tea clipper of her time (London-Melbourne 60 days) 🕵 . . . . . . JOHN BROOKE-LITTLE rounds up a couple more for the budding ballistician: **National Army Museum**, Royal Hospital Rd, SW3 ☎ (071) 730 0717 (*"rather neglected but very good for military things"*) and the **Royal Airforce Museum**, Grahame Park Way, Hendon, NW9 (*"very good"*) 🕵 . . . . . . Take the kids (and the kid in you) to the **Science Museum**, Exhibition Rd, SW7 ☎ (071) 938 8000, for 5 floors of scientific inventions, brilliantly set out in interactive and educational displays . . . . 🕵

space. Much loved by STEPHEN JONES, DUGGIE
FIELDS and CLARE FRANCIS.

THE SAATCHI COLLECTION, 98A
Boundary Rd, NW8 ☎ (071) 624 8299
Adman Charles Saatchi's ultramod gallery is
*"one of the most beautiful spaces for seeing art,
it's always such a treat to go there . . . very interesting shows"* – DUGGIE FIELDS. *"An amazing
collection"* – DAVID SHILLING. Rotating exhibitions of 3 to 4 artists focus predominantly on 20C
art – Andres Serrano's controversial *Pissed
Christ* and Mike Bidlow's life-size copies of
Picassos and Warhols among them.

SIR JOHN SOANE'S MUSEUM, 13
Lincoln's Inn Fields, WC2 ☎ (071) 2107
The eccentric 1813 house, designed and lived in
by Sir John Soane, is presented as was, complete
with violent yellow drawing room. Mammoth
hoard of sculpture, furniture, 30,000 architectural drawings, 10,000 books, Turners, Canalet-
tos and the famous Hogarth series, *The Rake's
Progress*. *"An incredible building, such an
English house where the imagination gets
moved"* – DOTT ROSA MARIA LETTS. *"A museum
which is itself a work of art with a coherence and
cohesion unmatched by any big, growing
museum"* – BRIAN SEWELL.

🏃 TATE GALLERY, Millbank, SW1
☎ (071) 821 1313
The national collection of British and modern
international art. A superb store of Stubbs,
Blake, Constable, Pre-Raphaelites and all the
key moderns and contemporaries – such as Carl
André's *Equivalent VIII* – a Pile of Bricks to
you and me. Annual rehangings give a fresh per-
spective on old favourites (the flipside, points
out BRIAN SEWELL, is: *"It's in a constant state of
upheaval so if you wanted to see, for example, a
Henry Moore, there's no guarantee it would be*

there"). The Clore Gallery houses the famous
Turner collection.

🏃 VICTORIA AND ALBERT MUSEUM,
South Kensington, SW7 ☎ (071) 589 6371
Glistening after its recent scrub, the V&A has an
equally polished collection. A feast of decorative
arts – silver, ceramics, glass, textiles, furniture,
costume, plus sculpture, the superb Indian
gallery, the Tsui Chinese gallery, the prized
Raphael Cartoons, prints, drawings, photographs and the largest collection of Constables.
The new European Ornament Gallery is a
brilliant lesson in the use of ornament in decorative arts, displayed thematically – a good place
to start your V&A tour. *"The new Indian Room
is wonderful"* – SERENA FASS. A firm favourite
of LORD MONTAGU OF BEAULIEU, JOHN BROOKE-
LITTLE, STEPHEN JONES and DAVID SHILLING.
Good shop and restaurant too.

🏃 WALLACE COLLECTION, Hertford
House, Manchester Square, W1
☎ (071) 935 0687
This compact Georgian house offers a celebrated
collection of French furniture, porcelain and 18C
paintings. Whimsical rococo paintings (Boucher,
Fragonard) plus Rembrandt (though nearly all
have been re-attributed), Rubens, Hals and co.
*"It is free which is wonderful – I think you
should go to a gallery just to see a few pictures
that you like"* – SIR CLEMENT FREUD. Clock the
1740 Astronomical Clock (tells the time anywhere in the northern hemisphere, the date,
month and signs of the zodiac) and the largest
collection of armour outside the Tower of London. *"Wonderful, a fabulous building and a
great collection"* – DUGGIE FIELDS. *"It works
extremely well – a really rich man's taste put
together by someone who had a great eye"* –
BRIAN SEWELL. At its nucleus is a pretty courtyard and fountains.

🏃 **Buzzz** Cultura Italiana: imbibe the
Italian ambiente at the delightful **Accademia Italiana**, 24 Rutland Gate, SW7 ☎
(071) 225 3474. Superb shows of top Italian artists plus the exemplary Orangerie Italiana (Dec) of priceless oggetti and pitture. Also delicious modern Italian nosh at the
café (Friends only) 🏃 . . . . . . Get handbagged by Margaret Thatcher or collared by Joan
Collins in the new walkie-talkie waxwork displays at **Madame Tussaud's**, Maryle-
bone Rd, NW1 ☎ (071) 465 0860 🏃 . . . . . . The neighbouring **London Planetarium**
☎ (071) 486 2242, offers sky-by-night shows and space exploration drama 🏃 . . . . . . As
temple to the designer decade, the **Design Museum**, Butlers Wharf, Shad Thames,
SE1 ☎ (071) 403 6933, displays design classics (then dive into the Blueprint Café for a
designer bite) 🏃 . . . . . . Photocall: happy snappers get exhibited and snapped up at
Hamiltons Gallery, 13 Carlos Place, W1 ☎ (071) 499 9493, a great favourite of
STEPHEN JONES 🏃 . . . . . . Photo opportunity: focus on ever-changing shows at the **Pho-
tographers' Gallery**, 5 & 8 Great Newport St, WC2 ☎ (071) 831 1772, and **Special
Photographers Company**, 21 Kensington Park Rd, W11 ☎ (071) 221 3489 . . . . 🏃

---------- *Arts centres* ----------

BARBICAN, Barbican Centre, EC2
☎ **(071) 638 8891**
The labyrinthine London base of the **Royal
Shakespeare Company** has its architectural
critics, but few cast aspersions on the drama
(watch the Bard and other heavyweights in the
2 main theatres and avant-garde plays in the
Pit, rated by NED SHERRIN). Nor do they slight
the strains of the **London Symphony
Orchestra** (also housed here), which constantly
thrills under conductor Michael Tilson Thomas.
"*I go for the very good quality of concert*" – MARC
BOHAN. Performance arts and ear-to-the-ground
exhibitions of painting, sculpture and photos
give the concrete caverns an arty buzz.

------------ *Ballet* ------------

🏃 **ROYAL BALLET COMPANY, Royal
Opera House, Covent Garden, WC2**
☎ **(071) 240 1066**
The company sizzles with vitality and spark and,
despite financial setbacks, stands among the
world's greatest. "*It has been injected with new
talent of world class and it's got some of the Bolshoi's star dancers as permanent members*" –
EDWARD THORPE. The brainchild of Dame
Ninette de Valois was nurtured by the legendary choreographer Sir Frederick Ashton,
who introduced the more lyrical, dramatic
English style. Productions are choreographed
by Kenneth MacMillan and David Bintley under
the directorship of Anthony Dowell.

---------- *Bars and cafés* ----------

BAR ITALIA, 22 Frith St, W1
☎ **(071) 437 4520**
Quaff great cappuccino and espresso in this jam-
packed caff. No imposters here – the folk
screaming at the football on the big TV screen
really are Italian. Good late at night, according
to SEBASTIAN SCOTT and SEAN MACAULAY.

MILDRED'S, 58 Greek St, W1
☎ **(071) 494 1634**
"*A wacky vegetarian (sometimes has fish)
restaurant with green Formica tables and lots
of posters – it is the best vegetarian food in the
centre of London*" – SEBASTIAN SCOTT. DUGGIE
FIELDS feels at home in this non-smoking, non-
licensed Soho arties' haunt.

OPEN HOUSE, 321 Portobello Rd, W10
No phone here. Lots of Fobos (faux Bohemians)
though, keeping out of touch in the multi-
layered, multi-media café-gallery. Walls smoth-
ered in silver foil, paintings for sale, bar codes
and post office symbols. Eat pancakes and
toasted sandwiches served by shaven-headed
art heads – DUGGIE FIELDS does.

┌─────────────────────────────────┐

Ballet High
🏃

Alternative dance companies are coming
on by leaps and bounds. EDWARD THORPE
offers his personal critique: **London City
Ballet**, a touring company based at
London Studio Centre, 42-50 York Way,
N1 ☎ (071) 837 3133, "*maintains an ever-
increasing standard – they've grown all
the time and have now got several permanent Russian stars with them*". **DV8
Physical Theatre**, *295 Kentish Town
Rd, NW5* ☎ *(071) 482 3631*, is "*more innovative, more exploratory than anything
else we have, at the forefront of avant-
garde modern dance. They address social
issues – the sex war, homosexuality, everything in the compass of modern society –
with wit and breathtaking physical ability.
One also has to mention* **Rambert
Dance Company**, *94 Chiswick High Rd,
W4* ☎ *(081) 995 4246, because the quality
of their productions is so high, even if one
doesn't like what they actually do*".

└─────────────────────────────────┘

------------ *Clubs* ------------

🏃 **ANNABEL'S, 44 Berkeley Square, W1**
☎ **(071) 629 3558**
The top. Established, Establishment, and exclusive – candidates have to be proposed and sec-
onded before paying the £500 annual fee –
Annabel's holds its place as the "*best nightclub
in the world*" – ANDREW LLOYD WEBBER. Court
cards a-plenty do the Berkeley Square shuffle
alongside film stars, plutocrats and potentates.
Members of all ages receive faultless service,
thanks largely to owner Mark Birley. "*He runs
it beautifully*" – GILES SHEPARD. And he knows
how to pick staff: "*Louis (Emanuelli, the manager) makes sure it is the best-run club
anywhere*" – DOUGLAS HAYWARD. "*The one that
anyone that matters in this country goes to*"
says RICHARD COMPTON-MILLER, who likes the
good food and top-quality champagne. "*Princess
Diana loves it,*" he adds. Not that anyone would
know it, thanks to a star-shielding doorman
rated by SEAN MACAULAY as "*a really nice guy.
It's in a different stratosphere. It's the Rolls-
Royce, it's so well run.*" Others, like ROBERT
SANGSTER, rave too.

THE BRAIN, 11 Wardour St, W1
☎ **071 437 7301**
Open all day (11am–3am), the psychedelic Mecca
for New Agers features a tarot workshop,

One Night Stands

The one night *thang* is still where it's at. Now 'house' is out and 'sexy' is in, according to SEAN MACAULAY: "*The asexual baggy clothes of acid house have been replaced by S&M outfits, erotic dancing and anything fetishistic – to compensate for safe sex.*" Apply a thin layer of rubber and get *Time Out* to find times and venues for **Moist**, **Orgasm** or **Tongue Kung Fu**. On Mondays **Kinky Gerlinky** is still going at the Empire, Leicester Square. Mellower affairs are **Recession Night** at the **Milk Bar** – dress well – and **Slow Motion** (a hit with SEBASTIAN SCOTT) at **Maximus**. Shoe-

horn back into leather for **The Porno House** on Wednesdays, but leave it at home on Thursdays for **Gaz's Rockin' Blues** at **Gossip's**. If you're not beating a path to the **Ministry of Sound** on Friday, you've got to be **High on Hope** at the **Rock Garden**, Covent Garden, and on Saturday choose from more **MOS**, or **Ophelia** at the **Gardening Club**, The Piazza, Covent Garden ("*chances are it'll be a good night*" – ROBERT ELMS), or delve into the New Age, new edge scene for **Serious Intentions** at **The Brain** and have yourself a psychoactive drink.

crystal healing sessions, hypnosis and The Brain Machine – a matter-relaxing helmet which plays music and flashes lights à la 60s spy movie. It's harder work at club time with house/garage/indie/techno/rare groove sounds as well as gay night on Thursday and live bands. "*Good if you're feeling wacky and you have a long stream of consciousness, and you like taking guarana*" – SEBASTIAN SCOTT. Also goes down well with STEPHEN JONES. Serious Intentions is London's serious Saturday-nighter.

CHELSEA ARTS CLUB, 143 Old Church St, SW3 ☎ (071) 376 3311
Redefining the word 'arts', the traditional Bohemian members-only haunt is filling up with PR, media and admen. But that's RICHARD COMPTON-MILLER's only carp. "*I think it's a tremendous success, really the best of its kind. It's got a wonderful garden, a good menu and a good bar, and you often meet faces in there.*" And there are ball games ("*a home for serious billiards and snooker*" – JOHN BROOKE-LITTLE), monthly art exhibitions and objets all over the place.

THE FRIDGE, Town Hall Parade, Brixton Hill, SW2 ☎ (071) 326 5100
No letting up from the 80s wonder club. The Fridge goes on and on playing whatever is hard and hip. "*I enjoy it because it is a big club and good fun to go to with lots of people*" says STEPHEN JONES.

FRED'S, 4 Carlisle St, W1 ☎ (071) 439 4284
The rock 'n' roll drinking club continues to pull in new members – generally by the pony-tail. Music, film and ad folk crowd the horseshoe bar and dance in the tiny basement. "*It still helps if you're wearing a leather jacket and a polo neck and drink your lager straight from the bottle,*"

advises SEAN MACAULAY – who thinks it's "*amazing*". STEPHEN JONES reckons barman Dick's cocktails are the best in the world.

GAZ'S ROCKIN' BLUES, at Gossips, 69 Dean St, W1 ☎ (071) 434 4480
In its 13th year, this is the one-nighter with stamina. DJ Gary (Gaz) Mayall spins ska, reggae, R&B, rockabilly tunes – while ravers of all ages and styles jive, skank and groove away their Thursday nights. SEAN MACAULAY would take his wide-eyed French cousin there for a night on the town. Why? "*They play songs you've heard of. It's very unaffected.*"

♠ THE GROUCHO CLUB, 45 Dean St, W1 ☎ (071) 439 4685
The centre of the universe as far as London's lunching, dining, drinking media types are concerned. High-profile hacks, publishers, film and music folk power through good modern fare in the 3 restaurants or lounge it in the low-lit easy-chaired bar. 11 bedrooms take care of the homeless, and private rooms host functions. "*You're likely to get what they call Groucho Neck – which is clocking all the celebs as they come in . . . Stephen Fry, Lenny Henry, Robbie Coltrane, John Sessions . . .*" – SEAN MACAULAY. Part-owner ED VICTOR launches books there, ALAN CROMPTON-BATT loves the atmosphere, SIR CLEMENT FREUD's been going since it opened, RICHARD COMPTON-MILLER wishes he'd invested in it and STEPHEN JONES finds it "*quite massaging to the brain*". ROBERT ELMS is grateful for its forbearance: "*It's my club and it's home and the staff are unerringly good to me no matter how drunk I get or how often I have erred.*"

HEAVEN, Under the Arches, Craven St, Charing Cross, WC2 ☎ (071) 839 3852
The gay Valhalla, Heaven is still throbbing and

thriving. Straights who want a look in on the hot house scene attend the **Rage** on Thursdays. The **Sound Shaft** operates as a one-nighter venue from the same building, with gay night on Saturday and other attractions throughout the week.

MILK BAR 12 Sutton Row, W1
☎ (071) 439 4655
Cool, diminutive, chic – whitewash and fatigued metal – with a clubby bar feel, life is hip and laid back in this Soho basement. "*It's for people who are sick and tired of slumming it in grimy clubs, who like to dress well and don't want to dance in a way that will give them a hernia. For 80s ravers who have matured a little*" – SEAN MACAULAY. STEPHEN JONES has matured a lot: "*Quite good . . . I tend to feel a bit like granddad.*" Live bands and DJs.

🐾 MINISTRY OF SOUND, 103 Gaunt St, SE1 ☎ (071) 378 6528
What could be more appealing than a teetotal nightclub? Not much, judging by this one's 1,500 groovers and the hours they keep (if you cop out before 9am you have no stamina). Vast industrial warehouse on New Yorker lines, with cinema, VIP lounge (for hip VIPs like Naomi Campbell) and juice bar. "*If you want to be somewhere at 7am, dancing to a brilliant sound system, then it rates*" – ROBERT ELMS. Fri and Sat nights are the ones to plug into.

RONNIE SCOTT'S, 47 Frith St, W1
☎ (071) 439 0747
The oldest and best jazz club in London with electromagnetic pull – this is the smoky room where the big names play. Over 30 years, saxophonist and raconteur Ronnie Scott has seen them all, and continues to host the likes of Andy Sheperd and Courtney Pine. Spot holidaying busman GEORGE MELLY. "*The crowd is knowledgeable and the artists are consistently of a very high standard but it's a bit grumpy*" – ROBERT ELMS. For this is serious stuff: sit and eat, but woe betide you if you talk – there's a quiet bar downstairs and a disco up for chinwaggers and shufflers.

SUBTERANIA, 12 Acklam Rd, W10
☎ (071) 960 4590
Edging Notting Hill, "*it has now established itself as the hip joint where everyone goes on a Friday night*" – SEAN MACAULAY. "*If you want to see the daughter of anyone who made a movie, was a model or went out with Mick Jagger in the 60s, go to Choice on a Saturday night*" – ROBERT ELMS. Funksters queue around the block to squeeze between the heavy black post-industrial-style walls, and stomp to heavy house sounds underneath the Westway. Mon-Wed, live bands. Thurs-Sat, DJs spin from a curved gallery looking down on the dance floor.

TRAMP, 40 Jermyn St, W1
☎ (071) 734 0565
Members only – film stars and glamour merchants, generally – get into this long-established nightclub, owned by co-founder John Gold. Less expensive than Annabel's, at £250 a year – Imran Khan, Liza Minnelli and Pamela Stephenson are among those who fork out. "*A less exclusive crowd, but on the other hand you're liable to see people like Michael Caine, Roger Moore, Sylvester Stallone and George Michael*" divulges RICHARD COMPTON-MILLER.

2 BRYDGES PLACE, WC2
☎ (071) 836 1436
Old world, new world – Brydges bridges the gap. The 10-year-old salon doesn't follow fashion, but Simon Callow, Lucian Freud and other low-key types follow their A-Zs to this narrow alley, to sit in comfy, homy, panelled rooms. "*I like it because it's eccentric and, as a connoisseur of alleys, it's up one of the world's narrowest*" – ROBERT ELMS. SEAN MACAULAY drops in.

WAG CLUB, 35 Wardour St, W1
☎ (071) 437 5534
London's long-standing, serious sounds club is still going strong. Big DJs like Fat Tony hold one-nighters there. SEAN MACAULAY notes "*Kylie Minogue popped up there recently, so it's still on the agenda*".

—— *Fashion designers* ——

ANOUSKA HEMPEL, 2 Pond Place, SW3
☎ (071) 589 4191
A luxurious, beswagged, bescented, Biedermeiered, beMozarted showcase for this demi-couture collection. Simple, elegantly structured evening wear of sumptuous fabrics, Montanaesque daywear, exquisitely matched shoes and hats and a few well-chosen items of furniture create the complete Hempel as experienced by her discreetly untouted royal clientele. BONNIE BROOKS admires.

ANTONY PRICE, 34 Brook St, W1
☎ (071) 629 5262; at A La Mode
An instant dose of over-the-top, show-stopping glamour. Still No 1 with jetsetters and rock queens for his sexy, structured couture evening wear: form-fitting, ruched, off-the-shoulder, or all of the above. Jerry Hall wears little else. He also sees daylight with daywear and men's suits.

🐾 ARABELLA POLLEN at Harvey Nichols, Harrods, Selfridges
Sharp, modern styling for grown-ups. Back in the fold after an over-trendy phase, Pollen's clothes make a statement with their uncompromising use of bold colour, big buttons, classy fabrics and impeccable tailoring. Pollen B offers affordable, witty, workable separates.

BELLA FREUD, 21 St Charles Square, W10 ☎ (081) 968 7579
A new young leading light, Freud has turned her multi-talented family inheritance to re-

creating the sweet and saucy little day dress. Neat, pale dresses and jackets land somewhere between Jackie O sophistication and baby-doll girlishness with suitably tiny, smart accessories.

BETTY JACKSON, 311 Brompton Rd, SW3 ☎ (071) 589 7884
Betty Jackson's shop celebrates the cohesion of her many looks under one roof. Suits everybody with her signature loose, generous shirts and jackets, plus her clinging knitwear. Those who dare, knot and bare, those who doubt, let the shirt hang out. A distinguishing bold print runs through her tightly edited collections.

Britain's Best Designers and Couturiers

I	VIVIENNE WESTWOOD
2	RIFAT OZBEK
3	CATHERINE WALKER
4	JASPER CONRAN
5	TOMASZ STARZEWSKI
6	KATHARINE HAMNETT
7	ARABELLA POLLEN
8	VICTOR EDELSTEIN
9	EDINA RONAY
10	CAROLINE CHARLES

BRUCE OLDFIELD, 27 Beauchamp Place, SW3 ☎ (071) 584 1363
A woman's man, whose sophisticated, beautifully cut and detailed day and evening wear makes the likes of MARIE HELVIN, JOAN COLLINS, Charlotte Rampling and Shakira Caine go weak at the knees. *"Truly glamorous clothes for glamorous women"* – DOUGLAS HAYWARD. On hand from the initial designing to the final fitting (which can take as little as 3-4 weeks) – little wonder his clientele is so devoted.

CAROLINE CHARLES, 56/57 Beauchamp Place, SW3 ☎ (071) 589 5850
Feminine occasion wear for the more mature woman, taking her in wool suits and silk frocks to Ascot and weddings. A resort wear line, too.

CATHERINE WALKER, Chelsea Design Company, 65 Sydney St, SW3 ☎ (071) 352 4626
Favoured by the chic royals (still No 1 on Princess Di's shopping list), this French couturier's very elegant, very expensive clothes whisper style through every clean seam and

uncluttered line. Beading is a current passion. *"She's inspired by all but makes the look her own. She's great, but who can afford her?"* – GAIL ROLFE. Also a bridal shop at 46 Fulham Rd, SW3 ☎ (071) 581 8811.

EDINA RONAY, 141 Kings Rd, SW3 ☎ (071) 352 1085; at Harvey Nichols
Ronay the tailor queen is one of the best around for sharp little suits and dresses that nod briskly to the 60s while striding through the 90s. The Duchess of York suits nothing better. Spot-on wool and cashmere separates wield *"a huge influence on the knitwear industry"* – DOUGLAS HAYWARD. *"My favourite clothes – expensive, but watch for the sales"* – JANE ASHER. CLARE FRANCIS sometimes finds a *"gem"*.

HARDY AMIES, 14 Savile Row, W1 ☎ (071) 734 2436
A wearable English institution, as sanctioned by HM. The ruling classes can still do a one-stop shop here for their little tweed suits, elegant evening wear and couture with clout, all of unimpeachable taste and quality.

JASPER CONRAN, 303 Brompton Rd, SW3 ☎ (071) 823 9134
Jasper has returned to what he does best: classic soft tailoring in cool neutrals, cut by a master. Column dresses of floor-length jersey and simply cut silk viscose travel suits have the Conran stamp and more than a touch of Lauren Bacall-like simple elegance. *"Back on the way up, doing simple, great clothes that people want to wear now"* – GAIL ROLFE.

JEAN MUIR, 59-61 Farringdon Rd, EC1 ☎ (071) 831 0691
Her puritanically pared-down look has eternal appeal. Sleek classics skim from bias-cut silk jersey to her famous knitwear, spun with Muir's exacting eye for colour and tone. *"Outstanding"* – JOAN BURSTEIN. Jean Muir Studio allows the more impecunious into the fold.

KATHARINE HAMNETT, 20 Sloane St, SW1 ☎ (071) 823 1002; at Browns
In the shop's surreal, sub-aqueous atmosphere, Hamnett's separates have their feet firmly on street level with her signature of young-spirited sexiness. Her prolific collections typically feature stark black and white with flashes of colour. Alongside her main line are her denim and cool-wool *primavera* collections.

NICOLE FARHI, 193 Sloane St, SW1 ☎ (071) 235 0877; at Harvey Nichols; menswear 27 Hampstead High St, NW3; at Harrods
Perennial favourite for spirited modern classics, Farhi's appeal lies in her everyday wearability – easy, relaxed jackets over unfussy, earth-coloured knitwear, the perfect trousers, slip o' silk frocks, loose shawl-collared coats over the lot. She suits the tall and slender best. *"I've got*

clothes of hers that are 10 years old and they still look great" – MAUREEN LIPMAN. Menswear is similarly dateless, big square jackets and loose-cut trousers, chunky hand-knits and jersey blazers. JOHN GOLD likes her for *"casual suits".*

PASCALE SMETS, Unit 255, 99-103 Lomond Grove, SE5 ☎ (071) 703 6113
A newcomer who spurns the outrageous for the classical, creating simple and sensibly wearable gear in smoky blues, oatmeals and greys – wide trousers with long heavy tunics, fine viscose bodies with Capri pants. *"She's very good – great skirts, jackets and bodies, with a definite French influence"* – GAIL ROLFE.

PAUL COSTELLOE at Harrods, Liberty, Harvey Nichols
Eminently mixable Irish hand-loomed tweed and linen separates, with a line in shorter, snappy suits and beautiful summer shirts. Perfect for the wedding guest. 1992 saw Breakfast at Tiffany's gamine elegance in sherbet-bright shifts. The understated sister label, Dressage, carries on the classic theme of silk and linen in neutral shades of cream, navy and brown.

♠ RIFAT OZBEK at Browns, Joseph, Harvey Nichols
From the sexy little black dress through high-tech-cum-flower-power white, Ozbek has retained his magpie-like form with his far-flung borrowings of tassels and embroidery. *"An amazing collection last summer, very wearable, with beautiful embroidery. He's back on target"* – GAIL ROLFE. Girls swagger out in both embellished cavalry jackets and Native American suede fringed trousers. His diffusion line, Future Ozbek, has expanded and holds its own with a strong mix of stretchy athleticism and tailored modern classics.

ROLAND KLEIN, 7/9 Tryon St, SW3 ☎ (071) 823 9179
Klein's recent collections of grown-up, confident clothes throw him back into the limelight. Occasion wear: well proportioned, polished day suits, sharp shifts with flowing jackets – all in fab fabrics and with a sheen of couture.

♠ TOMASZ STARZEWSKI, 15-17 Pont St, SW1 ☎ (071) 235 0112
A young man of Polish descent, Starzewski is fashion's brightest rising star, and *"one of our serious hopes for the future. He has a strong work base and a design talent and originality"* – GAIL ROLFE. A dynamic colourist with a love of luscious fabrics, he dresses Princess Diana, Fergie and a host of loyal Ladies. Couture and ready-to-wear.

Man about Town

♠

It has to be said – the Englishman conjures up an altogether different image from his female counterpart. English woman? Think Husky jackets, dowdy tweeds and a sensible headscarf. English man? Think beautifully cut bespoke suits and shirts and handmade shoes – making him the best-dressed of his species worldwide. From where does he get this sartorial splendour? For shirts, there is only one choice: **Turnbull & Asser**, 71 Jermyn St, SW1 ☎ (071) 930 0502. *"A well-deserved reputation for shirts"* – DOUGLAS HAYWARD. BOB PAYTON *"would rather shop there than anywhere"*, ROSS BENSON keeps returning *"like a homing pigeon"* as do JOHN GOLD and DOUGLAS FAIRBANKS JR. GILES SHEPARD collars their ties. The jury is divided over the search for the definitive tailor. There's **Huntsman**, 11 Savile Row, W1 ☎ (071) 734 7441, the top of the grand old Savile Rowers: *"It is safer for me to go there – I do not like the idea of designer clothes for men"* – MARC BOHAN. **Douglas Hayward**, 95 Mount St, W1 ☎ (071) 499 5574, suits Ralph Lauren, LORD LICHFIELD, Roger Moore, JOHN GOLD and now BRUCE OLDFIELD: *"I've just started wearing bespoke suits, I quite enjoy the process."* Or there's dandy: **Tommy Nutter**, 19 Savile Row, W1 ☎ (071) 734 0831, where LORD MONTAGU OF BEAULIEU has staid suits fitted, others peacock in brocade waistcoats. Shoeing the thoroughbred hoof is an easier task: **John Lobb Bootmakers**, 9 St James's St, SW1 ☎ (071) 930 3664. Traditional, beautifully made shoes, handcrafted by artisans. Royal bootmakers to Princes Charles and Philip, beloved of GIORGIO ARMANI, ROSS BENSON and DOUGLAS FAIRBANKS JR, with one reservation: *"They are almost prohibitively expensive."* The finishing touch saves cash: *everyone* buys their socks at M&S.

🔱 **VICTOR EDELSTEIN, 3 Stanhope Mews W, SW7 ☎ (071) 244 7481**
Glorious evening wear for the upper 100. Elegant, precision-cut suits are the understated daytime sisters of sleek cocktail dresses and cascading ball gowns. The perfect little black dress is now available ready to wear (from Harrods, etc).

🔱 **VIVIENNE WESTWOOD, 430 King's Rd, SW10 ☎ (071) 352 6551; 6 Davis St, W1 ☎ (071) 629 3757**
Winner for the 2nd time running of the coveted British Designer of the Year award, Westwood is the grande dame of intelligent street-cred, always unpredictable, always at the cutting edge of European fashion. "*Outstanding, very directional*" – JOAN BURSTEIN. Out of punk hath well-bred tailoring grown – though always with a twist in the tail. "*The most intellectually stimulating clothes in London*" – DUGGIE FIELDS. "*Extraordinarily original, wonderful and humorous – my No 1*" – STEPHEN JONES.

WORKERS FOR FREEDOM, 4A Lower John St, W1 ☎ (071) 734 3766
Never adhering to fashion fads, WFF make their own strong statement for a very definite customer. Quirky tailoring, always well cut and beautifully detailed, neatly blending the hip and hippy for the style- and environment-conscious wearer (their look was spot on at the turn of the decade, but now the novelty has worn off for some). Night-time sees shaded chiffons, slashed and slit for comfort as well as drama.

———— *Film* ————

LONDON FILM FESTIVAL, National Film Theatre, South Bank, SE1 ☎ (071) 928 3232
The movie-goer's festival rather than a film mart, showing British and foreign premieres, the best of the new international films, multi-million-dollar movies, low-budget Third World films, archive flicks, and the Junior Film Fest for young 'uns. "*It's an assiduously run comprehensive event which underlines the work the National Film Theatre does throughout the year – bringing out films that wouldn't find their way in the commercial centre*" – IAIN JOHNSTONE.

———— *Hotels* ————

THE BEAUFORT, 33 Beaufort Gdns, SW3 ☎ (071) 584 5252
2 early-Victorian houses transformed into a pretty, pastelly small hotel with a welcome pricing structure that allows you to treat it as your London home. HILARY RUBINSTEIN likes the fact that everything is included, a 24-hour sitting-room bar, health club membership, Roux brothers *sous-vide* meals in your room (there is no restaurant); gratuities are *not* welcome. SIR CLEMENT FREUD likes it "*for being left alone in*".

THE BERKELEY, Wilton Place, SW1 ☎ (071) 235 6000
Finally come of age (it hits 21 in 1993), The Berkeley runs with the same smooth courtliness as its older siblings in the Savoy Group. All the right stuff for business travellers – private rooms, satellite foreign news, etc, is crowned by service that stamps The Berkeley with distinction. "*I think it is highly desirable that a hotel has an understanding of your personal character and I get that at The Berkeley. I can ring them up and ask for help even when I'm not staying there*" – SIR PETER USTINOV. "*The porters are absolutely fabulous*" – SERENA FASS.

BLAKES, 33 Roland Gdns, SW7 ☎ (071) 370 6701
Anouska Hempel's haute couture hotel, beloved of the celebrity traveller with jaded tastes. Each room is decorated in a different, opulent, manner – billowing pure white, black lacquer, the softest washed pink. "*An extraordinary boutique hotel*" – ROBIN LEACH. "*Contemporary and Bohemian, very special in its own way. Great comfort and style – my favourite is the white room*" – GIORGIO ARMANI. The outrageously expensive restaurant is equally eclectic.

CAPITAL HOTEL, 22 Basil St, SW3 ☎ (071) 589 5171
Small town-house hotel, blending rather grand fin-de-siècle style with Ralph Lauren furnishings. Precision performance under David Levin, "*one of the best hoteliers in the business*" says BOB PAYTON, and LISA BARNARD agrees. So does LIS LEIGH: "*Opulence without flamboyance, a light touch, exquisite service, you could imagine Mozart composing an opera here. And he'd have put in an aria for the restaurant.*" Now Michelin-starred, the restaurant under Philip Britten is top-rated. PAUL HENDERSON recommends: "*He worked under Nico [Chez Nico] for some years but has a lighter style.*" Certainly lighter on the pocket, the carefully chosen £25 set dinner menu is extraordinarily good value.

🔱 **CLARIDGE'S, Brook St, W1 ☎ (071) 629 8860**
Striding towards her 100th birthday without a falter, Claridge's is still No 1. Art Deco opulence is offset by the highest standards of personal service (staff outnumber guests 2:1) to warm the chill marble floors. "*Wonderful and imaginative room service*" – SIR CLEMENT FREUD. "*I love everything about Claridge's, to stay there, to eat there, where it is located . . .*" – KEN HOM. "*We like going home to Claridge's. Ron Jones has developed a tremendous esprit among the staff*" – PAUL HENDERSON. "*There aren't enough words to praise Claridge's – they've won so many awards and Ron Jones keeps getting better and better*" – BOB PAYTON. "*If I've had a frenetic week, it's a great treat to sit in the foyer at Claridge's with a little gentle music and a delicious lunch afterwards. I feel at peace and at home*" – LADY ELIZABETH ANSON. "*I spent my*

The Lungs of London

London is one of the greenest capital cities on the globe. That's not to say its citizens are the most ardent rubbish recyclers or catalytic converter-users, simply that London is blessed with a profusion of gardens and parks. One of the most charming is **Chelsea Physic Garden**, 66 Royal Hospital Rd, SW3, a peaceful, birdsong-filled walled botanic garden, one of Europe's oldest (founded 1673). **Kensington Gardens** and **Hyde Park** together account for over 600 acres of prime real estate. A Sunday stroll holds a mirror to the city: children with nannies at the Round Pond, Rastafarians playing football, politicians manqués blowing soap bubbles at Speakers' Corner. **Hampstead Heath** is the wildest, woodsiest park of London with concealing corners for poetry-reading Hampstead-dwellers and the gayest of gatherings. **Greenwich Park**, the oldest Royal Park, stretches from windswept Blackheath down to the river, with magnificent views of the city's skyline landmarks (St Paul's, Canary Wharf) and the 12C fallen oak that Queen Elizabeth I was said to have hidden in. The deer park at **Richmond Park** is about as rural and rugged as you get so close to a metropolis. The best planned of them all is the **Royal Botanic Gardens** at Kew, 300 acres of beautifully kept gardens, with over 50,000 plant types, beloved of MADHUR JAFFREY and LORD LICHFIELD, who recommends the 1st week in May and the 2nd week in Oct for anyone who loves colour, and mid-winter for tranquillity and the winter shrubs in bloom.

---

wedding night there . . . and I love their ballroom" – LISA BARNARD. BARBARA TAYLOR BRADFORD recommends the restaurant for *"a proper English meal".*

🏃 THE CONNAUGHT, Carlos Place, W1
☎ (071) 499 7070
This most civilized, exclusive, almost painfully low-profile (no brochures and absolutely no advertising) hotel never changes except to make imperceptible improvements which will not alarm long-standing guests, of whom it is inordinately protective. *"The Connaught is still the top in atmosphere and old-world values and standards"* – RICHARD COMPTON-MILLER. *"Still the best,"* echoes BARBARA KAFKA, with back-up vocals from LORD MONTAGU OF BEAULIEU and KEN HOM. *"The only public-school hotel – when I am there I feel properly in Mayfair"* – ALEXANDRE LAZAREFF. LIS LEIGH is won over by *"dignity without fuss, charm without effusiveness. A grown-up, civilized hotel".* The classic Connaught breakfast wins the favour of such hearty types as JULIAN LLOYD WEBBER and ED VICTOR: *"The best bacon and egg breakfast in the world."* The **Grill** continues to lap up praise: *"Excellent lamb chops and good English food – the atmosphere is wonderfully intimidating with waiters in tail coats and white gloves"* – GIORGIO ARMANI. *"A great treat"* – LADY ELIZABETH ANSON.

THE DORCHESTER, Park Lane, W1
☎ (071) 629 8888
Lavishly redecorated (to the tune of over £70 million), with acres of marble bathrooms, swathes of Gainsborough silk, a wealth of chinoiserie and pelmetted to within an inch of its life, the one-time home from home of Noel Coward is hoping to retake its place alongside the other London grandees. *"Really good, and Ricci Obertelli, the general manager, is terrific"* – BOB PAYTON. *"Doing extremely well and trying to get their service 100% right"* – LISA BARNARD. The **Dorchester Club** is stamping its aristocratic seal on the London club scene – it's so exclusive even hotel guests need the manager's permission to enter. **The Oriental** restaurant is highly rated: *"You can't fault the food or the service, but you feel uncomfortable spilling an egg roll on the table cloth"* – MARK MCCORMACK. Barbra Streisand and Michael Jackson have checked in (MJ into the £1,175-a-night penthouse suite).

DUKES HOTEL, 35 St James's Place, SW1
☎ (071) 491 4840
Small, rather clubby hotel with a solid St James's address. *"It's so olde worlde it's wonderful"* – JOHN GOLD. One of London's great concierges, too: *"If you suddenly need a morning suit for Ascot, Thom Broadbent can find you one at a very good price"* – BOB PAYTON.

FOUR SEASONS INN ON THE PARK, Hamilton Place, Park Lane, W1
☎ (071) 499 0888
More than a link in the chain, this Four Seasons runs with the group's expected smooth professionalism and without the oppressive formality

of some of the longer-established London hotels. Suites overlooking Hyde Park are at a premium. The restaurant is a cut above many rivals: "*My absolute best hotel restaurant. Bruno Loubet's appointment as chef was a rather radical appointment for an otherwise straight hotel – Loubet's a flair player in the kitchen. He was doing cuisine de terroir – earthy, peasant dishes – while others were getting caught up in the search for the perfect purée. They've got the best-briefed service staff in London. If you ask about any dish, they know it and can advise you*" – SEAN MACAULAY. ANDREW LLOYD WEBBER was pleasantly surprised: "*Fabulous food and it dares, it's very innovative.*" ALASTAIR LITTLE warms to the "*sensational game*" but warns, "*the wine is over-expensive*". LORD LICHFIELD adds his word of warning: "*Make sure Loubet is cooking when you go.*"

THE GORE, 189 Queen's Gate, SW7
☎ (071) 584 6601

In a narrow, labarynthine building near Kensington Gardens, it is one of London's most appealingly idiosyncratic hotels. Unlike its big sister, Hazlitt's, it houses not one but two terrific eateries (190 Queen's Gate and Bistrot 190, see Restaurants). All the antique prints and bits and pieces have been hunted out by the hoteliers, giving the whole a quirky, unproduction-like air. PS Want to awe a friend? Book them into the Tudor Suite, complete with minstrel gallery and mammoth 4-poster bed.

Britain's Best Hotels

1	CLARIDGE'S · London
2	THE CONNAUGHT · London
3	CHEWTON GLEN · New Milton
4	THE RITZ · London
5	ONE DEVONSHIRE GARDENS · Glasgow
6	THE SAVOY · London
7	GRAVETYE MANOR · East Grinstead
8	THE BERKELEY · London
9	INVERLOCHY CASTLE · Fort William
10	SHARROW BAY · Lake Ullswater

HALCYON, 81 Holland Park, W11
☎ (071) 727 7288

Town-house hotel with a flair for dramatic décor which appeals to celebrities such as Jack Nicholson, Kevin Costner and Michael Douglas. The **Halcyon Restaurant**'s eclectic menu under Robert Ridley finds favour with ALAN CROMPTON-BATT and SEAN MACAULAY.

THE HALKIN HOTEL, Halkin St, SW1
☎ (071) 333 1000

No country-house frills here – all is sleek minimalism, the work of Emporio Armani's creators, Lorenzo Carmellini and Rocco Magnoli, who got Armani himself to design the staff uniforms. Fax machines are just about the only décor in bedrooms, while wildly impressive marble bathrooms give modernism an edge of luxury. "*Very special: a European hotel with enormous Italian style*" – BOB PAYTON.

HAZLITT'S, 6 Frith St, W1
☎ (071) 434 1771

An unlikely location for a charmingly homy hotel, this group of three 1718 houses is an oasis of quiet amid Soho's seedy glitz, with much appeal for film crews. "*Il gives me great pleasure. It isn't especially chic but it has character and someone really cares about how they furnish the rooms*" – HILARY RUBINSTEIN. Sanguine management appeals: "*A friend of mine lost his keys and climbed in through the window and they didn't seem to mind at all*" – ROBERT ELMS. Fresh croissants in the morning but *le tout* Soho is your restaurant.

THE HYDE PARK, Knightsbridge, SW1
☎ (071) 235 2000

General manager Paolo Biscioni has yanked this rather overdecorated Edwardian fuddy-duddy into 90s shape and it's now one of the sharpest hotels around. "*An excellent general manager and it is one of the best hotels for breakfast*" – LISA BARNARD. LOYD GROSSMAN reckons the **Park Room** restaurant is "*One of the best Italians in London. Proper modern Italian food which is great to look at and is just simplicity elevated to the nth degree*". British fare is given the same treatment at the updated **Cavalry Grill & Bar**.

THE LANESBOROUGH, 1 Lanesborough Place, SW1 ☎ (071) 259 5599

After its much hyped opening, it remains to be seen whether Caroline Hunt's latest baby lives up to its birth notices: a bill of £1 million for fitting out each room, staff/guest ratio is 3.7/1 (it's the 0.7 that makes the difference), CD players and bullet-proof windows in every room. The transformed St George's Hospital has an untoppable address (opposite No 1 London, and with a bird's-eye view over the Queen's Garden at Buckingham Palace) and Paul Gayler's modern English cooking in **The Dining Room** is set to challenge London's established stars. "*The conservatory is very original and beautiful and I very much like the individuality of the bedrooms. The dining room is beautiful, with delicious food, particularly the Arbroath smokie mousse*" – LADY ELIZABETH ANSON.

THE LANGHAM HILTON, 1 Portland Place, W1 ☎ (071) 636 1000

The largest building in London on its 1865 opening, the Langham's guests have spanned

Dvořák, Toscanini and WWII soldiers. Now the grand old Langham has been re-created with suitable pomp and ornament – a pukka **Chukka Bar**, the Russian **Tsar's**, **Memories of the Empire** restaurant et al. KEN HOM thinks it hits the spot: *"The location is fantastic – you can walk everywhere . . . the management is committed, it's in an affordable price range, it has a nice luxurious feel without being over the top."* For BOB PAYTON, it's *"the best new corporate hotel. The concierge, Michael Wilson, can make anything happen for you in this town."* RICHARD COMPTON-MILLER marvels at the Charles Laughton Suite: *"amazing, the size of a lot of people's London flats."* Great location: *"It's a good place to meet a friend if you don't want to go right into town"* – MAUREEN LIPMAN.

🔥 THE RITZ, Piccadilly, W1
☎ (071) 493 8181
Over the choirs of cherubim and the glister of gilt, the cry goes up: 'The Ritz is once more a name to be reckoned with!' Now restored to the original over-the-top glamour that attracted guests as disparate as Edward and Mrs Simpson and Andy Warhol, the grand institution continues: tea in the Palm Court, dancing after the theatre. And under Terry Holmes, *"The staff are amazingly unstuffy and good-natured – he has a really upbeat attitude"* – BOB PAYTON. *"We stayed in a beautiful suite, all blue and gold, overlooking St James's Park – fabulous"* – SKYE MACLEOD. Other Ritzy guests include JOAN COLLINS, DOUGLAS FAIRBANKS JR, JOHN GOLD and MADHUR JAFFREY.

🔥 THE SAVOY, The Strand, WC2
☎ (071) 836 4343
Gilbert and Sullivan left the world two legacies: some hummable tunes and this grand old hotel,

built as a result of their success. Superb service, along formal but attentive lines, and a cracking view over Embankment Gardens and the Thames draw songs of praise from MADHUR JAFFREY, DOUGLAS FAIRBANKS JR, and ANDRE PREVIN. The **Grill** under Anton Edelmann is still the best for simple food that ignores the trends. *"It's been a great treat for me from childhood"* – SIMON WILLIAMS. Denis Thatcher, Norman Tebbit, David Frost, JOHN TOVEY and LORD LICHFIELD are stalwarts, as is MAUREEN LIPMAN: *"Very nice food and a civilized atmosphere for lunch."* After 6pm, chatter at the **American Bar** almost drowns out the piano; after 8am, kippers and kedgeree in the **River Restaurant** set you up for another day.

THE STAFFORD, St James's Place, SW1
☎ (071) 493 0111
Long-serving staff (concierge over 15 years, head barman over 30) give this quiet, small (by Cunard standards) hotel a warm, clubby atmosphere which appeals to LORD MONTAGU OF BEAULIEU. The cavernous 350-year-old wine cellars are remarkable.

─────── Music ───────

ENGLISH NATIONAL OPERA, London Coliseum, St Martin's Lane, WC2
☎ (071) 836 3161
Having gained a reputation for superb quality, imagination and experiment, in 1993 the ENO loses general director Peter Jonas and music director Mark Elder for TV man Dennis Marks and young conductor Sian Edwards. If the style is maintained, expect up-to-the-minute operas, re-interpretations of modern masters – the 1991 Brittens were triumphant – and reworkings of

🏃 **Buzzz** Shopaholics should shore up at the new **Chelsea Hotel**, 17 Sloane St, SW1 ☎ (071) 235 4377, with *"the best decorated lounge and restaurant in a London hotel. It's modern but in a non-threatening and non-self-conscious way"* – GLYNN CHRISTIAN 🔥 . . . . . . Popaholics should rock up at The **May Fair**, Stratton St, W1 ☎ (071) 629 7777, to starspot – Prince, Lisa Stansfield, Mick Hucknall, Chris de Burgh, Gloria Estefan, Elton John and Stevie Wonder are just a few May Fairweather friends 🔥 . . . . . . Message in a bottle: Rumour has it that the water used to soothe those overworked vocal chords around the table at **10 Downing Street** is **Abbey Well Natural Mineral Water** 🔥 . . . . . . Clubby appeal? **The Draycott Club** (née Hotel), 24–26 Cadogan Gdns, SW3 ☎ (071) 730 6466, calls its guests 'members' (Donald Trump, Sophia Loren and Bruce Beresford among them); a good faux panelled bar and a small staff that play multiple roles (barman/porter/waiter) 🔥 . . . . . . Blooming lovely: the **Academy Hotel**, 17–21 Gower St, WC1 ☎ (071) 631 4115, is *"an extremely sympathetic hotel in that Georgian Bloomsbury area which is mostly full of lookalike hotels of a tawdry nature. Small, with good food and a jazz pianist who actually plays exceedingly well"* – HILARY RUBINSTEIN . . . . 🔥

classics from Mozart to Richard Strauss. Singing is in English, stagecraft is always sophisticated. *"Just wonderful"* – CLARE FRANCIS. LEO COOPER rates it above Covent Garden for value for money; EDWARD THORPE just rates it.

HENRY WOOD PROMENADE CONCERTS, Royal Albert Hall, Kensington Gore, SW7 ☎ (071) 589 8212

Since 1898, when Henry Wood's concerts began, the Proms (July-Sept) have made top-quality music available to all: 67 concerts in 58 days. Atmosphere is informal, standing room is cheaper and more fun – promenaders come and go as they will. The Last Night sees Brits roused in patriotic frenzy as they chant *Land of Hope and Glory* and wave Union Jacks and umbrellas saying 'Hello Mum'.

ROYAL FESTIVAL HALL, South Bank Centre, SE1 ☎ (071) 928 3002

Britain's best concert hall. Home to the London Philharmonic, it presents more live music than anywhere else in the world in conjunction with **The Purcell Room** and **The Queen Elizabeth Hall**.

🎩 ROYAL OPERA HOUSE, Covent Garden, WC2 ☎ (071) 240 1066

Grand, prestigious and supremely expensive ("why *doesn't* the government cough up like they do in the rest of Europe?" wail opera-lovers), Covent Garden is home to the Royal Opera and Royal Ballet. The wealthy or lucky can see the best in the world sing (and dance) for another few years – renovations have been postponed until 1996. Nicholas Payne comes hot from top op co Opera North as opera director in 1993; Bernard Haitink's musical directorship is generally praised, though some have reservations. Despite the expense, MARC BOHAN, LORD MONTAGU OF BEAULIEU and KEN LANE go.

WIGMORE HALL, 36 Wigmore St, W1 ☎ (071) 935 2141

"It has the best acoustics in London, and it has the kind of atmosphere which is really hard to find – it's a hall with a real tradition. I think the standard of artists appearing there is very high." So says JULIAN LLOYD WEBBER.

——— *Restaurants* ———

See also Hotels.

ALASTAIR LITTLE, 49 Frith St, W1 ☎ (071) 734 5183

The hype might have died down and the fickle faddists moved on but Alastair Little remains constant in serving clever, eclectic food to his faithful following, KEN HOM and STEPHEN JONES among them. The stark interior discourages a few comfort-lovers; the food encourages all. *"After the initial novelty is gone, you still eat so well at Alastair's"* – LOYD GROSSMAN.

🎩 BIBENDUM, Michelin House, 81 Fulham Rd, SW3 ☎ (071) 581 5817

Wildly comfortable and still wildly fashionable, Bibendum is the focal point of Sir Terence Conran's beautiful Art Deco Michelin building. Watched by the Michelin man in his various eccentric guises, diners make like modern Marie-Antoinettes and tuck into French peasant food that has been transformed beyond the average *paysan*'s recognition. *"It's marvellous in every way – a lovely big room, the cooking is fine, Simon Hopkinson is marvellous – just a nice place to go to"* – ELIZABETH DAVID. A compliment from a fellow pro (and a pal): *"I had a lunch there that made me jealous by its flair and execution – just a confit of duck and then fish and chips"* – ALASTAIR LITTLE. *"It's such a joy to go there, it's an oasis of calm and quiet – a*

> **❝** *With modern English cooking, we have the techniques, the refinements that cuisine nouvelle brought to French cooking, and the sensibility of Italian cooking brought to bear on traditional English dishes* **❞**
>
> 🎩 MATTHEW FORT

wonderful way of escaping from the world into great food" – ELIZABETH LAMBERT ORTIZ. *"Honest food and the tables aren't banged together so you can have a conversation"* – SALLY BURTON. *"A beautiful and understated dining room, and Simon Hopkinson is confident enough not to muck around with the food. The cheapest things on the menu, like fish and chips, are the best"* – PAUL HENDERSON. Non-fish and chip eaters *"may have misgivings over the cost but it's still a wonderful place to go and eat"* – MATTHEW FORT. *"One of the best places I have been to, again and again"* – KEN HOM. Vigorous nods from SOPHIE GRIGSON, BRUCE OLDFIELD, JOHN TOVEY, JULIAN LLOYD WEBBER, MARCO PIERRE WHITE and LORD LICHFIELD, who also puts in a good word for **The Oyster Bar** downstairs – *"if you don't want to spend an arm and a leg".*

BISTROT 190, 190 Queen's Gate, SW7 ☎ (071) 581 5666

Younger, more casual sister of **One Ninety Queen's Gate**, it's a small step for chef Antony Worrall Thompson, a great step for London restaurants. The cooking is robust and unpretentious with hearty Mediterranean flavours and bistro staples given a fresh modern direction. Be prepared to settle into the bar for a long wait: only members and guests of The Gore hotel may book. *"One of the great successes of our time – jolly good food, ripping good atmosphere and a place with a real buzz about it"* – MATTHEW FORT.

GLYNN CHRISTIAN can't understand why there aren't more like it. JOHN GOLD agrees.

🦞 THE BRACKENBURY, 129 Brackenbury Rd, W6 ☎ (081) 748 0107

An absolute gem in a less than salubrious part of town, tucked away in an old wine bar on a side street. Adam Robinson's (ex-Alastair Little and 192) eclectic, honest cooking becomes ever-more confident and polished, while the prices, remarkably, don't change. "*Definitely wonderful. It's at the end of an uninteresting street which makes it surprising*" – LORD LICHFIELD. It is up there with the best of them for JONATHAN MEADES: "*Spell-bindingly good. Adam Robinson is very skilful and it's a pleasant place to eat as well, the staff have an intelligent idea about hospitality, they're not hovering over your wine glass all the time.*" ANDREW LLOYD WEBBER states firmly: "*The best restaurant I've been to in London for 5 years. I had a fabulous dish of tongue in lentils and a wild mushroom risotto with truffles for about £4.50 which I'd had the night before at Harry's Bar for £28. You practically have to put your child down at birth.*"

CHRISTOPHER'S, 18 Wellington St, WC2 ☎ (071) 270 4222

The latest magnet for media magnates, screenies and glossies (Sir Robin Day, Stephen Fry, etc), this glam steak and lobster house offers whopping T-bones and rumps, great chips, divine creamed veggies, smoked tomato soup and other mod dishes with a New York flavour. It has also made co-proprietor Christopher Gilmour *the* most desirable man about town.

CIBO, 3 Russell Gdns, W14 ☎ (071) 371 2085

"*One of the three modern Italians (along with Riva and River Café) cooking upmarket peasant food – young, fresh, exciting. Terrible pictures, but a good atmosphere*" – LORD LICHFIELD. "*Good earthy food*" reckons MARTIN SKAN. MARK MCCORMACK is another fan.

🦞 CLARKE'S, 124 Kensington Church St, W8 ☎ (071) 221 9225

The most sensible restaurant around and the cleverest. Sally Clarke cooks a 4-course, no-choice dinner and a small-choice lunch and always gets it right. Grilled quail with chilli-spiced lentils, or lamb with rosemary, Tuscan beans and puréed garlic might be on offer. "*I've never had a dish there that wasn't spot on*" – PAUL HENDERSON. "*You have to pretend you're going to someone's house for dinner but you're in very good hands*" – LADY ELIZABETH ANSON. Early training in top California restaurants shows in the robust simplicity of the menus, the freshest seasonal ingredients and the stunningly good breads, but dislocated Californianism this ain't. "*World class*" – BOB PAYTON. KEN HOM, GEOFFREY ROBERTS, BARBARA KAFKA and JOAN BURSTEIN love it, as does LIS LEIGH for "*freshness, warmth and charm*".

DELL'UGO, 56 Frith St, W1 ☎ (071) 734 8300

The latest on the fast-becoming-ubiquitous Mediterranean cuisine front is also the latest from f-b-u Antony Worrall Thompson, along with the f-b-u Simpsons of Cornhill gang (Alan Crompton-Batt, Roy Ackermann . . .). Named after a Tuscan olive oil, dell'Ugo graduates over 3 floors from Soho café to gents' club. Bistro 190-ish nosh – deluxe bruschetta, one-pot dishes such as fish stew.

🦞 THE GREENHOUSE, 27A Hay's Mews, W1 ☎ (071) 499 3314

Gary Rhodes's revolution in English cooking leads right back to England: "*He's a man with a mission*" – MARTIN SKAN. In a bright, airy room surrounded by pagan offerings of fruit, vegetables and foliage, diners re-acquaint themselves with the taste of good "*English cooking done with great style and panache. It's solid, substantial fare but it's zippy for all of that. He brings together things English and non-English: I had fried mackerel with a mustard sauce and lentils which was absolutely superb*" – MATTHEW FORT. "*With things like faggots and bread and butter pudding, Gary Rhodes interprets original dishes faithfully, which is actually incredibly exotic – it's easier to find good Gujerati than good English food*" – JONATHAN MEADES. JOHN TOVEY warms to the Greenhouse.

Star Fish
🦞

Where the vinegar ain't vintage, the chips are *not* frites and *The Sun* makes an indelible impression on hands if not minds . . . it can only be that venerable institution the British chippy. Where do the big fish swim for a better batter? **Geales**, 2 Farmer St, W8 ☎ (071) 727 7969, is "*the Caprice of fish shops, showbizzy clientele in a 50s tea-shop atmosphere and very good cheap champagne*" – LOYD GROSSMAN. STEPHEN JONES agrees, but gives higher marks to **The Seashell**, 49 Lisson Grove, NW1 ☎ (071) 723 8702 ("*absolutely delicious*"), as does JOHN GOLD ("*ultimate cod and chips*"), to the audible sniffs of purist fish fancier MAUREEN LIPMAN: "*It's very designer chippy now.*" Along with JONATHAN MEADES she votes for the chippy that's No 1, **Nautilus**, 29 Fortune Green Road, NW6 ☎ (071) 435 2532; and, for the complete kosher fish experience, **Grahame's Fish Restaurant**, 38 Poland St, W1 ☎ (071) 437 3788, where beer batter bows to matzo meal.

GREEN'S, 36 Duke St, SW1
☎ **(071) 930 4566**
Solid standby for traditional English food (with interesting departures in the specials). A club away from the club for besuited gentlemen, a canteen away from the canteen for the staff of Christie's. MARC BOHAN and LADY ELIZABETH ANSON are keen Greens. A second Green's has opened in Westminster (Marsham Court, Marsham St, SW1 ☎ (071) 834 9552), so *"now Heseltine and people can go out to Green's and have oysters and champagne and grouse – English, simple, rather aristocratic food"* – RICHARD COMPTON-MILLER.

Britain's Best Restaurants

I	LE MANOIR AUX QUAT' SAISONS · Great Milton
2	HARVEY'S · London
3	LA TANTE CLAIRE · London
4	L'ARLEQUIN · London
5	BIBENDUM · London
6	NICO AT NINETY · London
7	L'ORTOLAN · Shinfield
8	FOUR SEASONS INN ON THE PARK · London
9	THE GREENHOUSE · London
10	GIDLEIGH PARK · Chagford

HARRY'S BAR, 26 South Audley St, W1
☎ **(071) 408 0844**
Buzzing throughout the recession with young girls flashing AmEx cards and toying with lamb's lettuce, this elegant dining club is another winner from the Mark Birley stable. Princess Diana, LADY ELIZABETH ANSON, MARCHESA DI SAN GIULIANO FERRAGAMO, ANDREW LLOYD WEBBER, RAYMOND BLANC, SKYE MACLEOD, DOUGLAS HAYWARD, JOHN GOLD, ROBERT SANGSTER and JOAN BURSTEIN join the groupies for top-flight Italian cooking. And the food *is "very, very good. It's very elegant, a most bizarre, odd place – you wouldn't think a stained glass window would work but it does there. It is Mark Birley at his best doing what he is best at"* – ANOUSKA HEMPEL. *"The top Italian restaurant in London"* – MARK MCCORMACK. *"It's a great treat for me to go to any of Mark Birley's places – he runs them beautifully"* – GILES SHEPARD. *"Mark Birley is a very fastidious man – he goes to a lot of trouble to make sure things are right"* – MARTIN SKAN. Reaching this standard doesn't

come cheap: *"I like it very much but it's wildly overpriced"* – SIR TERENCE CONRAN.

🍴 **HARVEY'S, 2 Bellevue Rd, Wandsworth, SW17** ☎ **(081) 672 0114**
Now that Marco Pierre White's storm-raising is confined to the kitchen, there are fewer tales of the unexpected at Harvey's and more unstinting praise for his culinary genius. *"Just heaven. His oyster tagliatelle really is . . ."* sighs SOPHIE GRIGSON. *"Probably the best food in London – Marco's the man most on form"* – ALAN CROMPTON-BATT. *"I do think now it's the best food in London,"* echo LORD LICHFIELD and MATTHEW FORT: *"I think that Marco's cooking is more interesting than ever – very, very, very, very good."* JONATHAN MEADES, NED SHERRIN, LADY ELIZABETH ANSON, LISA BARNARD, JANE ASHER and GEOFFREY ROBERTS would have to agree.

THE IVY, 1 West St, WC2 ☎ **(071) 836 4751**
Another winner from Chris Corbin and Jeremy King who transformed Le Caprice, The Ivy reopened as *"a fashionable restaurant created almost overnight"* – ALAN CROMPTON-BATT. No fly-by-night though, it is run with the same seasoned, seamless efficiency and attention to detail as its big sister. *"Right on form because of the hands-on approach of those 2 boys – there's always one of them there"* – NED SHERRIN. *"Very impressive – good English stuff and it fills a need for a good post-theatre restaurant"* – ANDREW LLOYD WEBBER. Such staples as fish cakes and Caesar salad (*"the kind of food one wants to eat late at night"* – SALLY BURTON), though perfectly realized, won't challenge the post-theatre crowd, but the contemporary oil paintings (*"amazing boldness to commission works of art from the great British artists"* – LOYD GROSSMAN) and the people-spotting make food a secondary consideration. *"The wooden panels around the walls mean you can hide from other people but still observe them"* – SEBASTIAN SCOTT. *"Fittingly for the theatre district, they have created a restaurant which is an amazing piece of theatre but is still unpretentious and comfortable"* – LOYD G.

🍴 **KENSINGTON PLACE, 201 Kensington Church St, W8** ☎ **(071) 727 3184**
This eatery's stark interior provides a fitting foil against which media folk make themselves heard (*"Very good if you don't want anyone to hear what you are saying"* – SEBASTIAN SCOTT). The noise and bustle may vibrate the glass walls and discourage the faint-hearted but Rowley Leigh's eclectic, health-conscious cooking more than compensates. *"The best food in London,"* sighs his old chum JONATHAN MEADES. *"Light without being mingy and the flavours sing through"* – SOPHIE GRIGSON. MATTHEW FORT prefers less din during dins, but acknowledges, *"In terms of food it's in the same league as Bibendum and they turn out 350 meals a day of extraordinarily high quality"*. MARCO PIERRE WHITE drops in *"for a quick and simple dinner if*

World Food 1

Londoners are no longer prepared to accept bland approximations of other nations' cuisines. They want their food spicy, they want it authentic, they want it regional, they want it around the corner. A new school Thai recommended by SOPHIE GRIGSON is **Sri Siam**, 14 Old Compton St, W1 ☎ (071) 434 3544, who *"are conscious of getting things close to the original"*. ROBERT ELMS sighs for *"Sri Siam's fish wrapped in banana leaf with 2 dipping sauces"*. Thai-ing for second place are **Busabong Too**, 1A Langton St, SW10 ☎ (071) 352 7414, praised by LORD LICHFIELD, and **Benjarong**, 95 Fulham Palace Rd, W6 ☎ (081) 741 5808, where kanom jeep (dumplings) and mee krob (thin fried noodles in caramel and port) come hotly recommended. The Cantonese **Fung Shing**, 15 Lisle St, W1 ☎ (071) 437 1539, *"is a wonderful exploration of the exotic and is invariably delicious,"* says MATTHEW FORT, and ALAN CROMPTON-BATT agrees. Battling for Chinese domination in Lisle Street is **Mr Kong** at No 21 ☎ (071) 437 7341, where BOB PAYTON can tell you *"18 things you must eat"*. A little out of the way, **New Peking Restaurant**, 139 Northfield Rd, W13 ☎ (081) 579 9935, has *"roast belly mutton which is miraculous, crispy and wonderful"* – ELISABETH LAMBERT ORTIZ. For that Gujerati vegetarian meal, MATTHEW FORT points you towards **Kastoori**, 188 Upper Tooting Rd, SW17 ☎ (081) 767 7027, for *"a freshness and delicacy and sprightliness to be found in very few Indian restaurants"*. ELIZABETH DAVID's superior curry house is the Pakistani **Kundan**, 3 Horseferry Rd, SW1 ☎ (071) 834 3434, *"A lovely restaurant, not very well known."* And the list continues. . . .

I don't want to dress up". *"A little crowded, the tables are jammed together, it's noisy, friendly and very nice"* – MARK MCCORMACK. Good for New World wines and new food combos, *"trendy food and clients"* – RICHARD COMPTON-MILLER.

L'ALTRO, 210 Kensington Park Rd, W11 ☎ (071) 792 1066
Cibo's younger sister. In a crumbling Italianate courtyard setting, tuck into pasta, fish and seafood (magnificent octopus and lobster), dished in hand-painted ceramics. *"Eat one course and stagger out – huge and delicious portions"* – LORD LICHFIELD.

LANGAN'S BRASSERIE, Stratton St, W1 ☎ (071) 493 6437
Alternately puffed and criticized, Langan's still attracts the rich and glitzy, even if the menu does not always delight. *"Whatever anyone might say, it's still a great restaurant by any standards"* – ALAN CROMPTON-BATT. JOHN GOLD agrees, although GEORGE MELLY feels it's lost something since Peter Langan's death: *"It's still a very nice restaurant but I really liked the old monster – the point of it was the tension engendered by his appearance or non-appearance."*

🍴 L'ARLEQUIN, 123 Queenstown Rd, SW8 ☎ (071) 622 0555
Very French, very tasteful, very understated, Christian Delteil's restaurant maintains its high standards of serious cooking and service. *"Restrained, delicate but infinitely satisfying food"* – MATTHEW FORT. *"One of the most underrated restaurants in London; very close to Nico and Tante Claire in quality"* – PAUL HENDERSON. LADY ELIZABETH ANSON and MARCO PIERRE WHITE join the chorus. The assiette gourmande, or selection of puddings, recalls schooldays: *"six of the best"* cries SEAN MACAULAY.

🍴 LA TANTE CLAIRE, 68 Royal Hospital Rd, SW3 ☎ (071) 352 6045
No 1 on the chef's busman's holiday tour. *"It is a nice mixture of modern cuisine and traditional approach in a lovely environment where you can relax with very, very good food"* – RAYMOND BLANC. Pierre Koffmann's classic, impeccable French cooking places him squarely in London's top handful of chefs: *"A very good, serious cook"* – BARBARA KAFKA; *"the highest level of cooking"* – LOYD GROSSMAN; for PAUL HENDERSON, he's *"the best chef in the world with foie gras"*. FREDERIC RAPHAEL, ANDREW LLOYD WEBBER, LIS LEIGH, MARCO PIERRE WHITE and MATTHEW FORT marvel, as does JANE ASHER: *"Food to rival any in the world."* The set-price lunch (£23.50 for 3 courses, coffee and petits fours) makes the Koffmann magic accessible to the impecunious.

🍴 LE CAPRICE, Arlington House, 17 Arlington St, SW1 ☎ (071) 629 2239
Le Caprice has it all – glam backdrop, well-

World Food 2

Korean and Vietnamese are taking over from Thai as the cuisines to watch: **Jin**, 16 Bateman St, W1 ☎ (071) 734 0908, is a cut above all Korean rivals, while in the Vietnam camp, **Nam Long at Le Shaker**, 159 Old Brompton Rd, SW5 ☎ (071) 373 1926, *"feels like a caff but food is unexpectedly good"* – LORD LICHFIELD. **Salloos**, 62 Kinnerton St, SW1 ☎ (071) 235 4444, is the maharajah of Indian restaurants, *"for serious meat-eaters"* – LORD L. For an unserious Indian, ANOUSKA HEMPEL and DUGGIE FIELDS recommend **The Star of India**, 154 Old Brompton Rd, SW5 ☎ (071) 373 2901, where frescoed walls and soaring opera are the main attraction. **Suntory**, 72 St James's St, SW1 ☎ (071) 409 0201, remains the supreme Japanese experience, while **Caravan Serai**, 50 Paddington St, W1 ☎ (071) 935 1208, and **Buzkash**, 4 Chelverton Rd, SW15 ☎ (081) 788 0599, fight over the laurels for best Afghan; sample the mahi nan (spiced prawns in nan bread) or murgh hazara (creamy chicken) before casting your vote. **Royal China**, 13 Queensway, W2 ☎ (071) 221 2535, gets LORD L's approval for *"wonderful dim sum – but you have to queue at weekends"*. Check out **Now and Zen**, Upper St Martin's Lane, WC2 ☎ (071) 497 0376, for the most striking design yet by Rick Mather, and sizzling modern Chinese food. YAN KIT SO reveals her short but definitive list of Chineseries: **The Country Club**, 160 College Rd, Harrow-on-the-Hill ☎ (081) 427 0729, for *"authentic Shanghai food – noodles and dumplings and steamed meat buns, eel cut into sections and steamed with Chinese wolfberries"*; **Golden Chopsticks**, 1 Harrington Rd, SW7 ☎ (071) 584 0855, looks like nothing much but is a revelation: *"Mrs Choy's speciality is her chicken, hand-torn, poached in stock and cooked in stock and sesame oil and ginger, also deep-fried soft-shell crab"* . . .

executed, reliable food, smooth service and a devoted, high-profile following. *"If you enjoy saying 'Oh, look, there's so and so' it always comes up trumps"* – GEORGE MELLY. Praise all round for consummate professionals Chris Corbin and Jeremy King, *"everyone's favourite restaurateurs. It's a fantastic achievement that even 10 years later people are still talking about it as if it were the newest, trendiest place"* – LOYD GROSSMAN. *"I'm very fond of the Caprice, they don't make a performance out of dinner"* – VICTOR EDELSTEIN. *"Almost unbeatable for value and perfection"* – CLARE FRANCIS. *"My favourite café"* – JOHN TOVEY. *"The best chips, I have them with everything"* – SALLY BURTON. She has chef Mark Hix to thank for that: *"He is excellent, the food is really on form"* – JONATHAN MEADES. PAUL HENDERSON votes for the fish cakes and Caesar salad. ED VICTOR, MARK MCCORMACK, STEPHEN JONES, MARTIN SKAN, JOAN BURSTEIN, JEFFREY ARCHER and NED SHERRIN all let the whim take them at times.

LE GAVROCHE, 43 Upper Brook St, W1 ☎ (071) 408 0881

Albert Roux and *fils* Michel run Le Gavroche like a luxurious, smooth and expensive machine. A temple to gastronomy at which many worship (*"Michel Jr has really invigorated everyone"* – GEOFFREY ROBERTS), although the complex haute cuisine leaves others unconverted: *"A place to dine in once a year at most"* – CLARE FRANCIS. MARCO PIERRE WHITE is decidedly on the pro side: *"Without a doubt the best restaurant in Britain, it's in a league of its own from the moment you walk through the door until the moment you are served coffee – the whole lot smells professional. Michel Jr has grown into his father's shoes and I have great faith that Le Gavroche will have another 25 years of great success."* So is SIR CLEMENT FREUD: *"My favourite restaurant and my favourite dish is the soufflé Suissesse."* JONATHAN MEADES belongs to the other camp: *"It's had its day – there are so many restaurants doing more interesting food that are more of a pleasure to go to."* The set-price lunch is welcomed by those with tastes richer than their wallets.

LEITH'S, 92 Kensington Park Rd, W11 ☎ (071) 229 4481

Leith's is Leith's is Leith's. Not at the cutting edge of modern cookery, but the flagship of Prue Leith's business empire is relied on for topnotch classic nosh by many devotees: *"She is the Maria Callas of cooking – she seems to enjoy it so much which must be the secret"* – SIR PETER PARKER. *"Exceptionally good"* – SERENA FASS. *"A major influence in food . . . sad she's not open for lunch"* – LORD LICHFIELD.

LE PONT DE LA TOUR, 36D Shad Thames, SE1 ☎ (071) 403 8403

The Conran philosophy on a plate – dead simple and frightfully well done. Chef David Burke's origins (Irish, ex-Ballymaloe) reveal themselves in the Dublin Bay Prawns and Colcannon potatoes, while Sir Terence's emerge in the cool five-section 'Gastrodome': crustacea bar, grill, restaurant, cellar and salon privé, all decked out à la ocean liner. "*It sounds big-headed but I do think it is one of the best things in London*" – SIR TERENCE CONRAN. His biographer LOYD GROSSMAN might agree: "*Every time Terence does something he moves the goal posts for everyone else.*" The jury's still out, thinks MARTIN SKAN: "*The position is good and it's attractively decorated; the sommelier is excellent but the food uneven.*" No wild surprises on the menu, but a few on the wine list – generally on the weighty pounds and pence side of the page.

L'INCONTRO, 87 Pimlico Rd, SW1 ☎ (071) 730 6327

Sophisticated, urban Italian which bucks the trend set by its rustic compatriots. "*Northern Italian elegance, bravura cooking where the peasant has become king*" – LIS LEIGH. Sleek diners, steep prices. "*Langoustine which is beyond beautiful, the best Italian I have ever had in England*" – STEPHEN JONES. "*Stylish, good food (especially when white truffles are in season) and wine*" – PAUL HENDERSON.

MOSIMANN'S, 11B W Halkin St, SW1 ☎ (071) 235 9625

That you have to pay twice – once for membership and again for the dinner – doesn't deter Anton Mosimann's admirers. Take BOB PAYTON: "*It's really underrated, not only is Anton charming and likeable but he can bloody well cook.*" Or MARK MCCORMACK: "*One of the great geniuses of modern culinary art. His presentation, the food, his imagination and the whole room are quite extraordinary.*" Words of dissent from ANDREW LLOYD WEBBER and SIR TERENCE CONRAN go over the heads of fans JEFFREY ARCHER, ROBIN LEACH and SALLY BURTON, who powders her nose at "*the best ladies' room in the world, it's so pretty and has everything you need – phone, make-up remover, needle and thread, mouthwash and a fire going in winter. A wonderful restaurant for a grand occasion or for something simple*".

NEAL STREET RESTAURANT, 26 Neal St, WC2 ☎ (071) 836 8368

The mushroom man's smart and successful ristorante is so established, it tends to be overlooked. "*Part of life in London – one of the handful of Italian restaurants worth going to, largely thanks to Antonio Carluccio*" – LOYD GROSSMAN. RAYMOND BLANC is of the same mind: "*The best I've found.*" Modern, exciting food, expensive, but JILLY COOPER isn't deterred. Next door's **Carluccio's** (run by la Signora) sells sublime delicatessen fare.

♣ NICO AT NINETY, 90 Park Lane, W1 ☎ (071) 409 1290

Nomadic Nico has reached the pinnacle of the London restaurant scene and is staying on his throne. Powerful, exciting food, executed with great sophistication and served with the sort of effortless efficiency to which others aspire. "*The best cook is Nico*" – BOB PAYTON; "*Nico, Harvey's and Tante Claire rule the roost*" – MATTHEW FORT; PAUL HENDERSON expands: "*We have followed Nico from Dulwich to Battersea to Shinfield to Westminster and now to W1 and the cooking keeps getting better.*" DAME BARBARA CARTLAND, LISA BARNARD and TERRY HOLMES would follow him too.

Neighbourhood Restaurants
♣

Village London finds its tastebuds satisfied and its pockets remarkably unscathed at a rash of modern eateries, often occupying lofty rooms above pubs and other unlikely spaces. **Harvey's Café** (no relation to the Marco stable), 358 Fulham Rd, SW10 ☎ (071) 352 0625, a canary-yellow diner atop the Black Bull, offers fresh-baked warm bread, great salmon fish cakes,, and much of what's modish. Over the river in Barnes, **Riva**, 169 Church Rd, SW13 ☎ (081) 748 0434, is sailing in the wake of the River Café. "*It displays the wealth of Italian regional cooking*" – MATTHEW FORT. "*All the rustic stuff with a lot of flair*" – LOYD GROSSMAN. "*I once employed Andrea Riva . . . I wish I still did. Really good value*" – LORD LICHFIELD. Just round the corner, **Sonny's**, 94 Church Rd ☎ (081) 748 0383, offers cracking good value, gutsy food (rolled shoulder of lamb with flageolets, chocolate polenta with a blood orange sabayon), and is a favourite with ALASTAIR LITTLE. Still, in essence, a neighbourhood restaurant (for Earl's Courtiers), is **Lou Pescadou**, 241 Old Brompton Rd, SW5 ☎ (071) 370 1057; locals such as NED SHERRIN drop in on the off-chance. LOYD GROSSMAN's a regular: "*One of the best places if you want a late-night bowl of pasta or very good fish soup. It is vraiment français including rather aggressive service – like an instant holiday.*"

OAK ROOM, Le Meridien, Piccadilly, W1
☎ (071) 734 8000
This lavishly panelled and gilded hotel dining room scores even before the food arrives: *"The greatest dining room"* – GLYNN CHRISTIAN; *"one of the most beautiful lunchtime places in London"* – JULIAN LLOYD WEBBER. Not that what's on the plate doesn't register: *"I think it has some of the finest cooking. David Chambers is just bloody good; his sense of presentation and the refinement of his cooking is on the highest level in London. It's a great place for secret power lunching"* – LOYD GROSSMAN.

ORSO, 27 Wellington St, WC2
☎ (071) 240 5269
A buzzing hive of activity – media/theatre people compete for colour with primary painted plates, an open kitchen and nuova northern Italian cooking: *"Everything's out on show, including the people"* – RICHARD COMPTON-MILLER. Perennial stars are the miniature pizzas: *"Just heaven, marvellous olive oil and herbs on a lovely thin base"* – CLARE FRANCIS. LORD MONTAGU OF BEAULIEU pops in after the opera; STEPHEN JONES, SEAN MACAULAY and MAUREEN LIPMAN happily enter the fray. Credit cards not accepted, which infuriates MARK MCCORMACK.

🐟 RIVER CAFE, Thames Wharf, Rainville Rd, W6 ☎ (071) 381 8824
Sub-River Café Italians have sprung up all over London but this meticulously undesigned space remains numero uno: *"The one that broke the mould"* – LOYD GROSSMAN. The Ruth Rogers/Rose Gray team doesn't muck around with the recipe: top-quality ingredients given a straightforward treatment. *"The prices are rather ridiculous but the quality is always first-rate and the cooking has really gutsy, assertive flavours"* – SOPHIE GRIGSON. *"The food is excellent – Italian food at its best"* – SIR TERENCE CONRAN. *"The best Italian in London and a wonderful place to be – you run into a lot of friends"* – ED VICTOR. Others in the running are GEORGE MELLY, MARTIN SKAN, SKYE MACLEOD and STEPHEN JONES.

SAN LORENZO, 22 Beauchamp Place, SW3 ☎ (071) 584 1074
Glossy old-style Italiana which still pulls the international fash with cash – the Princess of Wales, BRUCE OLDFIELD, the Duchess of York, Jack Nicholson, Rifat Ozbek, JOHN GOLD, RICHARD COMPTON-MILLER, Twiggy and many more loyal lunchers.

SYDNEY STREET, 4 Sydney St, SW3
☎ (071) 352 3433
Australia is colonizing Britain via this chic tuckshop in Chelsea – note the boomerang bar and Aboriginalesque mural – serving modern Australian food. Reef fish is flown in fresh along with the odd esoteric import of emu steak and crocodile. No flies on chef Mary-Jane Hayward (ex-Berowra Waters, NSW), whose exciting and intelligent cooking draws on the best of the Orient and Occident. Kick off with a Cascade (Tassie beer) and continue in the same New World vein.

TURNER'S, 87-89 Walton St, SW3
☎ (071) 584 6711
Brian Turner's high prices and refined French cooking don't please everybody but the Yorkshireman has his staunch fans such as LADY ELIZABETH ANSON and BARBARA KAFKA: *"With Brian Turner I consistently have the best food in London. He does a ravishing brandade of sole – it's like silk."*

——— Shopping ———

Establishment international designers live in and around **New Bond Street** and **Sloane Street**. **Knightsbridge** has the top stores and classy high-street shops, giving way to bastions of old-fashioned boutiquery towards Hyde Park Corner. Young trendy fashion areas are **Floral Street**, **Beauchamp Place** and 'Brompton Cross', where Fulham Rd turns into Brompton Rd and some of the chic-est shops and caffs can be found. **King's Road** is still a major stomping ground on Saturday afternoon – Whistles, Jigsaw, Hobbs and co at the Sloane Square end,

🐟 **Buzzz Harvey's Canteen,** Chelsea Harbour, Marco Pierre White's second string in partnership with Harbour-dweller Michael Caine, has got Deals neighbour LORD LICHFIELD intrigued 🐟 . . . . . . Say it with flour: Ditch the roses and have delivered instead a basket of yummy home-baked mini muffins from **Beverly Hills Bakery**, 3 Egerton Terrace, SW3 ☎ (071) 584 4401. It's a café too 🐟 . . . . . . Britain comes back to London in meat 'n' fishy style at **The Quality Chop House**, 94 Farringdon Rd, EC1 ☎ (071) 837 5093, *"solely providing the best prepared food of its kind in London"* – MATTHEW FORT 🐟 . . . . . . Meaty 2: Albert Roux's **Boucherie Lamartine**, 229 Ebury St, SW1, is where MATTHEW FORT and SALLY BURTON further satisfy carnivorous desires 🐟 . . . . . . Restaurateur turns retailer 2: Pick up Sally Clarke's heavenly breads at **& Clarke's**, 122 Kensington Church St, W8 . . . . 🐟

second-hand chic at World's End, with over-priced designer boutiques for the boys in the middle. **Soho** remains the hotbed of new street fashion. The 'West Soho' bunch are centred on **Newburgh Street**. **St Christopher's Place** and **Covent Garden Market** are part-trendy, part-touristy, part-chi-chi. **Brick Lane** market (Sun, dawn) is for earnest bargain hunters; **Greenwich** (Sun) yields a few incredible finds among the junk; **Bermondsey** (Fri, daybreak) is the best source of antiques (where all the trade go). Hit **Camden Passage**, Islington, at weekends, for antiques, second-hand lace, clothes and jewellery; and trendsville **Camden Lock** for new crafty clothes and accessories.

A LA MODE, 36 Hans Crescent, SW1
☎ (071) 584 2133
Modish selection of big-name labels which varies according to the current collections. Expect to find Gaultier, Isaac Mizrahi, Antony Price, Christian Lacroix (clothes and baubles), Geoffrey Beene and Tomasz Starzewski.

AQUASCUTUM, 100 Regent St, W1
☎ (071) 734 6090
For almost 150 years, Aquascutum has been maintaining high British clothing standards of quality, immutability and ever-so-slight dreariness so successfully that they now export the same to NY, Paris, Montreal and Japan. Still the best place for raincoats, top coats and Margaret Thatcher. JEFFREY ARCHER reveals he wears nothing else.

ASPREY, 165 New Bond St, W1
☎ (071) 493 6767
The purple box of Asprey turns up in all the best houses, concealing such essentials as the perfect signet ring and the watch of watches. Upscale wedding list stuff too: silver, leather, china, tableware, clocks, luggage and antiques. SALLY BURTON and ANOUSKA HEMPEL brave the uniformed doormen.

BROWNS, 23-27 S Molton St, W1
☎ (071) 491 7833
London's designer fashion emporium – Joan Burstein and team show a tightly edited selection of collections from Azzedine Alaïa, Jil Sander, Moschino, Sonia Rykiel, Donna Karan, Romeo Gigli and Byblos. Those who strive for Brownie points include Madonna, JOAN COLLINS, Liza Minnelli, MARIE HELVIN, Elton John and Patrick Swayze. The Browns phenomenon is taking over South Molton St: under its umbrella are G Gigli at 38/39, The **Genny Boutique** at 18 and **Labels for Less** at 45.

BURLINGTON ARCADE, Piccadilly, W1
The best the Brits can offer, all under one covered arcade. Here's where you will find the finest linen, the best cashmere, monogrammed slippers, silk waistcoats . . . all the indulgences necessary to lady and gentleman. Heavenly scents from **Penhaligon's** the perfumier, beau-tifully crafted men's shoes from **Edward Green**, antique and Art Deco trinkets and jewels from **Demas**, every pen imaginable from **Pen Friends**. For cashmere, it's a soft tug-of-war between **N Peal** (gorgeous jewel-bright or muted colours), **Lord's** (the oldest inhabitant in the arcade, est 1774, Valerie Louthan cashmeres and classic knitwear), **S Fisher** (all sorts of woollens as well as socks and ties) and **Berks** (wonderful cashmere but also the best velvet slippers). At **Pickett** are Georgina von Etzdorf's hand-printed silk accessories.

BUTLER & WILSON, 189 Fulham Rd, SW3 ☎ (071) 352 3045; 20 S Molton St, W1 ☎ (071) 409 2955
Fabulous fakes to adorn the extremities of the fashion-conscious and the famous (Lauren Bacall, Ali McGraw, Jerry Hall). Fire-shot Venetian glass earrings and necklaces, a constellation of enamelled stars and planets, outsized faux pearl chokers and chunky metallic belts – jewellery of the times.

COLLINGWOOD, 171 New Bond St, W1
☎ (071) 499 5613
Royal jewellers to the Queen, the Queen Mother and the Prince of Wales, with a strong line in Edwardian and Victorian pieces, as well as more contemporary jewels.

THE CONRAN SHOP, 81 Fulham Rd, SW3 ☎ (071) 589 7401
Your one-stop shop for DIY designer chic. The subterranean base of the Art Deco Michelin building houses museum-piece ultra-modern furniture, furnishings, kitchenware, eatables, presents, the perfect sunglasses and anything else you might need to face the 90s. SIMON WILLIAMS and LOYD GROSSMAN are keen.

CRABTREE & EVELYN, 6 Kensington Church St, W8 ☎ (071) 937 9335 and branches
Smell your way through a misty blue floral haze to find such essentials as lavender shaving cream, lily-of-the-valley toilet water and tayberry and Drambuie liqueur preserves, all beautifully and old-fashionedly packaged.

DAVID SHILLING, 44 Chiltern St, W1
☎ (071) 487 3179
Picture hats and hats in which to be pictured. Sip coffee from gold-initialled cups as the latest collection flashes before you on video. By appointment only.

DINNY HALL, 200 Westbourne Grove, W11 ☎ (071) 792 3913, at Browns, Liberty, Harvey Nichols
Given greater design freedom by her new shop, Dinny is augmenting her production of signature sand-blasted resin and filigree silver necklaces and earrings with one-off commissioned pieces such as huge diamond rings and ruby brooches. See her designs adorning the apparel

Che Bello

Wining, dining, opining – it simply has to be W11 in these post-London Fields days. PortobelloGate has had a facelift, and trustafarians now swagger down the old 'Front Line' on All Saints Road where once the rastas strutted alone. A new wave of immigrants – writers, admen and mediafolk – have now settled. The Mangrove Centre – former planning base for the Notting Hill Carnival and focus of a generation of London black consciousness – is now the **Portobello Dining Rooms**, 6-8 All Saints Rd, where eavesdroppers can sneak previews of forthcoming Amis and Barnes novels. Other hyper-hyped eateries include **192** (Kensington Park Rd) and the **First Floor**, 186 Portobello Rd, where Groucho Club folk come for a snappy bite. España-lovers go to **Garcia's**, 248 P Rd, where *"it's so Spanish you can't even mention Gibraltar"* –

SEBASTIAN SCOTT. Hip bevvies are poured in pubs like the **Portobello Star** and the **Warwick Castle**, (171 and 225 respectively on the P road). Trendy punters slug post-Molotov cocktails at the fashionable **Market Bar**, 240A P Rd, and dine upstairs amid Moorish decorations. Afterwards they might join the queue outside cred club **Subterania** (see Clubs). LIS LEIGH moved here just to be close to her top 3: *"***Portobello Market***, where there's a stall with enough rare funghi to make Antonio Carluccio jealous;* **Tom's**, *226 Westbourne Grove (we all know he's a Conran but don't hold it against him) – a hand-picked, perfectly formed collection of gourmet desirables;* **Mr Christian's**, *11 Elgin Crescent, for the ultimate handmade sausage for les bangers et mash. Forget about baking your own bread and see how the pros do it here."*

of Rifat Ozbek and Bruce Oldfield. JOAN BURSTEIN thinks she's terrific.

FLORIS, 89 Jermyn St, SW1
☎ (071) 930 2885
Posies of zinnia, lilac and lavender form scented everything – bath oils, body milks, shaving soaps. Lacking only a perfumed rubber duck for the total bath experience.

🐾 FORTNUM & MASON, 181 Piccadilly, W1 ☎ (071) 734 8040
The place that's launched a thousand lunches: Britain's finest food emporium. Liveried doorman and black morning-coated attendants usher you in to view vast arrays of traditional English foods; mustards, preserves and chocolate, all smartly wrapped. KEN HOM, SIMON WILLIAMS, MARC BOHAN (*"I like it as a Frenchman"*) and LORD MONTAGU OF BEAULIEU (*"for the best smoked salmon in the world"*) enter the Fortnum's fray. Check out the fashion before the feast: Muir, Ronay, MaxMara, Ungaro. . . . And those who know find other delicious, inedible surprises: *"It's the best place to buy cosmetics – they've got all the regular brands but no one knows about it so you don't get jostled"* – SALLY BURTON.

GARRARD'S, 112 Regent St, W1
☎ (071) 734 7020
Grandly formal home of the crown jewellers.

"One tends to think, 'I couldn't possibly go in there because it looks so awe-inspiring', but actually Garrard's is wonderful" – SALLY BURTON. Wonderful windows, too.

GENERAL TRADING CO, 144 Sloane St, SW1 ☎ (071) 730 0411
The only place worthy of a Princely wedding list, GTC has been furnishing the glory boxes of Sloanes for over 25 years. All you could want for a tasteful home, plus toys for young Ruperts and Arabellas. It's where LORD MONTAGU OF BEAULIEU does all his Christmas shopping.

GEORGINA VON ETZDORF, 149 Sloane St, SW1 ☎ (071) 823 5638; **at Burlington Arcade**
Sensuous, romantic fabrics that you want to get close to: velvet smoking jackets, soft silk trousers, sculpted organza jackets, and flowing dressing gowns. Unifying the range are Georgina's powerful hand-printed designs, inspired by Klimt and the Cubists.

GILLY FORGE, 14 Addison Ave, W11
☎ (071) 603 3833
Detailed couture millinery as seen atop several royal coiffures. Huge picture hats and flowerbedecked straw for summer, velvet boaters and faux fur cloches in winter. Collections for Arabella Pollen, Jean Muir, Chris Clyne and Anouska Hempel.

GRAHAM SMITH, 22 Crawford St, W1
☎ **(071) 935 5636**
By appointment only, couture milliner hats with a French accent. BeSmithed Princesses include Alexandra and Margaret, and demi-royalty, Elizabeth Taylor. Hats all the racing ladies, too.

HACKETT, 65B New King's Rd, SW6
☎ **(071) 731 2790 and branches**
Everything a young man about town and country might need: leather overnight bags and hacking jackets for weekends away, sharp suits for the City, and dinner jackets for society bashes; ANOUSKA HEMPEL thinks it's all fun. Hackett is now exporting own-brand English understatement to Tokyo and Madrid. The cluster of shops in Fulham sell casual wear (65B New King's Rd), suits (65A New King's Rd), formal wear (117 Harwood Rd) and shirts, shoes and nightwear (1 Broxholme House, New King's Rd). Financial whizzes in a hurry will find the full range at 1/2 Holborn Bars, EC1, and 26 Eastcheap, EC3.

🐘 **HARRODS, Knightsbridge, SW1**
☎ **(071) 730 1234**
Follow the sheeplike stream of tourists out of the Tube and ye shall find Harrods, the most recognizable store in the world. The Harrods green and gold emblem is emblazoned everywhere, from their personal taxis, through umbrellas to the gold-roped caviare bags. *"Much though it is often frowned upon, I think it is the best for getting everything under one roof – whether it is food or shoes or clothes or stationery"* – SERENA FASS. Foot-fatiguing expanses of clothes space display the best of British (Muir, Ronay, Jackson, Galliano), Europe and USA (Rykiel, Lacroix, DKNY, Dior, Ferragamo and Lagerfeld; with Armani, Byblos, Cerruti and Ballantyne for the chaps). If something exists (a game, a perfume, a roll of material) Harrods has it – if you can find it. NED SHERRIN pops in *"for quick things"*, STEPHEN JONES *"for silk socks, own brand. I must have more than 100 pairs, every different colour, short and long."* The food halls are one of the greatest temptations of the modern world, but all departments should be avoided at sale time unless you value your sanity at nothing.

🐘 **HARVEY NICHOLS, 109–125**
Knightsbridge, SW1 ☎ **(071) 235 5000**
The most discriminating designer department store, rising through chic accessories to the big names of the fashion world: Armani, Cerruti, Calvin Klein, Complice, Conran, Dolce & Gabbana, DKNY, Gaultier, G Gigli, Krizia, Lauren, Muir, Montana, Ozbek, Rykiel. MAUREEN LIPMAN and CLARE FRANCIS fancy the fashion, SERENA FASS likes it *"aesthetically, for its window display but not for a diverse range"*, MARC BOHAN finds it *"amusing, the trendy fashion department store"*. Sassy stash of hats, gloves, bags and hosiery. Clubbable clobber for the chaps on the lower ground floor.

HATCHARDS, 187 Piccadilly, W1
☎ **(071) 439 9921 and branches**
It might have been taken over by the giant, Dillons, but Hatchards is *"still the place for the gourmet book-buyer. The assistants talk, even argue, with you and everyone who comes in looks as though they read the books they buy"* – LIS LEIGH. Among them might be JEFFREY ARCHER or GIORGIO ARMANI: *"Any kind of book you could possibly want, a place to spend hours browsing."*

Kitchen Cachet
🐘

Forget state-of-the-art food processors, blow torches and electric carvers, the essential utensil for every self-respecting foodie is hand-held, elbow-grease-powered and preferably unpronounceable. Kitchens heat up as the cooks expound upon their professional passions. *"I am most passionate about my mezza luna, those curved knives with two handles. I am thinking about buying another one as company for the first"* – SOPHIE GRIGSON. Mettles are tested over the virtues of ever-more deadly knives. Those of Japan (*"next year's instrument, you can cut a whisker in mid-air"* – MATTHEW FORT) clash against LADY MACDONALD OF MACDONALD's British-born Kitchen Devils. More cutting remarks from LOYD GROSSMAN: *"My mandolin, just a piece of wood with a single-edged blade, is the best thing in the world."* RAYMOND BLANC favours a kinder, gentler approach to cooking with *"a heavy cast-iron Le Creuset pan. You hold it and you feel like giving something for the family to share"*. Those in the know stock up at **The French Kitchen and Tableware Supply Company**, 42 Westbourne Grove, W2, which caters to the caterers; **Divertimenti**, 139 Fulham Rd, SW3, and 45 Wigmore St, W1; and the kitchenware department of **John Lewis**, Oxford St, W1. For instructions on how to use your new-found arsenal, browse at **Books for Cooks**, 4 Blenheim Crescent, W11, where SOPHIE G *"always tends to bump into other cookery writers, all swearing happily under their breath because they've spent three or four times as much as they'd planned"*.

HERBERT JOHNSON, 13 New Bond St, W1 ☎ (071) 408 1174
For SALLY BURTON, this classic English man's and woman's hatter is *"an old-fashioned name so you feel that you're stepping back in time, but they also have wonderful modern hats alongside the traditional panama that you can roll up and put in a box, and very nice gentlemen to serve you".* JILLY COOPER rolls up too.

JOSEPH, 26 Sloane St, SW1 ☎ (071) 235 5470; 77 Fulham Rd, SW3, and branches
At the sleek and chic summit of the Joseph Ettedgui empire is this pair of uncluttered, well laid-out spaces in London's two shopping hearts. Alongside Joseph's ever expanding own understated label hangs the best of modern British and European lines: Galliano, Moschino, Prada, Irie, Alaïa. The Sloane St shop is home to the chunky hand-knits and leggings of Joseph Tricot; less expensive athletic stretchies are at 124 Draycott Ave, SW3; **Equipment**, 26 Brook St, W1, finds Joseph shirty. MAUREEN LIPMAN and CLARE FRANCIS are keen. Joseph also caters for shoppers' internal needs with **Joe's Café** at 126 Draycott Ave, **L'Express** at 16 Sloane St and **Joe's** in Harvey Nichols, each one a testament to the designer generation.

🍎 LIBERTY, Regent St, W1 ☎ (071) 734 1234
The beautifully packaged English-cum-oriental store is redefining its image. The acres of silk scarves remain, as do the rolls of floral lawn, floral notebooks, floral umbrellas, floral flowers . . . but they also have a forward-thinking, carefully chosen modern jewellery collection (Pellini, Moschino, Herve van der Straeten, Billy Boy, Dinny Hall, Eric Beamon, Simonetta Starabba), good fashion, terrific leather goods and an ever-changing exhibition space in the basement where they help set the flavour of the month (or year) with authoritative displays of all things Japanese, Guatemalan or Upper Voltan.

LOUISE SANT, Studio enquiries ☎ (071) 278 8860; at Liberty, Fortnum & Mason
Eccentric, unclassic fashion jewellery with a strong line in bold variations on pearls and semi-precious stones. Organic shapes and Etruscan-inspired forms are given colour by Roman glass, amber, amethysts or cornelians. Also fine jewellery to order.

MANOLO BLAHNIK, 49–51 Old Church St, SW3 ☎ (071) 352 3863
Feet that have been fitted by Manolo thenceforth spurn lesser treatment. Individual, crafted footwear of the supplest kid, suede, satin, brocade and velvet encase the toes of the most exacting: Madonna, Bianca Jagger, the Duchess of York. SIR PETER USTINOV kisses the Blahnik stone: *"Superb quality, I bought a pair in New York and a pair in London and they were equally good. My wife is in seventh heaven because they're comfortable from the beginning."*

MARINA KILLERY, W11 ☎ (071) 727 3121
Hats to order by appointment only. In her discreet Notting Hill studio, Killery creates modern whimsies and wearable classics for the racy racing set and for the Princess of Wales.

🍎 MARKS & SPENCER, Marble Arch, 458 Oxford St, W1 ☎ (071) 935 7954 and branches
It is estimated that at any one time, one British woman in 3 is wearing M&S knickers. What better recommendation than that for the superstore? Jolly good basics – aforesaid lingerie, plain lambswool jumpers, men's chambray shirts, 3-packs of white cotton T-shirts. Even, says CLARE FRANCIS, shoes: *"One of the few shops where I can be sure of getting a size 3."* In the food department, MADHUR JAFFREY finds *"the fruit and vegetables quite wonderful. And I love their sandwiches."* STEPHEN JONES thinks it is all *"extraordinary. The quality of food is superb."* LORD LICHFIELD remains devoted.

🍎 Buzzz Social death on the fashion circuit is the lack of a cleavage. Get yours clamped in place via **Rigby & Peller**, 2 Hans Rd, SW3 ☎ (071) 589 9293, corsetiers to the Queen, and bespoke creators of impressive architectural supports for both the well-endowed and those in need of a push-up 🍎 . . . . . . Bespoke 2: **David** (we all know he's really a Viscount and the son of Princess Margaret and Lord Snowdon) **Linley** continues to carve a name for himself as a carpenter, trading at 1 New King's Rd, SW6 ☎ (071) 736 6886. Today's handcrafted one-off piece is tomorrow's priceless antique. *"My favourite furniture designer and that's that"* – ANOUSKA HEMPEL. SERENA FASS raves: *"So imaginative, absolutely fabulous"* 🍎 . . . . . . Booked up: If you require proper service from your book supplier, look no further, dear reader, than **Waterstones**, 193 Kensington High St, W8 ☎ (071) 937 8432, and branches. The classy, unfettered chain of bookshops has a mail-order service, out-of-print book search and staff who know their stuff and don't mind browsers . . . . 🍎

S J PHILLIPS, 139 New Bond St, W1
☎ **(071) 629 6261**
The finest antique jewellers stocking everything
but Priam's jewels. Anyone may view the
16C–19C silver, Renaissance gems and 18C–20C
jewellery, but only a handful of power-pur-
chasers can buy.

STEPHEN JONES, 29–31 Heddon St, W1
☎ **(071) 734 9666**
Quirky, witty and wearable, Stephen's latest
batch of hats finds inspiration deep in flamenco
country. Those keeping up with Jones include
the Princess of Wales and Azzedine Alaïa. Collections for Hanae Mori, Enrico Coveri, Rifat
Ozbek, Jin Abe, Katharine Hamnett, Claude
Montana and Hermès.

WHISTLES, 12 St Christopher's Place,
W1 ☎ (071) 487 4484 and branches
For fashion-forward separates with a wicked or
witty twist. The starting point for many young
designers, Whistles takes a progressive line in
its buy-ins: Helmut Lang, Moschino's Cheap and
Chic, Junior Gaultier, as well as less-known offbeat Parisians. Whistles's own label is strong
and decently priced.

Wine merchants

With the largest on-premises cellarage in London – stretching under St James's and Pall Mall
– **Berry Bros & Rudd**, 8 St James's St, SW1
☎ (071) 839 9033, delivers faultless service and a
remarkable variety of wine from around the
world. Italian expert David Gleave chooses
great Barolos, Chiantis, etc, for **Winecellars**,
153–155 Wandsworth High St, SW18 ☎ (081)
871 3979. The biggest importer of the great
Romanée Conti is **John Armit**, whose treasure
trove is at 190 Kensington Park Rd, W11 ☎
(071) 727 6846. **Haynes Hanson & Clark**, 17
Lettice St, SW6 ☎ (071) 736 7878, are specialists
in the 3 Bs – Bordeaux and burgundy on a Bud-

get. At **La Vigneronne**, 105 Old Brompton Rd,
SW7 ☎ (071) 589 6113, find some rare old bargains among Liz Berry MW's rare old wines.
Top-notch German and Alsatian wines reside at
O W Loeb & Co, 15 Jermyn St, SW1 ☎ (071)
734 5878. **Corney & Barrow**, 118 Moorgate,
EC2 ☎ (071) 638 3125 (and branches), has fabulous clarets – especially Pomerols and St Emil-
ions – at a price. **The Australian Wine Centre**, 50 Strand, WC2 ☎ (071) 925 0751, is just as
it sounds, and "*a real find*" for LORD LICHFIELD.
Brit-born trailblazer GEOFFREY ROBERTS's **Les
Amis du Vin**, 51 Chiltern St, W1 ☎ (071) 487
3419, is *the* place for California and North West
Pacific wines – it's a wine club too. The empire
stretches to **The Winery**, 4 Clifton Rd, W9 ☎
(071) 286 6475, for more New World wines. For
competitively priced wines from top domains,
follow grapies to **Bibendum Wine**, 113
Regent's Park Rd, NW1 ☎ (071) 722 5577. **Odd-
bins** is the pick of the chains – knowledgeable
staff, adventurous selections and consistent
quality. The wine connoisseurs' supermarket is
Waitrose, followed by **Sainsbury's** and
Tesco, while their warehouse is **Majestic
Wine Warehouses**. See also Rest of England.

——— *Theatre* ———

See also Arts centres.

ALDWYCH, Aldwych, WC2
☎ **(071) 836 6404**
Built in 1905, the Aldwych is an old favourite
among actors – both on- and off-stage. SIMON
WILLIAMS loves it: "*For beauty of theatre, you
really can't beat the Aldwich.*" Unless you go to
the **Garrick**, that is.

HAYMARKET THEATRE ROYAL,
Haymarket, SW1 ☎ (071) 071 930 8800
A gracious Regency building both outside and
in, with productions to match – fine trad theatre.
Go to see favourite wits (Shaw and Wilde), Euro

🕵 **Buzz** A feast for all senses: follow
your nose to **Fratelli Camisa**, 1A Berwick St, W1, and 53 Charlotte St, W1, for fresh
truffles, own-vineyard wine, stinging nettle sauce and "*the best selection of olive oils*" –
SOPHIE GRIGSON 🕵 . . . . . . Pâtisserie **Maison Blanc**, 102 Holland Park Ave, W11, is run by
Raymond Blanc's ex-wife Jane with unimpeachable precision and Frenchness 🕵 . . . . . .
HR Higgins, 79 Duke St, W1, is best for freshly roasted coffee ground to order 🕵 . . . . . .
Le minimal pâtisserie **Cannelle**, 166 Fulham Rd, SW10, and 221 Kensington High St,
W8, draws you in by the senses for mouth-watering gâteaux 🕵 . . . . . . **Jeroboams**, 24
Bute St, SW7, is where JULIAN LLOYD WEBBER finds sublime unpasteurized French and
English cheeses and SOPHIE GRIGSON finds "*jolly good sales people*" 🕵 . . . . . . **Neal's
Yard Dairy**, 17 Shorts Gardens, WC2, "*sells only English and Irish cheeses but is a
model of what a cheese shop should be*" – MATTHEW FORT . . . . 🕵

heavies (Anhouille), top contemps and first-rate thesps (Jacobi, Lindsay, Bates, Maggie Smith). You might see NED SHERRIN or JEFFREY "*I love the Haymarket Theatre*" ARCHER there too.

THE OLD VIC, Waterloo Rd, SE1
☎ (071) 928 7616
The inimitable Old Vic is still making class drama available at modest cost. Favourite among actors: "*Unquestionably the best theatre in London for playing in. It has a rehearsal room on top which very few London theatres have*" – MAUREEN LIPMAN.

OPEN-AIR THEATRE, Regent's Park, NW1 ☎ (071) 486 2431 end-May to mid-Sept); ☎ (071) 935 5884 (all year)
Where better to see *A Midsummer Night's Dream*? Bring cushions and blankets and settle down to watch the New Shakespeare Company perform on the grassy stage. 2 Shakespeares, another classic and a children's play to choose from each summer. Mulled wine and hot food on sale if you're too chilled out.

> **❝** *The National and the Barbican are both on very good form. I've seen wonderful things at the Barbican recently . . . enchanting* **❞**
>
> 🖊 NED SHERRIN

THE ROYAL COURT, Sloane Square, SW1 ☎ (071) 730 1745
Traditionally the angry young testing ground for new writers – John Osborne most notably. However, as Stephen Daldry takes over (oh so gradually) from Max Stafford-Clark as artistic director, there is barely a handclap to be heard. 'Where is the old risk and passion and raw talent?' ask theatre buffs. And yet . . . what other mainstream theatre stages new writers? Just hope tomorrow's Osborne will emerge. More at the **Theatre Upstairs** (☎ (071) 730 2554).

🖊 ROYAL NATIONAL THEATRE, South Bank, SE1 ☎ (071) 928 2252
With the RSC, the Royal National Theatre Company is a world-beater. Political and financial wrangling seldom detract from the consistent dramatic excellence of productions in its Olivier, Lyttelton and Cottesloe theatres. Intelligent productions for drama lovers come from a long line of directors, most recently, Richard Eyre. NED SHERRIN is impressed; MAUREEN LIPMAN admires its spirit – but not the building.

WYNDHAM'S, Charing Cross Rd, WC2
☎ (071) 867 1116
A family affair until a few years ago, Charles Wyndham's turn-of-the-century theatre continues to stage quality work. Watch modern clas-

sics – Orton et al – under the remarkable gilt ceiling as NED SHERRIN does.

F ringe theatre

Expect the unexpected. The quality varies, but at best is extremely high. And there's that rare element – spontaneity. Venues away from the bright lights – in back rooms, pubs and parlours – give an 'in the know' feeling. The more established attract well-publicized shows from reputed rep companies and celeb performers. See them in the round at the **Young Vic**, 66 The Cut, SE1 ☎ (071) 928 6363 (anything from A Winter's Tale to the Snow Queen with well known names like Redgrave and Mirren) and the **Riverside Studios**, Crisp Rd, Hammersmith, W6 ☎ (071) 748 3354 – for eccentric interpretations of classics – Aeschylus, Shakespeare, and BIG dance names like Michael Clark. Ben Kingsley has trodden the boards at the **Man in the Moon** at 392 King's Rd, SW3 ☎ (071) 351 2876. The bar at **King's Head** – 115 Upper St, N1 ☎ (071) 226 1916 – files upstairs at showtime to watch such illustrious companies as the RSC playing. Other top venues include the **Almeida Theatre**, Almeida St, N1 ☎ (071) 359 4404; **Hampstead Theatre**, Avenue Rd, Swiss Cottage, NW3 ☎ (071) 722 9301; **Gate Notting Hill**, above Prince Albert pub, 11 Pembridge Rd, W11 ☎ (071) 229 0706; **Tricycle Theatre**, 269 Kilburn High Rd, NW6 ☎ (071) 328 1000; **Battersea Arts Centre**, Old Town Hall, Lavender Hill, SW11 ☎ (071) 223 2223, and 2 MAUREEN LIPMAN choices, the newly refitted **Richmond Theatre**, The Green, Richmond, Surrey ☎ (081) 940 0088, and the **Hampstead Theatre**, Swiss Cottage Centre, NW3 ☎ (071) 722 9301.

OXFORD

Synonymous with the oldest and most famous university in Britain (founded c. 1167). Of the glorious golden-stone colleges, see **Merton** (whose Mob Quad and library are the oldest in Oxford), the majestic **Christ Church** (Wren's Tom Tower), **New College** (enchanting cloisters, magnificent hall), and **Magdalen** (cloisters, deer park and the landmark bell tower). Don't miss the 15C **Divinity School** in Broad St, the oldest lecture room in the city, or Wren's semi-circular Sheldonian Theatre.

—— *Art and museums* ——

The **Museum of the History of Science** has the finest collection of early astrological, mathematical and optical instruments in the world. **Christ Church Picture Gallery** is rich in Italian Renaissance drawings (Lippi, Mantegna,

Leonardo, Raphael) as well as Old Master paintings and portraits of eminent erstwhile members of college.

ASHMOLEAN MUSEUM, Beaumont St
☎ (0865) 27800

Allegedly the oldest public museum in Great Britain, part of the building dates back to 1683. An impressive collection of paintings, prints and drawings by Michelangelo and Raphael, Old Master paintings, Impressionists, Pre-Raphaelites, and the museum's most important piece of art, Uccello's *The Hunt in the Forest*. Riches don't end there – feast also on Eastern art and decorative works, archaeology, 17C and 18C English furniture, sculpture, silver, ceramics and porcelain.

———— Gardens ————

BOTANIC GARDENS, Rose Lane
☎ (0865) 276920

Set on the banks of the River Cherwell, these are thought to be Britain's oldest botanic gardens. Within the 4 acres there is beautiful woodland with a yew tree from the 1650s, a tropical greenhouse, water lilies, a cacti and succulent house and a palm house.

———— Hotels ————

THE OLD PARSONAGE HOTEL, 1
Banbury Rd ☎ (0865) 310210

This charmingly individual stone building is a much-needed addition to the Oxford scene (students' parents can heave a sigh of relief). *"It's run on extremely good lines, it's caring, it's centrally located, it has good food – unfortunately it's going to be very popular and very difficult to get in"* – HILARY RUBINSTEIN. Privately owned by the people who brought you the legendary **Brown's** restaurant, the 30 guest rooms are prettily, if chintzily, furnished and facilities are bang-up-to-the-minute.

· REST OF ·
ENGLAND

—— Art and museums ——

TATE GALLERY LIVERPOOL, Albert
Dock, Liverpool ☎ (051) 709 3223

Clore Gallery architect Sir James Stirling turned to native Liverpool for this dockside complex. 3 floors for exhibitions, a warehouse gallery for contemporary works, performance arts space, a restaurant and artists' studios. 20C works from its big bro in London and other galleries are hung in ever-changing exhibitions and long-term displays such as *New Realities – Art From Western Europe 1945–68* (until 1995), which features modern masters from Picasso through to Christo.

———— Ballet ————

🐾 THE BIRMINGHAM ROYAL BALLET,
Birmingham Hippodrome, Thorp St,
Birmingham ☎ (021) 622 2555

60,000 Midlands ballet-lovers packed into the Hippodrome for the former Sadler's Wells Royal Ballet's first season here. Reports have been more than encouraging: *"It has produced some productions which are absolutely unparalleled in the world, under the direction of Peter Wright, and is really a company of major importance now"* – EDWARD THORPE.

———— Clubs ————

CLUB 051, 1 Mount Pleasant St,
Liverpool ☎ (051) 709 9586

Functional basement warehouse setting for serious dancing to all sounds. Funk on down on Fridays; Saturday is harder-core keeping up with James Barton and Andy Carroll's DJ-ing.

THE ESCAPE CLUB, 10 Marine Parade,
Brighton ☎ (0273) 606906

Futuristic minimal interior with 2 dance floors – one for techno sounds, one for soul and oldies. Sat's the best night and it's licensed till 4am.

GOLDWYN'S, Suffolk Place, Queensway,
Birmingham ☎ (021) 643 6843

Vast steamy warehouse club with funky light show and wall projections. Throbbing music sets the beat for ravers who let it all hang out. Pop along for Crackle on Fri.

THE HACIENDA, 11–13 Whitworth St W,
Manchester ☎ (061) 236 5051

The BIG Manchester scene of the late 80s, all post-industrialism and serious lights, has reopened to the approval of SEBASTIAN SCOTT (*"still good, but be prepared for the full body search with metal detector at the door"*). House music lingers on for the chosen 1,200.

THE MARDI GRAS, Bold St, Liverpool
☎ (051) 707 1669

Liver birds turn to hippydom at G-Love on the last Thurs of the month, when flowers, fruit and sweets are handed out. Dancers emerge from their dream state to hop to happy house music.

———— Festivals ————

The **Three Choirs Festival** and the **Aldeburgh Festival** both sound good to JULIAN LLOYD WEBBER. The former (held Aug), the oldest music festival in Britain (265 years), alter-

In an English Country Garden

There is something about an English garden that touches the hearts of its countrymen. When journeying abroad, nothing evokes the homeland more than the memory of a humming summer's evening amid the green lawns, floral borders, rockeries, majestic trees and lichen-covered walls that characterize the mature country garden. Most of all, England glories in its gardens of the 18C landscape movement, when informal parkland settings were created as an ideal backdrop for the gentleman's country house. A fine example is Henry Hoare's rolling Arcadian landscape at **Stourhead House**, Stourton, Warminster, Wiltshire ☎ (0747) 840348, awash with colour in spring, with the rhododendron dells and camellias, so admired by SERENA FASS. Lord Lichfield's Palladian seat, **Shugborough**, Milford, Nr Stafford ☎ (0889) 881388, set in 900 acres of park and woodland, has perhaps the greatest collection of neo-classical monuments and follies in the country. The splendid gardens of **Newby Hall**, Nr Ripon, Yorkshire ☎ (0423) 322583, delight Yorkshire lass BARBARA TAYLOR BRADFORD and SERENA FASS ("*one of the best*"), while **Cholmondely Castle Gardens**, Cheshire ☎ (0829) 720383, entrance KENNETH J LANE ("*a beautiful house and gardens . . . wonderful*"); see the water garden, with islands, temples and bridges. **Sissinghurst Gardens**, Cranbrook, Kent ☎ (0580) 712850, grew up in an altogether different era, designed by Vita Sackville-West in the 1930s; see her White Garden and herb garden. A potted product of that age is **Charleston Farm House**, Nr Firle, Lewes, E Sussex ☎ (032183) 265, decorated from head to toe in liberal Bloomsbury fashion by former residents Vanessa Bell and Duncan Grant and pals, and nestling in a cottage garden.

---

nates between the cathedrals of Worcester, Gloucester and Hereford. The latter (June), an innovative musical feast, was founded by Benjamin Britten. The **Hay-on-Wye Literary Festival** attracts the literati en force, all spouting forth on their latest tome or field of knowledge and drinking copiously. "*A quite extraordinary event . . . it's in a magical part of the country. Hay is the bookshop town, second-hand bookshops everywhere, and you bump into all these people in a sort of family atmosphere*" – JLW. **Lichfield** Cathedral, Staffs (July); good fringe too. **Cheltenham** (July) is mostly contemporary music. **Salisbury** (Sept) offers music mainly at the cathedral, and theatre at the Playhouse. **Brighton** (May) is the largest festival in England. After the Regatta's over (July), dances, cabarets, fireworks, and a floating stage transform dozy **Henley**.

Historic buildings and gardens

Most country houses are open to the public from around Easter to the end of Oct. The **National Trust**, 36 Queen Anne's Gate, London SW1 ☎ (071) 222 9251, owns over 300 properties and gardens of historic interest or natural beauty. **English Heritage**, Fortress House, 23 Savile Row, W1 ☎ (071) 973 3000, is a similar body. Join both and get their handbooks and free entry to their properties.

BLENHEIM PALACE, Woodstock, Oxfordshire ☎ (0993) 811325
Built by Sir John Vanbrugh, Blenheim was the 1st Duke of Marlborough's reward for battle victories. The Marlborough Maze, the largest symbolic hedge maze in Europe, opened last year. Glorious water terraces flow into the lake and an arboretum stretches for over a mile. "*An amazing setting*" – DOTT ROSA MARIA LETTS. Birthplace of Sir Winston Churchill: 5 rooms of memorabilia include his slippers. Fabulous collection of 18C furniture, porcelain, bronzes and supreme paintings by Reynolds and Stubbs. Much loved by KENNETH J LANE.

BROUGHTON CASTLE, Banbury, Oxfordshire ☎ (0295) 62624
Family seat of the Lords Saye and Sele since 1447, "*a very perfect castellated house with a quiet and ancient atmosphere*" – JOHN BROOKE-LITTLE. A spectacular setting, 3-acre moat, 14C gate house, 17C oak furniture, and arms and armour from the Civil War in the Great Hall. In

the 18,000 acres of parkland lies *"a garden which is coming on beautifully, just getting better and better"* – JOHN B-L.

BURGHLEY HOUSE, Stamford, Lincolnshire ☎ (0780) 52451
The largest and grandest house of the Elizabethan age and the Cecil family home for over 400 years. Set in Capability Brown deer parks.

CASTLE HOWARD, York, N Yorkshire ☎ (065384) 333
Designed for Charles Howard, the 3rd Earl of Carlisle, by Sir John Vanbrugh in 1699, the palace is instantly recognizable as the setting for the series *Brideshead Revisited* (Waugh had it in mind too). Sebastian's teddy might have been auctioned off (along with nearly £1 million of bric-à-brac in a grand car boot sale) but the important pieces remain. The walls glow with works by Gainsborough, Romney, Rubens and Reynolds, and the waterworks, Atlas and Prince of Wales fountains, cascade and waterfall have been restored to their former glory. LORD MONTAGU OF BEAULIEU recognizes its worth.

CHATSWORTH, Bakewell, Derbyshire ☎ (024688) 2204
Set on the River Derwent, Chatsworth is one of Britain's most beautiful and important houses, built in the late 17C. Seat of the Devonshires, it is famed for its splendid interiors (magnificent library) and arts collection – Old Masters, sculptures, silver, inlaid furniture and wall hangings of tapestry and leather. Marvellous gardens and Capability Brown parkland. All that and *"the best country-house shop, full of first-class local and home-made produce"* – SERENA FASS.

HAREWOOD HOUSE, Harewood, Leeds, W Yorkshire ☎ (0532) 886225
In one of the finest Capability Brown parks stands this 18C house, with interiors by Robert Adam. 17 state rooms resplendent with paintings by Reynolds, Canaletto and Turner, Chippen-

dale furniture and Chinese and Sèvres porcelain make JOHN TOVEY *"feel marvellous"*. Wander through the rose and bird gardens, by ancient oaks and the royal rhododendron collection. Brace yourself for Epstein's love-it-or-hate-it sculpture of Adam (as in A & Eve).

HATFIELD HOUSE, Hatfield, Hertfordshire ☎ (0707) 262823
Magnificent Jacobean House, home of the Marquis of Salisbury, built in the early 1600s by Robert Cecil. The surviving wing of the royal palace is where Elizabeth I spent much of her girlhood. Rich in rare tapestries, fine furniture, paintings and historic armour.

> **"** *The particular quality of green that you find in the British Isles, in the farms and lawns and forests of Ireland, England, Scotland and Wales, I think is unique* **"**
>
> 🖌 DOUGLAS FAIRBANKS JR

HEVER CASTLE, Nr Edenbridge, Kent ☎ (0732) 865224
The childhood home of Anne Boleyn, dating back to 1270, was richly restored by the Astor family (and is now owned by a property company). Superb wood carving and plaster work, and a marvellous collection of paintings and furniture. Gardens are a blaze of colour and waterways; the Italian garden contains statues and sculptures from Roman to Renaissance times.

LEEDS CASTLE, Maidstone, Kent ☎ (0622) 765400
Originally a 9C wooden fortress, rebuilt in stone in 1119, the moated castle is one of the most ancient and romantic buildings in the country. Furniture of the 14C and 15C has been recreated, tapestries, paintings and magnificent

🖌 **Buzzz** Green craft: Art reflects nature at **Nature in Art**, Wallsworth Hall, Sandhurst, Gloucestershire ☎ (0452) 731422, which *"has exhibitions by artists who paint or sculpt animals and birds – few people realize how fascinating it is"* – JILLY COOPER 🖌 . . . . . . Green berets: JOHN BROOKE-LITTLE marches to the **Green Howards Museum**, Trinity Church Square, Richmond, N Yorkshire ☎ (0748) 822133, *"The best-organized military museum – the history of the regiment in uniforms, medals, that sort of thing, well selected and awfully nicely displayed"* 🖌 . . . . . . Decorative arts: SERENA FASS reckons **The Bowes Museum**, Barnard Castle, Co Durham ☎ (0833) 69066, is *"exceptional – porcelain, furniture and generally a wonderful collection beautifully labelled"* 🖌 . . . . . . Domestic arts: JOHN B-L tips the **Shaftesbury Museum**, Gold Hill, Shaftesbury, Dorset ☎ (0747) 52157, for *"a great collection of miscellanea – it goes from smocks to ploughshares – it's quite charming"* . . . . 🖌

furnishings add to the splendour. The parkland is a delight, with its streams, waterfalls, traditional English garden, 13C greenhouses, vineyard, maze and the new aviary and duckery. *"For conferences it is fabulous, wonderful"* – SERENA FASS.

LONGLEAT HOUSE, Warminster, Wiltshire ☎ (09853) 551
The Marquis of Bath's Elizabethan manor is perhaps better known for its safari park. Take a walk on the tame side indoors with Italian Renaissance art, 17C Dutch paintings, Flemish tapestries and beautiful Meissen porcelain. A first class example of Boulle's work can be seen in the brass and tortoiseshell inlaid cabinet.

PENSHURST PLACE, Penshurst, Tonbridge, Kent ☎ (0892) 870307
Viscount de L'Isle's country house has one of the finest medieval halls in the country and a magnificent 10-acre Tudor walled garden, subdivided by yew hedges.

──────── *Hotels* ────────

See also Restaurants.

THE CASTLE HOTEL, Castle Green, Taunton, Somerset ☎ (0823) 272671
"Competes with true country-house hotels even though their view is of Taunton bingo hall! The restaurant is very good and new chef Phil Vickery (ex-Gravetye) looks set to match the standards set by Chris Oakes and Gary Rhodes. The bedrooms are outstanding" – PAUL HENDERSON. Director Kit Chapman is the man to be congratulated for developing the bright young culinary sparks. NED SHERRIN would pat him on the back: *"They do look after you, I was there for some gourmet dinner and they gourmeted very well."*

🏆 CHEWTON GLEN, New Milton, Hampshire ☎ (0425) 275341
As the slickest, least rustic country-house hotel passes its quarter century, birthday greetings pour in from its peers: *"Martin Skan has now been setting standards for the rest of us for 25 years – the new health centre, pool and tennis courts are exceptional"* – PAUL HENDERSON. BOB PAYTON echoes: *"The best resort complex; beyond world class."* ALAN CROMPTON-BATT, LEO COOPER, CAROL WRIGHT and JEFFREY ARCHER concur, as does KEN HOM: *"One of the most superb places in the world. Terrific service, good food – everything is done with such discreet charm. It's very European yet it does have English touches."* Classic, seasonally based cooking under Pierre Chevillard is matched by a wine list spanning 400 bottles.

CLIVEDEN, Taplow, Berkshire ☎ (06286) 68561
Hard to imagine a whiff of the Profumo scandal ever touching this very stately home; after all,

Rule Britannia was composed here. The Thames-side mansion imposes its presence on 376 acres of National Trust Gardens, *"very special"* – LISA BARNARD. If topiary, livery and rococory overwhelm, body and spirit can be cleansed with Turkish baths, massage and Jacuzzi. Rumour has it that service is much improved too – less frigid but still unobtrusive.

THE FEATHERS HOTEL, Market St, Woodstock, Oxfordshire ☎ (0993) 812291
Under new (still private) ownership, this 17C town house hotel is *"better than ever"* – JONATHAN MEADES. LIS LEIGH has high praise: *"Few country hotels make you want to reserve a*

Battle of the Sommeliers
♟
──────────────

Pity the poor sommelier, diplomat of the dining room. His daily task is immense: one must sell the wine, of course, but not push expensive wine for its own sake; one must be knowledgeable without making the diner feel ignorant; one must offer suitable wines but when, finally, a meaty claret is chosen to wash down a dozen oysters, acquiesce gracefully; one must also stock the cellar, organize and price the wine list, and head a team of drinks waiters – and all this in a country where most people don't even know what a sommelier is. Let us redress the balance and applaud the skill and knowledge of those noble souls who lubricate fine dinners. **Bruno Asselin** of Le Manoir aux Quat' Saisons, **Joël Lauga** of Lucknam Park, **Peter Davies** of Le Gavroche and **Werner Wissman** of The Savoy scale the peaks of their profession. But any award for the best sommelier, as acknowledged by his catering peers and rivals, must go to **Gerard Basset** of Chewton Glen, Britain's most decorated wine waiter. Basset first came to England from France to watch a football match; that was 1976, now he competes *against* France in the international sommelier stakes and beats them at their own game. And the secret of his ability? 3 or 4 hours studying every day (he's even doing a chemistry course), an overwhelming passion for wine, and, most important, a nose for success.

permanent room – this one does. Hand-picked antiques, uncluttered design, not over-floral. The right degree of comfort without the ubiquitous Jacuzzi and all so beautifully run it can accommodate riotousness or intimacy. Excellent bar, interesting menu. The reverse of rus in urbe for the sophisticated townie who likes trees but doesn't know their names."

> **❝ Fleetingly fashionable and sometimes maligned, the English country-house hotels are in a class of their own for warmth and comfort ❞**
>
> 🖋 MICHAEL BROADBENT

🛁 GIDLEIGH PARK, Chagford, Devon
☎ (06473) 2367
Hidden in 40 acres of grounds within the rugged Dartmoor National Park, Gidleigh Park's Tudor veneer is its only fakery. Perfect, pleasantly distant service, tea in front of a blazing fire and croquet on the lawn; under Paul and Kay Henderson's guidance, this is what a country-house hotel is all about, as fellow hotelier MARTIN SKAN recognizes. Chef Shaun Hill's reworked classics ("cooking with his customary élan" – MATTHEW FORT) and the far-reaching cellar have been showered with rosettes and stars. "Gidleigh Park is the most wonderful place and Shaun, besides cooking my sort of food, is the funniest chef I know" – BOB PAYTON. "Cuisine and cellars above the hotel chain average" – MICHAEL BROADBENT.

🛁 GRAVETYE MANOR, Nr East Grinstead, W Sussex ☎ (0342) 810567
"The grand old man of country-house hotels," says HILARY RUBINSTEIN; it is certainly one of the longest established. Set amid glorious 100-year-old gardens, this 16C manor house is a bastion of rather formal good service and taste. "Still excellent" – MICHAEL BROADBENT. "The top hotel in my view, largely because of the remarkable Peter Herbert. He has very high standards, rather like an avuncular headmaster" – RICHARD COMPTON-MILLER. The wine list makes fascinating reading for those with a day or two to spare – "Fantastic" – LADY ELIZABETH ANSON.

🛁 HAMBLETON HALL, Hambleton, Oakham, Rutland, Leicestershire
☎ (0572) 756991
This comfortable, elegant, lakeside manor is still a front-runner in country-house hotels. Go huntin', shootin' and fishin' in the area then home to chef Brian Baker's justly famous seasonal menus. "Apart from the Manoir, Hambleton Hall has the best food in a hotel in the country" – ALAN CROMPTON-BATT. PAUL HENDERSON salutes his fellow hoteliers: "One of the most

intelligently run hotels in Britain. Tim and Stefa Hart's taste shows in everything they do." MARY ROSSI and LISA BARNARD think so too.

HARTWELL HOUSE, Oxford Rd, Aylesbury, Buckinghamshire
☎ (0296) 747444
Meticulously restored to its original ornate Gothic splendour by the Historic House Hotel group, Hartwell House once housed the exiled Louis XVIII and now appeals to the regal inclinations of TERRY HOLMES. More contemporary pleasures – spa, gym, pool – in the newly built Hartwell Spa. "My favourite country-house hotel because it is done with great style and is totally understated. I stay with my friend who is the chef there and we fish on this idyllic lake in the garden, which was designed by Capability Brown" – MARCO PIERRE WHITE.

LUCKNAM PARK, Colerne, Wiltshire
☎ (0225) 742777
When your Lucknam's in, speed down the M4 along with press barons and pop stars to this large early-Georgian deluxe; a classic English country seat updated with spa, solarium, gym, clay pigeon shooting and so on (and on). "Good food, splendid house, good service and high-profile clientele," witnesses ALAN CROMPTON-BATT.

MIDDLETHORPE HALL, Bishopthorpe, York, Yorkshire ☎ (0904) 641241
Built in 1699 this classic William and Mary House stands in 26 acres of park land overlooking York racecourse. A perennial favourite for LORD LICHFIELD: "Stunningly well done and a marvellous place to escape the bustle of York."

MILLER HOWE, Rayrigg Rd, Windermere, Cumbria ☎ (05394) 42536
Guests return like Canada geese to panoramic views over Lake Windermere and the Langdale Pikes and to John Tovey's much-celebrated 5-course dinner menu. Among them are JULIAN LLOYD WEBBER ("magical") and MADHUR JAFFREY: "it is wonderful, his food is gorgeous."

NANSIDWELL, Mawnan Smith, Falmouth, Cornwall ☎ (0326) 250340
Jamie and Felicity Robertson left Jamie's eponymous wine bar in South Ken to set up this idyllic 12-bedroom hotel in National Trust coastland. Home-made everything, from jam to sausages and home-smoked salmon, it's home from home for JULIAN LLOYD WEBBER: "a marvellous place, it goes right down to the sea. Excellent. Very, very good."

🛁 SHARROW BAY, Lake Ullswater, Penrith, Cumbria ☎ (07684) 86301
The one with the family atmosphere – some of the staff have been there for a quarter of a century. Who cares if it's a little brown around the edges? Great food and great hospitality more than compensate. "Superlative" says RICHARD

COMPTON-MILLER. PAUL HENDERSON's favourite in Britain: *"Brian Sack and Francis Coulson care so much about their clients, and the food is wonderful. The setting of Bank House is so spectacular that it is worth driving a mile to dinner. The best breakfast in Britain."* Others, like LADY MACDONALD OF MACDONALD, HILARY RUBINSTEIN, and BOB PAYTON, love it too. LADY ELIZABETH ANSON sounds a small caution: *"By golly, you've got to book."*

STAPLEFORD PARK, Nr Melton Mowbray, Leicestershire ☎ (057284) 522
American gusto meets old English grace at this converted 16C/17C stately home. Famous style-setters give their names to bedrooms they designed at current owner Bob Payton's behest. Past contributors include Capability Brown – the parkland – and Grinling Gibbons – the wood carving in the dining room. Hundreds of country things to do and Mark Barker's hearty, unpretentious cooking to come home to. *"One of the most fantastic country-house hotels"* – TERRY HOLMES. Get there before Bob sells up, when things may change....

STON EASTON PARK, Chewton Mendip, Bath, Avon ☎ (076121) 631
Period details of this high Palladian stately home have been preserved with academic precision – Georgian mouldings and Hepplewhite and Chippendale pieces make this an authentic (if slightly too formal) throwback to the golden age of English country living. *"The best conversion of a Georgian house to an hotel"* says PAUL HENDERSON. *"Ston Easton is the hotel near Bath"* for BOB PAYTON.

Music

OPERA NORTH, Leeds Grand Theatre, 46 New Briggate, Leeds ☎ (0532) 439999
International, independent and highly reputed, though it's all change in 1993 as director Nicholas Payne moves to Covent Garden. 3 annual seasons and tours each year feature classical works as well as modern and commissioned pieces from resident composer Robert Saxton.

🦟 GLYNDEBOURNE FESTIVAL OPERA, Lewes, E Sussex ☎ (0273) 812321
The highlight of the summer season for music buffs and socialites alike – spare tickets are traced as frequently as Halley's Comet – which is why they've knocked down the old Opera House and are currently expanding it to more than 1,000 seats (it should be ready by 1994). Attracts the great voices of the world to sing classic and modern works ... attracts KENNETH J LANE and LORD MONTAGU OF BEAULIEU to hear them. The interval is reminiscent of schooldays as you picnic on a rug in the bitter chill of an English summer. Leave the moulded plastic garden table and chair set with matching cutlery at home – but don't forget the smoked salmon and bubbly.

PAVILION OPERA, Thorpe Tilney Hall, Nr Lincoln, Lincolnshire ☎ (05267) 231
Classic opera done as you like it, where you like it. Freddie Stockdale's company sings in the round, à la carte, in the grandest drawing rooms at home and away (they performed for the Prince and Princess of Wales at the British

🦟 **Buzzz** Put a bookmark in your diary for the literary dinners at **The Angel Hotel**, Bury St Edmunds, Suffolk ☎ (0284) 753926, when such speakers as Ludovic Kennedy, Joan Bakewell, Sandy Gall and Edna Healey provoke debate among well-read locals. Make a weekend of it – the ivy-clad Angel is a heavenly base for visiting the wool towns of Suffolk 🦟 ...... And then there were none: **Burgh Island Hotel**, Burgh Island, Bigbury-on-Sea, S Devon ☎ (0548) 810514, is where Agatha Christie penned *Ten Little Indians*. *"You get there by sea-tractor and then the tide comes up ... all the suites have double beds and wonderful bird's-eye maple – lovely"* – MAUREEN LIPMAN 🦟 ...... Literary notes 3: LIS LEIGH points you towards **Painswick Hotel**, Kemps Lane, Painswick, Gloucestershire ☎ (0452) 812160, and hotelier Somerset Moore, *"if you like Laurence Sterne and our tradition of rollicking country squires, good cheer, good conversation and a host who becomes a friend"* 🦟 ...... CAROL WRIGHT chips in with her tip: **Charingworth Manor**, Charingworth, Nr Chipping Campden, Gloucestershire ☎ (038678) 555, *"has gorgeous rooms and a long thin dining room with alcoves – it's very private and you can sit outside and not see any other houses"* 🦟 ...... Another hotel gone west: The unpretentious **Summer Lodge**, Evershot, Dorset ☎ (093583) 424, continues to earn plaudits for wholesome country living and eating .... 🦟

Embassy in Paris). *"It is the best"* – SERENA FASS – for the all-round experience, at any rate.

——— *Restaurants* ———

ANNIE'S RESTAURANT, 3 Oxford St, Moreton-in-Marsh, Gloucestershire ☎ (0608) 51981
"An astonishingly good country restaurant, sophisticated, unpretentious and clean – lots of it and never a bad dish." So says PRUE LEITH of Anne Ellis's pretty little Cotswold restaurant and husband David's country fare. Lamb fillet in red leek sauce and treacle tart attract the serious noshers of Sloaneshire.

Music Box

Bad concert halls make JULIAN LLOYD WEBBER crotchety. Good ones have him quavering with delight – here are some of his favourites: The **Royal Concert Hall**, **Nottingham**, Royal Centre, Theatre Square ☎ (0602) 482626, is *"a very fine new hall, very good facilities, comfortable for the audience, and excellent for the artists"*. **St David's Hall**, **Cardiff**, The Hays ☎ (0222) 371236, is *"certainly very good. Still probably my favourite of all is the* **Usher Hall**, **Edinburgh**" (see Scotland). Meanwhile, if you're on the South Coast, there's no place better than the **Poole Arts Centre**, Kingland Rd, Poole ☎ (0202) 685222.

THE BEETLE AND WEDGE HOTEL, Ferry Lane, Moulsford, Oxfordshire ☎ (0491) 651381
It *is* a hotel and a very pretty one at that, but the food here is the drawcard, both in the dining room and the more casual Boathouse. *"It's an Elizabeth David sort of place with well-executed bistro-type food"* – JONATHAN MEADES. *"Marvellous grills – I prefer the Boathouse – it's more fun"* – ANDREW LLOYD WEBBER. *"Richard and Kate Smith, the proprietors, never fail. Amazing thoughtfulness, food is the best of British, good strong flavours, swans idling past on the river, roses in the garden – everything for sensuous pleasure"* – LIS LEIGH.

CARVED ANGEL, 2 South Embankment, Dartmouth, Devon ☎ (08043) 2465
Right on the Dart estuary, this little restaurant is right on for PAUL HENDERSON: *"our favourite restaurant in Devon"*. Chef Joyce Molyneux

prepares ultra-fresh ingredients with invention – brill brill with lime, garlicky provençale fish soup, guinea hen with an orange-onion marmalade. Fine wine list.

EPICUREAN, 38 Evesham Rd, Cheltenham ☎ (0242) 222466
Modern British cooking at its finest. Chef Patrick MacDonald studied under Anton Mosimann and now conjures delights like parsley soup with scallops and oysters and roast squab with mushroom ravioli. Pace yourself in order to crown your feast with a glass of Brown Brothers Australian Orange Muscat – yes he *has* got it – and lemon tart. ALAN CROMPTON-BATT and MARCO PIERRE WHITE rate it highly.

HEATHCOTE'S, 104–106 High Rd, Longridge, Preston, Lancashire ☎ (0772) 784969
In the vanguard of the modern British revolution, Paul Heathcote, who trained under Raymond Blanc, reworks empire-building classics: ravioli of lobster with deep-fried vegetables and lobster and tarragon juice; grilled fillet of Dornoch beef garnished with braised oxtail. *"Extremely stylish, very well done – unusual to find in that part of the country,"* says MATTHEW FORT, who tucks into bread and butter pudding with apricot jam and clotted cream. Heathcote selects wines himself, serves only British cheeses, and showers guests with canapés and petits fours. Set in the Ribble Valley in a converted row of cottages.

L'ORTOLAN, The Old Vicarage, Church Lane, Shinfield, Berkshire ☎ (0734) 883783
Infinitely complex cookery by the inspired John Burton-Race, the menu reads – in English – like a Bacchic encyclopaedia. Diners are astonished by the subtlety and complexity of flavours. *"L'Ortolan is as splendid as ever"* – MATTHEW FORT. *"It is not far behind the best"* – PAUL HENDERSON. *"Exceptional food in beautiful surroundings"* – DAME BARBARA CARTLAND. LISA BARNARD, MARY ROSSI and ANDREW LLOYD WEBBER rate it very highly (though the prices cause ALW to gulp a little).

LE MANOIR AUX QUAT' SAISONS, Church Rd, Great Milton, Oxfordshire ☎ (0844) 278881
World-beating. Chef Raymond Blanc conjures sublime tastes and textures to amaze critics and guests alike. Despite asking and fetching a small fortune, pilgrims flock in to his countrified hotel-restaurant. *"£150 there is better value than £75 in lesser places,"* advises JONATHAN MEADES. *"Still a terrifically good place, the food coming out of the kitchen is just brilliant. Top of the land"* – MATTHEW FORT. *"Le Manoir gets better"* – BOB PAYTON. *"One of the most extraordinary properties in the world – incredible food, the service, the ambience – without a doubt el primo"* – ROBIN LEACH. LIS LEIGH cautions: *"Make sure*

Raymond Blanc is cooking and go with food-lovers who can appreciate how brilliant he is." Best hotel food for ALAN CROMPTON-BATT, and SALLY BURTON suggests being driven there and back by taxi for guilt-free indulgence. PAUL HENDERSON would advise her to stay: *"The hotel is supremely comfortable. Raymond Blanc is driven to be the best."* Bedrooms don't quite hit the mark (*un peu nouveau*), but the kitchen garden does for LORD LICHFIELD. BARBARA KAFKA and ANDREW LLOYD WEBBER add their votes.

THE OLD WOOLHOUSE, Northleach, Gloucestershire ☎ (0451) 60366
The tiny restaurant – only 4 tables – seats 18 happy diners, who can then conk out in the 10 bedrooms. Cosy atmosphere in a Cotswold stone house with open fires in winter. Run by Jacques and Jenny Astic whose cuisine is pure classical French – no fads here. Fresh seasonal food given the full butter/cream treatment.

🍴 PROVENCE, Gordleton Mill Hotel, Silver St, Hordle, Nr Lymington, Hampshire ☎ (0590) 682219
Down-to-earth dining that has MATTHEW FORT waxing lyrical: *"Girt around by trout streams, it's a very pleasant environment and the chef, Jean-Christophe Novelli, has eschewed the influence of cuisine nouvelle for something altogether more substantial both in style and flavour."* *"An outstanding chef who does extremely good offal,"* offers JONATHAN MEADES. It's where MARCO PIERRE WHITE heads when he's out of town.

SEAFOOD RESTAURANT, Riverside, Padstow, Cornwall ☎ (0841) 532485
Assiettes de fruits de mer, lobster, and seafood ravioli set new standards for the West Country. The spacious, bright restaurant resides in an archetypal Cornish fishing village. *"Is there a better fish restaurant in Britain?"* asks PAUL HENDERSON. ROBIN HANBURY-TENISON thinks not: *"The standards are of the highest imaginable and Richard Stein's cooking is very, very imaginative – consistently wonderful."*

21 QUEEN STREET, Newcastle-upon-Tyne ☎ (091) 222 0755
Euro-trained Geordie chef Terry Laybourne impresses JONATHAN MEADES with his airy, modern restaurant: *"I think it is very important, extremely good."* Look out for cappuccino of wild mushrooms, and the fillet of turbot with lobster and asparagus gratin.

WATERSIDE INN, Ferry Rd, Bray, Berkshire ☎ (0628) 20691
Michel Roux's Thames-side restaurant pulls diners out of town and returns them out of pocket. *"A perfect place for a day out of London. It tends to get dismissed because it's been there a long time, but food is top league"* – LORD LICHFIELD. LISA BARNARD loves the *"very classical French cooking"*. A new clutch of rooms means you now don't have to brave the breathalyzer on the trip back.

WELL HOUSE, St Keyne, Liskeard, Cornwall ☎ (0579) 42001
New chef David Woodfall has pushed the Well House hotel's restaurant further up the foodie league with provençale-styled dishes such as roast escalope of sea bass on a bed of braised onion, anchovies, olives, and warm capers. Smoothly run by Nicholas Wainford, who keeps a good cellar. *"Most enterprising – Nick Wainford has created the most country sort of hotel in a very tranquil bit of Cornwall"* – ROBIN HANBURY-TENISON.

Wine merchants

At **Adnam's**, The Crown, High St, Southwold, Suffolk ☎ (0502) 724222, find Simon Loftus's wide selection of wines from around the world. Mail-order service. Also in East Anglia is **Lay & Wheeler**, 6 Culver St, Colchester, Essex ☎ (0206) 67261, with a very strong all-round list. Find Rhône and Loire specialists **Yapp Brothers**, at the Old Brewery, Mere, Wiltshire ☎ (0747) 860423 – they find favour with JONATHAN MEADES. **Hungerford Wine Co**, Unit 3,

🎩 Buzz Tastes of the countryside: rustic sophisticates and mail-ordering townies have the best choice of produce. **Colchester Oyster Fishery**, North Farm, East Mersea, Colchester, Essex ☎ (0206) 384141, is the place to buy the best English oysters and clams 🍴...... Savour smokin' hot goodies from Hugh Forestier-Walker's **Minola Smoked Products**, Kencot Hill Farmhouse, Filkins, Lechlade, Gloucestershire ☎ (0367) 860391. Top London restaurants snap up oak-smoked wild Scottish salmon and smoked green-lip mussels (Bibendum) and smoked unsalted butter (Langan's). Hugh F-W is even exporting to Bahrain and Dubai 🍴...... MICHAEL BROADBENT's sweet tooth leads him to **The Toffee Shop**, 7 Brunswick Rd, Penrith, Cumbria ☎ (0768) 62008, for *"the best vanilla fudge – we have a standing monthly order"*. Good toffee too – treacle or butter...................... 🍴

Station Yard, Hungerford, Berkshire ☎ (0488) 683238, receives LORD LICHFIELD's vote for Bordeaux both red and white. Cotswoldies flock to **Windrush Wines**, The Barracks, Cecily Hill, Cirencester, Gloucestershire ☎ (0285) 650466, to try Mark Savage's list of more than 135 worldwide wine producers – especially North Pacific ones. *"Quite superb"* says LADY MACDONALD OF MACDONALD – they introduced her fave bubbly, Billcart-Salmon, to the UK. Further west, at **Avery's**, 7 Park St, Bristol, Avon ☎ (0272) 214141, old burgundies, Spanish, German and Australian wines are well represented.

—— Theatre ——

Provincials on the boil are: **Royal Shakespeare Theatre**, Stratford-upon-Avon, – best company (**RSC**), best playwright, great riverside theatre complex, great artistic director in Adrian Noble, and advisory director in Sir Peter Hall, recently wooed back to stage starry productions. The **Bristol Old Vic** company play first-rate moderns and classics at the **Theatre Royal**, Bristol. The **Leicester Haymarket** and **Sheffield Crucible** are top-notch provs; the **Royal Exchange**, **Manchester**, set in the enormous Victorian cotton exchange, *"is in the round and that's really challenging; a delightful-looking theatre"* – MAUREEN LIPMAN. The **Chichester Festival Theatre** puts on established works throughout the year, and stages a festival, Apr–Sept.

—— Tours and properties ——

THE LANDMARK TRUST,
Shottesbrooke, Maidenhead, Berkshire
☎ (062882) 5925
The serious, architecturally minded trustees also have an eye for the deeply eccentric. Trust them to find you the perfect place to get away. Alongside grand Scottish castles with booby traps for the unwary are a Napoleonic fort, a converted pigsty sleeping two, and the gatehouse where Mary Queen of Scots spent her last night.

WOLESEY LODGES, 17 Chapel St,
Bildeston, Ipswich, Suffolk
☎ (0449) 741297
A non-profit-making company which groups loosely a selection of private country homes offering bed and breakfast and often dinner. *"They're always wonderful houses, I stayed in a 15C hall near Winnie-the-Pooh country. It's like being in a hotel only much nicer and much cheaper"* – RICHARD COMPTON-MILLER.

WORTHY INTERNATIONAL TRAVEL,
The Power House, Alpha Place, London
SW3 ☎ (071) 376 3550
The route to instant social ascent. Susie Worthy will arrange your private stay in various stately homes and country estates, whisk you into the events of the Season and throw in some culture via guided heritage tours.

SCOTLAND

—— Art and museums ——

BURRELL COLLECTION, 2060
Pollokshaws Rd, Pollok Country Park,
Glasgow ☎ (041) 649 7151
A delight for decorative arts enthusiasts. 19C shipping tycoon William Burrell's 800-piece collection is housed in a bright modern gallery. The cast includes Ming and Tang dynasty porcelain, French and Dutch masters, Elizabethan and Georgian furniture and collections of stained glass, tapestry and silver. *"Exceptional"* says SERENA FASS, and JOHN TOVEY agrees.

NATIONAL GALLERIES OF SCOTLAND,
The Mound, Edinburgh ☎ (031) 556 8921
The **National Gallery** houses paintings by Raphael, Titian, Rembrandt, Van Dyck, Constable, Gauguin, a Bernini bust, and Scottish works. Amid the neo-Gothic splendour of the **Portrait Gallery**, Queen St, are Scotland's great and good immortalized on canvas, in print and stone. Out of the centre is the **Gallery of Modern Art**, Belford Rd, for most major European and American 20C artists – Matisse to Moore, Picasso to Paolozzi. All galleries present excellent exhibitions.

—— Festivals ——

🏆 **EDINBURGH INTERNATIONAL**
FESTIVAL, 21 Market St ☎ (031) 225 5756
Most things to most men. Edinburgh gets insomnia during August – performers from the 4 corners flock to the Athens of the North, bringing theatre, opera, dance and music to culture vultures (though standards are ever-criticized by real buffs). Meanwhile the **Fringe**, 180 High St ☎ (031) 226 5257, is a lucky dip of more than 500 acts filling bars, clubs and pubs with cabaret/stand-up/musical/serious entertainment for 24-hour revellers. The best is seriously good, the worst is simply ghastly. At the **Assembly Rooms**, 50 George St ☎ (031) 226 5992, top comics and musicians keep the crowds on edge. The **Film Festival** shows some fairly wacky celluloid, there are **TV** and **Jazz** festivals, and it all rounds off with the famous **Tattoo** up at the Castle.

—— Historic buildings ——

CAWDOR CASTLE, Nairn ☎ (0667) 7651
Built by the Thane of Cawdor in 1370, this

moated, turreted castle is lived in by the family to this day. Marvellous walks in one of the finest and oldest woods in the whole of Europe, and glimpses of the sea. Shophound SERENA FASS votes this one *"the best in Scotland"*, while guidehound LORD LICHFIELD homes in on *"far and away the best and funniest guidebook of any stately home – you want to buy 6 and leave one in every loo."*

CRATHES CASTLE, Dee Valley
☎ (03304 4525)
The most beautiful and best-preserved 16C castle in Scotland, with painted ceilings of renown. Drive there through magnificent woodland – exquisite colours and roaming deer – then stroll through the famous walled garden (1720 yew hedges, herbaceous borders and roses) overlooking the Dee Valley. *"The gardens are absolutely outstanding. A marvellous part of the world"* – SERENA FASS.

——— *Hotels* ———

AIRDS HOTEL, Port Appen, Appen, Argyll ☎ (063173) 236
Run by the Allen family this 300-year-old former ferry inn rests on the side of Loch Linnhe. Strong foodie/grapie emphasis: Oban langoustines, lobster, oysters and turbot are cooked by mother and son, while father Eric looks after the huge wine cellar. MARTIN SKAN and LADY MACDONALD OF MACDONALD are both admiring.

ALTNAHARRIE INN, Ullapool, Highland
☎ (085483) 230
Fred and Gunn Brown's little 8-room inn by Loch Broom makes visitors feel like houseguests. Set meals of seafood, beef and game are cooked to the liking of LADY MACDONALD OF MACDONALD and PAUL HENDERSON.

ARISAIG HOTEL, Arisaig, Inverness-shire ☎ (06875) 210
Built in 1720, the 15-bedroom inn stands close to the White Sands beaches – filmed in *Local Hero* and *Highlander*. Janice and George Stewart deliver top-quality Scottish fare for breakfast and dinner – and no messing with sauces unless you ask for them. *"The best beaches in Great Britain are between Mora and Arisaig, and you can't find them unless you know where to look. And the food at the Arisaig Hotel is wonderful"* – LADY MACDONALD OF MACDONALD.

CALEDONIAN HOTEL, Princes St, Edinburgh ☎ (031) 225 2433
Edinburgh's grand hotel finds it's way back into favour with JULIAN LLOYD WEBBER: *"It's been refurbished, and also it's a very good place for a light lunch."* KEN HOM has some advice for them: *"The place looks wonderful but what is missing is the service – you have a young staff that has not yet been properly trained."*

INVERLOCHY CASTLE, Fort William, Highland ☎ (0397) 702177
Under Ben Nevis, Queen Victoria's favoured Lochside Scottish castle is *"as close as you can come to being perfect"* according to PAUL HENDERSON. *"People will scoff, but it's marvellous. Michael Leonard is quite the best managing director"* – LADY MACDONALD OF MACDONALD. *"Inverlochy Castle is still the best place"* – BOB PAYTON. LISA BARNARD agrees.

ISLE OF ERISKA HOTEL, Ledaig, Connel, Strathclyde ☎ (063172) 371
Robin and Sheena Buchanan-Smith continue to delight guests with home cooking and good malt whisky at their wild island home. *"It's quirky and eccentric, but they really know about country living"* – LORD LICHFIELD.

KINLOCH LODGE, Sleat, Isle of Skye, Highland ☎ (04713) 214
Lord and Lady Macdonald of Macdonald's quiet home has 10 bedrooms overlooking the craggy Skye-line. Fine seasonal cooking by Lady M, plus fishing, stalking and golf.

ONE DEVONSHIRE GARDENS, Glasgow ☎ (041) 339 2001
The best hotel in Scotland. Updated Victoriana – rich mahogany, cunning lighting, four-posters and stained-glass windows – combines with supreme service and attention to detail to make this a natural stop-off for cultured bon viveurs such as BRUCE OLDFIELD. *"It really is a great place – Ken McCullough is a genius, a terrifically stylish man, he's ace"* – BOB PAYTON. LORD LICHFIELD pays his respects: *"It has got even better and the staff are even more polished – I think it's as good as Claridge's in its way."*

THE ST ANDREWS OLD COURSE HOTEL, St Andrews, Fife ☎ (0334) 74371
On the world's oldest golf course, the swish old-timer has been brought up to date by a £16 million overhaul. *"They've done a marvellous job – it looks absolutely spectacular inside"* – MARK MCCORMACK. SALLY BURTON rates their health treatments: *"The most beautiful, luxurious spa, all the treatments are superb. Very nice girls who seem to have all the time in the world to look after you."*

——— *Music* ———

SCOTTISH OPERA, 39 Elmbank Crescent, Glasgow ☎ (041) 248 4567
Highly respected company which puts on all kinds of opera from Mozart to Britten under the directorship of John Mauceri.

USHER HALL, Lothian Rd, Edinburgh ☎ (031) 228 1155
"Still probably my favourite of all . . . they tried to knock it down a few times, but it's a wonderful hall" – JULIAN LLOYD WEBBER.

—— *Restaurants* ——

See also Hotels.

**CHAMPANY INN, Champany Corner,
Linlithgow, Lothian ☎ (050683) 4532**
The carnivore's delight – nothing gets in the
way of simple high-quality Scottish beef, salmon
and lobster in Clive Davidson's restaurant. *"The
best steaks in the country are probably at
the Champany"* – ALAN CROMPTON-BATT. BOB
PAYTON likes his raw.

**THE GRILL ROOM, Balmoral Hotel,
Princes St, Edinburgh ☎ (031) 557 6727**
*"The best new restaurant in Edinburgh,
undoubtedly. I think it's absolutely scrumptious
. . . it's not trying to be French, just using good
Scottish ingredients"* – LADY MACDONALD OF
MACDONALD. Look out for the sautéed calf's liver
with bacon and mashed potato and the warm
glazed apple tart.

**🐚 THE PEAT INN, Peat Inn, Cupar, Fife
☎ (033484) 206**
Blink and you'll miss it – this is the sum of the
village of Peat Inn. Chef David Wilson prepares
multi-coursed feasts using the best Scottish
ingredients with invention. Great game (pigeon
breast with wild mushrooms, noisettes of venison saddle in a red wine sauce) and seafood
(ragout of scallops, monkfish and pork belly)
make this a perennial favourite for DAME BAR-
BARA CARTLAND, who stays in one of the suites
at the back. *"David Wilson is such a great chef
and such a nice man. He completely negates the
image of the chef as being an egomanical prima
donna . . . the sort of chef every country should
have at least half a dozen of"* – LOYD GROSSMAN.
He gets the thumbs up from PAUL HENDERSON.

**🐚 LA POTINIERE, Main St, Gullane,
Lothian ☎ (0620) 843214**
Uncompromising as they are (dinner on Saturday only, one sitting, no-choice 4-course menu,
hard to book), David and Hilary Brown set rules
that top gastronomes are happy to obey. *"Super
– they're very nice people and she is a very good
cook"* – MARTIN SKAN. *"Food and wine – often
below auction prices – are astounding value for
money"* says PAUL HENDERSON, who chose it for
his 50th birthday. JOHN TOVEY thinks it has the
best wine list in the country.

**WATERLOO PLACE, Waterloo Place,
Edinburgh ☎ (031) 557 0007**
Edinburgh's newest and best restaurant according to SOPHIE GRIGSON: *"The cooking is very simple but absolutely right, done without pretension
but of really superb quality."* MATTHEW FORT
agrees: *"The food is very sensible and very good,
very sensibly priced, it's got good flavours
enlivened by original and unusual touches.
Extremely well thought-out with a very distinct
personal style."* Chef Andrew Radford taught

himself to cook, and has turned the Georgian
building into *"a very beautiful airy dining
room"* – SOPHIE G.

—— *Theatre* ——

Top of the Scots is the **Citizen's** in **Glasgow**
for value and great plays by Euro and
Scottish writers – Spense, Gray, Kelman. In
Edinburgh, it's the **Travers**.

WALES

*Historic buildings and
—— gardens* ——

**CASTELL COCH, Tongwynlais
☎ 0222 810101**
The 3 turrets of this red sandstone fairytale castle peer through the surrounding woodland on
the side of a mountain. Built by William Burges
for the Marquis of Bute, this is Victorian roman-
ticism at its peak, with every surface painted
with natural and heraldic scenes. Furniture, also
by Burges, completes the fable.

**POWIS CASTLE, Nr Welshpool
☎ 0938 554336**
This medieval castle stands in magnificent 17C
formal gardens and houses an incomparable
collection of Indian works of art, brought from
India by Lord Clive and his son. *"The most
wonderful garden. It has terraces up and down
the hill, one side leads to a wilderness and
tunnels of hedges"* – DUGGIE FIELDS. *"Lovely
gardens, absolutely exceptional"* – SERENA FASS.

—— *Hotels* ——
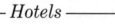

**BODYSGALLEN HALL, Llandudno,
Gwynedd ☎ (0492) 584466**
Wales's grandest hotel sits imposingly in formal,
landscaped gardens amid 200 acres of untamed
parkland. Stay in the 17C mansion or converted
outbuildings with the wilds of Wales without,
and warm, comfortable splendour within.

—— *Music* ——

**BRECON JAZZ FESTIVAL, Watton
Chambers, Brecon, Powys
☎ (0874) 625557**
80,000 jazz fiends descend on Brecon one weekend in August for over 100 sessions. The biggie
is always on Sunday afternoon – Sonny Rollins,
Jerry Mulligan and co. A definite GEORGE MELLY
winner.

WELSH NATIONAL OPERA, John St, Cardiff ☎ (0222) 464666
One of Britain's finest – certainly its least glitzy (people actually go to hear the *singing*). Heartfelt, exciting, sometimes shoestring productions. Tremendous team spirit and a great Welsh chorus. Based in the Cardiff New Theatre but regional tours win them fans, like LORD MONTAGU OF BEAULIEU, from all over Britain.

―――――― *Restaurants* ――――――

🐟 **WALNUT TREE INN, Llandewi Skirrid, Nr Abergavenny, Gwent ☎ (0873) 852797**
The pub-turned-foodie Mecca offers fabulous local produce imbued with Italian flair and oriental zip by chef-owner Franco Taruschio. "*Out of London, I would rather go there than anywhere else. A most enchanting place and it's still just a pub, a pub with white truffles with any luck. The tables and chairs are the same as they would be in a pub and Franco is behind the bar but the food, of course, is not a bit like pub food*" – ELIZABETH DAVID. "*The restaurateur's restaurant. Always hard to choose, but the hot seafood platter, Thai pork appetizer and porcetta are not to be missed*" – PAUL HENDERSON. "*An astonishing place to find in the middle of the hills*" – JULIAN LLOYD WEBBER. "*I don't think I've had a better meal anywhere for a long while. Worth driving from London just for lunch*" – SIMON WILLIAMS. SIR CLEMENT FREUD makes the trip: "*Wonderful and unpretentious and honest and different. Run by an Italian married to an English woman living in Wales*

with a Vietnamese adopted child so it's pretty international."

―――――― *Shopping* ――――――

VIN SULLIVAN, 4 Frogmore St, Abergavenny, Gwent ☎ (0873) 852331
John Sutherland's grown-up grocery supplies restaurants and hotels as far afield as Inverlochy Castle as well as catering for the needs of more immediate neighbours. An extraordinary array of seafood (fish, scallops, sea urchins . . .), local game from teal to ptarmigan and the finest fruit and veg.

CANADA

MONTREAL

―――――― *Bars and cafés* ――――――

ALEXANDRE'S, 1454 Peel St E ☎ (514) 288 5105
Très français bar – bistro tables and chairs on the street to watch the promenade.

L'ILE NOIR, 342 Ontario St E ☎ (514) 982 0866
The hot spot for spotting professional spotters – art directors, photographers – downing serious

 **Buzzz** Bingo! It's **Two Fat Ladies**, 88 Dunbarton Rd, Glasgow ☎ (041) 339 1944, a seafood restaurant as fresh and eccentric as its name. Owned and run by New Zealanders, who dish up fish with finesse (Brittany fish soup, grilled herring with wasabi and daikon, char-grilled mackerel with salsa) 🐟 . . . . . . Flower of Scotland: LADY MACDONALD OF MACDONALD thinks "*the best florist in Great Britain, never mind Scotland, is Thomas Maxwell of* **Maxwell Flowers** ☎ *(031) 226 2866. In a class of his own*" 🐟 . . . . . . Stocking up: **Jenners**, 48 Princes St, Edinburgh ☎ (031) 725 2442, is still the poshest department store in town, and a good source of top Caledonian produce – Speyside smoked salmon, smoked trout from Mull; also 70 different honeys, 68 cheeses, 112 teas 🐟 . . . . . . Scot stock 2: **Pinney's of Scotland**, Brydekirk, Annan, Dumfries & Galloway ☎ (05763) 401, offers the real McCoy – local salmon, oak-smoked on the premises and additive-free (supplies top shops like Fortnum's). Also gravad lax, smoked trout, mackerel and eel, available if you call in, or by mail order 🐟 . . . . . . Chock-a-block stock: **Valvona and Crolla**, 19 Elm Row, Edinburgh ☎ (031) 556 6066, is the best Italian deli this side of the border, crammed with 100 different olive oils, 600 Italian wines, nearly 200 cheeses, 40 to 50 salamis, macaroons, biscuits, pannetone – a "*superb place*," says SOPHIE GRIGSON. For LADY MACDONALD OF MACDONALD it's "*the best delicatessen in Great Britain*" . . . . 🐟

Scotch whiskies from the Highlands, Midlands and Lowlands menu.

LUX, 5220 St Laurent Blvd
☎ (514) 271 9272
Round-the-clock drop-in centre for Montreal's fashionable, intellectual insomniacs, this café/bookshop meets the needs of body and soul with coffee and Kafka.

Clubs

LE BELMONT, 4483 St Laurent Blvd
☎ (514) 845 8443
Zip along to see modish Montrealers getting down in French fashion. The disco beat throbs here to 'soft alternative' music that pulls a classily turned-out crowd on to the dance floor. Quiet room, too, for tête-à-têtes.

L'ESPRIT, 1234 Mountain St
☎ (514) 397 1711
Spirits of the past and present groove together in this high-tech multi-level club within a 19C cathedral-like building. Capacity for 1,200 high-energy boppers.

METROPOLIS CLUB, 59 E St Catherine's St ☎ (514) 288 2020
2,000 technoboppers can pack into this huge revamped Art Deco cinema for a sweaty groove. With 6 bars and acres of dance floor it's the largest club in Canada.

Fashion designers

HILARY RADLEY, 7101 Ave du Parc, Suite 304 ☎ (514) 273 9171
At the sharply cutting edge of Canadian design, for wonderfully modern structured coats for men and women. *"Very important"* for BONNIE BROOKS and *"a little lower key than some of the others but excellent"* for VALERIE GIBSON.

JEAN CLAUDE POITRAS, 400 Maisonneuve, Suite 1150
☎ (514) 849 8331
Tasteful timeless classics – dresses, suits – which appeal to such style-leading mesdames as Mila Mulroney.

MICHEL ROBICHAUD, 5253 Ave du Parc, #525 ☎ (514) 273 1567
Expanding empire of classy women's and children's wear and cosmetics to cover most of modish Montreal's needs.

SIMON CHANG, 555 Chabanel St W, Suite 1407 ☎ (514) 384 9203
Chang's only detractors say that he is too successful; those without green spectacles say *"he does clothes that every woman wants but with a little colour and dash. Wearable, colourful clothes for working women"* – VALERIE GIBSON.

Film

MONTREAL WORLD FILM FESTIVAL, 1455 blvd de Maisonneuve E
☎ (514) 933 9699
An influential festival of over 200 films, held annually in Aug/Sept. Make or break for Canada's innovative film industry and important in the wider world.

Hotels

HOTEL DE LA MONTAGNE, 1430 de la Montagne St ☎ (514) 288 5656
Rather plush French hotel with individually decorated rooms. The main restaurant, **Lutétia**, might be the height of gastronomic refinement but, unless you like singles bars, enter **Thursday's** at your risk.

 HOTEL VOGUE, 1425 rue de la Montagne ☎ (514) 285 5555
Chic newcomer to downtown Montreal. *"The rooms are wonderful, the food is good, it's centrally located: just terrific"* – KAREN KAIN. **Société Café** has established itself as *the* place to be seen to eat.

LE QUATRE SAISONS, 1050 Sherbrooke St W ☎ (514) 284 1110
The sort of smooth-running machine one expects from the Four Seasons group now has North America's first **Zen** restaurant, designed with glittering, icy precision by Rick Mather.

RITZ-CARLTON, 1228 Sherbrooke St W ☎ (514) 842 4212
The *grande dame* of Montreal sits with dignity in her fashionable setting. Small by city standards, with staff that are numerous and personal enough to dispel the ritzy grandeur of high, embossed ceilings, expanses of brass, etc. *"You can go for tea there in the afternoon, which is very pleasant, but as the day goes on it becomes more interesting and full of political people in the bar"* – MADELEINE POULIN. **Bar Maritime** is where city folk converge after work for drinks and terrific seafood.

Music

FESTIVAL DE JAZZ DE MONTREAL, 355 St Catherine St W, Room 301
☎ (514) 871 1881
An international street party in the heat of summer (June/July) with maestro musos playing up a storm in clubs and outdoors. *"Fantastic!"* – MADELEINE POULIN.

MONTREAL SYMPHONY ORCHESTRA, 85 St Catherine St W, Suite 900
☎ (514) 842 3402
The glorious Place des Arts is home to Canada's

finest orchestra, under revered conductor Charles Dutoit.

—————— *Restaurants* ——————

BEAVER CLUB, Queen Elizabeth Hotel, 900 Blvd Rene Levesque W
☎ (514) 861 3511
The place to watch the power-brokers beavering away over lunches that mean business. More than competent, high-quality (and -priced) French cooking, but in essence a hotel restaurant.

CHEZ DELMO, 211 rue Notre-Dame
☎ (514) 849 4061
A sea-foodie institution since 1910 – its reliable food and easy atmosphere keep the regular clientele (judges, lawyers, journalists) happy. "*I like going there on my birthday and always have the same thing – poached salmon with hollandaise*" – MADELEINE POULIN.

Moseying Montreal
—————————♠—————————

Montreal is a city which spurns not the pedestrian. Amble along the canal from Atwater Market to the historic greystone houses and cafés of Old Montreal or see the seasons change on Mount Royal from autumn scarlet to winter white. "*Walking on Mount Royal in the winter time is fantastic. There are no leaves on the trees so you can see the city and you have hard white snow underfoot. You walk along to Beaver Lake and there are little children skating and tobogganing . . . you see it all but don't hear it because the snow muffles everything*" – MADELEINE POULIN.

LA MAREE, 404 Place Jacques Cartier
☎ (514) 861 8126
Long-standing, consistently good French seafood restaurant. No 1 for romance buffs: it's in old Montreal but transports you to Paris.

LE PARIS RESTAURANT, 1812 St Catherine W ☎ (514) 927 4898
An institution for over 40 years, slightly down-at-heel but with reliable French food and some of the most loyal customers in the business: "*Full of old habitués. It's a family-type place, they know us and we know them*" – MADELEINE POULIN.

🐟 LES HALLES, 1450 Crescent St
☎ (514) 844 2328
Well-bred classic French cooking from long-time

chef Crevoisier Dominique, attracting a lively night-time crowd. Drawcards on the food front might include duck breast with a Cumberland sauce or fillet of beef with foie gras.

LES MIGNARDISES, 2035 Rue St Denis
☎ (514) 842 1151
Ex-Les Halles Jean Pierre Monnet applies similarly high standards of food and service to this expensive, élite restaurant.

PREGO, 5142 St Laurent Blvd
☎ (514) 271 3234
Contemporary, imaginative Italian in a happening Art Deco-rated dining room. Beautiful table settings and slick service.

🐟 RESTAURANT LALOUX, 250 Ave des Pins E ☎ (514) 287 9127
One of the greats. Uncluttered décor concentrates diners' minds on the elegant, Parisian cooking.

—————— *Shopping* ——————

Sherbrooke Street is still *the* area for grown-up fashion and glossy galleries, **Notre Dame St** for antique-browsing.

GREGE, 2130 Crescent St
☎ (514) 843 6228
Showcase for the more innovative design wonders such as Yamamoto, Comme des Garçons, Dolce & Gabbana, Kenzo.

HOLT RENFREW, 1300 Sherbrooke St
☎ (514) 842 5111
Holt's leads Canada's fashion direction as always. Beautifully displayed and carefully chosen, the collection features most of the world's sharpest designers (Lagerfeld, Montana, Karan, Armani, Ferré, Byblos) alongside top Canadians (Alfred Sung, Jean Claude Poitras). MADELEINE POULIN always finds something in the Armani boutique.

LES CREATEURS, 1444 Sherbrooke St W
☎ (514) 284 2102
Hip and fun clothery features creatures on the avant-garde edge of design – Jean-Paul Gaultier, Azzedine Alaïa, Junko Koshino, Jean Charles de Castelbajac.

LISE WATIER'S SPA, 392 Laurier St W
☎ (514) 270 9296
Everything a woman needs for her serious beauty regime, from facials and manicures to body wraps. Lise Watier has her own line of cosmetics (find them in department stores, etc) and is importing Montreal chic to Paris via her own boutique.

OGILVY'S, 1307 St Catherine St W
☎ (514) 842 7711
Department store par excellence with spacious,

well laid-out floors and the exclusive on Valentino, Joan & David, Escada and Perry Ellis. *"They choose their brands well in all categories and price ranges"* – MADELEINE POULIN.

REVENGE, 3852 St Denis St
☎ **(514) 843 4379**
A trendy boutique full of civic pride and the pride of Quebec's young design talent. Exactly who is in stock changes, but they will always be at the cutting edge of fashion: Jean-Claude Poitras, Michel Desjardins, Marie St Pierre . . .

L'UOMO, 1452 Peel St ☎ (514) 844 1008
For the designer man about town, stocking all the big boys: Basile, Byblos, Armani, Gaultier, Valentino, Cerruti, Gigli.

TORONTO

—— Art and museums ——

THE ART GALLERY OF ONTARIO, 317 Dundas St W ☎ (416) 977 0414
A splendidly diverse international collection with a strong line in contemporary Canadians and sculpture: *"The best Henry Moore collection in the world – magnificent"* – TONY ASPLER.

—— Ballet ——

♟ NATIONAL BALLET OF CANADA, 157 King St E ☎ (416) 362 1041
A fine company under director Reid Anderson, who brings the Royal Ballet tradition to Canada. Dancers such as Karen Kain and Rex Harrington match the best in the world. EDWARD THORPE would put them in his world top 10.

—— Bars and cafés ——

RODNEY'S OYSTER BAR, 209 Adelaide St E ☎ (416) 363 8105
A tiny room tucked in a basement in downtown Toronto, *"you enter it and feel like you've been transplanted to the coast. Great!"* – BONNIE BROOKS. That coastal feeling could be eastern or western – the oysters come from both.

SANTA FE BAR AND GRILL, 129 Peter St ☎ (416) 345 9345
Here, life is beautiful: the hippest place around to see, be seen, snack Santa Fe/Mex style and root for racing iguanas.

—— Clubs ——

BAMBOO, 312 Queen St W
☎ **(416) 593 5771**
The eccentric, energetic mix of reggae music,

Thai food and socialite owner Patty Habib still draws 'em in.

♟ GO-GO, 250 Richmond St W
☎ **(416) 593 4646**
Capacious 4-storey dance club, with a lounge bar, the Theater Room for high-energy hijinks, the White Room (all white, see, with Roman columns and statuary), an art gallery in the basement and a patio on the roof, with fountains and summer barbecues. Wed is gay/transvestite night; from Thurs thru Sun, Toronto's zippiest (mixed) 1,000 line up to get down.

STILIFE, 217 Richmond St W
☎ **(416) 593 6116**
Glitzy, high-energy dance-club for models, rock stars and wannabes. Rod Stewart and George Michael have been spotted when in town. Enter on Duncan St.

TOP O' THE SENATOR, 249 Victoria St
☎ **(416) 364 7515**
"The Ronnie Scott's of Canada" according to DANIEL STOFFMAN. Great jazz bar above the Senator (see Restaurants) where jazz greats mooch about and jam. *"Wonderful"* – TONY ASPLER.

—— Fashion designers ——

ALFRED SUNG, 55 Avenue Rd
☎ **(416) 968 8688**
Easy, wearable, loose-cut separates softly tailored in uncluttered lines. Great little cocktail numbers too. *"Wonderful clothes: practical, simple and good for my lifestyle"* – KAREN KAIN. Good for VALERIE GIBSON's, too.

COMRAGS, 410 Adelaide St W
☎ **(416) 360 0056**
Athletic gear along innovative, body-conscious lines, highly esteemed by BONNIE BROOKS.

LIDA BIDAY, 70 Claremont St, Studio 200 ☎ (416) 368 7661
A newish name in the Toronto fashion stakes. Contemporary dresses for day and evening, a favourite for BONNIE BROOKS. *"Beautifully tailored dresses in great fabrics for executive women"* – VALERIE GIBSON.

ROGER EDWARDS, 339 Queen St E
☎ **(416) 366 2501**
No longer at his boutique but definitely not out of the action. Still the best place for leather, from the perfect jacket to glamour numbers as worn by Linda Evans. Buy them direct from the studio.

STEPHAN CARAS DESIGN, 720 King St W, Suite 801 ☎ (416) 868 6929
Sexy, ultra-feminine evening wear for glamorous women. *"I love it and wear a lot of it"* – VALERIE GIBSON. Also dressy daywear with soft design lines in a classic palette – navy, grey.

WINSTON KONG, 158 Cumberland St
☎ **(416) 924 8837**
Haut-prix haute-couture for knock-'em-dead occasions – weddings, parties, anything.

―――――――― *Film* ――――――――

🏶 **TORONTO FESTIVAL OF FESTIVALS, 70 Carlton St** ☎ **(416) 967 7371**
The film world holds its breath for 10 days in Sept when a constellation of stars descends on Toronto for premieres and face-the-audience sessions. Offbeat European and Latin American offerings as well as mainstream blockbusters. *"If you watched movies for 24 hours a day, you still couldn't see them all. A tremendous production"* – STEVE PODBORSKI. *"The new up-and-coming festival – most of the top English and American critics prefer it to Venice, which is on at the same time. It's better run, bigger, more imaginative and it has the top films. It really is second only to Cannes"* – IAIN JOHNSTONE.

―――――――― *Hotels* ――――――――

🏶 **FOUR SEASONS, 21 Avenue Rd, Yorkville** ☎ **(416) 964 0411**
Canada's finest hotel, and certainly its most smoothly run under Isadore Sharp (*"hotelier extraordinaire"* – ROSEMARY SEXTON). SIR PETER USTINOV goes further: *"One of my favourites in the world. They have all sort of ingenious things like early-morning coffee and croissants in the foyer if you have to catch an early flight. And the best, relaxed coffee-shop type of restaurant, which is so charming I wouldn't mind taking a main meal there."* Indoor and outdoor pools and the haute French **Truffles**.

🏶 **HOTEL INTER-CONTINENTAL, 220 Bloor St W** ☎ **(416) 960 5200**
Brand new and smart with it – the established leaders are having to clutch their laurels more tightly. *"It's really beautiful and the restaurant,* **Signatures**, *is getting raves"* – VALERIE GIBSON. ROBERT RAMSAY echoes: *"Making its niche and has a wonderful first-class restaurant."*

KING EDWARD HOTEL, 37 King St E
☎ **(416) 863 9700**
Renovated to its original, rather formal grandeur (the British royal family stays here when in town), the King Eddy is making its mark once more. *"A fabulous tradition of superb service and excellent business facilities, and the restaurant is one of the finest in the city"* – STEVE PODBORSKI. ROBERT RAMSAY would pick **Chiaro's** as the place *"you'd take your grandmother for her birthday"* – unthreatening but perfectly turned-out French cooking.

🏶 **SUTTON PLACE HOTEL, 955 Bay St**
☎ **(416) 924 9221**
Glamorous hotel with a glitzy client-list. *"Sutton Place has come of age as the premier hotel in town, largely because of its manager, Hans Gerhardt. He really pampers his VIP guests and all that hard work has paid off"* – ROBERT RAMSAY. The pay-off includes Marlon Brando, Kathleen Turner, Vaclav Havel and MC Hammer (*"very nice and polite,"* according to head butler Werner Jankowsky).

―――――――― *Restaurants* ――――――――

See also Hotels.

CENTRO, 2472 Yonge St ☎ **(416) 483 2211**
Airy, West-Coast style restaurant, with modern Cal-Ital food and a where-its-at crowd. *"A very good place, very solid. Probably the best wine list in the city with a lot of Italian wines that aren't available anywhere else in Toronto"* – DANIEL STOFFMAN. BONNIE BROOKS approves, as does the entire Canadian ice hockey team.

Canada's Best Restaurants

1	SPLENDIDO BAR & GRILL · Toronto
2	LOTUS · Toronto
3	LES HALLES · Montreal
4	NORTH 44 · Toronto
5	UMBERTO IL GIARDINO · Vancouver

IL POSTO, York Square, 148 Yorkville Ave ☎ **(416) 968 0469**
Il Posto's imaginative *nuova cucina* has its supporters among the cognoscenti, BONNIE BROOKS for one. Detractors too: *"Overrated"* yawns DANIEL STOFFMAN.

🏶 **LOTUS, 96 Tecumseth St**
☎ **(416) 368 7620**
Tiny, beautifully elegant dining room, where tiny, beautifully elegant diners nibble on Asian/French/Canadian cuisine that answers to the same description. What's more, the flavours live up to the presentation.

MASANIELLO, 647 College St
☎ **(416) 533 7046**
A rare Italian restaurant that doesn't come via California. Authentic food and plenty of it with an accent on freshness and simplicity rather than fashion.

🏶 **NORTH 44, 2537 Yonge St**
☎ **(416) 487 4897**
Post-Pronto, Mark McEwan has *"transformed a store, put in huge soaring ceilings and large windows and it's now the North Toronto in-*

spot" – ROSEMARY SEXTON. Eclectic, world-influenced food on work-of-art plates finds favour with ROBERT RAMSAY (*"a miraculous combination of Pacific Coast plus American south-western cooking and very well managed"*) and VALERIE GIBSON (*"famous for their appetizer platters; very innovative with interesting combinations of tastes"*).

PRONTO, 692 Mount Pleasant Ave ☎ (416) 486 1111

Hip, hyped-up northern Italian food with a great bar and great staff. *"If I want an evening with the utmost in service and a serene atmosphere, I go to Pronto"* – STEVE PODBORSKI. TONY ASPLER does too: *"Very good."*

SCARAMOUCHE, 1 Benvenuto Place ☎ (416) 961 8011

One of the tops for classical, immaculately presented French food and its attendant hovering service. A favourite for TONY ASPLER and KAREN KAIN but the formality grates a little for DANIEL STOFFMAN and BONNIE BROOKS, who prefers the more casual pasta bar.

SENATOR, 249 Victoria St ☎ (416) 364 7517

A jazzy trio: the bar on top (see Clubs), an imitation diner with the best hamburgers in town, and a rather eccentric, elegant, 20s-style restaurant. *"The diner has really down-to-earth food and the décor is really authentic"* – DANIEL STOFFMAN. TONY ASPLER likes the upscale side of things: *"You dine in curtained booths and if you need service, you press a button. Very discreet."* KAREN KAIN is keen.

🦪 SPLENDIDO BAR & GRILL, 88 Harbord St ☎ (416) 863 9700

From the king of Toronto restaurateurs, Franco Prevedello (Centro, Pronto . . .), comes another jewel for his crown. Wonderfully warm terracotta interior, great grill-type Italian cooking under Hungarian-born Arpi Magyar and the most fashionable scene in the city: *"Hard to get in even on a Monday or Tuesday"* – DANIEL STOFFMAN. *"Very exciting décor and the best northern Italian food"* – BONNIE BROOKS. *"Loud, bistroish, great fun and good food though it's known more for its crowd"* – ROBERT RAMSAY. *"Italian high-tech"* – TONY ASPLER. *"The newest hot spot"* is ROSEMARY SEXTON's tip.

———— Shopping ————

Bijou **Yorkville**, with **Hazelton Lanes**, **Avenue Road** and **Cumberland Street**, is the smart area to shop, dine and promenade in your furs. Nearby, glossy **Bloor Street** (west side only) boasts the best stores. **Queen Street** (west side again) is the funkiest drag in town – street vendors selling artistic jewellery and bags, wild Bohemian boutiques, great cafés. There's also miles more shopping underground.

ANDREWS, Hazelton Lanes, 55 Avenue Rd ☎ (416) 920 0990

Wonderful new store with directional buying. All the grandees (Montana, Versace, Donna Karan, Valentino, Ungaro) for grand budgets. *"They have all the designer names but are also forward-thinking, with interesting, less well-known things"* – BONNIE BROOKS.

CHEZ CATHERINE, 55 Avenue Rd ☎ (416) 967 5666

Catherine Hill has European fashion sewn up in her ultra-swish boutique – Basile, Ferré, Valentino, Versace, Krizia, Lange.

CLASSICA UOMO DONNA, 150 Bloor St W ☎ (416) 961 0683

Chic European clobber for men – from classic Ferré to Gaultier. Now some women's wear as well.

DAVIDS, 66 Bloor St W ☎ (416) 920 1000

All of Toronto's well-heeled step out in Davids' designers: Bruno Magli, Maud Frizon, Mario Valentino, Andrea Pfister. . . . Leather accessories too – bags, luggage and belts.

FETOUN'S, Hazelton Lanes, 55 Avenue Rd ☎ (416) 923 3434

In a lush pink boudoir to the tinkling of the piano and under the watchful eye of her faithful boxer dog, Fetoun, or Fifi as she is known, supplies elaborate couture confections for big clients' big occasions.

HARRY ROSEN, 82 Bloor St W ☎ (416) 972 0556 and branches

Ladies and gentlemen find major labels – Valentino, Byblos, Lagerfeld – in the green marble and glass fashion district flagship store. City males trip downtown to the **Scotia Plaza** shop for a more traditional look.

HAZELTON LANES, 55 Avenue Rd ☎ (416) 968 8600

Glitzy glass shopping complex stuffed with the BIGGEST names in the smallest boutiques. Armani, Ungaro, Valentino, Krizia, Ferré, Alfred Sung, Ralph Lauren, Lagerfeld, Hermès, Saint Laurent and heaps of others grace the poshest mall in town. Galleries, restaurants and jewellers also. The best for TONY ASPLER.

HOLT RENFREW, 50 Bloor St W ☎ (416) 922 2333

The swanky marble and glass store which had the first exclusive Armani boutique in Canada has opened its doors to le fashion monde. She mightn't work there any more but BONNIE BROOKS reckons it's *"still the No 1. Holt's have everybody, they've added 10 new designers, they really have all the designers in the world now."*

IRA BERG, 1510 Yonge St ☎ (416) 922 9100

A local institution, Ira Berg has been dressing

the smartest Toronto ladies in Valentino, Ungaro, Givenchy for more than 60 years. Armani, Genny, Byblos, Artwear and Fratelli Rossetti keep chic customers coming back for more.

MAREK, 110 Bloor St W ☎ (416) 923 5100
The wacky emporium has Europhile stylies queuing up for colourful ties and innovative shoes, designed in-house.

ROOTS, 195 Avenue Rd ☎ (416) 927 8585
A global warming to Roots' green teen gear has brought Don Green and Michael Budman's earthy clothes stores to cities across the world. Shoes, coats, sportsgear – the stuff that (American) dreams are made of.

SPORTING LIFE, 2665 Yonge St ☎ (416) 485 1611
Crowd control is a priority here: as shoppers scrum down to grab top sports gear the store's own policeman directs the parking lot. Inside well-informed staff explain the latest in tennis rackets, pump-action shoes, skis, etc. Choose from hip names – Patagonia, Lauren, Fila, Sun Ice, Descente, Head, Rossignol, Ellesse. STEVE PODBORSKI rates it *"in terms of the best service and in terms of sporting goods"*.

Theatre

Two top festivals are worth the detour: **Stratford Shakespearean Festival**, PO Box 520, Stratford ☎ (416) 363 4471, held May-Nov, for the Bard and other playwrights including contemporaries; and **Shaw Festival**, PO Box 774, Niagara-on-the-Lake ☎ (416) 361 1544, Apr-Oct, for Shaw and other 20C classics.

ELGIN WINTER GARDEN THEATRE, 189 Yonge St ☎ (416) 594 0755
A double-decker theatre that has risen from the ashes of an old vaudeville house with plenty of greenery and plenty of big shows. *"All the detailed work and craftsmanship has been redone – it was great and it's still great"* – STEVE PODBORSKI. DANIEL STOFFMAN likes *"the old-fashioned atmosphere"*, ROBERT RAMSAY the quality of shows and location.

PANTAGES THEATRE, 244 Victoria St ☎ (416) 362 3218
A fine old 20s theatre restored to its gilded, mirrored and ornamented original splendour. It reopened with *The Phantom of the Opera* and it looks like that particular ghost will be haunting this particular theatre for a long while yet.

ROYAL ALEXANDRA THEATRE, 260 King St W ☎ (416) 593 4211
Faithfully restored Victorian building where all the blockbusters show. *"A definite first place to go if you're in town"* – BONNIE BROOKS.

VANCOUVER

Bars and cafés

See also Restaurants.

DELILAH'S, 1906 Haro St ☎ (604) 687 3424
Famous for their Martinis and all-round hot spot for drinks. Overstuffed chairs, low lighting and decent fixed-price menu make it difficult for lounge lizards to leave.

JOE FORTES SEAFOOD HOUSE, 777 Thurlow St ☎ (604) 669 1940
Fab fish restaurant with a great bar where the Vancouver vanguard converges after work.

PELICAN BAY, 1253 Johnston St, Granville Island ☎ (604) 683 7373
View the big city's bright lights through the glass wall or look down on the world from this bar/restaurant/club for Masters of the Universe.

SANTOS TAPAS, 1191 Commercial Drive ☎ (604) 685 3288
Tapas has reached Vancouver, and there is no better, more authentic, more crowded place to graze than this.

Clubs

🍎 **GRACELAND, 1250 Richards St ☎ (604) 688 2648**
Vancouver's biggest, maddest scene in a converted warehouse with 1,600 sq ft of dance floor. Anything goes atmosphere – wild clothes, wild music, ravy crowd. The best discs from the dance clubs of Europe and the USA.

RICHARDS ON RICHARDS, 1036 Richards St ☎ (604) 687 6794
Still the most popular club in the city, you'll have to queue for hours on Fri and Sat nights – the live bands are in vogue in Vancouver.

Fashion designers

ABBY KANAK, 307 W Cordova St ☎ (604) 683 4820
Vancouver's best-known and most interesting designer. Colourful, luxurious clothes in wonderful fabrics walk out of her elegant salon, wrapped around Canada's best bods.

Film

OMNIMAX AND SCIENCE WORLD, 1455 Quebec St ☎ (604) 687 8414
The biggest and best wraparound cinema, built

for Expo '86. The dome-shaped Omnimax is 7 screens high. See travel and nature films there and go next door to **Science World** to see robotic and natural history exhibits.

—————— *Hotels* ——————

**FOUR SEASONS, 791 W Georgia St
☎ (604) 689 9333**
Smoothly run, modern hotel with the customary Four Seasons trimmings – acres of fresh flowers, antiques and well-appointed rooms. See also Restaurants.

Canada's Best Hotels

I	FOUR SEASONS · Toronto
2	SUTTON PLACE · Toronto
3	HOTEL VOGUE · Montreal
4	CHATEAU WHISTLER · Whistler
5	BANFF SPRINGS HOTEL · Banff
6	PAN PACIFIC HOTEL · Vancouver

**🐚 PAN PACIFIC HOTEL, Suite 300, 999
Canada Place ☎ (604) 662 3223**
Nothing olde worlde about the Pan Pacific – it takes up 4 floors in the space-age Vancouver World Trade Center. If you like lift carpets with the day of the week woven into them – changed each night – this is your kinda place. 500-plus rooms, a business centre, spa, pool and 4 restaurants – **Five Sails** is one of the best in town. Spectacular views over the harbour and the Coast Range Mountains: *"We stayed in a very nice suite overlooking the harbour"* – ANDREW LLOYD WEBBER. Great terrace bar at the back, from which Vancouverites gaze at the seaplanes and ocean liners.

**WEDGEWOOD HOTEL, 845 Hornby St
☎ (604) 689 7777**
Eleni Skalbania's low-key Euro-flavoured hotel has fewer than 100 rooms and suites – tastefully decorated with florals and stripes. *"Small and elegant and fairly formal"* – ROSEMARY SEXTON.

—————— *Music* ——————

**DU MAURIER INTERNATIONAL JAZZ FESTIVAL, c/o Coastal Jazz & Blues Society, 203/1206 Hamilton St
☎ (604) 682 0706**
In June and July Vancouver rattles and hums to jazz and blues as bright sparks on the way up rub shoulders with the kings. More than 400 trad, contemporary, blues, fusion and ethnic artists hold court.

—————— *Restaurants* ——————

BRIDGES, 1696 Duranleau, Granville Island ☎ (604) 687 4400
Still the seafoodies' favourite – the BC grilled fresh salmon is a must. Glam dockside setting, *fresh* fish, and a good California/Pacific NW wine list reel in a chic crowd as well as quaffers from the pub next door, where the deck is Vancouver's most happening place of a summer's eve.

**CAFE SPLASH, 1600 Howe St
☎ (604) 682 5600**
Modern, buzzing, trendy joint with West Coast food and best coast location.

CHARTWELL, Four Seasons Hotel, 791 W Georgia St ☎ (604) 689 9333
Sophistiqués enjoy the gentleman's clubby bit – leather armchairs, walnut panelling, open fire, old-world atmosphere and top French cooking.

**🐚 FLAMINGO, 7510 Cambi St
☎ (604) 325 4511**
Vancouver's No 1 Chinese, in DANIEL STOFFMAN's book – and that's saying something: *"Vancouver may have the best Chinese food in the world. Flamingo is authentic Cantonese food, a good, very reliable, big restaurant."*

**IL BARINO, 1116 Mainland St
☎ (604) 687 1116.**
Great modern Italian (mainly northern) receiving innumerable plaudits. *Piatti* such as grilled mixed mushrooms with balsamic vinegar and a pear and goats' cheese salad show the direction. Frescoed, fresh and flower filled.

**THE LANDING, 375 Water St
☎ (604) 688 4800**
Dreamy restaurant in a converted turn-of-the-century building in the Gastown district. The best Canadian ingredients – West Coast seafood, Alberta beef – and gasp-inducing ocean/mountainscapes make this the place for anniversary, holding-hands-across-the-table sort of dinners.

**🐚 LE CROCODILE, 818 Thurlow St
☎ (604) 669 4298**
Still among the best – foodie folk go for excellent Alsace-leaning French food, authentic French accents, and exclusivity (they only seat 42).

🐚 UMBERTO IL GIARDINO, 1382 Hornby St ☎ (604) 669 2422
Top of Umberto's trio of nosheries (**Umberto's** at 1380 is the original, for northern Italian cuisine; **La Cantina di Umberto** at 1376 serves fresh local seafood) – the best Italian food in Vancouver. Wild game, wild funghi, wildly fresh pasta in a glassed-in garden dining room. Watch out for the symptoms of Il Giardino neck – you'll always be craning to spot the *face* that just walked in.

Shopping

South Granville is *the* fashion street. Take a walk there (especially between 9th and 14th Aves) and tick off the best boutiques – Bacci, Byblos, Bratz, Boboli. **Granville Island Market** is great for gastros.

BACCI, 2788 Granville St
☎ **(604) 732 7317**
The chicest spot for the snappiest dressers, who choose from Genny, Gigli, Complice and Montana, and consider Fratelli Rossetti, Romeo Gigli and Robert Clergerie worthy of covering their feet. The entire Byblos range for ladies and gents is stocked at Bacci's Byblos boutique, next door at 2790 ☎ (604) 737 0368.

BOBOLI, 2776 Granville St
☎ **(604) 736 3458**
With its black façade and cool collection of Euro labels for men and women, this is the trend merchants' No 1 spot in town. See them trotting smugly down the street with their glossy black boxes tied with gold bows.

GEORGE STRAITH'S, 900 W Georgia St
☎ **(604) 685 3301**
Top-to-bottom blue-blood classics from Europe – cover up with a Burberry mac, step out in Bally shoes, or shuffle through Hermès and Liberty prints. Drop other names like Ballantyne and Valentino. Fine French lingerie, too.

LEONE'S, 757 W Hastings St
☎ **(604) 683 1133**
Nuova Italia. Crammed with everything from cappuccino to Versace by way of Pavarotti. Fashion fiends fly from as far away as San Francisco to try on Valentino, Ferretti, Mondrian and Armani. Amazing shoe store.

MARK JAMES, 2941 W Broadway
☎ **(604) 734 2381**
Another Italian fave for the regular stars – Armani, Versace – lined up with more casual stuff from Girbaud, Marcel Dachet and C17. Weary shoppers take sustenance in the minimalist **Fiasco** restaurant, the happening place for a hip crowd on Thursday evenings.

· REST OF ·

CANADA

Art and museums

NATIONAL GALLERY OF CANADA, 380 Sussex Drive, Ottawa ☎ (613) 990 1985
Moshe Safdie's massive building is worth the trip in its own right. The most comprehensive collection of Canadian art, including the Group of Seven, hangs out with American and European exhibits.

Hotels

HASTINGS HOUSE, PO Box 1110, Ganges, BC ☎ (604) 537 2362
Anglicized island retreat on Salt Spring Island off the coast of British Columbia with contrasting décor for each room. *"It's right on the shore, a Tudor-style dwelling in a lovely setting. You are able to look out to sea. It's very English"* – ROSEMARY SEXTON.

MILLCROFT INN, Box 89, John St, Alton, Ontario ☎ (416) 791 4422
A much-loved country hotel which has expanded to include the 19C knitting mill's next door Manor House. The Manor House's 10 rooms are the most luxurious (those of the Croft units are more modern and utilitarian), kitted out in Canadian antiques. Swiss chef Freddy Stamm might have moved on but the team he trained remains to wow tastebuds with Euro-Canadian fusions such as venison loin with spatzle (German noodles). Over 200-strong wine list spans France, Ontario, California, NZ and Australia.

THE SHERWOOD INN, Port Carling, Muskoka, Ontario ☎ (705) 765 3131
Homy hotel with a New England feel (white clapboard with green shutters). Stay in the inn itself or in a beachfront cottage and strike a balance between health (new club with spa, exercise equipment, etc) and hedonism (6 courses nightly of most definitely *un*-nouvelle cuisine). Lake Muskoka, north of Toronto, is *"the vacation land for the rich in Canada. The lake area is surrounded by million-dollar cottages. Pretty, immaculate, elegant and very quiet. Skating and cross-country skiing in the winter and boating off a sandy beach in the summer"* – ROSEMARY SEXTON.

SOOKE HARBOUR HOUSE, 1528 Whiffenspit Rd, RR #4, Sooke, BC ☎ (604) 642 3421
A relaxed inn set in stunning country on Vancouver Island. Rooms are in Californian West Coast style with picture windows, Indian blankets and round wooden bath tubs. *"It looks out on the Pacific and is well known for the Californian food, with edible flowers on the plates"* – ROSEMARY SEXTON. Food and flowers come fresh from the organic garden.

Restaurants

GRANNAN'S, Smythe St, Market Square, St John, New Brunswick
☎ **(506) 634 1555**
Excellent seafood restaurant based in a converted old warehouse. *"Delicious fresh fish. It is*

one of the best in St John" – ROSEMARY SEXTON.
Tuck into a Seafarer's Platter (broiled scallops,
scrod, salmon and half a lobster) or a mind-bog-
glingly large Captain's Platter for two.

———— *Ski resorts* ————

BANFF/LAKE LOUISE, Alberta
Set in some of the world's most awesome countryside, getting to this part of the Rockies is half
the experience: by train from Vancouver (*"the
scenery is so gorgeous"* – CAROLINE HUNT) or by
car, from British Columbia (*"just an incredible
drive"* – STEVE PODBORSKI). No bum skiing here
– ski bums are serious: runs at **Mount
Norquay** are notorious (face the Face or Widow-
maker) and **Lone Pine** hurtles down to the
Great Divide into BC. **Sunshine Peak**, just
down the highway, is a high-bowl ski area with
the best snow. Some 30 miles on, **Lake
Louise**'s mind-blowingly beautiful trails cascade across 4 mountain faces (and the view
across Ten Peak Valley is spread across the
back of a Canadian $20 note). It's all national
parkland – major development is prohibited.
The best hotels are massive, old and stately.
Live like a lord at the baronial **Banff Springs
Hotel**, PO Box 960, Spray Avenue, Banff ☎
(403) 762 2211, or the near century-old **Château
Lake Louise**, Lake Louise ☎ (403) 522 3511,
with its fine **Edelweiss** restaurant. The **Post
Hotel**, Lake Louise (considered one of the city's
top restaurants), and **Giorgio's** on Banff
Avenue keep gastros happy.

WHISTLER and BLACKCOMB, BC
Soaring up to more than 5,000 ft, Whistler and
Blackcomb mountains stun skiers with the best
skiing, the biggest vertical drop in North America (5,280 ft) and the fastest lifts – *"you don't
have the queues and you are not sitting up there
dangling in the air, rather than skiing"* –
DANIEL STOFFMAN. It's one of STEVE PODBORSKI's
2 favourites in the world (the other's Vail, USA):
"Heli-skiing is always No 1." It's not all downhill – tennis, swimming, paragliding, glacier air
tours, trail skiing and nightlife keep most spirits
high. **Château Whistler**, PO Box 100 ☎ (604)
938 8000, at the foot of Blackcomb, is *"definitely
No 1"* – ROBIN LEACH; **Whistler Resort**, PO
Box 1400 ☎ (604) 932 3982, has condos, chalets
and pensions comme les Alps.

———— *Tours* ————

See also Travel Directory.

**CANADIAN MOUNTAIN HOLIDAYS, PO
Box 1660, Banff, Alberta ☎ (403) 762 4531**
Top heli-skiing tours to top spots – the
Monashees, Gothics, Galena, Ravelstocke and
Valemont and heli-hiking as well in the Buga-
boos, Cariboos, Adamants and Bobbie Burns.
Expert guides, introductory weeks for first-

Canadian Watercolours

*"The best drive in the world is from Banff,
Alberta, to Jasper, BC. You see some of the
greenest and bluest lakes, like emeralds
and amethysts – it's because the water has
so many minerals in it from melted
glaciers. And there are the mountains,
young mountains, so they are all sharp
peaks, and the light is shining across from
the west, and you are driving along and
you can just see the colour changes
between the rivers and lakes. Fabulous!"* –
STEVE PODBORSKI.

---

timers. Luxury lodges (accessible only by heli-
copter in winter) have saunas, pastry chefs, bars
and masseurs to soothe the muscle-shocked.

**CANADIAN OUTWARD BOUND
WILDERNESS, PO Box 116 Station S,
Toronto, Ontario ☎ (416) 787 1721**
Wilderness survival trips for townies who wish
to face the challenge of a lifetime. Get in training, don your hiking boots (don't forget the
sticking plasters) and off you go. Physically
tough and demanding, pitting you against the
elements and encounters of the wild kind, Outward Bounding draws forth resources you never
knew you had. Humour, too, provided your tent-
mates are outward-going rather than bounders.

CARIBBEAN

ANGUILLA

Peaceful coral island – an old British colony – in
the jade seas at the northern tip of the Leewards. *"The place to be seen – no other
Caribbean island has so many pluses: postcard-
perfect beaches, haute food, room to move"* –
ELISE PASCOE.

**CAP JULUCA, Maunday's Bay
☎ (809) 497 6666**
Moreish Moorish-style villas stretched out
across the mile-long private beachfront – marble
bathrooms, some with double baths, some with
headrests and racks for champagne glasses – the
works. 2 restaurants, waterskiing, sunfish sailing, sailboarding, day and night tennis are all at
your fingertips. ELISE PASCOE approves.

Our Man in Havana

"Havana is stately," says DAN TOPOLSKI. *"There is a sense of the past, it's elegant, but it's all a bit crumbling. The people are well educated and intelligent – if the Poles lived in the Caribbean, it would be like Havana!"* Montecristos count for little here – go underground to find the best baccy in town. *"In the basements of the hotels as well as the piano bars at the* **Presidente**, *First Ave and G St* ☎ *(07) 327521, and* **Ingleterra** ☎ (07) 97561 *(the best hotels), there will be a little old lady rolling cigars on the inside of her thigh. They're very good cigars – and they'll put* them in a gift box for you if you want. Cigars are definitely part of Cuban life, they take them very seriously." Find shapelier thighs at the open-air **Tropicana Floor Show**, where *"the mulatto girls are 6 ft tall and very beautiful, approachable and very friendly."* Best bar? **La Bodegita del Medio**, in the old town. Best beach? **Varadero Beach**, *"where the Cubans would like to go, but can't – it's too expensive."* Sensational May jazz festival – salsa, congas, brass galore; eat in the Miramar quarter – **El Bosque** and **Cecelia** are tops for TOPOLSKI.

COVECASTLES, PO Box 248, Shoal Bay West ☎ (809) 497 6801
Set out on salt flats, a private modern beach-house resort with elemental views of the sea rolling in. No-holds-barred freebies (gratis champagne – Dom Pérignon with caviare for those returning a third time), top-notch French restaurant (will deliver to villas), sunfish, wind-surfing, snorkelling, etc.

🐧 MALLIOUHANA HOTEL, PO Box 173, Maids Bay ☎ (809) 497 6111
Exclusive, arched marble hotel, sitting aloof on a clifftop. *"I love the weather, the service, the food, the little bungalow we had, the beach, the quality of the sand – like walking on satin sheets – everything about it"* – DOUGLAS FAIRBANKS JR. 3 freshwater swimming pools linked by waterfall, 2 miles of white beaches, 4 tennis courts and Michel Rostang's seafood dishes keep RAYMOND BLANC happy too: *"It was brilliant . . . one lives in a milieu of excellence and one likes to find that excellence somewhere else. Here there was this beautiful energy and amazing service . . . and the food was magnificent. The best experience in the Caribbean in every possible way."* ELISE PASCOE agrees: *"The wine list and cellar would be at home in a 3-star establishment in France. Great setting, fabulous food."*

ANTIGUA

COPPER & LUMBER STORE, PO Box 184, St John's ☎ (809) 460 1058
Former warehouse in English Harbour, done up in Georgian style – bare brick walls, 18C antiques, Persian carpets, etc. Ideal base for scuba diving, yachting – day charters available – and eating fish and chips out of the *Sunday Times* with a pint of English beer.

CURTAIN BLUFF, PO Box 288, Old Rd, Curtain Bluff Peninsula, St John's ☎ (809) 462 8400
Out at sea on a sandy peninsula. Guests swim, sail, waterski, dive, pitch, putt, play tennis, squash, and groove on down to calypso sounds at the beach club and BBQ on Sun and Wed. Suites have private gardens. A beach either side, one placid, the other swell.

JUMBY BAY, PO Box 243, Long Island ☎ (809) 462 6000
This private island 2 miles north of Antigua forms a Disney World of hibiscus, gardenia and bougainvillaea. Get away from it all in villas scattered around the 300 acres, rejoin other escapees for top-class cooking at the **Estate House**. *"It's fun, quiet, but you need a boat to ferry you"* – DAVID GOWER.

BARBADOS

St James Beach is where Who's Who-ers hang out – Elton John, Paul McCartney, Mick Jagger, Princess Margaret, LORD LICHFIELD, and Omar Sharif among them. ROBERT SANGSTER looks forward to blackened fish at **Raffles** and the *"good location and very good service"* at **Carambola**. Book ahead, they're the best.

COBBLERS COVE HOTEL, Road View, St Peter Parish ☎ (809) 422 2291
One of the most authentic hideaways in the Caribbean – an old house with self-contained

chalets. Food is streets ahead, service absolutely charming. Own beach, upmarket guests.

THE COLONY CLUB, St James
☎ (809) 422 2335
Pied-à-terre for the likes of Bryan Ferry. Set in 7 acres of tropical gardens overlooking St James Bay, with waterskiing, sailing and snorkelling.

CRANE BEACH HOTEL, St Philips
☎ (809) 423 6220
Away from the hubbub of St James, on the Atlantic coast, "*Crane Beach is on top of a cliff which overlooks the beach – the water tends to be a bit more exciting down there than on the west coast*" – DAVID GOWER. 4 hard tennis courts, Roman-style pool with classical columns (oft-featured in Vogue) and fresh fish from the reef.

ROYAL PAVILION, St James
☎ (809) 422 4444
Younger sister to neighbouring **Glitter Bay**, the spectacular haute-colonial-style hotel is bang on the beach. Beautiful tropical gardens, water, racket and bat sports, good dining at the **Palm Terrace**, and a happy DAVID GOWER: "*It's now been completely overhauled. . . . Very pleasant, very friendly too.*" LORD LICHFIELD says aye.

BARBUDA

Antigua's little-known little sister boasts a spectacular pink beach at Cedar Point. Not pale or blush, real *deep* pink – it's not sand but minute shells. Check in at the super-luxe, super-expensive **K Club** ☎ (809) 460 0300, right on the beach with all the Caribbean water activities and some right royal pampering thrown in.

BERMUDA

CAMBRIDGE BEACHES, Mangrove Bay, Sandy's Parish ☎ (809) 234 0331
Dating back to the 17C, this is the original cottage colony. The modern resort, begun in 1929, is full of antiques and Bermudan works of art. It sits out on a peninsula with a bay of its own and 5 wild ocean-swept beaches.

GRENADA

Less flashy than some of its more opulent and manicured neighbours, the southernmost island in the Grenadines holds on to its straightforward natural beauty. The capital, St George's, has 18C architecture and splendid restaurants serving produce from the island's fertile soil. Lay down your head at the small **CALABASH** hotel, L'Anse aux Epins, Box 382, St George's ☎ (809) 444 4234 – pretty rooms, delicious food; or the **SPICE ISLAND INN**, St George's ☎ (809) 444 4528, bang on Grand Anse Beach.

GRENADINES

MUSTIQUE
Real private, real exclusive. Royals, aristos, rock and Hollywood stars create the Mustique mystique – most have their own colonial or oriental-styled houses built especially. You might spot Princess Margaret, Lord Lichfield, Prince Rupert Löwenstein or David Bowie hammocking on their verandahs. Know one of them, or book ahead at the **COTTON HOUSE** ☎ (809) 456 4777. Otherwise, rent via **Mustique Villa Rentals** (see Travel Directory).

❝*I'm not a great heat person but I like Caribbean heat – there's always a lovely breeze blowing* ❞**

LADY ELIZABETH ANSON

PALM ISLAND
130 idyllic acres with the **PALM ISLAND BEACH CLUB**'s 24 cottages sprinkled around the quiet north beach (book one on ☎ (809) 458 8804). Yachts can put in on the other side of the island. Charter a sloop for a day trip, go deep-sea fishing in the powerboat and eat what you catch in the restaurant – spiced up à la creole or plain grilled.

PETIT ST VINCENT RESORT
☎ (809) 458 8428
If you *really, really, really* want to get away this island resort is the place. Completely unspoilt 113 acres of privately owned palm-covered land – no telephones or other distractions. Mini Mokes, the only traffic, act as room service to the 22 villas. Up goes the yellow flag and a Moke will arrive within 15 minutes; hoist the red one, and they'll keep away.

HAITI

LE RELAIS DE L'EMPEREUR, Petit Goave ☎ (509) 340 258
The place to stay in Haiti. Private, palatial, exotic, it is run by the flamboyant Olivier Coquelin with the help of his Burmese leopard

Sheba. The aim is to materialize the whims of guests before they are expressed. Olympic pool, deserted beach and lovely gardens.

JAMAICA

THE HALF MOON CLUB, PO Box 80, Montego Bay ☎ (809) 953 2211
Named after its slice of Montego Bay, the established, high-colonial club stands on over 400 acres of seaside land. The Robert Trent Jones championship golf course is top hole, the mile of private beach, 13 tennis and 4 squash courts ain't bad either.

JAMAICA INN, Ocho Rios ☎ (809) 974 2514
At the birthplace of reggae. A small, swinging retreat with rooms in 3 grand wings – twirling ceiling fans, palms, verandahs, freshwater pool and private cove.

ROUND HILL, PO Box 64, Montego Bay ☎ (809) 952 5150
It claims to be the first Caribbean resort, and has certainly hosted some famous guests, such as Noel Coward and Leonard Bernstein. Whitewash and timber villas, tennis, golf, yachting, and lively dancing.

SANS SOUCI, PO Box 103, Ocho Rios ☎ (809) 974 2353
Tucked between 2 headlands in a private cove with tropical gardens, gazebos and grottoes. Spring-fed mineral health spas, saunas, whirlpool baths, oceanside pool, golf, tennis club, and water sports to boot.

TRYALL GOLF, TENNIS & BEACH CLUB, PO Box 1206, Montego Bay ☎ (809) 952 5110
Overlooking Montego Bay, the fab 2,200-acre estate is centred around the 1834 Great House,

with tennis, water sports and 18-hole championship golf course. Scattered with 40 sea- or hillside villas – each with private cook, chambermaid, laundress, gardener and swimming pool.

ST BARTHELEMY

A twist of Gallic flavour in the same group as Anguilla and St Martin in the Leewards. *"It combines superb beaches and French restaurants, what better? Moreover, the small and dangerously exciting airport can only take the smallest amount of passenger aircraft. So no jumbo package tours"* – MICHAEL BROADBENT.

MANAPANY HOTEL, PO Box 114, 97133 St Barthélemy, French West Indies ☎ (590) 276655
Swish hotel/cottage resort with 2 restaurants – serving haute French and Italian – and all the trimmings. It remains one of ROBERT SANGSTER's favourite stop-offs – *"St Barts is superb. We've stayed at the Manapany twice and I can't better it."*

ST KITTS & NEVIS

2 remote volcanic islands, separated by the 3-mile Narrows.

GOLDEN LEMON, Dieppe Bay, St Kitts ☎ (809) 465 7260
Extra-special retreat sitting beneath the spectacular volcanic peak of St Kitts. Hear the tree frogs chirping as you dine in the gallery, then stroll around the 17C Great House. Sports include tennis, snorkelling and Kennedy-spotting.

MONTPELIER PLANTATION INN, PO Box 474, Nevis ☎ (809) 469 5462
Although rebuilt only a quarter of a century ago,

Buzz All aboard for the Caribbean cruise. Best waters are the **Grenadines** (as DAVID GOWER vouches), best style is a chartered yacht, picked up in St Vincent ...... Sailor 2: Find hot yachts and cool crews at **Nicholson's Yacht Charter**, English Harbour, Antigua ☎ (809) 460 1530, and **Charter Services**, PO Box 9997, St Thomas, US Virgin Islands 00801 ☎ (809) 776 5300 ...... Sailor you: Take the helm from **The Moorings**, Tortola ☎ (809) 494 2331 – a rare treat (provided you know main from your genoa) ...... Sailor crew: TERRY HOLMES rates his **Sea Goddess** (see Travel Directory) for reaching the ports other cruisers can't squeeze into: *"really like a private yacht"* ...... Sail adieu: Wave to the mainsail set, who take to the waters for **Antigua Race Week** at the end of April ...... **Pina Colada:** The best in the Caribbean are mixed at the idyllic resort **Guanahani**, Grand Cul de Sac, St Barthélemy ☎ (590) 276660, votes ELISE PASCOE .....

the Mount Nevis-side Great House looks and feels genuine 18C. Run by the Gaskells, it's more like a house party than a hotel – library, card room, home-grown veg and home-made marmalade, bread and pastries. Stay in one of the 8 cottages or 17 rooms, walk the slopes of the mountain or drive to the private beach.

ST LUCIA

Twin Peaks – St Lucia is famed for the 2 spectacular volcanic Pitons which soar up from the sea. Neighbourhood volcano La Soufrière is surrounded by hot sulphur springs – good for a soothing bathe. Do little in Dolittle Bay – moor there and locals will bring out fresh fruit to your boat – do a bit more on Thursday nights, when the main town Castries bursts into party mood, with bands and dancing in the streets.

JALOUSIE, 16 Bay St, Soufrière
☎ **(809) 454 7288**
Lord Glenconner's stunning new 320-acre resort nestling between the Pitons. Once you're there, it's cash free: open bars, restaurants, spa programme, scuba diving, and horse riding are all in. The ultimate in luxe.

LA TOC HOTEL, PO Box 399, Castries
☎ **(809) 455 3081**
Ritzy resort – among the Caribbean's smartest, with private cottage/suites dotted around the hillside. TERRY HOLMES declares an interest, but goes on: *"Luxury living in the Caribbean. Most of the houses have a little plunge pool outside so you can roll out of bed into it."*

TOBAGO

MOUNT IRVINE BAY HOTEL & GOLF CLUB, PO Box 222 ☎ (809) 639 8871
All-action resort – 18-hole golf course, water-skiing, snorkelling and diving – 200 yards from the private beach. Cottages dotted along the seafront, converted sugar mill restaurant.

VIRGIN ISLANDS

PETER ISLAND, British Virgin Islands
Rod-flexers and Windies windies head for the **PETER ISLAND HOTEL & YACHT HARBOR**, PO Box 211, Tortola ☎ (809) 494 2561, for top-notch marina and big-game fishing. The club owns almost all the island, and is among the smartest in the Caribbean. The best villa is the hilltop **Crow's Nest**; best bay, Deadman's Bay.

ST JOHN, US Virgin Islands
Chalk-white beaches, sensational scuba – note the fish, flora and coral formations at Trunk Bay – and utter cleanliness (the whole island is a National Park) keep St J top of the USVI. **CANEEL BAY**, PO Box 120 ☎ (809) 776 6111, is dead smart – 7 beaches, 7 tennis courts, old sugar mill restaurant.

TORTOLA, British Virgin Islands
Surf hard on the Atlantic coast, chill out on the gentle Caribbean, scuba all over the dazzling coral off the largest (18 x 5-mile island) in the BVI. Serious sailing – hop from island to island, 20 minutes a leap with the wind up. Get over-awed and overshadowed in the rainforest, and overdressed at the summer carnival. Poshest place to stay is **Prospect Reef**, PO Box 104, Road Town ☎ (809) 494 3311.

VIRGIN GORDA, British Virgin Islands
2nd in size to Tortola, the 'Fat Virgin' has 1,000 inhabitants. Stay at Caneel Bay's sister resort **LITTLE DIX BAY** – a 300-acre paradise with stilted thatched cottages, marina, open-air dining room, and cruises and sailing offshore.

CHINA

BEIJING

—————— *Hotels* ——————

JIANGUO, Jianguomenwai Rd
☎ **(1) 500 2233**
Partly done up in 1991, its good service, clubby surroundings and central location are welcomed by frequent travellers. Expats hang out in **Charlie's Bar**.

PALACE HOTEL, Wang Fujing St
☎ **(1) 512 8899**
Large, grand hotel in the thick of the Beijing action – Tiananmen Square and the Forbidden City are 10 mins walk, the Wangfujing shopping district is on the doorstep. Chinese, Japanese, French, German and Italian food can be worked off at the health club or disco.

SHANGRI-LA, 29 Zizhuyuan Rd
☎ **(1) 831 2211**
Top o' the range in Beijing, and well up there in the pan-Chinese ratings, the large (786-room) modern block has health club, business centre, antique and craft shops and tennis courts. Out of the centre – half an hour to Tiananmen – it nevertheless draws in the business folk.

China Mooning

DAN TOPOLSKI joins the People in their Republic and reports back: "*It is nothing like as difficult to travel around China as it was 10 years ago, and it is terribly rewarding. A fascinating trip would be a train journey from Hong Kong to Canton and on to Shanghai and Peking, travelling soft seat (first class – they don't like to use the word 'class') in a rather luxurious couchette. Out of the towns it's a world where people don't speak English, French or German. Of course, you can arrange tours via hotels or before you go, and you can have a permanent guide, but I prefer to travel on my own. Although it is more complicated to get yourself understood, it is quite surprising how someone will emerge from the crowd to interpret for you. In Peking, I met some students on the train, and the discussions, though limited by language, were quite intense . . . they were so knowledgeable about classical music, literature, politics. One is amazed at how articulate and well versed they are, much more so than kids of their age in the West. We'd hire bicycles and join this tide of Peking people cycling around the city. It was absolutely joyful.*"

Restaurants

DONGLAISHUN FANZHUANG, 16 Donghuamen/Dongfeng Market
☎ (1) 550069
This Eastwind Market complex offers Peking duck (no surprises there) but also shuanguangrou, prosaically translated as Mongolian hot pot – a Chinese fondue of lamb and stock.

❝ *I like the market in Shanghai – it's open, with provisions from vegetables to live eels* ❞

🕵 YAN-KIT SO

FANG SHAN RESTAURANT, Beihai Park
☎ (1) 441184
A grand old restaurant with bipartisan roots. Once the favourite of Chairman Mao, its elaborate food is cooked to unworkmanlike recipes from the old imperial kitchens: sesame-seed biscuits stuffed with minced pork or goldfish and duck web, for example.

SICHUAN FANDIAN, Rongxian Hutong, No 51 ☎ (1) 656348
Beautifully decorated and laid-out restaurant comprising several pavilions linked by traditional cobbled courtyards. Fiery Sichuan specialities such as lantern chicken and hot sauce noodles.

TINGLI GUAN, Summer Palace
☎ (1) 258 1955
On the shores of Kunming Lake in the former private theatre of the Dowager Empress Ci Xi, it's one for the tourists, but then who else could afford the prices? Typically northern dishes such as chicken velvet (finely minced chicken cooked in soup) with dumplings and fish that you can choose from the aquarium.

· REST OF ·

CHINA

Hotels

GOLDEN FLOWER HOTEL, 8 West Changle Rd, Xian, Shaanxi Province
☎ (29) 332981
Among the best in China; come here when you visit the spectacular archaeological site of the Terracotta Army. Two splendid restaurants – one of China's best Sichuans, one for homesick occidentals – service is as good as you can expect in the People's Repub.

SHANGHAI HILTON INTERNATIONAL, 250 Huashan Rd ☎ (21) 255 0000
Service that works – perfect spoken English; on call 24 hours a day. That's quite something in the land of the red tape. Facilities to match include upbeat gyms and exercise machines, and fabulous restaurants. Try the spectacular **Sichuan Court** – better than Hong Kong's best; **Suiyuan** for Cantonese; and **Shanghai Express** for local cooking and a great Sunday brunch with jazz band thrown in.

WHITE SWAN HOTEL, Shamian Island, Guangzhou ☎ (20) 886968
No man is an island . . . but some hotels are – this is China as it's rarely seen. Set out on a little isle encircled by the Pearl River there are beautiful

riverside gardens, 2 pools, an indoor water garden with its own waterfall and a skylit atrium. Flawless service too.

DENMARK

COPENHAGEN

Ballet

 **ROYAL DANISH BALLET, The Royal Theatre, Kongens Nytorv, PO Box 2185, DK-1017 ☎ 3314 1002**
High-flying ballet. Under director Frank Andersen the 200-year-old company has leapt up to join Paris, Russia, New York and London in the premier league, performing new pieces and the works of Denmark's great choreographer August Bournonville. Current top tiptoers Alexander Koeptin and Rose Gad trained, like all RDB dancers, at the company's school. Other former pupils include luminaries Peters Schaufuss and Martins. In EDWARD THORPE's top 3.

Hotels

HOTEL D'ANGLETERRE, Kongens Nytorv 34 ☎ 3312 0095
A Copenhagen landmark since 1755, and its best hotel too, in a lovely setting near the harbour. Antique décor, fine furniture, a first-class restaurant and top-notch service keep it at No 1.

Restaurants

CAFE LUMSKEBUGTEN, Esplanaden 21 ☎ 3315 6029
A long-established restaurant in a charming old port-authority building near the harbour. Diplomats mix in with the artsy, Bohemian types, who feel at home amid quirky old furniture and memorabilia (such as a 1930s photo of the Danish Queen Mother in Girl Guide uniform). Danish cuisine with French nouvelle keynotes – beef tartare with Russian caviare, sugar-marinated salmon and marinated vegetables.

KONG HANS KAELDER, Vingårdsstraede 6 ☎ 3311 6868
Named after the medieval Scandinavian king, this magnificent vaulted Gothic cellar was once his, and the street was his 'vineyard'. The first Danish restaurant to shoot to Michelin stardom thanks to Alsatian chef Daniel Letz, who smokes his own salmon, has a dozen artful ways with oysters, concocts the lightest duck-liver mousse, and rounds it off with such delicacies as millefeuilles with apples in rosemary.

SAISON, Skoyshoyed Hotel, 267 Strandvegen, 2920 Charlottenlund ☎ 3164 0028
Erwin Lauturbach blazes the trail for inventive Danish cooking, his fish and vegetarian menus leading the pack. Such wizardries as sautéed Jerusalem artichokes with black truffles, cabriot with oysters and smoked pork and fish with herb-scented oil send gastrocentric visitors, such as ALASTAIR LITTLE, wild. Set on the seafront a few miles north of Copenhagen, the restored hotel retains a whiff of the old days when this was a fashionable resort.

Czech it Out

In Prague, it's been springtime since 1989 and it seems the thaw's in for good. The plinth that once supported an official statue of Stalin now houses unofficial all-night raves; every second person on the street is a budding entrepreneur (a tour guide, a newspaper publisher, an art gallery owner) – suddenly Prague has become the city of endless possibility. Of course, it has always been *"the most beautiful city in Europe"*, as ROBIN HANBURY-TENISON recognizes; in fact, all Czechoslovakia *"has the most incredible palaces, castles, stately homes and suddenly it is possible to talk about, photograph and go and see them"*. The only snag is staying there – despite all efforts, Prague's housing and hotel standards will take years and an enormous cash injection before they reach those of the West – pensions are cheap and cheerful, but most travellers would be better off in somewhere like the **Hotel Inter-Continental**, 5 Curieouysh Square ☎ (02) 231 1812 (*"it's very near the Vltava river, very central, and much better than I expected"* – JULIAN LLOYD WEBBER), or the **Hotel Palace**, Panská 12 ☎ (2) 236 0008, with its Art Nouveau elegance, fine French food, Western facilities, and a good position by Wenceslas Square.

DUBAI

— Hotels —

**HATTA FORT HOTEL, PO Box 9277, UAE
☎ (4) 660311**
A cluster of small, bougainvillaea-covered chalets in the foothills of the Hajar Mountains. *"A most interesting drive from the city through the desert; we passed herds of camels and goats and verdant oases. I had a very good luncheon with a wonderful view"* – BETTY KENWARD. Jutting over the pool is a bedouin tent-styled café, white muslin walls wafting in the breeze.

HYATT REGENCY HOTEL, PO Box 5588, UAE ☎ (4) 221234
"The biggest and best Hyatt Regency hotel I have ever stayed in. You enter and it is fantastic – marble everywhere and mirror-glass – you think you're in a world quite out of this world. Bedrooms are frightfully comfortable, plenty of space and cupboard room – really every comfort. Excellent service. Downstairs is an ice-skating rink, which is the last thing you expect to find in Dubai" – BETTY KENWARD.

INTER-CONTINENTAL, PO Box 476, Bin Yass St, UAE ☎ (4) 227171
Swish modern hotel in Dubai's ever-expanding business district. Priorities are in order here – it boasts 11 eateries including an 'English' pub complete with pub grub and the highly rated **Fishmarket** for fresh-as-it-comes, cooked-as-you-like-it Arabian seafood.

— Restaurants —

See also Hotels.

THE WORLD TRADE CLUB, Dubai International Trade Centre, PO Box 9292, UAE ☎ (4) 394500
39 storeys above Dubai is the most upmarket restaurant in town. *"A frightfully good restaurant with a truly magnificent view. What was extraordinary was the quality of everything –*

an abundance of fresh fruit, good salads and delicious vegetables. There are 4 private dining rooms all done differently with very nice furniture and pictures" – BETTY KENWARD.

EGYPT

— Art and museums —

EGYPTIAN MUSEUM OF ANTIQUITIES, Eltahrir Sq, Cairo ☎ (02) 757035
Unparalleled collection of Egyptology and antiquity plotting the history of the great Pharaoh dynasties. The legendary treasures of Tutankhamen are the most famous; other pieces, dating back to around 4000 BC, are no less spectacular. Don't miss the remarkably contemporary-looking sycamore figure of Sheikh-el-Beled, carved a mere 4,500 years ago.

— Hotels —

MENA HOUSE OBEROI, Pyramid Rd, Giza, Cairo ☎ (02) 387 9444
Once the empire-builder's weekend haunt, now a smooth operation run by the Oberoi group. Palatial building set in 40 acres of park, with a 9-hole golf course, and views of the pyramids.

 CAIRO MARRIOTT, Saraya El Gezira St, Zamalek, Cairo ☎ (02) 340 8888
The best in the capital. Beautiful former palace built for Empress Eugénie on an island in the Nile. Over 1,000 rooms, stupendous ballrooms and dining rooms a-glitter with weighty chandeliers, plus tennis courts, restaurants, casino, nightclub, pool and flourishing gardens.

SALAMLEK, Kasr Al-Montazah, Alexandria ☎ (03) 860585
A right royal retreat, in a converted wing of the Al-Montazah Palace, former summer residence of King Farouk. Set above a beautiful beach on the eastern tip of Alexandria, it's surrounded by gardens and a massive forest.

Buzzz BETTY KENWARD takes us on a sporting tour of Dubai. First stop for pukka chukkers at the **Dubai Polo Club** (most days from Oct to end-Apr), where play is fast and furious on sandy ground ♣ . . . . . . No betting but plenty of action at the **camel races:** *"Great fun with a very nice members' stand, and men in white gloves and uniforms come around with cold drinks and cake"* ♣ . . . . . . **Gulf golf:** tee off at the first grass championship course in the UAE, **The Emirates Golf Club:** *"As good as any I've seen in the world"* ♣ . . . . . . Wind down, 40 minutes from downtown Dubai at the lush coastal resort of **Jebel Ali:** *"If I was coming to Dubai purely for a holiday in the sun I would stay here"* . . . . ♣

Tours

Do the Nile in style, or go native in a felucca – flowing along the 40 million-year-old lifeblood that pumps through Egypt is *the* way to see the sights. As you glide upstream, children gather and climb trees, waving and cheering; men and boys whistle and make bird calls. As the light fades, the only sound is that of fishermen smacking the water with their oars, chasing the fish into their nets. SKYE MACLEOD loved it: *"We went up the Nile in a houseboat from Luxor, which was wonderful."* In and around Luxor are the most stupendous ancient monuments, the **Temple of Karnak** (real *Death on the Nile* stuff, with tall, menacing columns stark against cloudless skies), **Temple of Luxor**, **Valley of the Queens**, and the **Valley of the Kings** (where scores of tombs are cut deep into the rugged limestone rockface, and painted hieroglyphics, cartouches and images of gods are incredibly preserved. Don't miss the tombs of Tutankhamen and Rameses VI).

Last stop is Aswan, where Cairenes come for mellow winter breaks. Take a dawn flight from here to **Abu Simbel** for the towering Temples of Rameses II and Queen Nefertiti – moved in their entirety to a new location to make way for the controversial Aswan dam.

Posh trips from **Abercrombie & Kent** (tasteful cruising boats of their own, plus balloon trips); Egypt specialists **Bales Tours** have the widest varieties of tours from basic to the luxury cruiser MS *Ra*; **Serenissima** and **Voyages Jules Verne** take the academic approach – complete with own lecturer; **Kuoni** do the full range. See Travel Directory.

FIJI ISLANDS

THE REGENT OF FIJI, PO Box 9081, Nad ☎ 70700
Hottest of the main island resorts. The expected efficiency and comfort of the Regent group with a laid-back Fijian patina: open architecture; villas dotted through paradisiacal gardens; firewalkers, singers and tropical feasts. If communal cheer palls, take a picnic to the island of Akuilau for blissful, Regent-exclusive isolation.

TOBERUA ISLAND, PO Box 567, Suva ☎ 26356 (office); 49177 (island)
A microdot undetected by rainclouds and mosquitoes. Stay in serious peace in one of only 14 private thatched bures (cottages). Eye-boggling tropical feasts; their own boat ('the Love Boat') for honeymoon escapes.

TURTLE ISLAND, PO Box 9317, Nadi ☎ 72921
Very private island for 14 well-heeled but bare-

The Spice of Life

The streets of Cairo are among the most chaotic in the world. Oblivious to the din, men lounge at roadside bars smoking shishas (hookahs) and clicking dominoes. Street vendors are keen on specialization – a loofah, perhaps? Or a tangerine? Or how about a 6-inch twig, which, when stripped and splayed at one end serves as a toothbrush? **Khan al-Khalili** bazaar is the place for practising your haggling technique. In a maze of narrow streets, tumbledown workshops spill with brassware, gold and silver jewellery, inlaid boxes and furniture, wooden dolls, exquisite glass scent bottles and perfume. Behind wooden latticework windows, craftsmen are busy doing their thing – goldsmiths a-hammering, jewellers a-polishing, fez-makers a-blocking. **Aswan** street market is perhaps the most enticing in Egypt. Carts weave in and out, piled high with just one product – aubergines, marrows, tomatoes, chillis, lemons, figs. But it is the brilliant array of spices that takes the biscuit: finely ground powders are heaped in brilliantly hued pyramids – red chilli pepper, sunshine yellow saffron and turmeric, crimson karkadeh (hibiscus flowers), and, in an inedible rogue pyramid, indigo dye.

foot couples. A beach for each and, if the white sands and turquoise waters look familiar, cast your mind back to 1979's *Blue Lagoon*. Once island-bound, it's cash-free: wash down your lobster with unlimited champagne. *"The best escape is the No 1 bure which has 360° views of the Pacific"* – WARWICK VYNER.

VATULELE ISLAND RESORT, c/o International Booking Office, 16 Moncur St, Woollahra, NSW 2025, Australia ☎ (02) 326 1055
The Pacific's most stylish newcomer, product of Oz film producer Henry Crawford. 12 Santa Fe-style whitewashed villas tucked among palm groves by a white-sanded beach. *"Combines tropical sun, waving palms and the warmth and charm of the Fijians themselves – the local culture is very much a part of it. In the emerald-tiled bathrooms you almost feel you're bathing outdoors yet there's privacy. Food is fresh and imaginative, a Thai feast one night, Italian wood-fired pizzas the next. Breakfasts of banana*

or coconut pancakes with views of the lagoon are a pure delight" – CLAUDIA ROSSI HUDSON. *"I like the laid-back sophistication. It's got everything you want and you don't have to ask for it . . . so much to do but you don't have to do anything at all. My favourite is when you want room service and you have to raise the flag . . . heaven"* – MARK PATRICK. SHARYN STORRIER-LYNEHAM favours barefoot chic, as does MARY ROSSI: *"Henry Crawford has used his flair as a film-maker to create an architectural gem."*

FRANCE

PARIS

—— *Art and museums* ——

The best international touring exhibitions – as queues testify – are staged at the **Grand Palais**, ave du Général Eisenhower, 75008 ☎ (1) 4289 5410. The **Petit Palais**, opposite, at ave Winston-Churchill ☎ (1) 4265 1273, holds 2 major exhibitions each year, in addition to a permanent collection of antiquities to 19C art.

CENTRE GEORGES POMPIDOU, place Beaubourg, 75004 ☎ (1) 4277 1233
Richard Rogers and Renzo Piano's famous building holds the Musée National d'Art Moderne – from Matisse and the Post-Impressionists to the end of WWII – and lots of contemporary art and photography exhibitions. *"Brilliant. It is worth the escalator ride to the top, which is a happening in itself – just wonderful, fab."* – DAVID SHILLING. Good reading library and shop

for hip postcards and posters. Walk out on to a piazza full of mimers and buskers.

INSTITUT DU MONDE ARABE, 23 Quai St Bernard, 75005 ☎ (1) 4051 3838
Jean Nouvel's 1987 feat of architectural daring continues to flourish as a home for all things Arab. Video lab, library, cinema, art and antiquities are housed in a building that mixes modernist planes and spirals with Arab styles: one part of the building sharpens to a dagger-like point, the south façade has Moorish geometric apertures that control the sunlight. There's homage to Lloyd Wright too – the library is a continuous spiral curve, comme le Guggenheim.

PALAIS DE TOKYO, ave du Président-Wilson, 75116 ☎ (1) 4723 3653
Central to the Paris scene, the restyled Palais is where a lot of arty chinwagging goes on. The right wing is the **Musée d'Art Moderne de la Ville de Paris** ☎ (1) 4723 6127, which recently wowed the art world with the largest-ever Giacometti retrospective (fans of old applaud as they see standards approaching once more the famed exhibitions of the early 70s – Man Ray, Rothko, etc); the left wing is the Palais – national centre for photography (the largest exhibition/archive space in the world) and for cinema (4 projection rooms with the last word in modern tech. And then there's the library, brasserie, bookshop and views over the Seine.

MUSEE CARNAVALET, 23 rue de Sévigné, 75003 ☎ (1) 4272 2113
See the history of Paris, as told through art, maps, memorabilia and a series of reconstructed Louis XIV, XV and 18C rooms. Don't miss the beautiful boiseries (panelling) by Ledoux and Mucha's original Art Nouveau interior of the shop Fouquet. Also housed in the 17C Hôtel Carnavalet and the neighbouring Hôtel Le Peletier de Saint-Fargeau is art from the

🐾 **Buzzz** Branch out into the 16th to the **Musée Marmottan**, 2 rue Louis-Boilly ☎ (1) 4224 0702, *"a charming museum housing fine Renaissance, Consular and First Empire collections, and a spectacular and surprising collection of Monet's later work painted at his home in Giverny, including his famous Sunrise"* – MARGARET KEMP; another drawcard is France's finest collection of Water Lilies 🐾 . . . . . . DAVID SHILLING thinks shop at the **Musée des Arts de la Mode**, in the Louvre's Pavillon de Marsan, 111 rue de Rivoli ☎ (1) 4260 3214, the first national costume museum in France, and a treasury of fashion fripperies for sale: *"Fabulous for exhibitions, costumes and clothes"* 🐾 . . . . . . Find him also next door at the **Musée des Arts Décoratifs**, 107 rue de R, checking out the furniture, ceramics, jewellery, and reconstructed room sets 🐾 . . . . . . JEAN-MICHEL JAUDEL goes out of town to the **Musée d'Art Brut la Racine**, Parc de l'Hôtel de Ville, Neuilly sur Marne ☎ (1) 4309 6273, *"a tiny museum of art made by loonies from loonybins; mad paintings by butchers . . . a very interesting museum"* . . . . 🐾

Jeu de Paume

The revamped Jeu de Paume (rather grandly renamed the **Galeries Nationales du Jeu de Paume**, place de la Concorde, 75001 ☎ (1) 4703 1250) is yet another of President Mitterrand and Culture Minister Jack Lang's Grands Projets. Having kicked off to a good start with a smashing Dubuffet retrospective, the first of its size for this major artist, the gallery will continue to hold shows of modern artists rather than housing a permanent collection (the old Impressionists who'd hung there for decades are now at the Musée d'Orsay). Now the most contemporary faces look out from the opened-out space on the equally rejuvenated Tuileries (regreened by brilliant young landscape designer Louis Benech). A minor quibble – having removed the partitions, the vast spaces demand paintings on an equal scale: *"It's great for Bacon but not for Freud"* – ANNE-ELISABETH MOUTET.

Revolution. Collections from antiquity and the Middle Ages are soon to go on display.

🦢 MUSEE DU LOUVRE, 34 quai du Louvre, 75001 ☎ (1) 4260 3926
The magnificent gallery is still something of a construction site as renovations continue for the 'Grand Louvre', to be unveiled officially in the bicentenary year of 1993 (though in reality completion won't be until 1995, with some parts waiting till 1997). Herein lies one of the greatest collections of art in the world, entered by I M Pei's landmark glass pyramid. Escalators lead from this skylight to an underground plaza with arteries to 200-plus galleries. *"It's a great institution for getting your teeth into the whole of European culture – the only trouble is people go to see the dreary things like the Mona Lisa whereas they should be wandering around the antiquities"* – BRIAN SEWELL. The awesome collection covers Egyptian, Greek (*Venus de Milo*, etc), Roman and Oriental antiquities; objects and furniture; and countless master works of sculpture and painting of the European schools, including Michelangelo's noble marble *Slaves*, Rubens's 21-strong series for Marie de Medici and Géricault's *Raft of the Medusa*.

🦢 MUSEE D'ORSAY, 62 rue de Lille, 75007 ☎ (1) 4549 4814
A temple for the golden era of French art – the Impressionists and their predecessors, followers and friends. Gae Aulenti's remodelling of the soaring mid-19C steel and stone Gare d'Orsay is now universally admired. Queue up to see Courbets and Corots galore, Manet's scandalous *Déjeuner sur l'Herbe* and *Olympia*, Degas's dancers, Monet's garden, works by Rodin and Redon, Cézanne and Sisley, Gauguin and Van Gogh. Superb collections of sculpture and dec arts (especially the Art Nouveau), a smart restaurant and a chic café behind the glass clock-face. The revamped bookstore is brilliant for art books in all languages – and you can bypass the museum entry fee.

MUSEE PICASSO, Hôtel de Salé, 5 rue de Thorigny, 75003 ☎ (1) 4271 2521
A delightful little museum, based in a lovely 17C hôtel with fine stone carving. An airy space with lighting by Diego Giacometti, brother of the sculptor. Follow Picasso's life through his work – paintings, statues, ceramics, book illustrations, manuscripts, sketches, even little owls by Picasso over doorways. Those In The Know call Yanou Collart (TITK are the only ones with her number) to arrange tours with Paloma P.

MUSEE RODIN, Hôtel Biron, 77 rue de Varenne, 75007 ☎ (1) 4705 0134
The Kiss, The Thinker, they're all represented, amid the calm of Rodin's pretty 18C house and garden, as the sculptor intended. Also working drawings and sketches.

Arts centres

THEATRE DES CHAMPS-ELYSEES, 15 ave Montaigne, 75008 ☎ (1) 4720 3637
Hosts not only opera, ballet, music and mime but an auction house (an offshoot of Drouot), where top francs are paid for top-drawer art.

Ballet

🦢 L'OPERA BALLET, Palais Garnier, 8 rue Scribe, 75009 ☎ (1) 4001 1789
The world's oldest ballet company, developed from the Académie Royale de Musique, founded in 1669 by Louis XIV. The stellar corps is given fresh sparkle regularly by graduates of the excellent ballet school. 10-12 productions annually. Housed in the mighty Second Empire opera house, the largest in the world with room for 450 artists on stage, much admired by EDWARD THORPE, as is the troupe itself, *"in terms of age and standing and heritage"*.

Bars and cafés

ANGELINA, 226 rue de Rivoli, 75001 ☎ (01) 4260 8200
"An elegant, old-fashioned café which does the most marvellous Mont Blanc – rich and deli-

cious. *All these very elegant Parisian women sit there sipping their hot chocolate taking little spoons full of their chestnut Mont Blanc. A place to go if you've been doing hard shopping or sightseeing, and want a little rest in elegant circumstances*" – SOPHIE GRIGSON. Paris wouldn't be Paris for JUDITH COOK without collapsing here for hot chocolate.

AUX DEUX MAGOTS, 6 place St-Germain-des-Prés, 75006 ☎ (1) 4548 5525
Famous Left Bank arty meeting place, thus on the tourist trail – but don't let that put you off. Get there early in the morning for a croissant and a petit noir.

CAFE DE FLORE, 172 blvd St Germain, 75006 ☎ (1) 4548 5526
Former talking shop for Rive Gauche intelligentsia – Sartre, Simone de Beauvoir, Camus and Picasso – next to Aux Deux Magots. "*For me the best breakfast café. I have scrambled eggs and good coffee*" – ALEXANDRE LAZAREFF.

HOTEL RAPHAEL, 17 ave Kléber, 75116 ☎ (1) 4428 0028
Euro-filmies pack into this English-style bar to drink, chat and look at the original Turner by the bar. It's the place that fanned the flames for Claire Chazal and Patrick Poivre d'Arvor during their famous affair.

L'ECLUSE, 15 Quai des Grands-Augustins, 75006, and branches
Top wine-bar chain – devour an assiette autour de l'oie and a glass of Sauternes in unfussy, minimal surroundings.

WILLI'S, 13 rue des Petits-Champs, 75001 ☎ 4261 0509
Trendy wine bar with a splendid list of more than 100 wines – particularly strong on Rhônes. The food's good too – spinach tarts, pork with fennel . . . owner Mark Williamson keeps the British end up.

——————— Clubs ———————

🏊 CASTEL'S, 15 rue Princesse, 75006 ☎ (1) 4326 9022
Top of the Paris pile, this is the suavely clubbish club to get into – though you'll find it tough unless you know Jean Castel or he knows of you. Castel's folk know each other well – you'll probably recognize them too: Roger Vadim, Christopher Lambert, Jean-Paul Belmondo . . . "*There is only one club where people like us can go, where a son can meet his father, both with their girlfriends. Good style of life, easy money, feast, love. When a family gets a baby, the owner, Jean, lays down a bottle for them and gives it to them for their 21st*" – ALEXANDRE LAZAREFF. Nothing changes, but that's the way ROLAND ESCAIG likes it, as does JOHN GOLD: "*I just love the ambience and everything about it, very*

Hijinks and High Kicks

As much a part of Paris as the Eiffel Tower, the vaudeville shows captured on canvas by Toulouse-Lautrec are still steaming ahead today. The scantily-clad, frilly-knickered troupers, singers, clowns, trapeze artists et al are cheered now by a largely foreign/provincial audience, who just *love* what they see. **Lido**, 116 bis ave des Champs-Elysées, 75008 ☎ (1) 4076 5610, is, for DAVID SHILLING, "*the best thing in Paris. I only just discovered it . . . it's just brilliant. Just wonderful. Just extraordinary. I have never seen so many feathers, it outdoes Las Vegas. When you see the ice rink come out of the floor, you don't mind being a tourist. It's camp and crazy but absolutely outstanding.*" More famous still is **Le Bal du Moulin Rouge**, 82 blvd Clichy, 75018 ☎ (1) 4606 0019, where LaToya Jackson is currently wowing audiences, displaying the right blend of dazzling vulgar-chic and true trouper qualities. Stage-mates variously appear bare-breasted, dancing le ballet, and fighting a crocodile in a water tank.

warm and welcoming with no neon flashing lights and things like that. They serve good food there too and there's a very nice clientele."

LA LOCOMOTIVE, 90 blvd Clichy, 75018 ☎ (1) 4257 3737
Faites la locomotion ici, or the twist, jive, skank, groove or anything else that comes to mind – do it comme les hippies at **Ashram**, on Sundays. 3 levels, mixed crowd and a good location next to the Moulin Rouge.

LA NOUVELLE EVE, 25 rue Fontaine, 75009 ☎ (1) 4526 7632
End-of-week raves for the snootier youth of Paris – young BCBGs come for the cocktail of rumba, cha-cha, swing and house.

LE KEUR SAMBA, 79 rue la Boëtie, 75008 ☎ (1) 4359 0310
Black beat boîte that loosens up as the night goes on. Late on it's the hip place to be – Jagger, Yannick Noah, Rupert Everett cruise in.

🏊 LES BAINS, 7 rue du Bourg-L'Abbé, 75003 ☎ (1) 4887 0180
Louche douche – get steamed up in the con-

verted baths; dress sparingly and you could actually get in. Models, photographers, filmies hang out here; so does JOHN GOLD: "*The younger crowd – a lot of fun. You eat on the ground floor, and then down in the basement, it's all still the white tiles with flashing lights and a lot of young model boys and girls.*"

LE TANGO, 13 rue au Maire, 75003
☎ (1) 4272 1778

A must for Afro and Latino groovers and shakers. Serious dancing – go there to get sweaty and smoochy. Hip party venue: the one organized by the satirist group Jalons to honour the 30th anniversary of the Cuban revolution was a rip-roarer.

NEW MORNING, 7–9 rue des Petites-Ecuries, 75010 ☎ (1) 4523 5141

Live music club for the best Latin, trad and modern jazz acts in town – names like Astrud Gilberto. House and rap too – you're just as likely to get Queen Latifah et al. Dark room, no added extras, just pure soul.

🍴 REGINE'S, 49 rue de Ponthieu, 75008
☎ (1) 4359 2160

One of the greats of the club world, the disco queen still packs 'em in. Film stars, aristos, the works come along: Anthony Delon, Prince Henri de France, Duke of Vendôme, Michael J Fox, Liza Minnelli and ROLAND ESCAIG. Regine's no fool – junior club cards ensure a whole new generation of big spenders.

SHEHERAZADE, 3 rue de Liège, 75009
☎ (1) 4874 8520

Have an Arabian Night here – well-preserved cabaret venue decked out in red, purple and gold stucco, Aladdin's lamps and whatnot. Glitter-crowd groove the night away to rap, soul, salsa and rai . . . .

—— *Fashion designers* ——

AGNES B, 6 rue du Jour, 7500
☎ (1) 4508 5656; menswear at No 3, children's at No 2; and branches

Casual chic for young bods – or young-at-hearts. Skirts, shirts, trousers, leggings for well-dressed well-knowns – Kevin Kline, Philippe Starck, Nastassja Kinski . . . .

🍴 AZZEDINE ALAIA, 7 rue de Moussy, 75004 ☎ (1) 4272 1919 (boutique); 18 rue de la Verrerie, 75004 (studio)

Modern master of sexy, figure-skimming, sharp-cut jackets, skirts and dresses. "*He gave us back the shape of the female body after the Japanese bag-lady look. He is the one designer since Dior launched his New Look in 1947 to have had a lasting impact on the way we look*" – GAIL ROLFE. Nipped-in waists, cleavages and broderie anglaise frills have been hitting the sidewalks of late, but his lasting title is as lord of Lycra –

nobody does the 'if you've got it, flaunt it' look better, as AMANDA DE CADENET testifies: "*I've worn it since I was about 12 years old – really stretchy, sexy, practical clothes, you can throw the whole lot in your bag and it won't get crumpled.*" Other admirers are DAVID SHILLING ("*for people who have got the figure, just brilliant*") and SKYE MACLEOD ("*wonderful*").

CERRUTI 1881, 3 place de la Madeleine, 75008 ☎ (1) 4265 6872 (men); 15 place de la Madeleine ☎ (1) 4742 1078 (women)

Spot-on tailoring – classic day and evening suits, in cotton for summer; impeccable blazers and trousers for men and women. Perfect flop-around casual clothes, too.

🍴 CHANEL, 31 rue Cambon, 75001
☎ (1) 4286 2850 (couture); 42 ave Montaigne, 75008 ☎ (1) 4723 7412 (boutique)

Karl Lagerfeld's synthesis of the classic Chanel look with his own wit and style is of perennial interest to fashion's arbiters, and of perennial buyability for fashion's clothes horses. "*Never loses its appeal – it's aspirational for younger women, and suits older women perfectly. Value for money gets better, too – for quality it's hard to beat*" – GAIL ROLFE. "*One of my 2 favourites, along with Armani. For his pure cheek of taking the understated ideas of Coco Chanel and turning them into these outrageous, show-stopping jobs that he does today, yet still keeping the signature of Chanel*" – BRUCE OLDFIELD. Now that Inès de la Fressange is out of Lagerfeld's life – though she is a neighbour on the avenue – he concentrates on the detailing and updating that keeps Chanel at the top for Jackie Onassis, Princess Caroline, Queen Noor of Jordan, Ann Getty, SKYE MACLEOD, JENNY KEE and AMANDA DE CADENET: "*Chanel is Chanel. They make great designs . . . I wear Levi's every day of my life with a Chanel jacket or something.*"

🍴 CHRISTIAN DIOR, 11 rue François 1er, 75008 ☎ (1) 4073 5444 (couture); 32 ave Montaigne, 75008 (boutique)

One that's on the move – in the right Diorection. Gianfranco Ferré (Golden Thimble award winner for his first 2 Dior collections) has reinterpreted the classic house style and come up with a new New Look. He loves white collars and cuffs, high heels with trousers, the perfect pants suit, and "*amazing, feminine evening dresses – he's softened up a lot*" – GAIL ROLFE. Daryl Hannah, Isabelle Adjani, Grace Jones and Ivana Trump all adore Dior, so does DAVID SHILLING. Chaps keep an eye out for excellent menswear; ladies slip into the best lingerie and furs.

🍴 CHRISTIAN LACROIX, 73 rue du Faubourg St Honoré, 75008
☎ (1) 4265 7908

Hyper-vamped couture from the exuberant, inventive and extravagant M Lacroix. Dead alluring frocks for all feline fatales – the kittens, leopards and tigresses of glam soc. Wildly impractical multi-textured creations come in satin, velvet, damask, leopard-print silk, tulle, with embroidery, beading, quilting, lace, tassels, fringing, swirls – *tout ensemble, alors!* Yet the effects of his catwalk shows filter down, much diluted, on to the streets. Femmes with attitude choose Lacroix couture: Madonna, Maryam D'Abo, Bette Midler, Ivana Trump, Faye Dunaway, CAROLINE LOCKHART. For those without FF100,000-plus to spend, the Luxe collection is half the price, and the prêt-à-porter is almost sensible. Get dazzled by his haut-fakery – huge rocks, spangled chandelearrings.

♠

France's Best Prêt-à-Porter

1	KARL LAGERFELD at Chanel
2	AZZEDINE ALAIA
3	CLAUDE MONTANA
4	LOLITA LEMPICKA
5	YVES SAINT LAURENT

♠ CLAUDE MONTANA, 31 rue de Grenelle, 75007 ☎ (1) 4549 1302
Beloved of the upbeat classicists – Montana's sophisticated tailoring is universally admired, his imaginative little twists set him apart. Look for clever use of colouring, pleated trousers, clever leather. KEN HOM does. *"Refined and simple – navy and white with silver buttons, red and pink together – he is a definite force in fashion"* – GAIL ROLFE.

EMANUEL UNGARO, 2 ave Montaigne, 75008 ☎ (1) 4723 6194 (couture); 58 rue du Faubourg St Honoré, 75008 ☎ (1) 4742 1606 (boutique)
Though his vision doesn't tally with those on the fashion front line, Ungaro offers sizzling style for women who want to be noticed – Nastassja Kinski, JOAN COLLINS, Anouk Aimée, Ivana Trump. Trained under the great Balenciaga, Ungaro is master of power prints, saturated colours, svelte shapes and clear cuts.

♠ JEAN-LOUIS SCHERRER, 51 ave Montaigne, 75008 ☎ (1) 4359 5539 (couture); 31 rue de Tournon, 75006 ☎ 4354 4907 (boutique)
Couturier to Euro royals and political wives, such as Madame Giscard d'Estaing. Beautifully composed cocktail and evening wear splashed with detail – embroidery in 18-carat gold thread, diamanté sequins, feathers – show to advantage on statuesque daughter-turned-model Laëtitia.

"I always love it – terribly feminine, terribly wearable. He always picks a country to be inspired by, and recently it was Africa, with wonderful tribal embroidery and headdresses" – GAIL ROLFE. The best in the world for MARY ROSSI. Go bargain-hunting at 29 ave Ledru-Rollin, 75012 ☎ (1) 4628 3927, for one of last season's designs at half price or less.

JEAN-PAUL GAULTIER, 6 rue Vivienne, 75002 ☎ (1) 4286 0505
Still thought of as the iconoclast, fashion wit and entertainer, Gaultier is not quite the force that he was at the end of the last decade. Nevertheless, his tailoring remains exemplary, and his style intelligently eclectic – social realism, ecclesiastics, punk, fetishism – he'll use them all in Lycra, rubber and metal on the one hand, gabardine, satin and velvet on the other. The Junior Gaultier line makes it all more attainable – SKYE MACLEOD goes for it.

KARL LAGERFELD, 17–19 rue du Faubourg St Honoré, 75008 ☎ (1) 4266 6464
The designer's designer, admired by all for his fashion hat-trick (his own line, Chanel and Fendi). However, the statement is weaker, the clothes less desirable here than at Chanel. His power lies both in incredible detailing and broad conception. Sharp-lined, beautifully tailored suits for female execs line up with a new groovier mood, casual and chic. Accessories variously adorn the best shoulders, feet and ears.

LANVIN, 22 rue du Faubourg St Honoré, 75008 ☎ 4471 3333 (femmes); 3 rue Cambon, 75001 ☎ (01) 4260 3883 (hommes)
A couture house to watch, with the relatively inexperienced Dominique Morlotti (late of Dior menswear) at the design helm. (Fashion-gazers still mourn the non-renewal of Claude Montana's contract after his enchanting spring collection for Lanvin.)

♠ LOLITA LEMPICKA, 2 rue des Rosiers, 75004 ☎ (1) 4274 4294
Ever more a classic name, ladylike Lempicka attires les jeunes sophistiquées in well-cut little crêpe dresses and suits in clever colours and shapes. Her handbags and gloves are becoming indispensable. She gets SKYE MACLEOD's and GAIL ROLFE's votes.

MADAME GRES, 422 rue St Honoré, 75008 ☎ (1) 4260 7200
Nonagenarian Madame Grés has now retired, but her style lives on under a creative design team. Swathes of silk jersey have the fluid Grecian goddess look wrapped up by night; sportswear, daywear, jewellery, too.

MARTINE SITBON, 6 rue Braque, 75003 ☎ (1) 4887 3747
Retro progress – here's the lady who's put the

bite back into catsuits. The kinkier bits from the 60s – tight fits for the body-conscious, bare midriffs and minis – get the heads turning.

PHILIPPE VENET, 62 rue François 1er, 75008 ☎ (1) 4224 5522
One-time Givenchy student, now fashionable Paris's best-kept secret. *"He cuts structured clothes like a dream"* – ANNE-ELISABETH MOUTET. *"A coat by Venet is simply in a different class from anything else"* – JEAN-MICHEL HENRY. Discreet, old-money clientele – the Comtesse de Paris and Queen Noor of Jordan among them – guarantees a profit.

SONIA RYKIEL, 6 rue de Grenelle, 75006 ☎ (1) 4222 4322; 70 rue du Faubourg St Honoré, 75008 ☎ (1) 4265 2081
Chic, wearable knitwear which Rykielites simply adore – some things never change. Flowing designs with understated detail and understated tones. Beautiful children's wear.

THIERRY MUGLER, 49 ave Montaigne, 75008 ☎ (1) 4723 3762; 10 place des Victoires, 75002 ☎ (1) 4260 0637
On the way back as the anti-promiscuous, standoffish mood of late wanes, chic shocker Mugler is getting the girls to give the come-on again. *"Wild . . . but he does the perfect Hollywood suit, beautifully cut"* – GAIL ROLFE. DAVID SHILLING'S all for it: *"I like his last collection – it's fun."*

France's Best Couturiers

1	GIANFRANCO FERRE at Dior
2	YVES SAINT LAURENT
3	CHRISTIAN LACROIX
4	KARL LAGERFELD at Chanel
5	JEAN-LOUIS SCHERRER

🏆 YVES SAINT LAURENT, 5 ave Marceau, 75016 ☎ (1) 4723 7271
It looks as if the king has finally been deposed. The founder of modern fashion design, his name is legendary, his quality is always supreme, but his latest collections have failed to bring in the plaudits they once did. However, for *his* first ladies (Mitterrand, Gorbachev, Deneuve, PALOMA PICASSO, CAROLYN LOCKHART, DOTT ROSA MARIA LETTS, Baroness Marie-Hélène de Rothschild) there is no one else. Hear NANCY PILCHER: *"My favourite, I have a very soft spot for him, I cry at the shows when he comes out at the end, I can't believe I am looking at this man – in years to come he is not going to be with us. He's a genius, like a God, very private."* YSL

20-20 Vision

The latest arrondissement on everybody's lips is le 20e, Belleville. A working-class area, it's always had a certain artsy je ne sais quoi – Maurice Chevalier and Edith Piaf were vingtième-dwellers. Now it's become the happening place for decidedly undesigner working artists such as Jérôme Ménager, Bezie and De Villeglé. At the centre of the arty community are 2 galleries: **Galerie Climats**, 84 rue Pixérécourt ☎ (1) 4797 7503, run by Patrice Moine, who shows the abstract artists Brooker, Espilit and Ostier; and **Orfila**, 80 rue Orfila ☎ (1) 4797 8499. As yet, the hip-for-hip's-sake crew haven't moved in. The character of the quartier comes from its thriving Chinatown (the Chinese supermarket in rue de Belleville is a hot place to shop), quiet Arab area and a chunk of old-fashioned village Paris. Feel the heartbeat around the place des Fêtes, absorb the atmos in any one of the local cafés and excellent ethnic restaurants.

---

has perfect taste in line and shape; down in the annals of fashion go his V-necked navy suit, the short, sharp skirt and *le smoking*.

Hotels

HOTEL BALZAC, 6 rue Balzac, 75008 ☎ (1) 4561 9722
Just off the Champs Elysées, an alternative to the big names (and the grand scale). *"An old hotel that I like a lot, smaller and much more intimate than the grand ones"* – MEREDITH ETHERINGTON-SMITH. Great Italian food at **Bice**, cousin of the famous Milanese eaterie. The film world flocks – Christopher Lambert and Diane Lane stayed for 6 months and Jane March (star of *L'Amant*) hid from the press here.

🏆 HOTEL DE CRILLON, 10 place de la Concorde, 75008 ☎ (1) 4265 2424
Live here *comme le roi*. 18C splendour in every vista – marble, crystal, polished glass, silver and gilt. *"Wonderful,"* lauds LISA BARNARD, *"a great hotel"*, raves ROBIN LEACH, *"the best hotel in Europe"*, mews MARK MCCORMACK, *"the essence of French chic"*, claims CLAUDIA ROSSI HUDSON. More eulogies from KEN HOM, NANCY PILCHER and MARK PATRICK, *"because I love Paris so much . . . it's so incredibly chic, yet you can wear jeans, the attitude is so worldly."* PETER BLAKE,

too: "*I can only add to how wonderful it is, mainly because we ordered room service for our little daughter, who was then two, and two waiters brought spaghetti in a silver server. So the service is absolutely wonderful.*" So is the food at **Les Ambassadeurs**, the glittering dining room under chef Christian Constant.

HOTEL DE L'ABBAYE SAINT-GERMAIN, 10 rue Cassette, 75006 ☎ (1) 4544 3811

Leafy solace off the great chatter-houses on the boulevard. Great for seekers of a dozy retreat such as JUDITH KRANTZ – try for a ground-floor room leading to the bird-filled garden.

HOTEL DE LA TREMOILLE, rue de la Trémoille, 75008 ☎ (1) 4723 3420

Tucked behind the Plaza Athénée and under the same ownership. "*A marvellous hotel, old-fashioned, elegant, chic, very elegant. The clientele is a combination of businessmen and rock stars, somewhere between Blakes and Browns*" – JEAN-MICHEL JAUDEL.

HOTEL LANCASTER, 7 rue de Berri, 75008 ☎ (1) 4359 9043

Quiet charmer with a very private feel – antiques and art are collected with discrimination, and the service is quiet and solicitous. "*You can't beat the Lancaster, it is the best*" – JOHN TOVEY. JULIAN LLOYD WEBBER liked it, bar the infernal lift ("*there's no way that at night you can get away from the noise of that lift – it really shakes the place to pieces*"), but CAROLYN LOCKHART zooms in on its strongest suit: "*I love the courtyard, it is charming, you are very conscious of it, it's very French.*"

🦞 HOTEL LE BRISTOL, 112 rue du Faubourg St Honoré, 75008 ☎ (1) 4266 9145

Quietly glamorous stop-off for those power men and women – politicians, diplomats – who want to avoid the limelight. Fine antiques, crystal, tons of marble, and famously discreet service. It's MEREDITH ETHERINGTON-SMITH'S bed for the night: "*I reckon it's the best hotel in Paris – it's got a swimming pool and it's full of very quiet, rather old-fashioned people, no noise, no glitz.*" It puts RAYMOND BLANC in sunny mood: "*It's really lovely, they've got a lovely conservatory, a garden within the house, it's very clever. Beautiful furnishings as well.*" BARBARA KAFKA dips in: "*It has the most charming swimming pool, indoors and outdoors, designed to look like the stern of a big yacht. And there's a mural that looks like Eden Roc. It's a very good hotel as well, but it's worth staying just to use the charming pool.*" And to dine in style.

HOTEL MEURICE, 228 rue de Rivoli, 75001 ☎ 4260 3860

This is the one that Salvador Dali chose as an address in Paris for 30 years – he reigned from the Royal Suite. Look out on to the Tuileries from the gorgeous gilt salons, ballrooms and dreamy creamy bedrooms. WARWICK VYNER chooses it too: "*I love the Meurice.*"

HOTEL MONTELAMBERT, 3 rue Montelambert, 75012 ☎ (1) 4548 6811

The traditional Bohemian haunt in the heart of literary Paris is attracting style fiends since its revamp by design hero Christian Liaigre. Rather plain modern elegance (navies and creams and spare lines) are the biz for SIR TERENCE CONRAN: "*I think it is very, very nice. It was a place I always used to stay, then it was redesigned, and now it's really an excellent place in Paris to stay.*" NANCY PILCHER, SHARYN STORRIER-LYNEHAM and BONNIE BROOKS are of one accord. "*The best hotel in Paris right now – it's really beautiful, beautifully decorated, very special, very small, very full, especially at fashion time*" – BB. Writers such as Nina Bouraoui, from the nearby publishing house Gallimard, prop up the **Bar Montelambert**.

HOTEL PLAZA ATHENEE, 25 ave Montaigne, 75008 ☎ (1) 4723 7833

All you would expect of a grand hotel that caters to the well-heeled (and the downright flashy) who march the shopping avenues of Paris. It spells glamour for JOHN GOLD ("*a very good hotel*") and gastronomy at **Le Régence** for LISA BARNARD ("*fantastic . . . it has a good restaurant*") and DAVID SHILLING ("*for lunch it's the best. It's just great*"). Flower-filled courtyard and one of the sleekest penthouse suites in town, all black lacquer and cream carpets, with a roof terrace.

HOTEL RITZ, 15 place Vendôme, 75001 ☎ (1) 4260 3830

One of a handful of Paris addresses that speak volumes, move mountains and send devotees into delirium – such as DAME BARBARA CARTLAND ("*still the most romantic and most comfortable hotel in the world*"), DOUGLAS FAIRBANKS JR, LORD MONTAGU OF BEAULIEU, ROBIN LEACH and LISA BARNARD. DAVID SHILLING confesses "*I am very old-fashioned and stay at the Ritz, but I shouldn't*". Fab location, marble, crystal ad infinitum, that amazing crested baroque bed in the Impériale suite – everything is uncompromisingly opulent, as only the French can be. "*I like it, there's a very nice nightclub, they have some wonderful facilities, magnificent rooms, beautiful antiques in the rooms and a fabulous restaurant*" – JOHN GOLD. ED VICTOR takes the plunge downstairs too: "*I like having tea in that wonderful garden, and it's got the best pool certainly – it's amazing because you don't feel at all that you are in a basement – you feel as though you are in Ancient Rome.*" RAYMOND BLANC picks up the watery theme: "*The bathrooms are absolutely stunning with lots of space and steam showers in some of them – it's the sort of thing no one normally does.*" Sip before dinner at the famous **Hemingway Bar**, then tuck in at the excellent **L'Espadon** restaurant. Retire afterwards to the suave Annabel's-like **Club du Ritz** – civilized and exclusive.

HOTEL ST REGIS, 12 rue Jean Goujon, 75008 ☎ (1) 4359 4190
Small hotel in the heart of fashionland, where BARBARA KAFKA stops off: "*It's just been completely redone. There are little rooms which look out over the rooftops and they have little balconies where you can have breakfast outside. It's been made into an absolutely charming hotel.*" And so say the flocking frock trade.

LA VILLA, 29 rue Jacob, 75006 ☎ (1) 4326 6000
Chic little designer hotel near St Germain des Prés, done up in stripped-down style by Starck-influenced Marie-Christine Dorner. "*It's Paris's mini-Royalton, really lovely, very quiet, modern but not aggressive*" – ANNE-ELISABETH MOUTET. George Michael and Joan Baez stay; writers flock to the bar, and cool types to the jazz club.

——— Music ———

CENTRE DE MUSIQUE BAROQUE, 16 rue Saint Victoire, 72000 Versailles ☎ 3949 4824
Echoes of concerts, opera and ballet in the château, in the park and throughout the town.

FEP FESTIVAL ESTIVAL DE PARIS, 20 rue Geoffroy-l'Asnier, 75004 ☎ (1) 4804 9801
Summertime classical music festival held around the churches and auditoria of the capital.

🐟 L'OPERA BASTILLE, 2 bis place de la Bastille, 75012 ☎ (1) 4001 1616
Carlos Ott's controversial and disliked modern building is now established as home to the **Paris Opera**, helped by an extraordinary Kabuki-style production of *The Magic Flute* last year, directed by the American avant-garde guru Bob Wilson. Under the baton of Korean conductor Myung-Whun Chung, the company aspires to the top international league.

THEATRE MUSICAL DE PARIS, 2 place de Chatelet, 75001 ☎ (1) 4261 1983
Highly regarded and funded hall for recitals and musicals that attracts the best conductors and orchestras from around the world (they have an agreement with the British Philharmonia among others). Also puts on major opera productions from time to time.

VERSAILLES FESTIVAL OPERA, c/o Syndicat d'Initiative, 7 rue des Réservoirs, 78000 Versailles ☎ 3950 3622
An early summer gem – a week of opera and concerts in May/June. The climax is the baroque opera in its original setting in the opera house at the Château de Versailles, built by Gabriel as a monument to the marriage of the future Louis XVI to Marie Antoinette.

——— Restaurants ———

See also Hotels and Shopping.

AMPHYCLES, 78 ave des Ternes, 75017 ☎ (1) 4068 0101
Gastronomic showcase for Philippe Groult, "*a bright young chef bred by Robuchon, who has been influenced for the best without copying him. It has taken him 2 years to establish himself. A great up-and-coming chef*" – ALEXANDRE LAZAREFF. BARBARA KAFKA seconds that, and adds "*he's young, and he does the best jus de boeuf I've ever had*". A stellar gelée de foie de veau as well.

🐟 APICIUS, 122 ave de Villiers, 75017 ☎ (1) 4380 1966
Sleek restaurant, spiffing, unintimidating cooking, and the good-looking chef M Vagato. "*I think he's superb, he has two stars, but I think he's a real comer, and he does particularly nice homy dishes, taking them up to the next level*" – BARBARA KAFKA. ROBERT NOAH agrees: "*Humble dishes that are transformed.*"

🐟 CARRE DES FEUILLANTS, 14 rue de Castiglione, 75001 ☎ (1) 4286 8282
Southwestern cooking brought to the capital by the inspired Alain Dutournier. "*Smashing. The most delicious white gazpacho, and he is one of the very few chefs who buys meat and then lets it mature. Absolutely delicious, best regional food in Paris*" – ALEXANDRE LAZAREFF. Really special specilities: ravioli stuffed with foie gras and truffles or with lobster; wild salmon cooked with smoked bacon. A chorus of approval from GILLES PUDLOWSKI and JONATHAN MEADES.

CAVIAR KASPIA, 17 place de la Madeleine, 75008 ☎ (1) 4265 3352
A pre-Revolutionary display of silver and memorabilia matched by a non-rationed selection of caviares to top blinis and be washed down by icy vodka or champagne.

DODIN-BOUFFANT, 25 rue Frédéric Sauton, 75005 ☎ (1) 4325 2514
Smart bistro (Mitterrand's favourite local) with a strong line in fish – more than 500 lbs daily. John Dory with oysters and leeks is a stand-out and the raspberry soufflé is legendary.

DUQUESNOY, 6 ave Bosquet, 75007 ☎ (1) 4705 9678
Bourgeois setting for bourgeois cuisine. "*A pretty little, intimate, romantic restaurant on the Left Bank, with excellent food*" – DAME BARBARA CARTLAND "*Very pretty and pleasant to eat in*" – BARBARA KAFKA.

FAUGERON, 52 rue Longchamp, 75016 ☎ (1) 4704 2453
Cuisine artistique – order the bavarois aux asperges or curry de jarret de veau aux

Sauternes et onions confit – and see why SIR PETER USTINOV is dumb-struck with admiration. Classy, classic cooking.

FOUQUET'S, 99 ave des Champs-Elysées, 75008 ☎ (1) 4723 7060
Ever-fashionable, even if prices have entered the stratosphere. So beloved of the Canned crowd that when threatened with closure it was declared a national monument of the film industry. La Veranda is the place to sit.

♠ GUY SAVOY, 18 rue Troyon, 75017 ☎ (1) 4380 4061
Remains closest to many foodies' hearts for his continuing invention and style. GILLES PUD-LOWSKI's for example: "*My favourite, because his cooking is the most personal and the lightest, the most surprising – he is always surprising.*" Just what the doctor ordered for GP are l'anguille aux poireaux (eel with leeks) and filet de sole à l'oseille (sole with sorrel sauce). ROLAND ESCAIG thinks Guy produces "*very good French cooking, not traditional, inventive – though maybe not as creative as before*". Serious service, with dishes under silver cloches.

♠ JAMIN (ROBUCHON), 32 rue de Longchamp, 75116 ☎ (1) 4727 1227
Perhaps the best restaurant in the world. Joël Robuchon's kitchen turns out masterpieces, every one checked by JR himself – he is the culinary world's most enlightened despot. And how they taste! "*One of his most famous dishes is the*

crème of cauliflower with caviare, served in a little porcelain bowl. You take the porcelain top off and it looks like it is still porcelain underneath – a gorgeous porcelain-thin layer of cauliflower cream, wonderful aspic and caviare. The mashed potato is simply potatoes cooked in their skins and mashed . . . nobody makes it as good as he does" – ROBERT NOAH. It's RAYMOND BLANC's No 1, it's in GILLES PUDLOWSKI's pantheon, ROLAND ESCAIG casts his vote, for ROBIN LEACH it's one of the "*extraordinary restaurants*", and it's a favourite of JILL MULLENS. DAVID SHILLING says: "*Yes – because it's brilliant and you are bound to see people you have been avoiding for weeks.*" All this comes at a price – FF1,000 a head, sans vin, for the top menu, and a lot of patience – book months, not weeks ahead. KEN HOM says: "*It is a place I have to eat at least 3 or 4 times a year just to get inspired,*" but for ALEXANDRE LAZAREFF moderation is the answer: "*I only go there once a year. It is perfection and I do not want to spoil my idea of perfection.*"

LA MAISON BLANCHE, 15 ave Montaigne, 75008 ☎ (1) 4723 5599
Newcomer on top of the Champs-Elysées Theatre of which SIR TERENCE CONRAN approves: "*Fantastic. A spectacular view down over the Seine and the Eiffel Tower and a really good modern interior, and there are not many restaurants in Paris that are blessed with that. Really high standards of service – it's a special place, it's got a lot of glamour that people dress up for,*

♠ **Buzzz** For true Parisian atmos, you can't beat a good bistro or brasserie. Here's where to join the squeeze: **Benoit**, 20 rue St Martin, 75004 ☎ (1) 4272 2576, where fans of informal, hearty French cooking whoop in ecstasy. "*It's of the old line of bistros that is for real, and it has this great thing of being open Saturday lunchtime and dinner*" – BARBARA KAFKA. The Lyonnaise food and burgundies on the wine list please JEAN-MICHEL JAUDEL, DOMINIQUE PIOT and MARK MCCORMACK ♠ . . . . . . **Chez André**, 12 rue Marbeuf, 75008 ☎ (1) 4720 5957, where BARBARA TAYLOR BRADFORD and Roman Polanski tuck in ♠ . . . . . . trad old **Chez Georges**, 1 rue du Mail, 75002 ☎ (1) 4260 0711, where you might see Joseph or the British Ambassador to Paris of an evening ♠ . . . . . . **Chez Edgard**, 4 rue Marbeuf, 75008 ☎ (1) 4720 5115, where media mix – gossip circulates via amicable host Paul Benmussa to cabinet ministers to celebs to assorted hacks to broadcast folk – and food is spot on (the perfect steak frites) ♠ . . . . . . **L'Oulette**, 38 rue des Tournelles, 75004 ☎ (1) 4271 4333, a winner for old-fashioned, decently priced cooking ♠ . . . . . . **Le Muniche**, 22 rue Guillaume Apollinaire, 75006 ☎ (1) 4633 6209, la même brasserie in a new location, for bright chitter-chatter, swift service and good shellfish; and its little sisters **Le Petit Zinc**, 4 rue Saint Benoit, 75006 ☎ (1) 4633 5166, and **L'Echaudé**, 21 rue de l'Echaudé, 75006 ☎ (1) 4354 7902 ♠ . . . . . . **Chez Géraud**, 31 rue Vital, 75016 ☎ (1) 4520 3300, ANNE-ELISABETH MOUTET's favourite for "*marvellous, unpretentious family cuisine with ultra-fresh produce from the country and a great wine list*". . . . . ♠

and when people dress up in Paris it's quite a thrill." But vrai Parisians are not necessarily of one accord – some find it too contrived.

France's Best Restaurants

1	JAMIN (ROBUCHON) · Paris
2	L'ARPEGE · Paris
3	TAILLEVENT · Paris
4	LOUIS XV, Hôtel de Paris · Monte Carlo
5	LES AMBASSADEURS, Hôtel de Crillon · Paris
6	LA COTE D'OR · Saulieu
7	L'AUBERGADE · Puymirol
8	L'AMBROISIE · Paris
9	LES PRES ET LES SOURCES D'EUGENIE · Eugénie-les-Bains
10	CARRE DES FEUILLANTS · Paris

L'AMBROISIE, 9 place des Vosges, 75004 ☎ (1) 4278 5145
Book way ahead to get into the carefully redecorated 17C former hall of the Hôtel de Luynes – one of France's oldest families. Chef Bernard Pacaud creates dishes in the nouveau classique vein: pièce d'agneau aux fèves fraîches, jambonette de grenouille avec sauce cressonnette aux morilles. RAYMOND BLANC recognizes the best when he sees it and MARQUIS DOMINIQUE DE LASTOURS reckons *"the place has weathered its success very well".* He approves of the décor.

L'AMI LOUIS, 32 rue du Vertbois, 75003 ☎ (1) 4887 7748
A true gourmanderie, going strong since its heyday under the late, great Antoine Magnin (1899–

1987). *"Here they do not believe in nouvelle helpings, but give you literally steaks of foie gras for starters"* – ANNE-ELISABETH MOUTET. Marlene Dietrich, Judy Garland, Liza Minnelli, Cardinal Roncalli (later Pope John XXIII) used to go; these days it's Robert De Niro and Barbra Streisand. The dingy décor has been touched up to look the same as ever (brown and yellow paint, old deal chairs). For MARTIN SKAN, it offers *"very wholesome and well-cooked food, using only the finest ingredients; enormous portions, wonderful atmosphere in a bad area."*

L'ARPEGE, 84 rue de Varenne, 75007 ☎ (1) 4705 0906
Tip-top tucker – young chef Alain Passard is stunning gastrocentric Parisians such as GILLES PUDLOWSKI, ROLAND ESCAIG and ALEXANDRE LAZAREFF: *"He is the only chef who deserved to cook for my wedding, and that was the best meal of my life."* Out-of-town questers of the foodie grail such as MATTHEW FORT love it too. ROBERT NOAH eulogizes: *"The food is very, very good ... some things are just amazing, so simple, but marvellous. For the duck, he uses a recipe of his grandmother's, very laborious and old-fashioned. And he has marvellous sole with candied lemon. Spectacular."*

LA TABLE D'ANVERS, 2 place d'Anvers, 75009 ☎ (1) 4878 3521
Christian Conticini and his creations send ROLAND ESCAIG into ecstasies: *"Superb – grande table, grand chef, superb, extraordinaire. The most inventive cooking with a lot of perfumes, spices and so on, most extraordinary. He's wonderful, wonderful, wonderful, wonderful. The most inventive in France."* ANNE-ELISABETH MOUTET finds a similar breath of fresh air in the unchic neuvième – *"unexpectedly creative"*; dishes such as rabbit stewed with chestnuts and liver in a sharp sauce bear her out.

LA TOUR D'ARGENT, 15 quai de la Tournelle, 75005 ☎ (1) 4354 2337
The snootiest haut-dinery in the foodie capital has recently bucked up on the cooking front – classic dishes with consistency and flair. Service continues in the 'aren't you lucky to be here'

Buzz If poisson's your poison, you'll flip at **Le Divellec**, 107 rue de l'Université, 75007 ☎ (1) 4551 9196, where BARBARA KAFKA finds, from autumn to early spring, *"the best seafood extravaganza of raw and barely cooked fish I have ever had. It is the most glamorous thing like that I know."* MARY ROSSI says aye to that ...... Claude Terrail's second string, **La Rôtisserie du Beaujolais**, presides next door to his famous La Tour d'Argent, at 17 quai de la Tournelle, 75005 ☎ (1) 4354 1747, and dishes up Lyonnaise delectables ...... Crowd scene: **La Palette**, 43 rue de Seine, 75006 ☎ (1) 4326 6815, is packing 'em in to its old-fashioned checked-cloths paintings-on-walls hustle-bustle dining room. Students from the nearby Beaux-Arts, writers and publishers converge for honest family cuisine ...

vein; the view (over Notre Dame) and the wine list (encyclopaedic) compensate in DON HEWITSON's eyes: *"I am not sure if I go there for the food or for the view or for the wine. It really is spectacular, on the banks of the Seine, and the wine cellar is wonderful."* BARBARA TAYLOR BRADFORD is another river-gazer. Star-gazers can turn to the walls for autographs of famous diners – Churchill, de Gaulle, Roosevelt.

LE COCHON D'OR, 192 ave Jean-Jaurès, 75019 ☎ (1) 4208 3981
Paris's best pig-out – come here when you've got a *big* hole to fill. Slabs of tender steak seared and pink, bricks of foie gras – that sort of hole.

LE GRAND VEFOUR, 17 rue Beaujolais, 75001 ☎ (1) 4296 5627
Staggeringly beautiful restaurant set in an 18C building next to the Palais Royal. Generous but light cooking based on classic French techniques – the chef trained under Robuchon for 5 years. LORD MONTAGU OF BEAULIEU is delighted to light upon another 3-star to his pleasing.

LE JULES VERNE, Tour Eiffel, Champ de Mars, 75007 ☎ (1) 4555 6144
Hautest rooftop cuisine in the world – no second-rate stuff here – food, view, clientele (chic, chic). *"Doing very well, it really is a night restaurant, because of the lighting"* – ROBERT NOAH. Cooking is fab (try the veal with lemon and vanilla); getting up there is a breeze – arrive by private glass lift. It's got it all for ALEXANDRE LAZAREFF: *"Perfect for a first visit in Paris. A romantic place, overlooking all of Paris, extremely good food, and it is very Parisian"*; JOHN TOVEY comes to the point: *"Superb."*

LES COLONIES, 10 rue Saint-Julien-le-Pauvre, 75005 ☎ (1) 4354 3133
Intelligent, sophisticated cooking in one of the Left Bank's most elegant restaurants. Influences from France's former colonies: caraway in the ragoût, raisins in the chicken, divine okra beignets. *"The first time I ever wanted to copy all the decoration in a restaurant: pale yellow rag-rolled 18C panelling, latticed parquet, tapestry undercloths like the ones in Vermeer paintings"* – ANNE-ELISABETH MOUTET.

LUCAS CARTON, 9 place de la Madeleine, 75008 ☎ (1) 4265 2290
Light, bright, contemporary cooking from Alain Senderens, served in listed Art Nouveau surroundings, eaten by glamorous fellows like ROBIN LEACH. Reports filter through that the cooking can be uneven, but the warm liver wrapped in a cabbage leaf is a sure bet.

MAXIM'S, 3 rue Royale, 75008 ☎ (1) 4265 2794
Same as it ever was – beautiful Art Nouveau dining room, starry eaters (JOAN COLLINS, Claus von Bülow), fair cooking, monstrous bill. Have lunch in the front, dine round the back, and dress up. MEREDITH ETHERINGTON-SMITH calls the window table the most glam in Paris.

MICHEL ROSTANG, 20 rue Rennequen, 75017 ☎ (1) 4763 4077
Here, the celebrated eponymous chef presides in the super-gourmet league. In common with other foodie bigwigs, he's opened a string of second strings, including the fashionable **Bistrot d'à Côté**, round the corner at 10 rue Gustave-Flaubert ☎ (1) 4267 0581.

MIRAVILE, 72 quai de l'Hôtel de Ville, 75004 ☎ (1) 4274 7222
Gilles Epié's old Miravile used to be a slightly grey place, a touch of the old KGB dining room – plush, discreetly gloomy. Now he's swopped banks and gone flashier, and is pulling the punters back for excellent food. BARBARA KAFKA recognizes *"a very good cook"*.

PAVILLON DES PRINCES, 69 ave de la Porte d'Auteuil, 75116 ☎ (1) 4743 1515
Inventive cooking by Patrick Lenôtre, nephew of smart caterer Gaston Lenôtre. *"In my mind it is way above any of the Paris 3 rosettes except Taillevent"* – ANNE-ELISABETH MOUTET.

PHARAMOND, 24 rue de la Grande-Truanderie, 75001 ☎ (1) 4233 0672
Authentic belle époquerie in branché Les Halles, with authentic specialities from Normandy – tripes à la mode de Caen (a pre-WWI recipe), pig's trotters, andouillette – and authentic power men – President Mitterrand is frequently spotted at the banquette of the best table downstairs (opposite and slightly left of the wrought-iron staircase). It's a fave for JULIAN LLOYD WEBBER: *"Very good, quite old-fashioned, the kind of place that seems almost to have vanished now."* ANNE-ELISABETH MOUTET reckons *"it is that rarity: a true provincial bourgeois island in the centre of Paris"*.

RESTAURANT JACQUES CAGNA, 14 rue des Grands Augustins, 75006 ☎ (1) 4326 4939
One of the maître-chefs of France and a wizard with poissons. Start with petits escargots surpris, follow with fillet of sea-perch stuffed with oysters or gougeonettes of sole and red mullet, and finish with a deliciously wicked pâtisserie.

🍴 TAILLEVENT, 15 rue Lamennais, 75008 ☎ (1) 4561 1290
Jean-Claude Vrinat's ambitious, ingenious cooking, a tremendous wine list, clairvoyant service and splendid setting in an old 2-storey town house mean it's *always* packed (with politicians, media and artsy types). Tuck in to the spectacular lobster and turtle ravioli, go for duck and ask for the cheese tray – it's massive. The best 3-star in Paris for ANNE-ELISABETH MOUTET, while ROLAND ESCAIG rates it primarily *"for the service and for the house"*. Book 6 weeks ahead and reconfirm the day before.

VAL D'ISERE, 2 rue de Berri, 75008
☎ **(1) 4359 1266**
A 60s après-ski-style bistro with the original mellow stripped pine furniture and fitting food – fondue, raclette, etc. *"It's a marvellous, atmospheric place: you expect the young Roger Vadim, Brigitte Bardot or Sophia Loren to jump out of a Facel Vega 2-seater and turn up anytime"* – CHARLES HEIDSIECK. Realistically, you might see AMANDA DE CADENET, who gushes: *"We always have the same thing, the speciality, which is tagliatelle and steak and this yummy kind of creamy sauce all mixed up together."*

VIVAROIS, 192 ave Victor Hugo, 75116
☎ **(1) 4504 0431**
One of those first-class restaurants that have been going on quietly in the leafy, bourgeois seizième, totally unfazed by fashion, turning out brilliant, imaginative (but not quite nouvelle) cuisine. Serious foodies, like GILLES PUDLOWSKI, are letting the cat out of the bag.

—————— *Shopping* ——————

See also Fashion designers.

Fashion's pearly portals open on to the **rue du Faubourg St Honoré** and **avenue Montaigne**: find Chanel, Lagerfeld, Dior, Lacroix, Ungaro, Saint Laurent, Laroche. Snoop out the mavericks in and around the **place des Victoires** – Gaultier and the Japanese gang. **Le Marais** is back-street bazaar – Alaïa, Lempicka, etc, sit among the jewellery and objet shops, tea houses, cafés, dress shops and topping Jewish delis. In **place Vendôme** diamonds are forever. Trip off the **blvd St Germain des Prés** into jostling boutiques and cafés along rue Bonaparte, rue de Tournon, rue de Four and nos 1-60 rue Grenelle for chic youth culture.

Best bargains in town are at the puces – flea markets – the biggest is **Saint Ouen**, at **Porte de Clignancourt**, where everything's been worn in for you (seek out **Malik** and **Marché Biron** for antique clothes); keep your eyes peeled for art and artefacts on the stalls at **Porte de Vanves**, **Marché Aligre**, between place de la Bastille and ave Ledru-Rollin in the 12e (also a fruit and veg market), and **Marché du Temple**, housed in Haussmann's carreau du Temple, rue Eugene-Spuller in Le Marais.

ALLIX, 6 rue de Surène, 75008
☎ **(1) 4265 1079**
A close-kept secret – fabulous finishing trifles for trifling amounts. FF250 might get you a pair of fine black leather gloves or chunky gold earrings studded with fake hematites.

BARRIER ET FILS, 20 ave Franklin D Roosevelt, 75008 ☎ **(1) 4289 0529**
Beautiful jewellery made to order with your own stones or 'off the peg'. *"A friendly jeweller in Paris, they're actually friends of mine, but it's a very welcoming place"* – JEAN-MICHEL JAUDEL.

BOUCHERON, 26 place Vendôme, 75001
☎ **(1) 4260 3282**
The jeweller dazzles on, on famous faces and other places – Joan Collins, Margot Hemingway, Queen Noor of Jordan.

CHARLES JOURDAN, 86 ave des Champs-Elysées, 75008 ☎ **(1) 4562 2928**
Feet-in-the-clouds glamour for the smart set. Glossy shoes with a bit of come-on . . . designer ranges from Lagerfeld and Coveri go down well with JOAN COLLINS.

Dairy Box

The big cheeses around Paris are causing a stir in foodie circles. Take JEAN-MICHEL JAUDEL's reaction to **Cantin**, 2 rue de Lourmel, 75015 ☎ 4578 7058: *"A wonderful cheese shop, their camembert moved me to tears"*. Blink back the emotions and find your way to **Androuet**, 41 rue d'Amsterdam, 75008 ☎ (1) 4874 2690, for super-galactic lactics from all over France, stored in the cheese cellars below the shop. Collected by cheese and wine master Pierre Androuet, there are more than 400 types. But perhaps the grandest fromagistes head for **Barthélemy**, 51 rue de Grenelle, 75007 ☎ (1) 4548 5675, and 92 rue Grande, Fontainebleau ☎ 6422 2164. Chock up your fat content for the day at **La Maison du Chocolat**, 225 rue du Faubourg St Honoré, 75008 ☎ (1) 4227 3944, and 52 rue François 1er, 75008 ☎ (1) 4723 3825, with rich, rich, rich chocolat chaud with cream (at rue François 1er). *"I go there all the time, it is one of my favourite places"* – KEN HOM. Cool off at **Berthillon**, 31 rue St Louis en l'Ile, 75004 ☎ (1) 4354 3161, which licks the rest of the glaceries flottant on the île (but sneakily avoid ginormous queues by sussing out neighbouring stalls that display the name in their window).

CHARVET, 28 place Vendôme, 75001
☎ (1) 4260 3070
Poplin palace – the No 1 shirt shop in France for the straight-down-the-line look, from a very wide selection of fabrics. Politicians earn their stripes here – de Gaulle, Giscard d'Estaing – they can also go to bed in Charvet nightshirts and pyjamas. Owns the rights to the Dufy prints – get one on a huge silk scarf.

DALLOYAU, 99 rue du Faubourg St Honoré, 75008 ☎ (1) 4359 1810
Perennial pleaser of the Parisian palate, which still manages to feel like a neighbourhood pâtisserie. *"The best caterers in Paris, the macaroons are a triumph"* – ANNE-ELISABETH MOUTET. *"Absolutely fantastic pâtisserie, boulangerie . . . and it's incredibly elegant as well, all the girls are in uniform and it's very chic"* – VICTOR EDELSTEIN. Pleasantly unchic is the upstairs *salon du thé*, where the nice ladies of the huitième sip tea and nibble macaroons.

DEHILLERIN, 18 rue Coquillère, 75001
☎ (1) 4236 5313
A foodie's dream: professionals' shop devoted to anything needed to cook, serve and eat food. ROBERT NOAH gets kitted out: *"Knives, pots, pans of heavy copper lined with tin, the best conductor of heat. I buy everything there."* DOMINIQUE PIOT says he has to steer clear of the place or he'll go bankrupt: *"Everything you buy here is long-lasting and made to be used by people who work in a kitchen instead of just prancing from time to time around it."*

♠ FAUCHON, 26 place de la Madeleine, 75008 ☎ (1) 4742 6011
Probably Paris's best-known and grandest food emporium. Goodies from France and around the world. *"The best food shop in Paris – good, even if you're not buying, just for sightseeing. They have one of the best fruit and veg departments.*

It's not huge but the quality is extremely good. I found a wonderful vegetable, chervil root, which I haven't found anywhere else – it's quite delicious. Everything is beautifully packaged and prepared and for people who want to buy food souvenirs, everything comes in very chic Fauchon packages. You can get lovely coffee, and just across the road is the Fauchon pâtisserie, which makes you feel very greedy indeed" – SOPHIE GRIGSON.

GALERIES LAFAYETTE, 40 blvd Haussmann, 75009 ☎ (1) 4282 3456
An Art Nouveau building – complete with stained-glass roof – containing ultra-chic petites boutiques. Get couture or prêt-à-porter from Dior, Saint Laurent, Alaïa, Gaultier, Lacroix, Chantal Thomass, Ralph Lauren and Yohji Yamamoto. In-house gear and accessories are groovy too.

HEDIARD, 21 place de la Madeleine, 75008 ☎ (1) 4266 4436 **and branches**
A cut above in the smartest circles, this is the place to say you've been. Less touristy than Fauchon, its produce is deemed by swankier foodies to be superior. Everything gastronomic is crammed in here, including their own spices, oils, vinegars and splendid wines.

♠ HERMES, 24 rue du Faubourg St Honoré, 75008 ☎ (1) 4017 4717
Still riding high, the place that started as a saddle-maker and found fame with the Kelly and Birkin bags and the silk square. Rifle through the wonderful luggage and leather goods, and look out for new designs from in-house Claude Brouet, as Hermès continues to update its style. Pop into the museum of original designs and see Napoleon's overnight case. JEREMIAH TOWER came out of the shop with something special: *"Hermès boxer shorts made from a scarf of your choice. I have the only ones."*

♠ Buzzz Follow in MARCHESA DI SAN GIULIANO FERRAGAMO's footsteps around the best antiquaires: **François Giraud**, 76 rue de Seine, 75006 ☎ (1) 4326 0761, for *"very beautiful old and modern engravings and books"*; **Nicole Mugler**, 2 rue de l'Université, 75007, for *"very particular antiques"*; **Akko Van Acker**, opposite at No 3 ☎ (1) 4260 2203, for *"beautiful engravings, it's rather an unusual antique shop"*; **Amidon**, 19 rue des Francs Bourgeois, 75004 ☎ (1) 4278 7230, for *"drawings, modern design, various amusing things"*; **Jean Pierre Besenval**, 32 rue de Sévigné, 75003 ☎ (1) 4277 5460, for *"painted furniture – not antique, but well done and with very good taste"* ♠ . . . . . . Anglophile JEAN-MICHEL JAUDEL pops into **Reels on Wheels**, 35 rue de la Croix Nivert, 75015 ☎ (1) 4567 6499, *"something unique – a video club which has exclusively English films in English, not dubbed as they usually are. Also it delivers and picks up, which is extraordinary in Paris"* ♠ . . . . . . Formal soirée, no black tie? You *shall* go to the ball, in a *smoking* hired from **Au Cor de Chasse**, 40 rue de Buci, 75006 ☎ (1) 4362 5189. . . . . ♠

INES DE LA FRESSANGE, 12 ave Montaigne, 75008 ☎ (1) 4723 0894
The ex-Chanel girl has had an instant hit on the great road, with ultra-simple, classic pieces – blazers, trousers, evening suits at reasonable prices. Also wacky dog accessories such as gold-studded leashes. *"She epitomizes the feeling of the moment. What she's done is make eclectic clothes, make what everyone wants to wear – the best navy blazer, the best velvet slipper, not a label, all the pieces you want. She's sold out"* – NANCY PILCHER. The grand opening blocked traffic all the way to the Champs-Elysées. Edith Cresson pops in, as do Princess Caroline of Monaco and CATHERINE ROUSSO.

JAR'S, 7 place Vendôme, 75001 ☎ (1) 4296 3366
Dazzlingly original baubles on commission for the chic élite – eg Baroness Marie Hélène de Rothschild. Rings for fingers and ears, necklaces, all a-glitter with precious stones.

LA MAISON DE LA TRUFFE, 19 place de la Madeleine, 75008 ☎ (1) 4265 5322
Price is no object here – 24-carat truffles, the best caviare, foie gras any which way – squeeze it all in a hamper and kiss goodbye to that size 8.

L'ECLAIREUR, 26 ave des Champs-Elysées 75008 ☎ (1) 4562 1232
Clothes and furniture store for the boys, with up-to-the-second names – exclusive in France for Fornasetti furniture, fabrics, porcelain, etc – Philippe Starck designs, glassware from Czech master Borek Sipeck. *"Marvellous for very sophisticated sportswear and leather clothes. They're interestingly chosen, very different to most places that just have the same things with different labels. It also does handbags, shoes, penknives, ashtrays. A big effort has been put in to make it different"* – JEAN-MICHEL JAUDEL. Ladies shop at 49 ave Franklin D Roosevelt to grab the best of Moschino, Antony Price, Vivienne Westwood, Dolce & Gabbana, Ozbek.

LES CAVES TAILLEVENT, 199 rue du Faubourg St Honoré, 75008 ☎ (1) 4561 1409
Grapies' Eden. Massive selection of the best wines from around France. Close by the restaurant Taillevent, it's run by Valérie, daughter of the great taster Jean-Claude Vrinat (he selects the wines, which puts them ahead by a nose).

LIONEL POILANE, 8 rue du Cherche-Midi, 75006 ☎ (1) 4548 4259
Hot as ever, the celebrated maître boulanger – mentor for the LA designer breadmen – turns out his world-beating sourdough pain de campagne from the wood-fired ovens.

LOUIS VUITTON, 54 ave Montaigne, 75008 ☎ (1) 4562 4700 (boutique); 78B ave Marceau, 75008 ☎ (1) 4720 4700 (luggage)
While trying to design its way off the luggage racks (drafting in Philippe Starck and Gae Aulenti to do new bags, pens, etc), LV has kept a loyal following. KEN HOM for one: *"It is sometimes used as a cliché but they do make some of the best stuff in the world. I think what a lot of people don't understand is that people want quality."* ANOUSKA HEMPEL has her own Love affair: *"Louis Vuitton's travelling desk and tiny stool are quite lovely. They fold up in a trunk and the side of the trunk opens up and the legs come out and you've got a writing desk."*

MARCEL BUR, 138 rue du Faubourg St Honoré, 75008 ☎ (1) 4256 0389
Building suits around the most powerful frames for the last 50 years – this is where diplomats and politicians come for a 'demi-mesure' – said to fit as well as many others' tailor-made, at a snip of the price.

MARCEL LASSANCE, 17 rue du Vieux Colombier, 75006; 21 rue Marbeuf, 75008 ☎ (1) 4548 2928
Boys' stuff. *"They do sportswear and suits, very good quality"* – JEAN-MICHEL JAUDEL. Also own-name luggage, briefcases, belts, ties, etc, and shoes from America by Alden. The place which made Mitterrand's image – for better or worse.

MAUD FRIZON, 81-83 rue des Saints Pères, 75006 ☎ (1) 4222 0693
Fabulous footwear for les femmes – known everywhere for beautiful design, top hides (calf, suede, patent) and handmade soles. JOAN COLLINS and Jean Muir have slipped into them. Bags at 7 rue de Grenelle, 75006.

NOEL, 49 ave Montaigne, 75008 ☎ (1) 4070 0239
A fabulous tradition of hand-worked linens, painstakingly made in the last of the world's old convents. A lace and organza embroidered tablecloth might take a good 200 hours.

PALOMA PICASSO, 5 rue de la Paix, 75008 ☎ (1) 4265 1079
Beautiful, distinctive and very expensive – but then she did have a huge decoration bill from Jacques Grange. Picasso has bold designs on silk scarves, jewellery, croc handbags, luggage, all eminently stylish and barely affordable.

PAUL B . . . , 4 rue Marbeuf, 75008 ☎ (1) 4720 8626
Bitter-sweet teeth make a beeline here: Paul Benmussa's additive-free confections – dark-coated smoked almonds, pralines, filled chocolates, biscuits, etc – are the cogno's choice. Next to Chez Edgard, it's chocs away after lunch.

PETROSSIAN, 18 blvd Latour-Maubourg, 75007 ☎ (1) 4551 5973
The name in caviare – top-quality in the classic tin that everyone's got to have. Other oh so simplicities include fine smoked salmon, foie gras, fresh blinis and Russian pastries.

RAFFI, 60 ave Paul-Doumer, 75016
☎ **(1) 4503 1090; 60 rue Lafayette, 75009**
☎ **(1) 4770 1292**
Smarter brother of the original Armenian grocer at rue Lafayette – get Middle Eastern gems – salty olives, blocks of sweet almondy halva, spices and dried fruits.

ROBERT CLERGERIE, 5 rue du Cherche-Midi, 75006 ☎ (1) 4548 7547
Puts his best foot forward, and keeps ahead of the field in fashion shoes. Square-heeled black suede platform stompers will keep you in step.

WALTER STEIGER, 83 rue du Faubourg St Honoré, 75008 ☎ (1) 4266 6508; 7 rue de Tournon, 75006 ☎ (1) 4633 0145
Classic shoes for la vrai Parisienne. Take in a snippet of fabric and they will make pumps to order, for a price.

RIVIERA

—— Art and museums ——

ATELIER CEZANNE, 9 ave Paul Cézanne, Aix-en-Provence ☎ 4221 0653
The Cézanne experience – his wee studio and ramshackle garden, complete with cherub statue and the descendants of his oft-painted apples.

FONDATION MAEGHT, 06570 St-Paul-de-Vence ☎ 9332 8163
Twin pink buildings outside the town contain a wonderful collection of modern art. Works by Miró, Chagall, Matisse, Bonnard, Léger, etc, stained-glass windows by Braque and Ubac, Giacometti sculpture and more . . . .

MUSEE PICASSO, Château Grimaldi, place du Château, 06600 Antibes
☎ **9334 9191**
Picasso donated his prolific output from the second half of 1946 to this museum. Paintings, ceramics, prints and drawings on a large scale, drawn from his life in and around Antibes.

MUSEE RENOIR, Les Collettes, Cagnes-sur-Mer ☎ 9320 6107
The house where Renoir lived *en famille* from 1907 to his death in 1919 has been preserved, along with the studio and gardens, just as he left them. Recent additions to the collection of his work include *Les Grandes Baigneuses* and landscapes of the countryside around Cagnes. See the bronze *Venus* among the ancient olive trees, some more than 1,000 years old.

VILLA EPHRUSSI DE ROTHSCHILD, ave Denis Semeria, 06230 St-Jean-Cap-Ferrat ☎ 9301 3309
Baroness de Rothschild's large collection of 18C French art is housed in a turn-of-the-century Italianate villa. Important examples of Sèvres and Meissen porcelain, French rococo paintings such as Boucher's *La Femme et l'Enfant*, Oriental decorative arts and Savonnerie carpets, including one from the Royal Chapel, Versailles. Splendid gardens, laid out in Florentine, Spanish, Japanese and French styles; peep through the palms to the sea.

—— Casinos ——

MONTE CARLO CASINO, place du Casino, 98007 ☎ 9350 6931
Gamble à la James Bond here – 24-carat glamour in the world's most (in)famous belle époque salons. Play European roulette, 30-40 and slot machines in the first one or, in the private salon,

🦅 **Buzzz** Parisian bijoux light the eyes of MARC BOHAN: *"I love the jewels of a young French girl,* **Dominique Aurentis**. *She does part of my jewellery for the show and evening bags"* 🦅 . . . . . . Jewels 2: Young **Billy Boy**, best known for his coutured collection of Barbie Dolls, also designs baubles for grown-up girls, available at Galeries Lafayette and in favour with DUGGIE FIELDS 🦅 . . . . . . Kilojoules: Tone that body at the membership-only **Le Cercle Foch**, 33 ave Foch, 75116 ☎ (1) 4501 7576: *"Swim, pump iron, fence, work out, practise a bit of judo or watch an avant-premiere movie in one of the city's best kept secrets"* – MARGARET KEMP 🦅 . . . . . . The sun always shines on **Soleil du Midi**, 6 rue du Cherche-Midi, 75006 ☎ (1) 4548 1502, a stash of oils, soaps, honeys, etc, from down south 🦅 . . . . . . If your bed is dear to you, treat it to the best linen, from **Porthault**, 18 ave Montaigne, 75008 ☎ (1) 4720 7525, made to their own designs, and a firm favourite for BARBARA TAYLOR BRADFORD 🦅 . . . . . . **Fauchon** (see page 164) is the only place in France with a stash of **Succession JL**, the latest cognac from Courvoisier, at FF20,000 a bottle . . . . 🦅

faites vos jeux on British roulette, blackjack, craps, baccarat or punto banco. (There's free entry across the road at the public casino in the touristique Café de Paris.)

Clubs

BEACH CLUB, Monte Carlo Beach Hotel, route du Bord de Mer, 06190 Roquebrune-Cap-Martin ☎ 9378 2140
Chill out by the pool with the Grimaldis – enthroned and bodyguarded in their green and white tent – and assorted loungers. There's jetskiing, waterskiing, swimming (out to the raft) and paragliding, and marvellous feasts for lunch on the leafy terrace.

JIMMY'Z D'HIVER (winter), place du Casino, 98007 Monte Carlo ☎ 9350 8080; JIMMY'Z D'ETE (summer), Monte Carlo Sporting Club, ave Princesse Grace ☎ 9326 1414
Monte folk and their rich kids cram in to Monaco's best. They dance beneath the stars in summer, thanks to the Sporting Club's retractable sliding roof. "*Still Jimmy'z, though·I don't actually think it's as good as when Régine was handling it*" – JOHN GOLD.

LES CAVES DU ROI, Hotel Byblos, ave Paul Signac, 83990, St Tropez ☎ 9497 0004
The top bop in San Trop, where you might bump into JOHN GOLD: "*Very good, a very chic nightclub. Josephine's special enclave is the place to sit if you can manage it.*" RICHARD COMPTON-MILLER's on the case: "*That's where you're going to find every sort of interesting Hollywood star from Warren Beatty to Joan Collins, George Hamilton and lots of bimbos – you need a lot of money because it's very expensive.*"

PARADY'Z, Monte Carlo Sporting Club, ave Princesse Grace, 98000 Monte Carlo ☎ 9330 6161
Mid-summer boppery for moneyed pre-Jimmy'z Teenies. Full of hairstyles, bronzed legs, ripped jeans, etc: "*For 17-year-olds and suchlike, very swinging*" – JOHN GOLD.

Festivals

FESTIVAL MONDIAL DE JAZZ D'ANTIBES, Maison du Tourisme d'Antibes, place Charles-de-Gaulle, 06600 Antibes ☎ 9333 9564
The great American jazzmen love playing in the South of France and the French love great American jazz. Thus, for 2 weeks in July, Antibes and Juan les Pins are abuzz with the best sounds from the USA – Sarah Vaughan, Ella Fitzgerald, Ray Charles and Fats Domino have all flown the flag.

Film

CANNES INTERNATIONAL FILM FESTIVAL, c/o 71 rue du Faubourg St Honoré, 75008 Paris ☎ (1) 4266 9220
The most important celluloid bazaar, where the seriously big biz kids decamp in May, and *Marathon Man, Nasty Girl* and *Problem Child* get *Truly, Madly, Deeply Shattered* after round-the-clock screening, preening, posing and partying. Yes, but is it art? Over to IAIN JOHNSTONE: "*It gets stronger and stronger, it's the best festival in the world, and the reason is everybody goes. Last year they focused on Madonna. It got front pages round the world. But Cannes really combines art with commerce artfully, in a clever way. It runs the most contentious arts festival – the best films made that year in the art house category tend to come along to Cannes and its supremacy is unlikely to be challenged for that reason. Also it is physically the most agreeable film festival to attend due to the fact that Cannes is rather a nice resort on the Mediterranean, the food is good, and the weather is hot at that time of year.*" Mega stars (Madonna, Cher) put up at the **Hotel du Cap-Eden-Roc** – you know you're in when you get an invitation there. The **Majestic**'s the place for lunch, **La Palme d'Or** at Hotel Martinez, and **La Plage Sportive** (IAIN J's choice) are hot too. After midnight make it to **Le Petit Carlton**, rue d'Antibes.

Hotels

CARLTON INTER-CONTINENTAL, 58 La Croisette, 06406 Cannes ☎ 9368 9168
The famous belle époque festival rendezvous continues to draw £35 million deal-sealers who chat on the terrace over cocktails and dinner. However, some feel it's too far from the action now that the fest is focused on the other end of town. Try the new 13-room suite with private limo, and butler if you've got the dosh.

CHATEAU DE LA CHEVRE D'OR, 06360 Eze Village ☎ 9341 1212
A rambly medieval stone house with sky-high outlook, 1,200 ft above the Med, pool terrace and rooms all facing seaward. "*If you don't mind climbing it's got an excellent restaurant and a superb view all around*" – BARBARA KAFKA.

🦐 HOTEL BEL-AIR CAP FERRAT, blvd de Général de Gaulle, 06290 St-Jean-Cap-Ferrat ☎ 9376 0021
New name, new and trendy crowd, the beautifully restyled Grand Hotel is bagging the people who count, including ANDREW LLOYD WEBBER: "*Everyone's going there this summer, they've all switched over from the Voile d'Or.*" A sensational looker, outside and in (£20 million well spent), it has tennis courts, a funicular down to the seaside Club Dauphin, and a pool

that seems to flow into the sea (non-swimmers will be able to drop the 'non' after a few sessions with legendary instructor Pierre Gruneberg). "*It is excellent*" – LISA BARNARD. ALEXANDRE LAZAREFF rolls up dutifully: "*It is the place you have to be – lovely setting, right on the sea.*"

HOTEL BYBLOS, ave Paul Signac, 83990 St Tropez ☎ 9497 0004
Swish hotel complex in 3 parts – the main, grand building, and 2 sets of villas overlooking the sea. "*An excellent hotel with very high standards. It's got a wonderful pool in the middle of the hotel so you can have breakfast by the pool. It's very close to St Tropez town but above it, so it has a sort of rarefied atmosphere, but near enough to the hurly burly*" – RICHARD COMPTON-MILLER. "*It's extremely good*" – JOHN GOLD.

HOTEL DE PARIS, place du Casino, BP 2309, 98007 Monte Carlo ☎ 9350 8080
The most glamorous hotel in Monte. Authentic Louis Quinzerie: gilt, marble, crystal galore. ROBIN LEACH checks in, so does LISA BARNARD: "*It is just the hotel, very over the top. Incredibly grand. The man who runs it is brilliant. Excellent chef – a jetsetter hotel.*" ANDREW LLOYD WEBBER raves too: "*The grand hotel that is fabulous, the whole works.*" Dine in style at **Louis XV** (see Restaurants).

🐟 HOTEL DU CAP-EDEN-ROC, blvd J F Kennedy, Cap d'Antibes, 06604 Antibes ☎ 9361 3901
Impossibly glamorous, hugely romantic, the approach to this *belle* hotel would humble the brightest star. A real sense of history – the likes of F Scott Fitzgerald and Noel Coward have stayed – is updated by the glitteriest of 20C guests. Fab marble-floored hallway – look out to sea from the beautiful gardens, and, during festival time, rub shoulders with the glitziest crowd around. Take lots of cash (no cheques or cards accepted), for prices are stratospheric. "*There's a splinter festival out at the Cap, where all the big stars put up, but I think they feel lonely out there . . . .*" says a green-eyed IAIN JOHNSTONE. ROBIN LEACH is impressed, as is LISA BARNARD: "*Really good.*"

HOTEL MAJESTIC, 14 La Croisette, 06407 Cannes ☎ 9368 9100
This is where it really happens in Cannes – the movers and shakers lunch here on the terrace, by the heated pool. Conveniently, it's right by the Palais du Festival. "*That's where you would expect to meet somebody – everybody's there. It really is just a question of chutzpah, entering the Majestic swimming pool area – if you're carrying a camera, they'll wave you through, there's nothing the French love more than publicity*" – IAIN JOHNSTONE.

HOTEL NEGRESCO, 37 Promenade des Anglais, 06000 Nice ☎ 9388 3951
Gilded, belle époque and grand, this is *the* place to stay in Nice. Eat at **Chantecler**, where chef Dominique le Stanc is charming Rivierites such as ANDREW LLOYD WEBBER: "*It's looking very good.*"

LA COLOMBE D'OR, 06570 St-Paul-de-Vence ☎ 9332 8002
Perched on a hillside in a medieval town, this gem is legendary for the art that covers the walls, floors, courtyards, partout. Picasso, Dufy, Matisse, Miró, Utrillo and Braque paid their bills with their paintings, sculptures, painted glass, decorated cushions and lamps. "*Ah, my favourite place in the world, my ultimate, I just love it with a passion. It's still as wonderful as ever, run by the family Roux, who have maintained these wonderful standards since 1946. To sit on their terrace and have a meal (and see the Léger mural) is one of the pleasures of the world we live in*" – JOHN GOLD. For STEPHEN BAYLEY, "*the atmosphere's perfect, dining on the terrace, not in the restaurant*".

LA RESERVE DE BEAULIEU, 5 blvd Général Leclerc, 06310 Beaulieu-sur-Mer ☎ 9301 0001
Revamped with a new poolside kitchen, the secluded resort hotel still seduces South of Francers. The restaurant terrace overlooks the small private harbour – a scene VICTOR EDELSTEIN likes to sop up over lunch or dinner: "*It's incredible, you don't mind how long it takes – on holiday you've got all evening or all afternoon, so that's wonderful.*"

LA VOILE D'OR, 06230 St-Jean-Cap-Ferrat ☎ 9301 1313
On the harbour, this old fave still draws sun-seeking actors and celebs. "*I love it, it's lovely, it's on the point, looking out over the harbour and the port of Cap Ferrat – a good exciting hotel*" – JOHN GOLD. But ANDREW LLOYD WEBBER finds it a shade passé.

LE CHATEAU EZA, 06360 Eze Village ☎ 9341 1224
Rustic medieval hilltop hotel with a handful of rooms and great cooking from André Signoret (ex-Hôtel de Crillon). "*We do like Château Eza*" – ANDREW LLOYD WEBBER.

────── *Restaurants* ──────

See also Hotels.

DON CAMILLO, 5 rue des Ponchettes, 06300, Nice ☎ 9385 6795
Nice nosher in nasty Nice – where Niçoises-in-the-know nibble Franck Cerutti's mix of local and Italian cooking and *cuisine de terroir*. ANDREW LLOYD WEBBER stumbled upon it, and is rather glad he did: "*Marvellous modern food – things like anchovy bouillabaisse and a marvellous courgette risotto made with courgette flowers, quite delicious.*"

LA CHAUMIERE, blvd du Jardin Exotique, 98000 Monte Carlo ☎ 9325 2299
Dead fashionable dining off the Grand Corniche. Josephe Zuccarelli's provençale cooking agrees with BARBARA KAFKA: "*They have this huge fireplace and they're one of the last places to do grilling over an open fire with really good meat – beef, lamb. Wonderful. And the first courses just come to you, crudités and sausages and pâté.*" ROBERT SANGSTER is a regular.

LE PROVENCAL, 2 ave Denis Semeria, 06230 St-Jean-Cap-Ferrat ☎ 9376 0397
Ultra-imaginative cooking from Jean-Jacques Jouteaux enchants celebs and foodies alike. Great seafood, though don't expect traditional provençale dishes – try John Dory roasted in fig leaves with beef marrow juice. "*Absolutely super, he's using provençale ingredients, but he's making them lighter and more elegant. He was one of the darlings of nouvelle cuisine. You're liable to see a rather chic crowd in off the boats*" – BARBARA KAFKA. "*Service is not too good, but they specialize in things like deep-fried lettuce leaves, very clever, and it's probably the best around*" – ANDREW LLOYD WEBBER.

🍤 LOUIS XV, Hotel de Paris, place du Casino, 98000 Monte Carlo ☎ 9350 8080
The awe-inspiring gilt and frescoed dining room, fabulous service and Alain Ducasse's cooking weaken CAROL WRIGHT's knees: "*He's producing divine food, which is Provence with sort of Italian ideas. It's so terribly ornate, yet he serves quite simple food if he feels like it. There's a trolley of 14 different kinds of bread and chocolates with edible gold paper. Tablecloths are ironed on the tables every day and they put out 2 different kinds of butter.*" ROLAND ESCAIG thinks "*it is one of the 3 best, very inventive, imaginative cooking with new flavours*".

LE MOULIN DE MOUGINS, Quartier Notre-Dame de Vie, 434 chemin du Moulin, 06250 Mougins ☎ 9375 7824
Ever-popular in the sunny Sud (despite crits in French foodie circles of over-commercialism), Vergé's place puts stars in ROBIN LEACH's eyes, DAME BARBARA CARTLAND reckons it's "*the best food in the South of France*" and ROBERT SANGSTER remains loyal. IAIN JOHNSTONE whizzes up from Cannes with the film crowd: "*It's still the place to go and Roger Vergé provides food like nobody else, he doesn't let you down,*" and it gets the thumbs-up from English foodie PRUE LEITH: "*It bucks the French trend by having terribly grand food but very friendly staff, from the kitchen porters up. And a very good cookery school.*"

TETOU, blvd des Frères Roustan, Golfe Juan 06220 ☎ 9363 7116
The Lourdes of the Côte d'Azur, for all things fishy and provençale – sea bass, grilled crayfish and the speciality, bouillabaisse. "*It's excellent for lunch or dinner on a Sunday – I've seen Arnold Weinstock in there and Adnan Khashoggi. It's a very French, family-run, purely fish restaurant*" – ROBERT SANGSTER.

Verge Away from Vergé 🍤

Branch off the beaten foodie trail, eat très well and come home with change from a fistful of francs. You can savour Mougins without ever mentioning the word 'Moulin', reckons ROBERT SANGSTER. Follow his lead to **Le Bistrot de Mougins**, place du Village ☎ 9375 7834, par example: "*You must book because it gets very full. It's a very attractive and very reasonable place, you stick to a specialist menu.*" Torte aux blettes, rascasse (fish) aux anchois et olives, fromages, and gâteau glacé au chocolat is a fixture. Then there's **Le Relais à Mougins**, place de la Mairie ☎ 9390 0347, run by André Surmain (ex-Lutèce, NY): "*That is excellent, probably a bit more sophisticated than the Bistrot, and a very good restaurant in the village.*" MARGARET KEMP picks up the trail, which leads her to Jean-Paul Battaglia's neighbouring restaurant, **Le Feu Follet**, place de la Mairie ☎ 9390 1578, for "*quality-priced menus that have them lining up around the picturesque 16C place Commandant Lamy. Henri Leconte, Stefan Edberg and Alain Prost are regulars.*" BARBARA KAFKA heads off to Juan-les-Pins to her new find, **Bijou Plage,** blvd Charles Guillaumont ☎ 9361 3907: "*It's got superb fish, very good fish soup, and the people are very nice and it's still got windows that open.*"

· REST OF ·

FRANCE

Festivals

CHOREGIES, BP 180, 84105 Orange ☎ 9034 2424
Chic operaholics make the July pilgrimage to this festival, where one-off productions, concerts and recitals are played, bellowed and trilled by

the most famous performers in the Théâtre Antique – an old Roman amphitheatre.

FESTIVAL D'AVIGNON, Bureau de Festival, BP 92, 84006 Avignon ☎ 9082 6708
Founded by celebrated French thespian Jean Vilar, this is an exciting and important drama fiesta in July-Aug. Look out for comic, experimental, fringe, mime, all-night and ethnic theatre; dance, lectures and exhibitions.

FESTIVAL MUSICAL DU PERIGORD NOIR, 53 rue du Général Foy, 24290 Montignac ☎ 5351 9517
The south-west's most notable music fest, and its largest. Thematic programmes usually start with early music and progress to chamber, all played in the Romanesque churches of Périgord.

FESTIVAL INTERNATIONAL D'ART LYRIQUE, Palais de l'Ancien Archevêché, 13100 Aix-en-Provence ☎ 4217 3400
Exuberant celebration of the arts which animates the whole medieval town in July – churches fill with concert and recital audiences, jazz and rock bands play in the squares while lunchers and diners listen from the outdoor bars and cafés. Opera buffs love it for the series in the open-air Théâtre de l'Archevêché (in the Archbishop's palace).

——— *Film* ———

DEAUVILLE FESTIVAL DU CINEMA AMERICAIN, c/o Promo 2000, 33 ave MacMahon, 75017 Paris ☎ (1) 4267 7140; or Office de Tourisme, Deauville ☎ 3188 2143
Small but *very* in – this one attracts big names (Liz Taylor, Tom Cruise, Jodie Foster, Spike Lee) with screenings of American films and James Bonds. Dine at **Chez Mioque** (good tucker and the splendid patron, M Mioque) or **Les Vapeurs** in nearby Trouville; take post-prandials at the **Normandy** (to see French vedettes) or the **Royal** (American stars).

——— *Hotels* ———

AUBERGE DE NOVES, 13550 Noves ☎ 9094 1921
A hotel restaurant with modern interpretations of traditional dishes by chef M Lalleman. "*Extra rooms have not spoilt the tranquillity of this beautiful hotel, where the food is consistently excellent*" – DAME BARBARA CARTLAND.

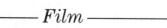 BOYER LES CRAYERES, 64 blvd Henry-Vasnier, 51100 Reims ☎ 2682 8080
Champagne château with brilliant cooking and 16 rooms, all beautifully detailed with massive bathrooms. Superlatives count here. "*It is the*

old Pommery family château. I think the only word that you could ever use is exquisite*" – DON HEWITSON. PRUE LEITH was delighted: "*So good (both food and service) you'll even forgive them for charging a fiver for 6 postcards of the hotel, and £70 for a key ring (the door keys are silver vine-leaves and grapes!).*" LISA BARNARD, IRVING SMITH KOGAN, PAUL HENDERSON, MARY ROSSI and ROBIN LEACH rhapsodize.

HOTEL DU PALAIS, 1 ave de l'Impératrice, 64200 Biarritz ☎ 5924 0940
Imperial in scale and grandeur, right on the Atlantic shore. Built under Napoleon III when Biarritz became a fashionable resort thanks to Empress Eugénie, it has formal gardens, a putting green and a splendid restaurant. A word of caution to light sleepers: the hotel was built before the advent of cars and mopeds – you can't hear the sea for the traffic.

HOTEL MIRAMAR, 13 rue Louison-Bobet, 64200 Biarritz ☎ 5941 3000
A hotel/spa where the modish go to get in trim. "*The sea-water therapy is supposed to do all sorts of wonderful things to you. There are 2 restaurants – one Michelin-starred, very good French, and the other low calorie. They've also got a cooking school so you can learn how to make the calorie-counted food*" – CAROL WRIGHT.

HOTEL ROYAL, blvd Cornuché, 14800 Deauville ☎ 3198 6633
The gottabethere address for the American Festival, this is to Deauville what the Majestic is to Cannes (and lo, it's run by the same man – Lucien Barrière). Anyone who's anyone will be round the kidney-shaped pool at festival time. It's pure showbiz – the suites are decorated in honour of Hollywood's greats.

🥄 LES PRES ET LES SOURCES D'EUGENIE, 40320 Eugénie-les-Bains ☎ 5851 1901
Foodies, healthies, bon vivants and long vivants don't mince their words about Michel Guérard's famous hotel/health spa/restaurant in another of Empress Eugénie's favourite towns. PAUL HENDERSON is one: "*We took the waters, a minceur lunch and a gourmand dinner for 3 days, and left totally refreshed. Unpretentious service.*" MICHAEL BROADBENT another: "*Heaven on earth. Beautiful, spotless perfection in the middle of nowhere.*" And GILLES PUDLOWSKI makes 3. A resort so elevated that the *Financial Times* is used to kindle fires.

OUSTAU DE BAUMANIERE, Le Vallon, 13520 Les-Baux-de-Provence ☎ 9054 3307
Beautiful scenery and haute cuisine in haute Provence, never far from RAYMOND BLANC's thoughts: "*You have the mountain and all sorts of rocks – rocks in beautiful shapes, some of them carved by artists. And this beautiful old 16C farmhouse which has been transformed into a hotel with the very, very best service. The food*

is good, not great but good, very provençale, it's 2-star Michelin. When one wants rest, one doesn't want somewhere too hectic . . . to me it could be one of the 7 marvels of the world."

—————— *Restaurants* ——————

GEORGES BLANC, 01540 Vonnas
☎ 7450 0010
Established 3-starrer: *"I can't go past this one . . . give me Blanc's 7-course menu découvert partnered by wine from Azenay vineyards"* – SUSAN KUROSAWA. The flower-filled garden is an idyllic setting for such masterly creations as quenelles de langoustine aux cresson (watercress) et tapioca.

🏊 LA COTE D'OR, 2 rue d'Argentine, 21210 Saulieu ☎ 8064 0766
Nouvelle's old hat, so they say. Le chef Bernard Loiseau would not agree, and neither would the Michelin men – he recently got his 3rd star. Dishes like frogs' legs, the special Sandre fish and pain d'épice with honey ice cream have convinced GILLES PUDLOWSKI too. For QUENTIN CREWE: *"He has a wonderful vegetarian menu – the best vegetarian food in the world."*

🏊 L'AUBERGADE, 52 rue Royale, 47270 Puymirol ☎ 5395 3146
Still stunning the gastroscenti. Presiding over his restaurant an hour from Bordeaux, Michel Trama is *"the best of the up-and-coming French chefs who are knocking on the door at the moment. I had salt cod with crispy bacon, the home-made charcuterie, and an amazing breakfast – the normal French stuff but better, much better – I think there were 8 types of brioche and pain au chocolat and croissants. Actually I've been getting bored with high-class French cooking, but this was amazing"* – ALASTAIR LITTLE. Remember to order the special nibbles – a prune wrapped in bacon, a pastry of oxtail and leeks. *"A very good one,"* says ROLAND ESCAIG, but FREDERIC RAPHAEL advises: *"You shouldn't go there if hungry – he's a good cook but rather tight. The waiters are*

unbelievably garrulous." STEPHEN BAYLEY is undeterred: *"For gastronomy I'd go to L'Aubergade."*

L'ESPERANCE, St Père, 89450 Vézelay
☎ 8633 2045
They call it 'sexual cuisine'. Marc Meneau's famous plats hit the spot – like the cromesquis de foie gras – cubes filled with liquid foie gras which erupt in your mouth, and his oysters preserved in a jelly of sea water. Not all seasoned palates can take the pace: GILLES PUDLOWSKI admits, *"yes, it's good, but it is rich"*. DOMINIQUE PIOT is fascinated by Meneau's constant experimentation.

LEON DE LYON, 1 rue de Pleney, 69001 Lyons ☎ 7828 1133
The full Lyonnaise experience – cuisine, clientele and ambience (warm and woody, in a room with stained-glass windows). Jean-Paul Lacombe dishes up salade Lyonnaise, ravioli à la Lyonnaise with cardoon (a green vegetable) and fresh truffles, and pied de porc.

L'HERMITAGE DE CORTON, RN 74, 21000 Chorey-les-Beaune ☎ 8022 0528
Chef André Parra prepares his menu de terroir and his inventive modern *carte* to the liking of DAME BARBARA CARTLAND: *"The Burgundians take their food and wine very seriously. Here there are large meals of exceptional quality."*

🏊 PAUL BOCUSE, 50 quai de la Plagne, 69660 Collonges-au-Mont-d'Or, Lyons ☎ 7822 0140
One of the pillars of modern French cooking, Bocuse is unimpeachable to many eyes – though he's not always in the kitchen, torn as he must be among the many outposts of his global empire. However, his black truffle soup is legendary and the cheeses, desserts and wines are astonishing. ROBIN LEACH applauds: *"An extraordinary restaurant."*

PAVILLON DES BOULEVARDS, 120 rue de la Croix de Seguey, 33000 Bordeaux ☎ 5681 5102
Top-notch Bordelaiserie serving traditional fare

🏊 **Buzzz** In Cognac country, visit the **Musée Courvoisier** ☎ 4535 5555, next to the Château Courvoisier at Jarnac, to see Napoleon's hat and watch a futuristic slide-show, showing the mysterious progress of grape to nectar, in a pitch-black cellar to the strains of Jean-Michel Jarre 🏊 . . . . . . Next to a beautiful stone church in the hills behind Draguignan is the little hotel-restaurant **Le Vieux Fox**, 83630 Fox-Amphoux ☎ 9480 7169, a sly retreat for crafty South of Francers in the know, such as STEPHEN BAYLEY: *"My real favourite, a tiny place in a village on top of the hill, it's a knocked-about crusader castle, with one dining room with wonderfully rough, robust food."* Hearty terrines and the house speciality of lamb with tarragon are balanced with lighter dishes such as brouillarde de morille (a mousse made with crème fraîche and local wild mushrooms). . . . . 🏊

Cuisine d'Alsace

Something's cooking in the region of Alsace, and if there's a man who can sniff out a good Alsatian, it's GILLES PUDLOWSKI. Hearty flavours and a strong sense of the seasons infuse the menus. The region's top-ranking restaurant needs no introduction – it is **Auberge de l'Ill**, rue de Collonges, Illhaeusern, 68150 Ribeauvillé ☎ 8971 8323, a long-established winner in foodiedom (and in touristdom). The pretty riverside restaurant has a delightful flower garden and wonderful combinations of haute cuisine with rustic influences from regional Alsace. *"The best auberge in France,"* declares GP, with back-up from PAUL HENDERSON and DAME BARBARA CARTLAND: *"The Haeberlin brothers provide the best food in France and it is worth making a long journey to go there."* **Hostellerie du Cerf**, route du Général de Gaulle, Marlenheim ☎ 8887 7373, offers masses of goodies – foie gras, choucroute with suckling pig and, a real speciality, preskopf de tête de veau, prepared by chefs Michel and Robert Husser. Opposite the European Council, set in a 17C Alsatian house, is **Restaurant Buereheisel**, 4 parc de l'Orangerie, 67000 Strasbourg ☎ 8861 6224, which completes the GP top trio with such revelations as a sweet fish stew with Riesling, matched by a wine list reaching back to a 1928 Gewürtztraminer.

---

updated with an Oriental twist – a speciality is the chinoiserie de pigeonneau, starting with pigeon skin in a crêpe, with honey and spices, followed by roast leg and slices of pink breast. *"A very good restaurant, with a young chef, very, very good indeed. There's a slight Japanese influence"* – FREDERIC RAPHAEL.

PIC, 285 ave Victor Hugo, 26000 Valence ☎ 7544 1532
Choosiest diners pick this one – and Jacques and Alain Pic's food is paramount according to PAUL HENDERSON: *"A place to eat rather than to be seen."* LISA BARNARD goes too.

RESTAURANT MILLION, 8 place de la Liberté, 73200 Albertville ☎ 7932 2515
In the centre of Olympicsville, a deux-étoiles with traditional Savoyard dishes from chef Philippe Million. Try the local lake fish, fera, any way it comes, and the petit gris escargots à la menagère, cooked to an ancient recipe in a meat/chicken bouillon with basil, parsley, mint, orange zest, etc. STEPHEN BAYLEY skis in.

TROISGROS, place Jean-Troisgros, 42300 Roanne ☎ 7771 6697
Legendary name in cooking, with a place named after them. Creators of the famous salmon with sorrel dish, the brothers are also responsible for such delights as foie gras with rhubarb. Unpretentious, bourgeois cooking at its finest.

Ski resorts

CHAMONIX
Not just a resort, but a lively French town in the shadow of Mont Blanc. One for serious skiers and daring mountain climbers. Pros on the slopes reckon it offers the most thrilling skiing in Europe – take the cable car to Aiguille du Midi and ski down the Vallée Blanche glacier through breathtaking scenery, or shoot down the famous off-piste Pas de Chèvre, a fearsomely steep drop of some 6,500 ft.

MEGEVE
Very French, very chic, a charming village resort set in a beautiful wide valley, ensuring longer daylight hours than most of its Alpine neighbours. Inès de la Fressange, tribes of Rossignols (of *the* ski label) and other ultra-smart natives go. Hotter on nightlife than skiing – it's too low to be sure of snow all season. Best hotel: **Chalet Mont d'Arbois** (best food, too).

MERIBEL
Attractive chalet resort at the heart of the Trois Vallées, and the best base for off-piste skiing. Frequented by many smart, private British, who bring their social life with them in self-contained parties. Extensive skiing at the hub of one of the major ski-lift systems of Europe. Small airport for private planes.

VAL D'ISERE
Star of the recent Winter Olympics, this is arguably the finest ski area in the world, one for the pros. A good all-rounder – daredevil off-piste skiing, mogul-bashing and even nursery slopes. Largely British and Swedish influx (the Brits are the ones at the Members' Bar of **Dick's T-Bar** – a sophisticated nightclub). Best hotel: **Hotel Savoyard**. Best wine bar/restaurant: **Au Bout de la Rue**.

Wine

Alsace

A narrow strip of vineyards on the steep slopes of the Vosges mountains – in the historically contested French/German borderlands – whose light, spicy, aromatic wines reflect both countries' styles. 3 major grape varieties, a few top producers. Riesling (NB in Alsace it generally makes *dry* wines): "**TRIMBACH**, *definitely, I'd go with* **KREYDENWEISS** *and* **KIENTZLER**, *both small owners making stunning, top-quality Riesling*" – LIZ BERRY. Gewürztraminer: best producer is **THEO FALLER**, whose wines repay long ageing; LIZ B tips makers big (**HUGEL PERE ET FILS**), medium (**ZIND-HUMBRECHT**) and small (**KIENTZLER**). Pinot Gris (aka Tokay in Alsace): "*Can be superb, the dry being excellent dinner wines, the late-picked sweet wines inimitable*" – MICHAEL BROADBENT. Again, LIZ B chooses the **ZIND-HUMBRECHT**, **HUGEL** and **FALLER**.

A word of advice from MICHAEL BROADBENT: "*Alsace is undervalued and one should take advantage of 3 recent superb vintages of 1988, 1989 and 1990 – the top* vendange tardive *wines of* **HUGEL** *and* **SCHLUMBERGER** *being superb*". Overall, SERENA SUTCLIFFE adores the style and breed of **TRIMBACH** and **ZIND-HUMBRECHT**.

Bordeaux

Accustomed to the abundant riches of the 1988, 89 and 90 vintages, claret lovers could be disappointed with the 91 – a frost across France in April decimated the young crop. The 80s was a great decade with only 2 blots on the landscape – disastrous 84 and 87, the latter redeemed by decent dry white wines and lighter reds for young drinking. 81, 83 and 88 all good, 82 and 86 superb, and the 85 and 89 are MICHAEL BROADBENT's favourite recent vintages.

THE MEDOC

A somewhat bleak landscape dotted with châteaux and covered with the quick-draining soil essential for growing the best claret grapes. Greatest here is the Cabernet Sauvignon, which forms the backbone of Médoc red wines. Cabernet Franc, Merlot and Malbec provide variations on a theme. In 1855, Médocs were classified into 5 *grands crus classés*. LIZ BERRY starts at the top: "*Obviously, the 1ers are superb, the best of the best.*" 4 of the 5 1st growths are Médocs, 3 from the village of Pauillac – Châteaux **LAFITE ROTHSCHILD**, **MOUTON ROTHSCHILD** and **LATOUR**. The fourth is **CHATEAU MARGAUX** from the village of the same name. Great vintages for MICHAEL BROADBENT: **Lafite** 1899 and 1953; **Margaux** 1900 and 1961; 1929 and 1945 **Latour** and 1949 **Mouton**. SIMON LOFTUS thinks the

1945 **Mouton** is "*an absolute humdinger of a wine*". Of younger years, SERENA SUTCLIFFE thinks **Mouton** 1985 is "*exquisite*" and **Lafite** 1989 and 90 "*ethereal – but for the future.*" In general, ventures SERENA S, "*1985 Médocs could be like 1953s, delicious throughout their whole life; 1986 Médocs are bigger and tougher.*"

1st-growth second wines are a good scoop – **LATOUR**'s is **Les Forts de Latour**; **LAFITE**'s **Moulin des Carruades**, and **MARGAUX**'s **Pavillon Rouge**.

Among the best *2ème crus* are the St Julien brothers, **CHATEAU LEOVILLE BARTON** (classic, rich claret, a bargain) and **CHATEAU LEOVILLE-LAS CASES** (for real power and longevity). **GRUAND-LAROSE** is "*luscious*", opines SERENA SUTCLIFFE. **CHATEAU COS D'ESTOURNEL** is top flight – its bizarre chinoiserie tower is worth a visit if you are passing through St-Estèphe. Try **LATOUR**'s worthy Pauillac neighbour **CHATEAU PICHON-LALANDE** – don't confuse it with newly named **PICHON-LONGUEVILLE** across the road – although it wouldn't be the worst mistake, since new ownership has

---

"brought this property back to the heights in 1988, 1989 and 1990" – SERENA SUTCLIFFE.

As for the *3èmes*, Margaux's the place to be: 61 **CHATEAU PALMER** makes the *premiers* blush and SIMON LOFTUS very happy; delicate **CHATEAU D'ISSAN** charms LIZ BERRY. Venture over to St Julien for Japanese-owned **CHATEAU LAGRANGE**. Don't underestimate the *5ème* Pauillacs – **GRAND-PUY-LACOSTE** and **LYNCH-BAGES**.

GRAVES

Now partially absorbed by Bordeaux's urban sprawl, Graves is notable for 2 things: the best of the region's dry white wines and the only 1st growth outside the Médoc – **CHATEAU HAUT-BRION**. Its formidable wines of 45 and 61 astound MICHAEL BROADBENT. Other Graves goodies are **DOMAINE DE CHEVALIER** (needs keeping – worth the wait) and HB's competitor (though under the same ownership), **LA MISSION HAUT-BRION**.

Best whites are **Haut-Brion Blanc** and **LA MISSION's Laville Haut-Brion** and *"Domaine de Chevalier, with fast-rising exotic* **CHATEAU FIEUZAL. CHATEAU LA LOUVIERE**, *both red and white, is still very good value"* – SERENA SUTCLIFFE.

ST-EMILION

Prettier than either Médoc or Graves. Uses higher proportions of Merlot and Cabernet Franc than the Médoc. There is a similar cru system, though it is neither as old nor as rigid – here there are *premiers grands crus classés, grands crus classés* and *grands crus.*

The two grandest PGCCs are **CHATEAU CHEVAL BLANC** – MICHAEL BROADBENT's choice for *"quality and consistency"* (SIMON LOFTUS puts in a vote for the 1947, SERENA SUTCLIFFE for the *"faultless"* 1982) – and **CHATEAU AUSONE** (SIMON L reaches for the 1864). DON HEWITSON goes for 1982 **CHATEAU CANON**: *"Gloriously rich, a voluptuous wine with a wonderful degree of natural ripe fruit, and the intensity hits you on the palate."* Keep your eyes out for **PAVIE**, too. LIZ BERRY's kept hers on some GCCs – Châteaux **FONROQUE** and **DASSAULT** for example. SERENA SUTCLIFFE watches **CHATEAU TROPLONG-MONDOT** (in the same hands as Pavie), *"which should be a candidate for elevation to PGCC status".*

POMEROL

Tiny, hilly, sun-drenched neighbour to St-Emilion, with a similar style. The best are known for taste and price; **CHATEAU PETRUS**, the only 1er cru, is a legend for both. **CHATEAU TROTANOY** is reckoned to be No 2. **LA FLEUR PETRUS, LA FLEUR** and **CONSEILLANTE** lead the rest of the field. But for MICHAEL BROADBENT, it simply is **PETRUS** and SIMON

LOFTUS can only say the 1929 is *"pretty bloody marvellous"*. LIZ BERRY treads more warily: **"VIEUX-CHATEAU-CERTAN** *is, I think, a better wine in many vintages."*

SAUTERNES/BARSAC

Of the sweet wines made here primarily from the Sémillon grape, **CHATEAU D'YQUEM** is unbeatable, the only *1er grand cru.* Owned for over 100 years by the Lur-Saluces family, the wine world raves – MICHAEL BROADBENT rates the 1847 as one of his greatest ever wines. Running behind are **RIEUSSEC** (owned by Lafite), **CLIMENS** (*"a close second for reliability and richness"* for MICHAEL B) and **LAFAURIE-PEYRAGUEY**. Try **FARGUES**, too, adds SERENA SUTCLIFFE and *"save up for the 88s, 89s and 90s as there have never before been 3 great Sauternes vintages in a row".*

Burgundy

Home of the capricious Pinot Noir grape, which can make some of the greatest red wine in the world when it feels like it (and when the unpredictable weather capitulates), but which is also unsurpassed in disappointing those who seek the grapie grail. Whites are made from Chardonnay; the best are simply the best and more reliable than the reds. More difficult to classify than Bordeaux: *"In Bordeaux if you have Château Lafite, it's Lafite and that's the end of it because it's made by one person. The problem with a burgundy is that you might have a magnificent 1985* **Corton** *from one grower and a poor one from another"* – JOHN ARMIT.

The most famous area is the Côte d'Or, which splits, uncomfortably, in two. The northern part, the Côte de Nuits, produces most of the greatest reds; the southern part, the Côte de Beaune, the whites. But there are many notable exceptions.

RED BURGUNDY

CÔTE DE NUITS

It's a one-horse race, according to JOHN ARMIT: *"The* **DOMAINE DE LA ROMANEE CONTI** *is probably acknowledged to be the greatest wine estate in the world. Very small production of Pinot Noir.* **LA ROMANEE CONTI** *itself is the grandest, the least of it is made and it is very expensive indeed. The next is* **LA TACHE**, *then* **RICHEBOURG**, *then* **ROMANEE-ST-VIVANT**, *then* **GRAND ECHEZEAUX**, *then* **ECHEZEAUX**. *Generally price and quality in that order, though it does vary."* MICHAEL BROADBENT has **LA ROMANEE CONTI** down as a great, especially the 1937, while SIMON LOFTUS prays for a 71 **La Tache** to come his way. SERENA SUTCLIFFE says the 1921 *"could be the wine of my life – sheer magic".* JOHN ARMIT adds a few more: *"In the very top is* **Clos de La Roche** *from the grower* **DUJAC**, *then* **Chambertin** *from a grower called* **PONSOT** *(I'd add their* **Clos St Denis** *as well) and then the* **Bonnes Mares** *from a négociant called*

LOUIS JADOT, *rich, intense, voluptuous wine. I think the area of Morey-St-Denis is absolutely brilliant".* SERENA S considers Charles Rousseau (**DOMAINE ARMAND ROUSSEAU**) in **Gevrey-Chambertin** *"a genius".*

CÔTE DE BEAUNE
Two big names – the villages of Pommard and Aloxe-Corton. Look for **Corton les Bressandes** among the latter, and listen to JOHN ARMIT for the former – he tips **Pommard** 1er cru from **RIOUGIENS**. He also goes for a **Volnay Clos des Ducs** from **D'ANGERVILLE**. SERENA SUTCLIFFE favours **DE MONTILLE** from **Pommard** and **LAFARGE** from **Volnay**.

WHITE BURGUNDY

MONTRACHET
The most famous and strictly eponymous **Le Montrachet** from **DOMAINE DE LA ROMANEE CONTI** or **MARQUIS DE LAGUICHE** sets the standard for MICHAEL BROADBENT, whose favourite recent vintages are 1985 and 1989. JOHN ARMIT thinks: "**Le Montrachet** *is the greatest of all and that has got to be a* **DOMAINE DE LA ROMANEE CONTI**, *or another grower,* **RAMONET**, *whose wine is opulent, exotic and complex.*" SIMON LOFTUS plumps for the latter's 1982 (*"fantastic"*). LIZ BERRY's choice is the **Chevalier Montrachet** from **LOUIS JADOT**.

MEURSAULT
Softer and smoother than the **Montrachets**. "*A domaine called* **MATROT**, *which makes* **Meursault Charmes**, *would be my No 1*" – JOHN ARMIT. LIZ BERRY's favourite is **LAFON** (he has the deepest cellars in the village). SERENA SUTCLIFFE's is "**COCHE-DURY**, *a very great winemaker and yummy wines*".

CORTON-CHARLEMAGNE
Real power here – from the predominantly red-wine regions around Aloxe-Corton – very rich and long-lived. JOHN ARMIT goes for "*either* **LOUIS LATOUR** *or* **TOLLOT BEAUT**";

Nom de Vin

Gather round close as JOHN ARMIT recounts tales of derring-do in the world of wine. *"Perhaps the greatest white-wine estate in the world is* **DOMAINE LEFLAIVE**, *they are absolutely the top, and there the greatest wines are, first,* **Puligny Montrachet Les Pucelles** *and then* **Bâtard Montrachet** *and* **Chevalier Montrachet**. *This is how they were named. . . . During the Crusades, the Chevalier Montrachet was the lord of the area and one day he spied a pretty girl in a field and exercised his droit de seigneur there and then. Then he went off to the Crusades and when he returned he found that from this liaison a child had been born. Since he was a decent chap he acknowledged the child and hence the* **Pucelles**, *the virgin, which is the best of the vineyards, next door to the* **Bâtard**, *the bastard, and another called the* **Bienvenue Bâtard Montrachet,** *the welcome bastard. And the* **Chevalier**."

SERENA SUTCLIFFE plumps for **BONNEAU DE MARTRAY**: *"Prime nectar in the glass."*

Champagne

A generally white wine made from generally red grapes, Pinot Noir, although Blanc de Blancs is made from Chardonnay.

BILLECART-SALMON
A relatively unknown maker with a growing reputation. LADY MACDONALD OF MACDONALD seeks it out: *"It really is delicious."*

Buzzz Crus Bourgeois: For LIZ BERRY, St-Estèphe's **Château Haut-Marbuzet** and **Château Sociando-Mallet** are classy unclassed; Margaux's **Château Monbrison** is another one that's a buzz word in France at the moment ...... **Château de Pez** from St-Estèphe's a brill buy, **Château Labégorce-Zédé** is DON HEWITSON's fave rave: *"They've done it all up, dramatic improvement in the quality of wine, superb and great value"* ...... SERENA SUTCLIFFE divulges that **Château d'Angludet** of the 80s is *"on top form"* ...... Moving Burgundy way, LIZ BERRY reckons the **Dr Barolet** wines are tops: *"An old gentleman doctor who was very keen on wine used to buy it in the barrel and do his own bottling and there are wines still available – superb wines from the 20s, 30s, 40s, 50s"* ....

BOLLINGER

Favourite among the non-vintage brands and No 1 for DAVID GOWER. The luxury marque, **RD**, is among the best. 1985 is LIZ BERRY's choice.

CHARLES HEIDSIECK

Non-vintage champagne that appeals to MICHAEL BROADBENT. Not to be confused with . . .

HEIDSIECK DRY MONOPOLE

"Not one that's generally as well thought of, but their vintage is always of superb quality" – LIZ BERRY. And so is their prestige cuvée, **Diamant Bleu**, tips SERENA SUTCLIFFE.

KRUG

Grand Cuvée is Krug's non-vintage champagne, and it is talked of in the same breath as everyone else's vintage or prestige marques. For MICHAEL BROADBENT, it is "peerless". LIZ BERRY just says: "Of course." SERENA SUTCLIFFE is keen on the 1945.

LANSON

The Black Label and Rosé continue to add sparkle to the lives of the chattering classes. Lanson Vintage champagnes are at the top end of the market – seek out the much-vaunted 1979, or make straight for the 1983, one of the best bargains around.

LAURENT PERRIER

Light and delicate non-vintage wine with a loyal following of grapies, SIMON LOFTUS among them: "**Laurent Perrier Ultra Brut, Laurent Perrier Grand Siècle** and, in summer, pink 1982 **Cuvée Grand Siècle Alexandra** – the sexiest champagne I have ever come across."

LEGRAS

A small champagne house, only making Blanc de Blancs and a favourite with SERENA SUTCLIFFE.

MOET & CHANDON

Dom Pérignon is the one here. Perhaps the best-known name in the biz, the vintage wine is named after the man who 'invented' champagne. A very good 1973 and 1958, according to SERENA SUTCLIFFE. "**Tête de Cuvée** is still one of the best-value champagnes, absolutely excellent" – FREDERIC RAPHAEL.

POL ROGER

Famous as Churchill's favourite – their luxury cuvée is the **Cuvée Sir Winston Churchill** – the vintage goes down very well with MICHAEL BROADBENT. SERENA SUTCLIFFE finds the **Blanc de Chardonnay** slips down a treat.

ROEDERER

This is MICHAEL BROADBENT's favourite non-vintage champagne, but it's **Cristal** that stirs violent passion in vintage champagne drinkers. SERENA S would "kill for Cristal Rosé".

TAITTINGER

Old and very well-respected house which is "my

Southern Shiners

Provence, Languedoc and Roussillon are the rising viticultural stars, sans doute. Here's why: "There are some very good young winemakers; there are many under 40 coming in and starting up new estates. Languedoc and Roussillon produce superb wines, such as **MAS DE DAUMAS GASSAC. MAS JULIEN** is another, owned by a 25-year-old, making some really stunning wines" – LIZ BERRY. Around Languedoc, **Daniel Domergue** is the name to know. SIMON LOFTUS rates him: "An absolutely brilliant winemaker – a stunning Syrah, a sensational Mourvèdre (one of the classic Rhône varieties giving a dark, intensely flavoured wine which needs a lot of bottle age) and the best Pinot Noir in the south of France." LIZ B agrees. In Provence it would be Henning Hoesch, who has **DOMAINE RICHAUME**. "His wines are not only delicious but organic, and he makes a Cabernet with a bit of Syrah and a Syrah with a bit of Cabernet and both are stunning" – SIMON LOFTUS. Moving on, SL says: "I'm keen on **DOMAINE PECH CELEYRON**, which is run by Jacques de St Exupéry, a relative of the writer. It was a volcanic region in prehistoric times which gives a certain flavour to the wines. He has an experimental wine, available only in very small quantities – a mixture of Viognier, Sauvignon, Sémillon and Altesse – because there is no appellation, it is simply called **Blanc des Cépages de France**. Again it's going to be a marker for the future." SERENA SUTCLIFFE goes to south-west France, to the foothills of the Pyrenees, and raves about Alain Brumot's **Madiran**, CHATEAU MONTUS **Cuvée Prestige** – "like deep velvet, with hidden fire".

The Sweet Smell of Succession JL

An objet d'art or a drink? Succession JL, a very old, very rare and very fine Grande Champagne cognac, is both. Released by Courvoisier in a limited edition of only 595, with a market price of over £2,000, Succession JL comes in traditional, heavy cognacaise bottles, individually signed by the bailiff that watched each one being filled, stamped with his seal in 18-carat gold, and accompanied by a parchment certificate. But if the packaging isn't enough to seduce you into buying a little portion of history, try to resist the poetic appreciation of the Master Blender: " . . . exotic perfumes of vanilla and spices associated only with very old and mature Grande Champagne cognac. It explodes in the mouth with an array of luscious flavours. It is a round, smooth cognac, full of finesse and delicacy, with an exceptionally long aftertaste."

---

ultimate favourite champagne" – LADY MACDONALD OF MACDONALD. LIZ BERRY goes for their special cuvée, **Comte de Champagne**.

VEUVE CLICQUOT
La Grande Dame is LIZ BERRY's choice (with a stunning new bottle). SERENA S thinks the NV is *"marvellous at the moment"*.

Loire Valley

Loire wines are thought of as dry and light – **Muscadet**, **Sancerre** and **Pouilly Fumé**, all from the Sauvignon Blanc grape, are splendid examples of this style. But MICHAEL BROADBENT has some advice: *"The Loire has been blessed with 3 great vintages – 1988, 89 and 90. In these marvellous years go for the richer* **Vouvray***s and excellent botrytis-affected* **Coteaux de Layon**.*"* All made from the Chenin Blanc grape, **HUET** is the big name in Vouvray. SIMON LOFTUS recommends the Montlouis area as an alternative: *"The 1989 and 1990 were spectacular."* LIZ BERRY echoes vintage wisdom: *"89 and 90 have been wonderful years for the botrytis wines, very, very hot news in the Loire."*

The Loire is not known for reds but SIMON LOFTUS likes them. *"Red Loire uses the Cabernet Franc grape, fresh, flavoursome, good summertime grapes – drink them cooler. Red*

Chinon is the most exciting, most of them have punch and great depth of flavour."

Rhône Valley

These are France's BIG Rabelaisian wines, the reds generally made from the Syrah grape, producing earthy, purple wines.

COTE ROTIE
The most refined and delicate of the Rhônes. Best growers and makers: **GUIGAL**, **ROSTAING** and **JASMIN**. **CLUSEL & ROCHE** is *"fairly new, quite young growers, the son of one winemaker and the daughter of another, they've been making top-quality wines over the last few years"* – LIZ BERRY.

HERMITAGE
Big brother – here is the Rhône's power house. Wines of huge muscle but with delicacy too. They behave like clarets and should be kept in the bottle for as long – 10–15 years *at least*. Look for **PAUL JABOULET** (**Hermitage La Chapelle**) and **GERARD CHAVE**. Wines from the Cornas area are a good buy, neighbouring to Hermitage but less expensive.

CONDRIEU
Made from the expensive Viognier grape, this is an aromatic, unusual and delicious wine. Try those of **VERNAY** or heed LIZ BERRY: *"This year, for the first time they've got people like* **CHAPOUTIER**, **JABOULET** . . . *very exciting at the moment."* Other names to look for are **GUIGAL**, **PINCHON** and the very pricy **CHATEAU GRILLET**.

FRENCH POLYNESIA

BORA BORA
Postcard-perfect island with a series of hotels and resorts nestling in tropical greenery, each with its own stretch of beach. **HOTEL BORA BORA** ☎ 482600, has the most idyllic spot on a promontory. Thatched bures among the flowers or floating on stilts – some have glass floors so you can spy on the fish; outrigger canoes, sunset cruises, beach barbecues and lessons in such essential Polynesian activities as pareu-tying.

HUAHINE
Increasingly popular little island with unspoilt crystalline beaches. Two great resorts: **HOTEL BALI HAI HUAHINE** ☎ 561352, with Polynesian bures set among canals, lily ponds and a tropical lagoon; and **SOCIETEL HEIVA** ☎ 688686, favoured by JEAN-MICHEL JAUDEL: *"There are bungalows on the water and it is heaven but sophisticated – a place for people who don't want to leave running water behind."*

MARIHI, Tuamotu Islands
Primitive but paradisiacal; stay at **KAINA VIL-LAGE** ☎ 964273 – you don't have much choice. *"The only thing on the island is this group of 10 bungalows, so obviously it is very private. Marvellous, traditional Polynesian food"* – JEAN-MICHEL JAUDEL.

Papeete par Nuit

Nightowl JEAN-MICHEL JAUDEL swoops in on the capital after dark. *"There are some very good restaurants in Papeete. One is* **Acajou** ☎ 428758, *which is on the water-front with marvellous traditional Polynesian food accorded the seriousness of French cooking. Very good service – the waiters are all transvestites, which is quite common. Another is the* **Dragon d'Or** ☎ 429612, *which is Chinese Hakka. Hakka are the Chinese equivalent of gypsies and, imported to Polynesia, they became very successful and powerful, as always. Afterwards, the only nightclub in the world worth going to is* **Tamure Hut** ☎ 420129. *It's mostly full of natives dancing the Tahitian waltz or the foxtrot. There is no sexier sight than a handsome Tahitian couple waltzing."*

RANGIROA, Tuamotu Islands
An hour's flight from Tahiti, this flat atoll (the rim of an ancient volcano) is named Rangiroa, 'boundless sky'. Unbeatable powerboating and sailing to uninhabited islands, where you feast on freshly speared fish. Stay in an individual thatched bungalow at the **KIA-ORA** ☎ (689) 428672, small, private and beautifully run. Splendid food and the perfect springboard for exploring the surrounding atolls.

GERMANY

BERLIN

— *Film* —

BERLIN INTERNATIONAL FILM FESTIVAL, Budapester Strasse 50, 1000 Berlin 30 ☎ (030) 25489
Traditionally one of Europe's top film fests,

Berlin has always been a vehicle for trumpeting East-meets-West – a propagandist flurry of W glamour amid E austerity. Now it's been thrown into turmoil, unsure of which path to take (for the first time, films from Armenia, Lithuania, etc, vie with those from America). IAIN JOHNSTONE assesses the fest: *"It was artificially fortified financially by the Senate to make the West glorious in the eyes of the East, but now with the Wall tumbling down it loses a bit of its raison d'être. They made their first mistake last year in transferring all the press showings to the* **Congresshalle**, *away from the centre."*

— *Hotels* —

 BRISTOL HOTEL KEMPINSKI, Kurfürstendamm 27, 1000 Berlin 15 ☎ (030) 884340
Berlin's finest with the impeccable service required by visiting members of the arts community. *"I really enjoy staying there"* – JULIAN LLOYD WEBBER. Famous (and infamous) grill room, *"where Goebbels used to eat; if it's good enough for Goebbels, it's good enough for us. Very international, indistinguishable perhaps from the Savoy Grill – people have to go elsewhere for their sauerkraut"* – IAIN JOHNSTONE.

GRAND HOTEL, Friedrichstrasse 158–164, 1080 Berlin ☎ (030) 23270
A substantial, rather imposing hotel on Berlin's east side. Built in an updated Jugendstil style and chocker with repro antiques alongside modern necessities such as health spa, hairdresser and 7 eateries.

HOTEL INTER-CONTINENTAL, Budapester Strasse 2, 1000 Berlin 30 ☎ (030) 26020
Where the film world lets its hair down after the festival. *"The place to stay because all the big film companies are there, especially the Americans. It also has one of the best hotel swimming pools in the world, where you can get a real swim"* – IAIN JOHNSTONE. Eat at the **Zum Hugenotten**.

— *Music* —

PHILHARMONIE, Natthaikirch Strasse 1, 1000 Berlin 30 ☎ (030) 254880
A well-respected venue for the much-vaunted Berlin Philharmonic, directed by the great Claudio Abbado. *"An outstanding modern hall"* – JULIAN LLOYD WEBBER.

— *Restaurants* —

APHRODITE, Schönhauser Allee 61, Prenzlauer Berg, 1058 Berlin ☎ (030) 448 1707
One of the best in what was the East, given free

rein now the Wall has crumbled. Chef-restaurateur Benno Ferch sets a warm tone to his dining room, and delivers warming fare to his diners – roast pork en croûte, duckling breast with lamb's lettuce. An ever-expanding wine cellar.

**BAMBERGER REITER,
Regensburgerstrasse 7, Wilmersdorf,
1000 Berlin 30 ☎ (030) 218 4282**
Glamorous restaurant with a feeling of old Germany – all stripped wood and mirrors. Sensational creative cuisine, a blend of French, German and Austrian, such as lobster with baby kohlrabi, mousse of calf's sweetbreads, ragout of seafood and baby vegetables.

**🐾 ROCKENDORF'S RESTAURANT,
Düsterhaupstrasse 1, Waidmannslust,
1000 Berlin 28 ☎ (030) 402 3099**
Vying with the best in the old West for the pan-German top slot, this one is a little way from the city centre, but, as MICHAEL BROADBENT advises, *"well worth the taxi ride"*. Set in an Art Nouveau villa with a superb cellar and a perfectionist menu of Teutonic-Gallic nouvellerie. Siegfried Rockendorf conjures truffles, lobster, shitake mushrooms and goose liver into heavenly combinations such as breast of squab and foie gras with apple salad and brioche.

MUNICH

—— Art and museums ——

**🐾 ALTE PINAKOTHEK, Barerstrasse 27,
8000 Munich 2 ☎ (089) 2380 5215**
Commissioned by Ludwig I, the gallery holds one of the world's greatest collections of Old Masters – north to south, Flanders and Germany to Italy. Hot on early Renaissance art of northern Europe, with a fine representation of Dürer (see *The Four Apostles*). Rubens is also there en force, with some 65 works, including his self-portrait with his wife, Isabella Brant.

**NEUE PINAKOTHEK, Barerstrasse 29,
8000 Munich 40 ☎ (089) 2380 5195**
Stunning building opposite its elder brother, housing 18C–19C European art, from German Romantics to French Realists.

**🐾 STAATSGALERIE MODERNER
KUNST, Prinzregentenstrasse 1 (Haus
der Kunst), 8000 Munich 22
☎ (089) 292710**
One of the world's major school rooms. Top-of-the-form artists from most major 20C schools hang here – Cubists, Fauves, Surrealists, Abstract Expressionists, Minimalists – from Spain (Picasso), Germany (Klee, Marc, Beckmann) and Italy (de Chirico, Boccioni, Burri).

—— Hotels ——

**HOTEL VIER JAHRESZEITEN
KEMPINSKI, Maximilianstrasse 17, 8000
Munich 22 ☎ (089) 230390**
Glossy schloss on the smartest street in town. This is Munich's best hotel – legendary for once handling the King of Siam's 1,320 pieces of luggage – built in 1858 for Bavarian high society. Fine **Waterspiel** restaurant, indoor pool, gym.

**RAFAEL, Neuturmstrasse 1, 8000
Munich 2 ☎ (089) 222539**
Classy conversion of a neo-Renaissance ballroom into a town pad with rooftop swimming pool. *"The owner, George Rafael, is obsessed by bathrooms, he thinks they are just as important as bedrooms. In hotels you often get a nice big bedroom and a tiny little bathroom. Not here – they're big and marble"* – LISA BARNARD. Claudia Schiffer is among the beauties to swan in.

—— Music ——

**🐾 BAVARIAN STATE OPERA,
Maximilianstrasse 11, 8000 Munich 22
☎ (089) 221316**
Tops in Germany and one of the best companies in the world. Their rendition of Richard Strauss's *Der Rosenkavalier* is sublime, as are the lavish sets. A night at the opera here is a dressy affair, where gilded Muncheners quaff champagne in gilded surroundings.

**MUNICH OPERA FESTIVAL,
Festspielkasse, Bayerische Staatsoper,
Maximilianstrasse 11, 8000 Munich 22
☎ (089) 221316**
Grand opera festival featuring Wagner, Strauss, Mozart, Verdi and pals, held in the Nationaltheater and the Altes Residenztheater in July.

—— Restaurants ——

**🐾 DIE AUBERGINE, Maximiliansplatz 5,
8000 Munich 2 ☎ (089) 598171**
The best in Munich, if not all Germany. Chef Eckhart Witzigmann, who studied under Paul Bocuse, dreams up fabulous Franco-German treats – if the veal in cherry sauce is on the menu, snap it up, likewise the semolina soufflé. Inspirational stuff that has tempted the King and Queen of Sweden.

**TANTRIS, Johann-Fichte-Strasse 7, 8000
Munich 40 ☎ (089) 362061**
Dazzling cooking, daunting décor. Heinz Winkler's artful dishes – such as red carp fillets in saffron sauce, crab and tomato mousse, and apple tart in rum sauce – are eaten on modern tables and chairs in a jet black/orange/yellow dining room housed in a concrete bunker-style building. The emphasis is on food.

· REST OF ·

GERMANY

—— *Art and museums* ——

STAATSGALERIE, Konrad-Adenauer-Strasse 32, 7000 Stuttgart
☎ **(0711) 212 5108**
Brit architect James Stirling's ground-breaking PoMo building houses an extensive collection of 19C and 20C art from Impressionism to the present day. The German Expressionists (Grosz, Beckmann and friends) and Bauhausers are strongly in evidence here.

WALLRAF-RICHARTZ-MUSEUM/MUSEUM LUDWIG, Bischofsgartenstrasse 1, 5000 Cologne
☎ **(0221) 221 2379**
Mixed bag of goodies – 2 collections are hung in the Rhineland's largest gallery. The first goes from medieval through 16C–18C European art and Impressionists; the second covers 20C Surrealists, Expressionists and contemporists.

—————— *Hotels* ——————

BREIDENBACHER HOF, Heinrich Heine Allee 36, 4000 Düsseldorf 1
☎ **(0211) 13030**
Established in the top league, the 157-year-old hotel has top-notch everything from the marble baths to the gilt-mirrored drawing rooms. *"It is very, very good, the best hotel in Düsseldorf"* – LISA BARNARD.

BRENNER'S PARK, An der Lichtentaler Allee, Schillerstrasse 6, 7570 Baden-Baden ☎ **(07221) 3530**
Classic turn-of-the-century water-taking venue and hotel – some of Europe's healthiest nobles have been here over the years. Spa, hotel and Lancaster Beauty Farm are set in beautiful gardens; shootin', coach-'n'-fourin' and tea-takin' are all still done with old-time airs and grace. *"Masses of gardens, very picturesque, you go there to get pampered"* – LISA BARNARD. ROBIN LEACH thinks it one of Europe's 2 best health spas, MARY ROSSI is keen.

SCHLOSS CECILIENHOF, Neuer Garten, 1561 Potsdam ☎ **332 3141**
Set in the splendour of the Hohenzollern family's 1913–17 Prussian version of an English country house. Half is a museum, the other half a hotel. *"Marvellous architecture, a palace that looks like a Tudor manor in Surrey. It's where, at the end of the war, Churchill, Stalin and Truman met. It's not very glossy, but so pretty and you can stay in Princess Cecilia's bedroom and it's only 45 minutes from Berlin"* – CAROL WRIGHT.

 HOTEL VIER JAHRESZEITEN, Neuer Jungfernstieg 9–14, 2000 Hamburg 36
☎ **(040) 34941**
Best in Germany – though taken over by Japanese in 1989, it retains the flavour of a private hotel. There's an old-world feel about the place – wood panelling, tapestries and antiques. ROBIN LEACH, LISA BARNARD and MARK MCCORMACK sing its praises and relish the hovering service. The **Haerlin** is a very good restaurant.

SCHLOSSHOTEL KRONBERG, Hainstrasse 25, 6242 Kronberg im Taunus ☎ **(06173) 7011**
Medieval style all over here – Beowulfian halls hung with tapestries, panelled dining room, all within a castle in a forest. Fairytale stuff.

—————— *Music* ——————

BAYREUTH FESTIVAL, Postfach 100262, 8580 Bayreuth 2 ☎ **(0921) 20221**
Only one word that counts here. Wagner. His opera house (he designed it), his music, his descendants run it and his devotees attend it. Tickets are among the hardest to find for a public event anywhere in the world. Some tips: get a programme at end-Oct and apply for tickets by mid-Nov. When this fails, try to marry into one of the festival-going families. When this fails, infiltrate a pan-European extortion organization. End-July to end-Aug.

—————— *Restaurants* ——————

 GOLDENER PFLUG, Olpener Strasse 421, Merheim, 5000 Cologne 91
☎ **(0221) 895509**
One of the best in Germany, for special-occasion dining on imaginative French-German wizardry. A former tavern sparked up with lots of gold bits – gold chairs, gold curtains, gold ceiling.

 LE CANARD, Elbchaussee 39, Hamburg 50 ☎ **(040) 460 4830**
Le Canard has flown. But the whatever-takes-his-fancy cooking from the effervescent and brilliant Josef Viehhauser remains consistent – superb seafood, nouvelled up, regional cooking. **Bistro Canard** is at Martinistrasse 11, where big brother used to be.

LE MARRON, Provinzialstrasse 35, 5300 Bonn 1 ☎ **(0228) 253261**
Warm, rustic, suburban dinery serving bigwig diners with fab fare. Nouvellish German/French/Italian food – try roast baby boar in noodle crust.

—————— *Wine* ——————

German wines still suffer from an image problem, though they can be some of the world's finest. Over-production and a succession of disastrous vintages (up to 88 that is) are partly to blame; garish labels and the ubiquity of the infamous Blue Nun probably have more to do with it. Because of this, *"wines from the top estates are still woefully underrated and underpriced"* – MICHAEL BROADBENT. German wines are not necessarily food wines in the way of the great French wines – they are often less alcoholic and less dry. The German ideal is a balance between fruit and acidity, and wines are categorized by the natural sugar content of the grapes before harvesting. Tafelwein doesn't attempt to be more than an easy quaffer; Quälitätswein bestimmer Anbaugebiete (QbA) is a step up and the top category, Quälitätswein mit Prädikat (QmP), subdivides by sweetness into Kabinett, Auslese, Spätlese, Beerenauslese and the great Trockenbeerenauslese, in ascending order.

Baden

Large area in the south west dotted with vineyards producing predominantly food wines. LIZ BERRY draws attention to **KARL-HEINZ JOHNER**, who is *"labelling his wines Pinot Noir rather than the official German name Spätburgunder, which upsets the authorities, but they are rich, powerful and very un-Germanic. His Pinot Blanc is oak aged and he's got everything in Burgundian bottles."*

Mosel-Saar-Ruwer

"Deservedly popular and marvellous drinks – as against food wines – are the ripest from the Mosel-Saar-Ruwer, of recent vintages 1988, 89 and 90 (the 76, 75 and 71 Auslesen and sweeter wines are still fabulous)" – MICHAEL BROADBENT.

DEINHARD is one of the best names in Germany, thanks initially to its 1900 acquisition of a portion of the Mosel's best vineyard: **Doktor** at **Bernkastel**. All its wines meet a very high standard.

EGON MULLER-SCHARZHOF is the best name in the Saar: **Scharzhofberger** Riesling is a world-class wine of penetrating perfume and vitality. The 1988 and 1989 **Auslesen** are sublime, as their gold capsules indicate.

MICHAEL BROADBENT's favourites from the area are **MAXIMIN GRUENHAUSER** (from **Von Schubert**) and **RAUTENSTRAUCH's** Eitselbachers. **DER BISCHOFLICHEN WEINGUTER** is one of the most famous old estates, charitably run but unreliable. **J J PRUM's Sonnenuhr** wines are among the Mosel's most voluptuous. In the middle-Mosel, MICHAEL B and LIZ BERRY praise **DR LOOSEN** in unison. *"The son, Ernst Loosen, is the one to watch"* – LB. MICHAEL B targets the 1988 **Wehlener Sonnenuhr Auslese**.

Rheingau

The Rhine's great vineyard region, producing fine Rieslings.

SCHLOSS VOLLRADS is one of Germany's greatest private estates (and their labels harbour, in smaller print, one of the wine world's best names: owner Graf Matuschka-Greiffenclau). From their cellars came one of MICHAEL BROADBENT's all-time Rhine wines: a 1947 **TBA.**

Among the other top Rheingau estates are the **RHEINGAU STATE DOMAIN** at Eltville, **SCHLOSS SCHONBORN, VON SIMMERN** and **WEGELER-DEINHARD**.

Nahe

The best Nahe wines are often said to be between those of the Mosel and Rhine in character, balanced and clean. Among the most delicate and hypnotic in Germany are the wines of **CRUSIUS, HANS and PETER**, and the **STATE DOMAIN OF NIEDERHAUSEN-SCHLOSS BOCKELHEIM**.

Rheinhessen

Large, but second-league, wine-making region. **BALBACH** is the dominant name of this area, making wines of enormous appeal.

Rheinpfalz

Another vast region, south of Rheinhessen and, with it, a chief source of **Liebfraumilch**, although capable of producing wines of great richness. The 3 Bs, **VON BUHL, BASSERMANN-JORDAN** and **BURKLIN-WOLF**, are among the names to go for.

🐕 **Buzzz** Hot dog: **Frankfurt** captures the imagination of top travellers, such as DAVINA JACKSON, who votes it *"the best city for modern art and architecture.* **The Museum of Modern Art** *is a brilliant building which encourages 60s and 70s conceptual art; strange and wonderful exhibitions by Warhol, Lichtenstein, etc. Along the river 5 or 6 museums and galleries have developed; wander from Richard Meier's* **Museum of Arts and Crafts** *to OM Ungers'* **Museum of Architecture** *to the neo-constructivist* **Postal Museum"** 🐕 ..... More down-to-earth, DAN KOMAR reckons Frankfurt has *"the best airport to wait for a connecting flight – it lets you stay near the fun bits and doesn't sequester you like others"* .... 🐕

GREECE

ATHENS

—— Festivals ——

**ATHENS FESTIVAL, Voukourestiou St 1
☎ (01) 323 0049**
Classy productions of classical and modern
drama, ballet, opera and music against a stunning ancient backdrop – the Acropolis and the
floodlit Parthenon. Take a cushion – the AD 161
Theatre of Herodus Atticus does not have
padded seats.

—— Hotels ——

**ASTIR PALACE, Vouliagmeni, PO Box
1226 ☎ (01) 896 0211**
Lavish complex half an hour's drive from
Athens, for out-of-town men-about-town,
leisured ladies, and serious high-livers. 3 hotels,
77 bungalows, 7 restaurants and every conceiv-
able facility – tennis, private beaches, etc . . . .

**GRANDE BRETAGNE, Platia
Syntagmatos ☎ (01) 323 0251**
Grand old pile (open since 1872) with a colourful
history (Greek political intrigues and espionage
plots are traditionally hatched here) and guest
list, including Churchill, Eisenhower and
Richard Strauss. Just across from the parliament in the centre of town, it has served as the
Royal Palace's guest house – suites were considered fit for crowned heads and top brass. Things
have not changed.

—— Restaurants ——

KAFENEIO, Loukianou 26 ☎ (01) 722 9056
A gracious and intimate restaurant in a 19C-
style house in the smart Kolonaki district.
Here the array of starters is mind-boggling –
choose 4 or 5 *mets* from some 40 platters. Not
only is the cuisine more refined than in the
standard taverna, but service is a cut above
the rest.

**KOKKINI VARKA, Akti Koumoudourou
50 ☎ (01) 417 5853**
A delightful little restaurant on seafood strip – a
row of seaside establishments by the yacht
harbour of Mikrolimano, near the port of
Piraeus. This one has a fishing smack suspended
from the ceiling. You pick your plump fresh fish
from the day's catch, then return to your
outdoor table to dine amid much chatter and
clinking of masts.

VASSILENA, Etolikou 72 ☎ (01) 461 2457
The true Greek experience, set in an old grocery
store in the port of Piraeus. A parade of predominantly seafood dishes is brought on for starters
(though they might finish you off). The former
royal family of Greece used to drop in of an
afternoon to dine on the rooftop terrace.

· REST OF ·

GREECE

—— Hotels ——

**AKTI MYRINA HOTEL, Myrina, Lemnos
☎ (0254) 22681. Outside May–Oct, c/o
Athens office ☎ (01) 413 8001**
Tops for marine boys and girls. A laid-back
resort with stone villas bang on the beach of one
of the less-spoilt Greek islands. Good food –
splendid picnics in the gardens – and water
sports.

HOTEL ALIKI, Simi ☎ (0241) 71665
Neo-classical splendour (a restored and updated
mansion) on the unspoilt seafront of the Island
of Simi near Rhodes. Charming roof gardens,
tables on the waterfront.

**HOTEL MIRANDA, Hydra
☎ (0298) 52230**
18C house full of antiques, painted ceilings and a
chic Athenian crowd – this former captain's
mansion is where it's done to be seen on high
days and holidays. Set above a picture-book
port, in narrow, uncongested streets (cars are
banned).

**VILLA ARGENTIKON, Chios, c/o The
Best of Greece, see Travel Directory**
A trio of villas, containing just 4 suites, stand in
this gorgeous private Italianate estate. Lush,
scented gardens have pergolas, arbours and
mosaic paths. White-gloved waiters attend your
every whim, superb cuisine is dished up in the
courtyard, and sailing trips along the nearby
Turkish coast can be arranged.

—— Restaurants ——

**IL CANTUCCIO, Sunset Path, Firo
Stefani, Santorini ☎ (0286) 22082**
Italian trat run by Franco Tirletti and his
French partner Gilles, set on the 'Sunset Path', a
corniche that runs along the almost sheer cliff-
side between Fira and Merovigli, with fab views
over harbour and dramatic sunsets. The place to
eat on this glitzy island – media types, antique
dealers, even the Greek Italian consul go – for
super-fresh pasta with clams, seafood or porcini
mushrooms, great antipasti and French puddings. Lovely frescos from the island have been
reproduced in natural, earthy colours.

Tours and villas

CV TRAVEL (see Travel Directory) are the best villa people in Corfu and Paxos – privately owned pads with private maid, cook and swimming pool. Tours and yachting. **THE BEST OF GREECE** (see Travel Directory) can direct you to the best of the rest of the country.

HONG KONG

Art and museums

HONG KONG MUSEUM OF ART, 10 Salisbury Rd, Tsimshatsui ☎ 734 2167
A controversial newcomer, whose permanent collection houses many pieces belonging to arch shopper/collector TT Tsui of V&A fame. *"If you thought the Cultural Centre was utilitarian, take a look at the Museum of Art next door, which takes the word bland to new extremes architecturally. Another superb harbourfront site has been wasted with a cross between a public loo and a multi-storey car park. Hong Kong is not known for its voracious appetite for visual art . . ."* – CATHERINE GAYNOR.

Arts centres

HONG KONG CULTURAL CENTRE, 10 Salisbury Rd, Tsimshatsui ☎ 734 9011
Ironically opened by the Prince and Princess of Wales in 1989, this is not a traditionalist's architectural dream come true. Intended to suggest the wings of a bird/sails of a ship, it's an ultra-modernist blot on the harbourfront landscape. But it has among the best arts facilities in Asia – the 2,100-seater high-tech Concert Hall, Grand Theatre, fringier studio and exhibition space has brought in voices like Norman and Sutherland, twirlers like the Royal Danish Ballet, top-class puffers and fiddlers and Chinese opera.

Bars and cafés

ASAHI SUPER DRY, Bank of America Tower, 12 Harcourt Rd, Central ☎ 521 0309
Wilder beasts' watering hole – the front runner of the new wave of serious drinking bars in Hong Kong, named after an extra-potent Japanese beer. *"A huge barn of a place, a super beer restaurant"* – SAUL LOCKHART. Inside it's a 2-level, 20,000 sq ft rabbit warren – rooms are decked out in marble, wood and tatami screens. Fri's the big night – eat Japanese and slug the eponymous beer with money-go-rounders and briefs – if they're not at their desks after 5.30, this is where they'll be.

THE CHAMPAGNE BAR, Grand Hyatt, see Hotels
First fizzy bar in Hong Kong, with 39 marques to choose from. Art Deco black lacquer and brass décor, bluesy/jazzy singer and soft lighting. *"The biggest range of champagne, available by the glass and by the bottle, has made it an immediate hot spot. And so it should"* – GLYNN CHRISTIAN.

THE GODOWN, Admiralty Tower II, Harcourt Rd, Central ☎ 866 1166
Now settled down after the move from its former, demolished, premises, the celebrated bar/restaurant is still in. The funky image – live jazz on Wednesdays, disco during the week – goes down well with get-on-downers.

MANDARIN ORIENTAL, see Hotels
The most important drinks venue for money-makers. They choose from 4. The **Chinnery Bar** is where top Swire's and other business folk move and shake. Caviare fetishists head upstairs to the new **Petrossian** counter at the **Harlequin Bar** – centred around a vast slab of Carrara marble which was winched up the building; the **Captain's Bar** still has an influential pull on the influential and the **Clipper Lounge** is the best goldfish bowl in town.

SPEAKEASY, 38 Windham St, Central ☎ 522 5566
On top of the nightlife area of Lan Kwai Fung. *"As the name implies, good music and action. It is one of the few places to get a late-night supper"* – SAUL LOCKHART. Last call 2.30 am.

Casinos

MACAO CASINO, Lisboa Hotel, Avenida da Amizade, Macao ☎ 77666
Pandemonium. Don't dust off the black tie to go here, it's rough and ready. The whole place just buzzes, punters bet staggering amounts of money on all the usual games – roulette, pontoon – and on weird and wonderful ones from Japan that no one understands. Stanley Ho's Crazy Paris Show still has the dancers kicking their legs up high and frolicking with feather boas.

MANDARIN ORIENTAL CASINO, Avenida da Amizade, Macao ☎ 567888
The only dressy casino in Macao. Stakes are higher – minimum bets HK$50 and HK$100 – than the normal HK$10, and noise is lower, but the word is it ain't as much fun.

Clubs

See also Bars and cafés.

B BOSS NIGHT CLUB, 14 Science Museum Rd, Tsimshatsui ☎ 369 2883
Probably the world's biggest nightclub. Under-

statement is foreign to its nature: there's a line-up of 1,000 hostesses and an electric Rolls-Royce, which drives around taking orders. *"Provided you can afford it, this is one stop on the 'you won't believe this' tour"* – SAUL LOCKHART. Provided you're a man, that is.

CALIFORNIA BAR AND GRILL, 30–32 D'Aguilar St, Central ☎ 521 1345
Been around for a while but it still happens in a big way early evening. Loadsamoney (portable phones galore), hearty tucker (hamburgers, etc), hip disco and a singles bar to boot.

CANTON, 161–163 World Finance Centre, 19 Canton Rd, Harbour City, Tsimshatsui ☎ 721 0209
Groovespot extraordinaire – Chinese hipsters make it happen here to the best sound system in HK; good visiting bands mime the night away. Very packed.

CATWALK, 18F, New World Hotel, 22 Salisbury World, Kowloon ☎ 369 4111
Night prowlers strut their stuff in this high-tech combination of dance club, karaoke room and bars. Would-be models flaunt it on the walk-way that circles the dance floors.

HOT GOSSIP, World Finance Centre, 19 Canton Rd, Tsimshatsui ☎ 721 6884
High-tech space filled with beautiful people who aren't next door at Canton. Good sounds, lasers and dancing.

JJ's, Grand Hyatt, see Hotels
A new R&B outfit has replaced regular band CC Riders, but JJ's is *"still the hottest spot in town, people still queue on a Monday night to get in."*

Multi-themed and cavernous, but glamorous" – CATHERINE GAYNOR.

JOE BANANAS, 23 Luard Rd, Wanchai ☎ 529 1811
Bar/diner/rock 'n' rollerie chocker with *really* fun expats getting down to grooves ancient and modern (50s onwards) and live sounds. It's a port of call for US/UK sailors when the boats come in – you have been warned.

NINETEEN 97, 9 Lan Kwai Fong ☎ 810 0613
The protean nightclub/singles bar/bistro/restaurant/disco has undergone massive plastic surgery and has come up with yet another identity – probably its 10th in as many years. Music's now Nina Simone, Billie Holliday, more sophisticated rock and classical as befits one of the longest surviving clubs in town.

—— *Fashion designers* ——

DIANE FREIS, Shop 258, Ocean Terminal, Harbour City, Kowloon ☎ 721 4342 and branches
Freis's one-size patterned dresses grace the best curves – Diana Ross's, Shirley MacLaine's, Victoria Principal's. Nighties and undies too. Factory outlet at Chung Nam Centre, 414 Kwun Tong Rd, Kwun Tong, Kowloon ☎ 343 6275.

EDDIE LAU, Shop 6, GF, Central Bldg, Pedder St, Central ☎ 877 3100
Silk for the slick set – ball dresses, cocktail minis (*very* figleaf) – teased into bold shapes for unretiring types. More down-to-earth for day-to-day gear, see him at Chinese Arts & Crafts.

🕴 **Buzzz Members lounge:** And where better to lounge than the new **China Club**, 13F, Old Bank of China Building, Bank St, Central ☎ 521 8888, opened by playboy David Tang to a closed membership (invitation only) that includes Brit MP Michael Heseltine and Chinese premier Li Peng. Atop the Bank of China building, a rare remaining pre-war building in HK, *"it has the ready-made atmosphere of a crusty gentlemen's club – worn-in leather armchairs, old retainers, faded curtains and covers"* – CATHERINE GAYNOR 🕴 . . . . . . The **Hong Kong Club**, Jackson Rd ☎ 525 8251, remains the place for food and service despite reservations over the new location 🕴 . . . . . . It's dollars that count at the **Royal Hong Kong Jockey Club**, Sports Rd, Happy Valley ☎ 583 7811, where social butterflies flutter on the gee-gees (more than HK$30 billion turnover) 🕴 . . . . . . Doodle dandies get into the **American Club**, 47F Tower Two, Exchange Square ☎ 842 7400, one of the tops in town with glorious country club in Tai Tam on the south side of the island 🕴 . . . . . . Puffed hacks head for the **Foreign Correspondents' Club**, 2 Albert Rd ☎ 521 1511, and sit around the circular bar – open 24 hours – swapping stories 🕴 . . . . . . The **Aberdeen Marina Club**, 8 Deepwater Bay Rd, Aberdeen ☎ 555 8321, pulls in the wealthies for billiards, bridge, mah-jong, etc, and boasts the best marina in Asia . . . . . 🕴

Festivals

HONG KONG ARTS FESTIVAL, c/o 13F, HK Arts Centre, 2 Harbour Rd, Wanchai ☎ 529 5555
Mostly Western festival held annually – opera, dance, symphony concerts, mime – you name it. Asian arts too – don't miss Chinese theatre. Ask your concierge to book the tickets.

HONG KONG FOOD FESTIVAL, 35F, Jardine House, 1 Connaught Place, Central ☎ 801 7111
Foodie fiesta – Hong Kong's kitchens great and small go crazy once a year. *"It's getting bigger and better every year and it's now gaining worldwide attention. Held at the end of winter, late March/early April, it's to highlight Hong Kong's position at the crossroads of the world and at the culinary heart of Asia. You can eat any cuisine of the world but, when in Hong Kong, do as the Chinese do"* – ELISE PASCOE.

Hotels

🐟 GRAND HYATT, 1 Harbour Rd, Wanchai ☎ 588 1234
Sleek flagship of the Hyatt group, poised somewhere between the glamorous and the outrageous. *"Quite one of the world's most spectacular new hotels, not only the site, right on HK harbour, but the extraordinary lobby, which has more black marble than all of Italy. The ballroom is spectacular, you walk up a ramp through free-standing columns of light and it's like Ancient Rome come to the East. The bedrooms appear a little pale, but then you realize you have a full wall of glass and HK at your feet. But the real thing is the bathrooms, which are marble and mirror and gold plate – there's not a single part of your body that you cannot see from several angles"* – GLYNN CHRISTIAN. Firm up first in the fabulously large outdoor swimming pool or on the rooftop tennis courts (watch those balls). The total package appeals to LISA BARNARD (*"amazing"*) and ELISE PASCOE. A brace of the best eateries around (see Restaurants) completes the picture.

🐟 MANDARIN ORIENTAL, 5 Connaught Rd, Central ☎ 522 0111
Consistently outranks the rest. Good central location, understatedly opulent surroundings and uncannily prescient service: *"I didn't want it to be the best hotel in the world, but it is. From the moment they bring you a wonderful pot of tea, plus your personalized notepaper, your fax number, a bottle of champagne and you slip between the sheets, you are in seventh heaven"* – IAIN JOHNSTONE. *"My favourite among favourites. It's pulled back against stiff competition – and it's the only one in the middle of Central"* – LORD LICHFIELD. Chic comes in a black marble lobby with gold temple carvings, chic

chinoiserie rooms and the most soporific of bedding, but it's the extraordinary attention paid to each guest that keeps them coming back. *"I don't know how they do it. Every time you go out, somebody comes in and straightens the bed and puts new fruit in the basket"* – SIR CLEMENT FREUD. *"They remember your name and what you would like to drink at bedtime"* – SERENA FASS. *"Spectacular, it has the discretion, the grandeur of, say, Claridge's, but with all the things the Oriental is famous for, the service and the unbelievable food"* – STEPHEN JONES. It's WARWICK VYNER's favourite for *"old-world atmosphere, 21st-century efficiency"*, which may be why LISA BARNARD and ED VICTOR re-Orient themselves. See also Restaurants.

🐟 THE PENINSULA, Salisbury Rd, Kowloon ☎ 366 6251
Dowager duchess of the Hong Kong hotels, the 1928 landmark has lost none of her class and few of her following. Beautifully renovated in 1988, it's the little things that count: the fleet of high Rollers, the English antiques, Portuguese marble bathrooms .... *"Impeccable service, check-in processed in your room. Hermès soaps, the best bathrooms in the world, white chocolate truffles, civilized afternoon tea in the lobby. Friendly without being familiar and service, service, service. Great shopping too – you need never leave the hotel"* – JILL MULLENS. SUSAN KUROSAWA says aye to all that. Good conduct counts for ANDRE PREVIN: *"An amazingly beautiful, luxurious, deeply personal hotel."* High-tech essentials – fax, CD, etc, in your suite – are as wel-

---

Comfort Eating

🐟

Had it with Hunanese? Does Peking pall? When you can't face one more goose web or fish maw, follow SAUL LOCKHART's advice and find French food to soothe the soul. *"The volatile owner/chef of* **Café de Paris**, *30-32 D'Aguilar St, Central ☎ 868 5100, Maurice Gardette, is probably more famous than his food, which is excellent. A bistro-style French restaurant called* **La Rose Noire**, *8-13 Wu On Lane, Central ☎ 526 5965, is one of the best value in town. Part of the attraction is the late-night piano playing of owner Michel Emeric (his wife used to be a cabaret singer). Set in a turn-of-the-century building,* **The Fringe**, *2 Lower Albert Rd ☎ 877 4000, has arguably some of the best French food in town, all the energy is concentrated on the limited menu."*

come but understated as the 3:1 staff:guest ratio, factors which rate with ED VICTOR and KEN HOM.

🏖 THE REGENT, Salisbury Rd, Kowloon
☎ 721 1211
No resting on laurels here – the Regent continues to update and re-update itself – rendering its No 1 position unassailable. And position is all – lapped by the harbour, facing the lights of HK. *"It really is the hotel with the view – just incredible. Brilliant bathrooms, the standard of service is impeccable"* – LISA BARNARD. Choose the view for you: from the 146×60 ft panoramic lobby window, from one of the exemplary dining rooms (see Restaurants), from your terrace suite's private outdoor Jacuzzi. *"I still think it's great, the most glamorous in Hong Kong . . . it has a whole forest of trees with lights on, it is just wow. Totally plastic, I love it"* – DAVID SHILLING. *"Tops everybody's best"* – ROBIN LEACH. Renovations are bringing the latest in audio-visual technology to the rooms, and, as GLYNN CHRISTIAN sees it, the health club couldn't be bettered. *"I've seen nothing like it in the world – rather than sharing them, you have a complete set to yourself, sauna, steambath, whirlpool – it's the best time I've ever had."*

SHANGRI-LA, 64 Mody Rd, E Tsimshatsui ☎ 721 2111
Polished, modern harbourside hotel, a favourite with business travellers. Just a touch of soullessness about the vast marble lobby but all mod cons are spot-on: jet-controlled pool, well-equipped business centre, even remote-control curtains from your bed. The exclusive Club 21 doubles the effort with personalized stationery, free limo service and morning papers delivered. See also Restaurants.

———— Restaurants ————

🏖 FOOK LAM MOON, 459 Lockhart Rd, Causeway Bay ☎ 891 2639
Still the best for non-hotel Chinese dining, drawing the most elevated of locals, who are over the moon about dishes traditional (shark's fin and abalone) and off-the-wall (civet cat).

🏖 GRAND HYATT, see Hotels
Grissini, a modern Italian restaurant, is *"the real Hong Kong hot spot. The most spectacular full wall of window, the best example of soft high-tech decoration, magnificent wooden panelling, lots of wrought iron and truly world-class food"* – GLYNN CHRISTIAN. ELISE PASCOE sniffs out the speciality: *"The feature is the bread oven in the reception area – you're greeted by fabulous aromas when you enter. Grissini [bread sticks] at least 2 ft long come straight from the oven to your table."* The split-level Cantonese restaurant **One Harbour Road** is now a sacred site for the international food pilgrim. *"Absolutely wonderful. I had little snow pea shoots"* – MADHUR JAFFREY. *"A fantastic*

restaurant – I was very impressed by the quality of food" – KEN HOM. GLYNN C is too: *"A revelation of Chinese restaurant design and food."*

🏖 HUNAN GARDEN, The Forum, Exchange Square, Central ☎ 868 2880
Hunan is where it's at culinarily, as ELISE PASCOE points out: *"It's taking over from Sichuan cooking and it's going to be hot hot hot. An elegant, upmarket Chinese restaurant, the best value for money outside the hotels."* *"A terrific restaurant, the food is really, really excellent"* – KEN HOM. Try duck's tongue in mustard sauce.

Hong Kong's Best Restaurants

1	LAI CHING HEEN, The Regent
2	ONE HARBOUR ROAD, Grand Hyatt
3	FOOK LAM MOON
4	MAN WAH, Mandarin Oriental
5	GADDI'S, The Peninsula
6	CAPRICCIO, Ramada Renaissance

🏖 MANDARIN ORIENTAL, see Hotels
If you've got a sturgeon urge on, go to **Petrossian**, the new caviare bar in the **Harlequin Bar**: *"It's terribly special, they have a range of caviare, and Jurg Munch, the chef, is always creating new dishes using caviare"* – GLYNN CHRISTIAN. CAROLYN LOCKHART has the same craving: *"Absolutely over-the-top luxury – gold-plated spoons, carpet is blue with gold medallions."* ELISE PASCOE rates the **Man Wah** as *"one of the 2 finest Chinese restaurants in HK"* – the other's in the Regent. Hong Kong's glamorati go to the French **Pierrot**, and lovers of simplicity love the etched-glass, split-level **Grill** for the freshest Welsh lamb, Scottish steaks and *"the most sumptuous spread for your morning repast"* – SAUL LOCKHART. *"The best plain food in a city of exotica"* – LORD LICHFIELD.

MICHELLE'S, Ice House St, Central ☎ 877 4000
A breath of fresh air in a city dominated by formal hotel restaurants, Melbourne-born owner Michelle Garnaut runs *"the closest Hong Kongers get to designer dining"* – CATHERINE GAYNOR. Cooking combines influences from the Med and the East; décor is quirky baroque including muscular frescos and rather perilous 3-legged chairs. A hit with locals.

NORTH SEA FISHING VILLAGE CO, Auto Plaza, Tsimshatsui E ☎ 723 6843; GF, 445 King's Rd, N Point ☎ 563 0187
Twin restaurants based around a floodlit junk

aswim with tanked fish, just waiting to be eaten. Chose your own – prawn and octopus are t'riffic, shark's fin and dim sum are good too.

🐧 THE PENINSULA, see Hotels

For visual and culinary feasters – the surroundings and Western food at **Gaddi's** are splendid. Sit in pomp – mirror-panelled walls, corniced ceilings, a carved wooden screen, c. 1670, created for the summer palace – and order specialities like lobster tartare with caviare, or king prawns with mussels in a sesame paste. Maître d' Rolf Heiniger is still the man to know and be known by, his sommelier will help you through the enormous wine list. JILL MULLENS says: *"It's a stand out."* The **Spring Moon** has upmarket Cantonese served à la Pen.

🐧 RAMADA RENAISSANCE, 8 Peking Rd, Tsimshatsui ☎ 375 1133

Capriccio is decked out in neo-Renaissance style – oils, frescos – with the best northern Italian food and wine (cooked and stocked by staff from the palatial Florentine eatery Enoteca

---

Pascoe on the Pulse

🐧

Feeling hungry but off-colour? Follow ELISE PASCOE to **Vassar Health Desserts Specialist**, 1F, Man Hee Mansions, 12 Johnston Rd, Wanchai ☎ 529 0009: *"It sounds awful, but it really is clever, subtle marketing. It is almost Scandinavian-looking, with bare wooden tables and clinical white décor. Most of us don't really like Chinese desserts – too sweet. But you go here so that you will feel better the next day. It's all soups, sort of sloppy custards with herbal mixtures, all tasting marvellous. The owner, Simon Chan, will ask what you need help with and then prescribe what you need – cream of peanut with mariuda root for kidney and skin problems, for example. There are 6 things on the menu and 3 nightly specials."* She's also rapt with **Grappa**, 132 The Mall, Pacific Place, 88 Queensway, Central ☎ 868 0086, *"because when you're in the gloom looking at small writing, they give you tiny, rimless lorgnettes which they call peeper-keepers, presented in a little case with the restaurant's name on them. It's the restaurant's gift to you. All the locals in the know have their peeper-keepers."*

Pinchiorri) in town. Mouthfuls of spiced-up pasta – fettucine with sautéed prawns and a light cream sauce flavoured with fennel and lemon chive – rare wines and grappa. Great Cantonese cooking in **T'ang Court**.

🐧 THE REGENT, see Hotels

Lai Ching Heen remains one of the very best in the East, and word's got around: *"It's the talk of Australia, anyone who enjoys Chinese food can't go to HK without going there"* – ELISE PASCOE. It's tops for chefs KEN HOM (*"for me still No 1 as far as food is concerned"*) and MADHUR JAFFREY: *"It is wonderful, wonderful, fabulous. I had a dish of chopped squid and green pea shoots, all stir-fried. Another one is a pear and a scallop put together with a piece of ham and then they deep-fry it very quickly and it is gorgeous. I tried to make it, but there is a secret that they won't give away."* Equally refined is **Plume**, which continues to soar in the Euro dining stakes.

🐧 SHANGRI LA, see Hotels

If you're after crystal glasses, a deep cellar, great service and imaginative nouvelle-inspired Western cooking, book a table at **Margaux**. There's fine Japanese at **Nadaman** and Chinese at **Shang Palace**.

SUNNING UNICORN, 1 Sunning Rd, Causeway Bay ☎ 577 6620

If cruelty to crustacea leaves you unmoved, this is the best place to try the Sichuan speciality, drunken prawns. Chinese yellow wine is poured over live prawns; when sozzled they are frazzled at your table. *"A wonderful place to eat, it is fabulous"* – DAVID SHILLING.

YUNG KEE, 32–40 Wellington St, Central ☎ 523 1562

Famous for the 'one-dish meal' – roast goose and rice – it's packed with locals night after night.

ZEN CHINESE CUISINE, LG/1 The Mall, Pacific Place, 88 Queensway, Central ☎ 845 4555

Beating the Hong Kong Chinese at their own game, Michael Leung, of the London Zens, has gone down like a house on fire in the colony. Fab Cantonese specials include sautéed prawns with sweet walnut and dry chilli. *"Absolutely unique in Hong Kong"* – SAUL LOCKHART.

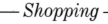

——— *Shopping* ———

The market place of the Orient – shoppers the world over come to buy the best from East and West, tax free. A top spot for antiques, works of art, jewellery, ceramics, porcelain, jade, pearls, gold, silk, embroidery, designer labels, made-to-measure suits, furs, ivory (import licences required), rugs, carpets, cameras, electronic and consumer goods – just about everything.

On HK Island, the **Mandarin** arcade has a

select coterie of local bests (Kai-Yin Lo, A-Man Hing Cheong, David's Shirts, Mayer Shoes) and foreign glamour (Chaumet, Fendi, Ferragamo). A network of walkways leads to the ritziest, shiniest shopping complexes, **Pacific Place** (swanky stores – superb Seibu, Lane Crawford), **The Landmark** (Ralph Lauren, Buccellati, Bulgari, Chanel, Ungaro, Vuitton, Loewe, Hermès, Joyce Boutique, The Swank Shop), **Prince's Building** (second-rung Euros) and **Swire House** (the pick of the Japs).

Kowloon is home to the swish arcades of the **Regent** (Diane Freis, Basile, Lanvin, Nina Ricci) and **Peninsula** (Joyce Boutique, Marguerite Lee, Hermès, Gucci), and impressive mega-centres like **Ocean Terminal, Harbour City** and **Ocean Centre** (the best lines from around the globe).

Choice Chinese goods can be found at department stores such as **Chinese Merchandise Emporium, China Products** or **Yue Hwa Chinese Products Emporium**. On HK Island, **Pedder Building** is a must for knock-down young designer wear. The newly renovated **Western Market**, HK's answer to Covent Garden, is home to many of the old 'Cloth Alley' salesmen. The **Lanes** between Queen's Road Central and Des Voeux Road bristle with little stalls for all sorts of bargains and fakery. **Stanley Market** remains a ritual gweilo haunt on a Sunday (shop, lunch at Stanley's, shop), but requires grit to cut through tourists and tat and find the real bargains (from Reeboks to jumbo jeans). On Kowloon, **Nathan Road** and all roads off to the east are bursting with jewellery, embroidery and electronic goods. **Kaiser Estate**, Phase I-III, Hung Hom, contains factory outlets for silk, linen, sportswear, etc – not necessarily high fashion, but dependable and cheap. NB Bargain-hunters should check out prices back home before embarking, and only shop where the HKTA sticker is displayed.

A-MAN HING CHEONG, M4, Mandarin Oriental, Central ☎ 522 3336
In the highest rank of Hong Kong tailors and shirtmakers – his quality and style are almost up to Savile Row. Prices are high for Hong Kong, but that doesn't deter Barry Humphries, LORD LICHFIELD or NICHOLAS VILLIERS.

BOLWIN COMPANY, GF, 43B Mody Rd, Tsimshatsui ☎ 366 1038
"The most stunning silk sheets that everyone can afford. They make silk shirts as well" – ELISE PASCOE.

CHINESE ARTS & CRAFTS, Star House, Kowloon ☎ 367 4061; Silvercord Bldg, 30 Canton Rd; Shell House, Wyndham St, Central; and branches
Silks, semi-precious stones and jewellery – jade, lapis lazuli – beaded bags by Kai-Yin Lo, Eddie Lau's silk micro dresses, embroidered and appliquéd linenware, cashmere, porcelain . . . top

quality in quantity, with government-controlled prices and standards.

THE SHOWROOM, 1203 Central Bldg, Pedder St ☎ 525 7085
Jewellery wholesaler Clare Wadsworth has all the right craftsmen connections in HK. Cognos love her South Sea black pearls and Colombian emerald creations. Special orders as well as off-the-peg pieces.

DAVID'S SHIRTS, M7, Mandarin Oriental, Central ☎ 524 2979; GF, 33 Kimberley Rd, Tsimshatsui ☎ 367 9556
Collaring the Hang Sengers – and anyone else who wants a well-made city shirt. Monogrammed initials on the breast for people who want other people to know who they are.

DORFIT'S, Sands Bldg, 17 Hankow Rd, Tsimshatsui ☎ 721 3938
"For sweaters, angora and cashmere, just the best value and good sizes, which is important when most of the Chinese are so small. Very good texture and colours, top quality. I went with Glynn Christian, and he bought cashmere like there was no tomorrow" – ELISE PASCOE.

FASHIONS OF SEVENTH AVENUE, Kaiser Estate, Block M, Hok Yuen St, Hung Hom, Kowloon ☎ 365 9061; 12A Sing Pao Bldg, 8 Queens Rd, Central ☎ 868 4208
Shipments of Donna Karan clothes arrive here from time to time with the labels cut out. When they do, all hell breaks loose among fashion-conscious bargain-hunters, who know what's what.

FLORINDA-HATTONS, Shop 11–12, Central Bldg, Pedder St ☎ 521 2565
Art Deco knick-knacks, Biedermeier furniture (the real McCoy), 20s and 30s Asprey objets all bought at auction in London and shipped out to Hong Kong by local barrister Ada Wong. *"Satisfying the cravings of seriously moneyed Europhiles"* – CATHERINE GAYNOR.

K S SZE & SONS, M6, Mandarin Oriental, Central ☎ 524 2803
Custom-made jewellery by Mr Sze, done any way you choose. Fine inlaid work, it's all good stuff in the eyes of the HK establishment.

KAI-YIN LO, M1, Mandarin Oriental, Central ☎ 524 8238; The Peninsula
Her name means 'dazzling revelation', her client list is just that – Hanae Mori, British royals, Arianna Stassinopoulos, Natalia Makarova. They choose from unrestrained modern designs made from semi-precious stones, antique bone, carved beads, concocted with characteristic Lo flair.

LEATHER CONCEPT, 11F, Union Hing Yip Bldg, 20 Hing Yip St, Kowloon ☎ 388 9338
Number 1 for factory-outlet leather in HK.

Jackets and separates by in-house designer Hannah Pang line up with the internationals – Calvin Klein and YSL. Hidden away, so ask your concierge to write down the address in Chinese for the taxi driver.

MARGUERITE LEE, Shop 210–211, Gloucester Tower, The Landmark, Central ☎ 525 6565 and branches (The Peninsula, Prince's Bldg)
Sexy stuff – lingerie by Anne Lewin, La Perla et al, and flexy stuff – swimsuits and hosiery.

MAYER SHOES, M16, Mandarin Oriental, Central ☎ 524 3317
Pay through the nose for the best for your feet – handmade, in whatever leather. Bags too, and other *objets de cuir* . . . JEREMIAH TOWER goes: *"Choose your own skins, leathers and dyes."* So does ELISE PASCOE: *"The best shoes are here, the man to see is Simon Tsui. Wonderful handmade shoes in about a week."*

OLIVER'S, Prince's Bldg, Chater Rd, Central ☎ 810 7710
Brill deli, *"the best international delicatessen in town – some of the outlets have a couple of tables and chairs so you can have a glass of wine and something to eat there. My favourite is the one in the Prince's Building. They have the finest wines, the best cheeses, the best olives, Bath Oliver biscuits, things you wouldn't expect to find. It shows what HK's best at – being the centre of the food universe"* – ELISE PASCOE.

ORANGE-ROOM, Shop 66, B1, New World Centre, Tsimshatsui ☎ 368 8051
Top Tsimshatshoe-erie with fab designs made in Japan. Ties and leather goods too.

PARIS SHOES AND LEATHERWEAR, Shop D5/6, BF, Sheraton Hotel, Kowloon ☎ 723 7170
Greased lightning – shoes, bags, briefcases, clothes made to measure in 10 hours – they last longer than that, but not forever.

RONALD ABRAM, Shop 128, Prince's Bldg, Central ☎ 845 2279
Repository for beautiful antique jewellery – Cartier, Van Cleef & Arpels – enter at your peril, resist if you can.

SAM'S TAILOR, Burlington Arcade, 92–94 Nathan Rd, Kowloon ☎ 367 9423
World-famous tailor, offering express value for money. His virtues are extolled by SIR CLEMENT FREUD: *"My favourite tailor is Mr Sam. He makes everything, my nightshirts mostly. I think nightshirts are important. He seems to have 10 or 12 people in the shop who can be swept aside when somebody he recognizes comes in. I have been going there for years and years."* So have Prince Charles, Denis Thatcher and countless other sar-Tories.

S P H DA SILVA, Shop 247, Pacific Place, 88 Queensway, Central ☎ 522 5807
Pearl of the South China Sea – you won't find them better than here. Also jade, diamonds, etc, made to measure and copied to order.

SIBA, GF, 22 Queens Rd, Central ☎ 525 1234
Big diamonds, more carats than Bugs Bunny's ever had.

TAK PAK, Room 301, Pedder Bldg, 12 Pedder St, Central ☎ 521 2547
Knock-out Anne Klein silkies from the makers at knock-down prices. Chantal Thomass too.

THE WORLD OF JOYCE, The Galleria, 9 Queens Rd, Central ☎ 524 6534
As if she didn't have enough shops in HK already (25 to date), local éminence grise of the fashion world, Joyce Ma, has immortalized herself with a 16,000 sq ft 'lifestyle' store. All her existing licensed fashion labels, such as Lacroix, Gaultier and Donna Karan, as well as providing the wherewithal to deck the apartment in similar style. Fornasetti flatware, contemporary ceramics and glassware by European and American designers, sourced out by Ma and therefore destined to become 'names'. Thoroughly user-friendly environment, which includes a health-food café, apothecary and organic florist. *"New Age consumerism at its most outrageous"* – CATHERINE GAYNOR.

HUNGARY

BUDAPEST

—— *Bars and cafés* ——

GERBEAUD, Vörösmarty tér 7 ☎ (1) 118 1311
Lofty coffee house with gilded ceilings, draped velvet curtains, marble-top tables, upholstered cane-back chairs and a clientele that looks distinctly wartime (a mix of Aryan youths, ageing intellectuals and lovers). Toppling ice creams, gooey hot chocolate, fine strudel.

—— *Hotels* ——

BUDAPEST HILTON, Hess András tér 1–3 ☎ (1) 175 1000
Arguably the best hotel in Budapest, up on Castle Hill in the old city of Buda, with views over the Danube. The architecture imaginatively incorporates the old Dominican monastery that once dwelled on this site.

HOTEL GELLERT, Gellért tér 1
☎ (1) 185 2200
If the hotel itself is rather drear, it's worth staying so you can pad down to the barrel-vaulted baths complex below, all a-glitter with mosaics of turquoise, sea green and terracotta. Mineral baths fed by natural hot springs have to be cooled before you can dip a toe in. An instant beautifying experience, where both body and ego are massaged – never will you have seen such lardy ladies in fold upon fold of pinko-white plasticine, or others whose aged flesh drapes like festoon blinds. Spa baths, saunas, steam baths and swimming pool (where everyone wears caps).

—————— *Restaurants* ——————

KELI, Mókus u 22 ☎ (1) 188 6938
Where those in the know go, in old Obuda on the Pest side, for trad Hungarian fodder in warm, friendly, mercifully untouristy surroundings.

KIS BUDA, Frankel Leó u 34
☎ (1) 115 2244
Small, cosy restaurant with a piano and violin to tug at your heartstrings and wooden loose-box seating. Food is hearty – try the huge helping of hot goose liver – but don't expect swift service.

Parker on Fish on Ice

In Iceland, SIR PETER PARKER puts on his parka and goes with the flow along **Laxà ì Kjos**, *"the top salmon river in Iceland. It is filled with glittering suicidal salmon and is so beautiful in the season. Fishing water is just unparalleled, truly Edenic with wild flowers thick on the banks.* **Asgardur** *is only 50 km from Reyjavik and it really is extraordinary, the runs of salmon are not polluted in any way so the area is not disturbed. At the lodge ☎ (91) 667002 itself, you live with the proper sense of dedication, nothing at all fancy, rods are up at 7 – marvellously hard work. The lodge has a stunning chef, who knows every way you can deal with a dead salmon. The salmon are plentiful and strong and those that end up in the kitchen are wonderfully dealt with by this astonishing chef. The views are formidable, the waters are quite dramatic, you could be in staggering roaring turbulence, just bellowing, and in another part be in an absolutely still slow flow – ravishing."*

INDIA

BOMBAY

 THE OBEROI, Nariman Point, 400021
☎ (022) 202 5757
A glossy twin hotel complex – the new atrium tower alongside the older Oberoi – with splendid views out over the Arabian Sea. Tons of polished red granite to tread on (bathe in marble in the Presidential Suite), a lengthy wine list in the **Rôtisserie**, and the smartest happy hour in town at the **Bayview Bar**. Soothing massages are a snip in the health club.

TAJ MAHAL INTER-CONTINENTAL, Apollo Bunder, Colaba, 400039
☎ (022) 202 3366
Enthroned by the gateway of India, the Taj group's standard bearer wins regular Raj-goers' unstinting loyalty. *"Very high quality"* – SERENA FASS. *"They've a number of brand-new, very high-specification hotels, but the Taj still has a bit of the old character about it"* – DAVID GOWER.

DEHLI

HOTEL OBEROI MAIDENS, 7 Sham Nath Marg, Old Delhi 110054 ☎ (011) 252 5464
Haute colonial edifice in Old Delhi, well out of the business centre of town. Wind down in the pool, dry off in the cool gardens, swing a cat in the massive rooms and get some *quiet* shut-eye.

 OBEROI NEW DELHI, Dr Zakir Hussain Marg, New Delhi 110003
☎ (011) 699571
Highest standards all round – service, décor and food . . . MARTIN SKAN is impressed: *"Easily the best there. The Oberoi people are truly professional and are outstanding among their Indian competitors."* Good French food at **La Rochelle**, super Sichuan **Taipan**.

TAJ MAHAL, 1 Mansingh Rd, New Delhi 110011 ☎ (011) 301 6162
Modern hotel with 5 restaurants and new AT&T telephone system. Swimming pool, health club, conference facilities . . . you name it. SERENA FASS gives it her stamp of approval: *"Very high quality."*

TAJ PALACE INTER-CONTINENTAL, 2 Sardar Patel Marg, New Delhi 110021
☎ (011) 301 0404
New business hotel in the heart of the dealdoing district, with all mod cons and 4 restaurants. *"It was good"* – SKYE MACLEOD.

JAIPUR

**JAI MAHAL PALACE HOTEL, Jacob Rd,
Civil Lines, 302006 ☎ (0141) 68381**
Built in 1839, the former palace of the Maharajah Mawai Mansingh is fit for kings occidental as well. Wonderful rooms, good Continental, Indian and Chinese food, barbecues on the lawn.

**HOTEL NARAIN NIWAS, Kanota Bagh,
Narain Singh Rd, 302004 ☎ (0141) 65448**
A bit of a museum piece – imagine Forsteresque linen suits strolling around the unrestored 1881 ochre and pink villa – a delight, if a little ragged at the seams. Decorative paintwork, four-poster beds, dhurries, portraits and weaponry are the genuine 19C articles; the peacocks aren't. Sited 8 miles up the road is a sister hotel, an old fort (18C) with 6 guest rooms, **Kanota Castle.**

🐘 **RAMBAGH PALACE, Bhawani Singh
Rd, 302005 ☎ (0141) 75141**
The best in town. *"It is what it says, an old palace converted into a hotel. Big suites and a fabulous setting"* – DAVID GOWER. Spectacular architecture – scalloped arcades, turrets and verandahs, pukka crowd at the **Polo Bar** (rub shoulders with the local Maharajahs). *"Peacocks on the lawn and wicker chairs on the terrace; drinks in the Polo Bar and curries in the town hall-sized dining room; absurdly cheap tariff and family retainer-style service. Star suite is the Princess with its own fountain and garden"* – SUSAN KUROSAWA.

**SAMOD PALACE HOTEL, Samod
☎ (0141) 42407**
Far away from the hubbub of Jaipur, some hour's drive north of the city, spin back in time to the palace of your dreams. *"Not for comfort but for romance – it is the most romantic place you could ever stay, where they filmed part of* The Far Pavilions. *It is so genuine still. They put on firework displays and you go for picnics on camels. It would be wonderful to have the honeymoon suite"* – SERENA FASS.

· REST OF ·

INDIA

**FORT AGUADA BEACH RESORT,
Sinquerim, Bardez 403515, Goa
☎ (0832) 7501; TAJ HOLIDAY VILLAGE
☎ (0832) 7515**
Where Goa-goers wind up when they've gone beyond shoestring hippydom. Impressive group of luxy villas huddled together on lush, terraced gardens overlooking the sea and miles of beach. Cottages stagger up the hill towards the **Aguada Hermitage**, an exclusive self-contained villa complex. Younger folk settle at the **Taj Holiday Village.**

**KIPLING CAMP, c/o Madhya Pradesh
State Tourism Development
Commission, Gangotri, TT Nagar, Bhopal
☎ (0755) 554339**
Tiger-spotting camp in Kanha National Park, run by Bob Wright of The Tollygunge Club. DAVID GOWER goes for the excitement: *"Kanha is one of these fabulous tiger reserves where you drive around in Land-Rovers to start with and then they send the trackers out, and if they find a tiger that is resting, they transfer you on to elephant back and you can get almost as close as you like. Unbelievable."* Look out for writer/adventurer Mark Shand's companion, Tara, the elephant that carried him across India (now enjoying a well-earned rest).

**MUGHAL SHERATON, Fatehabad Rd,
Agra 282001 ☎ (0562) 64701**
Top stop for the Taj Mahal and a favourite of SERENA FASS: *"It remains very high quality, a fabulous hotel with a lovely view of the Taj Mahal."* Weird and wonderful fruits and flowers in the rooms, good service throughout. Cool pool as well. Good base for forays to Fatehpur Sikri and the Bharatpur bird sanctuary.

**SHIVNIWAS PALACE, Udaipur 313001
☎ (0294) 28239**
Facing the Lake Palace, this is SERENA FASS'S choice: *"There you are, in the previous quarters of the late Maharajah, looking out on to the island and the mountains the other side. Absolutely stunning room with a view from dawn until sunset, just wonderful."* Extraordinary opulence inside – Belgian cut-glass armchairs and tables, carved ivory doors, glass inlay scenes of wildlife, a carved marble oval swimming pool. The most over-the-top suite is the Imperial, complete with circular bedroom, lounge and balcony for private dining.

**THE TOLLYGUNGE CLUB, Club House,
120 DP Sasmal Rd, Calcutta
☎ (033) 410616**
Old-style sporting, winding-down kind of club. *"For the nostalgia of the Raj. Absolutely lovely"* – SERENA FASS. DAVID GOWER thinks of it *"like a haven of green grass and almost clean air in among the grime of Calcutta. A golf course, horse riding. It's a lovely spot in Calcutta."*

**UMAID GHAWAN PALACE, Jodhpur
342006 ☎ (0291) 22316**
Labyrinthine palace, built between 1929 and 1942 by 3,000 artisans (it is very impressive). Dead luxurious too with indoor pool, 3 restaurants, and very few vacancies. Ergo book ahead.

Tours

**COX & KINGS, 404 Deepali, 92 Nehru
Place, New Delhi 110019 ☎ (011) 332 0067**
Old-timers who know what they're doing – they

kept the British Army shipshape in the Raj, so they'll keep you in good shape too. Tours or tailor-made itineraries.

KASHMIR HIMALAYAN EXPEDITIONS, Boulevard Shopping Complex, Dal Gate, PO Box 168, Srinagar 190001 ☎ (0194) 78698; 17 Indian Oil Building, Janpath, New Delhi ☎ (011) 332 3829
Adventurous treks in Ladakh, India and Nepal, rafting/elephant back and foot treks in the Himalayas, and camel safaris in Rajasthan.

TIGER TOPS MOUNTAIN TRAVEL, 1/1 Rani Jhansi Rd, New Delhi 110055 ☎ (011) 523057
Real high life – splendid Himalayan treks to mountain camps in Kashmir, Ladakh and Tibet, with the best Sherpas and cooks. Best tiger-spotting at Badhavgarh Jungle camp, central India, and the Kabini River Lodge in Karnataka. See also Nepal.

INDONESIA

BALI

🐚 **AMANDARI, PO Box 33, Kedewatan, Ubud ☎ (361) 95333**
A re-created Balinese village, luxurious beyond the dreams of most Balinese villagers. 27 walled garden pavilions overlook rice paddies 250 ft above the Ayung River gorge. *"Pretty fabulous, it really is out of this world. You sit in this pool which has no lip on it and it looks like you are sitting in the middle of a rice field"* – KEN HOM. Sliding window walls, marble floors and palm-thatched roofs lend coolness to the tropical heat. ROBIN LEACH agrees with the English translation: place of peace.

BALI OBEROI, Legian Beach, PO Box 351, Denpasar ☎ (0361) 51061
Lush tropical gardens splashed with coloured birds and dotted with thatched lanai cottages. *"A villa resort on the beach and you have your own lotus ponds and can sit out and there are statues of gods all over the place – gorgeous. Wonderfully designed gardens"* – CAROL WRIGHT. Presidential suites have their own pool.

KUPU KUPU BARONG, PO Box 7, Kedewatan, Ubud ☎ (0361) 35663
Luxurious hideaway built into the side of a canyon in the relative cool of Ubud. Separate, well-equipped bungalows, each with a very private, open-air bathroom.

TANDJUNG SARI, PO Box 25, Denpasar ☎ (0361) 88441
Tranquil family-run retreat on Sanur beach.

Into the Heart of Irian Jaya

🐚

You might not find a guide to take you and you need a police permit to allow you to stray from the tourist track but Irian Jaya, the western (Indonesian) half of the island of New Guinea, is one of the world's last wildernesses. *"The greatest journey is undoubtedly a walk through the wilds of Irian Jaya, the most remote, unexplored, tropical place on earth. No beds, no loos, no power, no nothing. We stayed in tents or slept in grass-roofed huts on mud floors, bathed in the rivers and walked. In the Baliem Valley, the remote villages don't even have the wheel. Truly a place where tourists never go. In one village, Manda, the villagers use stone axes and bamboo knives – they have no metal tools. One flies into Wanena then walks . . . no roads!"* – CAROL WRIGHT.

Airy thatched bungalows in palmy gardens appeal to Anaïs Nin and SHARYN STORRIER-LYNEHAM: *"The resort blends harmoniously with its surrounds. I like hotels that pick up on the mood of their environment."* Forward-thinking management supports local artisans and traditional dance – guests reap the benefits.

JAKARTA

HYATT ARYADUTA, Jalan Prapatan 44–48 ☎ (021) 376008
Expensively fitted-out new hotel containing only suites, plus the all-pampering Regency Club hotel-within-a-hotel.

JAKARTA HILTON INTERNATIONAL, Jalan Gatot Subroto, PO Box 3315 ☎ (021) 583051
Standard high-rise 70s block without, spacious and well designed within. The vast lobby's impressive ceiling replicates the Sultan of Jogjakarta's palace and the hotel's promotion of Indonesian handicrafts has earned high praise from President Suharto, no less. A plethora of bars, restaurants, tennis courts, pools, etc.

MANDARIN ORIENTAL, Jalan M H Thamrin, PO Box 3392 ☎ (021) 321307
In Jakarta's money belt, with the Mandarin's

customary insistence on immaculate service. Enormous suites, all carved teak and batik, and top-of-the-range sports facilities.

LOMBOK

SENGGIGI BEACH HOTEL, PO Box 2, Madaram ☎ (036) 423430
On the island neighbour of Bali (tipped by LORD LICHFIELD as *"the next Bali – as beautiful but far less spoilt"*). *"It's owned by Garuda and is really super. It's just modest bungalows with outdoor dining on your verandah and traditional Indonesian doorways and swimming pool. You have room service and because it's so nice and enclosed you don't feel like you're at a hotel"* – CAROL WRIGHT.

IRELAND

DUBLIN

—— Art and museums ——

NATIONAL GALLERY OF IRELAND, Merrion Square W ☎ (01) 615133
A splendid collection, balancing European masters and turn-of-the-century Irish painters. Rubens, Rembrandt, Poussin and Gainsborough hang alongside Jack B Yeats (WB's brother), Walter Osborne and William Leach. Also sculp-

ture, furniture and a strong community spirit – workshops, drawing courses and a free picture clinic. Take lunch at the excellent **Fitzers**.

—— Hotels ——

SHELBOURNE HOTEL, 27 St Stephen's Green ☎ (01) 766471
Very proper old-fashioned hotel with proper old-fashioned service. *"Still the place to stay in Dublin. Some of the rooms are right on St Stephen's Green – it's important to ask for a quiet room. A very fine old hotel"* – JULIAN LLOYD WEBBER.

—— Restaurants ——

🦐 THE COMMONS RESTAURANT, 85-86 St Stephen's Green ☎ (01) 780530
A rave new eatery in the basement of the restored Georgian treasure, Newman House. *"All the rage – and with reason. Not only is the location superb, the interior stunning and the sheltered terrace elegant, but it backs on to a hidden 5-acre garden, the food is imaginative and well cooked, service is excellent and it's unbelievably good value. Of course it's a hit"* – GEORGINA CAMPBELL. Dig into such delights as duck liver parfait with raspberry dressing, roast partridge with fig and honey sauce and warm fruit tartlette with orange sabayon. Extensive wine list accompanied by useful notes.

KING SITRIC, East Pier, Howth ☎ (01) 325235
Owner-chef Aidan MacManus has the distinction of running the longest-established fish restaurant in Dublin (it's just come of age at 21). *"It's better than ever. He keeps all the old favourites*

 **Buzzz** Write on: Based in 2 Georgian buildings, the **Dublin Writers Museum**, 18 Parnell Square, Dublin ☎ (01) 722077, traces the written word in Ireland from the 8C Book of Kells, via Swift, Wilde, Yeats, Shaw, O'Casey and Joyce, to the present day. Contemporary scribblers meet and work next door at No 19 in the **Irish Writers' Centre 🦐** ...... Pretty MOMA: The stunningly restored Royal Hospital, Kilmainham, houses the new **Irish Museum of Modern Art**, a showcase for the 20C's most influential artists 🦐 ...... King of the castle: In the wake of the K & Q of Denmark, Prince Rainier and Princess Grace and a host of Hollywood royals, take up your throne at **Luttrellstown Castle**, Clonsilla, Co Dublin ☎ (01) 213237, a lavish pile available for private rental only, with 14 bedrooms and a 560-acre estate 🦐 ...... Country estate 2: Shore up at 17C **Sheen Falls Lodge**, Kenmare, Co Kerry ☎ (064) 41386, amid lawns, woodland walks and semi-tropical gardens; spy waterfalls from **La Cascade** restaurant, go salmon fishing or riding, or wind down at the fitness centre 🦐 ...... International musos unite under Irish roofs as part of the June festival of **GPA Music in Great Irish Houses**, 14 Ashfield Rd, Ranelagh, Dublin ☎ (01) 962021 – smart concerts in such settings as Castletown House .... 🦐

on for faithful locals, but menus change daily with availability of fresh fish from the harbour. I love it" – GEORGINA CAMPBELL. Hook some smoked Irish salmon, Howth crab, or poached fish quenelles with lobster sauce.

OISINS IRISH RESTAURANT, 31 Upper Camden St ☎ (01) 753433

For traditional Irish food, cooked in an upscale manner and artfully presented. Dinner only, with a pricy set menu that offers "a wide range of dishes which are true to their origins but have a lightness of touch that is utterly modern" – GEORGINA CAMPBELL.

🍴 PATRICK GUILBAUD, 46 St James's Place, Lower Baggot St ☎ (01) 764192

Expense-account Dublin diner for the big boys of the banking biz. French to the letter, with a light, modern rendering of classics: Irish salmon baked under a potato pancake, ravioli filled with veal sweetbreads, casserole of black sole and prawns with an aromatic sauce. "A very today version of a French menu" – BARBARA KAFKA. "Simply the best for a decade, this star-spangled French restaurant has provided a benchmark for all others and is still going from strength to strength" – GEORGINA CAMPBELL.

🍴 THE WINE EPERGNE, 147 Upper Rathmines Rd ☎ (01) 962348

Tucked in an old Victorian shop, complete with mismatched antique furniture and family portraits, this one is "small and charming. Owner-chef Kevin Thornton and his wife Muriel are the young couple to watch in Dublin. Kevin [ex-Bocuse and Adare Manor] cooks with verve, dedication and rare finesse. But try to resist his irresistible breads or the day will be lost" – GEORGINA CAMPBELL. Ah yes, those breads . . . pistachio, walnut, olive oil, basil, fennel, brioche, pine kernel, rye or plain ol' white. Seasonal fare – loin of hare glazed with apple jelly and balsamic vinaigrette; roast mallard glazed with honey and pistachio with juniper and sloe sauce.

· REST OF ·

IRELAND

—— Hotels ——

ADARE MANOR, Adare, Co Limerick ☎ (061) 396566

Former pile of the Earls of Dunraven, a vast Gothic mansion with over 50 carved fireplaces and almost 900 acres of rolling green. "A very unusual building on a river, dating back to the 17C. Panelled ceilings, paintings . . . definitely worth a visit" – TERRY HOLMES. Time it for the fab July festival, which warms the hearts of classical music-lovers and socialites alike.

ARBUTUS LODGE HOTEL, Montenotte, Cork ☎ (021) 501237

Solid 18C house, once home to the Mayor of Cork, now to a handful of guests and a strong collection of modern Irish art. Wonderful terraced gardens but the restaurant's the thing, under Michael and Declan Ryan (Alain Chapel- and Troisgros-trained respectively). Traditional Irish dishes (bacon and cabbage or drisheen – blood sausage) are deftly reworked and matched, according to JOHN BOWMAN, "by French dishes and one of the best cellars in Ireland or Britain, not least for its quality and value in its choice of house wines". "You can eat informally out of doors or extremely well indoors, and they have a superb wine list" – BARBARA KAFKA.

ASSOLAS COUNTRY HOUSE, Kanturk, Co Cork ☎ (029) 50015

Charming riverside 17C manor house in beautiful gardens. 9 bedrooms only give fireside drinks or croquet a house-party air. The short menu might offer pigeon breast on braised cabbage and baked brill with balsamic vinegar.

🍴 BALLYMALOE HOUSE, Shanagarry, Co Cork ☎ (021) 652531

The family Allen's retreat, 2 miles from the coast, where hotel and foodie folk pick up their spirits and some pointers on how it's done. "It represents all the things I want in a hotel. It has such a sympathetic air and the caring of such a big family running it so well for so long. The food is marvellous . . . going from strength to strength" – HILARY RUBINSTEIN. BARBARA KAFKA abandons caution: "If you hear there's a buffet, don't hold back. It's divine." JOHN TOVEY waxes lyrical: "The best place in the whole of Ireland because it is run by all the family and the word that comes out every minute of every day is 'love'." Cookery courses are run by daughter-in-law Darina ☎ (021) 646785, with help from visiting chefs such as MADHUR JAFFREY: "I love it and I love the Allens."

BANTRY HOUSE, Bantry, Co Cork ☎ (027) 50047

Stay in one of 8 pretty bedrooms in the B&B wing of this splendid 18C mansion – the rest of the house, complete with the 2nd Earl of Bantry's fine collection of art and furniture, is a showpiece. Wonderful views over gardens to Bantry Bay, breakfasts set you up for the day.

MARLFIELD HOUSE, Gorey, Co Wexford ☎ (055) 21124

Charming Regency house, former dower house of the Earls of Courtown. "The most fabulous place to stay in the country, glorious décor, good art and some of the rooms are spectacularly big. There's a restaurant in a conservatory with French food" – BARBARA KAFKA.

NEWPORT HOUSE, Newport, Co Mayo ☎ (098) 41222

A fisherman's paradise. One of Ireland's most

beautiful country-house hotels, with immaculate interiors and a dining room that dishes up fish, fruit and veg from the estate.

🏛 PARK HOTEL KENMARE, Kenmare, Co Kerry ☎ (064) 41200

Country hotel with cracking views over Kenmare Bay, plenty of spirit, and an equal strength in arts visual and gastronomic. *"Owned and run by Francis Brennan. He loves his place, it is full of antiques that he has collected over the years. Fishing and golf nearby. Seafood's the speciality"* – TERRY HOLMES.

> **❝***Ireland is one of the great garden-viewing places of the world. Around Cork there are wonderful places . . . the forests are conservatories – people naturalize trees in the great spirit of the 19C* ❞**
>
> 🖋 BARBARA KAFKA

──── *Music* ────

GUINNESS JAZZ FESTIVAL, Cork. Tickets: Cork Opera House, Emmet Place, Cork ☎ (021) 270022

Jumping Oct festival touched by pure genius. For 3 days Cork bobs in a sea of over 600 musos and up to 100,000 jazz fiends. Venues range from pubs to the big names at the Opera House (Dave Brubeck, Dizzy Gillespie, BB King in recent years), making it one of Europe's biggest. It's music to GEORGE MELLY's ears.

WEXFORD FESTIVAL OPERA, Theatre Royal, High St, Wexford ☎ (053) 22240

Late Oct festival with a mission: to revive rare or neglected operas and put them in the world's ears – *L'Assedio di Calais* had critics wondering where it had been all their lives. A loyal following Europe-wide packs out the 550-seat theatre, the spill-over takes over Wexford for fringe events and recitals.

──── *Restaurants* ────

DRIMCONG HOUSE, Moycullen, Co Galway ☎ (091) 85115

17C estate house in 25 acres of lake, lawn and woodland. Chef Gerry Galvin is a strong supporter of local produce – he was a pioneer in the now ubiquitous all-Irish cheese board. *"A very good restaurant. All local ingredients like Galway fish and Connemara lamb; they grow their own herbs and vegetables"* – BARBARA KAFKA. Own chutneys and breads too.

ITALY

AMALFI COAST

──── *Hotels* ────

GRAND HOTEL QUISISANA, Via Camerelle 2, 80073 Capri ☎ (081) 837 0788

An imposing neo-classical sprawl in central Capri. Airy, tiled rooms with colonial accents, opening on to lovely gardens: *"Very beautiful"* – JOAN BURSTEIN. *"It's my home,"* says an enchanted PRINCESS PUCCI SALAMEH, *"the rooms are very big and I think it's the only hotel in Capri that has suites with 2 bathrooms. The buffet by the pool is lovely and the gardens are so well cared for."*

HOTEL PALUMBO, Via S Giovanni del Toro 28, 84010 Ravello ☎ (089) 857244

Clinging to the mountainside over the Gulf of Salerno, a charming hotchpotch of 12C, 17C and modern styles, Moorish and Med. The vine-covered terrace has sheltered the heads of VIPs from Wagner onwards, while the Swiss-Italian management results in some extraordinarily fine cooking.

🏛 SAN PIETRO, Via Laurito 2, 84017 Positano ☎ (089) 875455

Wildly glamorous resort hotel spilling down a cliff face to a tiny private beach. Cantilevered terraces, bougainvillaea-clad bars, a restaurant and spacious guest rooms where stay the world's romantics and ED VICTOR: *"Fabulous. It's carved out of a sheer cliff, so from every room you are looking out . . . a wonderful setting. They'll send a boat from the hotel – you'll be picked up on the rocks – to Capri. A very good restaurant."*

🏛 LE SIRENUSE, Via C Colombo 30, 84017 Positano ☎ (089) 875066

Low-key and old-fashioned with a charm unmatched by the flashier Amalfiites. Long-standing devoted guests such as GILES SHEPARD (*"I go every year – a marvellous small hotel. The staff has been there for years"*) and DOTT ROSA MARIA LETTS: *"A jewel, one of the greatest experiences. Positano has the most beautiful sea situation in the world, a tiny village with no cars. Very beautiful rooms, but more than that it is the atmosphere with the outside – you live on your terrace high above the village and there is this complete marriage between nature and the building – which is chic but not over-chic, old but beautifully kept up. It exudes elegance and mystery."*

FLORENCE

—— *Art and museums* ——

🏛 **GALLERIA DEGLI UFFIZI, Loggiato degli Uffizi 6, 50122 ☎ (055) 215721**
The richest collection in the world of Florentine and Sienese art from the 13C to the Renaissance, housed in Vasari's grand palazzo. The most oft-reproduced works of art revealed in their true colours – the wonders of Giotto, Fra Angelico, Lippi, Bellini, Mantegna, Raphael et al. *"The most important art gallery in the world"* states BRIAN SEWELL, *"because it is the great holding of Renaissance painting and also because it makes the connection between Florentine and Netherlands painting. If you want to learn about the Italian Renaissance you have to go to the Uffizi."* And for DOTT ROSA MARIA LETTS: *"It's the one I get the greatest satisfaction from because here are the great masters."* Dodge crowds of art students and tourists to glimpse Titian's glowing *Venus of Urbino*, Botticelli's *Birth of Venus* and *Primavera*, Leonardo's unfinished *Adoration of the Magi*, Caravaggio's *Bacchus* . . .

MUSEO ARCHEOLOGICO, Via del Colonna 36, 50121 ☎ (055) 215721
Undusty collection of antiquities from Egypt, Greek, Rome and Etruria. Must-sees include the Etruscan bronze *Chimera* and a treasure trove of Medici jewellery, revealed after 70 years' hiding.

MUSEO DEL BARGELLO, Palazzo Pitti, Via del Proconsolo 4, 50122 ☎ (055) 210801
Medieval palace given over to the celebration of sculpture and arts and crafts – works by Michelangelo, Donatello, Verocchio, Cellini, and Giambologna.

PALAZZO PITTI, Piazza dei Pitti ☎ (055) 213440
Familiar architectural landmark, dating from 1460, housing 4 museums, including the Royal Apartments and Silver Museum (fine and dec arts), Modern Art Gallery (19C–20C Tuscan art)

and the fabulously gaudy Palatine Gallery with its wonderful collection of Titian portraits, Rubens, Raphael and Italian Mannerists.

—— *Bars and cafés* ——

DONEY'S, Piazza Strozzi 18r, 50123 ☎ (055) 239 8206
Shoppers from the next-door Emporio rest their feet and crane their necks at this style-conscious, Armani-owned café. Chic cioccolata and cappuccino with clout.

GIACOSA, Via Tornabuoni 83, 50123 ☎ (055) 239 6226
Café-bar *con brio* attracting a highly groomed crowd to sample its (invented on the premises) Negroni and marvellous chocolate and pastry confections.

RIVOIRE, Via Vacchereccia 4r, 50123 ☎ (055) 214412
Grandly old-fashioned café on the edge of the perfectly proportioned Piazza della Signoria. Delicious pastries, pralines and chocolates.

—— *Clubs* ——

CENTRAL PARK/CAPITALE, Via del Fosso Macinato 2, Piazzale delle Cascine, 50100 ☎ (055) 7733 2723
In summer it's central, in winter it's capital; year-round it's packed with a crowd of the best-dressed young things in town. Different, progressive music styles each night.

🏛 **TENAX, Via Pretese 47, 50126 ☎ (055) 373050**
Tenaxiously hangs onto its top position as the club with the highest *cool* quotient. A vast (8,600 sq ft) and spartanly-converted warehouse with some of the most extreme Euro house sounds. Open Thurs to Sat.

VILLA KAZAR, Via della Vigna Vecchia 21r, 50123 ☎ (055) 293006
When relentless raving begins to pall, this is the place to go. *"It's really nice, an older crowd – yuppies of 25 to 40. It's got a disco on one level with glass that separates it from the piano bar*

🧥 **Buzzz** Capricious Capri: **La Capannina**, Via Le Botteghe 14 ☎ (081) 837 0732, (the little hut) is currently *the* one to nosh at 🧥 . . . . . . Slide your feet into fabulous handmade sandals and mocassins at **Canfora**, Via Camerelle 3 ☎ (081) 837 0487 🧥 . . . . . . Down the road, pick up amusing baubles from Lina and Federico at **La Campanina** (the little bell), where Onassis made the till chime for Jackie 🧥 . . . . . . More goodies for PRINCESS PUCCI SALAMEH: **Marcello Rubinacci**, Via Camerelle 9 ☎ (081) 837 7295, *"is best for cashmere sweaters and pants; I love the **Gelsomino di Capri** perfume from the Carthusian monks"*. . . . . 🧥

so you can have a quiet drink and conversation"
– SANDY WEYLAND.

Hotels

HOTEL BRUNELLESCHI, Piazza S Elisabetta 2, 50123 ☎ (055) 562068
Not the most glamorous of hotels but the offbeat charm of entering through a 9C church door and climbing to your room in a 6C tower is fair compensation.

🏊 HOTEL HELVETIA & BRISTOL, Via dei Pescioni 2, 50123 ☎ (055) 287814
Renovated to the nth degree (superb antiques, Carrara marble bathrooms with Jacuzzis), the 19C grandee has recovered the splendour that has attracted travellers from Stravinsky to the Danish Royal family. **The Bristol** matches set Tuscan menus with well-chosen wine.

┌─────────────────────────────────────┐

Frescobaldi's Firenze
🏊

MARCHESA BONA FRESCOBALDI searches alto and basso for the finest food in Florence: "**La Cantinetta di Rigagna**, *Badia a Passignano* ☎ (055) 854 4439, *where the Queen of Holland is a faithful client, lost in the beautiful hills near Florence with very simple tables under the trees*; **Trattoria La Baracchina**, *Via Scopetti S Andrea di Percussina* ☎ (055) 822 9600, *in the middle of the woods very close to Florence – its speciality is boiled meats.* **Ristorante Taverna del Bronzino**, *Via delle Ruote 25/27r* ☎ (055) 495220, *serves very good traditional Italian cuisine."*

└─────────────────────────────────────┘

HOTEL REGENCY, Piazza M D'Azeglio 3, 50121 ☎ (055) 245247
More a grand *casa* than an *albergo*, this conversion of two 19C villas in a peaceful residential square finds favour with those who bid for the understated luxury of overstuffed sofas, a warm, cosy library, and good regional Italian fodder at the **Relais le Jardin**.

LOGGIATO DEI SERVITI, Piazza SS Annunziata 3, 50122 ☎ (055) 239 8280
Charming small hotel behind a historic loggia opposite its twin, Brunelleschi's Ospedale degli Innocenti. Vaulted ceilings rise over terracotta floors and the prevailing atmosphere is of quiet calm. "*A very discreet hotel; there aren't a million faxes you can use for business, it is just charming and restful and the people are gorgeous. I love it there"* – STEPHEN JONES.

PENSIONE QUISISANA E PONTE VECCHIO, Lungarno Archibusiere 4, 50122 ☎ (055) 216692
The definitive room with a view (the set for the film as well), over the Arno to the red-tiled roofs and spires of Florence. Comfortable mahogany-furnished rooms and a roof terrace for prima colazione (breakfast).

🏊 VILLA SAN MICHELE, Via di Doccia, 50014 Fiesole ☎ (055) 59451
Fabulously faded ancient monastery whose façade and loggia are attributed to Michelangelo. Converted cells are far from monastic: all have Jacuzzis and all gaze either inwards on a charming courtyard or out across a sea of olive and cypress to Florence (some 15 minutes away). The stuff of romantic legends: Brigitte Bardot chose the villa for a honeymoon. LISA BARNARD loves it.

Restaurants

CANTINETTA ANTINORI, Piazza Antinori 3, 50123 ☎ (055) 292234
A hideaway wine bar on the ground floor of a Renaissance palace. Sample the Antinori family's own wine from their well-stocked cellar and mop it up with bread and sausage or a full 3-courser.

COCO LEZZONE, Via Parioncino 26r, 50123 ☎ (055) 287178
Self-consciously basic hole-in-the-wall trat just off Via Tornabuoni's style row. Fashion folk and die-hard shoppers love it for trad Tuscan pappa al pomodoro and bistecca fiorentina.

ENOTECA PINCHIORRI, Via Ghibellina 87, 50122 ☎ (055) 242757
The enoteca (wine merchant) has long gone but the cellar is still vast – as is the bill at this famous and smooth-operating restaurant. Tuscan, nouvelle and seafood menus, but take PAUL HENDERSON's advice and "*order the Tuscan menu, with a different wine by the glass with each course".*

IL CIBREO, Via dei Macci 118r, 50100 ☎ (055) 234 1100
Highly rated ristorante, long on Tuscan roast meats and vegetables, with a strict no-pasta ruling. Formal service and "*just extraordinary food; you think 'my God, how can they make simple things taste so delicious, where am I going wrong?'* " – STEPHEN JONES. **Cibrèo Trattoria** round the corner at Piazza Ghiberti 35 has similar nosh for less dosh and high table turnover.

OMERO, Via Pian dei Giullari 11r, 50100 ☎ (055) 220053
True Florence, a proper Tuscan trat, "*with a beautiful view of the city. You go through a grocery store to get in, it's a real family scene*

and they ladle olive oil out of a big terracotta jar" – FAITH WILLINGER.

SOR PAOLO, Via Cassia 40, 50100 ☎ (055) 828402
In a former casa colonica (farmhouse) on the outskirts of Florence, a charming restaurant in beautiful surroundings. Home cooking served on old sewing-machine tables – al fresco in summer.

TRATTORIA RUGGIERO, Via Senese 89r, 50100 ☎ (055) 220542
Where all the nobles hang out on a Sunday lunch, slumming at Ruggiero. *"Quintessential, leisurely and inexpensive with traditional Tuscan cuisine"* – FAITH WILLINGER.

──────── *Shopping* ────────

Via Tornabuoni is the smartest street, replete with Gucci, Valentino, Fendi, Armani, Versace, Ferragamo and the other classics. The more avant-garde shops live on tinier medieval streets – **Via Porta Rossa, Via della Vigna Nuova, Via Roma, Via Condotta**. **Via Maggio** is tops for antiques shops, while the daily market at **Santa Croce** yields the odd bargain. **Mercato delle Cascine** near Ponte della Vittoria (Tues mornings) is the best for food, ceramics, shoes and clothes both new and second-hand.

BELTRAMI, Via Tornabuoni 48r, 50123 ☎ (055) 287779
For all the timeless bits and pieces that make up the immaculate Florentine woman. Cashmere, of course, silk scarves, perfect separates and leather shoes, *certo*. Also at Via Calzaiuoli 31r and 44r.

CELLERINI, Via del Sole 37r, 50123 ☎ (055) 282533
Accessorize to kill. Hand-stitched, strongly yet delicately worked bags, belts, luggage and shoes for donna and uomo.

COLE-HAHN, Via della Vigna Nuova 77r, 50134 ☎ (055) 499940
Hard to beat for outsize feet. No 1 for US basketball players, Cole-Hahn will make shoes to order and airmail them anywhere in the world. Also the best, softest moccasins for women.

EMILIO PUCCI, Via de' Pucci 6, 50122 ☎ (055) 283061
Psychedelic revival? For Pucci, it never went away. Behind the fab façade of the Pucci Palace, Il Marchese shows no signs of tiring of the bold swirls that stamp the family's signature on the ties, dresses and scarves of the privileged.

FARAONE-SETTEPASSI, Via Tornabuoni 25r, 50123 ☎ (055) 215506
Long-time bejewellers of Florentine and other nobility. Expertly crafted gems, antique-styled silver and modern gold.

FARMACIA DI SANTA MARIA NOVELLA, Via del Escala 16, 50123 ☎ (055) 216276
Beyond a drug store, with *"perfumes, essences, all different kinds of soap and talcum powders. When you walk in you get an immediate scent of pot pourri and essences. It's been here for hundreds of years. The frescos on the ceiling are really amusing – a fabulous experience with crazy stuff like digestive liqueurs"* – FAITH WILLINGER. JEREMIAH TOWER sings praises of their acqua di rose.

GARBO, Borgo Ognissanti 2r, 50123 ☎ (055) 295338
Infinitely fragile, hand-worked silk, linen and lace foundation wear for women, embroidered and stitched on the premises. The same old-fashioned care goes into the making of wedding and christening gowns and kitchen linen too.

🕵 **Buzz** Florence's hotels are reviving their flagging reputation: **Hotel Berchielli** ☎ (055) 264061 has just been refitted and looks as good as its river view 🕵 ...... At the **Villa la Massa,** Via la Massa 6, Localita Candeli ☎ (055) 630051, BIJAN finds: *"I am able to enjoy the atmosphere of this ancient culture"* 🕵 ...... Restaurants speak to him in a similar tongue: a favourite is **Trattoria Le Tre Panche**, Via Pucinotti 32 ☎ (055) 583724, for *"primitive chic"* 🕵 ...... When STEPHEN BAYLEY's a local, his local's **Sostana**, 25r Via Porcellana ☎ (055) 212691, for *"Tuscan cooking, bread and tomato soup and Tuscan sausage"* 🕵 ...... YAN-KIT SO's is **La Baraonda**, Via Ghibellina ☎ (055) 660034, *"because every course was to the point – pasta, grilled chicken with rosemary, very thin apple tart. He came out to explain every single course with a beaming smile, so we were very taken with it"* 🕵 ...... MARCHESA DI SAN GIULIANO FERRAGAMO hotfoots it to **Vera Pizzicheria**, Piazza Frescobaldi 3r ☎ (055) 215415, to buy *"handmade ravioli, filled with mushrooms, salmon, cheese"* .. 🕵

LUISA VIA ROMA, Via Roma 19-21r, 50100 ☎ (055) 217826
The one-stop shop where fashionable Firenze dresses head to toe in the darlings of design. Clothes and shoes by Sybilla, Kamali, Kenzo, Gigli, Dolce & Gabbana, Matsuda, Byblos, Montana, you name it. At **Luisa Il Corso**, Via del Corso 56, they sell their own similarly forward-thinking designs.

MATUCCI, Via del Corso 46 (women) and 71 (men), 50100 ☎ (055) 212018
The total *rus in urbe* clothes-as-philosophy. Jodhpurs for Vespas and sheepskin for city wolves . . . Also **Beba Matucci** at No 36, for more of her designs.

RASPINI, Via Tornabuoni 25, 50122 ☎ (055) 213812; and branches
Insider Florentines come here for *"pretty good knock-offs of Prada, less expensive, and also top-line names like Kenzo. Good clothes and shoes"* – SANDY WEYLAND.

SALVATORE FERRAGAMO, Via Tornabuoni 12-16r, 50100 ☎ (055) 292123
The Ferragamo flag continues to fly under Salvatore's bizwise bambini and over this medieval palazzo. The world's best-fitting shoe has its slender-footed devotees worldwide: one pair of the low-heeled flat-buckled court shoes is never enough. Atop the shoe, sleek ensembles.

MILAN

—— Art and museums ——

CASTELLO SFORZESCO, Piazza Castello 1, 20121 ☎ (02) 870926
Enormous fairy-tale fortress containing the Municipal Museum of Art. Alongside the collection of Lombard oils, sculpture and decorative arts is Michelangelo's last work, the unfinished *Rondanini Pietà*. Also works by Lippi, Mantegna, Bellini and the Venetians.

MUSEO POLDI PEZZOLI, Via Manzoni, 20121 ☎ (02) 794889
Charming museum in a 19C villa with a small but perfectly formed collection of Renaissance masters – Piero della Francesca, Bellini, the Lombard and Venetian schools, plus antique watches and clocks and armoury.

🐾 PINACOTECA DI BRERA, Via Brera 28, 20121 ☎ (02) 8646 1924
Milan's major picture gallery and one of Italy's finest. Paintings up to the 20C but those of the Renaissance are the drawcard, among them Mantegna's famously moving *Dead Christ*. Strong support given by Raphael, Lotto, Piero della Francesca, Bellini and Tintoretto.

—— Bars and cafés ——

IL CIGNO NERO, Via della Spiga 33, 20123 ☎ (02) 7602 2620
The only bar on the street and, happily, *"the perfect place for a fuel stop during a hectic round of shopping"* – LOGAN BENTLEY. Lovely inlaid wood bar and wall panelling, tiny tables with delicate lace tablecloths, fresh flowers and soft lighting.

—— Clubs ——

NEPENTHA, Piazza Armando Diaz 1, 20123 ☎ (02) 8646 4808
Smart, members-only dinner and dancing club with unthreatening food (Milanese plus caviare and smoked salmon), and Top 40s-style music. *"The classic, institutional, the place that people who go once a year always pick"* -ALESSANDRO MODENESE.

PLASTIC, Viale Umbria 120, 20135 ☎ (02) 733996
As slick and black as PVC; it only gets into gear *very* late. *"A fun mix of young preppy types who go for excitement from the avant-garde music and the dark people who hang out there . . . a mixed bag"* – ALESSANDRO MODENESE.

—— Fashion designers ——

ALBERTA FERRETTI, Via Montenapolene 14, 20121 ☎ (02) 7600 4494
A woman who knows what women wants. Although she's been designing for years, she's suddenly hit the mark with her subtly seductive, feminine clothes. Cleverly cut, body-skimming dresses and separates that never overpower the wearer.

BYBLOS, Via Senato 35, 20121 ☎ (02) 702959
Youthful, exuberant clothes for men and women from ever-more-successful design partners Alan Cleaver and Keith Varty. Rich colours, extravagant fabrics and simple but effective embroidery transform basic mix 'n' match separates into covetable one-offs: *"Good for the very young"* – JOAN BURSTEIN.

🐾 DOLCE & GABBANA at Marisa, Via Sant' Andrea 10A, 20121 ☎ (02) 780793
Darlings of the design world with a finger on the pulse of youth. The Sicilian peasant signature now plays to a more swinging beat, with Hawaiian minis, beaded pinstripe suits and Madonna-wise sexy snippets. *"They do things like tight trousers and sexy beaded corsets and bra tops and they're really good"* – AMANDA DE CADENET. *"A beautiful collection, very pretty, very feminine – jewelled bodices and chiffon"* – JOAN BURSTEIN.

🐾 **GIANFRANCO FERRE, Via della Spiga 11–13, 20121 ☎ (02) 794864; menswear ☎ (02) 7600 0385**
Some feel Dior's design wonder is a little lost on home terrain, though not JOAN BURSTEIN. His is a serious approach to fashion, and he's best when sticking to it – the blouse that makes a statement, sharply tailored city suits and less structured, more glamorous evening gear. Classic menswear.

🐾 **GIANNI VERSACE, Via della Spiga 4, 20121 ☎ (02) 7600 5451; menswear Via Montenapoleone 11, 20121 ☎ (02) 7600 8529**
The rock 'n' roll master of creative tailoring has never been on better form nor more admired. Impeccably cut dresses and chic suits, eye-popping youthful gear, and printed men's and women's shirts that are collectors' items – devotees book them a season in advance. Grace Jones is a Versace virago; he also suits KEN HOM, Elton John, Chris Eubank and a zillion other discerning men. Prêt-à-porter and the cheaper Versus range lower the price without lowering the tone.

🎩 Italy's Best Designers

I	GIANNI VERSACE
2	GIORGIO ARMANI
3	DOLCE & GABBANA
4	GIANFRANCO FERRE
5	ROMEO GIGLI

🐾 **GIORGIO ARMANI, Via Sant' Andrea 9, 20121 ☎ (02) 7602 2757; EMPORIO ARMANI, Via Durini 11 ☎ (02) 7602 0306; MANI, Via Durini 23 ☎ (02) 7602 0306; GIORGIO ARMANI (CHILDREN), Via Durini 27 ☎ (02) 794248**
Fighting it out at the top with Versace, the cool Armani, with his hitherto unassailable sense of understatement, has been trying to play his glitzy rival at his own game. But his devotees love him for what he does best: *"Armani does this suit for the executive woman, very severe, but extremely feminine; short skirts, very big jackets, very beautiful soft blouses. And beautiful men's clothes"* – DOTT ROSA MARIA LETTS. Soft tailoring and muted, sludgy colours mean undatable elegance, and the gamut of lines (Emporio, Mani, White Label, Black Label) means widespread appeal. *"Armani all the way, rough stuff, ready-to-wear, couture, the whole thing. I like all his stuff. Very elegant and very disciplined"* – ANOUSKA HEMPEL. *"My favourite, along with Lagerfeld, the best – just total sophistication and restraint"* – BRUCE OLDFIELD. MARK PATRICK admires his simplicity, CAROLYN LOCK-

HART and SKYE MACLEOD covet the lot, Kim Basinger and Tina Turner give star approval. Tired of plain Armani, GAIL ROLFE prefers the fun, wearable Emporio collection.

KRIZIA, Via della Spiga 23, 20121 ☎ (02) 708429
Mariuccia Mandelli caters for a complete designer lifestyle with Krizia, Krizia Uomo, Krizia Baby and Krizia kitchen. *"Along with Armani, since the 80s and 90s, Krizia has been able to give perfect poise to the woman of the moment. An absolutely sober line – and sobriety is very important to me – and very feminine"* – DOTT ROSA MARIA LETTS.

MILA SCHON, Via Montenapoleone 2 and 6, 20121 ☎ (02) 701803
Neat, understated little suits and separates from the Austro-Hungarian Schon, with timeless appeal for modish Milan. Men are well catered for at No 3 ☎ (02) 701333. *"She really is one of the more reticent but top names in Italian design. All sorts of things from haute couture to popular wear. She's like an Italian Givenchy"* – SIR PETER USTINOV.

MOSCHINO, Via Sant' Andrea 12, 20121 ☎ (02) 7600 0832; CHEAP AND CHIC, Via Durini 14, 20122 ☎ (02) 7600 7605
Intelligent (though anti-intellectual) and deeply irreverent, Moschino is more prankster than designer. Appealing to the eccentric streak in people from Princess Di to Madonna, his early training with Versace means that, wild or no, at least the clothes are well made. The diffusion line, Cheap and Chic, guarantees affordability but not exclusivity, as two Smartie suit-wearing Ascot-goers found to their cost, and the photographers' delight.

🐾 **ROMEO GIGLI, Corso Venezia 11, 20121 ☎ (02) 7600 0271**
Now in his own shop, Italy's most dramatic designer shows his collection under one stylish roof. The baroque detailing that made him famous lends an ethereal quality to his clothes (loose, cocoon tunic tops, layered chiffon, waterfall pleating). *"Very glorious, different, lovely. Chiffon floating over other fitted materials and earthy, soft, subtle colours"* – JOAN BURSTEIN.

--- **Hotels** ---

EXCELSIOR HOTEL GALLIA, Piazza Duca d'Aosta 9, 20124 ☎ (02) 6785
The Art Nouveau Gallia, revamped by THF, is again a winner, especially with rag traders at collection time. A credit card's throw from the shopping streets and well equipped with health club, piano bar and Mediterranean restaurant.

HOTEL PRINCIPE DI SAVOIA, Piazza della Repubblica 17, 20124 ☎ (02) 6230
Grand old Lombardy, best loved for its service

and, by those with a taste for the OTT, its Presidential Suite (with indoor swimming pool). "*My favourite hotel, especially because of the people who work there. But,*" warns LOGAN BENTLEY, "*redecoration ordered by the new owner, the Aga Khan, is heavy-handed.*"

—————— *Music* ——————

LA SCALA, Teatro alla Scala, Via Filodrammatici 2, 20121 ☎ (02) 887 9211
The famous opera house, staging some of the world's most spectacular productions and starring the biggies – Pavarotti, Domingo et al. Mostly Italian opera, produced by equally luminous stars such as Franco Zeffirelli. The season (Dec-July) opens at fever pitch on 7 Dec, feast of Sant' Ambrogio, patron saint of Milan. Less frantic concert season (May-June, Sept-Nov); brief ballet season (Sept).

—————— *Restaurants* ——————

AIMO E NADIA, Via Montecuccoli 6, 20122 ☎ (02) 416886
Once a simple trat, now a rather smart and modern ristorante. A trek from the city centre but worth it for such innovations as gingered beef. BARBARA KAFKA recommends it, with a caveat or two: "*Very expensive, a touch overdone, but good.*"

ANTICA TRATTORIA DELLA PESA, Viale Pasubio 10, 20121 ☎ (02) 655 5741
A proper trattoria famiglia, unchanged by fashion, which is how fashionable Milan likes it. They tuck into hearty Milanese staples such as bollito misto, osso bucco and, of course, risotto milanese.

BAGUTTA, Via Bagutta 14, 20123 ☎ (02) 700902; (02) 702767
Cheerful Bohemian restaurant where the décor is as artfully arty as the clientele. Ever-changing and developing wall murals and fabulous, gutsy antipasti. Service, however, has been known to be high-handed: "*I went there with an American guest and was treated very badly. They know me but I was very disappointed*" – GIOVANNI SANTANGELETTA.

———————————————

Tourin' in Turin

SOPHIE GRIGSON tracks down some treats in Torino: "*The best bollito misto, a mix of stewed meats served with salsa verde and salsa rosso, is at* **San Giors**, *Via Borgo Dora 3* ☎ *(011) 521 1256 – I still think that's amazing and I've never had one better since. The* **Café Torino** *in the Piazza San Carlo is a marvellous turn-of-the-century grand café, with particularly good marrons glacés which arrive when you sit down. The other café in Turin is the* **Café Baratti e Milano**, *Piazza Castello 29, which has delicious pastries and corners you can hide away in. Off the track a bit is my favourite earring shop,* **An Atomyca**, *Via Po 3 – it alone makes your visit to Turin worthwhile.*"

———————————————

BICE, Via Borgospesso 12, 20121 ☎ (02) 795528
The one that started the chain (the Bice bug's bitten Paris, NY . . .), without losing its lustre. Fashion-leaders lead the way to the chic-est seats (close to the kitchen) – if you're in with the owner, there's always a table. Risotto with radicchio or simple pastas are perennial pleasures.

DON LISANDER, Via Manzoni 12A, 20121 ☎ (02) 7602 0130
Classically-rooted cooking in peaceful surroundings, especially in summer when you sit in the large garden. A favourite of bankers, business people and ALESSANDRO MODENESE.

LA TAVERNETTA, Via Fatebenefratelli 30, 20122 ☎ (02) 659 7610
Tuscan taverna with some Milanese injections such as osso bucco with risotto. INDRO MONTANELLI eats there almost every day. His regular table stands at the ready, as does a glass of Chianti.

Buzzz Meraviglioso Milano: everyone loves it but where do they stay? The new **Regent**, Via Gesu 10, might possibly be the top-grade hotel Milan's been waiting for. Unusually small (100 rooms) for the group, in a converted 14C convent ♟ . . . . . . NANDO MIGLIO wraps up the best of his town: "*Best bread – the* **Panificio** *on Via Cerva; best objects for the house –* **Giovanni Petrini**, *Via San Damiano; best traditional sportswear –* **Brigatti**, *Corso Venezia; best crystal and glassware –* **Vetreria Empoli**, *Via Verri; best gym –* **Francesco Conti** *on Corso Como; best flower stand – on the corner of Via della Spiga and Via Sant'Andrea* . . . . . ♟

LE IDEE DI GUALTIERO MARCHESI, Via Bonvesin della Riva 9, 20129 ☎ (02) 741246

The birthplace of la cucina nuova and the peak of modern Italian cooking. Marchesi has waged a war on the more-is-more school and his light, complex renderings of traditional dishes (aubergine with a sweet and sour sauce, for example) keep astounding critics and public. Book far ahead for a seat in the spare, somewhat charmless, dining room.

PAPER MOON, Via Bagutta 1, 20121 ☎ (02) 796083

Officially a pizzeria, more unofficially the fashion designers' guildhall. Versace is reputed to have a table permanently booked here; others, like ALESSANDRO MODENESE, have to queue. Best dish is robespierre, slices of almost raw beef topped with herbs and juices. Owner Pio Magrini commutes between Milan and the NY Paper Moon.

RISTORANTE PECK, Via Spadari 9, 20123 ☎ (02) 8646 1158

More all-encompassing than a mere nosherie, the peckish feeling takes in food shops and bars as well as the ristorante. It's ANTON MOSIMANN's favourite shopping experience, one of SOPHIE GRIGSON's too: "*I love it. The big shop is in the main area where you can buy cheeses, hams, prepared meals and chocolates. There's a separate cheese shop and fish shop and meat shop.*" LORD LICHFIELD is another Peck picker: "*It's amazing.*" Out of the bustle is the blond wood dining room – relax as do Milanese business execs over famously fresh northern Italian dishes such as ravioli stuffed with sea bass.

TORRE DI PISA, Via Fiori Chiari 21, 20124 ☎ (02) 804483

The place to be seen to lean. 3 homesick Pisan brothers run this Tuscan trattoria and all their ingredients, from the crostini Toscano to the spaghetti alla putanesca, come from Tuscany. A winner with Elio Fiorucci, JENNY KEE, and "*a lot of advertising people, young managers, it's an easy place for snobbish Milaneses*" – ALESSANDRO MODENESE.

—— Shopping ——

Milan is the shopping capital of Italy. **Via della Spiga** is still where its at for fashion and accessories. **Via Montenapoleone** is the established street for the major international names; **Via Sant' Andrea** and **Via Manzoni** are fashion-conscious, too. The best markets for antiques and some clothes are **Via Madonnina** in the young trendy Brera district (3rd Sat of the month) and the **Naviglio** along the canals of Porta Ticinese (last Sun of the month). For new clothes try **Fiera di Senegallia**, around Via San Luca (Sat), and **Viale Papiniano**, for knock-down designer gear.

ARS ROSA, Via Montenapoleone 8, 20121 ☎ (02) 7602 3822

A rose-tinted spectacle of silk and satin. Outer (wedding) and under wear, painstakingly embroidered and handmade. Divinely pretty children's clothes too – hand-smocked dresses, blouses, etc.

CAFFE MODA DURINI, Via Durini 14, 20122 ☎ (02) 7602 1188

Don't be fooled by the name, this is the city's top fashion store for all the big names from near (Ferré, Valentino, Krizia) and far. OK, there's also a little bar downstairs.

CARACENI, Via Fatebenefratelli 16, 20121 ☎ (02) 655 1972

Supremely elegant Italian tailoring from the master of cut and style. Some of the world's smoothest dressers are suited here, among them Agnelli and Lagerfeld; those with a few more rough edges go off-the-peg.

FRATELLI ROSSETTI, Via Montenapoleone 1, 20121 ☎ (02) 7602 1650

Outstanding in the competitive territory of shoe road. Rosettes rain down on their finely crafted leather footwear.

L'ORO DEI FARLOCCHI, Via Madonnina 5, 20123 ☎ (02) 860589

An Aladdin's cave of inspirational presents, antiques, objets and knick-knacks.

ROME

—— Art and museums ——

GALLERIA BORGHESE, Villa Borghese, Via Pinciana ☎ (06) 700 3888

Set in Rome's best-known park, the frescoed villa houses an important collection of Renaissance painting and sculpture. Many of the paintings are still not on view (will the renovations ever be complete?) but some of Bernini's most powerful sculptures are, notably *David, Apollo and Daphne* and *Pluto and Proserpine*. A wonderful view of the city from the gardens. Open mornings only.

GALLERIA DORIA PAMPHILI, Piazza del Collegio Romano 1 ☎ (06) 679 4365

La famiglia Doria's private collection of masters, one of Italy's finest, hung in their 17C palazzo. View Caravaggio, Carracci, Claude and Velázquez.

MUSEO CAPITOLINO, Piazza del Campidoglio ☎ (06) 678 2862

Europe's first public art collection, set up in the 15C by Pope Sixtus V in what was the centre of ancient Rome. Classical Roman and Greek sculpture is its strength – see eye to eye with Nero and Marcus Aurelius. The bronze *Spinario* (Boy with a Thorn) and moving marble *Dying Gaul* are highlights.

🏛 MUSEI VATICANI, Viale Vaticano ☎ (06) 698 3333
The extraordinarily rich papal palace's collection, built through donations and commissions. One of the suggested itineraries takes 5 hours to complete – your own might take double to find your way around the 4½ miles of works. *"One of the most important museums in the world and one of its most underrated. Everyone goes to see Michelangelo and Raphael, ignoring the museum's real strength, in classical Roman sculpture"* – BRIAN SEWELL. For most people, ignorance is bliss: renovation of Michelangelo's Sistine Chapel ceiling is now complete, the scaffolding removed and the frescos revealed in all their vivid, unearthly beauty. *The Last Judgement* is the next to be transformed. Impossible to list all the highlights but **Raphael's Stanze** and **Loggia** and the **Chapel of Nicholas V** frescoed by Fra Angelico rank among them. A fine picture gallery, and the largest collection of antique art in the world – don't miss the famous *Apollo Belvedere* and *Laocoön* that so influenced the Renaissance and baroque.

── Bars and cafés ──

ANTICO CAFFE GRECO, Via Condotti 86, 00187 ☎ (06) 679 1700
A stop-off on the European Grand Tour since its 1760 founding. SOPHIE GRIGSON carries on the tradition: *"I always love it. A very old-fashioned, famous literary café – literary people and politicians in the 19C and early 20C went there and their pictures are all over the wall. If you're feeling hot and weary, it's one of those places you long to get to because it's cool and comfortable and, sliding into one of those chairs, suddenly all the strains and stresses slip away."*

BABINGTON TEA ROOMS, Piazza di Spagna 23, 00187 ☎ (06) 678 6027
An anachronistic outpost of English Victoriana. Terribly civilized luncheon venue (proper tea and sandwiches) but be warned: *"This already high-priced place has increased its prices even more to keep out riff-raff"* – LOGAN BENTLEY.

HEMINGWAY, Piazza delle Coppelle 10, 00186 ☎ (06) 654 4135
All-nighter favoured by the film and fashion few. 3 themed rooms without a macho motif in sight – red Victoriana, green marble or Greek taverna.

── Clubs ──

GILDA, Via Mario de' Fiori 97, 00183 ☎ (06) 678 4838
Long-running, established disco/restaurant, where the man with the young girl might really be her father. The young prop up the bar, their elders gather near the stage.

NOTORIOUS, Via S Nicola da Tolentino 22, 00187 ☎ (06) 474 6888
Still one of the hippest clubs in un-nightclub-orientated Roma. Lives up to its name with its paparazzi-fodder crowd (Grace Jones, Simon Le Bon, most of the Italian film industry . . .).

OPEN GATE, Via San Nicola da Tolentine 4, 00187 ☎ (06) 482 4464
Unfaddish piano bar, restaurant and nightclub, *"an old favourite with the sophisticated crowd"* – LOGAN BENTLEY.

── Fashion designers ──

LAURA BIAGIOTTI, Via Borgognona 43, 00187 ☎ (06) 679 1205
The Queen of Cashmere reigns from her large, airy prêt-à-porter shop. Fabulous selection of the soft stuff in every colour and for every shape (cuts are generous). Give it extra oomph with her famous sunglasses, wristwatches, perfume, bags, scarves and shawls.

VALENTINO, Via Bocca di Leone 15–18, 00187 ☎ (06) 679 5862
Wonderful winner of hearts – the couturier who injects glamour into everything he does. For evening, fabulous fabrics, jewel-bright colours and technical wizardry mean that *"he is the most appealing to any woman, because he is, let's say, the Ferrari of clothing, but not for every day"* – DOTT ROSA MARIA LETTS. For Elizabeth Taylor's most recent float down the 'aisle', she wore little-girl flounces. Prêt-à-porter allows more women access to the Valentino touch and

 Buzzz Chic-er and quicker – dash into **Jean-Louis David**, Via Sant'Andrea 2 ☎ (02) 783245, for an appointment-free hairstyle. 9.30-6.30 non-stop 🏃 . . . . . . Or hare off to **Aldo Coppola**, Via Manzoni 25 ☎ (02) 8646 2163, cutter to Cindy Crawford and Linda Evangelista 🏃 . . . . . . Presents with presence: The best gift shop is **DOM**, Corso Matterotti 3 ☎ (02) 7602 3410, says SERENA FASS 🏃 . . . . . . The **flea market** that really jumps is outside Milan at Bollgate. It scratches an itch for ALESSANDRO MODENESE and RAFFAELLA CURIEL: *"Get there by 8am. I bought the most beautiful Venetian 16C ceiling"* . . . . 🏃

takes in neat little linen suits and shoes (designed by the brilliant Rene Caovilla).

—————— *Hotels* ——————

🛎 HOTEL HASSLER, Trinità dei Monti 6, 00187 ☎ (06) 679 2651

Swiss-run, unsurpassable location, discreet and personal, the revamped Hassler's still got it. Renovations have lent polish to glass-roofed lounge and green and white rooms, and meet the approval of MARK MCCORMACK: *"Finally getting to the 20C and it's very, very good." "At the top of the Spanish steps, fabulous and unique. One of the rare hotels where it is quite obvious who owns and runs it (the Wirth family). Dining at the Roof Restaurant you feel so much part of Rome – it overlooks the whole city"* – CATHY ROSSI HARRIS. Mother MARY and LISA BARNARD swell the chorus.

HOTEL INGHILTERRA, Via Bocca di Leone 14, 00187 ☎ (06) 672161

Charmingly run hotel in the heart of the shopping district, a favourite of fashion folk JENNY KEE and CARLA FENDI: *"It's where wives from the provinces stay when they come to town to go shopping. They are particularly protective of women alone, and the atmosphere in the bar and lobby is almost like that of a club."*

HOTEL LORD BYRON, Via G de Notaris 5, 00197 ☎ (06) 322 0404

Poetic sibling of Florence's Regency, with similarly high standards of comfort and style. The overhaul of the top 2 floors has created suites with stupendous city views – distant the city may be but the peace of smart suburbia weighs more heavily in the balance. **Relais Le Jardin** is one of Italy's most highly rated restaurants – a rare innovator in conservative Rome.

🛎 HOTEL MAJESTIC, Via Veneto 50, 00187 ☎ (06) 460984

The grand old Majestic, plushly refitted and flying high again under Silvano Pinchetti's (ex-Hassler) management. It has already played host to Pavarotti, Madonna (both of whom stayed – though not together – in suite 508-509 at the top, with the terrace), Whitney Houston (who brought an all-female posse of protectors and staff) and Jacques Delors. The smart Mediterranean restaurant spreads outdoors in the summer.

LE GRAND, Via V E Orlando 3, 00185 ☎ (06) 4709

Nothing misleading about the name here, either – it *is* grand, from the hand-painted wallpaper to the blue and gold carpets. The only place for jet-powered execs and Elizabeth Taylor, who hosted a thanksgiving dinner here. Downside: the location near the station. Upside: *"The best thing is the afternoon tea, Oct to May, which features a harpist, choice of 10 kinds of tea, finger sandwiches, scones with whipped cream, lemon tart, chocolate cake and other goodies, served in gilt-edged surroundings. There's a flat fee of 24,000 lire which I consider to be the biggest bargain in Rome"* – LOGAN BENTLEY.

—————— *Restaurants* ——————

See also Hotels.

ALBERTO CIARLA, Piazza S Cosimato 40, 00183 ☎ (06) 581 6668

Wealthy Rome's favourite fishery. Offbeat offer-

Dining Al Fresco

🛎

When in Rome, you want to do as the Romans, and not the tourists, do . . . tricky when you also want to eat outside. Here's where to get the best of both worlds. Once you've checked out the Bernini fountain on tourist-ridden Piazza Navona, slip round the corner to dine under big umbrellas at **La Maiella**, 45-46 Piazza S Apollinare ☎ (06) 686 4174, on gutsy Roman cuisine. Join the young, beautiful crowd tucking into pizzas at **Al Giardino del Gatto e la Volpe**, Via Buccari 14 ☎ (06) 325 1583. Leafy garden under the trees. **Dal Bolognese**, Piazza del Popolo 1/2 ☎ (06) 361 1426 has long been a jealously guarded secret of film stars, pop singers and aristos. A fine view of the piazza with its twin churches and a perfect plate of thin rare roast beef and mash when pasta begins to pall. Right off the tourist beat are the trio of restaurants with tables on the wide pavement of Viale Parioli: the two trads, **La Scala** at 79D ☎ (06) 808 3978 and **Celestina** at 184 ☎ (06) 807 8242, and the more modern **Caminetto** at 89 ☎ (06) 808 3946. Displace water with wine over long summer lunches outside **Archimede**, Piazza dei Caprettari 63 ☎ (06) 687 5216, where the absence of Roman traffic makes it the freshest of all al frescos.

ings (pasta with seafood and beans or fresh crab sauce) are matched by simple but fabulously fresh piatti – there's a page for oysters alone. Service can be a little *freddo*.

ANTONELLO COLONNA, Via Carsilina km 38300, 00030 LaBico ☎ (06) 951 0032
Small, family-run restaurant about 30 minutes from the city centre. *"Better than any food that exists in Rome – divine. Just fabulous, amazing food, rustic but glorified, with the heaviness taken out. I had the cabbage cooked with garlic and chilli pepper [which arrives under thinly sliced guanciale, cured pig's cheek]. A big, flavourful thing"* – FAITH WILLINGER.

🐷 CHECCHINO DAL 1887, Via di Monte Testaccio 30, 00153 ☎ (06) 574 6318
In the Mariani family for generations, a smart restaurant ominously based in the district of the old slaughterhouses, to the delight of offal-lover JONATHAN MEADES: *"The ultimate offal experience, spinal cord with brains, wonderful tripe. And, extraordinarily in Italy where you tend to find only local wines, it has a very, very good wine list. A wonderful barrel-vaulted room. It is, in fact, one of the world's outstanding restaurants."*

EVANGELISTA, Via de Voccolette 11, 00186 ☎ (06) 687 5810
The ultimate carciofi experience served with evangelical zeal, as FAITH WILLINGER testifies: *"Artichoke heaven. You can have them flat, in a soup, a risotto, pasta. The best is to have the artichokes smashed with a brick and then grilled."*

OSTERIA DEL ANTIQUARIO DI GIORGIO NISTI, Piazzetta S Simeone 27, 00186 ☎ (06) 687 9691
Classics updated with more delicacy than one would imagine from a former rugby player. An extensive cellar partners such dishes as tortelloni filled with cheese with asparagus and bresaola or duck stuffed with fennel. On warm summer evenings, sit at tables in the piazza.

PIPERNO, Monte de' Cenci 9, 00186 ☎ (06) 654 0629
Packed with charm and locals, Piperno is next to Palazzo Cenci in the old Jewish quarter. A light, delicate touch when frying shows in the carciofi alla Giudea (artichokes), filetti di baccalà (stockfish or dried cod) and fiori di zucca (pumpkin flowers).

——————— *Shopping* ———————

Via Condotti and **Via Borgognona** are the main seams of the area that sews up high fashion and jewellery, while the offbeat boutiques around **Trastevere** yield younger, more innovative wear. The flea market at **Porta Portese** is a good source of bargains and esoterica.

La Posta Vecchia

If you fancy living like a *conte*, or better still a multi-millionaire, the exclusive hotel **La Posta Vecchia**, 00055 Palo Laziale ☎ (06) 994 9501, could be the place to shore up. Some 40 minutes north-west of Rome, bang on the coast, this splendid villa was the former residence of J Paul Getty. With its stone fireplaces, coffered ceilings and heavy wooden doors, it *feels* authentic enough, but in fact it's a San Simeon-style folly de grandeur, created by Getty. Architectural relics and artefacts seamlessly transformed the shell of this 17C summer villa, which was itself built on the site of a Roman villa (a happy bonus for Getty, who unearthed the remains and created a mini-museum underground). Guests get to sleep in Getty's monogrammed linen, with the sound of waves crashing below, and the delicious scent of a specially blended pot pourri. With the fine restaurant, comfy library, indoor pool and little private beach, you might be tempted to take up permanent residence. . . . Just one snag – you'd have to be nigh on a multi-millionaire to do so.

BULGARI, Via Condotti 10, 00187 ☎ (06) 679 3876
The great jewellery designer with a 24-carat conscience – check out the new range inspired by (and supporting) the World Wildlife Fund. Extravagant pieces with a historical bent as well as bold modern designs too.

CAMOMILLA, Piazza di Spagna 85, 00187 ☎ (06) 679 3551
A well-dressed store with an eclectic selection of women's clothes. Italian film stars and Barbara Bach kit themselves out in the best of British (Helen Storey), US (Betsy Johnson), French (Chantal Thomass), Japanese (Yamamoto Kanazy), and home-grown talent. And shoes to match the bag to match the jewellery to match the outfit.

FEDERICO BUCCELLATI, Via Condotti 31, 00187 ☎ (06) 679 0329
Solid argent style from the master smithy. Intricately worked silver jewellery, cigarette cases and collectables have accents of white gold and platinum, pearls and diamonds. *"The greatest of all jewellers; not only his silver but his ordinary*

street jewels are absolutely unmistakable. High-class jewellery with an almost filigree technique – they look as if they are going to fly away at any moment. And if I were a burglar, they would" – SIR PETER USTINOV.

FENDI, Via Borgognona 39, 00187
☎ (06) 679 7641
You're an Italian woman, you buy a fur and that's that. And Fendi furs are the pinnacle – superlative pelts get Karl Lagerfeld's masterly treatment, stitched into classic capes or head-turning contemporary shapes. Also a vast array of accessories – check out the line of daytime bags embossed with Roman designs. This sleek shop's the supremo, the range spreads down the street: Fendissime at 4L, accessories at 4E, 36A and 38, and clothes at 40.

GUCCI, Via Condotti 8, 00187
☎ (06) 678 9340
Gucci's flagship is still afloat though its other vessel has sunk. The leaders of the worldwide mania for brand-stamping goods – the famous double Gs and red and green run rampant over keyrings, suitcases, handbags, wallets.... Avoid wearing your shop on your shoulder with non-emblazoned wares in leather of impeccable quality, plus scarves, umbrellas and more.

MAX MARA, Via Frattina 28, 00187
☎ (06) 679 3638
Everything from evening dresses to suits and coats by the many designers under the Max Mara umbrella. Another shop on Via Condotti, but *"this one's better lit and has a bigger selection as well as friendlier salesgirls"* – LOGAN BENTLEY.

RADICONCINI, Via del Corso 139, 00186
☎ (06) 679 1807
A slice of unradical tradition. Italy's oldest

milliners also have a hands-on approach to shirting: handmade and hand-monogrammed.

TANINO CRISCI, Via Borgognona 4, 00187 ☎ (06) 679 5461
For a well-crafted jodhpur boot or a low-heeled, wing-tipped pump, Tanino Crisci's classic shoes are *"tops. The more you wear these shoes the better they look"* – LOGAN BENTLEY.

VENICE
—— Art and museums ——

CA' D'ORO, Galleria Franchetti, Cannaregio ☎ (041) 523 8790
Fabulously ornate Gothic palazzo on the Grand Canal. Gilt and marble tracery run riot over the building, which houses works of art from the Venetian Renaissance as well as temporary shows.

CA' REZZONICO, Campo S Barnaba ☎ (041) 522 4543
The baroque palazzo beautifully displays its original exuberant Tiepolo frescos, 18C furniture and paintings.

COLLEZIONE D'ARTE MODERNA PEGGY GUGGENHEIM, S Gregorio 701, Dorsoduro ☎ (041) 520 6288
Those sated by the riches of the Renaissance revive spirits here in Guggenheim's grand palazzo and garden. An extraordinary collection of modern painting in its various stages, from Expressionism through Cubism and Surrealism (Guggenheim's main love) to the completely abstract. A canalside garden of contemporary sculpture too, notably by Moore, Marini and the Dadaist Arp.

Buzzz CARLA FENDI finds the best antiques at **Massimo Zompa**, via Fontanella Borghese 44, *"for refined details"*; at **Adalberto Arcidiacono**, via dei Delfini 33, in the Jewish ghetto (*"the most Roman and magic antique shop"*) and **Cirincione**, via del Clementino 92, *"for amusing discoveries"* ...... Follow her to the labyrinthine **Leone Limentani**, Portico d'Ottavia, to check out discounted top-brand crockery ...... No one can hold a candle to **Constantino Pisoni**, Corso Vittorio Emanuele 127 ☎ (06) 654 3531, for waxen delights: *"It's where the Pope buys his candles. You can choose from about 30 and they ask what length and width you would like. Beautiful colours – shocking pink and deep, dark green. The Pope obviously buys basic white"* – FAITH WILLINGER ...... Delving into the WILLINGER digest reveals a further personage of eggcellence: **Diego Percosse Papi**, Via S Eustachio 16 ☎ (06) 654 1466, a jeweller who fuses the baroque and contemporary. *"He has invented a new alloy that is not outrageously expensive. Fabergé have asked him to join them in creating some eggs. Usually semi-precious stones – just wonderful"*................................

⚓ GALLERIA DELL' ACCADEMIA, Campo della Carità, Dorsoduro ☎ (041) 522 2247
The city's finest picture gallery comprehensively illustrates Venetian painting, from the 14C onwards. The sweep of masterpieces takes in glowing Bellinis, Giorgione's mysterious *Tempest*, Veronese's mammoth *The Feast in the House of Levi*, Titians, Tintorettos and Tiepolos.

—————— *Bars and cafés* ——————

CAFFE FLORIAN, Piazza San Marco 56–59, 30125 ☎ (041) 528 5338
Fine old (1720) pasticceria, a gilded and frescoed bustle of Venetian social life. The *best* pastries, to be savoured over cups of macchiato ('smudge' – a dash of milk into a short black) or cappuccino. In summer, a small orchestra plays and you pay – once for the coffee and again for the view.

HARRY'S BAR, Calle Vallaresso 1323, 30124 ☎ (041) 523 6797
The world's most famous bar, home to the world's greatest cocktail, the bellini, and long-loved home from home of the fickle jetset. Sensational chicken sandwiches at the bar (especially if made by head barman Claudio) or sit alla tavola to tuck into fried shrimp, Venetian liver and "*chocolate cake which is as good as the one I make at home and I am very fussy about my desserts*" – LOGAN BENTLEY. Loved by NANDO MIGLIO, ROBIN LEACH, DOUGLAS FAIRBANKS JR and SIR TERENCE CONRAN: "*Still one of the great places . . . it's the quality of service, the almost casual way everything happens so perfectly.*" **Harry's Dolci**, Giudecca 773 ☎ (041) 522 4844, is sweeter on those with less in their pockets – prices about 30% less and you can buy the chocolate cake to take home.

—————— *Hotels* ——————

CASA FROLLO, Giudecca 50, 30100 ☎ (041) 520 8299
Literati in the know favour this small hotel on Giudecca island. The best bargain in Venice, with a priceless view of the Doge's palace and San Marco. Enormous, high-ceilinged rooms make the hotel "*full of charm*" – COUNT GIOVANNI VOLPI.

⚓ GRITTI PALACE, Campo S M del Giglio 2467, 30124 ☎ (041) 794611
More aristocratic home than brash hotel, with its own traghetto stop (for the cross-canal gondola). Public rooms are grand, guest rooms over-redecorated and a little hectic. Outstandingly personal service under terrific concierges, especially if you're a regular (like DOUGLAS FAIRBANKS JR); the **Club del Doge** dining room (with maître d' Mr Bovo, ex-Connaught) and terrace on the canal will always be star attractions.

⚓ HOTEL CIPRIANI, Giudecca 10, 30133 ☎ (041) 520 7744
The world's most hedonistic hotel, the water surrounding the island marking the divide between it and the less privileged world. Where to start listing its virtues? "*Fine linen sheets, approach by the private launch, the indulgence of the huge swimming pool where rich New Yorkers wind chiffon scarves about their throats before taking off in their stately breaststroke. Natale Rusconi is the best hotelier in the world and the Cipriani reflects this. Impeccable service – Cipriani staff understand the difference between a tip and a bribe*" – JILL MULLENS. DOU-

Italy's Best Hotels

1	HOTEL CIPRIANI · Venice
2	HOTEL HELVETIA & BRISTOL · Florence
3	LA POSTA VECCHIA · Palo Laziale
4	HOTEL HASSLER · Rome
5	VILLA SAN MICHELE · Fiesole
6	HOTEL VILLA CIPRIANI · Asolo
7	SAN PIETRO . Positano
8	HOTEL MAJESTIC· Rome
9	LE SIRENUSE · Positano
10	HOTEL SPLENDIDO · Portofino

GLAS FAIRBANKS JR, ROBIN LEACH, PRUE LEITH and SHARYN STORRIER-LYNEHAM would say aye to all that. For PAUL HENDERSON: "*The only way to relax from the bustle of Venice is to go in the winter or to stay at the Cip.*" GILES SHEPARD finds it "*excellent – it doesn't change, or rather, it is still improving*"; BETTY KENWARD agrees: "*Better than ever. You could not fault it anywhere.*" SKYE MACLEOD finds the pull magnetic: "*I didn't want to leave.*" NANDO MIGLIO reckons that "*Gianni and his group are the best concierges.*" He's also a lounger about the pool at its **Seagull Club**. The Cip's **Palazzo Vendramin dei Cipriani** applies similarly exalted standards to private home-style apartments. Some home.

HOTEL DANIELI, Riva degli Schiavoni 4196, 30122 ☎ (041) 522 6480
One of the landmark seafront hotels, a hop and a skip from San Marco. "*A 15C palace that became a boarding house for the likes of Dickens, Wagner and Ruskin in the 19C and has managed to maintain into the late 20C the mystery, the decadence and the obsession for detail that are the essential qualities of a great hotel*" – DAVID DALE. JENNY KEE's keen too.

208 ITALY · ROME · REST OF ITALY

--- *Music* ---

CHIESA DI S MARIA DELLA PIETA
Viva Vivaldi – in the church where he used to play – with regular concerts of his and other baroque music.

TEATRO LA FENICE, Campo S Fantin, 30124 ☎ (041) 521 0161; (041) 521 0336
One of Italy's oldest, most famous and most beautiful opera houses, under the directorship of John Fisher. The opera season last from Dec-May/June; concerts, ballet, recitals, etc, fill the house year-round (Aug excepted).

--- *Restaurants* ---

See also Hotels.

AI BARBACANI, Castello, San Lio 5746 ☎ (041) 521 0234
Charming ristorante close to San Marco. Immaculate food – the spaghetti alle vongole is a standout. "*Still very good*" – MARCELLA HAZAN.

ARCIMBOLDO, Castello 3219 ☎ (041) 528 6569
Classic Venetian cooking in a very stylish restaurant, designed by fashion journalist Luciana Boccardi. "*Off the regular tourist beat and not as expensive as most places in Venice*" – LOGAN BENTLEY. Star treatment for everyone: they'll send a little boat to pick you up and take you home. Dine outdoors in the summer.

🦞 DA FIORE, Calle del Scalater 2202, 30125 ☎ (041) 721308
Hard to find and becoming a little touristy but for culinary cognoscenti it's "*hands-down the best restaurant in Venice. Great seafood*" – BARBARA KAFKA. MARCELLA HAZAN seconds that: "*I still like it very much.*" ELISE PASCOE adds a third voice: "*The best food in Venice – very, very good. Everything was stunning, particularly the carciofini – tiny, raw, green artichokes, the first-picked of the season – which you have with green extra virgin olive oil and black pepper.*"

LOCANDA CIPRIANI, Torcello, 20012 ☎ (041) 730150
An unassuming inn whose food draws crowds to this peaceful island (and whose handful of rooms allow a chosen few to stay). Ernest Hemingway was a regular; following in his footsteps are the Prince and Princess of Wales, SALLY BURTON and JULIAN LLOYD WEBBER: "*One of the most romantic places in the world.*" LORD LICHFIELD would second that. He particularly loves it in Oct, when the whole island is ablaze with red creeper: "*It really is the most glorious sight.*" Closed mid-Nov to Mar.

RISTORANTE DA IVO, Calle dei Fuseri 1809, 30124 ☎ (041) 528 5044
A small and unpretentious find for BARBARA KAFKA: "*They do tiny fried shrimp in the shell and you can eat the whole thing – just wonderful. The man is not a cook by background but he does some wonderful things.*" Closed Jan.

RISTORANTE VINI AL COVO, Campiello della Pescaia, Castello 3968, 3012 ☎ (041) 522 3812
A charming, brick-walled ristorante with, as its name suggests, a good wine list – a rare find in Venice. "*Owned by a couple – he is Venetian and in the kitchen, she is Texan and looks after the tables. Very good food, Venetian with a touch of new things like carpaccio of brenzino, a type of bass*" – MARCELLA HAZAN.

--- · REST OF · ---

ITALY

--- *Festivals* ---

BATIGNANO MUSICA NEL CHIOSTRO, S Croce, 58041 Batignano (Grosseto) ☎ (0564) 38096
Late July-Aug festival revives forgotten or rarely aired operas. Held in the cloisters of a semi-ruined convent.

🎩 **Buzz** MARCELLA HAZAN shares the fruits of her shopping basket: "*In the market on Rialto, **Brissa** and **Il Parmiginano** have very good cheese; **Mascari** is good for dried mushrooms, fruit, marmalade and coffee; for bread, either **Carlon** or **Milani** in San Leo*" 🦞 ...... Good fortune: **Venetia Studium**, Largo 22 Marzo, S Marco 1997 ☎ (041) 523 6953, holds a stash of Fortuny dresses, bags and pillows. All is in silk, hand-dyed in vivid, natural colours. Fortuny lamps, too, and if an item loses its pleating, they'll restore it 🦞 ...... FAITH WILLINGER continues the shopping spree: **Jesurum**, 60/61 Piazza S Marco ☎ (041) 522 9864, is "*a classic, in a deconsecrated church, for the most beautiful table and bed linen you've ever seen in your life. I could only afford a handkerchief*" .... 🦞

Bol Beyond the Spag

If Rome is Italy's head and Florence her heart, Bologna is most definitely her stomach. Since the first Italian cookbook, *La Scienza in Cucina e l'Arte di Mangiar Bene* by Pellegrino Artusi, was published here in 1891, Bologna has been feeding on its deserved reputation for culinary excellence. It certainly has the right ingredients for success: Emiglia-Romagna is home of king cheese Parmigiano-Reggiano, balsamic vinegar, Parma ham and the world's best pasta. An early morning browse through the market off piazzas Maggiore and Nettuno turns up instant still lifes and specialist food stalls, like **Tamburini**, with over 30 different prosciutti, cannon-sized mortadella, butter, local cheeses, handmade tortellini . . . DIY or let the professionals take charge, as at **Ristorante Silverio**, Via Nosadella 37 ☎ (051) 330604, where, according to DAVID DALE: *"Silverio Cineri takes cooking to greater heights than any Frenchman has. Dishes such as tortellotti stuffed with truffles in a vegetable broth and caramelized radicchio in hazelnut cream, combined with warm, knowledgeable service from dedicated waiters, make a night at Silverio a lifelong memory. Like all geniuses, Silverio is somewhat eccentric and likes to give customers books of his poetry in which, among other flights, he compares a beautiful woman to a plate of steaming ricotta."* Stagger on to Bologna's finest hotel, **Baglioni**, Via Independenza 8 ☎ (051) 225445, where the wood fire in the foyer, linen sheets and charming staff make a stay most digestible.

🔱 **FESTIVAL DEI DUE MONDI, Via del Duomo 7, Spoleto ☎ (0743) 28120; tickets also from Via Margutta 17, 00187 Rome ☎ (06) 361 4041**
Italy's best performing arts festival (late June-July), founded by composer Gian Carlo Menotti. Spoleto rings to the sound of opera, concerts, theatre and ballet and the bravos of the itinerant culture crowd. The inspiration for copycat Spoleto festivals in South Carolina and Melbourne.

FESTIVAL PUCCINIANO, Torre del Lago Puccini, 55049 Viareggio ☎ (0584) 343322
An annual festival (July-Aug) to celebrate the work of the great 19C composer. The Puccini pack and football-loving opera converts gather at the open-air theatre of Lake Massacciuccoli.

ROSSINI OPERA FESTIVAL, Via Rossini 37, 61100 Pesaro ☎ (0721) 697360
Another one-man festival, held in Aug-Sept in the town Rossini honoured with his birth and Pavarotti with his summer home. Peerless productions, especially of lesser-known operas.

STRESA MUSICAL WEEKS, Settimane Musicale, Palazzo dei Congressi, Via R Bonghi 4, 28049 Stresa ☎ (0323) 31095
The charming lakeside town – all 19C architecture and greenery – is welcoming host to a splendid late-summer 4-week classical music festival. International big names and potential virtuosi perform in Stresa and in the baroque palazzo (where Napoleon and Mussolini have both stayed) on Isola Bella on Lake Maggiore.

—————— Hotels ——————

BORGO SAN FELICE, San Felice, 53019 Castelnuovo Berardenga ☎ (0577) 359260
The picturesque wine-producing hamlet of San Felice, near Siena, has been turned into an upmarket, ultra-discreet holiday village. Red-roofed medieval buildings have been restored to form the main hotel and suites. A few genuine villagers left in situ give an authentic air.

CERTOSA DI MAGGIANO, Via Certosa 82, 53100 Siena ☎ (0577) 288180
A mile outside the city walls, a small hotel built around the original 1314 cloisters and tower of Tuscany's oldest Carthusian monastery. The orchard-surrounded peace is beyond price, the fine cooking just pricey; sitting rooms are charmingly decorated by Lorenzo Mongiardino, which pleases PAUL HENDERSON, though he warns: *"The public rooms are better than the bedrooms."*

HOTEL CALA DI VOLPE, Porto Cervo, Costa Smeralda, 07020 Sardinia ☎ (0789) 96083
A villagy resort, its red-tiled roofs spilling down to the cove's wooden jetty. *"A little run-down, in need of refreshment however, a beautiful location on a beautiful cove"* – MARCELLA HAZAN.

HOTEL PITRIZZA, Porto Cervo, Costa Smeralda, 07020 Sardinia ☎ (0789) 91500
The finest and luxiest of the Aga Khan's clutch

of properties in Sardinia, where boat people stay in the handful of villas, lounge on the private beach, dip into the salt-water pool carved into of the rocks, and sail off to the nearby private island of Mortorio.

HOTEL POSTA MARCUCCI, Bagno Vignone, 53027 Siena ☎ (0577) 887112
Small family-run hotel in a tiny Tuscan hilltop village overlooking the Val d'Orcia (close to Montalcino and Montepulciano). Signora Marcucci keeps the rooms filled with fresh flowers; the heated outdoor pool means the hearty can swim all year round.

🏊 HOTEL SPLENDIDO, Salita Baratta 13, 16034 Portofino ☎ (0185) 269551
Once a private villa now an Italian Riviera resort hotel, holiday home of refugees from la dolce vita. The rose pink 20s building's bedroom terraces have views to the ocean and the enchanting fishing village of Portofino. Has discreetly cared for royalty both Hollywood and hereditary: Garbo, Bogart, the Duke and Duchess of Windsor. LISA BARNARD loves it.

❝Sardinia has some of the most beautiful, untouched forests in Europe. There are dwarf green oaks, some over 700 years old – dwarfs because sheep keep eating their tops ❞

 MARCELLA HAZAN

🏊 HOTEL VILLA CIPRIANI, Via Canova 298, Asolo, 31011 Treviso ☎ (0423) 952166
Luxurious 16C villa, the former home of Robert Browning, in the hillside hamlet of Asolo. More refined than racy (the Queen Mother is a fan), the hotel will accommodate guests' every whim. Attentive, unsnooty service and wonderful cooking using vegetables from the garden and *"white truffles in season, with risotto. What I remember most is the extraordinary manager, Giuseppe Kimenir, who tells these wonderful stories. Beautiful views of the Veneto from where you sit, drinking tiziano (sparkling Italian wine with grape juice). We had the time of our lives"* – RICHARD COMPTON-MILLER.

🏊 VILLA D'ESTE, Via Regina 40, 22010 Cernobbio, Lake Como ☎ (031) 511471
This historic hotel began life in the 16C as a cardinal's palazzo and has passed through the ownership of Jesuits, the estranged wife of George IV and a Russian tsarina. Still grandly imposing, set in marvellous gardens filled with temples and follies. Rooms with balconies overlooking the lake are among the world's most romantic. LISA BARNARD and ROBIN LEACH think it's fine.

── *Music* ──

ARENA DI VERONA, Ente Arena, Piazza Bra 28, 37121 Verona ☎ (045) 590109. Tickets: Arch 6 of the Arena ☎ (045) 596517
The vast 1C AD amphitheatre (one of the best preserved of Roman times) hosts a festival season of opera and ballet in July-Aug. Don't expect restraint from the audience (25,000-strong, roaring approval and singing in the intervals) or the productions, which tend to be along anything-with-crowd-scenes-and-elephants lines (*Aida* is the biz). NB Ancient amphitheatres were not built for comfort – bring cushions, picnics and anything else you might need during an evening of heroic scale and epic length.

TEATRO DI SAN CARLO, Via San Carlo, 80132 Naples ☎ (081) 797 2111
Fabulously gilded and stuccoed 18C opera house, stopping short just this side of gaudy. One of the grandest openings of the Italian season.

── *Restaurants* ──

BECCHERIE, Piazza Ancillotto 10, 31100 Treviso ☎ (0422) 540871
Rustic inn (all exposed beams, copper pans, you know the score), serving Venetian provincial dishes – pheasant liver with pepper sauce, crêpes with radicchio.

BOTTEGA DEL VINO, Via Scudo di Francia 3, 37121 Verona ☎ (045) 800 4535
Homy, atmospheric restaurant – all wood panelling and wine bottles – with good solid food and an extraordinary wine list (without too greedy a mark-up). A LOGAN BENTLEY discovery.

RISTORANTE LA FATTORIA DI GRAZZI, Via del Cerro 11, Tavarnelle Val di Pesa ☎ (055) 807 0000
Sensational rural ristorante with robust, flavoursome food which makes the best of Tuscan produce. Wonderful game and seasonal dishes – roast wild boar or suckling pig, home-made truffle ravioli and famous lightly fried sage.

RISTORANTE UMBRIA, Via S Bonaventura 13, Todi, 06059 ☎ (075) 882737
In gorgeous medieval Todi, this ristorante is a real find for ALASTAIR LITTLE: *"You must eat on the terrace. I had tagliatelle with truffles and it was outstanding."*

SAN DOMENICO, Via Sacchi 1, 40026, Imola ☎ (0542) 29000
The transformed 15C Dominican convent now converts worshippers (including Pope John Paul II) to its refined, elevated cooking. Chef Valentino (once pupil of the chef of the last king of Italy) creates outstanding dishes such as

mosaico di verdura, a layered concoction of puréed vegetables, sea bass with Beluga caviare, and lobster with black truffle sauce; expensive, naturally, but *"worth every luscious penny"* – LOGAN BENTLEY.

Supping in Sardinia

Isolated by sea, with its own climate, customs and dress, it's hardly surprising that Sardinia's food should also depart radically from the Italian norm. MARCELLA HAZAN rounds up the best of it: *"In Alghero, La Lepanto, Via Alberto 135 ☎ (079) 979116, has the freshest spaghetti with scampi. They have one dish that's very Sardinian – bottarga (the pressed salt eggs of a grey mullet) grated over pasta. Also tripe cooked in Sardinian wine. On the Costa Smeralda is Gallura, Corso Umberto 145 ☎ (0789) 24648, where chef/owner Rita d'Enza does dishes that you never have anywhere else. Wonderful soups – cranberry beans with mussels, chick-peas with clams. And lamb cooked with cauliflower. She's very creative, but always thinking about traditional cooking and she uses all the local and seasonal ingredients. Another I like, also on the Costa Smeralda, is Palau, Via Capo d'Orso ☎ (0789) 709558, where I have had the best pane carasau, bread which they also call sheet music, it's so thin, with chopped oregano, extra virgin olive oil and salt. Very good carpaccio of swordfish, porcetto arosto (roast suckling pig), and a ricotta that is served on top of pane carasau with honey – wonderful."*

TRATTORIA LA BUCA, Via Ghizzi 3, Zibello (Parma) 43020 ☎ (0524) 99214
Matrilineally-descended down 5 generations of chefs, the current of whom is Miriam Leonardi, this trat is a fine advertisement for the food of Parma: culatello, fettuccine con porcini, lingua in sugo di funghi (tongue in mushroom sauce) and their finale: caccio baverese, a semi-freddo concoction of biscotti, cocoa, eggs and sugar.

Ski resorts

CORTINA D'AMPEZZO
Swankiest of the Italian resorts – full of immacu-

lately coiffed and furred women who would never see a fall, mainly because they never mount the mountain. All the first families of Italy ski here: royals, the Pirellis, Buitonis, Cicognas. Enchantingly pretty scenery. Best hotels: **Miramonti Majestic**; **Cristallo**; **Hotel de la Poste** (bar and terrace are *the* hangout pre-dinner). Best restaurants: **El Toulà**, **El Caminetto**, the tiny **Il Meloncino** and the lakeside **Meloncino al Lago**.

Villas

THE BEST IN ITALY, Count Momi and Countess Simonetta Brandolini d'Adda, Via Ugo Foscolo 72, 50124 Florence ☎ (055) 223064
Rentals of luxury private villas and palazzos with swimming pools, tennis courts and staff. Also specialist, tailor-made tours for individual groups, always staying in grand private homes.

Wine

"There is a new Italian Renaissance, this time in wine" declares MICHAEL BROADBENT, *"1985 seemed a turning point. Enlightened owners, brilliant winemakers bringing even classic areas like Tuscany and Piedmont to renewed life."* The bad old days of the tired (and sometimes even oxidized) wines of the 70s have given way to a new order of freshness and experimentation, with exciting techniques and rediscovered grape varieties in the forefront.

Piedmont

The 80s were good in Piedmont, with 82, 85 and 86 standing out for DAVID GLEAVE. The big wines here are the red siblings from the fruity and tannic Nebbiolo grape: **Barolo** and **Barbaresco**. In the **Barbaresco** region, Angelo **GAJA** is *"king"* for MICHAEL BROADBENT: *"His 1961 is one of the finest-ever Italian wines, closely followed by his 1971. And the 1985 Gaia & Rey Chardonnay is now superb."* **BRUNO GIACOSA** is a fine maker of both of the big Bs.

Best makers of **Barolo** for DAVID GLEAVE are **ROBERT VOERZIO**, **GIUSEPPE MASCARELLO** (*"Monprivato has tremendous concentration, balance, complexity and length"*), Elio **ALTARE** (*"He's working with the best vineyards"*), **PIO CESARE** and, topping the lot, **ALDO CONTERNO**, who produces *"consistently outstanding wines. The 85 special selection, Gran Bussia is probably one of the finest Italian wines."*

SIMON LOFTUS points oenophiles towards the grape Dolcetto: *"The Italian equivalent of Beaujolais – capable of light wines and wines of grandeur."* The other two grapes to look for are Barbera, especially oak-aged (*"does wonders"* – SIMON LOFTUS), and Arneis, which makes a good, dry white, notably from **GIACOSA**.

Tuscany

Brunello di Montalcino is still, with **Barolo**, Italy's most celebrated red and, notes DAVID GLEAVE, "*it's no longer the case that it outprices any other wine.*" Producers he tips are the (still expensive), **CASTELGIOCONDO, TALENTI, ALTESINO, LISINI, CONSTANTI**, the enormous **VILLA BANFI** and **IL POGGIONE**.

SASSICAIA, Italy's great maker of Cabernet Sauvignon, leads the way forward in creating a Tuscan 'Bordeaux'. MICHAEL BROADBENT thinks the 79 "*outstanding*"; of the 80s, 81, 82 and 85 are showing great promise. **Tignanello** is the other 'Bordelaise' Tuscan. Made by Piero **ANTINORI**, from the ancient winemaking dynasty, its cellar partners are a fine **Chianti**, **Orvieto** and the 75% Cabernet Sauvignon, 25% Sangiovese **Solaia**.

Florence's **Chianti** area still produces those straw-covered bottles, and some fine, fruity wines. DAVID GLEAVE reckons the best is the 1985 **Montesodi Rufina Riserva** made by **FRESCOBALDI** (they only bottle the best years). The senior Chianti, **Chianti Classico**, is made best by **FELSINA**, says DAVID G. Chianti's **ISOLE E OLENA** makes tip-top Vino da Tavola (VDT) from the Sangiovese grape – other fine VDTs of the area include **AMA**, **FONTODI** and **FONTERUTOLI**.

Tuscan Chardonnays (a grape only recently permitted in the area) to note are **FRESCOBALDI**'s **Pomino il Benefizio, ISOLA E OLENA, FELSINA** and **CAPEZZANA**. DAVID GLEAVE's best years? 88 and 90, "*All of them except for* **Capezzana** *are quite rich and Burgundian, while it is unoaked and more like a Chablis*". **CASTELLO DI VOLPAIA** is making a fine red, **Coltassala**, which is "*a special blend, vinified in a very Italian way, but top-quality*" – LIZ BERRY.

Umbria

The most exciting producers in Umbria, tips DAVID GLEAVE, are **ADANTI** (**Sagrantino di Montefalco, Rosso d'Arquata**), **CAPRAI** and **PALAZZONE** (producers of fine Orvieto). "*Another producer in the Orvieto area is* **CASTELLO DELLA SALA** [owned by Antinori]. *The top white is* **Cervaro della Sala**, *rich and round and nutty.*" The big-business **LUNGAROTTI** brings up the rear strongly with its superb **Riserva Vigna Montecchio**.

Veneto

The Veneto has had a string of good years, 83, 85, 86, 88 and 90, according to DAVID GLEAVE. For **Soave**, "*it is best to drink the most recent vintage and* **PIEROPAN** *is consistent and reasonably priced.*" The Veneto's extraordinary winemaking techniques result in some pretty out-of-the-ordinary wines – hear SIMON LOFTUS:

"*One of my great passions is* **Recioto** – *the sweet red – and the potent, dry* **Amarone**. *The grapes are picked late and dried on bamboo racks, an old technique which was in danger of dying out.*" Names to look for? **QUINTARELLI, ALLEGRINI** and **TEDESCHI**. DAVID GLEAVE thinks **ALLEGRINI** is the pick of the bunch for **Valpolicella** too, especially in the good years of 85, 86 and 89.

JAPAN

KYOTO

—— *Hotels* ——

HIRAGIYA RYOKAN N,
Fuyacho-Aneyakoji-agaru, Nakagyo-ku
☎ **(075) 221 1136**
Splendid archetypal Japanese inn with delightful rooms overlooking traditional gardens. RAYMOND BLANC approves.

 TAWARAYA, Oike Fuyacho,
Nakagyo-ku ☎ **(075) 211 5566**
The best ryokan (inn) in Japan. Founded some 350 years ago, it's been in the family for 11 generations. Remove your shoes as you check in, then check out one of 18 beautifully simple bedrooms with screens and tatami mats, look out on to Zen gardens, take a searing hot bath and flake out on your futon. "*The best Japanese meal I've ever had. Soft-slippered maids bring food to one's room – feathery tempura prawns nestle in bamboo baskets, strips of buttery Kobe beef and green chillis are sizzled on white-hot rocks, fresh fruit is arranged with the symmetry of a geisha's fluted fan. Even the hand towels are fastened with silk ribbon like rare scrolls*" – SUSAN KUROSAWA.

—— *Restaurants* ——

CHIHANA, Nawate-higashi-iru,
Shijo-dori, Higashiyama-ku
☎ **(075) 561 2741**
Best Japanese food in town. Book ahead – it's a small kappo (top-grade, authentic restaurant), with trad Kyoto dishes.

—— *Temples and gardens* ——

ENRYAKU-JI TEMPLE, Mount Hiei
Tranquil cluster of temples standing on a sacred mountainside outside the town. Buddhists have come to the temple since before its Inextin-

guishable Dharma Light was set ablaze over 1,200 years ago. Take the local bus from Kyoto station to Shimeidake.

HEIAN SHRINE
Here bloom the famous cherry trees, into tiny pale pink and white confetti. Wonderful ponds and irises.

KINKAKUJI TEMPLE
The replica of the early 15C Golden Pavilion sits in peaceful water gardens. Don't miss the **Ryoanji Temple** nearby, with its pebble garden.

KIYOMIZU TEMPLE
Liltingly beautiful temple in the hills above the city, with glimpses of the real world of bustle below.

OSAKA

— Hotels —

THE PLAZA, 2-2-49 Oyodo-Minami, Kita-ku ☎ (06) 453 1111
Modern, massive, with *the works* – outdoor pool, 11 restaurants and bars (Japanese with teppanyaki, French and Chinese food), personal service, beauty parlour.

— Restaurants —

CHAMBORD, Royal Hotel, 5-3-68 Nakashima, Kita-ku ☎ (06) 448 1121
No 1 French restaurant with great seafood – try fresh crab tart with foie gras, sea bass with yams and fine herbs. Menu changes each month.

KICCHO, 2-6-7 Koraibashi, Chur-ku ☎ (06) 231 1937
New HQ for the best and most highly regarded restaurant in Osaka. *The* place for kaiseki ryori – the ultimate menu, meaning many small dishes. Try sashimi, soups and yakimono (baked fish). Beautiful presentation, objets and treasures.

TOKYO

— Art and museums —

HARA MUSEUM, 4-7-25 Kitashinagawa, Shinagawa-ku ☎ (03) 3445 0651
Hara Sensei's aesthetic pleasure-dome houses a collection of work by most major Western artists and up-to-date Japanese art. Curator Toshio Hara is the world authority on contemporary Japanese art. Good café.

HARA MUSEUM ARC, 2844 Kanei, Shibukawa-shi, Gunma-ken ☎ (0279) 246585
Spanking new gallery and museum designed by Arata Isozaki. *"Get out of Tokyo to see it ... one of the best in the country with the best in contemporary art"* – CLAUDIA CRAGG.

IDEMITSU MUSEUM OF THE ARTS, International Bldg, 9F, 3-1-1 Marunouchi, Chiyoda-ku ☎ (03) 3213 9401
A private collection of superb quality – fine and decorative art including ukiyoe (simple genre paintings of everyday life), Japanese prints and some of the world's finest porcelain.

NIHON MINKA-EN, 7-1-1 Masugata, Tamu-ku, Kawasaki-shi ☎ (044) 922 2181
Preservation halls – a collection of antique homes, 'Important Cultural Properties', brought here from all over Japan to be saved from destruction. See how merchants, village chieftains, horse-traders, etc, lived.

SUNTORY MUSEUM OF ART, Suntory Bldg, 11F, 1-2-3 Akasaka, Minato-ku ☎ (03) 3470 1073
Formidable display of all things Japanese – lacquered objects, painting, porcelain, textiles and kimonos a-plenty. Splendid exhibitions.

TOKYO NATIONAL MUSEUM, 13-9 Ueno Koen, Taito-ku ☎ (03) 3822 1111
Unsurpassed collection of the art of Japan, including lacquer works, painting, porcelain, prints and sculpture. Housed in 4 buildings in Ueno Park.

— Arts centres —

BUNKAMURA, 2-24 Dogenzaka, Shibuya-ku ☎ (03) 3477 9111
Impressive arts centre containing the **Orchard Hall**, Japan's biggest concert hall with 2,150 seats; the **Cocoon Theater**, for plays, small musicals and dance; the smaller **Franchise Theater** and 2 movie theatres in **Le Cinema**.

— Bars and cafés —

CAFE DE ROPE, 6-1-8 Jingumae, Shibuya-ku ☎ (03) 3406 6845
Melting pot for Japanese and Euro fleshpots - see the prettiest, chic-est crowd in town, feel pretty cool yourself.

CAFE LA RUE, JT Plaza B, 4-28-12 Jingumae, Shibuya-ku ☎ (03) 3746 2344
High among the new crop of ethnic eateries, *"an interesting new café, serving a blend of foods from north Africa, Vietnam, Tahiti and the Caribbean in a delightful atmosphere"* – CLAUDIA CRAGG.

RADIO BAR, 2-31-7 Jingumae, Shibuya-ku ☎ (03) 3405 5490
Every cocktail under the sun, imbibed by hip Japanese and gaijin. Worth tuning in.

RED SHOES, B1, Azabu Palace, 2-25-18 Nishi Azabu, Minato-ku ☎ (03) 3499 4319
Long-standing fave – over 10 years old and still pulling serious groovers and rock 'n' rollers, like the Stones. Open 12 hours, from 7pm, with music, videos and films – a wall-full of them.

SPIRAL CAFE, 6F, Spiral Bldg, 5–6 Minami Aoyama, Minato-ku ☎ (03) 3498 5791
Multi-layered, multi-purpose building with a great caff. Sit with a cuppa and watch the art world buzz in the gallery – up-to-the-second contemporary work. Up a flight on 2 is the **Spiral Market** (imported stationery, tableware, soaps, Japanese goods such as chopsticks); 3rd is a hall for fashion shows, and down in the basement there's a Thai restaurant and bar – **Cay** ☎ (03) 3498 5790. MIWAKO SATO is a regular.

—————— Clubs ——————

Roppongi, **Akasaka** and **Harajuku** are the trendy nightlife areas. The brassier **Shinjuku** and **Ginza** are packed, respectively, with gaudy gay and transvestite clubs and hostess bars.

AREA, 3-8-15 Roppongi, Minato-ku ☎ (03) 3479 3721
Low-key smart folks' joint. Chinese décor, Chinese food, housy sounds and a big dance floor.

CIRCUS, 64 7-14-8 Roppongi, Minato-Ku ☎ (03) 5474 4570
The club with a view in a penthouse. Look out over glitzy Tokyo, look around at the city's hip brigade, and look good on the dance floor.

ENDMAX, 3-4-18 Higashi Azabu, Minato-ku ☎ (03) 3586 0639
Groovy new dance venue, house music, big dance floor and bar. Loadsa gottabetheres.

GOLD, 3-1-6 Kaigan, Minato-ku ☎ (03) 3453 3545
Warehouse chic lives on in Tokyo. Ravers still make it out to the bay for all nighters in the funky 7-floor mega club. Big sound system, good light show and drinks machines operated by your very own special gold card.

LEXINGTON QUEEN, B1, 3rd Goto Bldg, 3-13-14 Roppongi, Minato-ku ☎ (03) 3401 1661
Big black hole that sucks in the super novae – Madonna, Michael Jackson, Tina Turner, Eric Clapton and Japan's best-known actor, Toshiro Mifune – proprietor Bill Hersey keeps them coming. Models, paparazzi and groupies too.

—————— Fashion designers ——————

COMME DES GARCONS, 5-11-5 Minami-Aoyama, Minato-ku ☎ (03) 3407 2480
Like most of the ground-breaking Japanese designers of late, Rei Kawakubo is consolidating what she's broken. Little change from the rigorous, bold silhouettes of her 'bag lady' look that won her the hearts and purses of Eastern and Western dress-me-ups. Men still love the outsized shapes of her **Homme Plus** line.

HANAE MORI, Omotesando, 3-6-1 Kita-Aoyama, Minato-ku ☎ (03) 3400 3301
Madame Mori is a craftswoman, a designer, above all a retailer. Printed silk dresses remain her signature, but she has a whole building devoted to her diversifications – couture, prêt-à-porter, accessories, bed-linen, jewellery. Purveyor of the Tokyo look and all things Japanese.

ISSEY MIYAKE, Tessenkai Bldg, B1, 4-21-29 Minami-Aoyama, Minato-ku ☎ (03) 3423 1408
Asymmetric cutting, origami shapes, wacky materials, outrageous colours – Miyake was in the vanguard of the haute-Japonnaise style revolution of the 80s. As uncompromising as ever, he's currently setting a rural theme, getting

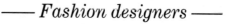 **Buzzz** Most gorgeous: **MZMZ** ☎ (03) 3423 3066, is the haunt of the latest willowy models to arrive on the Tokyo scene, clubbing it amid dead cool décor – granite, chrome and all that 👤...... Most enormous: **Juliana's**, 1-13-10 Shibaura, Minato-ku ☎ (03) 5484 4000, takes up 12 km of prime Tokyo space, with a vast body-sonic dance floor that packs in 2,000 bods 👤...... Most extortionate: A glass of **Courvoisier's Succession JL** cognac is poured for the princely sum of 12,000 yen in a Ginza bar – liquid gold 👤...... Best ramen: If you don't dare brave the street stalls for authentic, thick, Chinese-style noodles, go to **Keika**, 3-25-6 Shinjuku, Shinjuku-ku ☎ (03) 3352 4836 👤...... Best tempura: Pick from 18 varieties at the oldest tempura house in Tokyo, **Inagiku**, 2-9-8 Nihonbashi Kayabacho, Chuo-ku ☎ (03) 3669 5501, and branches .... 👤

back to basics. Less expensive **Plantation** and **Issey Sports** lines.

MATSUDA for MADAME NICOLE, Nicole Bldg, 3-1-25 Jingumae, Shibuya-ku ☎ (03) 3470 4821
Internationally known as Matsuda, this is a softer approach to haute. Wonderful tailoring and detailing – dresses, suits, separates in beautiful fabrics. Menswear for Narcissi.

TAKEO KIKUCHI, 6-6-22 Minami-Aoyama, Minato-ku ☎ (03) 3486 6607
Fashion and society wit – gets chaps into things chaps don't usually get into. See him about town too, visit him in his cheeky shop in his own TK building in Nishi Azabu.

> **❝** *Tokyo is a terrifyingly powerful city, brawling, teeming, wheeling and dealing but in it are extraordinary bits of beauty that escaped being bombed in the war* **❞**
>
> SIR PETER PARKER

TOKIO KUMAGAI, 3-15-10 Sendagaya, Shibuya-ku ☎ (03) 3475 5317
Weird and wonderful designs for men and women who want wackoid shoes and clothes with an incongruous juxtaposition of fabric. Another designer-about-town.

YOHJI YAMAMOTO, Maison Roppongi, 3F, 6-4-9 Roppongi, Minato-ku ☎ (03) 3423 3200
The original asymmetric geometric – leader of the big-on-shape movement, and maker of clothes that mould to your body, as though they were tailor-made. JENNY KEE remains loyal.

——— *Hotels* ———

CAPITOL TOKYU, 2-10-3 Nagata-cho, Chiyoda-ku ☎ (03) 3581 4511
One that satisfies the stars and DAVID GIBBONS: *"An older hotel, not the most luxurious, but so central. Great location, beside one of those little Japanese temples, so you can walk through the grounds at dawn and get over the jetlag. Food is very good."*

HOTEL OKURA, 2-10-4 Toranomon, Minato-ku ☎ (03) 3582 0111
Popular as ever, a city within a city – 8 restaurants, 4 bars, more than 40 shops, Japanese spa and massage, post office, photo studio, tea ceremony room. Service inspires loyalty in DOTT ROSA MARIA LETTS: *"Frankly it's an office, everyone stays there, and yet I find it very tasteful; you notice care in the service, the flowers, the*

music that they play as a little concert. Although Japan is in such a hurry, there seems to be no hurry here." LISA BARNARD and ANDRE PREVIN concur.

🏃 HOTEL SEIYO, 1-11-2 Ginza, Chuo-ku ☎ (03) 3535 1111
Japan's only boutique hotel – 80 rooms, highest staff:guest ratio (3:1), big English and American breakfasts, choice of 7 pillows, butler and secretary service, and in the fab bathrooms there's a TV and radio. Great food at the branch of Osaka's **Kiccho**. RAYMOND BLANC and MARY ROSSI approve, JEFFREY ARCHER's blown away: *"The best in the world – immaculate service, wonderful rooms, everything you expect."*

IMPERIAL HOTEL, 1-1-1 Uchisaiwaicho, Chiyoda-ku ☎ (03) 3504 1111
Prestigious address for finance folk – young Euro bods check in and hang out at the **Old Imperial Bar.** LISA BARNARD thinks it's the *"ultimate business man's hotel. Really brilliant, very, very grand".*

AKASAKA PRINCE 1-2 Kioi-cho, Chiyoda-ku, 102 ☎ (03) 3234 1111
Designed by Kenzo Tange, a cool 80s establishment. *"I just love the look of the place. It is extraordinary. The whole thing is in white marble, silver and purple. Quite an experience, it is very majestic, totally modern and space-age. It has the reputation for being an upper-class love hotel. Good food, I eat the sushi there. Enormous windows, light and airy"* – STEPHEN JONES.

MEGURO GAJOEN, 1-8-1 Shimo Meguro, Meguro-ku ☎ (03) 3491 4111
An old ryokan that sits somewhat incongruously with the modern blocks of the town centre. Japanese baroque interior.

——— *Music* ———

CASALS HALL, Ocanomizu Square 126, Kanda Surugadai, Chiyoda-ku ☎ (03) 3294 1229
Designed for chamber music, great acoustics and atmosphere. JULIAN LLOYD WEBBER loves to play there.

SUNTORY MUSIC HALL, 1-13-1 Akasaka, Minato-ku ☎ (03) 3505 1001
Modern, scientifically moulded acoustic technodrome. It cost the Japanese whisky giants a yen or two, but ANDRE PREVIN reckons it's worth it. Top orchestras, top batons.

——— *Restaurants* ———

CHOTOKU, 1-10-5 Shibuya, Shibuya-ku ☎ (03) 3407 8897
The place for udon (pasta-like white flour noodles). Served hot in dashi (fish-based stock)

with various toppings – try sansai (mountain vegetables).

EL TOULA, B1, From 1st Bldg, 3-10-5 Minami Aoyama, Minato-ku
☎ **(03) 3406 8831**
An Italian treat but not a trat – this one's formal, with a piano playing and offbeat dishes such as pasta with duck sauce or pumpkin-stuffed ravioli with sea urchin sauce. You're treated like kings, especially if it's your birthday or anniversary. Private dining room, too.

FUKUZUSHI, 5-7-8 Roppongi, Minato-ku
☎ **(03) 3402 4116**
Sensatonal sushi, tempura and chirashizushi (rice with raw fish laid on top). The most prestigious restaurant in town, high-powered business folk – gaijin and local – entertain each other; others can't afford to.

Blanc Mange

♟

"Japanese food is so much more visual – the sense of aesthetics, the flower arrangement, it's so sure, so much more unbelievably refined than in the West. The best fish markets in Tokyo are incredible, truly. Every sea creature in the world. I didn't see the Loch Ness Monster, but I wouldn't have been surprised. Things that I actually couldn't recognize, and all alive of course. I was mesmerized. Everything from shark to huge tuna fish to pieces of whale. They are very sensual about food, the Japanese, very purist. The purity brings them to the edge of cruelty when to get the ultimate experience they do things like eating live eels in vinegar, which creates a wonderful feeling in your stomach. This kind of refinement is sort of questionable" – RAYMOND BLANC.

HOTEL DE MIKUNI, 1-18 Wakaba, Shinjuku-ku ☎ **(03) 3351 3810**
Star chef Mikuni's restaurant combines light French cuisine with the Japanese art of presentation. Best value, as usual, is at lunchtime, when the sunny conservatory provides a delightfully different setting.

HOUSE OF 1999, 2-9-4 Shibuya, Shibuya-ku ☎ **(03) 3498 3001**
Another unusual setting for Tokyo, in a house with a covered entrance and a private pool club downstairs. Classic French cuisine, excellent

wine list – this is a rare establishment with a proper cellar. One for special occasions.

IL BOCCALONE, 1-15-9 Ebisu, Shibuya-ku
☎ **(03) 3449 1430**
Roman trattoria that's *"the hardest restaurant in town to get into, with exquisite food"* – CLAUDIA CRAGG. It's all cooked by Italians, and it's run and choreographed by the flamboyant 'everyone's my best friend' Silvano. Rustic setting, rustic nosh – delicious risotto in a half case of parmesan cheese.

INAKAYA, 7-8-4 Roppongi, Minato-ku
☎ **(03) 3405 9866**
The best robatayaki (roast-charcoal-grilled food) in Tokyo with some serious drama thrown in. The centrepiece is a U-shaped counter – 2 cooks in trad costume prepare prawns, fish, meat and fab veggie things, and waiters serve it all on long paddles. Ask for what you like the look of at the counter – loudly, or you won't be heard.

KISSO, B1, Axis Bldg, 5-17-1 Roppongi, Minato-ku ☎ **(03) 3582 4191**
Great food – tempura, kaiseki ryori – without the high formality of traditional Japanese service. Relaxed, modern and chic, gaijin make the most of it.

MAENAM, Togensha Bldg, 75, 1 & 2F, 1-70-3 Nishi Azabu, Minato-ku
☎ **(03) 3404 4745**
Terrific new Thai that's a fave with the likes of Janet Jackson, the Beach Boys and CLAUDIA CRAGG: *"Excellent chicken wrapped in pandanas leaves, Chinese vegetables Thai-style."* Japanese actor Hiroshi Taohi, a sort of Perry Mason-alike, goes too.

MAISON CAVIAR, 2-27-19 Minami Aoyama, Minato-ku ☎ **(03) 3470 0063**
Burgeoning sturgeonerie surging with Persian. Russian and Chinese too. Robert De Niro and Diane Lane succumb.

MAKIE, B1, 2-8-44 Kita Aoyama, Minato-ku
☎ **(03) 5474 6102**
An East-West mix that's perfect for Western palates. Tuck into Frenchified kaiseki (multi mini courses) served elegantly on makie (gold-embossed black lacquerware). Immaculate service and an unusually fine wine list.

PYRAMIDE, 6-6 Roppongi, Minato-ku
Little Italy, stacked up on 4 floors. *"One of the hottest places in Roppongi"* – MIWAKO SATO. Drink in the 3rd-floor bar, dine at the terrific **Trattoria** ☎ (03) 3746 0230, or **Il Forno**, ☎ (03) 3796 2641, along with ad/marketing types. Work off the pasta browsing in boutiques (Etoro, MaxMara), interiors shop and gallery.

SELAN, 2-1-19 Kita Aoyama, Minato-ku
☎ **(03) 3478 2200**
Another pan-Pacific success story – related to

LA's steamin' Chaya Brasserie – for steaks and seafood. Cool décor, cooler clients.

SUSHI BAR SAI, Langling Core Andos Bldg, 2F, 1-7-5 Jinnan, Shibuya-ku
☎ **(03) 3496 6333**
Sushi in the Western mode. Californian and Japanese cooking fuses to delight gaijin. Try tofu and vegetable sushi too.

TOSHIAN, 5-17-2 Shiroganedai, Minato-ku
☎ **(03) 3444 1741**
Tops for trad soba (light, buckwheat noodles), a popular lunch dish. Have them cold or hot, topped with tempura, scallops or eel and be sure to slurp them up, Japanese-style.

—— Shopping ——

Major stores are scattered here and there – find Matsuya, Mitsukoshi and Kanebo in **Ginza**, neighbouring **Yurakucho** has Hankyu and Seibu, **Nihonbashi** has Takashimaya, and **Shinjuku** Isetan. **Nireke-no-tori** "*is the very hottest fashion boulevard – sleeker than Omote-Sando, full of fashionable boutiques – Yohji, Comme des Garçons, Issey Miyake, Chantal Thomass, Emporio Armani*" – MIWAKO SATO. Find Ferré, Sonia Rykiel, Missoni and co in the **Sonet Aoyama Bldg**, and Gianni Versace, Cassina furniture and Verry in the **Colezione Bldg**.

AXIS, 5-17-1 Roppongi, Minato-ku
☎ **(03) 3587 2781**
Everything shouts 'design' here – the building, the shoppers and the products. Pick the most drawing-boarded furniture, tableware, kitchen goods, crafts, fabrics . . .

MATSUYA, 3-6-1 Ginza, Chuo-ku
☎ **(03) 3567 1211**
Fashion A to Z on floors 1-6, the best from Japan, Europe and the States. Get up to the 7th floor and you're in product design heaven.

NUNO, Axis Bldg, B1, 5-17-1 Roppongi, Minato-ku ☎ **(03) 3582 7997**
For trad fabrics you can't beat it. Hand-painted and silk-printed kimono silks, cut in lengths.

ORIENTAL BAZAAR, Omotesando, 5-9-13 Jingumae, Shibuya-ku ☎ **(03) 3400 3933**
Treasure trove of authentic Japanese goodies – furniture, ornate wedding kimonos in silk brocade (to hang on your wall), little lacquer bowls with chopsticks, hand-blocked prints, paintings and china.

PARCO, 15-1 Udagawa-cho, Shibuya-ku
☎ **(03) 3464 5111**
For shopaholics, this is *the* place. Part of the Seibu group, where chic modern Japan meets the consumer. Designers from around the world fit out the little shops, the coolest crowd in the

city saunters through. It even has its own exhibition space, cinema and theatre. Exit 6 from Shibuya Station (also for Seibu and Seed).

SEED, 21-1 Udagawa-cho, Shibuya-ku
☎ **(03) 3462 0111**
Studied designer building with floors devoted to Euro trendsetters, accessories, Japanese fashion for men, jewellery . . . and an English tea room called **Café Anglais**.

SEIBU, (Ginza), 2-1 Yurakucho, Chiyoda-ku ☎ **(03) 3286 0111; and branches**
Top department store. Famous old names have spaces here – Hermès, Vuitton, Rykiel, Lauren. So do the best Japanese – Comme des Garçons, Yamamoto. Any look you want, from shooting at Blenheim to grooving at the Lex. The foreign customer helpline is ☎ (03) 3286 5482.

VIVRE 21, Omotesando, 5-10-1 Jingumae, Shibuya-ku ☎ **(03) 3498 2221**
Junior fashion. Fab young Japanese – Shin Hosokawa, Takeo Kikuchi, Nicole, meet the wackiest from Europe.

WAVE, 6-2-21 Roppongi, Minato-ku
☎ **(03) 3408 0111**
CDs, pop videos, video laser discs, hifi, Filofaxes, bags . . . toys for today from the Seibu group.

· REST OF ·

JAPAN

—— Art and museums ——

HAKONE OPEN AIR MUSEUM, Kanagawa-ken ☎ **(0460) 21161**
Galleries and gardens showing the best sculpture from Japan and around the world – works by Takamura, Moore, Hepworth, Calder, Giacometti et al. Get there by the Romance Car, an open-top train from Shinjuku in Tokyo. Nearby hot springs to sit in afterwards.

—— Hotels ——

FUJIYA HOTEL, 359 Miyanoshita, Hakone ☎ **(0460) 22211**
Prettily placed near Mount Fuji, a Western-style hotel with a sense of eccentricity. If you prefer the native experience, book in advance at the annexe, a former imperial villa now run as a ryokan. Visit in May to see the azaleas in bloom.

MIYAJIMA LODGE, Miyajima
☎ **(0829) 442233**
A charming, traditional inn on the island on

Japan's inland sea. Solicitous service (steaming bath, personally cooked dinner . . .) and local attractions such as Empress Suiko's 6C Itsukushima Shrine, attract discerning rather than disco-ing types, such as Prince Charles.

---------- *Ski resorts* ----------

NAEBA
Choose this one if only to bathe away the aches and pains in a natural steam bath afterwards – hot springs surround the resort. The Emperor makes an annual trip.

SAPPORO
On the north island of Hokkaido, this one's bitterly cold, but offers good skiing and hot water springs. Japanese skiers arrive en force. The famous brewery's here (open to the public) and so is the annual Snow Festival.

ZAO
Wonderful skiing, scenic slopes, set in one of Japan's most beautiful natural parks.

KENYA

CHESHALA, c/o Tourist Promotions, PO Box 849, Malindi ☎ (0123) 21171
Remote beachside camp, reachable only by 4-wheel drive. 8 traditional bandas sleep 16 people. Yards from the Indian Ocean, it sweeps ED VICTOR away: *"One of my favourite hotels I've ever stayed in. It's just a collection of little huts, absolutely simple – the shower is a drum that is hauled by a little donkey and stuck up on your tent and the sun heats it so you get warm water. The beach is gorgeous, completely alone. All kinds of water sports and the food is quite wonderful – fish – they catch it, bring it in and grill it for you."*

LAKE NAIVASHA
Hippo gaze in the sparkling waters, but keep your distance – they can bite you in half. NICHOLAS VILLIERS lets you in on a secret: *"The Earl and Countess of Enniskillen have a ranch on the edge of Lake Naivasha called* **Mundu** (PO Box 1, Naivasha). *It's the most beautiful Kenyan house of the 20s. While the ranch is a full-time farm, they, on a very selective basis, almost by introduction only, have people to stay."*

LAMU
Africa's former link with Arabia, Lamu has a trading history dating back to the 10C. Completely unpolluted, here you travel by donkey-power or wind-power (by dhow). Stay at the **Peponi Hotel**, on an 8-mile beach, with deep-sea fishing, waterskiing, windsurfing and

snorkelling. Stroll along the sands to Shella, a little fishing village with minareted mosque, or charter the hotel's 35-ft dhow to the surrounding islands.

MASAI MARA GAME RESERVE
The staggering expanse of savannah extends from the Serengeti in Tanzania to form the greatest safari land in the world: a 9,600-sq-m ecosystem. See big game – elephant, lion, rhino – birds of prey and the massive migration of zebra and wildebeest between July and October. Stay at **Kichwa Tembo Camp**.

MOMBASA
Divine beaches protected from the crashing Indian Ocean by a reef. Secluded snorkelling, scuba, sailing, etc. **Serena Beach Hotel** ☎ (011) 485721 and **Serena Lodge** ☎ (011) 339800, are *"absolutely fantastic,"* sighs TERRY HOLMES.

 MOUNT KENYA SAFARI CLUB, PO Box 35, Nanyuki ☎ (0176) 33323
Superb hotel in the foothills of Mount Kenya, amid 200 acres of lawns and flower-beds with ponds, a walled rose garden and a mountain stream. *"In the colonial style, terrific rooms and excellent food. Lovely swimming pool. Horse riding into the foothills is spectacular"* – TERRY HOLMES.

SAMBURU GAME RESERVE
A semi-desert area bordering the Uaso Nyiro River. See rare species like the reticulated giraffe and Grevy's zebra. Birds too. Stay at **Samburu Lodge** or **Larsen's Camp**, both via Central Reservations Office, PO Box 47557, Nairobi ☎ (02) 335807.

TSAVO NATIONAL PARK
In southern Kenya, near the Tanzanian border, this was Kenya's first National Game Park. See snow-capped Mount Kilimanjaro on a clear day; game and other wildlife on an illuminated night. Best lodge, the first in Kenya: **Kilaguni Lodge**.

TREETOPS, c/o Central Reservations Office, PO Box 47447, Nairobi ☎ (02) 335807
The famous stilted, giraffe-high lodge where British royals and others view game-ridden water-holes by night, safe behind glass.

---------- *Tours* ----------

See also **Silk Cut Travel, Tempo Travel, Abercrombie & Kent** and **Tippett's Safaris** (see Travel Directory).

AIR KENYA, PO Box 30357, Nairobi ☎ (02) 501601 and SAFARI AIR, PO Box 41951, Nairobi ☎ (02) 501211
Get to the places others can't reach.

EAST AFRICAN WILDLIFE SAFARIS (see Travel Directory)
Here's a moveable feast; if you've had enough of lodges, hotels, etc, go by balloon or plane and sleep real peaceful – just like Caroline Kennedy and Charlton Heston.

LUXEMBOURG

LA BERGERIE, 1 Geyershof, Geyershof ☎ 79464
Hidden in the forest, some 25 km from the capital, this quiet low-key restaurant is chock-a-block with appreciative gourmets.

LE RELAIS ROYAL, 12 blvd Royal ☎ 41616
Part of the élite hotel of the same name. Chef Alain Thomas comes from Réunion Island and uses exotic spices and flavours to create unusual French cuisine – freshwater fish with thyme blossom and shallot and honey tartlet; lamb cakes with aubergine, courgettes and mash in port sauce. *"Has been named one of the world's top 50, an ideal place to dine in a discreet, distinguished and convenient setting"* – CHAMBERTIN.

SAINT MICHEL, 32 rue de l'Eau ☎ 223215
Opposite the Ducal Palace, Lysiane Guillou's charming restaurant is buckling under the weight of its infinite awards. French classics are reinterpreted with a modern touch in *"this sanctuary of perfection, good taste and distinction"* – CHAMBERTIN.

TIMES, 8 rue Louvigny ☎ 222722
The traditional 18C house belies the modern interior à la luxury liner of the 30s, with furniture by Philippe Starck. The chosen few (36 only, usually stars of media and film) choose from a small, frequently changing menu of market-led dishes; carpaccio with foie gras is unmissable.

MALAYSIA

EASTERN & ORIENTAL HOTEL, 10 Farquhar St, 10200 Penang ☎ (04) 375322
In colonial times you could find Somerset Maugham and Noel Coward strolling around here. Good mature gardens in which to take that constitutional, by the Indian Ocean, after which you'll be ready for an E & O Colada or an E & O Sling before dining in the splendid **1885 Grill**.

PENANG MUTIARA, Jalan Teluk Bahang, 11050 Penang ☎ (04) 812828
Fab resort and complex on the best beach in the somewhat tarnished pearl of the Orient. Great service, masses of water sports, tennis, fitness centre, Japanese, Chinese, and Italian restaurants, and pools with bars.

 **REGENT OF KUALA LUMPUR, 160 Jalan Bukit Bintang, 55100 Kuala Lumpur ☎ (03) 241 8000**
A mere toddler in age terms, the Regent's firmly established as a KL fave. Sleek mod cons – 469 business-minded rooms, massive duplex Regent Suite, health club, outdoor pool and 6 restaurants – with Japanese, Chinese, Malay and Western food.

SHANGRI-LA, 11 Jalan Sultan Ismail, 50250 Kuala Lumpur ☎ (03) 232 2388
Glitziest of the lot – and the biggest with 700-plus rooms on 28 floors. Brill food: **Restaurant Lafite** has some of the best French in town, **Nadaman** the best Japanese, **Shang Palace** for Cantonese. Sports and fitness fittingly catered for; special arrangements with local golf clubs.

MEXICO

LAS BRISAS, PO Box 281, 39868 Acapulco ☎ (748) 41580
Terraced into the hills spilling down to Acapulco Bay, a villa resort in groves of hibiscus and bougainvillaea. Each casita has its own or shared pool and, for exploring, *"you get given your own pink and white jeep. Everybody from Elizabeth Taylor to Princess Stephanie has stayed there. Acapulco is not so much beaches as views and nightlife"* – ROBIN LEACH.

HOTEL GARZA BLANCA, PO Box 58, Puerto Vallarta, Jalisco ☎ (322) 26944
Fabulously fashionable oasis in over-run Puerto Vallarta. Beachside suites on the still-white beach or little Mexican houses on the hillside with their own tiny pools and gardens attract the likes of Liz Taylor.

MOROCCO

EL MINZAH, 85 Rue de la Liberté, Tangier ☎ (9) 935885
Where the Med meets the Atlantic, a resort hotel with a cool, arcaded courtyard and Moorish red salon.

LA GAZELLE D'OR, PO Box 60, Taroudant ☎ (8) 852039
Sanctuary of winter sunshine near a fortified town in the Atlas mountains. *"An unexpected luxury hotel, with a nod to Berber tents. A cross-legged Arab makes you mint tea with thin sheets of sugar, fresh bunches of mint on to which is poured boiling water from a great height. Romantic Arabic touches like tented ceilings in your rooms; exotic gardens and lawns which are manicured with sickles"* – JILL MULLENS. Scene of *that* hol of the Duchess of York and Texan Steve Wyatt.

 LA MAMOUNIA, Ave Bab Djedid, Marrakech ☎ (4) 448981
Once Churchill's hideaway, now the most glamorous hotel in Morocco, sleek Art Decoesque (inlaid woods, chrome, M-motif carpets), with the odd OTT note (enormous chandeliers in the lobby). A quartet of fine restaurants (the Moroccan and Italian are tops); sensational buffet lunch by pool; lovely gardens; casino; chic nightclub. *"Very, very fashionable, ultra-ultra, élity"* – LISA BARNARD. Fab health and beauty facilities with hammam and sauna.

PALAIS JAMAI, Bab-el-Guissa, Fez ☎ (5) 634331
The Grand Vizier's old palace is a little jaded, but still offers scurrying service, deliciously cool gardens and wonderful Moroccan food (and a belly dancer to boot). Wake up to the Muslim call to prayer and look out over the medina. The faint-hearted should beware the hammam.

NEPAL

FISHTAIL LODGE, Pokhara ☎ (61) 221711
Travellers' rest: *"Not the most comfortable but just the best view, uninterrupted from you to the mountains. There's a really beautiful old Raj-style garden in front of you, then the lake . . . totally the most magical sight. Beyond that, lots of greenery and then the mountains, so close it is like looking the length of Sloane Street. The mountains are all covered in snow and so utterly beautiful you can't imagine anything more fantastic. You can hire an aeroplane and fly around Annapurna"* – SERENA FASS.

THE SOALTEE OBEROI, PO Box 97, Tahachal, Kathmandu ☎ (01) 272550
Nepal's swankiest hotel, boasting health club, 4 restaurants and the super-technology of CNN and direct-dial phones. The revamped Princep Wing has 110 deluxe rooms; the Himalayan is on its way to deluxedom.

TIGER TOPS JUNGLE LODGE, PO Box 242, Kathmandu ☎ (01) 222706
A cluster of thatched, stilted huts in one of Asia's richest wildlife sanctuaries, the Royal Chitwan National Park. Amateur Attenboroughs in this neck of the jungle include the British royal family. Travel by elephant in search of the great one-horned rhino or Royal Bengal Tiger, by boat through the river kingdom of the rare fish-eating gharial crocodile, or stay at the **Tiger Tops Tented Camp**: *"So beautifully run and so well organized. Absolutely the best thing in the world for seeing rhino, which are amazing, prehistoric"* – SERENA FASS. LORD MONTAGU OF BEAULIEU has his doubts: *"Very nice but a bit artificial. They tie a dead lion up to attract the tiger."*

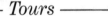 Tours

MOUNTAIN TRAVEL NEPAL, PO Box 170, Kathmandu ☎ (01) 414508
The oldest and best Himalayan trekking company, founded by ex-British Army officer, tiger expert and mountaineer Col Jimmy Roberts. Owners of the Tiger Tops clan that includes the

Buzzz Morocco bound: hope to come upon **The Swiss Café** (no address, no phone), on the coast between Oualidia and Safi: *"The best meal I have ever had, in an un-chic wooden pavilion on a lonely beach. Mussels and periwinkles were steamed in salt water while the staff went off to catch a fresh lobster. The lobster eventually appeared simply grilled with a squeeze of fresh lime juice. Food for the gods"* – JILL MULLENS . . . . . . Hole in the wall: Pop through this one near the casbah in Marrakech and a white-robed man, walking backwards, will lead you to Morocco's most spectacular restaurant, **Yakout**, 79 Sidi Ahmed Souissi ☎ (4) 441903. Sit on silk cushions in arcades strewn with rose petals, around a beautifully lit pool, and await your banquet . . . . . . Marrakech refuge 2: Duck out of the sandy-hued city by entering **Yves Saint Laurent**'s **Marjorelle Gardens**, Gueliz, a walled tropical paradise open to the public, with doors, window frames and pots painted in primary colours. . . . .

Jungle Lodge and Tented Camp (above), and the **Tharu Village** for only 16, staying in a traditional longhouse. Also the **Karnali Lodge** and **Tented Camp** in far western Nepal, with wildlife viewing by elephant and river rafting. Tailor-made treks with Sherpa guides.

NETHERLANDS

AMSTERDAM

—— *Art and museums* ——

REMBRANDTHUIS, Jodenbreestraat 6, 1011 NK ☎ (020) 6249486
Old Masters galore in the master's old house. More than 250 etchings (*The 3 Crosses, The 100 Guilder Print . . .*) in the 5 rooms and hallway. Drawings as well – not always exhibited.

RIJKSMUSEUM VINCENT VAN GOGH, Paulus Potterstraat 7, 1071 CX ☎ (020) 570 5200
Around 200 paintings by Van Gogh and others. See versions of the *Sunflowers* and *Irises*, *Vincent's Bedroom*, several self-portraits – one with severed earlobe, etc. Memorabilia too.

🍴 RIJKSMUSEUM, Stadhouderskade 42, 1071 ZD ☎ (020) 673 2121
The best in the world for 17C Dutch painting. Also 16C-19C painting, sculpture, and outstanding Delft pottery, ceramics, silver, glassware, lace and furniture. See Rembrandt's massive *Night Watch* and tender *Jewish Bride* while they're still attributed to him.

STEDELIJK MUSEUM, Paulus Potterstraat 13, 1071 CX ☎ (020) 573 2911
Fine national collection of modern and contemporary art from 1850 to the present. Impressive pieces from 1950 onwards.

—— *Hotels* ——

AMSTEL INTER-CONTINENTAL HOTEL, Professor Tulpplein 1, 1018 GX ☎ (020) 622 6060
Claims to be *the* royal resting place in Europe – more crowned heads have lain here than in any other hostelry. Built in 1866 and completely renovated in 1991, it's certainly a palatial stopover. Top-flight cooking in **La Rive** restaurant, overlooking the river.

THE GRAND, Oudezijds Voorburgwal 197, 1001 EX ☎ (020) 555 3111
A new deluxe hotel based in the former city hall,

sandwiched between two canals. After a megaguilder restoration, it's now as plush as can be, with health spa and Albert Roux-supervised **Café Roux** and **The Admiralty**.

HOTEL DE L'EUROPE, Nieuwe Doelenstraat 2–8, 1012 CP ☎ (020) 623 4836
19C Amstel-side hotel, semi-encircled by a canal. Spacious, pastel rooms with views, and the celebrated **Excelsior** French restaurant – piano, candelabra, Irish linen, the works.

HOTEL PULITZER, Prinsengracht 315–331, 1016 GZ ☎ (020) 523 5235
Prize hotel dreamt up by Joseph's grandson Peter. Converted from 24 17C–18C gabled canal houses, it's all corners, corridors, staircases and beams, plus interior gardens and an art gallery. Bizwise too (6 conference rooms), yet it feels like a private house.

—— *Music* ——

CONCERTGEBOUW, Concertgebouwplan 2–6, 1071 LN ☎ (020) 573 0573
One of the world's best concert halls for ANDRE PREVIN (*"great fun and very beautiful"*). Where the Royal Concertgebouw Orchestra bows, under the baton of the extraordinary Riccardo Chailly.

—— *Restaurants* ——

See also Hotels.

DE BELHAMEL, Brouwersgracht 60 ☎ (020) 622 1095
Bright and conscience-driven young English chef works wonders with organic meat and veg and smokes his own salmon. Bustly, fun atmosphere with young trendies and biz bods angling for a window table with views over the Herengracht canal.

DIE GOUDEN REAEL, Zandhoek 14 ☎ (020) 623 3883
Set in Amsterdam harbour, surrounded by boats and white swing bridges, this is a small, simple eatery with an elegant little daily-changing menu posted up on the wall. Pray that chalked up the day you go is the sensational entrée of 6 steamed fish.

TRECHTER, Hobbemakade 63 ☎ (020) 671 1263
Book way ahead to nab one of the 8 tables at this bestarred gastro-gnomic wonder. Chef-owner Jan de Wit is much praised for liquid innovations – endive soup with walnut and roquefort – and a light way with fish – red mullet with lentils and mussel juice, for example. Wine list as long and distinguished as the waiting list.

· REST OF ·

NETHERLANDS

—— Art and museums ——

FRANS HALS MUSEUM, Groot Heiligland, PO Box 3365, Haarlem
☎ **(023) 319180**
Authoritative collection of 17C portraiture, still lifes, landscapes and decorative art. Highlight, naturally, is Hals: 8 group portraits of militia companies and regiments. Modern works too, from the Dutch Impressionists to local working artists.

MAURITSHUIS, Korte Vijverberg 8, 2513 AB The Hague
☎ **(070) 346 9244**
A perfect example of Dutch Palladianism, built in 1636, now a perfect example of a small museum. Splendid collection of all the great 17C Dutch masters – Vermeer, Steen, Hals and Rembrandt.

RIJKSMUSEUM KROLLER-MULLER, Houtkampweg 6, 6731 AW Otterlo
☎ **(0838) 21041**
Make the trek – it's in the middle of a national park – to cop an astonishing collection of some 50 Van Goghs, including a *Sunflowers*, *The Weaver* and *The Potato Eaters*, as well as the best of the rest from Impressionism onwards. The sculpture garden trips through time from Rodin to Moore and Hepworth.

—— Hotels ——

HOTEL DES INDES, Lange Voorhout 54–56, 2514 EG The Hague
☎ **(070) 346 9553**
Grand, former baronial 19C palace, a favourite with diplomats visiting the nearby embassies. Classic French cuisine at **Le Restaurant**. Former guests include Mata Hari and Anna Pavlova, who expired gracefully here after a performance.

KASTEEL WITTEM, Wittemer Allée 3, 6286 AA Wittem-Zuid Limburg
☎ **(04450) 1208**
Historic medieval castle some 8 miles from Maastricht. 12 raftered bedrooms, including a suite in the tower. Once a strategic player in the 80 Years War (16C–17C), more recently hosted the strategic players in 91's Maastricht summit.

—— Restaurants ——

LE COQ D'OR, Van Vollenhovenstraat 25, 3016 BG Rotterdam ☎ **(010) 436 6405**
Has been laying *les oeufs d'ors* for some 30 years – highly regarded, expensive restaurant in a former trader's house in the old port district. Classic French cooking, surprisingly strong on vegetarian dishes. The crispy cod is a stand-out, those who know order it even when it isn't on the menu.

NEW ZEALAND

AUCKLAND

—— Hotels ——

THE REGENT AUCKLAND, Albert St, Private Bag 92125 ☎ **(09) 309 8888**
World-class polished performer. A reliable (invariably high) standard of service, facilities and food, plus little extras like the rooftop pool tip the balance for Rod Stewart and Rachel Hunter, Nigel Kennedy, Dire Straits and the English cricket team. Suites have harbour views. **Longchamps** restaurant treats local produce simply and well and matches it with a strong NZ wine list.

HYATT AUCKLAND, Cnr Waterloo Quadrant and Princes St ☎ **(09) 366 1234**
All rooms in Auckland's No 2 have views of

 **Buzzz** Dining with DON in Auckland: For breezy atmosphere and nice nosh, HEWITSON sails **Harbourside** ☎ (09) 307 0556: *"A magnificent setting in the old ferry terminal. Big, brash and bustling"* ...... He goes casual at **Killarney Street Brasserie** ☎ (09) 489 9409, for its *"skilfully selected wine list"* ...... Victuals with VIC: For food with a view, WILLIAMS heads for **Saints Waterfront Brasserie** ☎ (09) 575 9969, which boasts an all-women kitchen ...... **Columbus** ☎ (09) 358 3204 is his choice for an *"interesting mix of Cajun and Mediterranean cuisines from talented chef John Schwed"* ...... Over to **Ajo** ☎ (09) 358 1796, for an *"eclectic menu with Spanish/Italian leanings, in great surroundings"* – VW ...

harbour, city or park, and windows that actually open. Bon Jovi, Geoffrey Boycott, John Dankworth and Cleo Laine swear by it. Eat at the much-vaunted **Top of the Town**, or **Cloud's Café**, where Don and Phil Everly pigged out on black rice pudding.

SHERATON AUCKLAND HOTEL AND TOWERS, 83 Symonds St ☎ (09) 795132
Very 80s hotel, sleek and smooth-running. **The Towers** (super luxy 9th and 10th floors) keeps DON HEWITSON sweet: *"It has a butler service and a nice big lounge for meetings. Friendly, discreet service and excellent facilities – a guest lounge with a rarity: edible canapés. Excellent standard of wines."* Health club, too.

———— *Restaurants* ————

🐟 ANTOINE'S, 333 Parnell Rd, Parnell 1 ☎ (09) 798756
Auckland's best, housed in an early colonial building. Chef/owner Tony Astle still has a light hand with minceur combos such as rock oysters on raw salmon with chlorophyll sauce, though gutsier, recession-led farmhouse dishes (rabbit casserole, braised oxtail) appear more frequently. *"The finest, without a doubt"* – DON HEWITSON.

FRENCH CAFE, 210 Symonds St ☎ (09) 771911
Frankly one of the best in town, for super-fresh seafood, seasonal specials and decadent desserts. No borderland rivalry here – Spanish tapas are writ large on the menu. *"An award winner and deservedly so"* – VIC WILLIAMS.

VARICK'S, 70 Jervois Rd, Herne Bay ☎ (09) 376 2049
Chef/owner Varick Neilson is conjuring marvels with the very best of NZ produce – South Island salmon, Northland tua tua (a clam-like shellfish) and Canterbury venison. He recently pulled out of the hat lamb's loin, sweetbreads and brain, to win the 'best treatment of the national meat' award.

WELLINGTON

———— *Hotels* ————

PLAZA INTERNATIONAL, 148–176 Wakefield St ☎ (04) 473 3900
The one, with spectacular harbour views that draw Dire Straits, Shirley Bassey and Cliff Richard (who stays in the 8th-floor Presidential Suite). The elegant **Burbury's** restaurant (access for non-guests by exterior bubble lift) offers style on a plate, using NZ's best produce.

———— *Restaurants* ————

THE TERRACE COACHMAN, 97 The Terrace, PO Box 10682 ☎ (04) 473 8170
The Coachman's moved further into town and handed on the reins – Des Britten's son Dominic is now in charge of cooking. French dishes and South Island ingredients (venison with red cabbage confit, salmon wrapped in cabbage and white fish) keep DON HEWITSON suitably impressed.

PIERRE'S, 342 Tinakori Rd, Thorndon ☎ (04) 472 6238
Informal BYO bistro with super-fresh, simple dishes such as venison with pickled pear and bacon, char-grilled loin of lamb with stuffed onion and a garlic glaze, smoked South Island salmon flown in from Nelson. *"Remarkably consistent"* – DON HEWITSON.

ZINO'S, 351 The Parade, Island Bay ☎ (04) 383 8256
Mediterranean restaurant serving *"the best crayfish I have ever eaten – you'd be gasping if you had that. Absolutely brilliant"* – DON HEWITSON.

· REST OF ·

NEW ZEALAND

———— *Hotels* ————

🐟 HUKA LODGE, Huka Falls Rd, PO Box 95, Taupo, North Island ☎ (074) 85791
Fabulous fishing lodge on the banks of the Waikato. Deer hunting and trout fishing on your doorstep – present your bag/catch to the chef for transformation. HM and Prince Philip fell huka, line and sinker for it, as did HENRY CRAWFORD, ELISE PASCOE and CATHY ROSSI HARRIS: *"I could tuck up in bed with a book in one of those serene suites for a week and watch the river flowing by."* TERRY HOLMES chills out: *"One of the most beautiful places I have ever been, beside a raging river. You're away from everything including television. The food is all freshly caught and they have some of the best wines."* SUSAN KUROSAWA hotfoots it to *"NZ's most exclusive hideaway – timber guest cabins; décor combines French provincial with English manor; fine wine cellar".*

MOOSE LODGE, Whakatane Highway 30, RD 4 Rotorua ☎ (073) 627823
NZ's top trout lake is right on the doorstep. Anglers fly in for the ultimate getaway and some of the best fishing in the world. Great tucker and wines, hot mineral water pool, tennis, boating. The British royals have visited.

PARK ROYAL, Cnr Durham and Kilmore Sts, Christchurch ☎ (03) 365 7799
A frontrunner in the country for modern luxe and service – U2 and Princess Anne are satisfied guests. **Canterbury Tales** pleases foodie pilgrims.

SOLITAIRE LODGE, Lake Tarawera, RD 5 Rotorua ☎ (073) 28208
Idyllic lodge on a promontory on Lake Tarawera. Masses of things to do – guided fishing 'safaris', nature bush walks, climbs up Mount Tarawera, waterskiing, white-water rafting, riding, trips to the hot-water beach, geyser and boiling mud; heli-sightseeing, sailing . . . Good noshing, too – saffron chicken and ginger soup, venison marsala with pine nuts.

TIMARA LODGE, RD 2 Blenheim, Marlborough ☎ (057) 28276
Plum in the middle of grapies' paradise, the Marlborough wine region. Set in landscaped grounds planted at the turn of the century, with well-tended lawns and trees, there's a tennis court, pool and a man-made lake. Cooking is straightforward with ultra-fresh ingredients. Visit some of the best wineries, go fishing, cruising and skindiving in Marlborough Sound, or cruise down the coast to Kaikoura and watch some whales. Awesome.

Restaurants

YOU AND ME, 31 Pukuatua St, Rotorua ☎ (07) 347 6178
East, West, this one's best. "*A personal favourite, extraordinarily good. Chef/owner Kaname Yamamoto is the country's best exponent of 'fusion' cuisine, combining the best of Japanese and Western culinary disciplines. Try his tatake-rolled venison (farmed not far away) – fillets are rolled in garlic and ginger, seared, sliced thin and served with citric-flavoured ponza sauce, shaved daikon (Japanese radish) and ginger*" – VIC WILLIAMS.

Ski resorts

MOUNT COOK
Clear pistes, heli-skiing, the Harris Mountains *and* the adrenaline rush down the 8-mile Tasman glacier. Skiwis, Euro pros and dollarwise Aussies come for the world's freshest July-Aug skiing (and most affordable – passes and 'copter hire are much cheaper than in Oz). Stay in a chalet at **The Hermitage**, Mount Cook National Park, Private Bag ☎ (03) 435 1809, at the foot of the mountains.

MOUNT RUAPEHU
The crispest spring snow Down Under, bar none. Lay down your head at **Chateau Tongariro** ☎ (07) 892 3809 – the best hotel in the north. In the mountains with fab views and its own ski lodge, near magnificent National Parkland.

QUEENSTOWN
South Island's top base for skiiers – though the story doesn't end with the thaw. There's white-water rafting and jet boating on Shotover River, and plunging into Lake Wakatipu from slides on the surrounding mountains, the Remarkables. Stay at **Queenstown Resort Hotel**, Marine Parade ☎ (03) 442 7750.

Wine

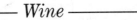

New Zealand continues to soar on the Sauvignon Blanc front. The South Island, in particular, has stripped the Loire of its honours by making the definitive crisp, intensely fruity Sauvignon Blanc. Meanwhile, other grapes are now finding a foothold on these unpredictable slopes – it seems the challenges of over-fertile soil, too much rain and too much sunlight spur makers on to find new, exciting techniques. So the cellars of NZ contain, alongside Sauvignon Blanc, fine Rieslings, Chardonnays, Pinot Noirs and Cabernet Sauvignons.

Best whites: One name stands out – the grab-it-while-you-can **CLOUDY BAY**. Its Sauvignon Blanc is a world model ("*they are making Cloudy Bay lookalikes now*" – SIMON LOFTUS), while its Chardonnay holds increasing appeal ("*my favourite, a more sophisticated wine*" – SL). DON HEWITSON tips: "*It will be interesting to watch the progress now they are owned by Veuve Clicquot*". Other South Island winners for MARGARET HARVEY are the white trio (Riesling, Chardonnay and Sauvignon Blanc) from **HUNTER ESTATE**, and **COOPERS CREEK**'s Marlborough Sauvignon Blanc.
Though based on the North Island, **MONTANA** pioneered winemaking in Marlborough. "*They've been amazing the world with their stunning* **Marlborough Sauvignon Blanc** *for years. Consistently excellent and affordable*" – DON H. In conjunction with Deutz of France, Montana produces the **Montana-Deutz Cuvée Marlborough**: "*Excellent méthode champenoise*" – MARGARET H; "*simply the best méthode champenoise made outside Champagne and better than a number of wines that carry the renowned appellation*" – DON H.
Moving north, the Sauvignon Blancs to nab are **NGATARAWA**'s unwooded and **BROOKFIELD**'s wooded version. Sauvignon/Semillon blends that find favour with MARGARET H are those made by **SELAK** and **MISSION VINEYARDS** ("*beautiful, the oldest winery in NZ and still run by the order of Marist Brothers*").
The North Island is making some of the world's best cool-climate Chardonnays, notably **TE MATA ESTATE**'s Elston Chardonnay and, the name everyone would like on their lips, the barrel-fermented **KUMEU RIVER**, admired by LIZ BERRY, MARGARET HARVEY and

Up the Creek in PNG

MICHAEL GEBICKI goes native in Papua New Guinea: "*One of the greatest journeys I ever made was up the Sepik River. At the beginning it's relatively civilized but as you go further upstream the villages become more and more primitive, and you can feel this incredible sense that the rules are changing, that layers of you are being stripped away, like the journey in Conrad's Heart of Darkness. The first time I did the trip I ended up staying with a crocodile hunter who'd married one of the local girls and set himself up on the riverbank, making a living from trading in jewellery that he made. He'd come there* *from Melbourne 20 years before and has never been back. His brother-in-law was staying also, a skinny young guy in a big cowboy shirt who didn't say a word, just smiled from a vinyl chair in the corner of the room and smoked Marlboros. I later found out he was the local witch doctor.*"

Twickers World (see Travel Directory) can arrange diving, bird-watching and cruising expeditions; **World Expeditions Ltd**, 8 College Rise, Maidenhead, Berkshire ☎ (0628) 74174, and **Trans Niugini Adventures**, PO Box 371, Mt Hagen, PNG ☎ (675) 521438, will send you on a wilder trek or down the river.

DON HEWITSON: "*Wonderfully fragrant. The 1987 was better than most highly touted Puligny Montrachets – and at a much lower price.*" The trophy-winning barrel-fermented Chardonnay from **VIDAL** in Hawkes Bay is also "*absolutely delicious,*" says MARGARET H, who adds **MILLS REEF** to the list for Chardonnay and an "*outstanding Gewürtztraminer,*" while the late-harvest Gewürtztraminer from **MATUA VALLEY** "*is heaven*."

The naturally sweet late-picked Riesling is, thinks GLYNN CHRISTIAN, NZ's strength. "*A perfect acid finish and a concentrated lemon flavour which is a real eye-opener*". MARGARET H tips a couple of nobly rotten 'stickies' – **NGATAWARA**'s Botrytis Selection and the **REDWOOD VALLEY ESTATE Botrytis Rhine Riesling**.

Best reds: Gaining momentum. Top of the pile are the Cabernet/Merlot blends from **VIDAL** and **TE MATA**: "*Te Mata's Coleraine is a refined, fruity classic. John Buck has created an individualistic wine which rates with the finest reds of the world and sets a benchmark for aspiring NZ red winemakers*" – DON HEWITSON. Other unusual blends to sniff out are the Cabernet/Syrah/Merlot of **ATA RANGI** ("*an award-winner*" – MARGARET H) and **GOLDWATER ESTATE**'s Cabernet/Merlot/Franc blend: "*Intensely herbacious with a delicious minty Cabernet flavour and real backbone*" – DON H.

The success of Pinot Noir is a new development and one name stands out: **MARTINBOROUGH** ("*the only really exciting Pinot Noir I've tasted outside Burgundy*" – DON H).

MARGARET H agrees, though she reckons that **RIPPON** and **ATA RANGI** have made the Burgundy breakthrough too.

PERU

GRAN BOLIVA HOTEL, Plaza San Martin 958, Lima ☎ (014) 276400
The best address in town. Spanish colonial landmark with most mod cons – it was redecorated throughout in 1991 but retains its glorious façade.

SUN RESORT LAS DUNAS, c/o Lima offices, PO Box 4410, Lima ☎ (014) 424180
Relaxed resort 180 miles south of Lima, in the coastal valley of Ica. *The* place to stay near the incredible Nazca lines (patterns of animals and astrological signs – some up to 400 yards long – cut into the landscape by the pre-Incan Nazcas around 2,000 years ago). See them by plane (the resort has its own airstrip). It also has 3 pools, horse riding, a Peruvian restaurant and plane trips to the Ballaspas Islands to see wildlife.

POLAND

Hotels

EUROPEJSKI, Krakowskie Przedmiescie 13, Warsaw ☎ (022) 265051
Grand old 19C building that retains some of its original structure and, it seems, original guests. The faithful are remembered and cosseted by long-time staff. Plain rooms, but many have lovely views.

MARRIOTT, Al Jerozolimske 65, Warsaw
☎ **(022) 306306**
Warsaw's only 5-star, built in 89, and with no serious contenders on the horizon . . . yet. Efficient, American-run, chintzily decorated and just a touch soulless. **The Chicago Grill** stuns the Poles with the prices of imported (US) steak; the fine wine list stuns all.

—————— *Restaurants* ——————

LERS, Ul Dluga 29, Warsaw
☎ **(022) 635 3888**
Where it's at in Warsaw, especially for the diplomatic pack. Comfortable, plush setting in the Old Town; hearty old Polish staples such as roast beef in a honey sauce with dumplings.

PORTUGAL

LISBON

—————— *Art and museums* ——————

CALOUSTE GULBENKIAN FOUNDATION, Avenida de Berna 45A
☎ **(01) 735131**
Up there with the big Gs (Getty and Guggenheim), Calouste Gulbenkian's personal collection runs to over 6,000 pieces. It spans 2,700 BC Egypt to early 20C. Chinese porcelain, European sculpture, master paintings and the famous collection of Lalique Art Nouveau jewellery.

—————— *Hotels* ——————

ALTIS, Rua Castilho 11 ☎ (01) 522496
Big, modern hotel that's big on facilities (indoor pool, health club) and dining. ELISABETH LAMBERT ORTIZ likes the rooftop restaurant: "*Exceptionally good, the sommelier knew more about Portugese wines than anyone I've ever come across. An attractive view and the food is superb – smoked swordfish is out of this world.*"

AVENIDA PALACE, Rua 1 de Dezembro 123 ☎ (01) 366104
Lisbon's ageing grandee, agleam with crystal, silk brocade and polished antique furniture. For traditionalists.

—————— *Restaurants* ——————

CERVEJARIA DA TRINDADE, Rua Nova da Trindade 20C ☎ (01) 342 3506
Buzzy, echoey tiled cavern, where politicos,

architects and intellectuals get noisily animated over plates piled high with bacalao (salt cod), hefty steaks, grilled sardines or steaming garlicky seafood. Beer (try the local brew Sagres) comes by the stein; inner courtyard.

PAP' ACORDA, Rua da Atalaia 57
☎ **(01) 346 4811**
Eat chicly and cheaply in the bustling Bairro Alto (old quarter). Fashionable, fun and full, it serves "*fantastic Portugese food, in a friendly environment – shellfish and pork*" – ALASTAIR LITTLE. Take the bread/egg/oil speciality Açorda with a pinch of salt, he warns: "*A horrible thing . . . like a bread porridge.*"

TAVARES RICO, Rua da Misericórdia 37
☎ **(01) 342 1112**
The grand old restaurant of Lisbon, mistress of the belle époque and a fave of Barry Humphries. The best of Portuguese cuisine in hale and hearty portions: partridge, hare or wild boar in winter, fresh fish all year (the ubiquitous bacalao and stuffed crab). Proudly xenophobic wine list.

Robin's Romania

"Romania is a wonderful place to travel because, although there are terrible things to see, a great deal of the country has remained untouched by the 20C. The more remote the area, the more wonderful Romania is, particularly the very north. The Maramures region is the last pure medieval society in Europe and they are the most hospitable people. I travelled there in the early 70s when you had to stay in a hotel and all the usual communist nonsense, but now anyone is only too delighted to let you stay. It's very primitive but comfortable: a cold tap in the yard, wonderful home cooking, peasant food. And the most colourful and friendly people, with embroidered waistcoats and clogs and ox-carts with wooden wheels. The **Inter-Continental** in Bucharest, Blvd Nicolae Balcescu 4, Sector 1 ☎ (0) 140400, is the best hotel, and deputy manager Dragos Onciulencu is a very special person who will organize anybody's life, from staying in one of the castles to fishing in the Danube or catching wild boar" – ROBIN HANBURY-TENISON.

Wine

Portugese table wines are largely overlooked. The best, most uncompromising, of the lot are the wines of **BUCACO**, made at the Palace Hotel in Buçaco and only available there and at its sister hotel in Lisbon. Quality varies but some old vintages, such as the 1945, rank alongside any first-growth Bordeaux. (LIZ BERRY tips Buçaco's old whites: *"Beautiful wines"*.) The port firm of **FERREIRA** makes one of Portugal's best reds, **Barca Velha**, made in very limited quantities. **QUINTA DA COTTO** makes *"very good table wines, very plummy, concentrated, aged in barriques"* – LIZ B.

Madeira

Vintage Madeira is among the world's best fortified wines, and will outlive vintage port. A vintage year, however, is rare. *"In the 18C, Madeira was, with claret, the most popular wine drunk by the British. Now, after years of neglect, we are seeing a revival.* **COSSART GORDON**'s 10-year-old **Verdelho** *is the perfect mid-morning glass. Old vintages are scarce but for age, quality and excellent value,* **BLANDY**'s **Malmsey Solera** *1864 is exquisite"* – MICHAEL BROADBENT. LIZ BERRY's top Madeira is the 1832 **TERRANTEZ**, followed closely by the *"absolutely superb"* 1952 **Verdelho** and 1863 **Malmsey** from **BLANDY**.

Port

"The standard of 20-year-old tawny port is so high that naming individual shippers is invidious," says MICHAEL BROADBENT, before naming **FERREIRA Duque de Bragança**. The advantage of a mellow old tawny is that one can dip into it for weeks, if not months, whereas vintage port should be consumed at one sitting. **TAYLOR'S** are the most famous shippers, for their rich, long-lived vintages and tawnies of stated ages. Other shippers to trust are **GRAHAM, FONSECA GUIMARAENS, DOW, WARRE** and the port house **QUINTA DO NOVAL**. MICHAEL BROADBENT has some vintage advice: *"Young vintage port is very undervalued, particularly the 1980, 1982 and 1983. The best vintages are 1985 for laying down; 1977 classic; 1970 undervalued with years more life; 1975 pleasant to drink now."*

RUSSIA

MOSCOW

Art and museums

ARMOURY PALACE, Kremlin
☎ (095) 221 4720
Supreme collection of opulence – fabulous Fabergé eggs and jewels, Russian gold and silver, rare 16C–17C English silver and diplomatic gifts from courts all over Europe.

PUSHKIN FINE ART MUSEUM, Ul Volkhonka 12 ☎ **(095) 203 7998**
Second only to the Hermitage for its comprehensive collection, spanning the ancients – Egyptologists love it – to the present. Strong on Impressionists and Post-Imps.

Hotels

🏨 **METROPOL, 1 Marx Prospeckt**
☎ **(095) 927 6002**
The best in town, opened in blaze of glory in 1991, and top of the list for visiting glitterati and bizmen. Managed by Inter-Continental, the opulent 1903 hotel has been restored to the tune of

🕵 **Buzzz** Dying swan? EDWARD THORPE explains why the **Bolshoi** is no longer a name to conjure with: *"For 15 years they've been under the direction of an iron-fisted KGB man Grigorvich, who has absolutely emasculated their major productions – the last ones in London were absolutely appalling, tacky and shabby. Secondly, over the upheaval of the perestroika years they've lost nearly all their world-class dancers. The whole company is in a state of flux – who knows if it will disintegrate?"* 🕵 . . . . . . Caviare for the lady? In the grand restaurants of Moscow, instead of selling roses at the tables, they sell **contraband caviare** and **homemade sausages** 🕵 . . . . . . **Inter-Continental** is the hotel group with muscle in Eastern Europe – 11 hotels in the major cities, and a new one due in **St Petersburg** in 1993 🕵 . . . . . . St P 2: The Communist Party's former private hotel is now smart travellers' HQ. **Mercury Hotel** ☎ (0812) 278 1154, has 16 rooms and warm service . . 🕵

$170 million. In the **Metropol** restaurant, dine under the glass-domed ceiling in the gilded room where Lenin used to give speeches. The **Evropeisky** restaurant has Romantic murals and excellent Georgian cuisine. Pool, health centre, nightclub and *smiling* service.

SAVOY HOTEL, Ul Rozhdestvenka 3
☎ **(095) 230 2625**
Post-thaw and top-drawer, restored recently to highest Western standards from the original 1912 building. Tough to get in – only 80 rooms – but worth it. Gilded ceilings, inlaid floors, room service, *plugs that fit*, Scando/Franco/Russian restaurant (classical cooking – bortsch, reindeer tenderloin – and good service) and a British pub/bar, the **Hermitage**, selling *draught* John Bull Export.

—— *Restaurants* ——

ARAGVI, Ul Gorkovo 6 ☎ **(095) 229 3726**
Grand Georgian restaurant – eat shaslik (kebab), chicken satsivi (with walnut and coriander sauce), drink champagne or the rapidly improving Georgian wines and listen to folk.

SLAVYANSKY BAZAAR, Ul 25-vo Oktyabrya 13 ☎ **(095) 221 1872**
The famous 19C restaurant – a meeting place for writers and artists – is always jam-packed. Usually there's fine traditional Russian food (though there are off days) – blinis, bortsch and zakuski (hors d'oeuvres) . . . Floor show too.

ST PETERSBURG

—— *Art and museums* ——

⚜ **HERMITAGE, Dvortsovaya Nab 34**
☎ **(0812) 212 9525**
Peter the Great's staggering 18C winter palace holds the largest art gallery in the world. Recently modernized, its immensely beautiful salons display some of Europe's greatest craftsmanship – in marble and precious stones, crystal, wood, plaster and gilt. Spanning early and primitive art, classical antiquity, the Renaissance and enlightenment to modernity, there are fabulous works by almost any *name* you care to mention – Titian, Raphael, Bernini, Rubens, Rembrandt, Bonnard, Degas, Matisse x 35 . . . Superb dec arts too.

—— *Ballet and opera* ——

⚜ **BALLET OF THE MARIINSKY THEATRE (Kirov Ballet), Mariinsky Theatre, Teatral'naya Pl 1**
☎ **0812 114 1211**
The Kirov has reverted to its pre-Revolutionary name but it still pleases EDWARD THORPE with its definitive and sublime classical performances: *"When they came over they still showed impeccable style, and their productions were much better [than the Bolshoi], and they still have some of their major stars."* Those they lost include Baryshnikov and Nureyev, but defections haven't stopped the company from touring – until recently the only way to see the best classical ballet in the world.

—— *Hotels* ——

GRAND HOTEL EUROPE, Ul Brodskovo 1–7 ☎ **(0812) 210 3295**
Top-class hotel by any standards. Formerly the Yevropeiskaya, St Petersburg's oldest hotel (opened in 1875) has welcomed Europe's great and good – Turgenev, Gorky, Strauss, Debussy and Shostakovich included. Completely refitted and jointly run with a Swedish company, it has a pool, sauna, laundry, VCRs and 4 restaurants.

SEYCHELLES

BIRD ISLAND
Splendid isolation – the untouched 120-acre island is home to squillions of Fairy, Noddy and Sooty Terns, a sesquicentarian giant turtle, and the 25 thatched cottages of **Bird Island Lodge** ☎ (248) 44449. An unbroken 3-mile white beach encircles the island. Creole (fish, garlic, chillis) and European cooking.

DENIS ISLAND
Peaceful privately owned paradise. Stay at **Denis Island Lodge** ☎ (248) 44143 – 24 bungalows, French/creole cooking – and go deep-sea fishing (world record catches here), snorkelling, scuba, windsurfing, Hobie Cat sailing, play tennis or go golf driving on the airstrip – preferably when it's not being used for landing aeroplanes.

SINGAPORE

—— *Clubs* ——

KHAMELEON DISCO, 31 Marina Park, Marina Village ☎ **227 4510**
Part of the Marina Village dining/entertainment complex, built on reclaimed land. Dance floor for 500, overlooked by a members-only lounge. Live bands and DJs. *"One of the hottest discos in town – all but displaced the old favourite Chinoiserie. Chic crowd"* – CH'NG POH TIONG.

TOP TEN, 400 Orchard Rd ☎ 732 3077
Top of the bops. A converted cinema, the show's now on the packed dance floor or the stage (live performances by biggies, great light show). DJs mix disco and house.

TORNADO, Hotel Phoenix, Orchard Rd ☎ 737 8666
Whirlwind into the hotel basement – all 9,000 sq ft of it – to check out Tornado's multi-functionality: disco, pub, café-bar, live bands, DJ music, bar billiards, darts, video clips, laser-disc video jukebox – it's like an underground theme park.

ZOUK, 17 Jiak Kim St ☎ 738 2988
Another multi-functional mammoth space – restaurants, club, bar and pub – designed along the lines of a Greek taverna. *"The whitewashed walls exude a Mediterranean seaside flavour. Young crowd"* – CH'NG POH TIONG.

——————— *Hotels* ———————

GOODWOOD PARK, 22 Scotts Rd ☎ 737 7411
Grand old colonialist renovated with taste. Ordinary rooms are enormous, suites gargantuan and the ballroom-sized Brunei suite is fit for a Sultan. The decoration and level of comfort are unassailable and it has a clutch of the best eateries in town (see Restaurants).

🔥 THE ORIENTAL, 5 Raffles Ave, Marina Sq ☎ 338 0066
Neck and neck with the Shangri-La for Singapore's best – as one of the Mandarin Oriental family, it would be surprising if it weren't. Spectacular 21-storey triangular harbour-fronter with a fabulous outdoor pool, swish health club and the expected jump-to service. 3-way view of city, harbour or surrounding park. See also Restaurants.

RAFFLES, 1–3 Beach Rd ☎ 337 8041
After S$160 million worth of renovations and incalculable hype, Raffles has re-opened to an unsurprisingly mixed response. The famous hotel of the 1890s, host to countless writers from Maugham to Malraux, is again a magnet for travellers, if only out of curiosity to see how they've replicated the ornate cast-iron portico or the **Long Bar** (home of the original Singapore Sling) or the 1,001 other bits of history. *"It's not exactly the Raffles many would have remembered, nevertheless, it remains a striking architectural achievement and gives a new meaning to hospitality"* – CH'NG POH TIONG. SERENA FASS and LISA BARNARD pass on ear-to-the-ground reports (*"I've heard it's absolutely great again by someone I absolutely trust"* – SF; *"I've had mixed reports, some very, very good"* – LB). But CAROL WRIGHT is disappointed: *"It's beautiful but they've taken all the soul and history out of it and it's frightfully commercial and hard."* Test out the **Tiffin Room**, **Raffles Grill** and **Writers Bar** before you cast your vote.

THE REGENT, 1 Cuscaden Rd ☎ 733 8888
The former Inter-Con's atrium hotel is looking better than ever. A polished performer from its marble floors to the staff's Hermès accessories, *"the Regent's attention to design and business needs is all there. The* **Tea Lounge** *in the Lobby is sumptuous yet discreet – a great place for a cup of Darjeeling. The bar on the second level is enchanting"* – CH'NG POH TIONG.

🔥 SHANGRI-LA, 22 Orange Grove Rd ☎ 737 3644
Still Singapore's leader; peerless in its facilities (especially when the S$90 million renovations are complete), setting and service. *"The service is incredible"* – ROBIN LEACH. Rooms in the Valley Wing are downright glamorous *and* you get a personal butler. CAROL WRIGHT thinks it's *"gorgeous – very nice and comfortable, and fantastic gardens"*. Great sports facilities. See also Restaurants.

——————— *Restaurants* ———————

BANANA LEAF APOLO, 56 Race Course Rd ☎ 293 8682
A Singaporean institution, albeit a messy one. Finger-lickin' good curries, fish-head or meat

🔥 Buzz Nicotine fiends in no-smoking city head to al fresco seafood restaurants on East Coast Parkway, such as **Singa Inn**, at No 920 ☎ 440 7128, for Thai food, satay and Chinese rojak 🔥 . . . . . . North Indian cooking is the current wow of Singapore – dig in at **Moti Mahal**, 18 Murray St ☎ 221 4338 🔥 . . . . . . Food wow 2: **Nonya cuisine**, food of the Baba or Peranakan culture, a blend of Malay and Hokkien Chinese. Try buah keluak ayam (chicken and black nuts in hot and sour gravy) at either **Guan Hoe Soon**, 214 Joo Chiat Rd ☎ 344 2761, or the lurid pink and green-fronted **Peranakan Place**, 180 Orchard Rd ☎ 732 6966 🔥 . . . . . . Food wow 3: **Peranakan cuisine**, a further refinement, blends Chinese with Indian or Malay. Sample it at **5 Emerald Hill** ☎ 732 0818, to the sound of soul . . . . . . 🔥

served on banana leaves – scoop them with your palms as CLAUDIA CRAGG does.

CHAO PHAYA, 4272-A, Block 730, Ang Mo Kio Ave 6 ☎ 456 0119
Terrific Thai – a little out on a suburban limb but worth the trek. Choose your victim from the display of fish, prawns, crab or lobster and watch the chefs transform it – into tom yam kung, green fish curry . . . .

DOMVS, Sheraton Towers, 39 Scotts Rd ☎ 737 6888
Domvs from domvs for hungry locals, who feast on authentic Italian home cooking (choose your own pasta/sauce combo, such as duck-filled ravioli with garlic, olive oil and red chilli). Unusually extensive list of Italian vinos.

GOODWOOD PARK, see Hotels
A fabulous variety of tastes, beautifully served, in swish surroundings. **Min Jiang** has splendid Sichuan, red/green décor, big Chinese lanterns and lightning service; so book. Wonderful fish – fresh, fresh, fresh – and dim sum at **Garden Seafood Restaurant**. Eat Shanghainese served in a Western style in **Chiang Jiang**; and beautifully presented Japanese at **Shima**. For steaks, American and Continental cooking, make for the **Gordon Grill**. End with a great coffee at **Café L'Espresso**.

LE RESTAURANT DE FRANCE, Hotel Meridien Singapore, 100 Orchard Rd ☎ 733 8855
Light, spacious, with a Parisian feel – and really top-class French cooking. Formal by Singaporean standards (wear a tie), with impeccable, friendly service.

MAXIM'S DE PARIS, The Regent (see Hotels)
A far cry from Paris, but carried off with Regent élan. *"A psychedelic stained-glass ceiling literally shines down on this celebration of the belle époque. Friendly staff"* – CH'NG POH TIONG.

THE ORIENTAL, see Hotels
A brace of fine restaurants – impeccable Sichuan and Hunan cooking in **Cherry Garden**, whose pebbled courtyard is a replica of that of a Ming nobleman. The Continental restaurant **Fourchettes** has a huge grill at the entrance and a table groaning under the display of hors d'oeuvres. Big biz lunch spot, with recession-beating set-price buffet.

🏊 SHANGRI LA, see Hotels
Tops for Singaporean food and great salads is the **Waterfall Café**, set amid lush tropical vegetation and running water. Smart international cuisine, spectacular lunchtime buffet and impressive wine list at **Latour**. **Shang Palace** serves dramatic Cantonese cuisine, and **Nadaman**, on the 24th floor, superb Japanese.

—— Shopping ——

Singapore designer-bargains are a myth. Electrical goods can still be a good buy but your Hermès tie will be much the same price the world over. Nevertheless, Singapore is still the place for shopaholics, with centres ever springing up.

Orchard Road is *the* shopping street: check out the new and massive **Ngee Ann City**, home to Gucci, Dunhill, YSL and other Euro labels, plus batik and Chinese curios; the Japanese store **Isetan**, crammed with designer labels; **Hilton Shopping Gallery**, for all you need for body, face and lifestyle – Valentino, Ferré, Frizon, Bulgari, Dunhill, Gucci, Vuitton, Lanvin, Davidoff, L'Ultima; opposite, the swish **Palais Renaissance**, *"something of a Faubourg St Honoré in one building. Chanel, Salvatore Ferragamo, Christian Lacroix, Karl Lagerfeld, Cartier . . ."* – CH'NG POH TIONG; **Centrepoint**, where expats and Anglophiles stock up on M&S necessities at **St Michael** (**Robinsons'**, the original 'English' department store, is there too, for terribly British presents, perfumes, tableware); and **The Promenade**, a non-stop source

> **❝ When Singaporeans are not shopping they're eating. In the morning, they don't ask 'how are you?' but 'have you had breakfast? ❞**
>
> 🏃 CAROL WRIGHT

of designer desirables (best boutiques are **Man & His Woman**, for Miyake, Byblos, Matsuda, Tokio Kumagai, and **Glamourette**, for Ozbek, Gaultier and co) . . . The Oriental's **Marina Square** claims to be the largest shopping complex in S E Asia. **Scotts Shopping Centre**, Scotts Rd, must be one of the grandest, developed at a cost of S$200 million. Find top accessories, a **China Silk House**; **Tang Studio** (for gimmicky/trendy clothes and accessories) and **Cost Plus Electronics**, one of the most reputable firms in the city (fixed price but guarantees). **Metro** (7 branches – the most up-market are M Grand and M Paragon), has cool designer boutiques and own-label quality gear. At **Peninsula Plaza**, N Bridge Rd, seek out **Allan Chai Fashion Design** ☎ 338 4330, for counterfeit couture from the master – give him your Chanel and Givenchy and go home with 2 of each. Undetectably true to the original.

Holland Village is an expat haunt for local handicrafts – try **Lim's Arts & Crafts**, Holland Rd Shopping Centre, for ceramics, wood carvings, chests, pictures, silk screens, etc; **Tanglin Shopping Centre** is still tops for Oriental antiques and carpets; also for **Justmens** ☎ 737 4800, *the* tailor to the expat and business community. Best place for jewellery and stones (prices and authenticity are regulated) is **South Bridge Centre**. And for electronic gadgetry (plus cosmetics, furnishings and more), the **Funan Centre**.

SOUTH AFRICA

———— *Hotels* ————

 CYBELE FOREST LODGE, PO Box 346, White River ☎ (01311) 50511
A small luxy lodge (22 guests) some 35 km from Kruger National Park, with thatched bungalows set in bluegum-shaded gardens. Paddock suites have their own pools. *"Open fireplaces, chintzy décor and an atmosphere that's pure Out of Africa"* – SUSAN KUROSAWA.

LONDOLOZI PO Box 1211, Sunninghill Park ☎ (011) 803 8421
DAVID GOWER's wild about this lodge: *"One of the best, a fabulous spot, with 3 camps: Main Camp, Bush Camp and Tree Camp. There's a private game park next door on the borders of the Kruger National Park in the Sabie Sand area. Very wild and very comfortable, lots of game. The food's very good – you get meat off the farm as it were – fresh antelope, which is beautiful, a bit sweeter than beef."*

MALA MALA, Rattray Reserves, PO Box 2575, Randburg ☎ (011) 789 2677
Less than 100 visitors are allowed into the 57,000-acre private game reserve at once, so you're assured of undisturbed watching.

MOUNT NELSON HOTEL, 76 Orange St, PO Box 2608, Cape Town ☎ (021) 231000
Rose-coloured row of villas in the shadow of Table Mountain. Renovations have removed all 60s and 70s carbuncles, and now the likes of the Duchess of Devonshire and Sir Laurens van der Post deem it fit for a visit. Colonial feel, beautiful gardens, attentive service.

THE PLETTENBERG, PO Box 719, Plettenberg Bay ☎ (04457) 32030
Originally a 19C holiday mansion in this fashionable resort, still drawing smart South Africans. *"Very grand. Good food, if about 2 years behind the times. Best view, right over the sea. Well decorated in a rather chintzy English country house way, which is rather nice at the sea. Good atmosphere"* – PRUE LEITH.

———— *Tours* ————

See also **Tempo Travel** (Travel Directory).

BLUE TRAIN, c/o Connex Travel, PO Box 1113, Johannesburg ☎ (011) 774 4504
Bijou choo choo – the Orient Express of South Africa – with brill food, a splendid wine list, private valets and real gold-tinted windows (to cut down the sun's glare.) Steam out of Cape Town at a sedate 40 mph, through the new Hex River mountain tunnel, across the Karoo to Jo'burg and Pretoria.

GAMETRACKERS, PO Box 4245, Randburg ☎ (011) 886 1810
Fly into Botswana from Jo'burg – choose your own itinerary from a list of camps and get worm's and bird's eye views of the Delta, Moremi and Chobe.

Buzzz SA wine may have some catching up to do, but DON HEWITSON has found an exception: *"Hamilton-Russell is making some superb wines, I think showing as much promise as anybody"* 🕴...... PRUE LEITH leaps into **Frog**, 376A Jan Smuts Ave, Craighall ☎ (011) 787 2304, for *"the most fashionable and nicest food in Johannesburg [fresh fish grilled with chilli, soy or tamarillos; piping hot 3 dough breads]. I must declare an interest – Sue Edelstein, who runs it, is ex-Leith's cookery school"* 🕴...... Leith leap 2: Between the sheets at the **Johannesburg Sun**: 84 Small St, Johannesburg ☎ (011) 297011, *"an amazing hotel – it has pairs of executive suites, one like a set from a very tasteful play – watercolours, muted furnishings; the other for the man who wants to have 5 girls at once in the Jacuzzi – black Jacuzzi, black sheets, leather bed cover"* 🕴...... And 3: **Cape Sun**, Box 4532, Strand St, Cape Town ☎ (021) 238844, *"a fantastic big hotel with the mountain on one side and Table Bay on the other. Everything brilliantly done, very professional"* 🕴...... Cape of Good Beaches: **Llandudno Bay, Camps Bay, Clifton Beach** on the Atlantic side for sunbathing only (strong undercurrents, icy water); **Muizenburg Beach** on the Indian Ocean side (warmer and safer waters).. 🕴

John Tovey – Cape Crusader

*"I spend my winters in Cape Town. I stayed at a small country house, **Greenways**, 1–5 Torquay Ave, Upper Claremont ☎ (021) 761 1792, with a side view of the mountain and a 12-acre garden full of flowers, just beautiful, so quiet. I climb the mountain every day at about 5.30 in the morning. The best restaurant in Cape Town is **Truffles**, 161 Main Rd, Heathfield ☎ (021) 726161; it's so good because he does the finest sauces and the finest pasta and the finest lamb I know."* [Peter Gravelius also does a good line in crustacea – lobster ravioli over a rich lobster sauce – and foie gras on fried apple with hanepoot sauce.] *"Another lovely one, run by a friend of mine, is **Freda's**, 110 Kloof St, Gardens ☎ (021) 238653, who does the most superb buffet, lots of Elizabeth David recipes, lots of Mediterranean dishes. The restaurant with the most wonderful view has got to be the **Blue Peter**, 1 Popham Rd, Bloubergstrand ☎ (021) 561956 – you just sit there looking at Table Mountain."*

HILTON ROSS, Box 32154, Camps Bay, Cape Town 8040 ☎ (021) 438 1500
Day tours of the wine route for groups or individuals. Drink and lunch your way round Stellenbosch (SA's second-oldest town), Boschendale, Franschoek Wine Estate and Paarl.

SOUTH AFRICAN AIR TOURS, PO Box 8, Lanseria 1748 ☎ (011) 659 2880
Whatever you want, wherever you want to see it, whenever it's convenient. Big game that is.

SPRINGBOK ATLAS SAFARIS, 179 Albert Rd, Woodstock, Capetown 8001 ☎ (021) 448 6545
Standard and specialist tours – for stud breeders, gemologists, botanists or sportsmen. Do the winelands, Table Mountain, Garden Route, wildlife or see the big cities – Durban, Jo'burg, Pretoria and Capetown.

SPAIN

BARCELONA

—— *Art and museums* ——

MUSEU PICASSO, Montcada 15–19 ☎ (93) 319 6310
Splendid pair of medieval palaces in the Gothic Quarter devoted to Barcelona's best-loved boy. A revelation to see the evolution of his work – represented through more than 900 paintings, engravings, drawings and ceramics – from the age of 9 to the end of his life. See his tribute to Velázquez's *Las Meninas*.

—— *Bars and cafés* ——

CAFE DE L'OPERA, Rambla 74 ☎ (93) 317 7585
Buzzy belle époque café opposite the Liceu opera house (sit inside, not on the Ramblas). Go for breakfast (light pastries, cornetti, etc), early evening or late-late. Excellent coffees.

L'ASCENSOR, Bellafila 3 ☎ (93) 318 5347
A mellow bar, where Barri Gòtic locals go for low-key, late-night drinks. The doorway is formed by an old wooden lift; the room is reminiscent of an old railway carriage of the Orient-Express era. Rattan chairs, iron tables, and a mean carajillo – half-coffee, half-cognac.

 TORRES DE AVILA, Marques de Comillas, Poble Espanyol ☎ (93) 424 9309
The mock-medieval gateway has been transformed by Alfredo Arribas and design wunderkind (he of Cobi the Olympic mascot fame) Javier Mariscal into *"one of the trendiest in town with a rooftop dining area and a dazzling overview of the city"* – DAVINA JACKSON. *"A hedonist's Disneyland where rooms revolve, glass lifts shoot you from floor to floor and a baffling nonsense language of Masonic and telluric symbols prevails"* – ROBERT ELMS.

UNIVERSAL, Mariá Cubí 182–184 ☎ (93) 200 7470
Lofty room, dominated by a designer bar snaking diagonally and a noisy, stand-up, artsy/media crowd. Upstairs is a taste of old Spain, with tall ceilings, original tiled floor, French windows and tables and chairs.

—— *Clubs* ——

OTTO ZUTZ, Lincoln 15 ☎ (93) 238 0722
Cavernous 3-level warehouse disco in the lively

Gràcia district, which vibrates to the hottest sounds and attracts the coolest crowds.

TICKTACKTOE, Roger de Lluria 40
☎ **(93) 318 9770**
In a former textile factory, a superb product of Catalan design – sweeps of gleaming honeyed woods, extraordinary lamps. *"A stylish combination of billiards room, restaurant, bar and nightclub with very good food"* – DAVINA JACKSON.

VELVET, Balmes 161 ☎ (93) 217 6714
One of *los bares de diseño* that sprang up over the last decade, from the Arribas/Mariscal team. *"A classic 80s nightclub, with long ramps leading to the 2 entrances and a rich and theatrical interior"* – DAVINA JACKSON. Sit on barstools with buttock-cheek seats; check out the loos and (men only) activate the strobe-lit urinals.

Modernisme

In Paris it was Art Nouveau, in Germany Jugendstil, in Britain Arts and Crafts. Barcelona's exuberant flourishing of art and architecture in the boomtime between 1900 and WWI boldly proclaimed itself Modernisme. Hallmarks of the style are superb craftsmanship, attention to (and abundance of) detail and a harking back to the organic forms of nature. Nouveaux riches provided the wherewithal, the Eixample – 'urban extension' – provided the area, and Modernisme provided Barcelona with a legacy of extraordinary buildings. The most distinctive is Gaudí's hurdy-gurdy **Casa Milà** (aka **La Pedrera**), Passeig de Gràcia, a rippling corner house inspired by marine life, down to the last barnacle-encrusted chimney-pot. Down the boulevard is Gaudí's hump-backed, dragon-skinned **Casa Batlló**; next door is Puig i Cadafalch's superbly crafted **Casa Amatller**, and at the end of the block, Domènach i Montaner's **Casa Lleó Morera**, a profusion of mosaic murals, porcelain reliefs, intarsia floors and ceilings and a wall of stained-glass window. The famed **Els 4 Gats**, Montsío 3 bis, where Picasso paid his bar bills in doodles, could prove the least stressful way to take in this most overwhelming of styles.

Hotels

♨ GRAN HOTEL HAVANA, Gran Vía 647
☎ **(93) 412 1115**
The latest from the Condes (see below) team, a superbly styled 5-star with an impressive glass-domed atrium. Arguably the quietest rooms (triple-glazed) and suavest interiors in town.

HOTEL COLON, Avinguda Catedral 7
☎ **(93) 301 1404**
An old charmer, right by the cathedral (nice view, shame about the bells). A favourite with old South American money and MEREDITH ETHERINGTON-SMITH: *"It's a rather old-fashioned Spanish hotel, rather 30s in feeling."*

♨ HOTEL CONDES DE BARCELONA, Passeig de Gràcia 75 ☎ (93) 487 3737
Beautifully adapted from a Modernista residence, a chic hotel in the best location (safer and smarter than the Barri Gòtic, but near the action and shops). Some rooms have inner balconies overlooking a quiet court. Gina Lollobrigida, Ursula Andress and Bob Geldof have stayed.

HOTEL RITZ, Gran Vía 668
☎ **(93) 318 5200**
Built just after WWI, a typically Ritzy institution that has housed most visiting VIPs: the Duke of Windsor and Mrs Simpson, Somerset Maugham . . . Vast rooms have been renovated with an abundance of gilt and rather hectic carpets. LISA BARNARD rates it.

Restaurants

AGUT, Gignas 16, ☎ (93) 315 1709
Bright, buzzy brasserie with whitewashed panelling, 20C paintings, and a devoted following among the Gòtic set. Little sister to the **Reial Club Maritím**, Moll d'Espanya ☎ (93) 315 0256, a classy, glassy, seafoody restaurant in the old port.

BELTXENEA, Mallorca 275, Entlo
☎ **(93) 215 3024**
The best Basque restaurant, where affluent Catalaned-out locals flock. Hidden away behind a private entrance (a maid or butler opens the door), this restaurant has a country-house atmosphere with a series of dining rooms, and log fires in winter.

CASA LEOPOLDO, San Rafael 24
☎ **(93) 241 3014**
Trad old Catalan haunt in the notorious Barrio Chino. *"A really great old restaurant, covered in tiles, at the end of a great alley – people wince when you say you're going because it's supposed to be dangerous. It sells the best rabbit with aioli that you will ever eat anywhere in all of your life"* – ROBERT ELMS.

Barcelona by Design

Barcelona has become synonymous with high design, from the chic-est bar down to the last door handle. **Bd Ediciones de Diseño**, Mallorca 291 ☎ (93) 258 6909, presents the best of contemporary design (tables, chairs, lighting, tea sets, glassware) from such Catalan braves as Oscar Tusquets and Javier Mariscal, as well as repro pieces by great masters such as Gaudí and Mackintosh. Based in the Casa Thomas, an old graphic arts company and a marvellous Modernista building. **Vinçon**, Passeig de Gràcia 96 ☎ (93) 215 6050, has a stylish stash of functional and fanciful designs, from mosquito nets to ironing boards to classic Catalan lamps with parchment shades.

EL TRAGALUZ, Passeig de la Concepció 5 ☎ **(93) 487 0621**
Designer dining in a glass-covered room, open in summer. *"Multi-floor restaurant with delightful painted frescos on the walls – the smart interior is by Sandra Taruella and Pepe Cortes. Food not always brilliant but this doesn't deter the chic clientele"* – DAVINA JACKSON.

MADRID

— Art and museums —

🏛 **MUSEO DEL PRADO, Paseo del Prado** ☎ **(91) 468 0950**
One of the leading galleries in the world, covering 12C–19C Italian art, 15C–18C Dutch, French, English and German art, and showcase, of course, to the old Spanish masters – Velázquez, El Greco, Goya . . . *"Do see the Dutch galleries – they're extraordinary: Breughel, Dürer, Vermeer, Bosch. They're little-visited because the punters all go to see Las Meninas, etc"* – MEREDITH ETHERINGTON-SMITH. BARBARA TAYLOR BRADFORD's a long-time fan.

— Clubs —

ARCHY, Marqués de Riscal 11 ☎ **(91) 410 7343**
Multi-functional (restaurant/bar/club) trendspot for late late-night drinking (arrive before 2 am and it's dead). *"Archy's is the place . . . pretty young Madrid of both sexes"* – ROBERT ELMS.

TEATRIZ, Hermosilla 15 ☎ **(91) 577 5379**
High design stretched to breaking point – Philippe Starck has left no knife, light or chair untouched by his dynamic hand. Sassy bar/club/restaurant with arty, light cuisine. *"It's full of rooms with no apparent function and the smallest discothèque in the world, about 8 x 6 ft, padded with black leather – it's so odd but very charming"* – ROBERT ELMS.

— Hotels —

🏛 **HOTEL RITZ, Plaza de la Lealtad 5** ☎ **(91) 521 2857**
Spain's finest, a belle époque beauty restored with care and integrity by THF. Each room has hand-woven bespoke carpets and many look over the Prado. Tops for VIPs, LISA BARNARD and MEREDITH ETHERINGTON-SMITH: *"It must be one of the best hotels in the world. Very beautiful and grand, also horrendously expensive. There is a formal garden with a marble floor, a Versailles kind of garden with hedges around it."*

MIGUEL ANGEL, Miguel Angel 31 ☎ **(91) 442 5320**
Teenager (1977-built) with ye olde worlde public rooms and old-fashioned service. *"Extremely well run and extremely kind and thoughtful service. Everyone was chirruping and happy. The indoor swimming pool is extremely good"* – ELISABETH LAMBERT ORTIZ.

— Restaurants —

HORCHER, Alfonso XII 6 ☎ **(91) 522 0731**
An unlikely fusion of German/Spanish cooking, Teutonically efficient service and a dash of Latin warmth. MEREDITH ETHERINGTON-SMITH thinks it's . . . grand: *"The grand restaurant and grand classical Spanish food like their 'zarzuela', a very grand fish stew with lobster."*

JOCKEY, Amador de los Rios 6 ☎ **(91) 319 2435**
Solid and clubby with the discreet hum of wheeling and dealing. Wildly expensive and, in spite of chef Clemencio Fuentes's retirement, still serving immaculate food (sea urchin soup, sea bass cooked with oil in a paper parcel). *"Very smart, as it is in Paris, the best club. Turn up for lunch,"* advises MEREDITH ETHERINGTON-SMITH.

LA DORADA, Orense 64 ☎ **(91) 570 2004**
As every Spaniard knows, seafood is as fresh in Madrid as in its coastal home. Simply cooked fish (Andalusian bream baked in a salt-crust is a must) in a whitewashed restaurant with fishing nets on the walls.

🦃 **ZALACAIN, Alvarez de Baena 4**
☎ **(91) 561 4840**
One of Spain's finest, most bestarred restaurants. Elevates north-eastern Spanish cooking to its Platonic ideal: roast duck might be partnered with sweetbreads and pepper sauce, red mullet roasted with olive oil and herbs. Smart, luxurious and not cheaply come by.

· REST OF ·

SPAIN

———— *Hotels* ————

🏨 **HOSTAL DE LOS REYES CATOLICOS, Plaza de España 1, Santiago de Compostela ☎ (981) 582200**
A 15C pilgrims' hostel, mooted to be the oldest hotel in the world. Now it's a 5-star and *"one of the most beautiful buildings in an extravagantly beautiful town. It's that old kind of Catholicism, the walls are thick stone and the floors wood, rooms with great antique furniture . . . and it's around a beautiful courtyard. But don't eat there"* – ROBERT ELMS.

🏨 **HOTEL ALFONSO XIII, San Fernando 2, Seville ☎ (95) 422 2850**
Sumptuous Mudéjar revival palace in the heart of town. *"A wonderful hotel, very grand and very Andalusian. It's where everyone stays for the Feria de Abril, the horse fair, and you start your day in the Alfonso with sherry, lots of it"* – MEREDITH ETHERINGTON-SMITH.

HOTEL EL CORSARIO, Old Town, Ibiza ☎ (071) 301248
So well known that it needs no street address. *"My new favourite hotel in the world. It is absolutely beautiful, only 2 star but more elegant than almost any 5 star I've ever stayed in. The bedrooms are exquisite, I had a very old mahogany four-poster bed and the ceilings are made of sandalwood so the fragrance comes down. A spectacular view and charming, charming people. The most beautiful dining room on a terrace overlooking the whole of Ibiza town. The food is excellent, the gardens exquisite"* – STEPHEN JONES.

HOTEL LA BOBADILLA, 18300 Loja, Granada ☎ (958) 321861
Luxy hotel that emulates a pueblo blanco (white village), in a lovely setting. *"Pretty, comfy and very Spanish. A mega pool, like a lagoon, and a very good restaurant"* – LORD LICHFIELD. King Juan Carlos stays too.

🏨 **LA RESIDENCIA, Deiá, Majorca ☎ (971) 639011**
A grand old 16C manor house in the mountains, done up with perfect simplicity. *"A hotel that's paradisiacal for those who can afford it"* – HILARY RUBINSTEIN. SOPHIE GRIGSON splashes out: *"My ideal hotel, so elegant and so relaxed and easy. It's in the most beautiful setting, among olive groves with great views from the terrace. I would happily stay there for ever. Beautiful bedrooms with lovely old wooden Majorcan furniture, white curtains, white hangings from the ceiling and four-poster beds."* ROBERT ELMS is equally taken: *"One of my favourite places in the world; very, very, very high quality. It's got the most beautiful pool I've ever seen, surrounded by pink mountains."*

———— *Restaurants* ————

🏨 **ARZAK, Alto de Miracruz 21, San Sebastián ☎ (943) 278465**
No 1 in Spain, and probably the best-value 3-

🦃 **Buzzz** Chasing el sol: For ROBIN HANBURY-TENISON, *the* way to get to Spain is by sea: *"Le Bretagne* [Brittany Ferries] *is a pearl among ferry boats, all elegance and space, Art Deco and haute cuisine"* 🦃 . . . . . . On the Costa, he drops in on **Robbie's** in Estepona ☎ (952) 802121 for *"quite the best food, most entertaining milieu and nicest host in southern Spain"* 🦃 . . . . . . Another moreish southerner is **Hotel Coral Beaches**, Ctra Cádiz-Málaga, Marbella ☎ (952) 824500, in Puerto Banus. *"It's got the most lovely Moorish restaurant. A really imaginative mix of food"* – CAROL WRIGHT 🦃 . . . . . . Rising star: One of the best young chefs in Spain is Hilario Arbelaitz, cooking at the farmhouse restaurant **Zuberoa**, at Oyarzun, near San Sebastián 🦃 . . . . . . **Best cerveza:** *The* beer to be seen downing from the bottle is Barcelona-brewed **Voll-Damm.** 🦃 . . . . . . **Best Cava:** LIZ BERRY declares **Juve y Camps** the best producers of méthode champenoise, and **Reserva de la Familia** their finest Cava. . . . . 🦃

❝One of the most exciting things to see is a bull-fight on horseback – the rider and the horse are as one. It's so dangerous and fast you can't believe what you're seeing ❞

 VICTOR EDELSTEIN

star in Europe. Juan Marí Arzak has done more to elevate the chef's profession than any of his countrymen. *"My favourite European-style restaurant, and one of the best in Europe. Almost exclusively fish . . . Basque cuisine, one of the great undiscovered cuisines of Europe. Merluza – hake – in a clam sauce is amazing, but the thing that will kill you is cheese-flavoured ice cream, which is magnificent"* – ROBERT ELMS.

——— *Wine* ———

Spain is beginning to rise above her reputation as producer of middle-of-the-road quaffable reds in large quantities. French grape varieties still dominate and LIZ BERRY notes a tendency to grow ever more Chardonnay, but Spain's future lies in the rediscovery of her old grape varieties, and a handful of pioneers are doing just that.

In Penedès, **TORRES** produce a portfolio of wines from different classic and native grape varieties. Their best is undoubtedly **Gran Coronas 'Black Label'**.

The Priorato area, in Tarragona, produces full-bodied reds as well as LIZ BERRY's favourite *"dessert wines of top quality"* (best makers are **DE MULLER** and **BARRIL**).

Ribera del Duero produces the renowned if rarely found **VEGA SICILIA**, which is 10 years in the making. **Valbuena**, the cheaper second wine, is considered by some aficionados a better wine, while **Unico** is *"the Lafite of Spain"* for MICHAEL BROADBENT, who advises the 1966 is at its peak. **Pesquera** from **BODEGAS ALEJANDRO FERNANDEZ** curries favour, too.

From the best-known region of Rioja, **MARQUES DE RISCAL** is the best-known name, especially among claret-lovers, though its elegant modern wines are almost too light. **MARQUES DE MURRIETA** is a more powerful and altogether more serious wine. **MARQUES DE CACERES** is more modern and very reliable. LIZ BERRY recommends **CVNE** across the board, **BODEGAS RIO-JANAS**, and the **Vina Ardanza Reserva 904** from **BODEGAS LA RIOJA ALTA**.

Sherry

Just as mouldy grapes make some of the world's best sweet wines, so mouldy white wine makes one of the world's best apéritifs: dry sherry. The thicker the fur of *flor* across the wine in cask, the drier the finished sherry. The most brilliant Finos and Olorosos are greatly undervalued, selling at a fraction of the price of their equivalents in Burgundy or Madeira. **Barbadillo's SANLUCAR MANZANILLA, Domecq's LA INA** and the famous **TIO PEPE** of **Gonzàles Byass** would make a Fino start to any meal (Gonzàles B's **APOSTOLES** – dry oloroso – is another treat). SERENA SUTCLIFFE also votes for **Valdespino's INOCENTE FINO** and joins LIZ BERRY in lauding the oldies of **Sandeman**.

SRI LANKA

THE GALL FACE HOTEL, Colombo 3
☎ **(1) 441010**
Vintage stuff from the Raj, the 137-year-old dame still flourishes. *"One of the best experiences I've had was staying in one of their suites, which are spectacularly huge, all teak floors, big fans, a marble bath, ocean view. Breakfas delivered by your barefooted butler is the best value in the world"* – GLYNN CHRISTIAN. *"An old-fashioned hotel which I liked very much, one of the remaining colonial hotels, excellent. Very pleasant people and huge bathrooms"* – QUENTIN CREWE. *"One should spend a few days there, wonderful"* – GIOVANNI SANJUST.

SWEDEN

STOCKHOLM

——— *Hotels* ———

GRAND HOTEL, S Blasieholmshamnen 8, PO Box 16424, S-10327 Stockholm
☎ **(08) 221020**
Stockholm's grandest, opened in 1874 and recently restored, *"has the best view of any hotel I know. It's right in the centre and it look over the Royal Castle with a sort of quayside in between – it's stunning, a very good, very beautiful hotel"* – JULIAN LLOYD WEBBER. First-rate French at **Franska Matsalen**, smorgasbord and home-made pastries out on the verandah. Suites at the adjacent Venetian-style Bolinder Palace, are the last word.

——— *Music* ———

DROTTNINGHOLM PALACE
☎ **(08) 759 0380**
More than just a musical experience, this out-

standing 17C palace, the Versailles of the North, is still the official residence of the Swedish royal family. See the follies in the grounds, the wood and iron 'tent' and the Chinese Pavilion. The 18C **Court Theatre**, built for Queen Lovisa Ulricha, remains unchanged – gawp at the original sets for *Die Zauberflöte*, *Cosi Fan Tutte*, still used, along with the antique instruments. The season lasts from late May to Sept, and JULIAN LLOYD WEBBER makes it if he can: *"It's the most beautiful place."* Apply to **Drottningholm Opera**, PO Box 27050 ☎ (08) 665 1100.

SWITZERLAND

GENEVA

—— *Hotels* ——

BEAU RIVAGE, 13 quai du Mont-Blanc, CH-1201 ☎ (022) 731 0221
Run by the Meyer family for over 125 years. Once home to the Duke of Brunswick, then home from home to the Duchess of Windsor. A winner with LISA BARNARD, and DAVID GIBBONS for lakeside dining: *"One of my favourite restaurants,* **Le Chat Botté**. *The food is haute cuisine, more French than Swiss. Tremendous service, beautiful wine list, great cheeses, great food."*

LE RICHEMOND, Jardin Brunswick, CH-1211 ☎ (022) 731 1400
A once-unassuming pensione, now more a private

mansion run for over a century by the Armleder family. The sort of luxury you can sink into from the moment the Rolls-Royce collects you from the station. The visitors' book gives a good overview of 20C culture: Colette, Miró, Walt Disney, Chagall ... ROBIN LEACH, DAVID SHILLING and LISA BARNARD add their signatures.

—— *Restaurants* ——

LA PERLE DU LAC, 128 rue de Lausanne, CH-1202 ☎ (022) 731 7935
Pretty lakeside restaurant with outdoor eating in summer. Views of the city and Mont Blanc and a specialization in *les poissons*.

TSE FUNG, Hotel Réserve, 301 route de Lausanne, CH-1293 Bellevue ☎ (022) 774 1741
In a modern hotel outside Geneva, this is, for SIR PETER USTINOV, *"arguably the finest Chinese restaurant in the world – a wonderful, wonderful restaurant. It's authentic and yet refined to our tastes. It has a wonderful sweet and sour soup and Mongolian meat things".*

ZURICH

—— *Bars and cafés* ——

CAFE SCHOBER, Napfgasse 4, CH-8001 ☎ (01) 251 8060
A coffee house since 1357, rambling and low-eaved. Sit outside with your napfkuchen (like a pound cake) and coupe Schober – apricot, strawberry and vanilla ice-cream swimming in rum, strawberry sauce and topped with fruit. They sell SIR PETER USTINOV's favourite Teuscher chocolates.

 **Buzzz** Meal ticket: Just outside Geneva proper is a simple workmen's café which attracts a most sophisticated clientele. **Le Buffet de la Gare de Céligny**, Fillistorf, Céligny ☎ (022) 776 2770, does *"the best filet de perche. Absolutely sensational, only served when it is fresh, so phone ahead. It's gone slightly upmarket but because it's an agricultural area you get workers coming in for their FF14 plat du jour"* – SALLY BURTON. NICHOLAS VILLIERS is in on the secret too: *"Renowned for its lake perch. A charming, local restaurant, very pretty indoors or out, the kind of place no one would know about unless they were told"* ...... SIR PETER PARKER finds his fish 'n' chips at a mystery café on the water's edge: *"A God's hostess runs it, beautiful to watch. Chaucer would have loved her"* ...... Cigar puff: **Gérard Père et Fils**, 12 quai du Mont-Blanc, Geneva ☎ (022) 326511, is *"the best cigar shop in the world, without a doubt. They are importers of Havana cigars, both father and son have been there for ever. Worth a stop for any connoisseur, for quality and selection. M Gérard has produced an encyclopaedia of cigars"* – NICHOLAS VILLIERS. ....

CONFISERIE SPRUNGLI, Am Paradeplatz, Bahnhofstrasse 21, CH-8001 ☎ (01) 221 1722
The richest, creamiest chocolates, brittlest bon-bons and most perfect pâtisseries to take away or to eat on the spot with a cup of aromatic coffee.

──────── *Hotels* ────────

BAUR AU LAC, 1 Talstrasse, CH-8022 ☎ (01) 221 1650
Grand old man of Swiss hotels, catering to the carriage trade. Smooth service (concierge Albert Ostertag is world-famous), though MARK MCCORMACK is aghast that it doesn't have 24-hour room service. Canal and lake views, Rolls-Royce airport pick-up and spacious suites are some compensation for ROBIN LEACH, BARBARA TAYLOR BRADFORD and LISA BARNARD.

DOLDER GRAND HOTEL, Kurhausstrasse 65, CH-8032 ☎ (01) 251 6231
Stately Swiss resort hotel on the mountainside above the city. Though highly reputed, some find it has a clinical air. But no one, ROBIN LEACH included, could fault the facilities: fine French restaurant, golf course, pool, ice skating.

──────── *Restaurants* ────────

AGNES AMBERG, Hottingerstrasse 5, CH-8032 ☎ (01) 251 2626
Fashionable, clever-boots food attracts an up-to-the-minute crowd. Taste combinations pack more of a punch than the frilly décor would suggest; try sautéed foie gras in cabbage with rock salt and Sichuan pepper.

🐟 LES VACANCES CHEZ MAX, Seestrasse 53, CH-8702 Zollekon ☎ (01) 391 8877
Max Kehl may have shot to stardom with his Franco/Asian fusion but he is by no means style-bound. After a long (and obviously inspiring) holiday, Chez Max has let its hair down, put on a beach shirt and now dances to the rhythm of a global culture. The menu could place Morocco alongside Greece, Italy and Switzerland; the cooking still smacks of Max to the max.

───────────────────

· REST OF ·

SWITZERLAND

──── *Art and museums* ────

THYSSEN-BORNEMISZA COLLECTION, Villa Favorita, CH-6976 Castagnola ☎ (091) 521741
A fresh face on the Old Masters. Reopening in 1993 after renovations and a rehang, Baron Thyssen's astounding private collection bows only to the Queen of England's in quality and scope, with some 1,350 works (Holbein, Van Eyck, Titian, 18C rococo, Impressionists, Picasso, Cézanne, Van Gogh, German Expressionists . . .). Some 150 works can be seen here in his beautiful lakeside villa; many more are on loan to the Villahermosa Palace in Madrid.

──────── *Hotels* ────────

HOTEL DREI KONIGE, Blumenrain 8, CH-4001 Basle ☎ (061) 261 5252
Regal hotel, privately owned, with some pretty kingly Louis XIV and XV furniture. The French restaurant is favoured by DAME BARBARA CARTLAND: *"Delicious food on a beautiful terrace overlooking the Rhine."*

HOTEL HAUS PARADIES, CH-7551 Ftan ☎ (084) 91325
Alpine retreat in the unbelievably verdant Lower Engadine, with great cross-country skiing when the valley turns white. Only 21 rooms (each with fireplace or stove), well-stocked library. PAUL HENDERSON asks: *"Does any hotel have a better view? Bedrooms are spacious and well appointed, each facing over the valley. Very good regional cooking, though the Lobster Menu seems contrived."* As crustacea are available all year from mountain reservoirs, one can forgive chef/manager Roland Jöri's enthusiasm.

🐟 RHEINHOTEL FISCHERZUNFT, Rheinquai 8, CH-8200 Schaffhausen ☎ (053) 253281
Tiny hotel/restaurant in a 15C German guild, right on the Rhine. A clutch of rooms sleeps barely a house party in hedonistic comfort; the restaurant comforts those who didn't book a room in time. *"Doreen Jaeger, who runs the restaurant, is Chinese, and her husband, André, the chef, is French – a very sophisticated couple with very good style. The whole place is alive with her personality, the flowers are a knock-out, the china is unbelievable and the glassware and cutlery and the whole place just sparkles. The food is some of the best I've ever eaten in Switzerland"* – MARTIN SKAN. PAUL HENDERSON picks up the baton: *"The only hotel where both the head and the foot of the bed can be raised at the press of a button. For jaded palates that have seen everything, this is the most interesting restaurant in Europe. The flower bill is treble the dairy account! Go for the fish buffet, run for one week in spring and one in autumn."*

──────── *Music* ────────

FESTIVAL DE MUSIQUE MONTREUX-VEVEY, ave des Alpes 14, CH-1820 Montreux ☎ (021) 963 0879
Small but worthy classical lakeside festival.

Chamber music, philharmonic orchestras, recitals and 20C sounds fill concert halls, churches and museums each Sept.

MONTREUX JAZZ FESTIVAL, Service de Location, Case 97, CH-1820 Montreux; tickets c/o Tourist Office ☎ (021) 631212
Stompin' rock and jazz festival every June, co-produced by Quincy Jones. Big names – Elvis Costello, Dizzy Gillespie – pack out the casino's hall; lesser-knowns tough it on the streets.

——— *Restaurants* ———

🏆 **GIRARDET, 1 rue d'Yverdon, Crissier, CH-1023 Lausanne ☎ (021) 634 0505**
One of the world's greatest star chefs. Impossible to sum up his brilliant but always well-judged flights of fancy – the menu will always be fresh and surprising: potato cake with black Périgord truffles, perhaps, or John Dory with ginger and tarragon. Or ignore the menu altogether: "*Let him devise one for you. Very Swiss and superb*" – SALLY BURTON. ROBIN LEACH recognises greatness when he tastes it.

STUCKI BRUDERHOLZ, Bruderholzallee 42, CH-4059 Basle ☎ (061) 358222
Classic French cooking under Hans Stucki. Devotees get stuck into such specialities as warm escalope of duck's liver and langoustine minestrone. Al fresco eating in the charming garden.

——— *Ski resorts* ———

CRANS
Chic resort, drawing royals and aristos from Benelux, Denmark and Italy. Spectacular views over the Rhône Valley; a south-facing town, it's bathed in sun for hours longer than most other ski resorts. Best Alpine shopping in rue du Golf.

GSTAAD
Famed more for après than ski, a charming rural village which once a year is loaded with glamour: Prince Rainier et famille, Audrey Hepburn, Roger Moore, the Texan Wyatts, Boucherons, Bulgaris and Buckleys. Most social hotel: **Palace Hotel ☎ (030) 83131**, favoured by LISA BARNARD and NICHOLAS VILLIERS, who also likes the **Olden** hotel **☎ (030) 43444** which has "*probably the oldest restaurant in Gstaad, good Swiss food and music. The most local of local restaurants.*"

KLOSTERS
Favourite resort of the PoW, who now sports an avalanche-survival balloon on his back when skiing. Small, smart, old-fashioned resort. Best choice of slopes and other icy sports at nearby Davos. Best hotels: **Wynegg** (excellent cuisine); the small **Chesa Grischuna**.

ST MORITZ
One of the best for the seriously sporty (and social): downhill and cross-country skiing, bob-sleighing, curling, heli-skiing and, on the frozen lake, cricket, racing, polo and the mad mountain sport skikjöring, where a 'jockey' is towed, waterski-style, behind a riderless horse. St Moritz would be a less sunny place without the Cresta Run: the British boys' tradition of hurtling down a toboggan run collecting 'Cresta kisses', ice lesions, at Shuttlecock corner. Feb is party month for jetsetters who wing in in their G3s and Falcon 50s – the Aga Khan, Agnellis, Rothschilds, Niarchoses, Guinesses. Best hotels: **Badrutt's Palace ☎** (082) 21101, a baronial-style lodge with the best nightclub, **Kings'**; **Suvretta House ☎** (082) 21121, the most discreet of the grand-scale hotels, out of town with Christmas card views; **Kulm**, with the best panoramic lunchspot for basking non-skiers (spot Koo Stark) at the **Sunny Bar**; the **Carlton**. Best Alpine nosh: **La Marmite ☎** (082) 36355, for dishes of chairlift-threatening richness; Hotel Schweizerhof's **Acla ☎** (082) 22171, "*the best restaurant in the world. A marvellous restaurant if you're very hungry and not poor*" – JEAN-MICHEL JAUDEL.

VERBIER
"*One of the top areas for right-to-the-limit, really extreme skiing*" – STEVE PODBORSKI. The Attelas and Mont-Fort sectors throw up a challenge to off-piste experts; thrilling black runs down to Tortin. Best hotels: **Rosalp, Rhodania** (dancing in the basement **Farm Club** – best nightspot in the Alps), **Le Mazot**. Best restaurant: **Upstairs at the Rosalp**. Best boozer: the raucous **Pub Montfort**.

> **❝** *Best skiing? I think it's a toss up between St Moritz and Zermatt* **❞**
> ROBIN LEACH

ZERMATT
Romantic setting beneath zer Matterhorn. Only horse-drawn sleighs and electric taxis allowed in town. Brilliant, varied skiing, some of the best heli-skiing in Europe. Best café-bar: **Elsie's Bar**. Best restaurant: **Le Mazot**. Best discos: at **Hotel Alex; Le Village** and the **Broken Bar** at the Hotel Post. Best nightclub: **Zermatt Yacht Club**. Best hotels: **Mont Cervin; Zermatterhof**.

TAIWAN

GRAND HYATT TAIPEI, 2 Sung Shou Rd, Taipei ☎ (2) 720 1234
The place to stay. 1,000 rooms and opulence as only Hyatt knows how. The glass-roofed atrium

with two curving galleries looks up to the Taipei World Trade Centre; 9 restaurants (Californian, Shanghainese, Japanese, English pub, etc), great fitness centre.

HILTON, 38 Chung Xsiao Rd West, Section 1, Taipei ☎ (2) 311 5151
High-riser that impresses JULIAN LLOYD WEBBER: *"The best Hilton I've stayed in. It moved me to write a little note to the manager. It's an excellent hotel, run incredibly efficiently in a very chaotic city. The rooms are large, all suites, very good indeed."* 5 restaurants, rooftop garden, sauna, Jacuzzi and health centre.

TANZANIA

Home to the famous Serengeti National Park, the incredible snow-capped, volcanic Kilimanjaro, and Ngorongoro Crater, refuge of many a rhino and lion. Watch the sun rise over the rim from **Ngorongoro Crater Lodge**.
In the port of Dar es Salaam, stay as DAVID SHILLING did at **Kilimanjaro ☎ (51) 21281**: *"The best hotel . . . the only hotel in the centre of town, that is the trouble. It's booked up for ever"* – DAVID SHILLING.
Folks say you can smell the 'Spice Island' of Zanzibar before you reach it by boat. Former hub of the East African slave trade, it was home for infamous trader Tippu Tip – and Dr Livingstone. Best hotel: **Bhawani**, PO Box 670 ☎ (054) 30200, big and modern.

THAILAND

BANGKOK

—— Art and museums ——

GRAND PALACE ☎ (02) 223 5172
The royal palace, a large complex of golden and coloured spires, wats (temples) and palace buildings. A fusion of Eastern and Western styles. See Thailand's most sacred images – the small **Emerald Buddha** (made of green jasper) on the altar of Wat Phra Kaeo, a traditional Thai monastery, and the 160 ft golden **Reclining Buddha**.

JIM THOMPSON'S HOUSE, 6 Soi Kasemsan 2, Rama 1 Rd
A wonderful collection of Thai fine art, porcelain and furniture. Displayed in 6 reconstructed tra-

ditional houses – stilted teak buildings – shifted from the ancient capital of Ayutthaya by silk sultan Jim Thompson. Don't miss the gardens.

—— *Clubs* ——

Nightlife centres on sleazy/glitzy/kinky **Patpong** (sex shows, massage parlours and go-go bars) and **Soi Cowboy**, off Soi 23 Sukhumvit Rd, a narrow back alley lined with lively bars. The less adventurous frequent **Silom Plaza**, with its café-bars spilling out on to a piazza.

BROWN SUGAR, 231/20 Sarasin Rd
A Bangkok landmark. Live bar with a cool crowd. Jazz and blues, relaxed atmosphere, friendly staff.

BUBBLES, Dusit Thani, Rama IV Rd ☎ (02) 233 1130
Mainstream hotel disco packed out with smarty pants. Go for a good dance. Easy to park – one reason why it's so popular.

NASA SPACEDROME, 999 Ramkhamhang Rd ☎ (02) 314 4024
Top Thai ravadrome. Do the shuttle shuffle underneath a model spaceship which flies over the dance floor. Big, bursting and bouncy bouncy.

ROME CLUB VIDEOTHEQUE, Soi 4, 90-96 Silom Rd ☎ (02) 233 8836
Kinky karaoke – groove till 1 am then watch the transvestite cabaret mime act. *"The best disco anywhere for dancing"* – JEREMIAH TOWER.

—— *Hotels* ——
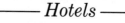

HILTON INTERNATIONAL, 2 Wireless Rd ☎ (02) 253 0123
Crescent-shaped, low-level riverside building in the 8-acre landscaped Nai Lert Park – complete with waterfalls, canals and bridges. Big bedrooms, Valentino-designed super suites. See also Restaurants.

🏆 THE ORIENTAL, 48 Oriental Ave ☎ (02) 236 0400
The best in Thailand, if not the Orient, if not in the world. PRUE LEITH, LISA BARNARD, SERENA FASS, WARWICK VYNER and ROBIN LEACH are bowled over. Legendary service: listen to KEN HOM: *"I still love it. I think it is really among the best in the world; it's not easy to do that kind of service anywhere else in the world. You are at a place where people can anticipate your needs, they know who you are and what your needs are. What is impressive about the Oriental, having been back there several times, is how it continues to improve, especially food-wise"* (see Restaurants). *"The best in the world"* for MICHAEL BROADBENT, who thinks *"the views are spectacular – surely the most endless bustling*

river frontage. *Staff not only efficient but courteous to an extraordinary degree, remembering and using one's name, above all, smiling and charming. World-class cuisine at its* **Normandie** *restaurant produced by an English chef.*" JENNY KEE stays in the Authors' Wing; book in there for a taste of the lazy old colonial days, or go swish in the modern block – the Oriental Suite has had a US$ 500,000 silk, marble, teak and crystal fit-up. "*Extremely soigné and very luxurious*" – DOTT ROSA MARIA LETTS. "*Just super, you can't fault it*" – and that's quite something from ANDREW LLOYD WEBBER.

Far East's Best Hotels

1	THE ORIENTAL · Bangkok
2	THE REGENT · Hong Kong
3	MANDARIN ORIENTAL · Hong Kong
4	GRAND HYATT · Hong Kong
5	HOTEL SEIYO · Tokyo
6	THE PENINSULA · Hong Kong
7	THE REGENT . Bangkok
8	SHANGRI-LA · Singapore
9	THE ORIENTAL · Singapore
10	OBEROI · New Delhi

🏃 **THE REGENT, 155 Rajadamri Rd**
☎ **(02) 251 6127**
Challenging the Oriental in every department (service "*still the best in the world*" – ELISE PASCOE, cooking and grandeur) and surpassing it for business-wise location. Set in lush gardens with ponds and fountains; soaring lobby with

amazing hand-painted silk murals on walls and ceiling, depicting Thai astrological legends. Sheer opulence in bedrooms – silk bedspreads, balconies decked out with flowers; brilliant food (see Restaurants).

—— Restaurants ——

BUSSARACUM, 35 Soi Pipat 2, Convent Rd ☎ (02) 235 8915
The place to eat old-style 'Royal Thai' cooking. Delicious hot, sour tom yam kung, beautifully presented starters shaped into birds, turtles, etc, and stunning steamed sea bass.

HILTON INTERNATIONAL, see Hotels
Nouvellish Continental fare at **Ma Maison** – also great if your teeth are itching for a real prime rib. The German chef has cooked for the King and Queen of Thailand. If you're dying for a Japanese, you can't better **Genji**.

LE BANYAN, Soi 8, 59 Sukhumvit Rd ☎ (02) 253 5556
Inventive French cooking from ex-Normandie cook Bruno Bishoff. Occasional Thai spice too – lemon grass, ginger, etc. Lovely setting in an old wooden Thai house; the main focus of the dining room is the silver duck.

🏃 **LEMON GRASS, 5/1 Soi, 24 Sukhumvit Rd ☎ (02) 258 8637**
Brilliant food in a charming Thai house, regional specialities from the south. "*I think it was the best Thai meal I've eaten, the cooking was absolutely exquisite and the flavours always perfect. The restaurant is several small rooms linked together and decorated with old Thai tapestry and artefacts*" – SOPHIE GRIGSON. There's a twin Lemon Grass in Chiang Mai.

MAYFLOWER, Dusit Thani Hotel, Rama IV Rd ☎ (02) 233 1130
Tuck into the best Cantonese cooking in town –

🏃 **Buzzz** After years of wrangling and indecision, Bangkok could get its long awaited **monorail** to relieve traffic nightmares – no more 5-hour drives to the airport 🏃 . . . . . . The capital's newest big hotel, the **Grand Hyatt Erewan** ☎ (02) 254 1234, opened last summer to exceedingly good reports 🏃 . . . . . . Movers drink shakers at the **Crowne Royale**, Patpong 2 – it's Bangkok's offbeat answer to Hong Kong's Captain's Bar 🏃 . . . . . . If the name fits: savour great Thai home cooking at **Cabbages and Condoms**, 8 Soi 12, Sukhumvit Rd ☎ (02) 251 0402, in the knowledge that proceeds go to the Population and Community Development Association for family planning education 🏃 . . . . . . SOPHIE GRIGSON went shopping in Chiang Mai: "*The best food market is* **Vararot**, *absolutely massive, indoor and outdoor, filled with things of which you have absolutely no idea what they might be. Extraordinarily exciting and bizarre, my hot favourite market*" 🏃 . . . . . . **The Royal Wing Hotel** in Pattaya is the place to find JEREMIAH TOWER in Feb . . . . 🏃

abalone and jellyfish salad is a grasp-the-nettle must. Modern décor, Chinese porcelain. And this is what's meant by service Thai-style: they keep a computerized record of your order so they know what you like for next time.

SEAFOOD MARKET AND RESTAURANT, 388 Sukhumvit Rd ☎ (02) 276 1810
Select a fish, buy it, have it cooked and tuck in. SOPHIE GRIGSON did: *"Sounds a bit gimmicky but it really works. You take a shopping trolley and there's this massive counter filled with all kinds of fish and shellfish, 5 types of lobster and God knows how many types of prawns and fresh sea bass that's still wriggling . . . When you arrive at your table a waiter glides up and looks at what's in your trolley and makes suggestions on how to cook it. It's extraordinary."*

THE ORIENTAL, see Hotels
The **Normandie**'s a winner for MICHAEL BROADBENT and CLAUDIA CRAGG: *"The best French restaurant in Bangkok, the service is discreet."* Great river view from the top floor. Sea-foodies make a beeline for **Lord Jim's**, sit in a 19C steamship stateroom-style dining room and eat fab fish. Traditional Thai at **Sala Rim Nam** across the river: *"The most spectacular Thai restaurant in town"* – CC – top tucker and Siamese dancing. Take tea in the **Authors' Lounge** and a cocktail on the **Riverside Terrace**.

THE REGENT, see Hotels
Splendid Euro/Gallic food at **The Regent Grill**. Sit around the tropical pool at the less formal **La Brasserie** and dine on Continental cuisine. ELISE PASCOE's choice is the mock bazaar-style **Spice Market**: *"Very, very good. The famous pomelo salad with river prawns and pork is very good and I love their deep-fried grouper with chilli sauce – the fish stands up grandly on the plate."*

THANYING RESTAURANT, 10 Pramuan Rd, Off Silom Rd ☎ (02) 236 4361
A calm restaurant filled with Asian antiques and serving Royal Thai cuisine – extraordinary iced rice with jasmine, sea bass with chilli sauce.

TUMNAK THAI, 131 Ratchadapisek Rd ☎ (02) 277 8855
Perhaps the largest restaurant in the world – a phenomenal 10-acre site which seats 3,000. Computer-run, with hundreds of roller-skating, walkie-talking staff, 150 cooks, trees, waterfalls, music, dancing and jolly good nosh.

——— Shopping ———

As Hong Kong is to men's tailors, Bangkok is to women – quick, and made to measure – chalk up designery gear at **Kai Guerlain**, 2–14 N Wireless Rd ☎ (02) 253 2998. Hipper gear on the 2nd floor of the **Charn Isala Tower**, Rama V Rd – look for society dressmaker **Teeraphan Wanarat, Daung Jai Bis, Urai Risa** and **Venick**.

For jewellery there's only one place – **Peninsula Plaza** in Rajadamri Rd. Find Princess Chailai's shop **Chailai**, an ethnophile's dream, with pieces from north Thailand, and society dazzlers **Bualaad Jewellery** and **Frank's Jewellery**. Chic shoppers also head for the **Oriental** and **Regent** arcades – find **Lotus** at the latter, a trove of delightful trinkets, semi-precious carved stones, embroidery, rugs and antiques.

Stay in the groove at the **World Trade Center**, the **Mah-Boon Krong** area, and the **Siam Center** – hundreds of boutiques and little shops. Go for fake designer goods around **Silom Village** in Silom Rd, street 'bazaars' between **Sois 7 and 11 off Sukhumvit Road**, and the **Gaysorn** area. Ethno crafts at **Thai Home Industries**, 35 Oriental Ave. Collect eccentric Thai antiques and bric-à-brac at the weekend market at **Chatuchak Park**, off Phalan Yothin Rd. 'Antiques' can be checked for authenticity by the Fine Arts Department ☎ (02) 233 0977.

JIM THOMPSON, 9 Surawong Rd ☎ (02) 234 4900
A respected name for iridescent dyes on floating

🧥 **Buzzz** Tuck into Turkish tucker at **Pandeli**, Misir Carsisi, Ermigan ☎ (01) 522 5534, *"an old restaurant in the bazaar, above the spice market. Looks like a men's club out of E M Forster. Very good traditional Turkish food, not a tourist restaurant"* – NICHOLAS VILLIERS 🧥 . . . . . . MARK BIRLEY heads out of town to **Urcan** at Sariyer ☎ (1) 420367, *"a very superior and charming restaurant, right by the Bosphorus. I cannot possibly recommend it too highly, they even have a huge tank full of live turbot; it's one of the few places remaining where you can have fresh as opposed to frozen whitebait".* 🧥 . . . . Site visits: See some of the most spectacular relics of antiquity at **Troy, Ephesus** and **Aphrodisias** 🧥 . . . . . . Turkish bath: Wallow in the natural limestone basins lapping with hot spring water at **Pamukkale** . . . . 🧥

silks – Parma violet, sky blue, emerald, peacock, flame. Other items too – *big* cushions, clothing and accessories.

KRISHNA'S, 137-6-7 Sukhumvit Rd (btwn Soi 9 and 11) ☎ (02) 254 9944

Oriental handicrafts from elephant chairs and Burmese rugs to pottery, lacquer and wood carving. Spread out over 3 floors. If you get too carried away, they'll arrange shipping home.

· REST OF ·
THAILAND

🐘 AMANPURI, Pansea Beach, Phuket
☎ (076) 311394

Live like Thai royalty in the most indulgent and glamorous hotel in the country. "*The 40 pavilion suites, all resembling tiny Thai temples, stretch over 20 acres of a coconut palm plantation. Each villa comes with its own private sun deck and sunken tub – it's pretty extraordinary and pretty exclusive*" – ROBIN LEACH. Your personal assistant manager to pamper you, and tennis, swimming pool, snorkelling, scuba, game fishing, etc, to energize you. "*One of my favourite hotels. Glamorous 30 m black-tiled pool; best views from suites 103 and 105*" – SUSAN KUROSAWA. "*A brilliant resort. Paradise*" – LISA BARNARD.

❝ *The night markets at Hua Hin are fabulous – they make duck soup and mussel omelettes with fresh mussels and duck eggs – marvellous stuff and extremely good value* **❞**

 ELISE PASCOE

DUSIT ISLAND RESORT, Chiang Rai, c/o Dusit Thani, Rama IV Rd, Bangkok
☎ (02) 236 0450

On an island in the Mai Kok River in the northern hills. "*An exceptionally good hotel with a very, very good Thai restaurant in the grounds. The best hotel swimming pool in the world – with the possible exception of Hayman Island – you've got 360° views over the river up to the Golden Triangle. You can go into the long neck villages, where the people stretch their necks, and you can go elephant trekking. The food in the markets has Laotian, Vietnamese and Burmese influences*" – ELISE PASCOE.

DUSIT RESORT AND POLO CLUB, Hua Hin, c/o Dusit Thani (see above)

In the royal seaside town, south of Bangkok, it's

caught ELISE PASCOE's attention: "*The rooms are wonderful – the Polo Suite is to die for. Two things on the menu really stood out – duck and grape soup and beef and pumpkin curry.*"

TURKEY

ISTANBUL

—— *Hotels* ——

HIDIV KASRI, Cubuklu-Kanlica
☎ (1) 331 2651

Look down on the Bosphorus from the fabulous former summer palace of the last Viceroy of Egypt. Inside it's everything from Art Nouveau to trad Turkish, the best pad is the Viceroy's Suite with its own terrace. Get there by boat from the city centre.

YESIL EV, Kabasakal Craddesi 5, Sultanahmed ☎ (1) 511 1150

Converted from a grand old Ottoman pavilion, the 'Greenhouse' gets NICHOLAS VILLIERS's vote: "*A 19C private house which has been transformed into a wonderful small hotel. Little garden which you can eat in, decorated with old Turkish furniture.*" Great location between Hagia Sophia and the Blue Mosque.

—— *Yacht charter* ——

"*Those in the know sail the Turkish coast rather than the Greek – it's the best unexplored part of the Med if you don't want grand luxe*" – LORD LICHFIELD. Experienced sailors go for **Top Yacht Charter** (see Travel Directory) – most sailing is unskippered 'bareboat', though there are crewed boats as well. Or try out a traditional wooden gulet.

VENEZUELA

HATO PINERO, Av La Estancia, Torre Diamen, Piso 1, Ofic 19, Chuao, Caracas 1060 ☎ (02) 916854

Set on a pre-Cambrian outcrop, flanked by rivers, the converted cattle ranch is a paradise for bird and game-watchers. 342 wingèd wonders are 'inventoried' in the environs. Down-to-earth folk include ocelot, jaguar, crab-eating fox, anteater, puma and capy bara – the world's largest rodent. Head out in May as the flowers bloom with the first rains, or in winter (up to Sept) for the best ornithology. Safaris and boat rides through the lagoons.

LOS FRAILES, c/o Avensa, Centro Comercial Tamanaco, Nivil C2, Caracas ☎ (02) 563 3020
In the mountains of Mérida, an hour's flight south of Caracas, then a winding drive 13,500 ft up in the clouds – with a sheer drop over the edge. Stunning views when you get there; stay in former monks' cells in this 17C monastery run as an inn.

ZAMBIA

Wildlife watchers find more species in greater numbers in the South Luangwa National Park than almost anywhere else in Africa.

KAPANI SAFARI LODGE, PO Box 100, Mufuwe ☎ (062) 45015
Thatched, native-style lodges with viewing platform overlooking a secluded lagoon. Relax over drinks on the verandah and keep your eyes peeled. The tiny nearby sister camp, **Louwi River Camp**, is one of the best in the bush, run by naturalist Norman Carr.

CHINZOMBO CAMP, c/o MRI (see Travel Directory)
A basic, no-frills safari lodge, and DAVID GOWER loves it: "*Thatched huts, on the edge of the Luangwa River. You view the game from the back of open land cruisers, drive into the national parks. It's good – they've got leopard, lion, and the big game, elephant, buffalo, etc.*"

ZIMBABWE
—— *Hotels and camps* ——

BUMI HILLS SAFARI LODGE, PO Box 41, Kariba ☎ (161) 2353
Fan-cooled rooms are set at the edge of a cliff overlooking Lake Kariba. Go fishing, game viewing or try a Water Wilderness safari in rustic houseboats that are purportedly insect-proof.

ELEPHANT HILLS HOTEL, Victoria Falls ☎ (13) 4691
After its illustrious inauguration (hosting the Commonwealth Conference) the trumpeting's died down. But this project by Zimbabwe Sun to challenge the Vic Falls Hotel is no Dumbo, as DAVID GOWER recognizes: "*They have a golf course that used to be a championship course, which is actually like a game park in itself. There's a classic photograph of people playing golf with elephants in the background. Green-keeping is a problem.*"

MEIKLES HOTEL, PO Box 594, Stanley Ave, Harare ☎ (4) 707721
Zimbabwe's first 5-star hotel, and still the best place to stay in the capital. 3 restaurants, rooftop pool deck, plenty of bars.

RUCKOMECHI CAMP, c/o Shearwater
Idyllic riverside camp, 10 cottages all with showers – though the bathroom that opens on to the river is a *must*. Walking, canoeing and driving safaris.

Foaming at the Mouth

For madmen, adrenalin junkies, and professional sportsmen only – whitewater rafting takes you through some of the world's most spectacular scenery, down bad-tempered rivers and, you hope, delivers you safely at the other end. Horror stories abound (being sucked down holes and spewed out again, men overboard, inexperienced guides – for which Nepal is notorious). But daredevil DAVID GOWER stays upright Down Under: "*The best thing to do in New Zealand is to go whitewater rafting. I've done it both times in the South Island – there are all sorts of rivers which are admirably suited to it, with differing grades of difficulty (the maximum is 8 or so). You go in an inflatable, so it's got a bit of flexibility, about 8 of you plus a guide – someone who knows what they are doing.*" But for real white-knuckle white water, Zimbabwe has his last word: "*The Zambezi below the falls is as good as you can get – they claim it's the best in the world, and a lot of people from the States and Australasia would back that up. Very white, one of the highest-graded whitewater rafting sections in the world. Go beyond that and you're talking impossible.*" Rafting operators **Shearwater** (see Tours and charters) will tell you all you need to know before steering you downstream towards the infamous rapid number 18 . . . .

VICTORIA FALLS HOTEL, PO Box 10, Victoria Falls ☎ (113) 4203
Famous old-world place – it opened in 1904 – with wide verandahs, peaceful gardens, a famous doorman, nightly African dance displays and a contented DAVID GOWER: *"The old traditional colonial venue, good fun."*

—— *Tours and charters* ——

See also Travel Directory.

SHEARWATER, 5th Fl, Karigamombe Centre, PO Box 3961, Harare ☎ (4) 735712
Zambezi adventuring with something for most folk. Go softly amid the blue water of the lower river in an Indian canoe; toughen up in a conventional canoe between Kazungula and Vic Falls; or frighten yourself witless on the whitewater rapids. Good tucker from the 'luxury' support team – eat at long tables under the acacia and ebony trees.

UNITED AIR CHARTERS, PO Box AP 50, Harare Airport, Harare ☎ (4) 731713
'Scenes so lovely they must have been gazed upon by angels in their flight . . . .' See what Livingstone saw, on the Flight of Angels: 5 separate waterfalls – the Devil's Cataract, Main Falls, Horseshoe Falls, Rainbow Falls and the Eastern Cataract – that make up the Mosi oa Tunya (Smoke that Thunders). Also air safaris over game parks.

TRAVEL DIRECTORY

—— *Airlines* ——

All airlines have their fans; here is a list of those that our contributors recommend. Inevitably there is a patriotic bias in their choice but some airlines fly beyond national boundaries.

AIR FRANCE
Famed for its food, and the *choix évident* for Frenchmen MARC BOHAN and JEAN-MICHEL JAUDEL.

AIR INDIA
Good value, good service and a good few non-stop flights to India every week.

AIR NEW ZEALAND
The kiwi that flies is known for wines which stand the test of altitude and fine business and first class services. Hear DON HEWITSON: *"I judge my airline first of all on the seat, second on good service and third on wine, and Air New Zealand is brilliant . . . and the seafood is just*

wonderful."

ALITALIA
A stylish worldwide carrier whose new staff uniforms and plane interiors have been designed by Giorgio Armani, no less, and whose first class consistently comes out top in surveys. MARCHESA DI SAN GIULIANO FERRAGAMO is a fan.

🛦 AMERICAN AIRLINES
Stripping stars off its US competitors, American Airlines is a winner for MARK MCCORMACK, ROBIN LEACH, CAROLINE HUNT (*"the service is excellent"*) and DAVID SHILLING: *"I think that they are trying really hard – really friendly and very hot on security"*. CAROL WRIGHT is *"particularly impressed by the presentation of the food, which was designed by an architect"*.

Virtuous Virgin

Branson's baby's growing up, up and away . . . breaking through the clouds as the 90s' highest-flying carrier. Virgin Atlantic has established an impeccable track record and a growing fan club as the airline that best serves the business traveller. First there's the service itself: *"It really is exceptionally good,"* says STEPHEN JONES. *"The stewardesses are helpful without being subservient, not too much in evidence but always there and refreshingly normal. First-class service at business-class prices."* Then there's the food: *"Virgin are brilliant, so brilliant that I work for them now, in charge of food. Branson has created something unique"* – RAYMOND BLANC. Then there's in-flight entertainment: Virgin was first to give *every* passenger at individual TV screen. Not to forget the complimentary Upper Class beauty therapist whose manicure and aromatherapy mean you're more likely to jet ahead than lag on arrival. And now full economy fare-paying passengers have their own first: Mid Class, which, with separate cabin, wider seats, priority check-in, etc, feels like business class. IAIN JOHNSTONE knows why there's nothing like a Virgin (*"the most comfy way to go"*), as do DOUGLAS HAYWARD, JOHN GOLD and JOHN BROOKE-LITTLE: *"Absolutely terrific. I did a tour of the plane and everybody seemed happy – quite a new experience."*

♠ BRITISH AIRWAYS

British is best for many discerning travellers; this high flyer has *"had its ups and downs but now it is on an up again"* – TERRY HOLMES. MADHUR JAFFREY (*"they're really perking up again"*) and MARK MCCORMACK (*"going from strength to strength"*) applaud their efforts too. AMANDA DE CADENET is their No 1 fan: *"If British Airways don't go there, I don't go there. Great service, they're reliable, they take off on time, the food is edible, I just like them."* Stiff-upper-lipped support from MARTIN SKAN (*"I'm very British minded and tend to support the firm"*) and JEFFREY ARCHER (*"one must support patriotic enterprises"*). The toss-up between first and club classes continues but the whole airline wins out for NICHOLAS VILLIERS (*"still doing the best job"*), SIR CLEMENT FREUD (*"I'm a fan"*), JULIAN LLOYD WEBBER (*"very reliable"*), JOHN TOVEY (*"for the consistency of the service and the standards – they really are trying"*), PAUL HENDERSON, LOYD GROSSMAN, DAN TOPOLSKI, JOHN GOLD, ROBERT SANGSTER, SERENA FASS, ROBIN LEACH and LORD MONTAGU OF BEAULIEU. Non-Brits JEREMIAH TOWER, ANDRE PREVIN, MARC BOHAN, KEN HOM and SKYE MACLEOD choose to take to the skies with BA, too.

♠ CATHAY PACIFIC

Hong Kong's airline, part of the Swire Group, is one of the best for food in the air and *the* best for service. *"It is the sort of attention they pay to you, for instance when you wake up dehydrated there is a glass of mineral water there. And they bend down to talk to you, so that they can look at you and ask, 'What can we do to make your trip comfortable?', without being obtrusive and obsequious"* – KEN HOM. ROBIN HANBURY-TENISON is equally keen: *"Cathay Pacific make you feel part of the family."* Eastern magic makes it happen for MARK MCCORMACK, DAN TOPOLSKI and JULIAN LLOYD WEBBER.

♠ CONCORDE

SIMON WILLIAMS sums up the intrinsic appeal of Concorde: *"I love the whole snob ethic of it: it reduces the amount of time you're up there sharing the air with people; the fact that the captain says 'If you look out your window on the port side, you'll see one of our subsonic friends', referring to a huge great jumbo a couple of miles beneath us."* It cheers TERRY HOLMES up too: *"No better way to fly to NY. The Americans are so jealous, especially when the captain says, 'we are ahead of schedule by 3½ seconds'."* DOUGLAS FAIRBANKS JR likes the fact that *"it's so fast and sleek and the service is great"*; MARC BOHAN and FREDERIC RAPHAEL just like it.

JAPAN AIR LINES

Efficient and reliable, winning votes from MARK MCCORMACK and ANDRE PREVIN. JULIAN LLOYD WEBBER is a dissenter: *"I don't like the food and they don't offer you an alternative dish."*

LUFTHANSA

High on security, punctuality and service, the flying German finds favour with SERENA FASS, MARK MCCORMACK and ROBIN LEACH. The food hits the mark too, pleasing culinary sticklers MADHUR JAFFREY and MARCELLA HAZAN: *"They are very nice and clean and the food is some of the best I've had on an airline."*

MERIDIANA

A new acquisition for the Aga Khan in late 1991, this Europe-only airline is *"really fantastic. Very, very nice, very well organized, very good service, very good food"* – MARCHESA DI SAN GIULIANO FERRAGAMO. A great point in favour: they fly into Florence rather than Pisa.

MGM GRAND AIR

New York to LA daily – in style. The converted 727s offer all 33 passengers first class luxe. Stand-up bar and lounge, squashy armchairs, private sleeping compartments, gourmet cuisine, choice of 6 movies, papers and mags, s-p-a-c-e. *"It is almost like your own luxury charter but it doesn't cost any more. Gourmet food, sometimes prepared by chefs from Spago and Le Cirque, is cooked fresh on the plane. They bake chocolate chip cookies to have with your tea. You are spoilt"* – ROBIN LEACH.

♠ QANTAS

Going from strength to strength, building a loyal coterie atop their impeccable safety record. SKYE MACLEOD doesn't *"care how much it costs, as long as I feel safe."* JILL MULLENS agrees, and finds the food and the service excellent. CAROL WRIGHT has the right priorities: *"They have marvellous Australian dessert wines and champagnes."* ROBERT SANGSTER, MARK MCCORMACK, ANTHONY HANSON, JULIAN LLOYD WEBBER, HENRY CRAWFORD and MICHAEL GEBICKI catch the spirit of Australia.

SAS (SCANDINAVIAN AIRLINE SYSTEMS)

The airline of Denmark, Norway and Sweden. Reliability is their watchword and who wants surprises or excitement when in the air? Not JULIAN LLOYD WEBBER. Linked with most top hotels in Scandinavia; checking in as you check out is a breeze.

♠ SINGAPORE AIRLINES

The ultimate in service airlines, whether you want to be pampered (*"the service couldn't have been more impeccable, they gave me great buckets full of caviare for the last leg because I was getting a bit tetchy by then"* – NED SHERRIN) or you want to be left alone: *"They actually listen to what you say and I don't want to be interrupted except for water and emergencies"* – CLARE FRANCIS. MICHAEL GEBICKI and MARK MCCORMACK applaud all that, however KEN HOM find the Singapore service *"a little bit obsequious"*. Nevertheless, no one could fault the airline's speed, spotlessness or efficiency.

♠ SWISSAIR

Very highly regarded (it's that inimitable Swiss

precision), with a comforting safety record. ROBIN LEACH and ANDRE PREVIN rate it (with Lufthansa) the best in Europe, DAVID GIBBONS reckons it is the best in the world: "*I have to say that because they own the hotel I manage but I also say it because the service is so good.*" LOYD GROSSMAN, SERENA FASS, MARK MCCORMACK and DAN KOMAR would say *ja* to that, as would SIR CLEMENT FREUD, "*but for the stewards smoking in their area and it all wafting back*".

—— *Cruises* ——

CLUB MED 1, Club Med, 106–110 Brompton Rd, London SW3, England ☎ (071) 225 1066
The moveable arm of the Club Med empire is the sleekest (and one of the largest) sailing yacht in existence: a 5-masted, 10,000-ton, 614-ft vessel, with 7 decks of Burmese teak. Yet she's still neat enough to enter small harbours and marinas. 425 guests lap up the usual Club Med fun and games and brilliant banquets. A platform descends to sea level to provide a sun deck and marina from which to windsurf, waterski, snorkel or scuba dive. Sister ship Club Med 2 caters to a Pacific-going Japanese market.

ROYAL VIKING LINE, 95 Merrick Way, Coral Gables, FL 33134, USA ☎ (305) 447 9660
Classy cruises all over the globe, from the Norwegian fjords to the balmy South Pacific. Go for a week, or opt for a 109-day world trip, visiting 36 ports. The 10,000 ton Royal Viking Queen is the swankiest cruiser on the seas, an all-suite vessel built at a cost of £50 million. Of intimate proportions that mean it can sail shallow waters – from the Seine to the Norwegian fjords – its stern turns into a marina for watersports. LORD LICHFIELD sails with the Vikings.

🕯 SEA GODDESS CRUISES, Cunard, South Western House, Canute Rd, Southampton, England ☎ (0703) 229933; 30A Pall Mall, London, SW1, England ☎ (071) 491 3930

More floating clubs than all-embracing cruisers, the 2 identical small ships carry about 100 guests each and almost as many staff. The compact size means "*it potters round to tiny ports. Very expensive but everything is included, as much champagne as you can stuff into yourself, nice wines and all your food (which is very good). If you want to eat in your cabin or on deck they set up a table with flowers and cutlery*" – CAROL WRIGHT. Comes with all the expected watersports, nightclubs, etc, but, thankfully, without any pressure to do anything but lounge.

—— *Rail* ——

PALACE ON WHEELS, Central Reservation House, 36 Chandralok, Janpath, New Delhi 110001, India ☎ (011) 322332
Grand old steam train, once belonging to the Maharajahs, which now takes in all the sights of Rajasthan, with overnight stops at top-class hotels. "*You see stunning desert and wonderful rock formations dotted with camels and sheep*" – MADHUR JAFFREY. JOHN TOVEY found the palatial experience "*superb*".

VENICE SIMPLON-ORIENT-EXPRESS, Sea Containers House, 20 Upper Ground, London SE1, England ☎ (071) 928 6000
The world's most famous train is much as she was in her 20s heyday. Still coal-stoked, still with charming cabins (polished mahogany, marquetry, brass fittings, glowing table lamps) and, for people who don't have to move a muscle for days, there is still *far* too much *very* good food served in the lovely dining cars. Added to the traditional Venice or Budapest to London trip is a new, equally luxurious Eastern Oriental train, running between Bangkok and Singapore. DOUGLAS FAIRBANKS JR thinks it's a "*wonderful train, the best I know of anywhere.*"

— *Tours, villas and agents* —

See also Australia, Brazil, Britain, Canada,

🕯 **Buzz** On track: The **Blue Train** from Cape Town to Johannesburg is "*just miles better than the Orient Express; it has bathtubs in the bedrooms and very good food*" – MARK MCCORMACK 🕯 ...... Hits back: still in South Africa (Pretoria to Nelspruit), "**Rovos Rail** *is 10 times better than the Blue Train; beautifully restored and with superb food*" – JOHN TOVEY 🕯 ...... Clacketyclack: DAVID GIBBONS advises, "*Take the train across Canada through the Rockies when there's a full moon and it is just incredible; a spectacular sense of travel*" 🕯 ...... Snack attack: "*In the dining-room of the Catalan Talgo Express from Narbonne in France to Barcelona in Spain, the chef managed to make a perfect omelette in the cramped kitchen, as well as grilled trout and sautéed veal with peppers. It's a lesson to all other rail operators*" – DAVID DALE .... 🕯

Caribbean, Egypt, Greece, India, Italy, Kenya, Malawi, Nepal, Seychelles, South Africa and Zimbabwe.

ABERCROMBIE & KENT, Sloane Square House, Holbein Place, London SW1, England ☎ (071) 730 9600; 1520 Kensington Rd, Oakbrook, IL 60521, USA ☎ (708) 954 2944
Exclusive, extensive and expensive, A&K is one of the world's best tour companies. Kenya is their forte. Hot air ballooning, champagne breakfasts; wing, camel and land safaris. Tailor-made or guided tours in Turkey.

AFRO VENTURES, Unit 2, Somerset, 11–13 York St, Kensington B, Randburg, South Africa ☎ (011) 789 1078
Specialists in overland tours in Zimbabwe and Botswana and Namibia. Rough it in tents or luxuriate in lodges.

BALES TOURS, Bales House, Junction Rd, Dorking, Surrey, England ☎ (0306) 885923 (brochures); 885991 (reservations)
Covering 43 countries but specialists in Egypt, the Middle East, China and Africa, from budget to luxury holidays.

BEST OF GREECE, 100 Week St, Maidstone, Kent, England ☎ (0622) 692278
As it says . . . the pick of Greece's resort hotels, neo-classical mansions, private whitewashed villas, even a private island – Argironisos – complete with cooks, maids and skippers.

BUSHBUCK SAFARIS, 48 High St, Hungerford, Berkshire, England ☎ (0488) 684702
When Bushbuck says individually tailored safaris, it means it. Itineraries (in Botswana, Zimbabwe and Zambia, Malawi, Kenya and Tanzania or Oman, Yemen and Madagascar) are carefully worked out to meet clients' inclinations and abilities. No brochures, no advertising, no groups.

BUTTERFIELD & ROBINSON, Suite 300, 70 Bond St, Toronto, Canada ☎ (416) 864 1354
The hiking and biking people do trips to Bali, NZ, Eastern Europe and the Rockies but best – and most cosseting – of all to Italy and France: *"In Bordeaux I was in the middle of a field with mustard poppies growing by the roadside, and we knew we had a lovely hotel to go to that night, baggage was being looked after and all we had to do was find a café. I threw my hands off the handlebars and said 'This is just where I want to be'"* – CLAUDIA ROSSI HUDSON.

CARIBBEAN CONNECTION, Concorde House, Forest St, Chester, England ☎ (0224) 41131; 93 Newman St, London W1 ☎ (071) 631 4482
Tailor-made, individual holidays to carefully vetted upmarket hotels and villas in the Caribbean.

CONTINENTAL VILLAS, 3 Caxton Walk, Phoenix St, WC2, London, England ☎ (071) 497 0444
Luxury villas, old and modern, mostly with pools, some with staff, in the South of France, Spain, Majorca, Ibiza, Italy, Portugal, Greece, Palm Beach and the West Indies.

CV TRAVEL, 43 Cadogan St, London SW3, England ☎ (071) 581 0851
The smartest villas (and villa girls) on Corfu and Paxos – the Duchess of Kent stayed in one. Also beautifully decorated privately owned villas in Southern Spain, the Algarve, the Riviera and Italy. Maids and often cooks available. Their **Different World** takes you to the best, most tasteful resort hotels in the Caribbean and Africa, and Indian Ocean.

EAST AFRICAN WILDLIFE SAFARIS, PO Box 43747, Nairobi, Kenya ☎ (02) 227217
Luxury, tailor-made safaris in Kenya, Tanzania, Zimbabwe and Botswana.

EQUINOX TRAVEL, 12 Beauchamp Place, SW3, England ☎ (071) 584 2244
Small company specializing in tailor-made tours for individuals in India, Pakistan, eastern Thailand and Burma. Good connections with maharajahs, so you can visit palaces and private villas. Adventure tours too (from camel to bicycle safaris) and VIP treks in Thailand.

EXPLORASIA, 13 Chapter St, London SW1, England ☎ (071) 630 7102
Pioneering treks in India, Nepal, Ladakh, Tibet, Ecuador and Peru. Celebrate the 40th anniversary of Everest's conquering in 1993 with a hike to Everest Base Camp.

GAMETRACKERS, PO Box 4245, Randburg, South Africa ☎ (011) 886 1810
Wing safaris in Southern Africa (SA, Botswana, Namibia and Zimbabwe), tailor-made from a choice of camps.

GREATWAYS TRAVEL, 100 Kercheval Ave, Grosse Pointe Farm, MI 48236, USA ☎ (313) 886 4710
Independent and international with itineraries for individuals, they're in with BOB PAYTON: *"Great – when they hear about a new place they get on a plane or boat or train to find out if it really is good or not."*

HEMPHILL HARRIS, 16000 Ventura Blvd, Suite 200, Encino, CA 91436, USA ☎ (818) 906 8086
Highly exclusive tours for rich fogeys, old and young, which guarantee the ultimate in luxury from hotels to transport. Trips all over the

world (except N America) include heli cruises, ballooning and a world tour in a private jet.

KUONI TRAVEL, Kuoni House, Dorking, Surrey, England ☎ (0306) 740888
Vast range of worldwide holidays, from lazing in a Caribbean club to searching for lions in Meru and taking in every continent in between.

MARY ROSSI TRAVEL, Suite 3, The Denison, 65 Berry St, N Sydney, NSW 2060, Australia ☎ (02) 957 4511
All arrangements for upmarket globetrotters are made by pioneering travel agent Mary and members of her extensive family.

MUSTIQUE VILLA RENTALS, Chartam House, 16A College Ave, Maidenhead, Berkshire, England ☎ (0628) 747733
For the cream of Caribbean villas owned by celebrated Mustique-philes.

SERENA FASS TOURS, 2 Chesil Court, Chelsea Manor St, London SW3, England ☎ (071) 352 9769
Tours of beauty, organized by Serena Fass (ex-Serenissima) and frequently accompanied by knowledgeable lecturers. Syria and Jordan, opera long weekends in Verona, painting and walking in southern India.

SERENISSIMA TRAVEL, 21 Dorset Square, London NW1, England ☎ (071) 730 9841
Cultural tours accompanied by a lecturer. Travel the waterways between St Petersburg and Moscow; follow a path from Thebes to rose-red Petra. NB Not all are cocoons of luxury.

SILK CUT TRAVEL, Meon House, Petersfield, Hampshire, England ☎ (0730) 265211
Combining upmarket (small group) tours, and hotels in the Caribbean and the Indian Ocean. Not tailor-made but flexible.

SPECIALTOURS, 81A Elizabeth St, London SW1, England ☎ (071) 730 2297
Cultural tours (often for Friends of museums and societies) of Europe, USA and the Middle East, taking in rare artwork, hidden museums, private houses and gardens.

TEMPO TRAVEL, Brunswick House, 91 Brunswick Crescent, London N11, England ☎ (081) 361 1131
African specialists, from Botswana to the Seychelles – safaris, cruises, simple lodges, first-class hotels. Particularly good on South Africa.

TIPPETT'S SAFARIS, PO Box 43806, Nairobi, Kenya ☎ (02) 332132; 14E Paveley Drive, London SW11, England ☎ (071) 223 3187
Private tented trips off the beaten track in Kenya and Tanzania.

TRAILFINDERS, 194 Kensington High St, London W8, England ☎ (071) 938 3939 (long-haul); (071) 938 3232 (transatlantic and Europe); (071) 938 3444 (first and business class); 42-48 Earl's Court Rd, London W8 ☎ (071) 938 3366
The full service for travellers. The cheapest reliable flights, on-the-spot ticketing, insurance, immunization and medical advice, travellers' cheques and currency, maps and books.

TWICKERS WORLD, 22 Church St, Twickenham, Middlesex, England ☎ (081) 892 7606
A massive selection of tours and treks to outlandish places with the accent on wildlife, wilderness, adventure, action and culture. Do an ecological tour of Galapagos and the Amazon; watch whales in the Hebrides and Canada; see Botswana on elephant back.

UNITED TOURING COMPANY, United House, 6 Park House, PO Box 2914, Harare, Zimbabwe ☎ (04) 793701
Largest tour operator in Kenya, with United Air Charters under its aegis as well. They'll also organize package or tailor-made safaris in Zimbabwe and book hotel accommodation.

VACANZE IN ITALIA, Bignor, Nr Pulborough, W Sussex, England ☎ (07987) 426
Superb privately owned villas and châteaux for hire in Italy and France (Vacances en Campagne ☎ 433). Also English Country Cottages (covering Scotland and Wales too) ☎ (0328) 851155.

WORLDWIDE JOURNEYS & EXPEDITIONS, 146 Gloucester Rd, London SW7, England ☎ (071) 370 5032
Upmarket tours and treks for ecologically (and financially) sound individuals and individually minded groups. Safaris throughout Africa and treks in the Himalayas and Andes.

─────── *Yacht charter* ───────

See also Australia and the Carribean

CAMPER & NICHOLSONS, 12 ave de la Libération, 06600 Antibes, France ☎ 9291 2912
Over 400 luxury crewed yachts, motor and sailing, modern and old-fashioned, steered where you will. Prices range between a paltry US$1,000 per day to a negotiable US$50,000.

TOP YACHT, Andrew Hill Lane, Hedgerley, Buckinghamshire, England ☎ (0793) 642640
With bases at buzzy Bodrum and tiny Gocek, they arrange bareboat and crewed yacht or gulet cruising in Greek and Turkish waters. Can be combined with self-drive mainland tour.

INDEX